BUZZCOCKS – ever fallen in love ...

(with someone you shouldn't've)

THE
ENCYCLOPEDIA
OF SINGLES

This edition published by Parragon 1999
Parragon
Queen Street House
4 Queen Street
Bath
BA1 1HE, UK

| Paperback ISBN | 0-75253-337-1 |
| Hardback ISBN | 0-75253-324-X |

Produced for Parragon by Foundry Design & Production,
Crabtree Hall, Crabtree Lane, Fulham, London SW6 6TY, UK.

AUTHORS

PHILIP DODD
Philip Dodd is a publishing consultant and writer specializing in music and popular culture. As a publisher with Reed Books and Virgin, he concentrated on books on rock 'n' roll and pop, and worked directly with acts ranging from U2 to Take That, Pink Floyd to Boyzone.

PAUL DU NOYER
Paul Du Noyer is a former editor of *Q* magazine, which he helped to launch, and of *Mojo*, which he founded. He remains Contributing Editor on both titles, as well as writing for a wide range of other publications. In 1997 he wrote the widely acclaimed book about John Lennon's solo songs, *We All Shine On*.

DAWN EDEN
Dawn Eden is a freelance rock writer and historian whose work has appeared in *Mojo*, *Billboard* and *Salon*. A shameless Sixties pop superfan, she has over 60 CD liner notes to her credit, including Harry Nilsson's *Personal Best*, the Hollies' *30th Anniversary Collection* and John Carter's *As You Like It, Volume 2*. She is single and has no children that she knows of.

EITHNE FARRY
Eithne Farry graduated from Goldsmiths' College in 1986 and has made London her home. She has worked as a freelance journalist and reviewer for various publications including *Time Out* and *Melody Maker*. She has also contributed to a series of educational books.

MICHAEL HEATLEY
Michael Heatley was editor of *The History Of Rock*, a ten-volume series on popular music (1981–84). Since then, he's written over 50 music, sport and TV books, contributed to *Music Week*, *Gold Mine (US)*, *Record Collector*, *Radio Times* and many other magazines. He is the founder of Northdown Publishing, producers of quality music books.

MARTIN NOBLE
Martin Noble is a writer/editor who has contributed to over 20 music books including the *NME Rock 'n' Roll Years* and written a dozen novels/novelizations including *Who Framed Roger Rabbit*, *Tin Men*, *Ruthless People* and *Trance Mission*. He has worked for over 170 British publishers and many writers worldwide, and can be reached at his web site www.demon.co.uk/aesop.

Additional contributions by: Graham Betts, Nigel Cross, Alan Kinsman, Ian Powling, Andrea Thorn, Suresh Tolat, Ian Welch and Nick Wells.

ACKNOWLEDGMENTS

We particularly acknowledge the assistance of Dave Bates who kindly gave us access to his research database; he is currently working on a book about the world's top music producers. Special thanks are due to Sean and all the staff at Helter Skelter music bookshop in London's Denmark Street; John Stickland; Valerie Pavett at St Martin's School of Art in London; Alastair Blaazar, Jim Brittain and Lorne Murdoch at MCPS; Jackie Da Costa at Re-Pro, The Guild of Recording Producers, Directors and Engineers; Bob Shannon, co-author of *Behind the Hits*, and Bill Pitzonka.

With grateful thanks to Frances Banfield, Kirsten Bradbury, Josephine Cutts, Claire Dashwood, Grant Duffort, Lucinda Hawksley, Helen Johnson, Penny Lane, Keeley Lawrence, Dylan Lobo, Lee Matthews, Ezra Nathan, Brian Nevill, Adrian Pay, Andrea Power, Ian Powling, Miguel Rosales, Chris de Selincourt, Mike de Selincourt, James Smith, Amanda-Jane Tomlins and the many record companies who patiently supplied us with information.

We would like to acknowledge the following sources which proved invaluable in cross-checking our research and would recommend as further reading: Jay Warner, *Billboard's American Rock 'n' Roll In Review*, Schirmer, 1997; Dave McAleer, *Encyclopedia of Hits: The 1960s*, Blandford, 1996; Paul Gambaccini, Jonathan Rice and Tim Rice, *Guinness British Hit Albums*, Guinness, 1994; Mark Lamarr (intro.), *Guinness British Hit Singles, 11th edition*, Guinness, 1997; Colin Larkin (ed.), *The Guinness Encyclopedia of Popular Music*, Guinness, 1994; Nick Logan and Bob Woffinden, *The Illustrated New Musical Express Encyclopedia of Rock*, Hamlyn, 1976; Patricia Romanowski and Holly George-Warren (eds), *The New Rolling Stone Encyclopedia of Rock & Roll*, Fireside, 1995; Dafydd Rees and Luke Crampton, *Q Encyclopedia of Rock Stars*, Dorling Kindersley, 1996; Dave McAleer, *The Warner Guide to UK and US Hit Singles*, Carlton/Little Brown, 1996; Dick Jacobs and Harriet Jacobs, *Who Wrote That Song?*, Writer's Digest Books, 1994.

PICTURE CREDITS

All artist photographs courtesy of Redferns. Album covers courtesy of:
8 Sony USA. 10 Virgin Records. 11 Artwork reproduced with kind permission of A&M Records Limited. 13 Parlophone Records. 16 EMI Records Limited. 17 EMI Records Limited. 20 By kind permission of BMG Entertainment International UK and Ireland Ltd. 23 Virgin Records. 25 By kind permission of BMG Entertainment International UK and Ireland Ltd. 27 Arista Records. 31 Queen singles are reproduced by kind permission of Queen Productions Ltd. 32 Sony USA. 33 MCA/Geffen Records. 34 WEA. 35 © 1990 Iron Maiden Holdings Ltd. 39 Beggars Banquet. 42l Mercury Records. 42r Island Records Ltd. 44t Warners. 44b Warner Bros. 47l Warner Bros. 47r Sony USA. 49 Sony USA. 50l EMI-Capitol Entertainment Properties. 50r Island Records Ltd. 52 Mercury Records. 56l Creation Records. 56r Island Records Ltd. 58 Sony USA. 59 WEA. 61 WEA. 62 Polydor Records. 63 EMI Records Limited. 66 Epic. 74l Chrysalis Records Limited. 74r Sony USA. 76 Polydor Records. 79 Arista Records. 81 Warner Bros. 83l EMI-Capitol Entertainment Properties. 83r Warner Bros. 85 © Apple Corps Ltd. 87 East West Records. 89 WEA. 90 Virgin Records Ltd. 93l Mercury Records. 93r Warner Bros. 95l Polydor Records. 95r Epic. 97 Columbia. 99 Queen singles are reproduced by kind permission of Queen Productions Ltd. 100 Atlantic Recording Corporation. 101 Arista. 103 Mercury Records. 107 Polydor Records. 108 Reproduction by kind permission of EMI Svenska. 109 EMI Records Limited. 110 BMG Entertainment International UK and Ireland Ltd. 114 Warner Bros. 115 Virgin Records Ltd. 117 WEA. 118t Pye Records. 118b Artwork reproduced with kind permission of A&M Records Limited. 121 Derek Boshier. 123 Warner Bros. 124 Warner Bros. 125 Reproduced with kind permission of Go! Discs Ltd. 126 Creation Records. 127 Mercury Records. 129 Photography, Typography and Design by Parched Art. 130 Parlophone Records. 131 WEA. 134 BMG Entertainment International UK and Ireland Limited. 137 Warner Bros. 138 Artwork reproduced with kind permission of A&M Records Limited. 139 Mercury Records. 140 Artwork reproduced with kind permission of A&M Records Limited. 141 BMG Entertainment International UK and Ireland Ltd. 142 Mercury Records. 144 © Apple Corps Ltd. 145 Mercury Records. 146 Warner Music UK Limited. 147 Polydor Records. 148l Chrysalis Records Ltd. 148r Warner Music UK Limited. 149 EMI Records Limited. 150 BMG Entertainment International UK and Ireland Limited. 152 MCA/Geffen Records. 153 Sony USA. 154 Virgin Records Ltd. 156 Reproduced by kind permission of Parlophone, EMI Records Limited. 157 Universal USA. 159 Parlophone Records. 161 Island Records. 163 Warner Music UK Limited. 164 Queen singles are reproduced by kind permission of Queen Productions Ltd. 165 CBS. 166 Sleeve designed by Malcolm Garrett. 167 WEA. 170 BMG Entertainment International UK and Ireland Limited. 173 Mercury Records. 174 Creation Records. 175 Artwork reproduced with kind permission of A&M Records Limited. 176t Mercury Records. 176b John Carder Bush. 179 Some Bizarre Records. 181 EMI Records Limited. 183 Parlophone Records. 185 Epic. 186 Mercury Records. 189 Queen singles are reproduced by kind permission of Queen Productions Ltd. 190 East West Records. 191 Reproduced by kind permission of EMI Records Limited. 193 Reproduced by kind permission of EMI Records Limited. 194 WEA. 199 Mushroom Records Ltd. 201t Epic. 201b Columbia. 203 Castle Communications. 205 BMG Entertainment International UK and Ireland Limited. 206l CBS. 206r Warner Music UK Limited. 210 Artwork reproduced with kind permission of Go! Discs Limited. 211 Sony USA. 212 Warner Bros. 213 © Aplle Corps Ltd. 214 Polydor Records. 217 CBS. 218l Polydor Records. 218r Chrysalis Records Ltd. 221t ZTT Records. 221b Reproduced by kind permission of EMI Records Limited. 223 Artwork reproduced by kind permission of A&M Records Limited. 225 Chrysalis Records Ltd. 226 Atlantic Recording Corporation. 228l Sony USA. 228r Mercury Records. 229 Artwork reproduced by kind permission of A&M Records Limited. 133l Queen singles are reproduced by kind permission of Queen Productions Ltd. 233r Sony USA. 235 EMI Records Limited. 237 Warner Music UK Limited. 238l 'When The Going Gets Tough, The Tough Get Going' by Billy Ocean, as featured on L.I.F.E. Love Is Forever, available on Jive Records. 238r EMI Records Limited. 240 Sugar Hill Records. 242 BMG Entertainment International UK and Ireland Limited. 243 BMG Entertainment International UK and Ireland Limited. 244 CBS. 245 Mercury Records. 248 Creation Records. 250 Parlophone. 252 The Hit Label.

THE ENCYCLOPEDIA OF SINGLES

Philip Dodd, Dawn Eden, Eithne Farry,

Michael Heatley and Martin Noble

General Editor: Paul Du Noyer

Introduction

The whole idea was that they were cheap. And being cheap, they were disposable. You could play a single until you were sick of it, and then you bought a different one to take its place. Built-in obsolescence was the assumption that underpinned the early pop business, a view you held whether you loved pop or despised it. But now we look back at four decades of pop singles and we see that things have turned out very differently. Like the plastic they used to be made of, these little singles have shown an unexpected resilience. Their durability is miraculous, and here is a book that celebrates it. Wander at will through our list of a thousand delights. Pause wherever you want. Reach out to that dusty stack in some neglected corner of your room, or maybe some cobwebbed recess of your mind, and rediscover the magic that lives inside those tiny grooves. If you don't possess these records already, and perhaps have yet to hear some of the songs at all, then take these pages as your guide.

It's a benevolent fact of our new, digital age that almost all popular music is once again available – whether on cheaply cheerful compilation discs or within the dignified bulk of grandly packaged box-sets. Great new singles are still being made – no doubt there is one being written in some humble garret even as we speak – but the special quality of a brilliant single, however old, is that it goes on giving pleasure for ever. The past refreshes the present, provided we are alive to it. That is where a book like this can help. Why do we love particular singles? And why do we revere the single in general? To the former question we each have our own answers, and to the latter I think this book can offer much by way of enlightenment.

An individual single is the most potent source of nostalgia ever devized, recalling to mind some moment of personal epiphany, excitement or deliciously poignant emotion. Singles that were hits have a communal aspect also. Far more than its earnest older brother, the album, the Top 20 smash enjoys its season in the sun by getting played on pub and coffee-bar juke-boxes, on the club dancefloor, on radios in shops, factories and offices, or maybe escaping from the wound-down windows of passing cars.

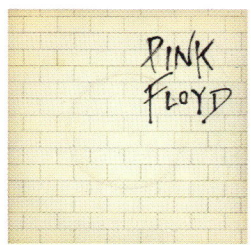

In recent times the pop single has actually become the focal point of quite profound national moods – beginning, I suppose, with the UK and US records made to promote the famine appeal that climaxed in Live Aid, right up to the 1997 release of Elton John's

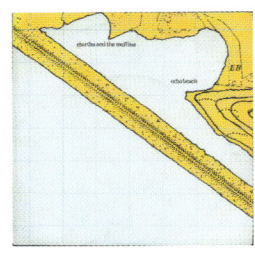

new *Candle In The Wind*, which became in effect the first public monument to Diana, Princess of Wales, and now stands as the biggest-selling single of all time. The single is truly the people's art-form, and it's far from obsolete.

The '45', to revive its pre-CD name, has been an icon of our lives since the early 1950s, when the American RCA company introduced it. Just seven inches across, the lightweight disc was conceived as a cheap alternative to the other vinyl format, the 12-inch $33^{1}/_{3}$ rpm 'long-player' pioneered by RCA's rivals at CBS. Housing only one track per side, the single was really a direct successor to the old shellac 78 disc, which it soon despatched to technology's graveyard. At first the new vinyl arrivals fought a 'format war' – not the first or last the recording industry has seen – until the advent of twin-speed turntables. And so it came to pass that albums and singles could happily co-exist, and in their vinyl form they became the two key carriers of popular music in the late 20th century.

Much less breakable than the 78, and by definition more suited to the pop song than to the stage musical or classical symphony, the single was quickly adopted by the young. American teenagers of the 1950s were the first to turn it into a sort of fetish object – early record sleeves would often feature naïve designs based upon the shiny black disc, as if it were a magic talisman. By the early 1960s, youthful consumers on both sides of the Atlantic were able to buy small, portable record players (of which the Dansette has become the connoisseur's favourite). With their parallel accessory, the tiny transistor radio, these fabulously modern machines became a symbol of consumer freedom, whether in suburban English bedrooms or on Californian beaches. They too cropped up on record sleeves, in the slick sketches of finger-popping party-goers, gaily jiving to lines of musical notes that snaked out of the speaker-grille.

The single and pop radio, of course, were made for one another. The rise of each has been dependent on the other; even today they are inseparable. One way or another, it was singles such as Elvis Presley's *Heartbreak Hotel* and Eddie Cochran's *Summertime*

Blues – you can, of course, read about them here – which defined the rock 'n' roll explosion as well as an entirely new way of life. By the 1960s the revolution was well advanced: now those Dansettes and transistors shook to such consummate mini-epics as Phil Spector's Ronettes hit *Be My Baby*, or Brian Wilson's superlative compositions for The Beach Boys like *God Only Knows* and *Good Vibrations*. The Beatles reigned across the whole decade: from *She Loves You* to *Hey Jude* and beyond, they revealed new possibilities for the medium with every release. In Detroit the self-styled 'hit factory' of Motown spawned an unstoppable flow of soul masterpieces including Stevie Wonder's *My Cherie Amour* and Smokey Robinson's *Tracks Of My Tears*. (All these, too, are featured here.)

The single has never looked back, but in the late 1960s it was eclipsed somewhat by the culture of the rock album, and has had to settle for junior status ever since. A new generation of artists, led by Bob Dylan but including The Beatles themselves, adopted albums as the badge of serious creativity. An emerging audience, older and more sophisticated, agreed. A kind of schism divided the music market, and remains to this day: the album is the broad canvas that offers artistic freedom and depth of expression, whereas the single is ephemeral, a place for kiddies' jingles. Ominously enough, some key acts of the 1970s – Led Zeppelin and David Bowie spring to mind – considered themselves 'album artists' above all (in fact Led Zeppelin scorned the seven-inch format altogether). And the 'single acts' like T. Rex, The Osmonds and Slade were relegated to lower divisions of hip esteem. This divide is more pronounced in America, where a single is hauled from the shelves as soon as it competes with its parent album. Britain has had a greater regard for the 45, being more fond of pop flash and whimsy, but also valuing its cheapness – for similar reasons of economy, EPs (or 'extended play' 45s of four or five tracks) were more common in the UK than in America.

Looking back, however, there are plenty of singles – let's just mention Abba's *Dancing Queen* and Queen's *Bohemian Rhapsody* – with a staying power superior to that of some highly-lauded 'serious' albums of the same era. Before the 1970s were over the single was once again triumphant, thanks to those ever-antagonistic bedfellows punk rock and disco. After such landmarks as The Sex Pistols' *Anarchy In The UK* and Chic's *Le Freak*, singles hit the 1980s on a high. Even that Cinderella format, the EP, lived on, evolving into the 12-inch 45 – the bigger disc was a club DJ favourite, especially in reggae and dance circles where it gave the extra playing time and packed a sonic boom to boot. The re-mixed track, the extended and alternative versions are all vestiges of the old 12-inch single that later made the transition to compact disc. In the hip-hop culture that began to flourish in New York, vinyl of all speeds and sizes was prized by pioneers of 'scratching'. In the final years of their market dominance, old-fashioned plastic singles erupted in a riot of coloured vinyl, picture discs and absolutely any shape of packaging the marketing teams could dream up.

The best pop singles might be immortal, but no one format lasts for ever. From the mid-1980s the vinyl 45 was steadily giving ground to the cassette single. And by the mid-1990s the CD had outstripped them both. Vinyl today is all but extinct in its seven-inch guise, and fading fast in 12-inch; cassettes accounted for a quarter of the market in 1996, but their share is also falling rapidly. The latest victors lack the tactile charm of their defeated rivals – and, conveniently for the industry, each new format costs you more than its forerunner – but that's no reflection on the vitality of singles themselves. Sales have been erratic in the last decade; in Britain, especially, the graph is a rollercoaster whose peaks are labelled with names such as Kylie Minogue and Jason Donovan, Bros, Take That and The Spice Girls. More generally, it's the dance market that supports the single and dominates the chart, interspersed with cover versions or classic revivals (the latter inspired by anything from a movie to a Levi's TV commercial).

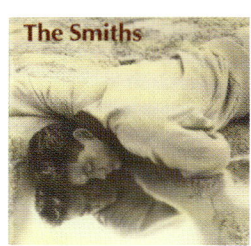

The most frustrating aspect of today's chart is its rapid turnover. Whereas a hit record used to spend weeks climbing to the top, modern media saturation, and the ultra-

sophistication of contemporary marketing, mean that a typical single will now hit its target audience straight away, plunging downwards swiftly thereafter. But the average chart is still a fiesta of variety and surprise, and singles have withstood the doom predicted for them at the hands of video and computer games. In 1984 the typical UK Number 1 sold just over 100,000 copies, and the figure slumped to 77,000 in the next four years. A chart-topper in 1997 needed to sell almost twice that amount – 145,000 – to reach the summit, which is a sign of the single's proud resurgence.

Let us then praise the single, and pray we need never bury it. In the following pages we refer to 1,000 examples of this glorious art-form. Each is lovingly detailed with information and opinion. We hope you will also catch the occasional germ of infectious enthusiasm, enough to make you ache to hear that single for yourself. You're bound to know some already, and there will be a few that you've laboured to forget (Father Abraham's *The Smurf Song*, anyone?) Naturally, there will be omissions that dismay you, but try to be forgiving – the sea of singles is enormous. A list of even its most dazzling examples is practically infinite, and far more difficult to compile than an equivalent list of albums. We used a variety of criteria to arrive

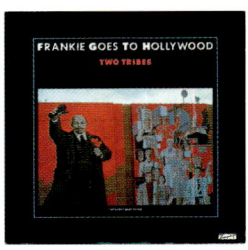

at our eventual choices. Commercial success was self-evidently a factor, because singles are nothing if not a commercial product. The single that is not designed to be popular is almost a contradiction in terms. Plenty of noble efforts have missed the mark, of course, and there have been some ghastly successes. But sales are one measure of a record's worth that it would be stupid to ignore. We therefore considered every record that has appeared in the UK or US Top 5 since 1953. We looked also at the English-language singles that have sold the most in other markets across the globe.

Further weight was given to the discs that have shown up in newspaper, magazine and radio polls down the decades, whether voted for by readers, listeners, critics or musicians themselves. Among the many sources consulted were the *Melody Maker* Readers' Polls since 1970, the *Mojo* '100 Greatest Singles' issue of August, 1997, and Capital Radio

listeners' all-time Top 100. We noted, too, the acclaim of the music industry, expressed through events like the Grammy, Brit and Ivor Novello Awards. And finally, to fine-tune the whole process, we've walked the halls of oblivion to rescue some of those hits-that-should-have-been; the songs that were overlooked at the time and yet, somehow, have gnawed away at our collective memories until they become recognized classics. (So welcome home, for example, Paul Simon's **50 Ways To Leave Your Lover**.)

In all, it was a complicated method, but we avoided the bias of an author's personal prejudices, and bridged the gap between 'expert' opinion and authentic mass appeal. Mourn the glories we have missed, by all means, but be reassured that nothing in here is without a powerful claim to its place. Our entries are listed alphabetically, by song title – an approach that offers you the serendipity of random dipping, yet gives ease of reference. Within each entry you can read of the people who made the music, and learn the story that lies beneath its grooves. All that remains is to wish you happy reading and – to follow, perhaps – some truly ecstatic listening. The single was really where pop music began, and though pop has changed beyond all recognition, the single is where its heart remains.

Paul Du Noyer

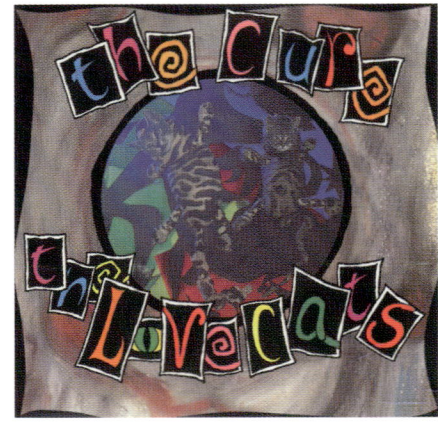

How to use this book

The encyclopedia is organized alphabetically by single title for ease of reference. To locate entries for a particular artist or group, refer to the Index of Artists, also at the back of the book. As part of the extensive research in the compilation of this encyclopedia, we consulted and cross-checked using a wide range of print, digital and microfiche sources. The following notes offer some background information, where appropriate, on our approach.

Release date: gives the date of a record's 'debut' – its first appearance in the world. According to sources used, this may be date of release or date of chart entry. Where the information was available we have given dates for both UK and US releases, otherwise we have provided a single date.

Writers and Producers: we have included as much information as was available to us at the time of publication, trawling a wide range of sources. Label: we provide the label of initial release, or both UK and US labels, where known. Wherever possible, we have endeavoured to provide a quote from the music press that helps to put the single in context. Ranging from adulatory to downright dismissive, these excerpts frequently offer an insight to a single's initial critical reception and work as a counterpoint to the contributors' entries. A small number of quotes compiled were written at the time of a record's re-release. For ease of reference, we have presented **Album Names** in bold and ***Single Titles, Songs*** or ***Tracks*** in italicized bold.

Abracadabra

ARTIST The Steve Miller Band **RELEASE DATE** June 1982 (UK)/May 1982 (US) **WRITER** Steve Miller **PRODUCER** Steve Miller, Gary Mallaber **LABEL** Mercury (UK)/Capitol (US) **UK CHART PEAK/WEEKS** 2/11 **US CHART PEAK/WEEKS** 1/25

Steve Miller is an accomplished musician with strong songs and a blues base. His 1972 **The Joker**, a sly piece of pop, brought him to the attention of the mainstream, but for the next few years he continued with a more rootsy sound. *Abracadabra* was more radio friendly pop, which wanted to 'reach out and grab yah', with softer vocals and rock instrumentation. Then Steve Miller returned to his old love, the blues, releasing the **Born To Be Blue** album in 1988.

Steve Miller has bounced back from last year's missteps and once again pulled off a hummable sleight of mind. **Steve Pond, Rolling Stone, July 1982**

Ace Of Spades

ARTIST Motorhead **RELEASE DATE** September 1993 **WRITER** Ian Kilminster, Eddie Clarke, Phil Taylor **PRODUCER** Vic Maile **LABEL** WGAF **UK CHART PEAK/WEEKS** 23/5 **US CHART PEAK/WEEKS** –

The singular mission of the 'Head, it seemed, was to strike fear into the hearts of mild-mannered music lovers everywhere. They succeeded gloriously in 1980 when *Ace of Spades* powered its way into the upper reaches of the UK charts, with the most un-chart-friendly of sounds, a kind of tightly controlled thrash. The combined talents of Lemmy (born Ian Kilminster), Fast Eddie and Philthy Animal Taylor appealed to metalheads everywhere and also won converts from the punk congregation, who grudgingly admired the band's sheer speed and aggression.

On the back cover of this sulphate madness the boys are lounging around in a sand pit clad in leather and ammo belts looking like Serge Leone extras. Gambling, women and drugs come into the scene somewhere, and as these are the central concerns of the universe why shouldn't they be understood? **Ian Pye, Melody Maker, November 1980**

Addicted To Love

ARTIST Robert Palmer **RELEASE DATE** May 1986 (UK)/February 1986 (US) **WRITER** Robert Palmer **PRODUCER** Bernard Edwards **LABEL** Island (UK & US) **UK CHART PEAK/WEEKS** 5/15 **US CHART PEAK/WEEKS** 1/22

Robert Palmer is a blue-eyed soul singer with a lounge-lizard smoothness, and a chameleon tendency to change the style of his music. He started out in Vinegar Joe, a soul rock group, but over the years he has dabbled in reggae, techno, hard rock and big band sounds. He is probably best known for the **Addicted To Love** video, which featured mini skirted models strumming guitars to Palmer's pared down pulsing vocals. It was slick and tacky, but effective.

Grunting and groaning, dream fella Bob shifts his poetic bulk onto another foot, music plays, and the singer begins to shake his ugly swollen body in what he assumes to be a rhythmic fashion. From the mouth region comes a sound that is akin to a bucketful of mud. **Mr Spencer, Sounds, April 1986**

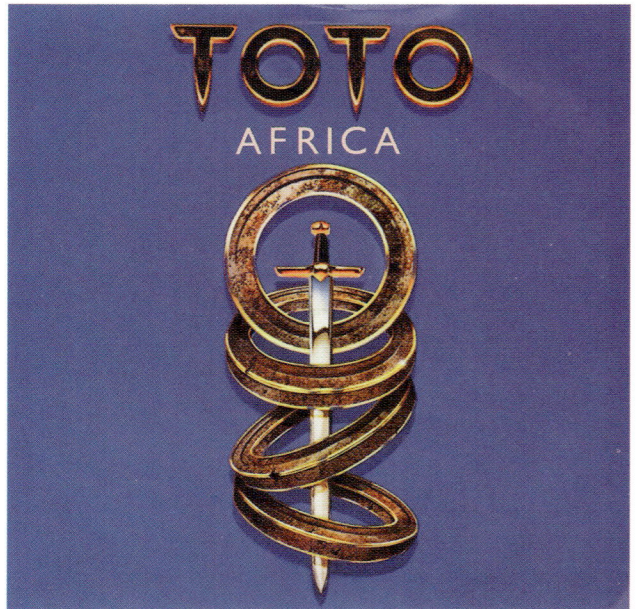

Africa

ARTIST Toto **RELEASE DATE** February 1983 (UK)/October 1982 (US) **WRITER** David Paich, Jeff Porcaro **PRODUCER** Toto **LABEL** CBS (UK)/Columbia (US) **UK CHART PEAK/WEEKS** 3/10 **US CHART PEAK/WEEKS** 1/21

The LA session players behind Toto: David Paich, the Porcaro brothers and Bobby Kimball, appeared on many releases by other acts from Steely Dan to Earth, Wind and Fire. In their own line-up they came up with a polished – maybe slightly anaemic as far as 'authentic' rockers were concerned – adult contemporary rock, which peaked in the early Eighties with *Rosanna* and the evocative *Africa*, written by Paich and the late lamented Jeff Porcaro.

… as far as 'Elevator Rock' goes Toto are in a class of their own and this is soft rock with a smooth filling, a tootling vibes-like synth figure making it the kind … that your mother would like. **Dave Lewis, Sounds, January 1983**

Agadoo

ARTIST Black Lace **RELEASE DATE** June 1984 **WRITER** Myra Simille, Michael Delancery, Giles Peram **PRODUCER** – **LABEL** Flair **UK CHART PEAK/WEEKS** 10/9 **US CHART PEAK/WEEKS** –

One of the most maligned hits of the Eighties, *Agadoo* was a victim of its own catchiness. Its critics would not have minded it so much were its chorus not so infectious. Black Lace were from Wakefield and started out as a quartet, but by the time of *Agadoo* they had been pared down to a duo. They first gained notice when they represented the UK in the 1978 Eurovision Song Contest, performing *Mary Ann*.

Against All Odds (Take A Look At Me Now)

ARTIST Phil Collins **RELEASE DATE** April 1984 (UK)/February 1984 (US) **WRITER** Phil Collins **PRODUCER** Phil Collins, Hugh Padgham **LABEL** Virgin (UK)/Atlantic (US) **UK CHART PEAK/WEEKS** 2/14 **US CHART PEAK/WEEKS** 1/24

Phil Collins wrote *Against All Odds* at the request of director Taylor Hackford, who needed a title for his film of that title. The song did quite a bit better than the film, becoming Collins' first US Number 1 as well as his first gold disc there. He adapted it from an out-take from his **Face Value** sessions, *How Can You Sit There?*

Although his vocal performance is magnificent the arrangement is far too safe, despite the booming bottom line synth; however, it's obvious that Phil has been asked to write for a particular market and to supply a suitable musical score as the credits roll. **Paul Strange, Melody Maker, March 1984**

Ain't No Mountain High Enough

ARTIST Diana Ross **RELEASE DATE** September 1970 (UK)/August 1970 (US) **WRITER** Nicholas Ashford, Valerie Simpson **PRODUCER** Nicholas Ashford, Valerie Simpson **LABEL** Tamla Motown (UK)/Motown (US) **UK CHART PEAK/WEEKS** 6/12 **US CHART PEAK/WEEKS** 1/14

Motown's huge financial investment in launching Diana Ross' solo career after she left The Supremes in 1970 paid off with *Ain't No Mountain High Enough* – it went to the top of the US charts. The soul classic, written and produced by Ashford and Simpson, was also included, together with another early solo hit, *Reach Out And Touch (Somebody's Hand)*, on **Diana Ross**, her debut solo album.

… like a baby's first cry, the smell of new-mown hay, the bleat of a new-born lamb, the touch of a young girl's lips … somehow Diana brings the sensation of life's beautiful moments into a heady distillation of melody and rhythm. **Chris Welch, Melody Maker, September 1970**

Albatross

ARTIST Fleetwood Mac **RELEASE DATE** December 1968 **WRITER** Peter Green **PRODUCER** Mike Vernon **LABEL** Blue Horizon **UK CHART PEAK/WEEKS** 1/20 **US CHART PEAK/WEEKS** 0/0

This languid instrumental, influenced by Santo and Johnny's 1959 US hit *Sleep Walk*, was a total departure for British bluesters Fleetwood Mac, who were more often seen laying down a 12-bar for ace guitarist Peter Green to solo at length over. It would prove the peak of their association with Mike Vernon's Blue Horizon label, for after topping the chart in January 1969 and following up with the May Number 2 *Man Of The World*, they quit for a short-lived stay with Immediate.

A delicate and technically exemplary guitar duet, supported by throbbing tom-toms, and electric bass, with distant slide-guitar and crashing cymbals, giving the effect of a soaring albatross. Excellent – but hardly chart material. **Derek Johnson, NME, December 1968**

Alison

ARTIST Elvis Costello **RELEASE DATE** May 1977 **WRITER** Elvis Costello **PRODUCER** Nick Lowe **LABEL** Stiff (UK)/Columbia (US) **UK CHART PEAK/WEEKS** 0/0 **US CHART PEAK/WEEKS** 0/0

Elvis Costello's second single, *Alison*, provided the title for his first album, **My Aim Is True**. Although it did not become a hit at the time, it is now a radio staple. The positive feedback he got upon its release encouraged him to quit his job as a computer operator. It was a risky move for a man with a wife and child, but his foresight of better things proved true within months as his popularity increased and **My Aim Is True** reached Number 14.

Reminds me strongly of mid-period Brinsley [Schwartz] ballad – which can't be bad. Too tasteful to be a hit … **Tom Lott, Sounds, May 1977**

Alive And Kicking

ARTIST Simple Minds **RELEASE DATE** October 1985 (UK & US) **WRITER** Simple Minds **PRODUCER** Bob Clearmountain, Jimmy Levine **LABEL** Virgin (UK)/A&M (US) **UK CHART PEAK/WEEKS** 7/9 **US CHART PEAK/WEEKS** 3/20

This cut from the **Once Upon A Time** album was the band's first release after the departure of bass player Derek Forbes, and rode on

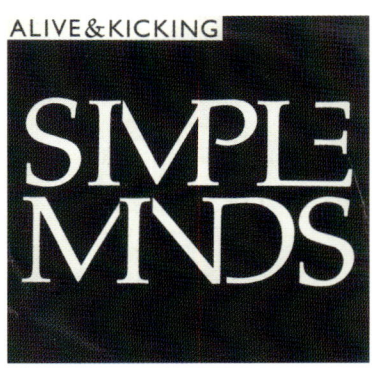

the back of the huge exposure they received when they appeared at the JFK Stadium as part of Live Aid. Purist fans thought the band had lost its edge as they headed towards a stadium and anthem rock reminiscent of U2, but mainstream fans, particularly in the States, responded well.

Designed to be haunting and mysterious, it is in fact dull and unmemorable, with Kerr's singing doing nothing special and surprisingly little chemistry from the Burchill/McNeil direction. You used to hear a Simple Minds song and know immediately who it was. This could be anyone. **Adam Sweeting, Melody Maker, October 1985**

All Along The Watch Tower

ARTIST Jimi Hendrix **RELEASE DATE** October 1968 (UK)/September 1968 (US) **WRITER** Bob Dylan **PRODUCER** Chas Chandler **LABEL** Track (UK)/Reprise (US) **UK CHART PEAK/WEEKS** 5/11 **US CHART PEAK/WEEKS** 20/9

Although Chas Chandler, his manager, had discovered him in New York, Jimi Hendrix had made Britain his launch pad to rock fame. His choice of Dylan's *All Along The Watchtower*, a track first heard earlier in 1968 on the **John Wesley Harding** album, was what broke Hendrix in America. The single sold more copies in the US than the Experience's previous four releases combined, breaching the all-important Top 20 and establishing him as a major star in the land of his birth.

This, for my money, is his best yet. It's a Bob Dylan song and, though Jimi occasionally seems to have a little trouble timing the lyrics to the backing, there are great dollops of magnificent Hendrix guitar. **Bob Dawson, Melody Maker, October 1968**

All Around The World

ARTIST Lisa Stansfield **RELEASE DATE** October 1989 (UK)/February 1990 (US) **WRITER** Ian DeVaney, Andy Morris, Lisa Stansfield **PRODUCER** Andy Morris, Ian DeVaney **LABEL** Arista (UK & US) **UK CHART PEAK/WEEKS** 1/14 **US CHART PEAK/WEEKS** 3/22

Rochdale's finest hit pay-dirt with this piece of sweet soul music, lovingly created by Stansfield and her writing and production partners Andy Morris and Ian DeVaney. September 1989's **This Is The Right Time** didn't do much, but this release from the debut album **Affection** was Number 1 in a dozen territories, winning an Ivor Novello Award and gaining Stansfield the Brit for Best British Newcomer. It also went to the top of the US R&B charts – only the second time a white artist had done so.

From her carefully crafted image, to the contents of her lyrics, to the production of her record, to her years of playing duets – the rise of Lisa Stansfield has relied as much on formula as your last Algebra class. **Dana Mayer, Melody Maker, April 1990**

All Day And All Of The Night

ARTIST The Kinks **RELEASE DATE** October 1964 (UK)/December 1964 (US) **WRITER** Ray Davies **PRODUCER** Shel Talmy **LABEL** Pye (UK)/Reprise (US) **UK CHART PEAK/WEEKS** 1/10 **US CHART PEAK/WEEKS** 7/12

Having got off the mark with **You Really Got Me**, the Kinks played it safe with the follow-up, which started its 14-week UK chart run just as its predecessor bowed out. The formula was exactly the

same: Shel Talmy's raw, exciting production building the tension through repeated hard guitar riffing and the gradual introduction of layered backing vocals. Still to show signs of the major songwriting talent he became, Ray Davies undoubtedly discovered the knack of producing exactly what the youngsters wanted to hear.

Ah, fond memories of the Weston-Super-Mare sea front where I first heard this, watching the bikers play the one arm bandits – I couldn't reach them. **Chris Bohn, Melody Maker, March 1980**

All I Have To Do Is Dream

ARTIST The Everly Brothers RELEASE DATE May 1958 (UK)/April 1958 (US) WRITER Boudleaux Bryant PRODUCER – LABEL London (UK)/Cadence (US) UK CHART PEAK/WEEKS 1/21 US CHART PEAK/WEEKS 1/17

Penned in a quarter of an hour by songwriters Felice and Boudleaux Bryant, *All I Have To Do Is Dream* gave Don and Phil Everly their first transatlantic chart-topper, which has since been covered by artists as diverse as Richard Chamberlain (1963), Glen Campbell and Bobbie Gentry (1970) and Andy Gibb and Victoria Principal (1981). Its companion tune on the single was a song called *Claudette*, written by a then unknown Roy Orbison about his wife.

The first Everlys single to reach Number 1 on both sides of the Atlantic. Dream was composed by the Everlys' regular song writing team: Felice and Boudleaux Bryant. **Roy Carr, NME, February 1976**

All I Wanna Do

ARTIST Sheryl Crow RELEASE DATE November 1994 (UK)/August 1994 (US) WRITER Sheryl Crow, Wyn Cooper, Bill Bottrell, David Baerweld, Kevin Gilbert PRODUCER Bill Bottrell LABEL A&M (UK & US) UK CHART PEAK/WEEKS 4/13 US CHART PEAK/WEEKS 2/33

Sheryl Crow's breakthrough hit, *All I Wanna Do*, was the culmination of years trying to succeed in the rock world. Born in Missouri, with a classical music degree from the state university, Crow moved to Los Angeles in 1986 to pursue a career in pop. Her first break came when she sang backup on Michael Jackson's Bad tour. She finally got a deal with A&M, resulting in her highly praised debut **Tuesday Night Music Club**, from whence this disc came.

This critical darling is poised for a long deserved Top 40 breakthrough with this breezy hand clapper. Crow has a friendly demeanour that adds extra bounce to a sweet instrumental setting of jangly guitars and toe-tapping beats. Live sounding jam is a filling to a day at the beach or speeding down the highway with the top down. **Billboard, 1994**

All Right Now

ARTIST Free RELEASE DATE June 1970 (UK)/August 1970 (US) WRITER Paul Rodgers, Andy Fraser PRODUCER Paul Rodgers, Simon Kirke, Free LABEL Island (UK)/A&M (US) UK CHART PEAK/WEEKS 2/16 US CHART PEAK/WEEKS 4/16

All Right Now is from Free's third album, **Fire And Water**. It's hard to believe, but one of the greatest rock anthems of all time was recorded by a band whose average age was just 20 but which had already taken rock in a new direction with its own personal blend of R&B, blues and bass-heavy boogie. Brilliant, soulful, unforgettable, and deservedly a huge hit on both sides of the Atlantic.

*Yeah, I know it sounds like **Honky Tonk Women**, and its vocalist grunts like he's been listening to too many Motown records, but it's currently Number 1 in England and there's a reason: It's good – good beat, good chorus, good guitar and good melody.* **Ed Ward, Rolling Stone, September 1970**

All Shook Up

ARTIST Elvis Presley RELEASE DATE June 1957 (UK)/April 1957 (US) WRITER Otis Blackwell, Elvis Presley PRODUCER – LABEL HMV Pop (UK)/RCA Victor (US) UK CHART PEAK/WEEKS 1/20 US CHART PEAK/WEEKS 1/30

Elvis's first Number 1 single in Britain, and the first of 17 British Number 1s. Recorded during a two-day session in January 1957 that included secular and gospel material, *All Shook Up*'s swinging, infectious rockabilly delivery established it as the biggest hit of 1957. Elvis received a co-writing credit with Otis Blackwell who had been challenged to write the song by his publisher, Al Stanton, when he entered Blackwell's office shaking a Pepsi.

Must have been a strong competition demoting Too Much, which has made Elvis Presley All Shook Up. **The Alley Cat, NME, June 1957**

All The Young Dudes

ARTIST Mott The Hoople RELEASE DATE August 1972 (UK)/September 1972 (US) WRITER David Bowie PRODUCER – LABEL CBS (UK)/Columbia (US) UK CHART PEAK/WEEKS 3/11 US CHART PEAK/WEEKS 37/11

Penniless and dumped by their record company, things weren't going well for Mott The Hoople in 1972. But the gift of a song to his 'favourite band' by one David Bowie was enough to turn things around. *All The Young Dudes,* written and produced by Bowie, was part pomp, part shimmery pop perfection: an exhortation to the 'glam-rock army' to carry the new sound to the masses. It did just that, catapulting Mott from oblivion to stardom, and enduring as a consummate teen anthem.

Bowie, who is as smart in the studio as he is flamboyant on stage, was employed to help Mott tie up its few loose ends with a much needed commercial boost by supplying them with a brilliantly written single.... **Bud Scoppa, Rolling Stone, December 1972**

All You Need Is Love

ARTIST The Beatles RELEASE DATE July 1967 (UK & US) WRITER John Lennon, Paul McCartney PRODUCER George Martin LABEL Parlophone (UK)/Capitol (US) UK CHART PEAK/WEEKS 2/11 US CHART PEAK/WEEKS 1/11

This was the anthem of 1967's 'Summer of Love'. Lennon & McCartney wrote it during their Maharishi days, when they felt the need to justify their pop star status by creating music that would bring the world together. Not that they weren't sincere, but the flower and drug-laden atmosphere that surrounded The Beatles seemed based on image as well as feeling. It was written for their appearance on *Our World*, the first live global satellite broadcast. Four hundred million viewers watched The Beatles perform it inside Abbey Road, joined by their invited guests, including Mick Jagger and Keith Moon.

The message is love and I hope everyone in the whole world manages to get it. The flip, **Baby You're a Rich Man**, *shows you the kind of wealth that will be yours if you get the message.* **Nick Davies, Melody Maker, July 1967**

Alone

ARTIST Heart RELEASE DATE June 1987 (UK)/May 1987 (US) WRITER B. Steinberg, T. Kelly PRODUCER Ron Nevison LABEL Capitol (UK & US) UK CHART PEAK/WEEKS 3/16 US CHART PEAK/WEEKS 1/21

Although the Wilson sisters were unhappy to sing outside material when they signed for Capital in 1984, they found themselves with two US Number 1 singles, *These Dreams*, and *Alone*, by the team that had already written chart-toppers for Madonna (*Like A Virgin*) and Cyndi Lauper (*True Colours*). Tom Kelly had been singing backing vocals for Survivor when producer Ron Nevison confided he was looking for a ballad to cut with Heart: the song, five years old, came out of his back pocket.

The pleasantly acceptable face of FM from the pleasantly acceptable faces of the Wilson sisters. The sort of thing that we would be able to see on Top Of The Pops. **The Stud Brothers, Melody Maker, May 1987**

Alone Again (Naturally)

ARTIST Gilbert O'Sullivan RELEASE DATE March 1972 (UK)/June 1972 (US) WRITER Raymond O'Sullivan PRODUCER Gordon Mills LABEL Mam (UK & US) UK CHART PEAK/WEEKS 3/12 US CHART PEAK/WEEKS 1/18

Gilbert O'Sullivan had a strange image for a grown man: a sort of giant Bisto kid. He wore short trousers, sleeveless jumpers and a flat cap, but his music was firmly in the crooning tradition. He wrote sentimental ballads. *Alone Again (Naturally)* is a melancholy meditation, chronicling the death of his parents to a piano accompaniment. It was his first American success. He soon discarded the cloth cap for the long curly haired look and a collegiate sweater.

O'Sullivan renders his tale in a Bee Gees/Brogue voice that is as charmingly tinny as a twenties coronet heard on a gramophone. The acoustic guitar breach is mellifluous and succinct and the entire tune comes off spectacularly. **James Isaacs, Rolling Stone, October 1972**

Along Comes Mary

ARTIST The Association RELEASE DATE June 1966 WRITER Tandyn Almer PRODUCER – LABEL Valiant UK CHART PEAK/WEEKS 0/0 US CHART PEAK/WEEKS 7/11

While the Association are known for sentimental ballads, their first release was anything but. Released in the spring of 1966, *Along Comes Mary* was an intense, avant-garde hybrid of folk-rock-jazz, and what was just beginning to be called 'psychedelia'. Its arrangement earned praise from Leonard Bernstein, who, on his ABC-TV special *Inside Pop*, used it to show how sophisticated rock had become. Radio programmers fretted over the lyrics – 'Mary' was marijuana – but the disc made the US Top 10 despite efforts to ban it.

One of America's top groups. **Derek Johnson, NME, March 1967**

Alright

ARTIST Supergrass RELEASE DATE July 1995 WRITER – PRODUCER Sam Williams LABEL Parlophone UK CHART PEAK/WEEKS 2/10 US CHART PEAK/WEEKS –

It took two goes for Supergrass to make it – their first manifestation as the Jennifers produced a single *Just Got Back Today* on Suede's label Nude Records, but they didn't crack it until they signed to EMI via fellow Oxford-based band Radiohead's management in 1994. *Alright* rode on the back of press glory, the release of their UK Number 3 album **I Should Coco**, a triumphant Glastonbury appearance and a Monkees-style video.

Three happy-go-lucky pranksters who spend their lives ambling mindlessly through an episode of the Banana Splits *… Alright gives much the same impression. The knockabout melody line and infectiously upbeat lyric makes you think of a Smurf's stag night …* **Ian Watson, Melody Maker, February 1996**

Always On My Mind

ARTIST Willie Nelson RELEASE DATE July 1982 (UK)/March 1982 (US) WRITER Johnny Christopher, Wayne Thompson, Mark James PRODUCER Chips Moman LABEL CBS (UK)/Columbia (US) UK CHART PEAK/WEEKS 49/3 US CHART PEAK/WEEKS 5/23

Willie Nelson's music was Texan Country, with a honky tonk swing, and his voice was bottom-of-the-class hoarse. He made his name with bittersweet ballads, which were sparse and intense, often just Willie husking out over his acoustic guitar. In the Seventies he took control of his own record career and established himself as a Country superstar, with a cowboy mythology to match. *Always On My Mind* is sung in a drifting, laid-back style, the regret elaborated by the strumming chords.

Willie Nelson is now beginning to sound like some country DJ: he's startlingly insincere, faking emotions instead of feeling them. Always On My Mind is a strictly paint-by-numbers product. **Paul Nelson, Rolling Stone, May 1982**

Amazing Grace

ARTIST Royal Scots Dragoon Guards RELEASE DATE April 1972 (UK)/May 1972 (US) WRITER John Newton PRODUCER – LABEL RCA (UK)/RCA Victor (US) UK CHART PEAK/WEEKS 1/24 US CHART PEAK/WEEKS 11/9

Tucked away on **Every Picture Tells A Story,** the monster hit album which in 1971 launched Rod Stewart's solo career after he left The Faces, was the track *Amazing Grace*. While Rod was enjoying both the album and the single *Maggie May* going to Number 1 in the UK and US charts simultaneously, the band of The Royal Scots Dragoon Guards were on their way to celebrating a hit single; their plaintive bagpipe version of *Amazing Grace* hit Number 1 in April 1972.

The thought of some hairy-legged, be-kilted Scotsman blowing down the pipes may not exactly turn you on, but it's certainly sent a large number of Joe Public scurrying to their record shops with 49p. **Julie Webb, NME, April 1972**

American Pie (Parts 1 & 2)

ARTIST Don McLean RELEASE DATE January 1972 (UK)/November 1971 (US) WRITER Don McLean PRODUCER Ed Freeman LABEL United Artists (UK & US) UK CHART PEAK/WEEKS 2/16 US CHART PEAK/WEEKS 1/19

Don McLean was a folk singer, who sang about ecological purity and American history. He was the state sponsored 'Hudson River Troubadour' and travelled up and down the water, giving impromptu concerts. His single *American Pie*, an eight minute, thirty-six second chronicle of American pop music, was imbued with a sense of history and nostalgia. Inspired by the aeroplane deaths of Buddy Holly and Richie Valens, it was a graceful elegy to 'the day the music died'.

When this record first came out I didn't think it was going to be a big hit. Maybe it is one that you have to hear a few times. **Eve Graham, Melody Maker, January 1972**

Amoureuse

ARTIST Kiki Dee RELEASE DATE November 1973 (UK)/July 1976 (US) WRITER Veronique Sanson, Gary Osbourne PRODUCER Clive Franks, Elton John LABEL Rocket (UK & US) UK CHART PEAK/WEEKS 13/13 US CHART PEAK/WEEKS 1/20

Kiki Dee had been making records since the Sixties, but her career didn't get going until Elton John signed her to his Rocket label. *Amoureuse* was not her biggest hit, but certainly a turntable one, charting in 1973 and again three years later. Her powerful voice was equally comfortable in soul and rock grooves. It would be no surprise if she were rediscovered once more.

One of the nicest records of the week. Kiki is one of those ladies whose vocal talents have been hidden for ages behind that off-putting TV producer's image of a girl singer: you know, immaculate make-up, discreetly sexy dress. **Rob Mackie, Sounds, September 1973**

Anarchy In The UK

ARTIST The Sex Pistols RELEASE DATE December 1976 WRITER Steve Jones, Paul Cook, Johnny Rotten, Glen Matlock PRODUCER Chris Thomas, Bill Price LABEL EMI UK CHART PEAK/WEEKS 38/4 US CHART PEAK/WEEKS –

The Pistols made their first appearance on UK TV performing *Anarchy,* their sneeringly scabrous debut release, on the music programme *So It Goes*. Shortly afterwards they ensured national notoriety for themselves with their famous appearance on Bill Grundy's chat show. EMI, under pressure from the media, were forced to withdraw the single, which by then had sold some 50,000 copies in the UK and reached the Top 40. Producer Chris Thomas found the tempo of the single – slower than most punk records – menacing, and Rotten's vocal 'chilling'.

In an attempt to perpetrate McLarenism, rather than tell the truth, the whole truth, and nothing but, the press release starts: 'recognizing a good rip off when they see one…'. **Melody Maker, December 1980**

And I Love You So

ARTIST Perry Como RELEASE DATE April 1973 (UK & US) WRITER Don McLean PRODUCER – LABEL Arca (UK & US) UK CHART PEAK/WEEKS 3/31 US CHART PEAK/WEEKS 29/16

The cardigan-sweater man made a surprise comeback in 1973 with this recording of a song by Don McLean. Perry Como's version of **And I Love You So,** which was originally a minor hit for Bobby Goldsboro of **Honey** fame, made a respectable Number 29 in the USA. In the UK, however, it was a much bigger smash, adding a different flavour to a Top 20 filled with glitter and glam.

Angel Eyes

ARTIST Wet Wet Wet **RELEASE DATE** December 1987 **WRITER** Tom Cunningham, Neil Mitchell, Marti Pellow, Graham Clark **PRODUCER** Michael Baker, Axel Kroll **LABEL** Precious Jewel **UK CHART PEAK/WEEKS** 5/12 **US CHART PEAK/WEEKS** 0/0

Taken from the Wets' Number 1 debut album **Popped In Souled Out**, *Angel Eyes* gave the Scots a first taste of the singles Top 5, which they followed up with a Number 1 three months later in the shape of **With A Little Help from My Friends**. *Angel Eyes* was an original, although Squeeze claimed that it used lyrics from their *Heartbreaking World* – an out-of-court settlement was made.

A dire few minutes of empty soul and a lesson in state-of-the-art blandness: this is soggy, soggy, soggy. Yuk! **Neil Perry, Sounds, November 1987**

Angie

ARTIST The Rolling Stones **RELEASE DATE** September 1973 (UK & US) **WRITER** Keith Richard/Mick Jagger **PRODUCER** Jimmy Miller **LABEL** Rolling Stones (UK & US) **UK CHART PEAK/WEEKS** 5/10 **US CHART PEAK/WEEKS** 1/19

Angie, an aching tender ballad of love on the rocks, was similar to earlier Stones singles releases such as **Ruby Tuesday** and **Lady Jane** – less of the Southern blues-rock idiom than something that might be more at home in St John's Wood. Much to the surprise of many critics, **Angie** shot to the top of the US charts and reached Number 5 in the UK.

*It is my considered opinion that **Angie** is one of the best vocal performances from Mick Jagger on record. Imbued with expression and emotion, he puts heart and soul into this laid-back ballad, giving the lyrics full attention.* **Chris Welch, Melody Maker, August 1973**

Angie Baby

ARTIST Helen Reddy **RELEASE DATE** January 1975 (UK)/October 1974 (US) **WRITER** Alan O'Day **PRODUCER** Joe Wissert **LABEL** Capitol (UK & US) **UK CHART PEAK/WEEKS** 5/10 **US CHART PEAK/WEEKS** 1/17

The Beatles' **Lady Madonna** inspired Alan O'Day to write **Angie Baby**. 'I thought, I'm going to write a song about somebody who's growing up with the radio playing in the background of their life,' he said later. The truth behind Angie's mysterious visitor in the song remains cryptic, but it caught the public imagination at a time when women were beginning to question their roles and identities. It was first offered to Cher, but she rejected it. It reached US Number 1 with Helen Reddy, who made it her own.

*From her upcoming album, we have **Angie Baby**: a strange, compelling tale of an introspective slip of a lass and her relationship with her transistor radio, garnished with brooding electric piano and Helen's own timbre.* **Nick Went, NME, January 1975**

Annie's Song

ARTIST John Denver **RELEASE DATE** August 1974 (UK)/June 1974 (US) **WRITER** John Denver **PRODUCER** Milton Okun **LABEL** RCA (UK) RCA Victor (US) **UK CHART PEAK/WEEKS** 1/13 **US CHART PEAK/WEEKS** 1/17

Although John Denver had many hit albums in Britain, the unabashedly romantic *Annie's Song* was his only Top 40 single. It not only hit Number 1 for him, but also hit Number 3 in a 1978 version by Irish flautist James Galway. According to legend, Denver wrote the paean to his wife Ann in 10 minutes, while riding a ski lift. The song helped heal a temporary rift in their marriage, but they divorced 10 years later.

Usual wallpaper music from one of the most innocuous of artists. Another dab of the cream-puff. One of those kinda songs about which you say 'that's OK, that's nice' and leave it at that. **Jeff Ward, Melody Maker, July 1974**

Another Brick In The Wall

ARTIST Pink Floyd **RELEASE DATE** December 1979 (UK)/January 1980 (US) **WRITER** Roger Waters **PRODUCER** Bob Ezrin, Pink Floyd **LABEL** Harvest (UK)/Columbia (US) **UK CHART PEAK/WEEKS** 1/12 **US CHART PEAK/WEEKS** 1/25

Pink Floyd not only survived the early loss of their singer, lead guitarist and songwriter Syd Barrett, they also prospered. Through the Seventies the Floyd built up a formidable reputation as an albums band, especially for the much fêted **Dark Side Of The Moon**. Its dark anthemic chorus hooked deep into the psyche of the record-buying public. It became a massive hit, Floyd's first single success since 1967's **See Emily Play**.

Floyd characteristics are there: ominous guitar/keyboard themes, this time fired by a scratchy guitar figure, sardonic peoples' voices singing and a smooth homogenized production – all effectively streamlined, in keeping with the times. **Chris Bohn, Melody Maker, November 1979**

Animal Nitrate

ARTIST Suede **RELEASE DATE** March 1993 **WRITER** Brett Anderson, Bernard Butler **PRODUCER** Ed Butler **LABEL** Nude **UK CHART PEAK/WEEKS** 7/7 **US CHART PEAK/WEEKS** 0/0

1992 had been Suede's breakthrough, landing a Melody Maker cover before releasing a single track and cracking the UK Top 20 with **Metal Mickey**. By the time of *Animal Nitrate* they had learnt how to stir up a bit of controversy: the single's title was a pun on amyl nitrate and the video featured men kissing. At the 1993 Brit Awards Suede performed *Animal Nitrate* and caused a furore when Brett Anderson whipped himself on the derrière with the microphone.

Oh how underwhelmed and irritated I was at first … Let me admit I've been howling along to it and thinking all the while how strange it is to play something for the first time and know gut-certain how glitteringly important it is. **Jennifer Nive, Melody Maker, February 1993**

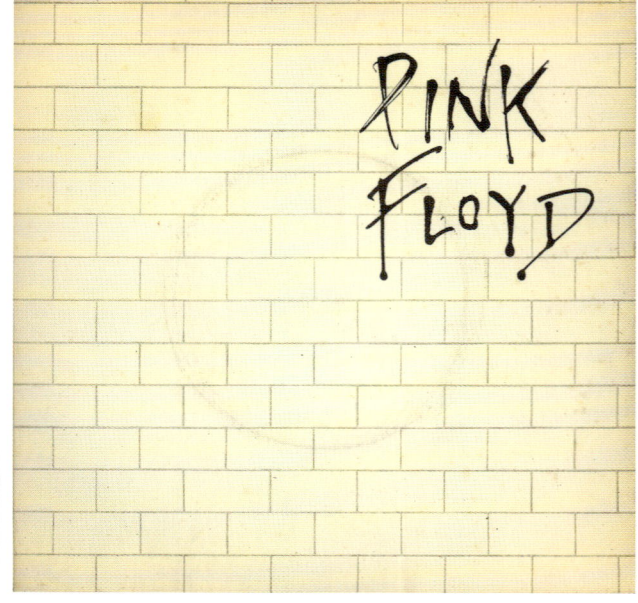

Any Dream Will Do

ARTIST Jason Donovan **RELEASE DATE** June 1991 **WRITER** Andrew Lloyd Webber, Tim Rice **PRODUCER** Nigel Wright **LABEL** Really Useful **UK CHART PEAK/WEEKS** 1/12 **US CHART PEAK/WEEKS** –

The first fruits of the Tim Rice and Andrew Lloyd Webber partnership was a 15-minute musical work entitled *Joseph And The Amazing Technicolor Dreamcoat* written for an end of term school concert in the late Sixties. It included two highlights, **Any Dream Will Do** and **Close Every Door**, and the duo later developed it into a full-scale musical but set it aside to concentrate on the biblical rock opera *Jesus Christ Superstar*. *Joseph* would eventually be revived, and when Australian soap star Jason Donovan took the lead role its West End success, however belated, was assured.

While Kylie went cred, Jason has gone cabaret – a kind of Tom Jones without the raunch. However, it is difficult to imagine the mums lining up outside the Palladium … throwing knickers at him, or the eight year old kids for that matter…. **Lucy O'Brien, Vox, October 1993**

Anyone Who Had A Heart

ARTIST Cilla Black **RELEASE DATE** February 1964 **WRITER** Hal David, Burt Bacharach **PRODUCER** George Martin **LABEL** Parlophone **UK CHART PEAK/WEEKS** 1/17 **US CHART PEAK/WEEKS** 0/0

The former Priscilla White became one of the biggest stars on Brian Epstein's formidable management roster with her version of the US hit that Bacharach and David penned for Dionne Warwick, **Anyone Who Had A Heart**. Her first Number 1, it sold over 900,000 copies, making it one of the all-time best-selling UK singles by a solo female artist. It was also the first Number 1 by a solo female artist since Helen Shapiro's **Walking Back To Happiness** in 1961.

*Cilla Black will become a star with **Anyone Who Had A Heart** – if she hasn't already made enough impact on the record buying public with her unaffected manner and down-to-earth temperament.* **Chris Roberts, Melody Maker, February 1964**

Apache

ARTIST The Shadows **RELEASE DATE** July 1960 **WRITER** Jorgen Longmann **PRODUCER** – **LABEL** Columbia **UK CHART PEAK/WEEKS** 1/21 **US CHART PEAK/WEEKS** –

Cliff Richard's backing band met **Apache's** composer, Jerry Lordan, when they appeared on the same bill during a 1960 tour of the UK. Lordan performed the number – already recorded but not released by guitarist Bert Weedon – on his ukulele and the Shadows re-

worked it to feature Hank Marvin's guitar, along with Cliff on bongos. Their first Number 1, deposing the boss's **Please Don't Tease** from the top, it was voted NME's Record Of The Year.

Apache *is the official A side, but for my money* **Quarter Master's Stories** *is much better –* **Apache** *goes on and on, a repetitive rock instrumental. Both numbers will be good for Juke Boxes and jiving, but neither will be very good for listening to at home.* **Keith Fordyce, NME, June 1960**

April Love

ARTIST Pat Boone **RELEASE DATE** December 1957 (UK)/October 1957 (US) **WRITER** Paul Francis Webster, Sammy Fain **PRODUCER** – **LABEL** London (UK)/Dot (US) **UK CHART PEAK/WEEKS** 7/23 **US CHART PEAK/WEEKS** 1/26

Pat Boone's fifth and last US Number 1 was **April Love,** the theme from the film of the same name, in which Boone starred. Although his character had an attractive romantic interest in the form of Shirley Jones, he refused to do any kissing scenes for fear of upsetting his wife.

The song is excellent, the melody appealing and distinctive. Pat Boone is at his best. I'll stake my reputation on this being a very big hit, without any reservations whatsoever. In other words this is a RAVE for Pat's latest on the London-American. **Keith Fordyce, NME, November 1957**

Aquarius

ARTIST The Fifth Dimension **RELEASE DATE** April 1969 (UK)/March 1969 (US) **WRITER** Gerome Ragni, James Rado, Galt MacDermot **PRODUCER** Dayton Bones-Howe **LABEL** Liberty (UK)/Soul City (US) **UK CHART PEAK/WEEKS** 11/12 **US CHART PEAK/WEEKS** 1/17

By merging two show-stopping numbers from the hippy musical *Hair* at the suggestion of their producer Bones-Howe, black soul vocal quartet the Fifth Dimension found themselves a major pop hit. It was edited down twice, from seven to five and finally three minutes, but the good-time feel of the track recorded in Los Angeles (instrumental) and Las Vegas (where the group added their vocals between live engagements) proved a smash hit from coast to coast and the year's second best-selling US single.

*We got **Aquarius** through one of those weird lucky accidents. The true story is that Billy lost his wallet in New York. It was found in a taxi, by Ed Gifford, one of the New York producers of Hair … We liked the songs and that was that.* **Marylin McCoo interviewed by Leonard Feather, Melody Maker, October 1969**

Are 'Friends' Electric

ARTIST Gary Numan And The Tubeway Army RELEASE DATE May 1979 WRITER Gary Numan PRODUCER – LABEL Beggars Banquet UK CHART PEAK/WEEKS 1/16 US CHART PEAK/WEEKS –

Gary Numan joined the Lasers as a guitarist and rapidly took over the helm of the punk band, who, with a name change to Tubeway Army, were signed to Beggar's Banquet in 1978 and released some suitably aggressive singles. But by the time they started work on an album, the synth had entered Numan's life, and he ditched the guitar completely. The rest of the band quit in disgust and Numan completed *Are 'Friends' Electric* with his uncle on drums.

Tubeway Army sound like Bill Nelson before he learnt to tie his judoka. **Ian Penman, NME, May 1979**

Are You Lonesome Tonight?

ARTIST Elvis Presley RELEASE DATE January 1961 (UK)/November 1960 (US) WRITER Roy Turk, Lou Handman PRODUCER Chet Atkins, Steve Sholes LABEL RCA (UK)/RCA Victor (US) UK CHART PEAK/WEEKS 1/15 US CHART PEAK/WEEKS 1/16

Originally a popular song of the silent movie era and part of Al Jolson's repertoire, *Are You Lonesome Tonight?* was transformed by Elvis into a piece of country Grand Guignol containing one of the most famous heartfelt monologues in pop history, culminating in the lines 'And if you won't come back to me/Then they can pull the curtain down'. In 1982 a live version, featuring Elvis laughing uncontrollably during the monologue, made the Top 40.

He has an extraordinary range for a pop singer, with resonant low tones, and an exciting change of texture in the upper register. There is more 'colour' in his voice than in his … oh-well, not rivals, because he doesn't have any. **Tony Brown, Melody Maker, January 1961**

Arthur's Theme (Best That You Can Do)

ARTIST Christopher Cross RELEASE DATE October 1981 (UK)/August 1981 (US) WRITER Carole Bayer Sager, Burt Bacharach, Christopher Cross, Pete Allen PRODUCER Michael Omartian LABEL Warner Bros. (UK)/Warner (US) UK CHART PEAK/WEEKS 7/15 US CHART PEAK/WEEKS 1/24

Christopher Cross earned his longest running US Number 1 with *Arthur's Theme*, from the movie that starred Dudley Moore and Liza Minnelli. *Arthur's Theme*, which won the 1981 Oscar for Best Song, was a flop when originally released in the UK in October 1981. It re-charted a few months later, after the film opened, and hit the Top 10.

The man is a genius. He makes a sound so septic that you could melt it down and make antiseptic, and it isn't rock music! And he has no scruples whatsoever! and I can be part of it! Without having to think. **Dave McCullough, Sounds, December 1981**

As Long As He Needs Me

ARTIST Shirley Bassey RELEASE DATE August 1960 WRITER Lionel Bart PRODUCER – LABEL Columbia UK CHART PEAK/WEEKS 2/30 US CHART PEAK/WEEKS –

Shirley Bassey enjoyed two Number 1s in the Sixties, but her biggest-selling hit was one that just missed the top spot: *As Long As He Needs Me*. The Cardiff-born singer's rendition of the song from the West End musical *Oliver* spent a total of 30 weeks in the charts. Although she enjoyed 12 Top 10 hits in the UK, her only song to go Top 10 in the US – the theme from *Goldfinger* – was not one of them.

It's high time we saw the name of Shirley Bassey on the hit parade. This song is a big ballad, slow and powerful, a perfect showcase for Shirley's terrific vocal impact. **Keith Fordyce, NME, July 1960**

Ashes To Ashes

ARTIST David Bowie RELEASE DATE August 1980 (UK & US) WRITER David Bowie PRODUCER David Bowie, Tony Visconte LABEL RCA (UK)/RCA Victor (US) UK CHART PEAK/WEEKS 1/10 US CHART PEAK/WEEKS 0/0

David Bowie's second Number 1 was a narrative sequel to his first. His previous chart-topper was the 1975 reissue of his 1969 single *Space Oddity*. Five years later, he continued the saga with *Ashes to Ashes*, although the song bore little similarity to *Space Oddity* other than its protagonist being Major Tom. It was the first single from his forthcoming album, **Scary Monsters**, which also hit Number 1.

Bowie doesn't make records, he paints sound pictures. On his latest effort the canvas is covered with a total entity – no parts or hooks leap out and bury themselves into your cranium, but the total sound is hypnotic and makes for compulsive listening. **Martyn Sutton, Melody Maker, August 1980**

At Seventeen

**ARTIST Janis Ian RELEASE DATE June 1975 WRITER Janis Ian PRODUCER –
LABEL CBS (UK)/Columbia (US) UK CHART PEAK/WEEKS 0/0 US CHART
PEAK/WEEKS 3/20**

A wistful portrait of the loneliness and insecurity experienced by
the less-than-perfect teenager in a world where looks and social
skills are everything, *At Seventeen* was an excellent example of
the singer-songwriter's art which enjoyed sustained success in the
first half of the Seventies. Amazingly, this delicate and
consummately realized effort failed to chart in the UK, despite a
fair amount of radio exposure, although in America it reached
Number 3 in the opening days of 1976.

At The Hop

**ARTIST Danny And The Juniors RELEASE DATE January 1958 (UK)/December
1957 (US) WRITER A. Singer, J. Medora, D. White PRODUCER – LABEL HMV Pop
(UK)/ABC Paramount (US) UK CHART PEAK/WEEKS 3/19 US CHART
PEAK/WEEKS 1/21**

Danny And The Juniors hailed from Philadelphia, home of
Dick Clark's hugely popular TV show *American Bandstand*. A
local independent label owner asked Clark's opinion of a
recording by them about a local dance craze: *Do the Bop*. 'Why
not make it 'At the Hop'?' he replied. His advice was ignored,
and *Do the Bop* flopped. Clark asked the group to perform it
again, but as *At the Hop*, on *Bandstand*. They did, ABC Records

was watching, and, within weeks, the song was Number 1 in
the nation.

*Probably the most interesting of the newcomers…. They went to Art
Singer for an audition, he liked what he heard and combined with them
to write* **At The Hop,** *which he recorded on his small independent label.*
Derek Johnson, NME, January 1959

Autobahn

**ARTIST Kraftwerk RELEASE DATE May 1975 (UK)/March 1975 (US) WRITER
Florin Elseden-Schneider, Ralf Hutter, Emil Schult PRODUCER Kraftwerk
LABEL Vertigo (UK & US) UK CHART PEAK/WEEKS 11/9 US CHART
PEAK/WEEKS 25/10**

The likes of Gary Numan, Ultravox and the Human League
were undoubtedly influenced by this single which took
synthesizers into the singles charts in early 1975. An edited
down version of an album title track, it still managed to convey
the synth-produced sounds of a German motorway (Autobahn)
journey. Its transatlantic chart placings opened the doors to
the coming electro-pop wave whose bands unanimously
declared their debt to the band led by Ralf Hutter and Florian
Schneider.

*Odd noises from percussion and synthesizer drift out from the
speakers without any comprehensible order while a few words are
muttered from time to time in strange tongue.* **Colin Irwin, Melody
Maker, May 1975**

Automatic

ARTIST The Pointer Sisters RELEASE DATE April 1984 (UK)/January 1984 (US) WRITER Brock Walsh, Mark Goldenberg PRODUCER Richard Perry LABEL Planet (UK & US) UK CHART PEAK/WEEKS 2/15 US CHART PEAK/WEEKS 5/20

Automatic was a sensual and passionate dance track from The Pointer Sisters. It used synthesizers to build up a steady, hearty beat, and the vocal style was sexy and mature. They were originally a Californian family group of close harmony scat singers, but by the mid-Seventies they had ditched the Forties nostalgia and the retro clothes for a witty, seductive image, and smooth rock-tinged pop. Their pre-disco dance sound and their tough, sparky lyrics were hard hitting and inspirational.

The Pointer Sisters are adequately described by their title. **Charles Shaar Murray, NME, April 1984**

Avalon

ARTIST Roxy Music RELEASE DATE June 1982 (UK & US) WRITER Bryan Ferry PRODUCER Rhett Davies, Roxy Music LABEL EG Roxy (UK)/Atco (US) UK CHART PEAK/WEEKS 13/6 US CHART PEAK/WEEKS 0/0

Roxy Music's final studio album, **Avalon,** topped the UK charts for three weeks. The title track, more perhaps than any other Roxy song, epitomizes the stylish, elegant, decadent feel of their later work. Written and sung by Bryan Ferry, *Avalon* has a fin de siècle quality, exquisitely textured by Phil Manzanera's guitar work and Andy Mackay's moody sax. Roxy were a peculiarly British phenomenon and never achieved a Top 20 hit in the US.

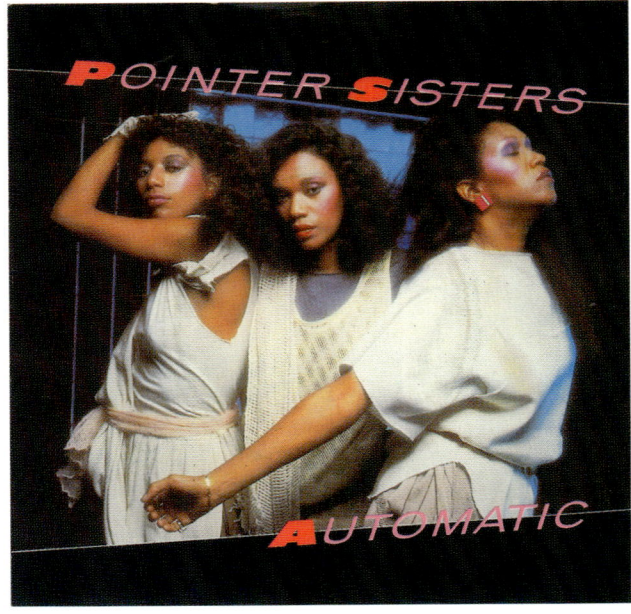

Babe

ARTIST Styx RELEASE DATE January 1980 (UK)/October 1979 (US) WRITER Dennis DeYoung PRODUCER Styx LABEL A&M (UK & US) UK CHART PEAK/WEEKS 6/10 US CHART PEAK/WEEKS 1/19

To many critics' horror, Styx were the most popular rock band amongst 13 to 18-year-old Americans in 1979. The Chicago pomp rock quintet, based around keyboard player Dennis DeYoung and lead guitar Tommy Shaw's falsetto yelping, was variously described as 'dire' or 'unlistenable'. *Babe* was a DeYoung power ballad that became their all-time best-selling release.

I started to hear **Babe** *on the radio and much to my surprise, after at first switching off, discovered that, bar the odd cringe, I could hum it. Later I could only manage the occasional wince, and after a while I actually found myself liking it.* **Geoff Barton, Sounds, February 1980**

Babe

ARTIST Take That RELEASE DATE December 1993 WRITER Gary Barlow PRODUCER Steve Vervier LABEL RCA UK CHART PEAK/WEEKS 1/10 US CHART PEAK/WEEKS –

The third Number 1 for Take That in five months, *Babe* was a chance for little Mark Owen to take centre stage on lead vocals with this tale of fatherhood. Owen was nervous, but the fragility and sincerity of his voice made it even more touching for their fans. It would have been the Christmas Number 1 by a mile, except for – as Gary Barlow was heard to mutter – 'Mr Bloody Blobby'.

I am not, Voodoo-Queen-like, jealous of Take That because they are prettier than me. Far from it. **Pray** *boasted a fantastic chorus and, besides, I am jealous because they are younger and richer than me.* **Babe***, however, is mush.* **Chris Roberts, Melody Maker, December 1993**

Babe I Love Your Way

ARTIST Peter Frampton RELEASE DATE September 1976 (UK)/June 1976 (US) WRITER Peter Frampton PRODUCER Peter Frampton LABEL A&M (UK & US) UK CHART PEAK/WEEKS 43/5 US CHART PEAK/WEEKS 12/16

The 'Face of '68' (as frontman of popsters the Herd) was still looking for solo stardom in 1976, but four polite studio albums and a lot of US touring paid off when his double album, **Comes Alive**, took off. This, the second single, became a soft-rock classic, but stalled in Britain outside the Top 40, though later covered in white reggae style by Big Mountain it got to Number 2. Frampton, who had fallen from commercial grace, doubtless appreciated the royalties.

Even though Frampton is grossing millions in the US, he has not done it over here, and if A&M keep saturating us with this dull middle-of-the-road rock, will he ever? **Caroline Coon, Melody Maker, October 1976**

Baby Come To Me

ARTIST Pattie Austin And James Ingram RELEASE DATE February 1983 (UK)/April 1982 (US) WRITER Rod Temperton PRODUCER Quincy Jones LABEL Quest (UK & US) UK CHART PEAK/WEEKS 11/10 US CHART PEAK/WEEKS 1/32

Patti Austin and James Ingram's **Baby Come to Me** was a flop on its first release, stalling at Number 73 on Billboard's Hot 100 in May 1982. Six months later, it returned to life after being featured on the popular US soap opera *General Hospital*. Even so, it faced an uphill climb, but finally made Number 1 in February after 18 weeks on the Hot 100. It was the first Number 1 for the 34-year-old Austin, the god-daughter of Dinah Washington.

Baby Got Back

ARTIST Sir Mix-A-Lot RELEASE DATE August 1992 (UK)/April 1992 (US) WRITER Sir Mix-A-Lot PRODUCER Sir Mix-A-Lot LABEL Def America (UK & US) UK CHART PEAK/WEEKS 56/2 US CHART PEAK/WEEKS 1/28

Though a Seattle native, Sir Mix-A-Lot is aligned with the Miami Bass sound of acts like 2 Live Crew. His 1992 album, **Mack Daddy**, had the requisite funky groove, and showed off the aggression of his rapping, but was laced with some wit. **Baby Got Back**, a lusty tribute to women with large backsides, got him into PC trouble, but he said he was really having a go at stick-thin supermodels and the abnormal ideals of beauty they represented....

Baby I Need Your Lovin'

ARTIST The Four Tops RELEASE DATE August 1964 WRITER – PRODUCER Lamont Dozier, Brian Holland LABEL Motown UK CHART PEAK/WEEKS – US CHART PEAK/WEEKS 11/12

Originally known as the Four Aims, the Detroit group formed in 1953 and learnt their trade touring with Billy Eckstine. They initially signed with Columbia, but had no chart success. In 1964 they signed with the new Tamla-Motown label: Berry Gordy asked songwriters Holland, Dozier and Holland to write for them and their first song met with instant success. **Baby I Need Your Lovin'** reached Number 11 in the US and was the first of a string of chart entries.

If you've got a winning formula, stick to it and you won't go far wrong – that seems to be the policy adopted by The Four Tops. **Derek Johnson, NME, January 1967**

Baby I'm-A Want You

ARTIST Bread RELEASE DATE January 1972 (UK)/October 1971 (US) WRITER David Gates PRODUCER David Gates LABEL Elektra (UK & US) UK CHART PEAK/WEEKS 14/10 US CHART PEAK/WEEKS 3/12

By the summer of 1971, Bread founder member Robb Royer had left to try his luck as a screenwriter in Hollywood. As a replacement the group recruited Larry Knechtel, a move widely regarded as a major coup since Knechtel was a highly regarded, multi-talented session musician who'd most memorably been the pianist at the heart of Simon & Garfunkel's *Bridge Over Troubled Water*. The new line-up's first recording sessions included *Baby I'm-A Want You*, which continued Bread's soft-rock chart success and maintained their trademark sound – an effortlessly laid-back ballad, full of major sevenths and showcasing David Gates' wistful, near falsetto, vocals.

And that is the right title. A beautiful song arranged and produced by Gates. Very romantic, if you have those kind of tendencies, and pure, and the kind of track that may produce a little peace of mind. **Penny Valentine, Sounds, November 1971**

Baby Love

ARTIST The Supremes RELEASE DATE October 1964 (UK & US) WRITER Edward Holland, Brian Holland, Lamont Dozier PRODUCER Lamont Dozier, Brian Holland LABEL Stateside (UK)/Motown (US) UK CHART PEAK/WEEKS 1/15 US CHART PEAK/WEEKS 1/13

This infectious Holland-Dozier-Holland song was Diana Ross – now singing lead – and company's follow-up to *Where Did Our Love Go*, and their only transatlantic Number 1. It also earned a place in the discographer's annals by being the first US Number 1

by an all female act, and the last by an all American female act until the Bangles' *Eternal Flame*.

Our singing is for night-clubs, but we enjoy doing a lot of different things. Everything we do on stage, including our movements, are all very carefully worked out beforehand. **Mary Wilson, Melody Maker, October 1964**

Back For Good

ARTIST Take That RELEASE DATE April 1995 (UK)/August 1995 (US) WRITER Gary Barlow PRODUCER Chris Porter, Gary Barlow LABEL RCA (UK)/Arista (US) UK CHART PEAK/WEEKS 1/13 US CHART PEAK/WEEKS 7/30

Premiered at the 1995 Brits and on Radio 1, Take That's new single racked up 300,000 sales in the first week of its release, the highest tally for 10 years. This was the sixth in their total of eight Number 1s and charted in the US Top 10 for the first time. Gary Barlow said it took him 15 minutes to write – and that was with a coffee break!

… the slow TT are unimaginative white boys ripping off slightly less unimaginative black boys with love, respect, attention to detail and the complicity of a reflexively racist music industry. **Jennifer Nine, Melody Maker, April 1995**

Back To Life (However Do You Want Me)

ARTIST Soul II Soul featuring Caron Wheeler RELEASE DATE June 1989 (UK)/September 1989 (US) WRITER P. Hooper, S. Law, B. Romeo, Caron Wheeler PRODUCER Nellee Hooper, Jazzy B LABEL 10 Ten (UK)/Virgin (US) UK CHART PEAK/WEEKS 1/14 US CHART PEAK/WEEKS 4/28

Caron Wheeler featured on Soul II Soul's breakthrough single **Keep On Movin'** in 1989, fronting the mobile sound system from north London that evolved organically into a musical collective, fashion label and way of life. The added value on their best songs always came from the additional singers: Wheeler, Victoria Wilson-James and Kym Mazelle. **Back To Life** got a Grammy for best R&B group performance, and established Jazzie B and Nellee Hooper as hot producers – for **Nothing Compares 2 U** and beyond.

The word irresistible doesn't do justice to the masterful combo of Caron Wheeler's soulful vocal bravado and Jazzie B's evocation of vintage Barry White with tender strings and a sultry rhythm. **Rolling Stone, December 1989**

Bad

ARTIST Michael Jackson RELEASE DATE September 1987 (UK & US) WRITER Michael Jackson PRODUCER Quincy Jones, Michael Jackson LABEL Epic (UK & US) UK CHART PEAK/WEEKS 3/11 US CHART PEAK/WEEKS 1/14

The title track of Michael Jackson's fifth album – and, more importantly, the follow-up to the record-breaking **Thriller** – was eagerly awaited as the summer of 1987 drew to a close. Five years had passed since its predecessor, and Jacko was once again aided by producer Quincy Jones. The video told the story of a student trying to avoid the clutches of a neighbourhood gang and was aired the day of the album's release.

Here's Jackson, the man who descended to Earth, determined to erase the borders of race and gender in his own person: an alien by alteration. He's a phenomenon too large, too placeless to retain any content. All there is is intensity.... **Paul Oldfield, Melody Maker, September 1987**

Bad Bad Leroy Brown

ARTIST Jim Croce RELEASE DATE April 1973 WRITER Jim Croce PRODUCER Tommy West, Terry Cashman LABEL ABC UK CHART PEAK/WEEKS – US CHART PEAK/WEEKS 1/22

Jim Croce's first US Number 1 was inspired by a frightening soldier he met while stationed with the army. He also had a genuine fear of junkyard dogs, having evaded many during his starving-artist years. His producers initially wanted to take out the 'junkyard dog' line, because they thought nobody would understand what it meant, but they wisely changed their minds. They did, however, come up with the piano intro, which they lifted from Bobby Darin's **Queen Of The Hop**.

A panoramic view of Croce's fantasy vision of the underside of society.... Jim Croce is the most blatantly commercial of the newest crop of folk singers, although in his case that is more compliment than criticism. **Jon Landau, Rolling Stone, April 1973**

Bad Moon Rising

ARTIST Creedence Clearwater Revival RELEASE DATE August 1969 (UK)/May 1969 (US) WRITER John Fogerty PRODUCER John Fogerty LABEL Liberty (UK)/Fantasy (US) UK CHART PEAK/WEEKS 1/15 US CHART PEAK/WEEKS 2/14

Bad Moon Rising, Creedence Clearwater Revival's follow-up to **Proud Mary**, likewise sold over two million copies and reached Number 2 on *Billboard*'s Hot 100. In England, it became the group's only Number 1, an irony considering they never had one in America. Thanks to Fogerty's cryptic delivery of the line, 'There's a bad moon on the rise', the song became one of rock's most famous cases of misheard lyrics. A surprisingly high percentage of listeners thought he was singing: 'There's a bathroom on the right'.

Tremendous! – a Buddy Holly-type rock beat, with driving and beautifully simple guitars and a well echoed vocal. This will be an enormous hit, and has already sold a million in the States. **Chris Welch, Melody Maker, August 1969**

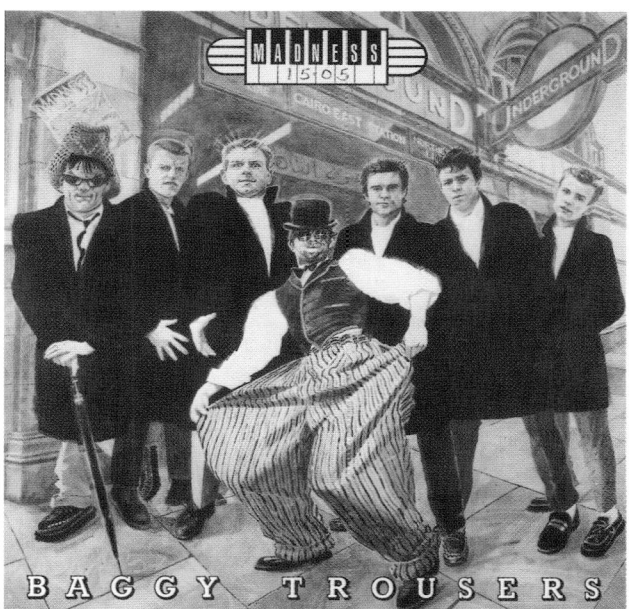

Baggy Trousers

ARTIST Madness RELEASE DATE September 1980 WRITER Graham McPherson, Chris Foreman, Mike Barson PRODUCER Clive Langer, Alan Winstanley LABEL Stiff Boy UK CHART PEAK/WEEKS 3/20 US CHART PEAK/WEEKS –

Madness mixed blue beat ska with their very own 'nutty sound': it featured speeded-up reggae rhythms and a kind of pub piano playing. The songs were witty and charming observational comedies about growing up in London in the Seventies. Suggs was the perfect front man, full of irony and witty sarcasm. His jerky dancing was fine too. Their imaginative videos added to their popularity.

If this be madness, there is method in it, or not. Madness recall schooldays in familiar skanking mode. Not quite my cup of tea chaps, but it will probably get them sand-dancing their way up the charts. **Patrick Humphries, Melody Maker, September 1980**

Baker Street

ARTIST Gerry Rafferty RELEASE DATE February 1978 (UK)/April 1978 (US) WRITER Gerry Rafferty PRODUCER Hugh Murphy, Gerry Rafferty LABEL United Artists (UK & US) UK CHART PEAK/WEEKS 3/15 US CHART PEAK/WEEKS 2/20

A smash hit around the world, *Baker Street* hit Number 1 in the US and peaked at Number 3 in the UK. Featuring a haunting sax hook played by Raf Ravenscroft, Rafferty's engaging love song smoothed its way past the vitriol of punk rock and became one of the few pop tunes that almost everybody can hum. Less well-known is the fact that one of Scots-born Rafferty's early musical collaborators was comedian/actor Billy Connolly, in a group called the Humblebums.

There is inspired use of sax here. Approaching the mix of sleaze and amateurishness that Bowie excels in, it adds the other side to Rafferty's cosy pop romanticism. Thickly textured, and Rafferty's smooth voice comes over strongly. **Ian Birch, Melody Maker, February 1978**

Ballad Of Bonnie And Clyde

ARTIST Georgie Fame RELEASE DATE December 1967 (UK)/February 1968 (US) WRITER Mitch Murray, Pete Callender PRODUCER Mike Smith LABEL CBS (UK)/Columbia (US) UK CHART PEAK/WEEKS 1/13 US CHART PEAK/WEEKS 7/14

The *Ballad Of Bonnie And Clyde* gave keyboardist-vocalist Georgie Fame his third and last UK Number 1 and was his only song to make the US Top 10. The song was inspired by the 1967 film *Bonnie And Clyde*. Fame would later team up with ex-Animal Alan Price and in the Nineties was a mainstay of Van Morrison's band.

This is such a good record, and Georgie sings so well, it must be a hit. Fashionable or not, it's probably Fame's best pure pop single yet, apart from **Sunny**, *produced by Mike Smith and written by Mitch Murray and Peter Callender.* **Chris Welch, Melody Maker, December 1967**

The Ballad Of Davy Crockett

ARTIST Bill Hayes RELEASE DATE January 1956 (UK)/February 1955 (US) WRITER Tom Blackburn, George Bruns PRODUCER – LABEL London (UK)/Cadence (US) UK CHART PEAK/WEEKS 2/9 US CHART PEAK/WEEKS 1/20

This novelty song from TV actor Bill Hayes spent five weeks at the top of the US charts in 1955 and narrowly failed to repeat the achievement in the UK the following year. Telling the story of US frontier folk hero Davy Crockett, it resulted in a mania for all things related to the name (e.g. 'coonskin hats). In the UK, three other versions of the song also made the Top 30 in 1956: Tennessee Ernie Ford's – Number 3, Dick James' – Number 29, and Max Bygraves' – Number 30.

Around six million Davy Crockett records have been sold in America. Of the twenty or so versions that go to make that total, Bill Hayes' version has sold over two million copies there – though, as a recording artist, Hayes meant little until **Crockett** *rocketed him into stardom.* **Don Wedge, NME, January 1956**

The Ballad Of The Green Berets

ARTIST Sgt Barry Sadler RELEASE DATE March 1966 (UK)/February 1966 (US) WRITER Barry Sadler, Robin Moore PRODUCER – LABEL RCA (UK)/RCA Victor (US) UK CHART PEAK/WEEKS 24/8 US CHART PEAK/WEEKS 1/13

There are few more clean-cut Number 1s in the history of pop. Vietnam veteran Sadler created this tribute to his comrades in the Special Forces and the release, originally destined solely for a military audience, was the US's biggest-selling single of 1966. An album of similarly patriotic material also reached US Number 1, but Sadler went AWOL from the charts thereafter. Nancy Ames sang an answer version, *He Wore The Green Beret*, which touched the US Top 100.

It is just propaganda. We do not need stuff like this in the pop charts. **John Lennon, Melody Maker, April 1966**

The Ballroom Blitz

ARTIST Sweet RELEASE DATE September 1973 (UK)/June 1975 (US) WRITER Mike Chapman, Nicky Chinn PRODUCER Phil Wainman LABEL RCA (UK)/Capitol (US) UK CHART PEAK/WEEKS 2/9 US CHART PEAK/WEEKS 5/25

The arrival of Nicky Chinn and Mike Chapman in the career of Sweet revolutionized the band's prospects, with the Chinnichap chaps writing and producing a sequence of songs where bubblegum met heavy metal glam. The hits kept coming from *Funny Funny* through to the first Number 1 *Blockbuster*, and *Ballroom Blitz*. There was a blitzkrieg of a break with Chinn and Chapman in 1974, after which Sweet wrote their own US Top 10 hit, *Fox*, but never regained their former success.

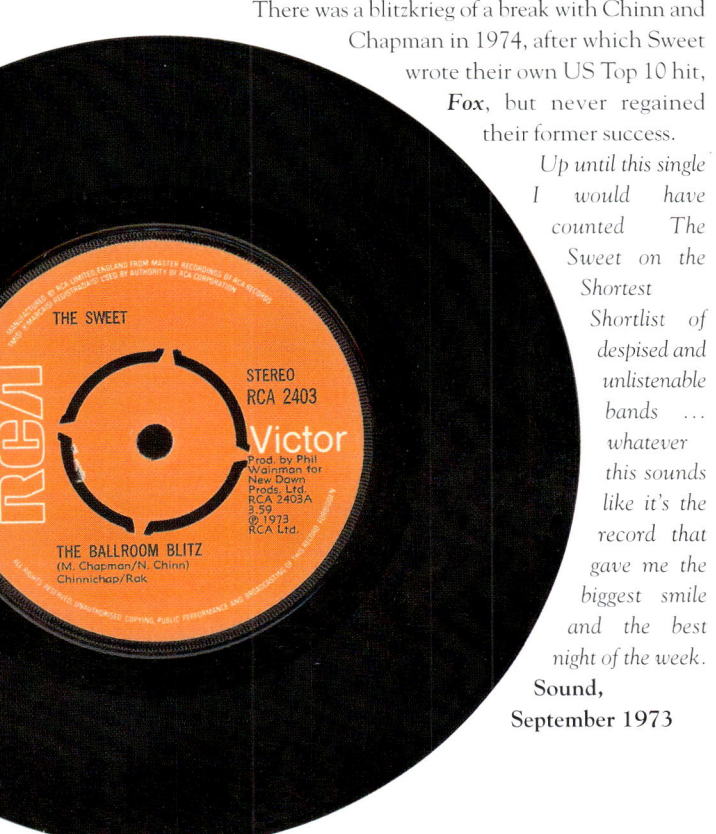

Up until this single I would have counted The Sweet on the Shortest Shortlist of despised and unlistenable bands ... whatever this sounds like it's the record that gave me the biggest smile and the best night of the week. **Sound, September 1973**

Band Of Gold

ARTIST Freda Payne RELEASE DATE September 1979 (UK)/April 1970 (US) WRITER Ronald Dunbar, Edythe Wayne PRODUCER Lamont Dozier, Brian Holland LABEL Invictus (UK & US) UK CHART PEAK/WEEKS 1/19 US CHART PEAK/WEEKS 3/20

Freda Payne was a cabaret and jazz singer before being taken under the wing of the mighty Holland, Dozier, and Holland. They made ephemeral golden music, creating three-minute 'symphonies for the kids', and Freda was given a pop make-over. *Band of Gold* had a driving bass and sparkling tambourines, and Freda's voice cascaded out. Heartbreak had been given the dynamism of gospel and the stomp of R&B, and through it all you could catch the pain in Payne's vocal.

A US chart-topper: it is a fine soul sound, with Holland-Dozier type changes – ideal for your local discotheque! **Chris Welch, Melody Maker, September 1970**

Band On The Run

ARTIST Paul McCartney And Wings RELEASE DATE July 1974 (UK)/April 1974 (US) WRITER Paul and Linda McCartney PRODUCER Paul McCartney LABEL Apple (UK & US) UK CHART PEAK/WEEKS 3/11 US CHART PEAK/WEEKS 1/18

After the release of **Red Rose Speedway** and the single **My Love**, McCartney was being dubbed the world's most talented jingle writer. He hit back at his critics with the album **Band On The Run**, essentially a McCartney solo set. The album threw up some great singles including **Jet** and the title track – a multi-sectioned mini epic.

You hear just about all the things that made Paul McCartney great. It starts soft and low, a beautiful melody introduced by guitar and electronics ... some beautiful, achingly beautiful harmonies. **John Peel, Sounds, July 1974**

The Battle Of New Orleans

ARTIST Johnny Horton RELEASE DATE June 1959 (UK)/April 1959 (US) WRITER Jimmy Driftwood PRODUCER – LABEL Philips (UK)/Columbia (US) UK CHART PEAK/WEEKS 16/4 US CHART PEAK/WEEKS 1/21

Taking his inspiration from an early 19th-century American folk song, **The Eighth Of January**, celebrating the defeat of the British in the last engagement of the War of 1812, teacher Jimmy Driftwood wrote the lyrics to **The Battle Of New Orleans** in 1955. By 1959, however, the song had been picked up by country singer Johnny Horton and would become a US chart-topper and Grammy-winner. Driftwood quit teaching and turned to music full-time.

It is not often that anyone can offer a serious challenge to Lonnie Donegan, but Mr Horton certainly does. Side drums provided a fast marching tempo of the sort that has a stronger appeal for American ears than for our own. **Keith Fordyce, NME, June 1959**

Be-Bop-A-Lula

ARTIST Gene Vincent And The Blue Chips RELEASE DATE July 1956 (UK)/June 1956 (US) WRITER Gene Vincent, Sheriff Tex Davis PRODUCER – LABEL Capitol (UK & US) UK CHART PEAK/WEEKS 16/7 US CHART PEAK/WEEKS 7/20

A Korean War veteran, Gene Vincent, in hospital after a bad motorbike smash, met a marine called Donald Graves, and together they created this song. Graves's writing interest was later bought out for $25. Vincent jammed with WCMS house band The Virginians; *Be-Bop-A-Lula* caught the attention of DJ Tex Davis and eventually the song reached Capitol Records. This was real rock 'n' roll, and so like Elvis that Mrs Presley rang her son to congratulate him on his new hit.

Quite different is the studied affection of Gene Vincent. A newcomer to Capitol who, it seems, is falling over himself to give a faithful impression of Elvis Presley. The emotion in Vincent's renderings of Be-Bop-A-Lula ... seems almost mechanically contrived. **Laurie Henshaw, Melody Maker, July 1956**

Be My Baby

ARTIST The Ronettes RELEASE DATE October 1963 (UK)/August 1963 (US) WRITER Jeff Barry, Ellie Greenwich, Phil Spector PRODUCER Phil Spector LABEL London (UK)/Philles (US) UK CHART PEAK/WEEKS 4/13 US CHART PEAK/WEEKS 2/13

An early and prime example of Phil Spector's 'Wagnerian approach to rock 'n' roll' was the work he produced with The Crystals and The Ronettes. The latter, comprising sisters Veronica (who later married Spector) and Estelle Bennett and their cousin Nedra Talley, had already recorded five singles without success when in 1963 Spector produced the two singles which sold a million each,

Be My Baby and *Baby I Love You*. Brian Wilson of The Beach Boys called *Be My Baby* 'the most perfect pop record of all time'.

'It's all the work of our new record boss, Phil Spector,' said Ronnie. 'He's just a genius. We stand in the middle of a recording studio, in a glass box, like goldfish, and the place is packed with musicians. We just sing what he tells us to.' **Ronnie Bennett interviewed by Ray Coleman, Melody Maker, January 1964**

Beat It

ARTIST Michael Jackson RELEASE DATE April 1983 (UK)/February 1983 (US) WRITER Michael Jackson PRODUCER Michael Jackson, Quincy Jones LABEL Epic (UK & US) UK CHART PEAK/WEEKS 3/12 US CHART PEAK/WEEKS 1/25

Beat It followed *Billie Jean* to the top of the US charts, a one-week residency by Dexy's Midnight Runners with *Come On Eileen* separating the two *Thriller* tracks. One of the first videos to bring Jackson the dancer to the world, *Beat It* – at a cost of $160,000 – included a choreographed sequence which utilized real street gang members and Eddie Van Halen on guitar.

Another track from **Thriller,** *this is a touchingly anti-macho song winningly designed to set off the new slightly more macho Jackson stance as revealed in recent videos and sleeves.* **Charles Shaar Murray, NME, April 1983**

Because The Night

ARTIST The Patti Smith Group RELEASE DATE April 1978 (UK & US) WRITER Patti Smith, Bruce Springsteen PRODUCER Jimmy Levine LABEL Arista (UK & US) UK CHART PEAK/WEEKS 5/12 US CHART PEAK/WEEKS 13/18

Rock 'n' Roll was a religion to Patti Smith, to which she devoted the power of her guitar chords and the fractured eloquence of her

voice. Originally she pursued a literary career, influenced by Rimbaud and Camus, Genet and Dylan. But she turned her poetry into music, creating art-rock, with careening vocals and abrasive guitars. The stand-out track on her **Easter** album was *Because The Night*, an elemental folk song, co-written with Bruce Springsteen; it was also her only international hit.

After six months in a neck brace the lady returns to resuscitate the dead ... The lyrics are simpler, the voice more confident than ever. **Melody Maker, April 1978**

Ben

ARTIST Michael Jackson RELEASE DATE November 1972 (UK)/August 1972 (US) WRITER Walter Scharf, Don Black PRODUCER The Corporation LABEL Tamla Motown (UK)/Motown (US) UK CHART PEAK/WEEKS 7/4 US CHART PEAK/WEEKS 1/16

Jackson's first US chart-topper at the age of 14, *Ben* was written about a young boy's relationship with a rat for the 1972 film of the same name. With the lyrics to *Born Free* already under his belt, Don Black utilized some of the dialogue from the film and the resulting theme was offered to Michael. Ever the animal lover, Jacko had no hesitations and was rewarded with his fourth solo hit.

The brilliant little fellow turns his solo talents to a slow number that, while it tends to sound a bit white, couldn't have been handled better by anyone. He emotes all over the place and I foresee it in the charts before you can blink. **Penny Valentine, Sounds, November 1972**

The Best

ARTIST Tina Turner RELEASE DATE September 1989 (UK & US) WRITER Holly Knight, Mike Chapman PRODUCER D. Hartman LABEL Capitol (UK & US) UK CHART PEAK/WEEKS 5/12 US CHART PEAK/WEEKS 15/14

The Turner anthem – later adopted as a theme tune by the likes of boxer Chris Eubank and strip squad the Chippendales – was a composition by Chinnichap's Mike Chapman and American Holly Knight, featuring a sax solo by Edgar Winter. The opening cut on Turner's **Foreign Affair** album, the single's promo video was directed by Lol Creme, late of 10 cc.

Persistent tune, typically full-blooded vocal. **Paul Elliott, Sounds, August 1989**

Best Of My Love

ARTIST The Emotions RELEASE DATE September 1977 (UK)/June 1977 (US) WRITER Maurice White, Albert McKay PRODUCER Maurice White LABEL CBS (UK)/Columbia (US) UK CHART PEAK/WEEKS 4/10 US CHART PEAK/WEEKS 1/23

Emotions, a three-piece Chicago vocal group formed in the late Fifties as a gospel act, found themselves at the top of the US chart with *Best Of My Love*, co-written by Earth Wind and Fire's mainman Maurice White, and diced with Bee Gees brother Andy Gibb. The girls repaid the favour by adding their vocals to EW&F's storming *Boogie Wonderland* in 1979. By the mid-Eighties they had defected from White's Kalimba Productions to Motown.

Even Sister Sheila, whose songs used to flirt with double rhymes and sly rhythms, is into wham-bam funk like the rest. Everything's up front ... one riff after another. Oh what a relief it is – when it's over. **Ariel Swartley, Rolling Stone, October 1978**

The Best Things In Life Are Free

ARTIST Luther Vandross and Janet Jackson RELEASE DATE August 1992 (UK)/May 1992 (US) WRITER M. Bivins, R. Devo, James Harris III, Terry Lewis, Ralph Tresvant PRODUCER Jimmy Jam, Terry Lewis LABEL Perspective (UK & US) UK CHART PEAK/WEEKS 7/7 US CHART PEAK/WEEKS 10/20

Vandross, the great lover man of contemporary R&B, whose impeccable touch usually avoided schmaltz, had R&B chart success throughout the 1980s but only hit the mainstream charts in 1990 with *Here And Now*. This 1992 duet with Jackson from the movie *Mo' Money* was only kept out of the UK Number 1 position by Snap's *Rhythm Is A Dancer*. In 1994 Vandross repeated the duet formula with Mariah Carey on *Endless Love*, a transatlantic Top 3 hit.

Vandross and Jackson vocally swerve and weave around each other like they have been singing together for years ... The true kudos, however, goes to the masterful Jimmy Jam and Terry Lewis, who have crafted a slammin' track that would work no matter what. **Billboard, May 1992**

It's a folk saga of a strong, silent miner who saved his mates' lives at the expense of his own. Treatment is compelling, and Jimmy Dean sings with simple virility. **Melody Maker, November 1961**

Big Girls Don't Cry

ARTIST The Four Seasons RELEASE DATE January 1963 (UK)/October 1962 (US) WRITER Bob Crewe, Bob Gaudio PRODUCER Bob Crewe LABEL Stateside (UK)/Vee-Jay (US) UK CHART PEAK/WEEKS 13/10 US CHART PEAK/WEEKS 1/16

Recorded at the same session as their debut chart entry *Sherry*, it had been a topic of discussion as to which should be released first. In the end, it mattered not as they both shot to the peak of the US charts within the space of five weeks. The similarly styled ***Big Girls Don't Cry*** had been inspired by a Clark Gable line watched on the big screen by writers Bob Crewe and Bob Gaudio, and was tailor-made for Frankie Valli's expressive falsetto.

When John Wayne walked out on Joan Crawford in one movie scene and the line 'Big girls don't cry' was uttered, Bob's reaction was instinctive. He reached for his manuscript paper and ran for the piano. **Ian Dove, NME, January 1963**

Bette Davis Eyes

ARTIST Kim Carnes RELEASE DATE May 1981 (UK)/March 1981 (US) WRITER Donna Weiss, Jackie DeShannon PRODUCER Val Garay LABEL EMI America (UK & US) UK CHART PEAK/WEEKS 10/9 US CHART PEAK/WEEKS 1/26

The first time Kim Carnes hit the Hot 100, in 1972, it was as a cartoon bear: *You Are the One* was credited to the Sugar Bears, an Archies-style cartoon group which was part of a campaign for a breakfast cereal. It would be nine more years until she hit Number 1 with ***Bette Davis Eyes***, and stayed on top for a staggering nine weeks – topping the charts in 20 other countries and earning both the Record of the Year and Song of the Year Grammys.

So they tell me that you are big in the States, may I suggest that you stay there, one Elkie Brooks is more than enough, thank You. **Steve Sutherland, Melody Maker, May 1981**

Big Bad John

ARTIST Jimmy Dean RELEASE DATE October 1961 (UK & US) WRITER Jimmy Dean PRODUCER Don Law LABEL Philips (UK)/Columbia (US) UK CHART PEAK/WEEKS 2/13 US CHART PEAK/WEEKS 1/16

Country star Jimmy Dean wrote ***Big Bad John*** on a plane ride to Nashville when he realized he needed a fourth song for his recording session there. His inspiration was one John Mentoe, a 6 ft 5 in actor he knew back when he used to do summer stock. Floyd Cramer, a hit-maker in his own right, helped with the mine sound effects, banging on a piece of steel normally used to weight TV cameras.

Billie Jean

ARTIST Michael Jackson RELEASE DATE January 1983 (UK & US) WRITER Michael Jackson PRODUCER Quincy Jones LABEL Epic (UK & US) UK CHART PEAK/WEEKS 1/15 US CHART PEAK/WEEKS 1/24

Telling the story of a woman who claims Jackson is the father of her illegitimate baby, *Billie Jean* was the second single to be extracted from the mega-successful **Thriller** album which would go on to sell more than forty million copies worldwide. With Jackson's vocals recorded in one take, the song boasted a video which enjoyed enormous television attention and undoubtedly added to his already impressive reputation. It also inspired Lydia Murdock's answer hit, **Superstar.**

Billie Jean is engaging enough … Nowhere near in the league of **Off The Wall** *though.* **Danny Baker, NME, January 1983**

Billy Don't Be A Hero

ARTIST Paper Lace RELEASE DATE February 1974 (UK)/April 1974 (US) WRITER Peter Callender, Mitch Murray PRODUCER – LABEL Bus Stop (UK)/Mercury (US) UK CHART PEAK/WEEKS 1/14 US CHART PEAK/WEEKS 96/3

Paper Lace got their pop break after appearing on Hughie Green's TV talent-spotting show *Opportunity Knocks*. The band, based in Nottingham, took its name from one of its local industries: lace. The song is about a young man's determination to sign up for the army, and his girlfriend's desperate pleas of 'Billy, don't be a hero', so that he can come back and make her his wife. It has an American Civil War feel to it, with a call-up drum roll and a penny whistle solo.

The performance is unimaginative and delivered with nary a sense of humour or conviction. **Charlie Walters, Rolling Stone, October 1974**

Bitter Sweet Symphony

ARTIST The Verve RELEASE DATE 1997 WRITER Mick Jagger, Keith Richard, Richard Ashcroft PRODUCER Andrew Loog Oldham, Youth, The Verve LABEL Hut UK CHART PEAK/WEEKS – US CHART PEAK/WEEKS –

Out of Wigan, but far removed from Northern Soul, the Verve purveyed a cosmic sound with the improvized ambient feel of early Floyd. After two years the band broke up, and everyone thought that was that – until they re-emerged in 1997 with the album **Urban Hymns**: its opening track, and the come-back single, *Bitter Sweet Symphony* was a piece of elegant symphonic pop that set the tone for the rest of the suite of songs.

Richard Ashcroft sounds less blissed out with every record which can only be a good thing. **Mark Luffman, Melody Maker, June 1997**

Black Or White

ARTIST Michael Jackson RELEASE DATE November 1991 (UK & US) WRITER Michael Jackson PRODUCER Bill Bottrell, Michael Jackson LABEL Epic (UK & US) UK CHART PEAK/WEEKS 1/14 US CHART PEAK/WEEKS 1/20

Ever the consummate video performer, Jacko lost the plot somewhat with the 11-minute John Landis-directed epic for this taster for the **Dangerous** album. Its simultaneous première on MTV and two other US channels was followed by edits of scenes of crotch-rubbing and violence. Musically *Black Or White*, a plea for racial tolerance, was developed from a **Bad** out-take and given guitar icing by Guns N' Roses' Slash, with echoes of Eddie Van Halen's contribution to **Beat It**.

Slash has the guitar intro to The Bitch Is Back. Jacko squeals like a pig with piles and a four year silence ends – with a noisy bland flourish. The rapping is workaday and you get to thinking of all the trademark bits out of the Prince and George Michael records. **Stuart Bailie, NME, November 1991**

single of all time. It melded together dance beats, with a melodic tang, and was coloured with a melancholy vocal line.

I'm really getting VERY tired of records that don't admit to having one good (in theory) and one bad (in theory) side – in the future I plan to review the worst one on purpose. **Blue Monday Mark 2** *is a moody papist chant, for all you little Damiens out there who like that sort of thing.* **Julie Burchill, NME, 12 March 1983**

Blue Moon

ARTIST The Marcels RELEASE DATE April 1961 (UK)/March 1961 (US) WRITER Lorenz Hart, Richard Rodgers PRODUCER Stu Phillips LABEL Pye Int (UK)/Col Pix (US) UK CHART PEAK/WEEKS 1/13 US CHART PEAK/WEEKS 1/14

The Marcels are best known for their sparkling cover of **Blue Moon**. Their sound was a retro mix of R&B and Doo-Wop classics. On **Blue Moon** they tried something new: they speeded it up and added an infectious introduction by bass singer Fred Johnson. His 'dang a dang dang, ding a dong ding' hooked in DJs and record buyers, and the floaty harmonies were instantly appealing. In 1982 it was featured on *An American Werewolf In London* over the closing credits.

I was entertained by **Blue Moon** *as interpreted by the Marcels.* **Keith Fordyce, NME, June 1961**

Blinded By The Light

ARTIST Manfred Mann Earth Band RELEASE DATE August 1976 (UK)/November 1976 (US) WRITER Bruce Springsteen PRODUCER Michael Mann LABEL Bronze (UK)/Warner (US) UK CHART PEAK/WEEKS 6/10 US CHART PEAK/WEEKS 1/26

Manfred Mann continued with the girl group theme for a while, recording The Shirelles' **Sha La La**. The band underwent many changes over the years – practically the only consistent element was the keyboard player, Manfred Mann himself. When singer Paul Jones left their sound became more poppy. The line-up changed again, and the name extended to Earth Band. This time they introduced jazz elements to rock numbers. Their cover of Bruce Springsteen's **Blinded By The Light** was another big hit.

An office rave. Manny's version of the Springsteen song is stylistically close to the original, replete with response chorus harmonies and stirring strings. The essence of Springsteen, it builds and soars in a dazzling series of hooks and tempo changes and musical gimmickry. **Vivien Goldman, NME, August 1976**

Blue Monday

ARTIST New Order RELEASE DATE March 1983 WRITER Stephen Morris, Peter Hook, Bernard Dicken, Gillian Gilbert PRODUCER New Order LABEL Factory UK CHART PEAK/WEEKS 9/38 US CHART PEAK/WEEKS –

Joy Division was a new wave band, fronted by Ian Curtis, whose records were closed up with depression and paranoia. Following the death of Curtis the band became New Order. Influenced by Kraftwerk and the New York dance scene, they added synthesizers and sequencers to their guitar and drums. **Blue Monday** was their breakthrough record, and went on to be the best-selling 12 inch

Blue Suede Shoes

ARTIST Elvis Presley RELEASE DATE May 1956 (UK)/April 1956 (US) WRITER Carl Perkins PRODUCER Steve Sholes LABEL HMV Pop (UK)/RCA Victor (US) UK CHART PEAK/WEEKS 9/10 US CHART PEAK/WEEKS 20/12

After hearing a dancer declare, 'Man, don't step on my suedes', Carl Perkins was inspired to write his rock classic which hit the charts hard on the heels of Elvis's *Heartbreak Hotel*, making the Top 3 of the pop, country & western and R&B charts. Even after 13 takes by producer Steve Sholes, Elvis still felt their version could not rival the original. Even so, within a week the Presley version had entered the charts and, after Perkins met with a car accident, it was Elvis who performed it on *The Ed Sullivan Show*.

No good my starting a society for the suppression of Elvis Presley; it seems that I would be the only member. Sales wise **Blue Suede Shoes** *has proved another winner.* **Laurie Henshaw, Melody Maker, July 1956**

Blue Velvet

ARTIST Bobby Vinton RELEASE DATE September 1990 (UK)/August 1963 (US) WRITER Bernie Wayne, Lee Morris PRODUCER Bob Morgan LABEL Epic (UK & US) UK CHART PEAK/WEEKS 2/10 US CHART PEAK/WEEKS 1/15

A hit for Tony Bennett in 1951, *Blue Velvet* gave Vinton a US Number 1 although the singer thought it was too sweet for a hit – its use as the title tune in David Lynch's 1986 film of the same name proved just how wrong he was. Recorded in Nashville with top local session musicians, and arranged by Burt Bacharach, the song showed off Vinton's nasal vocals. Re-released in 1990 on the back of a Nivea TV ad, the single made UK Number 2.

Blueberry Hill

ARTIST Fats Domino RELEASE DATE November 1956 (UK)/October 1956 (US) WRITER Al Lewis, Larry Stock, Vincent Rose PRODUCER – LABEL London (UK)/Imperial (US) UK CHART PEAK/WEEKS 6/15 US CHART PEAK/WEEKS 2/27

Unusual by being recorded in Los Angeles rather than in Fats Domino's native Crescent City, *Blueberry Hill* was in all other respects typical of a man who, by the time Elvis first entered the Sun studios, already had five years of recording under his substantial belt. Including the R&B as well as the pop charts, Fats notched up 58 hits between 1950 and 1960, of which 18 sold a million.

He arrived at the top of the hill - **Blueberry Hill** *to be exact – for that's the title of his fantastic nit record which causes gasps and screaming the moment he goes into the first notes on a one-night stand.* **Leonard Feather, Melody Maker, January 1957**

Bohemian Rhapsody

ARTIST Queen RELEASE DATE November 1975 (UK)/January 1976 (US) WRITER Freddie Mercury PRODUCER Roy Thomas Baker LABEL EMI (UK)/Elektra (US) UK CHART PEAK/WEEKS 1/17 US CHART PEAK/WEEKS 2/41

With stunning nine-part harmony vocals, a full six minutes in length, this was Number 1 in the charts for nine consecutive weeks. *Bohemian Rhapsody* is a phenomenal tribute to the eminence of Queen and of writer/performer Freddie Mercury. Combining almost kitsch operatic pretensions with grunge-like heavy metal, it was recorded towards the end of the Progressive Rock era but, like so much of Queen's output, has managed to hold up through the changes in music fashion, helped, no doubt, by their exploitation of the eclectic nature of pop.

Superficially impressive pastiche of the incongruous music style, Bohemian Rhapsody is full of drama, passion and romance and sounds rather like one of those mini opera affairs. **Allan Jones, Melody Maker, November 1971**

Boogie On Reggae Woman

ARTIST Stevie Wonder RELEASE DATE January 1975 (UK)/November 1974 (US) WRITER Stevie Wonder PRODUCER Stevie Wonder LABEL Tamla Motown (UK)/Tamla (US) UK CHART PEAK/WEEKS 12/8 US CHART PEAK/WEEKS 3/7

Wonder won a 1975 Grammy for best R&B vocal performance for this up-tempo single from **Fulfillingness' First Finale**, his first album after suffering serious injuries in a 1973 car accident. The single wasn't quite reggae but, hey, it was close enough for the mainstream market.

… may not be reggae, but it certainly has the word in the title. **Brian Harrigan, Melody Maker, February 1975**

Boogie Oogie Oogie

ARTIST A Taste Of Honey **RELEASE DATE** June 1978 (UK & US) **WRITER** Janice Johnson, Perry Kibble **PRODUCER** Fonze Mizell, Larry Mizell **LABEL** Capitol (UK & US) **UK CHART PEAK/WEEKS** 3/16 **US CHART PEAK/WEEKS** 1/23

West Coast soul-cum-disco outfit Taste Of Honey was a genuine band, led by Janice Marie Johnson and Hazel P. Payne on lead vocals (and bass and guitar respectively). It took three months for the group's get-down-and-boogie track to work its way to the top of the US charts, where it saw off Frankie Valli's *Grease*. Winners of the 1979 Grammy for Best New Artist – usually a poisoned chalice – they managed one more Top 5 success, a cover of Kyu Sakamoto's *Sukiyaki*.

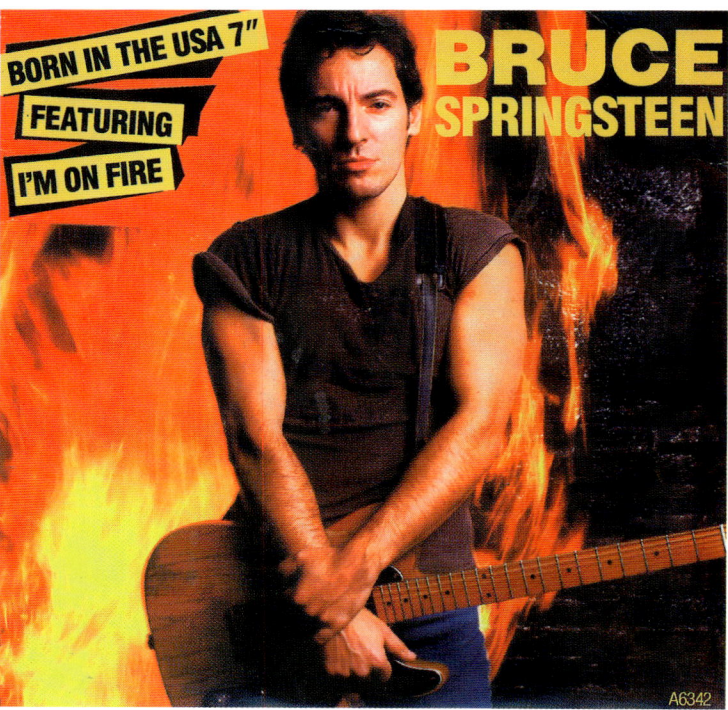

Born In The USA

ARTIST Bruce Springsteen **RELEASE DATE** June 1985 (UK)/November 1984 (US) **WRITER** Bruce Springsteen **PRODUCER** Chuck Plotkin, Steve Van Zandt **LABEL** CBS (UK)/Columbia (US) **UK CHART PEAK/WEEKS** 5/12 **US CHART PEAK/WEEKS** 9/17

Born In The USA was a highlight of the album of the same name which most listeners, to Springsteen's annoyance, assumed was a patriotic battlecry – in fact the message was one of despair about the state of the Union. Chrysler read it the wrong way and wanted it as their theme tune: Springsteen turned down an offer of $12 million. But he did allow 2 Live Crew to sample the track for 1990's *Banned In The USA*.

In the past he has come off as prolix, unpretentious and generally retrogressive. This song, however, confirms the legitimacy of his vision beyond reasonable argument. Even an Englishman could get into this one. **Editor, Rolling Stone, December 1984**

Born Slippy

ARTIST Underworld **RELEASE DATE** May 1995 (UK & US) **WRITER** Rick Smith, Karl Hyde, Darren Emerson **PRODUCER** Underworld **LABEL** Junior Boys Own (UK)/Sire (US) **UK CHART PEAK/WEEKS** 52/2 **US CHART PEAK/WEEKS** 0/0

The experimental electronica trio – ex-Freur members Karl Hyde and Rick Smith teamed with hot young DJ Darren Emerson – merged guitars and vocals with techno pulses on their 1994 crossover, post-rave comedown album **Dubnobasswithmyheadman.** The single *Born Slippy* received its ultra-credible ticket to mass exposure through its place at the heart of the Trainspotting soundtrack, even opening up the American market, so long resistant to the UK's dance scene.

Born To Be Wild

ARTIST Steppenwolf **RELEASE DATE** June 1969 (UK)/July 1968 (US) **WRITER** Mars Bonfire **PRODUCER** Gabriel Mekler **LABEL** Stateside (UK)/Dunhill (US) **UK CHART PEAK/WEEKS** 30/9 **US CHART PEAK/WEEKS** 2/13

Its inclusion on the soundtrack of *Easy Rider* virtually guaranteed that *Born To Be Wild* would become the definitive biker's anthem, and like much of the lore surrounding biking, there was a lot more below the surface here. *The Pusher*, another Steppenwolf classic, and *Snowblind Friend* were anti-drugs songs at a time when the mood was all for exploration.

They haven't changed much since they began as a chemically-propelled freak band a few years ago. For one thing, Steppenwolf is frequently imitated – especially by 16-year-olds who live down the block and rehearse in a garage after school. **David Gancher, Rolling Stone, July 1970**

Born To Run

ARTIST Bruce Springsteen **RELEASE DATE** May 1987 (UK)/September 1975 (US) **WRITER** Bruce Springsteen **PRODUCER** Mike Appel, Bruce Springsteen, Jon Landau **LABEL** CBS (UK)/Columbia (US) **UK CHART PEAK/WEEKS** 16/4 **US CHART PEAK/WEEKS** 23/11

Born To Run was first performed in Cambridge, Mass., the gig that Jon Landau saw and reviewed for *Rolling Stone* with the albatross quote about Springsteen being the future of rock 'n' roll. With that pressure on him, Springsteen kept tinkering away with the recording, bringing Landau in to help on the production, but finally reverting to the power and intensity of the original recording session – an arrangement as big in its own way as Phil Spector's wall of sound.

… it reached a point where it was a nightmare, we were not getting close [to perfection]. Then John Landau came in and he was able to say 'Well you're not doing it because of this, and this…'. Me, you know, I just want to hear it, I don't want to know. **Bruce Springsteen interviewed by Lisa Robinson, NME, March 1977**

The Boxer

ARTIST Simon & Garfunkel **RELEASE DATE** April 1969 (UK & US) **WRITER** Paul Simon **PRODUCER** Roy Hallee, Paul Simon, Art Garfunkel **LABEL** CBS (UK)/Columbia (US) **UK CHART PEAK/WEEKS** 6/14 **US CHART PEAK/WEEKS** 7/10

1969 was a relatively quiet year for Simon & Garfunkel. **Mrs Robinson** had charted at US Number 1 in 1968 and brought them a new level of success, but **The Boxer** was their only release the following year, and the first 16-track recording that Columbia Records had undertaken. In 1970, the year the song was included on the **Bridge Over Troubled Water** LP, Bob Dylan covered it on his **Self-Portrait** album.

This song will impress instantly with its gentle rhythms and delicate voices; lyrical meaning will be deduced only after repeated plays, and perhaps it isn't so important anyway. If pop is art, then this is pop, and a hit. **Chris Welch, Melody Maker, April 1969**

The Boys Are Back In Town

ARTIST Thin Lizzy **RELEASE DATE** May 1976 (UK & US) **WRITER** Phil Lynott **PRODUCER** John Alcock **LABEL** Vertigo (UK)/Mercury (US) **UK CHART PEAK/WEEKS** 8/10 **US CHART PEAK/WEEKS** 12/17

After a number of changes in the group, with two new guitarists, the Californian Scott Gorham and Scot Brian Robertson, the Irish

hard rock act developed their version of Seventies laddism around Phil Lynott's striking presence and voice on the **Jailbreak** album, getting their rewards when **The Boys Are Back In Town**, a bittersweet rocker with biting guitars, became an acclaimed hit.

A lilting Phil Lynott song, radiating warmth and hooliganism, sung by the man who is heir to Van Morrison's Irish soul, cascading words over a tricky eight-bar line: each one a different picture … punched along by unexpected power chords. sharp shooting bass and strutting guitar chords. **Phil McNeill, NME, May 1976**

The Boys Of Summer

ARTIST Don Henley **RELEASE DATE** February 1985 (UK)/November 1984 (US) **WRITER** Don Henley **PRODUCER** Greg Ladanyi, Don Henley, Mike Campbell, Danny Kortchmar **LABEL** Geffen (UK & US) **UK CHART PEAK/WEEKS** 12/10 **US CHART PEAK/WEEKS** 5/22

The one-time Eagles' singing drummer made his own emphatic mark with this single, following his million-selling **Dirty Laundry** into the US Top 5 and giving him his first solo British hit. The song told of seeing 'a Deadhead sticker on a Cadillac', and insisting that

you shouldn't look back – an apt sentiment for someone who once said his former multi-platinum group would re-form only 'when hell freezes over'. Needless to say, it did just that in 1994!

The Boys of Summer is a loveable, unpretentious single – something about as common as black faces on the Melody Maker front pages. That shows how to grow old with grace. Better than just about anything the Eagles put out and should be a hit. **Lynden Barber, Melody Maker, February 1985**

Brand New Key

ARTIST Melanie RELEASE DATE January 1972 (UK)/October 1971 (US) WRITER Melanie Safka PRODUCER Peter Schekeryk LABEL Buddah (UK)/Neighborhood (US) UK CHART PEAK/WEEKS 4/12 US CHART PEAK/WEEKS 1/18

Melanie was an idiosyncratic singer, with a quirky folk style. She was a symbol of the peace and love generation with her appearance at *Woodstock* and her hippy philosophizing. *Brand New Key* was a slightly risqué song about a pair of roller skates and an adjustment key. It was mercilessly parodied by The Wurzels: their version stated: 'I've got a brand new combine harvester...'. She faded with the flower power era.

Galumping Melanie puts on her wellies and bounces along the street with her dolly. I like Melanie, and when I'm grown up I'm going to marry her. **Chris Welch, Melody Maker, November 1971**

Brass In Pocket (I'm Special)

ARTIST The Pretenders RELEASE DATE November 1979 (UK)/February (US) WRITER Chrissie Hynde PRODUCER Chris Thomas LABEL Real (UK)/Sire (US) UK CHART PEAK/WEEKS 1/17 US CHART PEAK/WEEKS 14/22

This moody, rocking single gave the band its first US hit, thanks in part to a classy black and white video featuring Chrissie Hynde as a seductive waitress. The album **Pretenders** launched them on the road to becoming one of the premier international stadium bands of the 1980s, with their combination of R&B roots, superb songs and tight, modern rock. By 1982, the rock 'n' roll dream would become a bad reality with the tragic deaths through drug overdoses of both guitarist James Honeyman-Scott and bassist Pete Farndon.

*I hated **Brass In Pocket** with a vengeance. F***in' AOR. I hated it so much that if they started to play it in Woolworths, I would have to leave the store.* **Chrissie Hynde interviewed by Chris Salewicz, NME, October 1980**

Breaking Up Is Hard To Do

ARTIST Neil Sedaka RELEASE DATE July 1962 (UK)/June 1962 (US) WRITER Howard Greenfield, Neil Sedaka PRODUCER Don Kirshner, Al Nevins LABEL RCA (UK)/RCA Victor (US) UK CHART PEAK/WEEKS 7/16 US CHART PEAK/WEEKS 1/14

Breaking Up's up-tempo feel delivered Neil Sedaka's third million-seller. When the Brits invaded the States after 1964, his style of music began to slither down the charts, but he came back in the early Seventies, writing a hot streak of three US Number 1s in 1975: *Laughter In the Rain*, *Bad Blood* (with Elton John) and Captain & Tennille's *Love Will Keep Us Together*. In 1976 he re-recorded *Breaking Up* as a ballad, but most critics dismissed it as a pale imitation of the original.

Bridge Over Troubled Water

ARTIST Simon & Garfunkel RELEASE DATE February 1970 (UK & US) WRITER Paul Simon PRODUCER Roy Hallee, Paul Simon, Art Garfunkel LABEL CBS (UK)/Columbia (US) UK CHART PEAK/WEEKS 1/20 US CHART PEAK/WEEKS 1/14

By 1970 there were disagreements brewing between the duo after long hours working on a new album and over Garfunkel's acting commitments. But when Garfunkel heard the gospelly demo he knew it was great, and thought it was a song for Simon to sing, but, 'No,' said the writer, it was a vehicle for Garfunkel's tenor. The song swept the 1971 Grammy Awards and was both commercially and critically successful, but by then the pair had parted.

That's Paul Simon and it's a great record. I don't believe that Art comes in until right at the end … The record has been fantastically produced – like all their records. **Sandy Denny, Melody Maker, February 1970**

Bright Eyes

ARTIST Art Garfunkel **RELEASE DATE** March 1979 **WRITER** Mike Batt **PRODUCER** Mike Batt **LABEL** CBS **UK CHART PEAK/WEEKS** 1/19 **US CHART PEAK/WEEKS** 0/0

Written by Wombles songwriter Mike Batt about a rabbit, this song gave American Art Garfunkel his second UK chart-topper after a revival of the oldie **I Only Have Eyes For You** had established an ocular theme to his career four years earlier. Art was not keen on including the film theme for the animated *Watership Down* on his forthcoming album **Fate For Breakfast**, but when his record label showed him queues of fans waiting to see the movie he changed his mind.

Bright Eyes is still a manipulative heart puller, but I have to confess that every time it comes on the air, my heart is not pulled. I gave away my review copy and I shall have to buy another. **Simon Frith, Melody Maker, April 1979**

Bring Your Daughter To The Slaughter

ARTIST Iron Maiden **RELEASE DATE** January 1991 **WRITER** Bruce Dickinson **PRODUCER** Martin Birch, Steve Harris **LABEL** EMI **UK CHART PEAK/WEEKS** 1/5 **US CHART PEAK/WEEKS** –

Granted a UK chart-topper simply by releasing the track in numerous formats which the fans bought in their droves, Iron Maiden registered their only Number 1 with … **Slaughter**. Written by singer Bruce Dickinson for the *Nightmare On Elm Street 5* film (1989), it was the second single from their 1990 **No Prayer For The Dying** album. Dickinson was replaced by Blaze Bayley (ex-Wolfsbane) after his 1994 departure for a solo career.

*Bruce Dickinson is loving every second of it. 'Ha, Ha, Ha! What a F****** result. The fact that it was Cliff we replaced is really sweet! Sorry Cliff me old mate. Ha, Ha, Ha.'* **Terry Staunton, NME, January 1991**

Brown Eyed Girl

ARTIST Van Morrison **RELEASE DATE** June 1967 **WRITER** Van Morrison **PRODUCER** Bert Berns **LABEL** London (UK)/Bang (US) **UK CHART PEAK/WEEKS** – **US CHART PEAK/WEEKS** 10/16

Van the Man was still a youthful 22 when he scored this solo hit, only a year after quitting Them. As the band's vocalist and harmonica player he had helped create the classic R&B

double A-side **Baby Please Don't Go** and **Gloria**. But this was different – **Brown-Eyed Girl**, an up-tempo ballad with a superb melody and some faultless sha-la-la-ing, was perfect blue-eyed soul. Van Morrison had arrived.

This track is the earliest memory I have of being knocked out by Morrison, just before he left for America … He eases his cutting voice around the lyrics with the kind of marvellous tight backing work he has become famous for. **Penny Valentine, Sounds, April 1971**

Brown Sugar

ARTIST The Rolling Stones **RELEASE DATE** April 1971 (UK)/May 1971 (US) **WRITER** Mick Jagger, Keith Richard **PRODUCER** Jimmy Miller **LABEL** Rolling Stones (UK & US) **UK CHART PEAK/WEEKS** 2/13 **US CHART PEAK/WEEKS** 1/12

While **Sticky Fingers** is now regarded as the classic 'decadent' Stones album, with Jagger's singing on **Dead Flowers**, **Sister Morphine** and **Wild Horses** a superb rendering of exhaustion, **Brown Sugar** is a blistering up-tempo blues rocker celebrating the delights of a nameless black woman, and driven by Keith Richard and saxophonist Bobby Keyes. It shot to Number 1 in the US and Number 2 in the UK.

*The song that introduced the Rolling Stones' label to the world exists in different mixes and takes … **Brown Sugar** was released as a sleeved maxi-single in Britain, together with **Bitch** and a 'live' in Leeds workout of Chuck Berry's **Let It Rock**.* **Bob Woffinden, NME, February 1976**

Bus Stop

ARTIST The Hollies RELEASE DATE June 1966 (UK)/July 1966 (US) WRITER Graham Gouldman PRODUCER Ron Richards LABEL Parlophone (UK)/Imperial (US) UK CHART PEAK/WEEKS 5/9 US CHART PEAK/WEEKS 5/14

The Hollies were the cream of Manchester, and this is a fine example of their harmony-packed Sixties output. The peerless vocal trio of Clarke, Hicks and Nash – the latter, taking the top line, would be sadly missed from 1968 on – could turn anything into gold, and this tale of teenage love on public transport, written by future 10 cc stalwart and fellow Mancunian Graham Gouldman, was no exception. It featured their new bass player Bernie Calvert, who had replaced founder member Eric Haydock.

Paul: 'Hollies singing in Indian I am sure…. It's a good record. I would like to hear it a few more times.' Barry: 'It is not as good as their last one.' **Ryan Twins, Melody Maker, June 1966**

Bye Bye Baby (Baby Goodbye)

ARTIST The Bay City Rollers RELEASE DATE March 1975 (UK & US) WRITER Bob Crewe, Bob Gaudio PRODUCER Phil Wainman LABEL Bell (UK)/Arista (US) UK CHART PEAK/WEEKS 1/16 US CHART PEAK/WEEKS 0/0

If anyone was unaware of Rollermania at the start of 1975, the fresh burst of pubescent pandemonium accompanying the release of *Bye Bye Baby* opened their eyes. The Bay City Rollers scored their first and longest held Number 1 with the cover of the decade-old Four Seasons tune. Today they are remembered as the band that inspired millions of young girls to wrap themselves in tartan.

California Dreamin'

ARTIST Mamas & Papas RELEASE DATE April 1966 (UK)/January 1966 (US) WRITER John & Michelle Phillips PRODUCER Lou Adler LABEL RCA (UK)/Dunhill (US) UK CHART PEAK/WEEKS 23/9 US CHART PEAK/WEEKS 4/12

The Mamas & Papas were funky and dirty and sang like angels. Their four-part harmonies were hippy visions of the Summer of Love. They took their name from Hells Angel terminology, and *California Dreamin'* was their hymn to the West Coast. It was a joyous cascade of harmonies, the women's voices sweetening out the deeper tones of the men. It ended with a flute solo and was THE song of San Francisco's hip Haight Ashbury.

Like flying to the moon … like attending the NME Poll Winners Concert … like meeting John Lennon at Disney Land…. The Mama's and Papa's almost defy description! and they come in all shapes and sizes too! **Ann Moses, NME, May 1966**

California Girls

ARTIST The Beach Boys RELEASE DATE September 1965 (UK)/July 1965 (US) WRITER Brian Wilson PRODUCER Brian Wilson LABEL Capitol (UK & US) UK CHART PEAK/WEEKS 26/8 US CHART PEAK/WEEKS 3/11

Mike Love's lyrics for *California Girls* were inspired by the many young women he had met in his travels with the Beach Boys. Its unique piano intro hinted at Brian Wilson's growing desire to incorporate non-rock influences such as Nelson Riddle and George Gershwin into his music. It reached Number 3 on *Billboard*'s Hot 100 in 1965, the same position that David Lee Roth would reach with his cover version nearly 20 years later.

Call Me

ARTIST Blondie RELEASE DATE April 1980 (UK)/February 1980 (US) WRITER Debbie Harry, Giorgio Moroder PRODUCER Giorgio Moroder LABEL Chrysalis (UK & US) UK CHART PEAK/WEEKS 1/9 US CHART PEAK/WEEKS 1/25

The theme from *American Gigolo*, the aggressive **Call Me** was the fourth of Blondie's five Number 1s. It was the only Blondie hit produced by Giorgio Moroder, who also co-wrote the song with Deborah Harry. While Moroder was known for his slickly produced disco records, he was equally adept with rock.

Great. This time they sound like adults (and a group again) and a lot more comfortable for it. Moroder's concocted an expansive, clean-cut movie theme (it's from the American Gigolo soundtrack) and Harry torches it up front. **Chris Bohn, Melody Maker, March 1980**

Can't Get Enough

ARTIST Bad Company RELEASE DATE June 1974 (UK)/August 1974 (US) WRITER Mick Ralphs PRODUCER Bad Company LABEL Island (UK)/Swan Song (US) UK CHART PEAK/WEEKS 15/8 US CHART PEAK/WEEKS 5/15

Bad Company's first hit, **Can't Get Enough** was the second chart-buster to feature Paul Rodgers on lead vocals. Rodgers had previously been in Free, as had drummer Simon Kirke; other alumni of chart acts were Mick Ralphs of Mott the Hoople and Boz Burrell of King Crimson. Although they were an extremely successful album act in Britain, they enjoyed their greatest singles success in America, where both **Can't Get Enough** and **Feel Like Makin' Love** made the Top 10.

Bad Company felt like it was going to be a good band before we had heard the first note at the Rainbow a couple of Thursdays ago. They produced one of the most exciting concerts I've seen for ages. **Bob Harris, Sounds, May 1974**

Can't Give You Anything (But My Love)

ARTIST The Stylistics RELEASE DATE July 1975 (UK & US) WRITER Hugo Peretti, Luigi Creatore, George Weiss PRODUCER Van McCoy LABEL Atco (UK & US) UK CHART PEAK/WEEKS 1/11 US CHART PEAK/WEEKS 51/6

Much of The Stylistics' early material had been provided by the celebrated Philadelphia-based duo of Thom Bell and Linda Creed, but now their music was in the hands of Van McCoy, who, critics felt, swamped the subtle touch of Thom Bell with a super-saccharine overload. **Can't Give You Anything** brought the group their biggest UK hit, but the States had tired of McCoy's over-production and it didn't even make the Top 50.

Cosy, harmonic groove that's the Stylistics' particular forte. Masses of orchestral backing to carry through the boys and their high pitched voices, dripping with romance.... **Colin Irwin, Melody Maker, July 1975**

Can't Help Falling In Love With You

ARTIST UB40 RELEASE DATE May 1993 (UK & US) WRITER Hugo Peretti, Luigi Creatore, George Weiss PRODUCER UB40 LABEL Dep Int (UK)/Virgin (US) UK CHART PEAK/WEEKS 1/16 US CHART PEAK/WEEKS 1/29

The song had originally been released by Elvis Presley in 1961 and its appearance on the soundtrack of the movie *Sliver* gave UB40 the necessary exposure to earn a Number 1 in the UK and US. In fact the track had originally been recorded for the movie *Honeymoon In Vegas*, but had been replaced by a version from U2's Bono.

Oh, do it yourself. You have got the ingredients. You know Presley's classic, throbbing testament to the fearless and matchless mystery of love. You know the grey funereal, grim plod which is UB40's entertainment style. **Ian Griffith, Melody Maker, May 1993**

Can't Take My Eyes Off You

ARTIST Frankie Valli RELEASE DATE May 1967 WRITER Bob Crewe, Bob Gaudio PRODUCER Bob Crewe LABEL Philips UK CHART PEAK/WEEKS 0/0 US CHART PEAK/WEEKS 2/16

Francis Castelluccio had already recorded for Mercury as Frankie Valli before joining The Four Seasons, who released their first singles in 1962 – Valli did not sing solo again for another three years. **Can't Take My Eyes Off You**, a mid-tempo ballad, was his first big hit, and from then on he would keep his solo career running in tandem with his role as leader of The Four Seasons. The single was a million-seller in the US, but saw no chart action in the UK.

Valli speaks with a slow, precise diction, every sentence composed to emit the maximum emotion and feeling. For a small guy, he sure packs a heap of sincerity into his conversation. **Allan Jones, Melody Maker, January 1975**

Candle In The Wind

ARTIST Elton John RELEASE DATE March 1974 & September 1997 (UK & US) WRITER Elton John, Bernie Taupin PRODUCER Gus Dudgeon, George Martin LABEL DJM UK CHART PEAK/WEEKS 11/9 & 1/40+ weeks US CHART PEAK/WEEKS –

A tribute to screen goddess Marilyn Monroe, this song only reached Number 11 when first released in 1974. In the US, **Candle In The Wind** was relegated to the B-side in favour of the R&B-styled **Bennie And The Jets**, a decision proved to be correct when that song topped the US charts for one week. A live version of the song recorded in Australia was issued in 1988 and reached Number 5, but the 1997 version released as a tribute to Princess Diana has since become the UK's biggest-selling single of all time.

Hats of to E. J., the man who has kept pop music sane, fun and nice to know. One of the most beautiful songs from the classic **Yellow Brick Road** *album....* **Chris Welch, Melody Maker, March 1973**

Careless Whisper

ARTIST George Michael RELEASE DATE August 1984 (UK)/December 1984 (US) WRITER George Michael, Andrew Ridgeley PRODUCER George Michael LABEL Epic (UK)/Columbia (US) UK CHART PEAK/WEEKS 1/17 US CHART PEAK/WEEKS 1/21

George Michael and Andrew Ridgeley were Wham! boys with Ibiza suntans and rolled up jeans. Their image was of Young Guns 'going for it', hedonistic and part of the disco nation. But George, the song writer of the duo, had more serious intentions in mind, and he released **Careless Whisper** as a solo effort. It was a tuneful, hushed number, white soul delivered silkily and professionally and it paved the way for his solo career when Wham! split in 1986.

Synths waft by on fluffy white clouds, a Spanish guitar dedicatedly spells romance, and George bears his soul rather than his breast. The strangest thing is that it works. There will not be a pair of dry knickers in the house. **Colin Irwin, Melody Maker, July 1984**

The Carnival Is Over

ARTIST The Seekers RELEASE DATE October 1965 WRITER Tom Springfield PRODUCER – LABEL Columbia UK CHART PEAK/WEEKS 1/17 US CHART PEAK/WEEKS 0/0

Formed in 1963, the Seekers finally fell into shape when they brought lead singer Judith Durham into the line-up and they became Australia's first major pop export. **The Carnival Is Over**, an end of romance number, was written by their Svengali Tom Springfield, who borrowed some of the melody from a traditional Russian folk song called **Stenjka Razin**.

They have benefited, like Cliff Richard, by the adding of strings and a more lush sound. As a production this is the best they have done. Their harmony is spot on. As a fellow Aussie, three British cheers for them. **Alan Freeman, Melody Maker, October 1965**

Caroline

ARTIST Status Quo RELEASE DATE September 1973 WRITER Francis Rossi, Robert Young PRODUCER Francis Rossi, Rick Parfitt LABEL Vertigo UK CHART PEAK/WEEKS 5/13 US CHART PEAK/WEEKS –

After their late Sixties psychedelic-ish, Lowry-influenced *Pictures Of Matchstick Men* (their only US hit), Status Quo completely re-thought their act in 1972 and transmogrified into the down-the-line, 12-bar boogie band we all know. *Caroline*, written by guitarist Francis Rossi and Bob Young, the band's tour manager and co-writer of many of their hits, was a typical barnstormer, with driving guitar, waistcoats and long hair nodding.

Nicely out of tune guitars, a hint of feedback, the oldest riffs in the book and you all's got Status Quo…. It's pub rock with pints of lager swilling over the sawdust, elbows digging into ribs and close range B.O. attacks. **Chris Welch, Melody Maker, September 1973**

Cars

ARTIST Gary Numan RELEASE DATE September 1979 (UK)/February 1980 (US) WRITER Gary Numan PRODUCER Gary Numan LABEL Beggars Banquet (UK)/Atco (US) UK CHART PEAK/WEEKS 1/11 US CHART PEAK/WEEKS 9/25

Gary Numan sang futuristic songs and surfed into the British charts on a wave of synthesizer music. Born Gary Webb, he had been influenced by Bowie, Bolan and Ferry and went from Webb to Numan, the name of a plumber in the telephone directory. He originally made sub-punk records with Tube Way Army. *Cars* is electronic sci-fi, with a robotic vocal over atmospheric haunting keyboards. In 1996 it became popular again when used in a beer commercial.

*He hasn't changed a winning formula. The callous, digital memory backing is as smooth and soullessly seamless as ever but there is none of the McDowell tension that made **Down In The Park** so compelling. A hit, of course.* **Max Bell, NME, August 1979**

Cathy's Clown

ARTIST The Everly Brothers RELEASE DATE April 1960 (UK & US) WRITER Don Everly, Phil Everly PRODUCER Wesley Rose LABEL Warner Bros. (UK)/Caden (US) UK CHART PEAK/WEEKS 1/18 US CHART PEAK/WEEKS 1/17

The Everly Brothers' harmonies had brought them nine hits by the time they fell out with Cadence Records over royalties and musical direction. Uncertain of their future, they signed with the fledgling Warner Brothers label for $1 million and, under immediate pressure to produce a hit for their new bosses, released *Cathy's Clown*. Don had conceived the embryonic idea for a song and within two days the pair had the finished item. It became the first single ever to simultaneously top the UK and US charts.

Cathy's Clown was a Don Everly composition, only the second self-composed number they had chosen as an A-side…. Cathy's Clown was Number 1 on both sides of the Atlantic in 1960 and remains a collector's item as its catalogue number is WB1. **Roy Carr, NME, February 1976**

Celebration

ARTIST Kool And The Gang RELEASE DATE November 1980 (UK)/October 1980 (US) WRITER Ronald Bell, Claydes Smith, George Brown, Robert Bell, James Taylor, Eumir Deodato, Robert Mickens, Carl Toon Junior, Dennis Thomas PRODUCER Eumir Deodato LABEL De-Lite (UK & US) UK CHART PEAK/WEEKS 7/13 US CHART PEAK/WEEKS 1/30

Kool And The Gang broke into the big league when vocalist James Taylor and producer Deodato joined them. The new team scored almost immediately with *Ladies Night* and further success was expected with the second album **Celebration**. As well as being played at innumerable weddings and birthday parties, this song was used at the 1981 Superbowl as the theme song for the Oakland Athletics baseball team, and was also played when the American hostages held in Iran were returned home.

Get Dooown – it's party time. At last, that's the idea. A riff in search of a tune that sounds like nothing at all without a big high powered bass bin and the odd flashing light or two. **Pete Silverton, Sounds, November 1980**

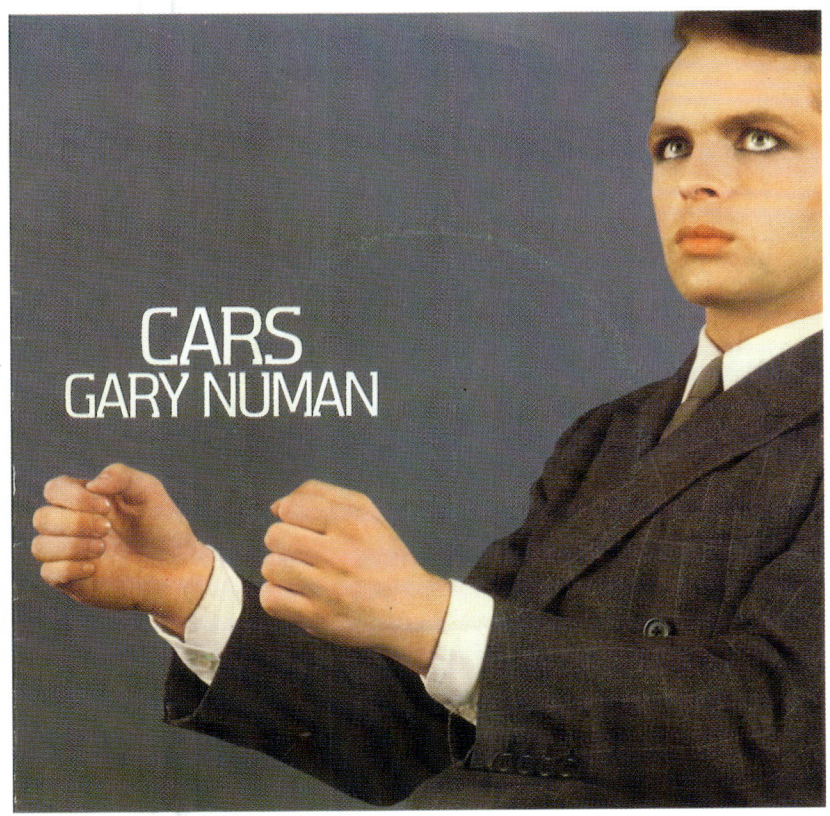

Centerfold

ARTIST The J. Geils Band **RELEASE DATE** February 1982 (UK)/November 1981 (US) **WRITER** Seth Justman **PRODUCER** Seth Justman **LABEL** EMI America (UK & US) **UK CHART PEAK/WEEKS** 3/9 **US CHART PEAK/WEEKS** 1/25

Every red-blooded US male knew what a centerfold was, and though the girls in the video kept their nighties on, the inference was clear. Geils and his boys had been playing hard-edged R&B to a moderate-sized but dedicated audience, but the **Freeze Frame** album, combined with a support tour with The Rolling Stones, helped up their profile – maybe naked ambition was what they had lacked?

Chain Reaction

ARTIST Diana Ross **RELEASE DATE** January 1986 (UK)/November 1985 (US) **WRITER** Barry, Robin and Maurice Gibb **PRODUCER** Barry Gibb, Albhy Galuten, Karl Richardson **LABEL** Capitol (UK)/RCA Victor (US) **UK CHART PEAK/WEEKS** 1/17 **US CHART PEAK/WEEKS** 95/3

Written and co-produced by Barry Gibb and The Bee Gees, **Chain Reaction** very consciously whisked Diana Ross out of the disco-land/Vegas fodder she had been producing since the mid-1970s and recreated a high-energy, if somewhat ersatz, pastiche of the catchy Sixties Motown numbers of The Supremes' golden period. This single gave the Gibb brothers their sixth UK Number 1 as writers and won an Ivor Novello award for Most Performed Song.

Ross, now a trademark more than a talent, is with Barry Gibb; she has been for the last few vinyl outings, an airbrushed bloodless blur, here battered by the dreaded syndrome-D. Ross for the dynasty danceteria. **Gavin Martin, NME, January 1986**

A Change Is Gonna Come

ARTIST Sam Cooke **RELEASE DATE** January 1965 **WRITER** Sam Cooke **PRODUCER** – **LABEL** RCA Victor **UK CHART PEAK/WEEKS** 0/0 **US CHART PEAK/WEEKS** 31/7

Sam Cooke's **A Change Is Gonna Come** was a landmark in the history of soul songwriting. Here was a pop and soul singer, normally known for singing about neglecting his 'science book' and 'twistin' the night away', singing a hard-hitting protest song inspired by Bob Dylan's **Blowin' In The Wind.** Sadly, Cooke did not live to see any change as he was murdered shortly after recording the song. But his composition lived on. It made the US Top 40 and was covered by Otis Redding on **Otis Blue**.

'I'm emotional myself,' he continued. 'You have got to move some emotions to get to know music. If you can make emotions then you home free.' **Sam Cooke interviewed by Ray Colman, Melody Maker, July 1964**

Chapel Of Love

ARTIST Dixie Cups **RELEASE DATE** June 1964 (UK)/May 1964 (US) **WRITER** Phil Spector, Ellie Greenwich, Jeff Barry **PRODUCER** Jeff Barry, Jerry Leiber, Mike Stoller, Ellie Greenwich **LABEL** Pye Int (UK)/Red Bird (US) **UK CHART PEAK/WEEKS 22/8 US CHART PEAK/WEEKS 1/13**

The only American group to break the British, especially The Beatles', stranglehold on the pole position in the US charts during the first half of 1964, the Dixie Cups were little more than one-hit wonders. Written by husband and wife Jeff Barry and Ellie Greenwich together with Phil Spector, *Chapel Of Love* had originally been included on **Presenting The Ronettes** and gave Joan Marie Johnson and sisters Barbara Ann and Rosa Lee Hawkins a chart-topper with their debut entry.

Cherish

ARTIST The Association **RELEASE DATE** August 1966 **WRITER** Terry Kirkham **PRODUCER** Kurt Boettcher **LABEL** Valiant **UK CHART PEAK/WEEKS 0/0 US CHART PEAK/WEEKS 1/14**

Association producer Curt Boettcher thought their recording of **Cherish** was too slow and too long to be a hit. When they insisted it be their follow-up to **Along Comes Mary**, he reluctantly went back and made it more radio-friendly. He sped it up and lied about its timing, listing it on the label as '3:00' – the longest radio would tolerate – instead of 3:27. It worked: **Cherish** topped *Billboard*'s Hot 100 for three weeks.

Recently back from their European tour, Terry of the Association said, 'I must say, the most rewarding experience we had in London was doing Top of the Pops, *They looked after us very well.'* **Ann Miles, NME, June 1968**

Cherry Pink And Apple Blossom White

ARTIST Perez Prado And His Orchestra **RELEASE DATE** March 1955 (UK & US) **WRITER** Mack David, Loui Gay **PRODUCER** – **LABEL** HMV (UK)/RCA Victor (US) **UK CHART PEAK/WEEKS 1/17 US CHART PEAK/WEEKS 1/26**

Smooth, handsome charmer Prado was already king of the mambo throughout Latin America in the early 1950s when he spearheaded the invasion of sexy Latin sounds into the US. He spent ten weeks at the top of the US charts during the mid-Fifties. The Mexican could transfix teenage girls with his voice, but it was one of the best trumpet solos of modern popular music on **Cherry Pink** that captivated an audience beyond the dancing, dreaming popster.

The last time I saw Perez was in a Jane Russell film called Underwater. *It wasn't a good film, but it has provided him with the biggest hit tune, and the biggest hit record of his entire career.* **Mike Butcher, NME, May 1955**

Chirpy Chirpy Cheep Cheep

ARTIST Middle Of The Road **RELEASE DATE** June 1971 **WRITER** Harold Scott **PRODUCER** – **LABEL** RCA **UK CHART PEAK/WEEKS 1/34 US CHART PEAK/WEEKS –**

Chirpy Chirpy Cheep Cheep was almost a novelty record, but not quite. The song is shrill, and chirpy but has a certain repetitive charm, with its call and answer vocal lines, and bird words chorus. The band were aptly named because the song is definitely easy listening, with tack value.

The catchy item, now Number 1 in England, is the RCA version … it is also well done by The Kissoons, with equal play, sales and chart potential. **Billboard, 1971**

Cinderella Rockefella

ARTIST Esther And Abi Ofarim **RELEASE DATE** February 1968 (UK)/March 1968 (US) **WRITER** Mason Williams, Nancy Ames **PRODUCER** – **LABEL** Philips (UK & US) **UK CHART PEAK/WEEKS 1/13 US CHART PEAK/WEEKS 68/6**

Cinderella Rockefella was a bizarre little song, featuring husband and wife team Esther and Abi Ofarim. It had speedy, overlapping vocals sung almost like a music hall number. It was coy and cute, and a star attraction in Israel. They were brought to the attention of the British public when they appeared on the Eamonn Andrews show.

This is a great record – absolutely fabulous. It's so different, and such a quaint record, and Esther has such a wonderful voice. I bet they had fun making this. **George Best, Melody Maker, April 1968**

Close To You

ARTIST The Carpenters **RELEASE DATE** September 1970 (UK)/June 1970 (US) **WRITER** Burt Bacharach, Hal David **PRODUCER** Jack Daugherty **LABEL** A&M (UK & US) **UK CHART PEAK/WEEKS** 6/18 **US CHART PEAK/WEEKS** 1/17

In which the pop world is introduced to the angel-pure voice of Karen Carpenter. Although Karen started out as a not-bad drummer in brother Richard's band, it soon became clear that singing was her greatest talent. With **Close To You**, she took a song that Burt Bacharach and Hal David had written in 1963 for Dionne Warwick and infused it with so much warmth and intimacy that listeners could not help but be charmed. Top 10 in the UK, in their home country it would become their biggest single ever, topping the Hot 100 for four weeks.

*The Carpenters make good singles. **Close To You** was Bacharach & David music at its best. Karen Carpenter's lead vocal was soulful, while the arrangement was exceptionally sharp middle of the road music.* **Jon Landau, Rolling Stone, June 1971**

Come On Eileen

ARTIST Dexy's Midnight Runners **RELEASE DATE** July 1982 (UK)/January 1983 (US) **WRITER** Kevin Rowland, Jim Paterson, Kevin Adams **PRODUCER** Clive Langer, Alan Winstanley **LABEL** Mercury (UK & US) **UK CHART PEAK/WEEKS** 1/17 **US CHART PEAK/WEEKS** 1/23

A new Dexy's line-up fronted, as ever, by Kevin Rowland came up with a new 'gipsy-style' image with dungarees replacing donkey-jackets. For this single, their second in the new incarnation, they joined a group of fiddlers called the Emerald Express and credited them equally on the record. The song topped the UK charts for four weeks in 1982 and the US charts for one week the following year, becoming the UK's best selling single of 1982.

*Come On Eileen is good enough to give them another Number 1 record. It's spry and merry, cobbled together from fine plucked mandolins, sawn fiddles and tack piano and still retains that **Geno**-style northern soul refrain from the chorus.* **Danny Baker, NME, June 1982**

Come Softly To Me

ARTIST The Fleetwoods **RELEASE DATE** April 1959 (UK)/March 1959 (US) **WRITER** Gary Troxel, Barbara Ellis, Gretchen Christopher **PRODUCER** Bob Reisdorff **LABEL** London (UK)/Dolphin (US) **UK CHART PEAK/WEEKS** 6/8 **US CHART PEAK/WEEKS** 1/16

When childhood friends Barbara Ellis and Gretchen Christopher joined forces with Gary Troxel, the group Two Girls and a Guy was born. After performing Come Softly at school events, they were persuaded to record it. After they changed their name to the Fleetwoods, the track became the debut release on the newly formed Dolphin label. The title was extended to **Come Softly To Me** to avoid any innuendo possibilities.

Come Softly To Me, America's current Number 1 song hit, has leapt into the British best sellers at Number 20, and has thus brought international recognition to a hitherto unknown trio of US high school students calling themselves the Fleetwoods. **Derek Johnson, NME, April 1959**

Common People

ARTIST Pulp **RELEASE DATE** June 1995 **WRITER** Pulp (lyrics by Jarvis Cocker) **PRODUCER** Chris Thomas **LABEL** Island **UK CHART PEAK/WEEKS** 2/13 **US CHART PEAK/WEEKS** –

Jarvis Cocker and his crew had been trying to make it since 1981. They toured, they made singles, they played small radio shows. They crafted simple, effective rock songs in the mode of the Kinks. Then they released **Common People** with its acerbic, witty take on the seedy titillation of reverse social climbing and suddenly they emerged in the middle of 1990s Britpop-mania with more credibility than Oasis and Blur put together.

… anthemic, gigantic new single whose relentlessly intense rhythm … recalls the demonic, supersonic, electronic mo-mo-momentum of Eno-era Roxy Music and whose juggernaut keyboard and vitriolic sex-geek lyric smack of Elvis Costello at his most deliciously wicked. **Paul Lester, Melody Maker, May 1995**

Cool For Cats

ARTIST Squeeze **RELEASE DATE** March 1979 **WRITER** Glen Tilbrook, Chris Difford **PRODUCER** Glen Tilbrook, John Wood, Squeeze **LABEL** A&M **UK CHART PEAK/WEEKS** 2/11 **US CHART PEAK/WEEKS** –

South-east London's streetwise, musically inventive chaps had emerged from the pub circuit and established the tone of their articulate, witty, melodic pop by the release of their album **Cool For Cats** in 1979. This typically smart Squeeze number, from the Difford-Tilbrook team, and with Jools Holland's tasty keyboards, was only kept from the UK Number 1 slot by Art Garfunkel's **Bright Eyes**.

Deceptively fine…. **Dave McCullough, Sounds, May 1979**

Could It Be Magic

ARTIST Barry Manilow **RELEASE DATE** December 1978 (UK)/June 1975 (US) **WRITER** Barry Manilow, Adrienne Anderson **PRODUCER** Ron Dante, Barry Manilow **LABEL** Arista (UK & US) UK CHART PEAK/WEEKS 25/10 US CHART PEAK/WEEKS 6/18

After a series of fairly unsuccessful singles Take That decided to try cover versions. Manilow's **Could It Be Magic** was chosen. Barry had based the swoonsome ballad on Chopin's *Prelude In C Minor*, and he worked a subtle keyboard spell. Take That went for a more straightforward pop approach, with vocal harmonies and swish instrumentation, which took it to the top.

Barry's notion of vocal dynamics is to sing increasingly louder as the song goes along: he seems to feel that if he sang softly, it would kill his momentum. **Don Shewey, Rolling Stone, May 1978**

Country House

ARTIST Blur **RELEASE DATE** August 1995 (UK & US) **WRITER** Damon Albarn, Graham Coxon, Alex James, David Rowntree **PRODUCER** Stephen Street **LABEL** Food (UK & US) UK CHART PEAK/WEEKS 1/12 US CHART PEAK/WEEKS 0/0

Country House won a highly publicized chart battle with Oasis' **Roll With It**, which was released on the same day. While the song was intended to rib the rich, its video was unintentionally ironic, depicting Blur living in council housing while the protagonist had a mansion. In fact, with the success of their previous album, **Parklife**, Blur were themselves millionaires.

Musically … it's too oikishly bouncy for me this time, something for people to jump up and down to, stop jumping up and down for a minute in the middle and then jump up and down towards the end. **David Stubbs, Melody Maker, August 1995**

Crazy

ARTIST Patsy Cline **RELEASE DATE** December 1990 (UK)/October 1961 (US) **WRITER** Willie Nelson **PRODUCER** – **LABEL** MCA (UK)/Decca (US) UK CHART PEAK/WEEKS 14/11 US CHART PEAK/WEEKS 9/11

Patsy Cline's ability to rebound was remarkable. As a child, she suffered a throat infection so serious that she had to spend time in an oxygen tank. Upon her recovery, she discovered that her voice had grown to booming, Kate Smith-like proportions. Years later, in June 1961, she experienced near fatal head injuries when thrown through the windshield in a head-on car crash. Yet, just two months later she recorded **Crazy** – on crutches. She died in a plane crash in 1963.

*Some newcomers make life a little bit more bearable, **Crazy**, on the other hand, does a little bit more than that – Patsy Cline has got one of the most spine chilling voices ever and this is a heart-melter.* **George Berger, Sounds, December 1990**

Crazy

ARTIST Seal **RELEASE DATE** December 1990 (UK)/June 1991 (US) **WRITER** Seal **PRODUCER** Trevor Horn **LABEL** Ztt Zang (UK)/Sire (US) **UK CHART PEAK/WEEKS** 2/15 **US CHART PEAK/WEEKS** 7/19

The Eighties had been a long decade of playing the pub and club circuit in London for Seal (Henry Samuel), and he'd also suffered a case of lupus, leaving him with distinctive facial scarring. His break came when he wrote lyrics for Adamski's **Killer**, and its success made Seal a hot prospect: Trevor Horn snapped him up for ZTT records. **Crazy** helped spur his eponymous album to UK Number 1, and brought him two prestigious Ivor Novello awards for songwriting in 1992.

Seal's debut solo effort builds from a mild ache to a passionate throb, channelling its pristine energy into several different directions. After starting out life as a slow lament, **Crazy** *becomes remarkably fresh, bumping and grinding like Prince after a cold shower and massage.* **Paul Mardlet, Sounds, December 1990**

Crazy For You

ARTIST Madonna **RELEASE DATE** June 1985 (UK)/March 1985 (US) **WRITER** John Bettis, Jon Lind **PRODUCER** John Benitez **LABEL** Geffen **UK CHART PEAK/WEEKS** 2/15 **US CHART PEAK/WEEKS** 1/21

Crazy For You featured in the film *Vision Quest*, starring Matthew Modine. It was a breathless love song, with sweeping strings and a dreamy chorus. Madonna's voice is husky, full of little sighs and catches that give the record a shivery intimacy. Later on in that year Madonna married the actor Sean Penn, whom she described

as 'the coolest guy in the universe'. Unfortunately things cooled between them fairly quickly.

What's that smell? Only Geffen Records and the big money movie men undergoing some serious internal combustion as they race to get Madonna contributions to the Vision Quest soundtrack onto the streets in a glorious single. **Barry McIlheney, Melody Maker, June 1985**

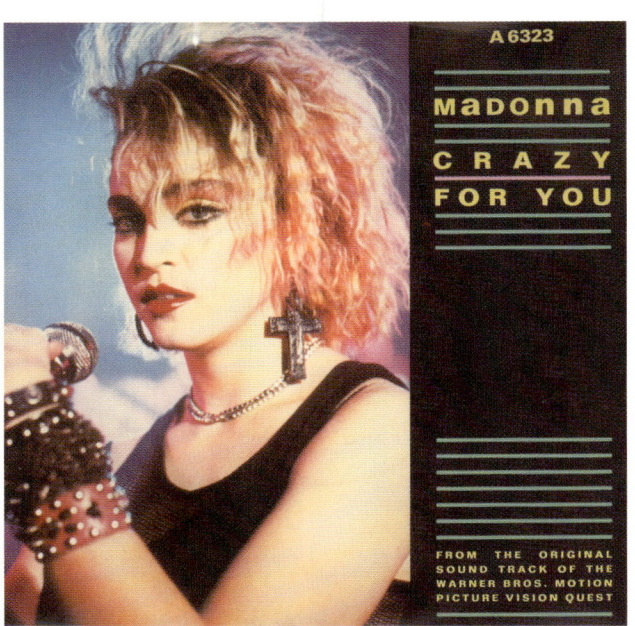

Crazy Horses

ARTIST The Osmonds **RELEASE DATE** November 1972 (UK)/October 1972 (US) **WRITER** Alan Wayne, Merrill Osmond **PRODUCER** – **LABEL** MGM (UK)/MGM Kolob (US) **UK CHART PEAK/WEEKS** 2/18 **US CHART PEAK/WEEKS** 14/12

Crazy Horses was a bit of a gallop away from The Osmonds' usual clean cut pop: it had wild guitars, the chords strummed to sound like horses whinnying, a pounding drum beat, and deep rock-out vocals, which repeated 'crazy horses', over and over again. It was probably their one opportunity to let loose musically in a busy year, which saw the release of **Puppy Love**, Little Jimmy's **Long Haired Lover From Liverpool**, and the hysteria of Osmond-mania in the UK.

Quite, quite ghastly. The vocals are mixed well back, and from what you can hear that is just as well. Heavy music one side, and slushy ballad the other, it is pure unadulterated pap, and a million seller no doubt. **Steve Peacock, Sounds, November 1972**

Crazy Little Thing Called Love

ARTIST Queen **RELEASE DATE** October 1979 (UK)/December 1979 (US) **WRITER** Freddie Mercury **PRODUCER** Mac Reinhold **LABEL** EMI (UK)/Elektra (US) **UK CHART PEAK/WEEKS** 2/14 **US CHART PEAK/WEEKS** 1/22

A sparse, stylish piece of neo-rockabilly, **Crazy Little Thing Called Love**'s release was accompanied by a camp pop video featuring a leather-clad Freddie Mercury delivering an Elvis-like vocal sandwiched between assorted females on a Harley Davidson. It was the first recorded track on which guitarist Brian May used a Fender Telecaster. The single became Queen's first US Number 1.

It's the Mercury Men back in action with what I imagine they intend to be a genial pastiche of late-Fifties boogie. The picture bag, which has the quartet looking sturdy in battered leather, bears this out. **Ian Birch, Melody Maker, October 1979**

Creep

ARTIST Radiohead **RELEASE DATE** September 1993 (UK)/June 1993 (US) **WRITER** – **PRODUCER** Paul Kolderie, Sean Slade **LABEL** Parlophone (UK)/Capitol (US) **UK CHART PEAK/WEEKS** 7/6 **US CHART PEAK/WEEKS** 34/20

Unlike some of their more musically insecure Britrock contemporaries, Radiohead were slow to find success and **Creep** was a miserable failure on its first outing, picking up interest only when the college circuit in the US started to play it endlessly. This slowburner from their first album **Pablo Honey** then became one of the most heavily-played singles in the US. Singer Thom Yorke's anguished, almost murderous, wail is broken by startling, nightmare guitar crunches which build into a terrifying picture of the crippling awkwardness of youth.

Creep itself is a stormer, a perfect monster of malevolent pop song…. Sharon O'Connell, Melody Maker, September 1992

Creep

ARTIST TLC RELEASE DATE January 1995 (UK)/November 1994 (US) WRITER Dallas Austin PRODUCER Dallas Austin LABEL LaFace (UK & US) UK CHART PEAK/WEEKS 22/14 US CHART PEAK/WEEKS 1/32

Pebbles, the R&B performer, brought this trio together when Tionne 'T-Boz' Watkins and Lisa 'Left-Eye' Lopes signed with her production company in 1991. Adding Rozonda 'Chilli' Thomas gave them a name (based on the initial letters of their three nicknames), a sound, and a deal with LaFace Records. After a US Number 6 with **Ain't 2 Proud To Beg** and a US Number 2 with **Baby-Baby-Baby**, this sensuous track got them the Number 1 slot, and a Grammy for best R&B performance.

The vocals are tightly woven and rife with raspy grit – a nice contrast to wafting horn sample and quivery guitars. A gem that seems destined for instant approval. **Billboard, November 1994**

Crocodile Rock

ARTIST Elton John RELEASE DATE November 1972 (UK)/December 1972 (US) WRITER Elton John, Bernie Taupin PRODUCER Gus Dudgeon LABEL DJM (UK)/MCA (US) UK CHART PEAK/WEEKS 5/14 US CHART PEAK/WEEKS 1/17

This was the first release from Elton's LP **Don't Shoot Me, I'm Only The Piano Player** which became his first UK Number 1 LP and second in the US. The song was another Taupin/John composition with heavy 1950s influences and a falsetto vocal reminiscent of Pat Boone's 1962 hit **Speedy Gonzales**. It was performed on the *Royal Variety Show* just before UK release, but it was the US audience that gave him his first singles chart-topper.

Cryin'

ARTIST Roy Orbison RELEASE DATE September 1961 (UK)/August 1961 (US) WRITER Roy Orbison, Joe Melson PRODUCER – LABEL London (UK)/Monument (US) UK CHART PEAK/WEEKS 25/9 US CHART PEAK/WEEKS 2/16

The Big O's soulful tenor was perfectly suited to the mini-tragedies he committed to vinyl during the Kennedy years. **Cryin'** only reached Number 25 on the UK charts but it became an enduring classic, reaching Number 1 when it was covered by Don McLean in 1980, and charting again when Orbison himself duetted with kd lang in the late Eighties. On the original version, Orbison's voice climbs towards heartbreak over a sombre drumbeat and strummed guitar, backed by strings and heavenly choirs.

*The melody line of **Cryin'** seems too discursive to make this another **Only The Lonely** for Orbison. The Flip side is repetitive – and dull.* Melody Maker, September 1961

Crying In The Chapel

ARTIST Elvis Presley **RELEASE DATE** May 1965 (UK)/April 1965 (US) **WRITER** Artie Glenn **PRODUCER** – **LABEL** RCA (UK)/RCA Victor (US) **UK CHART PEAK/WEEKS** 1/15 **US CHART PEAK/WEEKS** 3/14

Recorded in 1960, Elvis's revival of The Orioles' 1953 million-selling gospel ballad was originally released to coincide with Easter, but finally hit the Top 3 in June 1965, becoming his first US Top 10 hit since **Bossa Nova Baby**. In spite of the British invasion, spearheaded by The Beatles, which had largely banished most of Elvis's contemporary rockers from the charts and drastically affected Elvis's record sales, it managed to sell one million copies. It also became a UK Number 1.

Elvis' sexy voice. What's he keep putting out rubbish for? I feel sorry for the Elvis fans. I used to like him, and I don't anymore. **Sandy Shaw, Melody Maker, May 1965**

Cum On Feel The Noize

ARTIST Slade **RELEASE DATE** March 1973 (UK)/May 1973 (US) **WRITER** Noddy Holder, Jim Lea **PRODUCER** Chas Chandler **LABEL** Polydor (UK & US) **UK CHART PEAK/WEEKS** 1/12 **US CHART PEAK/WEEKS** 98/2

Slade were on a roll in the early Seventies. **Coz I Luv You** marked their first Number 1, and with songs like **Cum On Feel The Noize** and **Gudbuy T'Jane** they kept up the momentum over six number 1s in the UK. They were much of a muchness as singles, but the formula was always fun and the band engendered enduring loyalty. In 1983 US heavy metal band Quiet Riot reached US Number 5 with a cover version.

D'you Know What I Mean

ARTIST Oasis **RELEASE DATE** 1997 **WRITER** Noel Gallagher **PRODUCER** Owen Morris, Noel Gallagher **LABEL** Creation (UK)/Epic (US) **UK CHART PEAK/WEEKS** – **US CHART PEAK/WEEKS** 0/0

A well-crafted driving rock song with a strong hook and the arrogant but excellently daft chorus, 'All my people, right here, right now, D'you know what I mean?' Many probably hadn't a clue, but it was still a welcome release after a long period of silence, imposed by the industry's need to properly milk the old material, and not from any lack of creativity on the part of the band's prolific songwriter, Noel Gallagher.

D.I.S.C.O.

ARTIST Ottawan **RELEASE DATE** September 1980 **WRITER** Daniel Vangarde, Jean Klugar **PRODUCER** – **LABEL** Carrere **UK CHART PEAK/WEEKS** 2/18 **US CHART PEAK/WEEKS** 0/0

It was difficult to know if Ottawan were sublime or ridiculous. Certainly the kitsch factor was high, but **D.I.S.C.O.** was cute and inventive, if somewhat tacky. The group from Guadeloupe used each letter of the title to describe the infuriating and loveable qualities of a girl: 'She is D, desirable, she is I, incredible.' It was of course a H.I.T. They also charted with **Hands Up, Give Me Your Love,** before heading off the dance floor.

D.I.S.C.O, (D) dislikeable. (I) incomprehensible. (S) superficial, (C) such a cop-out, (O) … oh forget it. **Paul Du Noyer, NME, November 1980**

D.I.V.O.R.C.E.

ARTIST Tammy Wynette **RELEASE DATE** June 1975 (UK)/June 1968 (US) **WRITER** Bobby Braddock, Curly Putman **PRODUCER** – **LABEL** Epic (UK & US) **UK CHART PEAK/WEEKS** 12/7 **US CHART PEAK/WEEKS** 63/6

When Wynette headed to Nashville to find fame she hooked up with two men who would play leading roles in her eventful life: producer and writer Billy Sherrill, with whom she developed a new, smoother country sound, and George Jones, the hell-raising country singer who married her. Although their marriage (her third) hit the rocks just about the time the single was released, this song was a number of years old. In 1975 it made the UK Number 1 slot.

Being brave and manly about it, I can't really see it storming the charts, delightfully corny as it is. The silent majority is unlikely to adopt the sentiment. **Colin Irwin, Melody Maker, June 1975**

Da Ya Think I'm Sexy

ARTIST Rod Stewart **RELEASE DATE** November 1978 (UK)/December 1978 (US) **WRITER** Rod Stewart, Carmine Appice **PRODUCER** Tom Dowd **LABEL** Riva (UK)/Warner (US) **UK CHART PEAK/WEEKS** 1/13 **US CHART PEAK/WEEKS** 1/21

After the raw honesty of **Maggie May** critics spurned any song they thought showed Rod Stewart sliding towards hokum – and for many this was the pits. But the pumping, flaunting disco hit, written by Stewart and legendary drummer Carmine Appice, went to Number 1 both sides of the Atlantic. Songwriter Jorge Benjor sued Stewart, claiming it was based on his **Taj Mahal**, but that didn't stop Rod singing it in the United Nations in 1979, sending the royalties to UNICEF.

Disco fever filters through to the Bel Air Mansion and Rodney drags himself onto the floor with the whole disco chic. The lyric is the usual boy-meets-girl and gets her knickers off, spread mighty thin over a pumping bass and swirling synthesizer. Monotonous. **Alan Lewis, Sounds, November 1978**

Dancing In The Dark

ARTIST Bruce Springsteen **RELEASE DATE** May 1984 (UK & US) **WRITER** Bruce Springsteen **PRODUCER** Chuck Plotkin, Jon Landau, Steve Banzant **LABEL** CBS (UK)/Columbia (US) **UK CHART PEAK/WEEKS** 4/23 **US CHART PEAK/WEEKS** 2/21

The **Born In The USA** album delivered seven Top 10 singles, including the title song, **Cover Me** and **Glory Days.** Its predecessor, **Nebraska,** had been stripped down and folky, but now with songs like **Dancing In The Dark** Springsteen was back with strong, hook-driven, even danceable material. For this release he also

ventured for the first time into the world of the promo clip, directed by Brian De Palma and notable for featuring Courtney Cox in pre-Friends days.

Well, sorry to disappoint you old chap, but this missive from the camp is frankly a load of old twaddle…. A flat-footed beat carries no momentum and the vocals sound like the death throes of a strangled wino. **Helen Fitzgerald, Melody Maker, May 1984**

Dancing In The Street

ARTIST Martha & The Vandellas **RELEASE DATE** October 1964 (UK)/August 1964 (US) **WRITER** William Stevenson, Marvin Gaye, Ivy Hunter **PRODUCER** William Stevenson **LABEL** Stateside (UK)/Gordy (US) **UK CHART PEAK/WEEKS** 28/8 **US CHART PEAK/WEEKS** 2/14

Dancing In The Street was a Motown classic that sizzled through the charts. Martha Reeves' voice is a clarion call of soul and passion, soaring above hand claps, finger clicks and swinging saxophones. The Vandellas provided stylish backing vocals and the percussion laid down a beat that demanded foot stomps. Reeves started work as a secretary in the Brill Building, but soon switched from typewriter to microphone. The Vandellas were one of the hottest female acts at Motown.

*They have so far failed to crash Britain, and **Dancing In The Street** (Stateside) is in their familiar style of wailing voices and all happening backing. This is messy and no hit.* **Keith Richard, Melody Maker, October 1964**

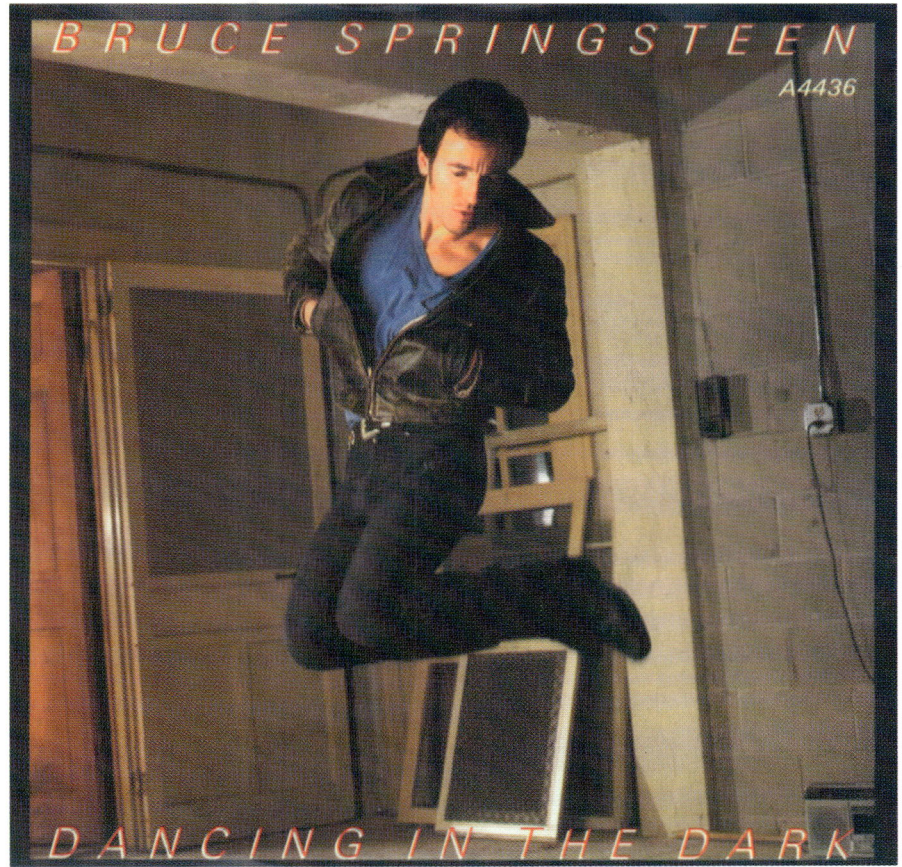

Daniel

ARTIST Elton John RELEASE DATE January 1973 (UK)/April 1973 (US) WRITER Elton John, Bernie Taupin PRODUCER Gus Dudgeon LABEL DJM (UK)/MCA (US) UK CHART PEAK/WEEKS 4/10 US CHART PEAK/WEEKS 2/15

Although lyricist Bernie Taupin wrote *Daniel* as an oblique comment on the Vietnam war, its message was diluted by having a final verse chopped off for being too long when Elton John set it to music. The song became Elton's fifth Top 10 hit in the US, spending one week behind Paul McCartney/Wings' *My Love* and nearly emulating its chart-topping but less enduring predecessor *Crocodile Rock*. In the UK, the song became his fourth Top 10 hit.

A warm, attractive song that grows in its appeal with each hearing. Set to a Calypso beat, Elton uses electronic piano and lends a kind of steel drum effect to a fine song and a convincing hit. **Chris Welch, Melody Maker, January 1973**

Day Tripper

ARTIST The Beatles RELEASE DATE December 1965 (UK & US) WRITER John Lennon, Paul McCartney PRODUCER George Martin LABEL Parlophone (UK)/Capitol (US) UK CHART PEAK/WEEKS 1/12 US CHART PEAK/WEEKS 5/10

The lyrics of *Day Tripper* were generally interpreted to be about what was then known as a 'loose woman', but those in with the counterculture recognized its inspiration. Although John Lennon had yet to take an LSD trip, he had heard about tripping and was fascinated with the concept. In Britain the song was released as a double A-side with *We Can Work It Out*. America had *Day Tripper* marked as the A-side, though the flip also charted.

I liked this immediately. The trouble is, what can you say about The Beatles? They just go on producing great records. **Eric Burdon, Melody Maker, December 1965**

Dancing Queen

ARTIST Abba RELEASE DATE August 1976 (UK)/December 1976 (US) WRITER Benny Anderson, Bjorn Ulvaeus PRODUCER Benny Andersson, Bjorn Ulvaeus LABEL Epic (UK)/Atlantic (US) UK CHART PEAK/WEEKS 1/15 US CHART PEAK/WEEKS 1/22

A disco classic, *Dancing Queen* hearkens back to a time when dance records were orchestrated, not synthesized. It became Abba's third straight UK Number 1, selling over 850,000 copies. In America it caught on slowly, creeping to the top over a four-month period. During that time, sales built up so fast that it went gold before reaching the Number 1 spot.

The title is using the word 'dancing', which is as hip as were all those earnest hacks of last year when to have rock 'n' roll in the title somewhere in your phrase book was a guarantee of covering studio time and pressing costs. The word 'Queen', too, is closely associated with money. **Fluff, NME, August 1976**

Daydream Believer

ARTIST The Monkees RELEASE DATE November 1967 (UK & US) WRITER John Stewart PRODUCER Chip Douglas LABEL RCA (UK)/Colgems (US) UK CHART PEAK/WEEKS 5/17 US CHART PEAK/WEEKS 1/12

Daydream Believer is a lovely, melodic ballad, sung simply and openly by Davy Jones. The instrumentation is sparse and floaty,

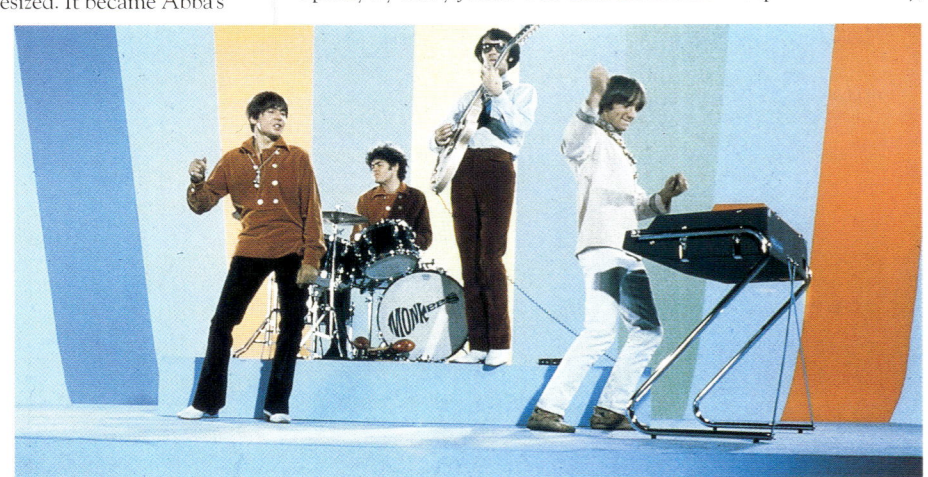

giving the record an elegant, thoughtful quality. It sounds as if Jones means what he's singing, but in the recording studio he had difficulty interpreting the lyrics, forcing the engineer to resort to the use of codes for different versions. Jones laughingly asks: 'What number is this?' and The Monkees reply 'Seven A' – the conversation was kept as the intro on the record.

It's a good song, and after all, the Monkees could hardly be allowed to make a bad record or there would doubtless be a chain of firing throughout the organisation. **Chris Welch, Melody Maker, November 1967**

Dead Ringer For Love

ARTIST Meat Loaf RELEASE DATE November 1981 (UK & US) WRITER Jim Steinman PRODUCER Stefan Galfas LABEL Epic (UK & US) UK CHART PEAK/WEEKS 5/17 US CHART PEAK/WEEKS 0/0

Meat Loaf somehow combines light opera with heavy rock. It is probably a hangover from his days in *The Rocky Horror Picture Show*. Some releases have been dramatically long: *I'd Do Anything For Love (But I Won't Do That)* which was seven and a half minutes and counting. *Dead Ringer For Love*, his uncredited duet with Cher, was a snappier rock out. The guitars surged along nicely and Meat Loaf's vocal was coy and growly at the same time.

This has to be Meat Loaf, this has to be dreadful – sorry, I can't share the joke. Everything sounds speeded up, to make it sound more urgent, or then again to get it over with a bit quicker. **Melody Maker, October 1981**

December 1963 (Oh What A Night)

ARTIST The Four Seasons RELEASE DATE January 1976 WRITER Judy Parker, Bob Gaudio PRODUCER Bob Gaudio LABEL Warner Bros (UK)/Warner Curb (US) UK CHART PEAK/WEEKS 1/10 US CHART PEAK/WEEKS 1/27

New Jersey's Four Seasons were the first group in the early Sixties to have three consecutive US chart-toppers. They returned to the charts in 1975 with a song originally written about the repeal of prohibition and set in 1933. However, the lyrics were rewritten by Bob Gaudio and Judy Parker and the song went to Number 1 on both sides of the Atlantic. In 1996, the track was updated by Clock under the title of *Oh What A Night* and made the UK Top 20.

Dry, punchy brass, incandescent synths, phasing vocals and rippling bass, which two bars of socking drums and four bars of funky Honky Tonk piano hook you in even before Frankie Valli gets a chance to pour his unique voice over this sweet surrender of a track. **Caroline Coon, Melody Maker, January 1976**

Deck Of Cards

ARTIST Wink Martindale RELEASE DATE December 1959 (UK)/September 1959 (US) WRITER T. Texas Tyler PRODUCER – LABEL London (UK)/Dot (US) UK CHART PEAK/WEEKS 5/29 US CHART PEAK/WEEKS 7/17

Wink Martindale, a DJ and a TV host, with a voice full of smoke, half sang, half recited this hokum sermon about a deck of cards, a young soldier and a church. The soldier is disciplined for having a deck of cards open during a church service, but nope, he isn't practising a sly poker hand, he's really praying. Each card represents something religious; the pack is an emblem of his Christian faith. The word kitsch springs to mind.

With Deck Of Cards Wink has made a lasting impression on both sides of the Atlantic. Against a slow rock backing of guitar, organ and voices, he tells the story of a soldier bringing out a pack of cards in church – a deadly sin in the eyes of his sergeant. **Ifor Griffiths, NME, December 1959**

Delilah

ARTIST Tom Jones RELEASE DATE February 1968 (UK)/March 1968 (US) WRITER Les Reed, Barry Mason PRODUCER – LABEL Decca (UK)/Parrot (US) UK CHART PEAK/WEEKS 2/17 US CHART PEAK/WEEKS 15/15

This dramatic recording by Welsh balladeer Jones spent two weeks at Number 2 in the UK, his third consecutive release to peak just short of the summit. The song was a worldwide success; in Germany it was Number 1 for nine weeks while a cover by Peter Alexander was Number 1 there for a further fortnight. In 1975, the song was covered by the Sensational Alex Harvey Band and gave the Scots rock group their only UK Top 10 hit.

Just as Samson came in for a few knocks via his relationship with Delilah, the same tempting lady is now stirring it up and creating a bit of bovver for our own Tom Jones. Single Delilah is being criticized for bad taste by a number of critics. **Alan Smith, NME, March 1968**

blondie

denis
contact in red square
kung fu girls

Denis

ARTIST Blondie **RELEASE DATE** February 1978 **WRITER** Neil Levenson **PRODUCER** Richard Gottehrer **LABEL** Chrysalis **UK CHART PEAK/WEEKS** 2/14 **US CHART PEAK/WEEKS** 0/0

From New York City, Blondie hit the charts in the UK before they made it in their native country. *Denis* was the perfect debut, a song which gave singer Deborah Harry the opportunity to display her unique talent while at the same time showing her, uh, roots. It was a gender-switched version of *Denise,* originally a hit in 1963 for another New York quintet, Randy & the Rainbows.

Debbie Harry sings beautifully and everybody at London Airport whistles this tune already. Consequently this is up for high placement…. Denis does not wear tight trousers that make his balls look soppy, and have poetic hair, and he IS French. A hit. **Ian Dury, NME, February 1978**

A Design For Life

ARTIST Manic Street Preachers **RELEASE DATE** April 1996 **WRITER** James Dean Bradfield, Sean Moore, Nicky Wire **PRODUCER** Mike Hedges **LABEL** Epic **UK CHART PEAK/WEEKS** 2/11 **US CHART PEAK/WEEKS** –

The Manic Street Preachers used punk and poetry to fuel their music and help them escape from the gloom of their working class backgrounds in a small Welsh town. In 1994, they were devastated by the disappearance of Richey Edwards, their guitarist. His abandoned car was found at the Severn Bridge. The band continued and released *Design For Life*, an anthemic critique of working-class culture, and a best-selling album **Everything Must Go**. Richey was never found.

I did detect a certain 'millencholia', a deep millennial angst trembling there in the thunderclap chords and marshalled tumult. In fact, the song's

effect has been immeasurably positive, returning to the Manics that hunger and immense pride that first inspired and galvanised the band. **Taylor Parkes, Melody Maker, June 1996**

Devil Woman

ARTIST Cliff Richard **RELEASE DATE** May 1975 (UK)/July 1976 (US) **WRITER** Terry Britten **PRODUCER** Bruce Welch **LABEL** EMI (UK)/Rocket (US) **UK CHART PEAK/WEEKS** 9/8 **US CHART PEAK/WEEKS** 6/22

With his career seeming almost stalled after the early 1970s, Richard responded with the ironically titled **I'm Nearly Famous**, produced by long-time friend Bruce Welch of the Shadows. From this surprise hit album came the single *Devil Woman*. Although the song's lyrical implications may have raised eyebrows among some devotees of clean-cut Christian Cliff, it nevertheless hit Number 9 in the UK charts and went gold in the States.

Diana

ARTIST Paul Anka **RELEASE DATE** August 1957 (UK)/July 1957 (US) **WRITER** Paul Anka **PRODUCER** Don Costa **LABEL** Columbia (UK)/ABC-Paramount (US) **UK CHART PEAK/WEEKS** 1/25 **US CHART PEAK/WEEKS** 1/29

Paul Anka was rock's first teenage prodigy, writing and singing his first release, the world-wide smash *Diana*, when he was only 15. It was an ode to one Diana Ayoub, who baby-sat for his younger brother and sister. Many of his later hits would also be inspired by real life events, most notably *Puppy Love*, which was about his romance with Annette Funicello, five years his senior and inaccessible.

Paul Anka is another singer of the drool-school…. Diana has a 'little darlin'' motif in the accompaniment. This is also a sure bet. **Laurie Hernshaw, Melody Maker, August 1957**

Disco 2000

ARTIST Pulp RELEASE DATE December 1995 WRITER Pulp (lyrics by Jarvis Cocker) PRODUCER Chris Thomas LABEL Island UK CHART PEAK/WEEKS 7/11 US CHART PEAK/WEEKS –

One of a string of hits to follow in the wake of the 1990s Britpop boom and taken from Pulp's hugely successful album **Different Class**. **Disco 2000** is Jarvis Cocker at his camp and sniping best, a sly, rhythmic comment on the gritty, yearning angst of inner-city youth. The agonizingly sensitive lyrics are swelled by the pulsing, foot-tapping riffs, retrospectively hurtling its shy teenage hero through the confusion of his pre-pubescent nightmare.

Disco 2000, like Pink Glove before it, shows that what fuels his vindictive bitterness is actually a deep romanticism…. Jarvis' fantasy of meeting an old flame and reversing time – romanticism, remember, is equal parts dreaming of what could be and what could have been. **Simon Price, Melody Maker, November 1995**

Distant Drums

ARTIST Jim Reeves RELEASE DATE August 1966 (UK)/April 1966 (US) WRITER Cindy Walker PRODUCER – LABEL RCA (UK)/RCA Victor (US) UK CHART PEAK/WEEKS 1/25 US CHART PEAK/WEEKS 45/7

Distant Drums had already been released by Roy Orbison. The release of Jim Reeves' version, two years after his death, saw it rise to Number 1 in the UK. It was one of Reeves' 21 UK Top 40 entries and one of his 11 US Country Number 1s. Cindy Walker, the writer, became the first woman to achieve a UK chart topper with a solo composition.

Jim Reeves' smooth tones effortlessly glide through this country favourite, backed by strings, vibes and an underlying throbbing which stress the title. Very square but will appeal to all his fans, and may be a minor hit. **Derek Johnson, NME, July 1966**

Dizzy

ARTIST Tommy Roe RELEASE DATE April 1969 (UK)/February 1969 (US) WRITER Tommy Roe, Freddy Weller PRODUCER Steve Barri LABEL Stateside (UK)/ABC (US) UK CHART PEAK/WEEKS 1/19 US CHART PEAK/WEEKS 1/15

Because of his popularity in the UK, Roe moved to England in the mid-1960s where he and producer Steve Barri churned out a row of bubble-gum hits. Among these, the Buddy Hollyesque **Dizzy** was his most successful, though he had already sold a million records each with **Sheila** (1960) and **Everybody** (1963). In 1991 the British surrealist comics Vic Reeves and Bob Mortimer released a more or less straight cover version, which again took the song to Number 1 in the UK.

It's doing good in the States, it's Tommy Roe isn't it. It is good for a pop record – it's a beautiful pop record – but I wouldn't buy it. **Stevie Wonder, Melody Maker, July 1969**

Do It Again

ARTIST Steely Dan RELEASE DATE August 1975 (UK)/November 1972 (US) WRITER Walter Becker, Donald Fagen PRODUCER Gary Katz LABEL ABC (UK & US) UK CHART PEAK/WEEKS 39/4 US CHART PEAK/WEEKS 6/17

The first track on their debut album, **Can't Buy A Thrill**, was a weird, vaguely menacing tale of lost hope, addiction and obsession, featuring Donald Fagen's nasal twang, a boppy latin rhythm and a rare use of electric sitar and cheap electric organ for the solos. All the favourite Dan adjectives could be applied to the lyrics *Do It Again*: inscrutable, idiosyncratic. The US audience pushed it to US Number 6.

Do That To Me One More Time

ARTIST Captain And Tennille **RELEASE DATE** February 1980 (UK)/October 1979 (US) **WRITER** Toni Tennille **PRODUCER** Daryl Dragon **LABEL** Casablanca (UK & US) **UK CHART PEAK/WEEKS** 7/10 **US CHART PEAK/WEEKS** 1/27

After the Captain And Tennille's *You Never Done It Like That* made the US Top 10, they tried to follow it up with *You Need A Woman Tonight*. When that disc stalled at Number 40, they decided to go back to the 'do me' theme. That did it. **Do That To Me One More Time** not only hit Number 1 in America but also provided them with their only UK Top 10.

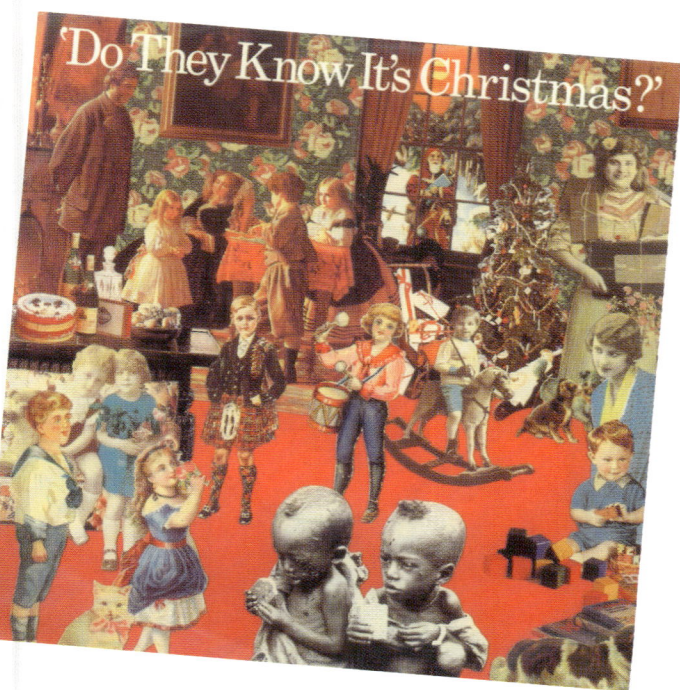

Do They Know It's Christmas?

ARTIST Band Aid **RELEASE DATE** December 1984 (UK & US) **WRITER** Bob Geldof, Midge Ure **PRODUCER** Midge Ure **LABEL** Mercury (UK)/Columbia (US) **UK CHART PEAK/WEEKS** 1/20 **US CHART PEAK/WEEKS** 13/9

Until Elton John's **Candle in the Wind 1997**, Band Aid's release was the biggest and fastest selling single in British history. In many ways, it paved the way for **Candle**, as it was the first benefit record from which neither artists, manufacturer, nor retailers took any profit. The man who convinced them to make this gesture was Boomtown Rats leader Bob Geldof.

Do Wah Diddy Diddy

ARTIST Manfred Mann **RELEASE DATE** July 1964 (UK)/September 1964 (US) **WRITER** Jeff Barry, Ellie Greenwich **PRODUCER** John Burgess **LABEL** HMV Pop (UK)/Ascot (US) **UK CHART PEAK/WEEKS** 1/14 **US CHART PEAK/WEEKS** 1/13

Do Wah Diddy Diddy was a glorious catchy song by Ellie Greenwich and Jeff Barry who had been responsible for some of the great Sixties girl group hits. The Exciters had released this first, but it didn't do anything despite its finger snapping, infectious style. Manfred Mann, whose usual fare was American uptown R&B, covered it and managed to oust The Beatles' **A Hard Days Night** from the top of the charts.

Our latest record, which we understand is doing quite well, was recorded about four or five weeks before it was released. **Do Wah Diddy Diddy** *is the first of our singles that has not been written by us.* **Manfred Mann, Melody Maker, August 1964**

Do You Really Want To Hurt Me

ARTIST Culture Club RELEASE DATE September 1982 (UK)/December 1982 (US) WRITER Roy Hay, John Moss, Michael Craig, George O'Dowd PRODUCER Steve Levine LABEL Virgin (UK)/Epic Virgin (US) UK CHART PEAK/WEEKS 1/18 US CHART PEAK/WEEKS 2/25

With Do You Really Want to Hurt Me, Culture Club made history. Never before had a rock group led by a full-time drag queen reached Number 1. Lead singer Boy George so successfully put across his asexual image that he appealed to children and even the middle-aged. He was cute and safe, like a teddy bear with mascara. Lifted by his soulful performance, the single kicked off Culture Club's short but memorable string of danceable, soul-inspired hits.

… on the cover Boy George is pictured doing that clumsy, embarrassing dance that our society's 'free-er' children always feel prone to…. **Danny Baker, NME, September 1982**

The Dock Of The Bay (Sittin' On)

ARTIST Otis Redding RELEASE DATE February 1968 (UK)/January 1968 (US) WRITER Steve Cropper, Otis Redding PRODUCER Steve Cropper, Otis Redding LABEL Stax (UK)/Volt (US) UK CHART PEAK/WEEKS 3/15 US CHART PEAK/WEEKS 1/16

The son of a Baptist preacher, Redding became the biggest thing since James Brown. His wistful ballad was recorded just before he flew with his band, the Bar-Kays, to an interview. The plane crashed in a lake in Wisconsin, USA, killing the 26-year-old phenomenon. *The Dock Of The Bay* became a million-seller in its first 30 days and has sold more than four million copies over the years. He was posthumously awarded two Grammys for Best R&B

Vocal Performance and Best Song. This, his best-remembered song, was successfully re-recorded by his sons Dexter and Otis III in 1982 and again by Michael Bolton in 1988.

Dominique

ARTIST The Singing Nun RELEASE DATE December 1963 (UK)/November 1963 (US) WRITER Noel Regney, Soeur Sourire PRODUCER – LABEL Philips (UK & US) UK CHART PEAK/WEEKS 7/14 US CHART PEAK/WEEKS 1/13

Secular success ultimately proved too great a temptation for Sister Luc-Gabrielle (born Janine Deckers), the Belgian nun who created this tribute song to the founder of the Dominican order. A surprise Christmas hit – there was also a Number 1 album – she collected a Grammy for the Best Gospel Or Religious Performance. Leaving the order in 1966, no follow-up hits ensued although she did try releasing a later rocked-up version. Janine committed suicide in 1985.

Surely the most unlikely hit parade material of all time – The Singing Nun. Already a chart-topper in the States, her **Dominique** *is now at Number 4…. The album that I would most like to see in 1964? The Singing Nun meets Thelonius Monk.* **Melody Maker, January 1964**

Don't Be Cruel

ARTIST Elvis Presley RELEASE DATE November 1956 WRITER Otis Blackwell, Elvis Presley PRODUCER Steve Sholes LABEL HMV Pop (UK)/RCA Victor (US) UK CHART PEAK/WEEKS – US CHART PEAK/WEEKS 1/27 (Double A Side with Hound Dog)

Sorting through acetate demos during the same sessions that produced *Hound Dog*, Elvis picked out an Otis Blackwell song. After one rehearsal producer Steve Sholes was ready to record but Elvis insisted on more rehearsal with guitarist Scotty Moore, pianist Shorty Long and the Jordanaires. By the 28th take, his vocal had evolved into an almost languid counterpart to the sprung rhythm – with additional 'snare drum' effect created by D. J. Fontana's use of a mallet on the back of Elvis's leather-covered guitar.

I think that **Don't Be Cruel** *and* **Hound Dog** *are the best R&R records to be made in years, and I cannot see any other record holding it when it is released in Britain.* **John Davidson, NME, August 1956**

Don't Believe The Hype

ARTIST Public Enemy RELEASE DATE June 1988 WRITER Carlton Ridenhour, Hank Shocklee, Eric Sadler PRODUCER Carl Ryder, Hank Shockley LABEL Def Jam UK CHART PEAK/WEEKS 18/5 US CHART PEAK/WEEKS –

Don't Believe The Hype was typical of hip-hop DJ rappers Public Enemy's aggressive machine-gun rasp of percussion and samples. As an object lesson in street-level sloganeering, the release confirmed them as the swaggering princes of rap, a chauvinistic ghetto band taut with trigger-happy homophobia and misogyny.

Another tedious tosh load of repetitive chanting, thoroughly devoid of sex and humour, labouring under the doughy idea that by utilising the word 'hype' they are pre-empting it from veering towards their own rock-hard foreheads. Yo, dumb mush on show. **Chris Roberts, Melody Maker, July 1988**

Don't Cry For Me Argentina

ARTIST Julie Covington **RELEASE DATE** December 1976 **WRITER** Tim Rice, Andrew Lloyd Webber **PRODUCER** – **LABEL** MCA **UK CHART PEAK/WEEKS** 1/18 **US CHART PEAK/WEEKS** –

Andrew Lloyd Webber and Tim Rice used to make a habit of releasing albums of their musicals before the actual musicals were produced. They did this with the **Jesus Christ Superstar** album, and they likewise scored big with their auditory preview of **Evita**. With Julie Covington, formerly of Rock Follies, lending sufficient drama to the role, the disc sold 980,000 copies in the UK alone, making it at the time the biggest-selling single ever by a female vocalist.

The moving main theme from Andrew Lloyd Webber's and Tim Rice's opera, Evita, about the life of Eva Peron. If you have not heard the whole work, the lyric will make no sense at all, though you have to admire the fine performance of Ms Covington, The Rock Follies lady. **Alan Lewis, Sounds, November 1978**

Don't Dream It's Over

ARTIST Crowded House **RELEASE DATE** June 1987 (UK)/January 1987 (US) **WRITER** Neil Finn **PRODUCER** Mitchell Froom **LABEL** Capitol (UK & US) **UK CHART PEAK/WEEKS** 27/8 **US CHART PEAK/WEEKS** 2/24

When Split Enz alumni Crowded House released their first album it was left to America to make **Don't Dream It's Over** a hit, although a few Brits did manage to drag it kicking and screaming into the lower end of the Top 30. Today, the song is widely recognized as a pop classic. Neil Finn wrote it at his brother Tim's house, where he had retreated following a marital spat. Listeners could tell it came from the heart.

Sounding a bit like a less glib version of Squeeze at its peak, Crowded House is a pure-pop lover's dream. This song is a craftily composed, romantic ballad that McCartney should be covering, if not have written. **Rob Tannewbawm, Rolling Stone, January 1987**

(Don't Fear) The Reaper

ARTIST Blue Öyster Cult **RELEASE DATE** May 1978 (UK)/July 1976 (US) **WRITER** Donald Roeser **PRODUCER** Sandy Pearman, Murray Krigmas, David Lucas **LABEL** CBS (UK)/Columbia (US) **UK CHART PEAK/WEEKS** 16/14 **US CHART PEAK/WEEKS** 12/20

Don't Fear the Reaper was the only Top 40 hit for this New York quartet, which began its career as Soft White Underbelly. Known more for their hard rock excursions than for the subdued, melodic **Reaper**, they were a very successful album act and a strong influence on many of today's metal acts.

This is a beautiful Donald Roeser song that adapts sound of the Byrds to that of BOC, with interweaving guitars, a totally seductive melody, energy held at bay and the usual strange lyrics. **Ian Birch, Melody Maker, May 1978**

Don't Give Up On Us

ARTIST David Soul **RELEASE DATE** December 1976 (UK)/January 1977 (US) **WRITER** Tony Macauley **PRODUCER** Tom Macauley **LABEL** Private Stock (UK & US) **UK CHART PEAK/WEEKS** 1/16 **US CHART PEAK/WEEKS** 1/19

The blond hunk who played Starsky's partner Ken Hutchinson had done a little folk singing before concentrating on acting. He built on the success of the cop show when it was at its peak, bringing his white-boy soul voice to bear on a number of, frankly, drippy ballads. **Don't Give Up On Us** was his only US hit, but he had another Number 1 in the UK with **Silver Lady** before turning in his chart badge.

Actually, he hasn't got a bad voice. But would you trust Lassky and Crutch to search your kid Brother. **Tony Parson's, NME, December 1976**

Don't Go Breaking My Heart

ARTIST Elton John and Kiki Dee **RELEASE DATE** July 1976 (UK)/August 1976 (US) **WRITER** Elton John, Bernie Taupin **PRODUCER** Gus Dudgeon **LABEL** Rocket (U K & US) **UK CHART PEAK/WEEKS** 1/14 **US CHART PEAK/WEEKS** 1/20

Although Elton John had to wait until 1989 for his first solo UK Number 1 with **Sacrifice**, this duet with Kiki Dee topped both the

UK and US charts in 1976. Dee was the first British vocalist to sign for Motown but had never reached the UK Top 10 before. The song was the second best selling single of 1976 in both the UK and US. In 1994, Elton recorded the song with female impersonator Ru Paul and again made the UK Top 10.

They're both quite good singers, but its a pity Orson & Blanch … didn't write them a more memorable song than this, which jogs along harmlessly. (He did write a good song in 73.) **Phil McNeill, NME, June 1976**

Don't It Make My Brown Eyes Blue

ARTIST Crystal Gayle RELEASE DATE November 1977 (UK)/August 1977 (US) WRITER Richard Leigh PRODUCER – LABEL United Artists (UK & US) UK CHART PEAK/WEEKS 5/14 US CHART PEAK/WEEKS 2/26

Born Brenda Gail Webb in 1951 and the youngest sister of country singer Loretta Lynn, Crystal Gayle scored her biggest US hit with this single, spending three weeks at Number 2 behind Pat Boone's daughter Debby's ten-week chart-topper *You Light Up My Life*. The song gave her a second chart-topper in the US country listings. It is also her biggest UK hit. In 1979, she became the first country artist to tour China.

Don't Leave Me This Way

ARTIST The Communards RELEASE DATE August 1986 (UK)/December 1986 (US) WRITER Cary Gilbert, Kenny Gamble, Leon Huff PRODUCER Mike Thorn LABEL London (UK)/MCA/London (US) UK CHART PEAK/WEEKS 1/14 US CHART PEAK/WEEKS 40/13

The Communards were masterminded by former Bronski Beat leader Jimmy Somerville. With musical partner Richard Coles, Somerville, who was always big on image, recruited a backing band, the main requirement being the possession of two 'x' chromosomes. After two unsuccessful singles, they brought the deep-voiced Sarah Jane Morris on board and hit the top with their cover of *Don't Leave Me This Way,* which was Top 5 for Harold Melvin & The Blue Notes in 1977.

Jimmy Somerville's vocals on this single hold none of the mystery and power they had in former days. The performance is Le-Pub Cabaret: showy, glitzy, temporary and artificial. The Communards own one of the finest voices in pop, but will they ever get to use it? **Neil Taylor, NME, August 1986**

Don't Let The Sun Go Down On Me

ARTIST Elton John & George Michael RELEASE DATE December 1991 (UK & US) WRITER Elton John, Bernie Taupin PRODUCER George Michael LABEL Epic (UK)/Columbia (US) UK CHART PEAK/WEEKS 1/10 US CHART PEAK/WEEKS 1/20

Originally released in 1974, this song featured Carl and Bruce Wilson (Beach Boys) and Toni Tennille (Captain and Tennille) on backing vocals, but it was when Elton teamed with ex-Wham! heart-throb George Michael that it became a UK and US chart-topper. Elton had shown up at a Wembley concert by George in 1991 and came on unannounced to duet with him: the version released was from this show.

*There are many elements to this single that you'll enjoy – faint and distant tambourines, those aforementioned f***ers on guitar– but it's the way these elements are fused together to produce a deceptively simple sound that is most impressive.* **John Peel, Sounds, June 1974**

Don't Look Back In Anger

ARTIST Oasis RELEASE DATE March 1996 (UK)/August 1996 (US) WRITER Noel Gallagher PRODUCER Owen Morris, Noel Gallagher LABEL Creation (UK)/Epic (US) UK CHART PEAK/WEEKS 1/21 US CHART PEAK/WEEKS 55/14

The album **(What's The Story) Morning Glory** was starting to take on the look of a greatest hits collection when **Don't Look Back In Anger**, the fourth single from it, was released. It had to wait in the wings for a while, however, until **Wonderwall** finally quit its chart residency. Basically a ballad, with a fine soaring chorus, it is especially notable because songwriter Noel Gallagher takes over lead vocal duties on the track, one of his personal favourites.

They didn't send me a copy, of course. Which wouldn't have stopped me reviewing it from the LP, but I can't be arsed…. I'll leave it for next week's Creation-approved reviewer to make it SOTW. I just wanted them to know I could've slagged it if I wanted, that's all. **Simon Price, Melody Maker, February 1996**

Don't Stand So Close To Me

ARTIST Police RELEASE DATE September 1980 (UK)/February 1981 (US) WRITER Sting PRODUCER Nigel Gray, Police LABEL A&M (UK & US) UK CHART PEAK/WEEKS 1/10 US CHART PEAK/WEEKS 10/18

1980 was a busy year for Police. They started their first world tour, which would take in 37 cities and 19 countries, before ending up in Sting's hometown of Newcastle. They also became the first Western group to perform in Bombay, India. The year was a learning experience, and this motif was continued in **Don't Stand**

So Close. It is sung as a teacher to a student, with a nod to Nabakov in its Lolita theme.

Scratching guitar, Sting's sex appeal and that inimitable mysterious build-up to that archetypal Police sing-along-with-Sting chorus. **Paulo Hewitt, Melody Maker, September 1980**

Don't Stop

ARTIST Fleetwood Mac RELEASE DATE April 1977 (UK)/July 1977 (US) WRITER Christine McVie PRODUCER Richard Dashut, Lindsey Buckingham, Chris Norris LABEL Warner Bros (UK)/Warner (US) UK CHART PEAK/WEEKS 32/5 US CHART PEAK/WEEKS 3/8

This track from 1977's multi-platinum **Rumours** album gained a new lease of life when it was adopted as the theme song for Bill Clinton's early-Nineties presidential campaign. The classic line-up that recorded it were persuaded to reconvene for a January 1993 performance at Clinton's presidential inauguration at the Capital Centre, Landover, Maryland. The lyric 'Don't stop thinking about tomorrow' seemed curiously inappropriate, however….

Immaculate though Mac are, producing a stream of mainstream rock at its most bearable, they don't seem to hit the right nerve over here. Will we love them here as much as they do in the States? Chart Potential. **Caroline Coon, Melody Maker, April 1977**

Don't Turn Around

ARTIST Aswad RELEASE DATE February 1988 WRITER Diane Warren, Albert Hammond PRODUCER Chris Porter LABEL Mango UK CHART PEAK/WEEKS 1/12 US CHART PEAK/WEEKS –

Seasoned songsmiths Diane Warren and Albert Hammond's **Don't Turn Around** first saw life as the B-side of Tina Turner's **Typical**

Male. Aswad – whose name means 'black' in Arabic – saw greater potential in the tune, retooling it to fit their reggae style. It became the first hit for the London trio, who had been together since 1975.

Don't You (Forget About Me)

ARTIST Simple Minds RELEASE DATE April 1985 (UK)/February 1985 (US) WRITER Keith Forsey, Steve Schiff PRODUCER Keith Forsey LABEL Virgin (UK)/A&M (US) UK CHART PEAK/WEEKS 7/20 US CHART PEAK/WEEKS 1/22

The Scottish band didn't originally want *Don't You* included on the soundtrack of *The Breakfast Club* but it gave them their breakthrough in the States, underlined by their appearance at the Philadelphia leg of Live Aid. Co-written by Billy Idol producer Keith Forsey, the song had been rejected by Idol and Bryan Ferry. Despite their initial reluctance Simple Minds made the most of their opportunity and the song entered the UK chart four times during 1985.

Jim Kerr's … capacious ego has produced too meagre a ration of enlightening signals, with too many crass gestures. **Ted Mico, Melody Maker, April 1985**

Don't You Want Me

ARTIST The Human League RELEASE DATE December 1981 (UK)/March 1982 (US) WRITER Philip Oakley, Adrian Wright PRODUCER Martin Rushent LABEL Virgin (UK)/A&M/Virgin (US) UK CHART PEAK/WEEKS 1/13 US CHART PEAK/WEEKS 1/28

Clean, perfect in every detail, infuriatingly catchy, not necessarily a musical triumph but as soon as you heard it you just knew it was going to be massive. *Don't You Want Me* dominated the dying weeks of 1981 and confirmed the Human League's status as world-beating pop stars. A chart-topper in America, New Zealand, Canada and even Israel, this was Number 1 in the UK for five weeks over Christmas, the perfect piece of escapism in an economically depressed Britain.

Classic heart-throbbing duo pop, like a synthesized, new romanticized Sonny and Cher. It underlines the Human League's arrival as purveyors of perfect pop singles.… And you thought **Love Action** *was good.* **Colin Irwin, Melody Maker, November 1981**

Donna

ARTIST 10 cc RELEASE DATE September 1972 WRITER Kevin Godley, Lol Creme PRODUCER 10 cc LABEL UK UK CHART PEAK/WEEKS 2/13 US CHART PEAK/WEEKS –

The Manchester foursome came together at Strawberry Studios in Stockport. Stewart, Godley, Creme and Gouldman did session work and generally noodled round on the equipment. One such noodle, 'Neanderthal Man', was put out under the name **Hotlegs** in 1970 and reached UK Number 2; two years later Stewart's friend Jonathan King signed them to his UK label – and they got serious. *Donna* was a pastiche of Fifties American doo-wop and rock 'n' roll and was typical of the referential and witty songs of early 10 cc.

Donna parodies Fifties teen ballads and The Beatles **Oh Darling** *at the same time.… Although currently recording for a plethora of labels under a variety of names, 10 cc is one group whose very last record is worth tracking down.* **Greg Shaw, Rolling Stone, November 1973**

Down In The Tube Station At Midnight

ARTIST The Jam RELEASE DATE October 1978 WRITER Paul Weller PRODUCER Vic Coppersmith-Heaven LABEL Polydor UK CHART PEAK/WEEKS 15/7 US CHART PEAK/WEEKS –

This single, arguably the Jam's first classic pop song, plugged the gap between a 1978 Reading Festival appearance and the Jam's third album **All Mod Cons** on which it would be the final track. Ironically the band had considered every track bar *Tube Station* a potential single, and in typically contrary fashion had chosen it to trailer the album! A BBC airplay ban due to its 'disturbing' nature halted chart progress, but it was a gem.

Tremendous, clever, talent-packed record from one of the best LPs ever made.… **Danny Baker, NME, January 1983**

Downtown

ARTIST Petula Clark **RELEASE DATE** November 1964 (UK)/December 1964 (US) **WRITER** Tony Hatch **PRODUCER** Tony Hatch **LABEL** Pye (UK)/Warner (US) **UK CHART PEAK/WEEKS** 2/15 **US CHART PEAK/WEEKS** 1/15

When 'Pet' Clark made her American debut in late 1964 with **Downtown**, she was seen as the latest in a succession of British female vocalists that included Cilla, Sandie, and Dusty. In fact, the 32-year-old singer had been a child star, nicknamed 'The Forces Girl' for the hundreds of shows that she performed for the troops. **Downtown** marked her 15th year as a recording artist. It was nonetheless an important hit as it brought her into the beat music era.

It is certainly the best song I have ever recorded in English, and I am very grateful to Tony Hatch who wrote the tune and the lyrics…. It has tremendous atmosphere. **Petula interviewed by Mike Hennessey, Melody Maker, November 1964**

Drama!

ARTIST Erasure **RELEASE DATE** September 1989 **WRITER** Vincent Clark, Andrew Ball **PRODUCER** Gareth Jones **LABEL** Mute **UK CHART PEAK/WEEKS** 4/8 **US CHART PEAK/WEEKS** 0/0

Amazingly for a group featuring the multi-talented songwriter Vince Clarke, ex-of Depeche Mode and Yazoo, electro-pop duo Erasure would only reach the Number 1 spot with a set of tongue-in-cheek Abba cover versions in 1992. By that time they had clocked up 17 Top 40 hits, of which **Drama!** reached Number 9. It was extracted from the chart-topping album **Wild!** at the end of a year in which their efforts had been recognized by a Best British Group award at the Brits.

It is never a good sign when you cannot work out which is the A-side of the single. Perhaps this is the world's first double B-side. Both tracks are useless. **Stuart Maconie, NME, September 1989**

The Dreamer

ARTIST Supertramp **RELEASE DATE** February 1975 (UK)/September 1980 (US) **WRITER** Richard Davies, Roger Hodgson **PRODUCER** Ken Scott **LABEL** A&M (UK & US) **UK CHART PEAK/WEEKS** 13/10 **US CHART PEAK/WEEKS** 15/14

Band founders Rick Davies and Roger Hodgson re-invented the band in 1973 and finally got some decent songs together. By 1975 the elements were in place and this single from the album **Crime**

Of The Century – an ersatz **Dark Side Of The Moon** – driven by electric piano and sax brought the group plenty of attention, although they didn't really chart until **The Logical Song** reached both the UK and US Top 10.

Featuring a lot of repeated open piano chords, harmonized vocals and some heavy tom-tom work by the drummer, this sounds like an Anglicized Beach Boys. **Brian Harrigan, Melody Maker, November 1974**

Dreamlover

ARTIST Mariah Carey **RELEASE DATE** August 1993 (UK & US) **WRITER** Dave Hall, Mariah Carey **PRODUCER** Walter Afanasieff, Dave Hall, Mariah Carey **LABEL** Columbia (UK & US) **UK CHART PEAK/WEEKS** 9/10 **US CHART PEAK/WEEKS** 1/29

Mariah Carey released **Dreamlover** shortly after returning from her honeymoon with the man who had made her dream of stardom come true, Sony Music president Tommy Mottola. The highly anticipated disc, her first original single in over a year, entered *Billboard*'s Hot 100 at Number 1. It was the first hit from her album **Music Box**, which would also provide another international smash, **Hero**.

Mariah Carey sings with consummate power, grace and range over a Janet-swing lagoon of a track, both languorous and sassy. She looks a million dollars and is in reality worth several million more. **Chris Roberts, Melody Maker, August 1993**

Dreams

ARTIST Fleetwood Mac RELEASE DATE July 1977 (UK)/April 1977 (US) WRITER Stevie Nicks PRODUCER Richard Dashut, Lindsey Buckingham, Chris Norris LABEL Warner Bros (UK)/Warner (US) UK CHART PEAK/WEEKS 24/9 US CHART PEAK/WEEKS 1/19

Yet another hit from the mega-selling **Rumours** album, *Dreams* would amazingly be the group's one and only US singles chart-topper in any of their many personnel configurations. The star of the show was singer and writer Stephanie ('Stevie') Nicks, a Melanie soundalike who had joined the band for the previous eponymous album.

This kind of super-sophisticated ballad schmaltz sends me to sleep. The blurb reckons that the yearningly sexy voice of Stevie Nicks shades every word with delicate shades of emotion. Balls, more like the sort of record that Hamburger joints used to get rid of their customers. **Max Bell, NME, July 1977**

Drive

ARTIST The Cars RELEASE DATE September 1984 (UK)/August 1984 (US) WRITER Ric Ocasek PRODUCER Robert John 'Mutt' Lange LABEL Elektra (UK & US) UK CHART PEAK/WEEKS 4/23 US CHART PEAK/WEEKS 3/19

Drive hit the Top 10 twice within one year. It first sped upwards in October 1984, when it reached Number 5, becoming the Cars' first hit in six years and their biggest since 1978's **My Best Friend's Girl**. The following August, after the song was used during Live Aid as background music for footage of African famine sufferers, it re-entered and went one point higher than before. At that point Ric Ocasek announced that he would donate all subsequent **Drive** royalties to the Band Aid Trust.

Dub Be Good To Me

ARTIST Beats International RELEASE DATE February 1990 (UK)/April 1990 (US) WRITER Norman Cook, James Harris, Terry Lewis PRODUCER Norman Cook LABEL Rhythm King (UK)/Elektra (US) UK CHART PEAK/WEEKS 5/11 US CHART PEAK/WEEKS 76/5

Formed by former Housemartins guitarist Norman Cook, Beats International scored a Number 1 their first time out with **Dub Be Good To Me**. It was essentially a reggae-style cover of former SOS band members Jimmy Jam and Terry Lewis's **Just Be Good To Me** combined with an instrumental sample from the Clash's **Guns Of Brixton**. Their only song

to reach the top, it appeared the following year on their first album, **Let Them Eat Bingo**.

*This is a terrific deep dub version of the SOS Band's fabulous **Just Be Good To Me**, the heart-quake synths of the original replaced by sensor beeps, with a lonesome 'Midnight Cowboy' harmonizing. Just Fine.* **Simon Reynolds, Melody Maker, 1990**

Easy

ARTIST The Commodores RELEASE DATE July 1977 (UK)/June 1977 (US) WRITER Lionel Richie PRODUCER James Anthony Carmichael LABEL Motown (UK & US) UK CHART PEAK/WEEKS 9/10 US CHART PEAK/WEEKS 4/22

In the summer of 1977 the Commodores attempted to align themselves with the disco craze, appearing with Donna Summer in the cash-in film *Thank God It's Friday*. However, smooth, slow ballads were still their forte, as shown by the international success of **Easy**, which hit Number 9 in the UK. The song charted even higher in 1993, when hard-rockers Faith No More's version made Number 3.

Easy *hovers over a gospel piano melody until it's scooped up in the metal talons of McClary's guitar. A great finale – and possibly the most likely single to succeed in Britain.* **Cliff White, NME, June 1977**

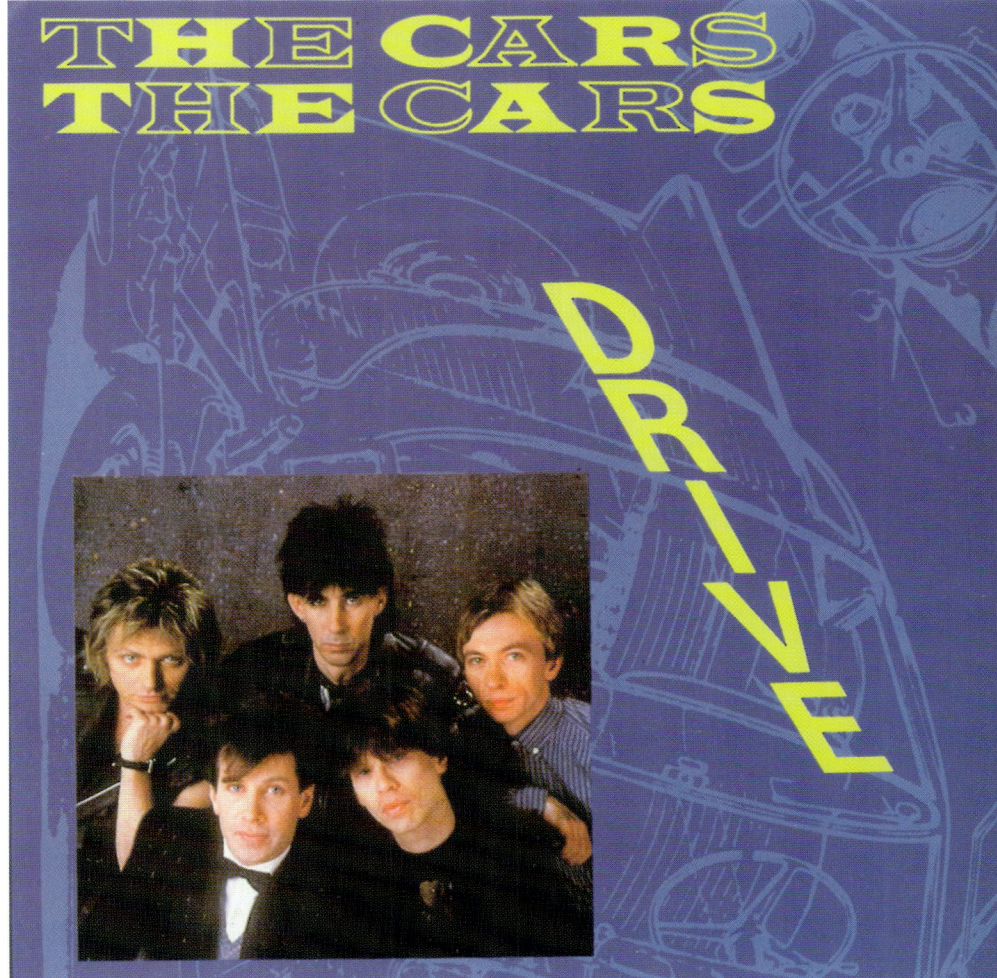

Easy Lover

ARTIST Philip Bailey With Phil Collins RELEASE DATE March 1985 (UK)/November 1984 (US) WRITER Philip Bailey, Phil Collins, Nathan East PRODUCER Phil Collins LABEL CBS (UK)/Columbia (US) UK CHART PEAK/WEEKS 1/12 US CHART PEAK/WEEKS 2/23

The only duet between two Phils ever to make the charts, *Easy Lover* was from the album Collins produced for Bailey, **Chinese Wall**, Bailey's first solo outing after leaving Earth, Wind and Fire. Although Collins had not released a solo single for eight months, *Easy Lover* marked the second time in five months that he played drums on a UK Number 1. The earlier one was Band Aid's **Do They Know It's Christmas?**.

*Easy Lover is still an unflawed display of Collins's skill at playing the same old cards of MOR disco, and brushing them up anew, putting on the edge that lights up his own **No Jacket Required**. Richard Cook, NME, March 1985.*

Ebeneezer Goode

ARTIST The Shamen RELEASE DATE September 1992 (UK & US) WRITER Colin Angus, Richard West PRODUCER The Shamen LABEL One Little Indian (UK)/Epic (US) UK CHART PEAK/WEEKS 1/10 US CHART PEAK/WEEKS 0/0

Stars of London's indie label One Little Indian, The Shamen were leaders of indie-dance crossover, using the sampling skills of Will Sinnott, and creating multi-media shows that fitted perfectly into rave culture. When Sinnott died in the Canary Islands in a drowning accident in 1991, founder Colin Angus carried on, after some soul-searching. After August 1992's **Love Sex Intelligence**, this UK Number 1 the following month created mild controversy over its punning lyrical suggestion that 'E's are good'.

Derry: 'I like the lyrics … Chips & Peas-er: Vera Lyns-Ships … I've always liked The Shamen. They have never really made a big single…. Mark: 'They never suck up to anyone and make clichéd commercial shit.' Mark and Derry from EMF, Melody Maker, August 1992

Ebony & Ivory

ARTIST Paul McCartney & Stevie Wonder RELEASE DATE April 1982 (UK & US) WRITER Paul McCartney PRODUCER George Martin LABEL Parlophone (UK)/Columbia (US) UK CHART PEAK/WEEKS 1/10 US CHART PEAK/WEEKS 1/19

John Lennon was murdered in December 1980, and Paul McCartney did not release anything for a year and a half. He returned to the pop scene with a sprightly ballad, recorded with Stevie Wonder. They wanted to promote racial tolerance and used the image of a piano keyboard as a musical image of this on **Ebony And Ivory**. It was an unchallenging melody, simple and tinkly, and it marked the beginning of a series of collaborations that Paul would make over the years.

Inspiration behind this opus is the realisation that there are black and white keys on a piano (No? Really!), an apparent excuse for dishing out some embarrassing McCartneyesque moments about racial harmony…. Listen carefully to this worthless ballad and you will hear someone choking on his own halo. Lynne Barber, Melody Maker, April 1982

Echo Beach

ARTIST Martha And The Muffins RELEASE DATE March 1980 WRITER Mark Gane PRODUCER Mike Howlett LABEL Dindisc UK CHART PEAK/WEEKS 10/10 US CHART PEAK/WEEKS 0/0

Martha and The Muffins were a playful Canadian new wave band. Their roots were in a mid-Seventies act, called Oh Those Pants, a 10 piece which did Sixties cover versions. *Echo Beach* was the Muffins's second single and their most successful. It was charming and catchy, with reverby keyboards, a jazzy saxophone and an un-ornamented vocal from Martha. The band recorded follow-up singles and a few albums, but none of them achieved mainstream success.

Another damp squib from a record label that seems to specialise in 'oddball' damp squibs. If the shirts were to write the soundtrack for a new, cheap beach movie, the result might sound something like Martha and her Muffins. Ian Birch, Melody Maker, January 1980

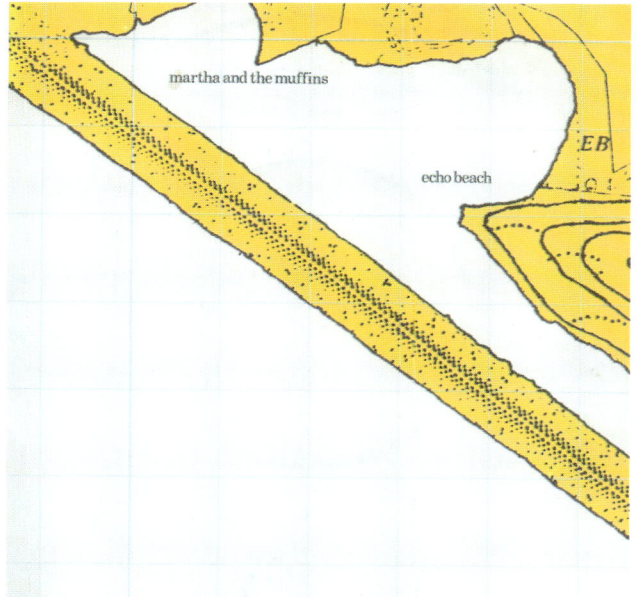

martha and the muffins

echo beach

Eight Miles High

ARTIST The Byrds RELEASE DATE May 1966 (UK)/April 1966 (US) WRITER Gene Clark, David Crosby, Jim McGuinn PRODUCER Alan Stanton LABEL CBS (UK)/Columbia (US) UK CHART PEAK/WEEKS 24/9 US CHART PEAK/WEEKS 14/9

With **Mr Tambourine Man**, the Byrds had added the word 'folk-rock' to the lexicon of rock. A year later, with **Eight Miles High**, they added the word 'psychedelia' as well. Although psychedelia was already familiar to hipsters, the Byrds's disc played a major part in bringing it into the mainstream. It would have gone Top 10 were it not the object of an airplay ban by some broadcasters who thought it was about LSD.

Eight Miles High, which really means 42,000 feet up in a jet. We like speed, man, and those jets give it to you. **Jim Crosby, Melody Maker, May 1966**

End Of The Road

ARTIST Boys II Men RELEASE DATE September 1992 (UK)/July 1992 (US) WRITER Babyface, L. A. Reid, Daryl Simmons PRODUCER – LABEL Motown (UK & US) UK CHART PEAK/WEEKS 1/21 US CHART PEAK/WEEKS 1/32

Boyz II Men's first Number 1 set a US record for the longest stay at Number 1 – 13 weeks. The triumph was bittersweet, however, as the downbeat song's title unintentionally reflected events in the group's life. Two months before the disc's release, their road manager was killed and their assistant road manager wounded by three assailants following a scuffle in a hotel elevator. Although the loss hit the Boyz hard, they themselves were far from the end of the road, with many more hits to come.

This pop/R&B tune is one of the many treats on the soundtrack to Boomerang. Those now recognisable harmonies glide over a swaying, doo-wop melody, making the track the perfect compliment to a romantic evening. Has the makings of a multi-format smash. **Billboard, July 1992**

Endless Love

ARTIST Diana Ross & Lionel Richie RELEASE DATE September 1981 (UK)/July 1981 (US) WRITER Lionel Richie PRODUCER Lionel Richie LABEL Motown (UK & US) UK CHART PEAK/WEEKS 7/12 US CHART PEAK/WEEKS 1/27

The most successful US single for Diana Ross, Lionel Richie and Motown Records, **Endless Love**, the title song of a Brooke Shields film, was the first recording to credit The Commodores's vocalist Richie by name. It stayed at Number 1 in the US for nine weeks, selling over two million. Richie himself wrote and produced the track at the same time as producing another US Number 1 hit in the country chart, Kenny Rogers' **I Don't Need You**.

Diana! What have you done? You have gone to Number One in the States with your Commodore pal with this movie title track. You have gone: syrupy, sentimental, superficial, unconvincingly romantic. You have made an escapist record for coffee-table couples, staring into their cups and wondering 'where did your love go?' **Carol Clerk, Melody Maker, September 1981**

An Englishman In New York

ARTIST Sting RELEASE DATE February 1988 (UK)/April 1988 (US) WRITER Sting PRODUCER Neil Dorfsman LABEL A&M (UK & US) UK CHART PEAK/WEEKS 51/3 US CHART PEAK/WEEKS 84/4

Quentin Crisp, the ex-pat 'queen' of England, was the inspiration for Sting's 1988 single, from his **Nothing Like The Sun** album, when the strong jazz flirtations that had marked his earlier solo outings with the likes of Branford Marsalis and Kenny Kirkland had given way to a broader based music with guest appearances from Andy Summers, Clapton and Knopfler. The haunting, sax-laced song was used as the title track to the film version of William Boyd's **Stars And Bars**.

… part self-referential but is in the main a tribute to one of the gay community's most celebrated elder statesmen: Quentin Crisp. **Alan 'Chopper' Jackson, NME, February 1988**

Enjoy The Silence

ARTIST Depeche Mode **RELEASE DATE** February 1990 (UK)/April 1990 (US) **WRITER** M. L. Gore **PRODUCER** – **LABEL** Mute (UK)/Sire (US) **UK CHART PEAK/WEEKS** 6/9 **US CHART PEAK/WEEKS** 8/24

Nine years after Depeche Mode released their first single, they scored their biggest hit yet with the international smash *Enjoy the Silence*, from their album **Violator**. It went on to win the 1990 Brit award for Best British Single. By that point they were working hard to stay ahead of the many bands who had adopted their pioneering synth-pop sound.

This group studiously keep their fingers on the pulse of contemporaneity (the synth's nod to the new age thang, the guitars to New Order), but somehow the glum, earnest sound in the singer's gullet makes this feel very dated: New Romanticism injected with C86 miserablism. **Simon Reynolds, Melody Maker, February 1990**

Enola Gay

ARTIST Orchestral Manoeuvres In The Dark **RELEASE DATE** October 1980 **WRITER** Andrew McCluskey **PRODUCER** Mike Howlett **LABEL** Dindisc **UK CHART PEAK/WEEKS** 8/15 **US CHART PEAK/WEEKS** –

Orchestral Manoeuvres In The Dark picked their name so they wouldn't be mistaken for a punk band. Their ambitious use of synthesizers was legions away from strum and spit. Andy McCluskey and Paul Humphreys were influenced instead by the pure, analogue sound of Kraftwerk. They created their cool bright electro pop of which *Enola Gay* is a fine example. It is a song about the plane which dropped the atom bomb on Hiroshima. The icy, haunting vocals echo across the keyboard soundscape.

The human interface between electronics and pop. Wry, oddly touching, fleetingly melancholic, Orchestral Manoeuvres stride forward with confidence and a sure sense of their own identity. **Allan Jones, Melody Maker, October 1980**

Eternal Flame

ARTIST The Bangles **RELEASE DATE** February 1989 (UK & US) **WRITER** S. Hoffs, T. Kelly, Billy Steinberg **PRODUCER** Davitt Sigerson **LABEL** CBS (UK)/Columbia (US) **UK CHART PEAK/WEEKS** 1/18 **US CHART PEAK/WEEKS** 1/19

The Bangles's only UK Number 1 was inspired by the flame that burns by Elvis Presley's grave. It focused on Susanna Hoffs's voice more so than had any of their other hits. This was a far cry from their early days, when the foursome fashioned themselves in The Beatles's egalitarian image. The single had barely left the UK charts when they split, ending the career of the most successful self-contained all-female rock group to date.

I don't think Susanna Hoffs has ever sung so badly as she has done on this limp MOR ballad. It seems strange that this foursome that was once fresh and forthright have become the female answer to REO Speedwagon. **Caren Myers, Melody Maker, January 1989**

The Eton Rifles

ARTIST The Jam **RELEASE DATE** November 1979 **WRITER** Paul Weller **PRODUCER** Vic Coppersmith-Heaven **LABEL** Polydor **UK CHART PEAK/WEEKS** 3/12 **US CHART PEAK/WEEKS** –

Singer and songwriter Paul Weller hit a personal high with **Setting Sons**, the Jam's fourth album that targeted suburban life, Britain's fast-fading colonial past and urban decay, in the style of the Kinks's Ray Davies. The anthemic *Eton Rifles* was taken from the album to give the band their first UK Top 10 single and signal three years of chart dominance that ended when *Beat Surrender* debuted at the top as Weller announced the band's demise.

Lovely, sharp, exciting, economical parody of sham 69-style class

warfare. Here the lads sup up their beer and take on Eton … the guitars clash, and the ruling class manoeuvres … **Simon Frith, Melody Maker, October 1979**

Eve Of Destruction

ARTIST Barry McGuire RELEASE DATE September 1965 (UK)/August 1965 (US) WRITER Phil F. Sloan, Steve Barri PRODUCER Lou Adler LABEL RCA (UK)/Dunhill (US) UK CHART PEAK/WEEKS 3/13 US CHART PEAK/WEEKS 1/11

Barry McGuire was a long-haired, fur-wearing folk singer on the LA scene. His single *The Eve Of Destruction* was a cynical attempt to cash in on 'protest singing'. McGuire had a shouty hoarse voice which he used to warn of the dangers of apocalyptic war. The guitars are overblown and pompous, and the whole single has a slick professional feel which was in direct contrast to the hippy ethos, where sincerity mattered more than polish.

I don't like this song very much: it seems to be cashing in on the trendy protest songs, which makes me concentrate on the lyric, which I don't like. **Paul McCartney, Melody Maker, October 1965**

Ever Fallen In Love (With Someone You Shouldn't've)

ARTIST The Buzzcocks RELEASE DATE September 1978 WRITER Peter Shelley PRODUCER Martin Rushent LABEL United Artists UK CHART PEAK/WEEKS 12/11 US CHART PEAK/WEEKS –

Seventies punk was a singles genre, and no band understood this better than the Buzzcocks. Although they never had a Top 10 hit, many of the singles they released during their prime are remembered more today than the songs that overpowered them in the charts at the time. A good example is *Ever Fallen In Love*, which has a positively baroque melody combined with urgent guitars and Kafka-on-amphetamines lyrics to produce a shotgun marriage of noise and melody.

Maybe that sibilant hiss above the guitars is meant to be a vocal. Hard to tell. This band are said to have made something of a name for themselves. On this evidence, they seem to be all buzz and not much of anything else. **Bob Edmonds, NME, September 1978**

Evergreen (Love Theme From 'A Star Is Born')

ARTIST Barbra Streisand RELEASE DATE April 1977 (UK)/December 1976 (US) WRITER Paul Williams, Barbra Streisand PRODUCER Phil Ramone LABEL CBS (UK)/Columbia (US) UK CHART PEAK/WEEKS 3/19 US CHART PEAK/WEEKS 1/25

Streisand had plenty of input to the success of this song – apart from vocal duties, she co-wrote the number with Paul Williams, an experienced writer of hits like *Rainy Days And Mondays* and

We've Only Just Begun, and she co-produced it with Phil Ramone, who had worked with the likes of Billy Joel and Simon & Garfunkel. Her first UK Top 10 single, it also won the Oscar for the best song from *A Star Is Born*, in which she starred.

'In these days of novelties, rock, freak instrumentals and all kinds of gimmicked music – I'm the first singer to sell with straight forward music' … 'It proves an important point,' says Barbra: 'Anything that's truly real, musically genuine, is commercial.' **Interviewed by Leonard Feather, Melody Maker, February 1964**

Everlasting Love

ARTIST The Love Affair RELEASE DATE January 1968 WRITER James Cason, Mac Gayden PRODUCER Mike Smith LABEL CBS UK CHART PEAK/WEEKS 1/12 US CHART PEAK/WEEKS –

Most of Love Affair did not actually appear on the single *Everlasting Love*. They were a teeny bop group and their instrumental talents were not that hot. Producer Mike Smith used session musicians to record the track, and actually admitted to it, which was unusual in the Sixties. Lead singer Steve Ellis's powerful and expressive voice WAS used and it carried the romantic song all the way to the top. The band had four more Top 20 hits before fading away.

A young British group, with ages ranging from 15 to 17, who, like The Monkees, were formed by answering a newspaper advert, and they have the same brand of youthful vitality and exuberance as the Monkees in this sparkling up-beat item. **Derek Johnson, NME, December 1967**

Every Breath You Take

ARTIST Police RELEASE DATE May 1983 (UK)/June 1983 (US) WRITER Sting PRODUCER Hugh Padgham, Police LABEL A&M (UK & US) UK CHART PEAK/WEEKS 1/11 US CHART PEAK/WEEKS 1/22

Every Breath You Take is Sting's great song of obsession. Police had become almost cocksure in their style – a little too complacent and lack-lustre. *Every Breath You Take* is not guilty of these things. It uses a crashed-out surf music rhythm reworked into something hushed and shimmery. Sting's voice isn't monumental or emotive: it is very quiet and silvery, yet manages to capture the essence of a love/hate relationship.

Having proved conclusively that he can't act, it's back to what he does best. Every Breath You Take, with its moody undercurrents and reserved crooning, is a welcome diversion, and next week I'll be singing it in the street, and the supermarket.... **Kirsty McNeill, NME, May 1983**

Every Little Thing She Does Is Magic

ARTIST Police RELEASE DATE October 1981 (UK)/September 1981 (US) WRITER Sting PRODUCER Hugh Padgham, Police LABEL A&M (UK & US) UK CHART PEAK/WEEKS 1/13 US CHART PEAK/WEEKS 3/19

In 1981 Sting was named songwriter of the year at the Ivor Novello Awards and the group began recording their fourth album at Montserrat in the Caribbean. They also released *Every Little Thing She Does Is Magic*, which is a breeze of a love song using simple words and a jaunty melody. They rounded off the year by playing a secret gig at The Marquee in London. Outside a blizzard was blowing, and only a few people turned up.

Typically well-crafted fodder from the camera-shy trio; more piano than guitar, nicely walloping chorus. Sting can't resist adding a few 'eeee-yo's at the end. **Melody Maker, October 1981**

Every Rose Has Its Thorn

ARTIST Poison RELEASE DATE February 1989 (UK)/October 1988 (US) WRITER Bobby Dall, C. C. DeVille, Bret Michaels, Rikki Rocket PRODUCER Tom Werman LABEL Capitol (UK)/Enigma (US) UK CHART PEAK/WEEKS 13/9 US CHART PEAK/WEEKS 1/21

Poison were heavily into spandex and big hair, they were glam metal, a pantomime of the gritty, dirty axe merchants. *Every Rose Has Its Thorn* is typical Poison: an overblown soft metal ballad, with flowery instrumentation and guitars which are too clean to rock. But they did live the life of metal monsters, with videos featuring peroxide babes, and ludicrous dressing room demands for vast quantities of pepperoni pizza, fried chicken and boxes and boxes of Trojan condoms. All of which were provided.

And then there's Poison with their US Number 1 – like I said, a lean week for metal. **Keith Cameron, Sounds, February 1989**

Everybody Wants To Rule The World

ARTIST Tears For Fears RELEASE DATE March 1985 (UK & US) WRITER Roland Orzabal, Ian Stanley, Chris Hughes PRODUCER Chris Hughes LABEL Mercury (UK & US) UK CHART PEAK/WEEKS 2/14 US CHART PEAK/WEEKS 1/24

Synth-pop with heart – Tears For Fears's most successful single release was written by Orzabal with their producer Chris Hughes. It was the first of two US Number 1s, but in Britain, ironically, USA For Africa's **We Are The World** kept it at Number 2. However, when the song was selected as the theme for Sport Aid's Race Against Time in 1986 – the title slightly rejigged to work as **Everybody Wants To Run The World** – it was another Top 5 entry in the UK.

*… marginally more palatable than the maudlin moodiness that has become their trademark. They might never make another **Change** but at least this is one soggy step up from abysmally dire **Shout**.* **Adrian Thrills, NME, April 1985**

Everybody's Talkin

ARTIST Nilsson RELEASE DATE September 1969 (UK)/August 1969 (US) WRITER Fred Neil PRODUCER Richard Perry LABEL RCA (UK)/RCA Victor (US) UK CHART PEAK/WEEKS 23/15 US CHART PEAK/WEEKS 6/12

Everybody's Talking was in a totally different vein to the lachrymose **Without You**. It was the theme song for *Midnight Cowboy*, capturing perfectly the drifting, lost soul feel of the film. Nilsson gave the Fred Neil-penned song a poignant simplicity, cruising along with affecting gentleness. Harry's own songwriting career had begun when he worked as a computer specialist at a bank. He did the night shifts and spent the day composing. John Lennon considered him one of his favourite American song writers.

Thank God somewhere within the ritualistic rock there's still room for Nilsson. **Jud Rosebush, Rolling Stone, May 1971**

Everyday People

ARTIST Sly & The Family Stone RELEASE DATE March 1969 (UK)/November 1968 (US) WRITER Sylvester Stewart PRODUCER Sylvester Stewart LABEL Direction (UK)/Epic (US) UK CHART PEAK/WEEKS 36/5 US CHART PEAK/WEEKS 1/19

The band Sly Stone put together was eclectic in background, mixing race and gender at a time when such cross-fertilisation was much less common. An appearance at the Woodstock Festival and subsequent film, the release of their album **Stand!**, all added to their profile, helping to make their single go gold. Sly followed up **Everyday People** with two more infectious hits that blended rock and soul and proved equally appealing to both the R&B and pop charts.

Sly & Co seem like a most unusual and interesting group, combining coloured soul with white-group sounds. The result is highly distinctive and ideal for your listening and dancing pleasure. One can utter 'too much' in both a seated and leg-wriggling position, depending on one's demands on popular music…. **Chris Welch, Melody Maker, January 1969**

(Everything I Do) I Do It For You

ARTIST Bryan Adams RELEASE DATE June 1991 (UK & US) WRITER Bryan Adams, Michael Kamen, Robert John 'Mutt' Lange PRODUCER Robert John 'Mutt' Lange, Bryan Adams LABEL A & M (UK & US) UK CHART PEAK/WEEKS 1/25 US CHART PEAK/WEEKS 1/22

In Britain, this disc is remembered for more than its sound. It spent a record-breaking 16 weeks at Number 1, trouncing the 11-week record that Slim Whitman set in 1955 with **Rose Marie**. The best-selling single of 1991, it was the first UK million-seller in six years, with total sales of over eight million copies world-wide. It came from the soundtrack of the Kevin Costner film *Robin Hood Prince Of Thieves*.

It's the sentimentalism of The Great British Public. I reckon girls were buying it to slip onto their boyfriends' stereos in the Ford Capri. The funny thing is he openly confesses to hating it now, as does the MD of A&M. **Miles Hunt, NME, December 1991**

Eye Level

ARTIST Simon Park Orchestra RELEASE DATE November 1972 WRITER Jack Trombey PRODUCER – LABEL Columbia UK CHART PEAK/WEEKS 1/24 US CHART PEAK/WEEKS –

Simon Park, who began playing piano at the age of five, was a music graduate from Winchester College, Oxford. He conducted **Eye Level** with its distinctive melody and bristling, jaunty instrumentation to the top of the charts. It was the first television theme tune to go to Number 1. The music was used for the detective series *Van Der Valk*. It was released twice and took a mere 380 days to peak.

Eye Of The Tiger

ARTIST Survivor **RELEASE DATE** July 1982 (UK)/June 1982 (US) **WRITER** Jim Peterik, Frank Sullivan **PRODUCER** Jim Peterik, Frank Sullivan **LABEL** Scotti Brothers (UK & US) **UK CHART PEAK/WEEKS** 1/15 **US CHART PEAK/WEEKS** 1/25

The hard rocking Chicagoans had their label, Scotti Brothers Records, to thank for introducing them to Sylvester Stallone, who was looking for a strong rock sound for the film *Rocky III*. Watching rough cuts of the movie, the band picked up on the phrase used by Rocky's trainer: 'Keep the eye of the tiger'. On its release the single sold two million in the US, 800,000 in the UK. The band also supplied **Burning Heart** for *Rocky IV*, reaching the Top 5 on both sides of the Atlantic.

The only problem with this well polished production is that it's really a demonstration of professional skill and experience, not the lustful risk-taking of youth. The urgency is contrived. **Mark Highling, Rolling Stone, September 1982**

Faith

ARTIST George Michael **RELEASE DATE** October 1987 (UK & US) **WRITER** George Michael **PRODUCER** George Michael **LABEL** Epic (UK)/Columbia (US) **UK CHART PEAK/WEEKS** 2/12 **US CHART PEAK/WEEKS** 1/20

Faith was the sign that George Michael had made the right decision. He disbanded Wham! when they were at the height of their commercial success, to go in his own direction. His first attempts were shaky. **I Want Your Sex** was mediocre, only interesting because it was banned by radio stations. **Faith** came good: it was a funky, sizzling number which George had written, arranged and produced. Not bad for a Wham! rapper.

George goes skiffle! Pop's most thoughtful superstar takes another u-turn in the canyons of his mind, slipping into an acoustic hand-jive that recalls a rather tasteful Shakin' Stevens. Not only that, but in various places he comes across like a hybrid of Boy George and Freddie Mercury (without the steroids). **Sean O'Hagan, NME, October 1987**

Fame

ARTIST Irene Cara **RELEASE DATE** July 1982 (UK)/June 1980 (US) **WRITER** Dean Pitchford, Michael Gore **PRODUCER** Michael Gore **LABEL** RSO (UK & US) **UK CHART PEAK/WEEKS** 1/16 **US CHART PEAK/WEEKS** 4/26

The one person who actually got famous from being in the movie *Fame* was Irene Cara, who not only acted in it but also got to sing its theme. Cara had acted since childhood, earning an Obie (the off-Broadway award) for her performance in *The Me Nobody Knows*. **Fame**, her breakthrough hit, was co-written by a relative of another female hitmaker, Michael Gore, brother of Lesley.

Irene Cara has a voice that's perfect for singing anthems for youthful striving.... It has a masked, unstudied, emotional appeal. **Don Shewey, Rolling Stone, March 1984**

Family Affair

ARTIST Sly & The Family Stone **RELEASE DATE** January 1972 (UK)/November 1971 (US) **WRITER** Sylvester Stewart **PRODUCER** Sylvester Stewart **LABEL** Epic (UK & US) **UK CHART PEAK/WEEKS** 15/8 **US CHART PEAK/WEEKS** 1/14

After bursting onto the scene in the late Sixties with their brand of soul/pop and a dash of jazz, the Family Stone went through a period of comparative slump. The word was that there were drug problems. But in 1971 Sly hit back: gone the happy hippy uplifting anthems – here was low key, brooding, introspective funk. **Family Affair** used a beatbox, Sly adding piano chords with Billy Preston dropping in some organ riffs. Brooding, but catchy.

Sly, sleazy and laid back, they've got all the ingredients that makes for commercial success, yet they're evil as hell and Sly's voice on this one hits such grit at times it makes your backbone freeze. Excellent. **Roy Hollingworth, Melody Maker, December 1971**

Fantasy

ARTIST Mariah Carey **RELEASE DATE** September 1995 (UK & US) **WRITER – PRODUCER** Dave Hall, Mariah Carey **LABEL** Columbia (UK & US) **UK CHART PEAK/WEEKS** 4/11 **US CHART PEAK/WEEKS** 1/25

With **Fantasy,** Mariah Carey became the first female singer ever to debut at Number 1 on *Billboard*'s Hot 100 singles chart. The first single from her album **Daydream**, which also debuted at Number 1, has a backing track that was built around samples from the Tom Tom Club's 1982 hit **Genius of Love**. Part of its chart momentum stemmed from the fact that, not counting her Christmas disc, her fans had waited a year for a new single, her last being **Endless Love**.

When a friend told me about this one, I actually thought they were trying to be funny. But it's real. The Ol' Dirty Bastard ... rapping for the Stepford Megababe with the Minnie Riperton range. **Simon Price, Melody Maker, September 1993**

Feels Like I'm In Love

ARTIST Kelly Marie **RELEASE DATE** August 1980 **WRITER** Ray Dorset **PRODUCER** – **LABEL** Calibre **UK CHART PEAK/WEEKS** 1/16 **US CHART PEAK/WEEKS** –

Jacqueline McKinnon, better known as Kelly Marie, was the beneficiary when Elvis Presley died and songwriter Ray Dorset gave this song to her instead of sending it to Graceland. He had also released it as a B-side with his own group Mungo Jerry; but this high-energy version, which took nine months to move from club hit to chart-topper, remains definitive and a staple of disco compilations.

Fernando

ARTIST Abba **RELEASE DATE** March 1976 (UK)/September 1976 (US) **WRITER** Benny Andersson, Stig Anderson, Bjorn Ulvaeus **PRODUCER** Benny Andersson, Bjorn Ulvaeus **LABEL** Epic (UK)/Atlantic (US) **UK CHART PEAK/WEEKS** 1/15 **US CHART PEAK/WEEKS** 13/16

Both the women in Abba had been solo stars in Sweden before they were in the group, and they continued their solo careers even as Abba was having international success. *Fernando*, a ballad set against the backdrop of the Mexican civil war, originally appeared on Frida's 1975 album **Frida Ensam** ('Frida Alone'). Done a year later by Abba, it became their third Number 1, their second successive single to reach the top.

Unadulterated pop, with lyrics written in English by Swedes, who have always had a slightly quaint conception of the English language and the pronunciation, that operate at the most basic level of childish/adolescent fantasy. **John Rockwell, Rolling Stone, March 1976**

Father And Son

ARTIST Boyzone **RELEASE DATE** November 1995 **WRITER** Cat Stevens **PRODUCER** – **LABEL** Polydor **UK CHART PEAK/WEEKS** 2/16 **US CHART PEAK/WEEKS** –

Father And Son was Boyzone's closest-yet brush with Number 1 when it hit the charts at the end of 1995. Eighteen-year-old Ronan Keating sang lead on the group's high-gloss version of the Cat Stevens classic. While Stevens dramatized the song's message by singing in one pitch as the father, and another as the son, Keating made no such attempt to distinguish one character's voice from the other. It sounded watered down compared to the original, but it nonetheless exposed a new generation to Stevens' music.

Ferry Across The Mersey

ARTIST Gerry And The Pacemakers RELEASE DATE December 1964
(UK)/February 1965 (US) WRITER Gerard Marsden PRODUCER George Martin
LABEL Columbia (UK)/Laurie (US) UK CHART PEAK/WEEKS 8/13 US CHART
PEAK/WEEKS 6/11

Gerry And The Pacemakers were the first act to have their first
three singles go to Number 1 in the UK charts. **Ferry Across The
Mersey** made the UK and US Top 10 in 1965. The song was
revived in 1989 to raise funds for the Hillsborough disaster fund
after the tragedy at the FA Cup Semi-Final between Liverpool and
Nottingham Forest. The re-recording was credited to 'Christians,
Holly Johnson, Paul McCartney, Gerry Marsden and Stock Aitken
& Waterman' and entered the UK charts at Number 1.

*The title song of the film is out on a new Columbia single, proving
that Gerry can slow the pace down as well as rave it up. Gerry wrote it,
and it's a good little song. Pretty, and a substantial hit.* **Paul
McCartney, Melody Maker, December 1964**

Fever

ARTIST Peggy Lee RELEASE DATE August 1958 (UK)/July 1958 (US) WRITER
John Davenport, Eddie Cooley PRODUCER – LABEL Capitol (UK & US) UK
CHART PEAK/WEEKS 5/11 US CHART PEAK/WEEKS 8/15

Peggy Lee endured an unhappy childhood, being on the end of
over a decade of beatings from her stepmother. Little wonder she
invested everything she sang with bittersweet emotion – not least
this cover of a 1956 hit for bluesman Little Willie John, otherwise

best known for **Need Your Love So Bad**. He died behind bars in
1968 having served two years of a manslaughter sentence. **Fever**'s
writer credit is disputed: Otis Blackwell has laid claim to it, while
others suggest John and Eddie Cooley were co-writers.

*Here's the Lee girl again – this time with a single that makes more of
an impact than any of the tracks on the recently reviewed* **Jump for Joy**
LP … she projects this telling number– a sort of cool, eerie **Frankie and
Johnnie** *– to an economical beat accompaniment….* **Laurie
Hernshaw, Melody Maker, July 1958**

50 Ways To Leave Your Lover

ARTIST Paul Simon RELEASE DATE January 1976 (UK)/December 1975 (US)
WRITER Paul Simon PRODUCER Paul Simon LABEL CBS (UK)/Columbia (US)
UK CHART PEAK/WEEKS 23/6 US CHART PEAK/WEEKS 1/17

When Simon split from Garfunkel in 1970 he began a phase of
exploring different styles – including gospel, Latin and world folk
musics – before returning to a more conventional singer-songwriter
approach on the album **Still Crazy After All These Years**. The
wry **50 Ways To Leave Your Lover**, which offers suggestions to
named males on how to dump a partner, used top session men to
create a polished, meaningful, jazz feel.

*Beautifully presented, carefully drawn, minimum of fuss type song,
packed with Simon's usual craft…. Lyrics never rise above rather banal
couplets.* **Caroline Coon, Melody Maker, January 1976**

Fire

ARTIST Crazy World Of Arthur Brown RELEASE DATE June 1968 WRITER
Arthur Brown, Vincent Crane, Peter Kerr, 'Finesilver' PRODUCER Pete
Townsend, Kit Lambert LABEL Track UK CHART PEAK/WEEKS 1/14 US CHART
PEAK/WEEKS –

One of pop's most memorable one-hit wonders, Arthur Brown was
a man with a gimmick – an enormous hat which he would set
alight during performances. It usually worked, but when it didn't

he was really in trouble. His stunt was enough to make the dense psychedelic rocker *Fire* a Number 1, but could not keep Brown's career on the boil for very long.

Who is this? I like this very much. Very exciting. Yeah I like that. It's not like other singers who get a style or arrangement imposed on them. I imagine Arthur Brown had quite a say in this. **Marty Feldman, Melody Maker, June 1968**

Firestarter

ARTIST The Prodigy RELEASE DATE March 1996 WRITER Liam Howlett, Keith Flint, Anne Dudley, J. J. Jeczalik, Paul Morley, Gary Langan PRODUCER Liam Howlett, Chaz Stevens LABEL XL XLS UK CHART PEAK/WEEKS 1/19 US CHART PEAK/WEEKS –

The first hot blast of success for the underground club collective from deepest Essex, *Firestarter* ignited an inevitable backdraft of complaints that helped to fuel massive sales both in the UK and in the US where they went on to storm past contemporary rivals Oasis. With roots as rave DJs with a large core following, Prodigy achieved international acclaim when their hard techno scratched at the raw nerves of a club culture over-exposed to a diet of MOR remixes.

A 60-Marlboros-a-day growl more suited to guitar-drenched cider punk than the Prodigy's fast and furious cyber punk … musically this cut finds the boys slamming through an exhilarating, breakbeat techno theme for snow-boarding freestylers. Half-pipe hard-core – you know the score. **Martin James, Melody Maker, March 1996**

The First Time Ever I Saw Your Face

ARTIST Roberta Flack RELEASE DATE May 1972 (UK)/March 1972 (US) WRITER Ewan McCall PRODUCER Joel Dorn LABEL Atlantic (UK & US) UK CHART PEAK/WEEKS 14/14 US CHART PEAK/WEEKS 1/18

Three years and two albums after Roberta Flack recorded *The First Time Ever I Saw Your Face* for her 1969 debut album **First Take,** Clint Eastwood, filming HIS directorial debut, *Play Misty for Me,* remembered the tender, majestic love song. Knowing it would be perfect to underscore the key romantic scene of the movie, he phoned Flack to ask permission to include it. Six weeks after the movie's release it reached Number 1 in the charts, where it stayed for another six weeks.

A beautiful, sensitive Ewan McCall number which, ironically for the girl long predicted to be Aretha's number one rival, isn't really a soul record at all. Though it is sung with great feeling, it's closer to Joan Baez than Aretha. **Roger St Pierre, NME, May 1972**

Flashdance … What A Feeling

ARTIST Irene Cara RELEASE DATE June 1983 (UK)/April 1983 (US) WRITER Keith Forsey, Irene Cara, Giorgio Moroder PRODUCER – LABEL Casablanca (UK & US) UK CHART PEAK/WEEKS 2/14 US CHART PEAK/WEEKS 1/25

Irene Cara got her big break in 1980 when her recording of the theme from the movie *Fame* made the US Top 5 (it would not hit Number 1 for another two years). It took her nearly two years to score another Top 10 hit, but she finally did it with the theme from Flashdance. While it stopped short of Number 1 in Britain, it topped *Billboard*'s Hot 100 for six weeks.

This is the theme from the forthcoming Paramount Picture Flashdance – Saturday Night Fever's Tony Manero with a sex change – and it's Giorgio Moroder going through the motions, Donna Summer sleepwalking…. **Tony Parsons, NME, June 1983**

Flowers In The Rain

ARTIST Move RELEASE DATE September 1967 WRITER Roy Wood PRODUCER Denny Cordell LABEL Regal Zonophone UK CHART PEAK/WEEKS 2/13 US CHART PEAK/WEEKS –

The Move had beat driven guitar and vocals, like The Beatles, but added a lick of pastiche. The Fab Four recorded **Sgt. Pepper's Lonely Heart Club Band**, but The Move went one step further and became ELO. In 1965 they were dressed as Chicago gangsters, despite the fact that they came from Birmingham, and smashed TV sets on stage. Their single *Flowers In The Rain*, a jaunty piece of twisted psychedelia, was the first pop record to be played on BBC Radio One.

The Moves' latest sound grows out of the clapping thunder and the pouring rain into an explosive, winning sound all the way. **Melody Maker, August 1967**

The Fly

ARTIST U2 RELEASE DATE November 1991 (UK & US) WRITER U2 PRODUCER Daniel Lanois LABEL Island (UK & US) UK CHART PEAK/WEEKS 1/6 US CHART PEAK/WEEKS 61/11

The Fly was the much awaited first release from **Achtung Baby**, and the promotional video gave a taste of what would become Zoo TV on the 1993/4 tour, including Bono's 'Fly' persona – all leather and shades. The sound was distinctly different too: stripped down, clangourous, definitely darker – Bono likened it to four men chopping down the Joshua Tree.

For those who have been weaned on INXS and other pale imitations … this is U2 back to prove who's boss. This dance-oriented … single takes on the juniors at their own game and inevitably triumphs. At what cost? **Simon Dudfield, NME, October 1991**

Fly Robin Fly

ARTIST Silver Convention RELEASE DATE November 1975 (UK)/October 1975 (US) WRITER Sylvester Levay, Stephen Prager PRODUCER Michael Kunze LABEL Magnet (UK)/Midlands Int (US) UK CHART PEAK/WEEKS 28/8 US CHART PEAK/WEEKS 1/17

Silver Convention was the brainchild of two Munich-based producers, Sylvester Levay and Michael Kunze. They had a UK hit with **Save Me** in 1975, then scored a US Number 1 with this release and collected a 1975

Grammy for Best R&B Instrumental, the song qualifying because it contained only two words: 'robin' and 'fly'. The pair expanded to include three German/Austrian female vocalists, Penny McLean, Linda Thompson and Ramona Wulf, and had a disco hit with **Get Up And Boogie** in 1976.

Those who like their music soulless, but with a heavy dancing beat, can do a lot worse than this … **Ray Coleman, Melody Maker, June 1977**

Fools Gold/What The World Is Waiting For

ARTIST Stone Roses RELEASE DATE November 1989 WRITER John Squire, Ian Brown PRODUCER John Leckie LABEL Silvertone UK CHART PEAK/WEEKS 8/19 US CHART PEAK/WEEKS –

Announcing the mainstream arrival of the Stone Roses, who along with fellow Mancunians Happy Mondays were starting waves in the music press about the Manchester baggy movement, *Fools Gold* already had the band's references – Byrds-like Gretsch and Rickenbacker guitars, Small Faces haircuts and sharp lyrics – in place. This funky groove was first released as a double A-side with **What The World Is Waiting For**, and then re-issued in 1990, to the annoyance of the band, by their original label Silvertone, reaching UK Number 22.

Wah-Wah guitars, thin laconic voices, deadly Clyde Stubblefield drums and drifting, human mix. Both sides are part of the same thing: buy the 12-inch and get 13 minutes of pure pleasure – which is a bit longer than the average orgasm. **Ian McCann, NME, November 1989**

For What It's Worth (Stop, Hey What's That Sound)

ARTIST Buffalo Springfield RELEASE DATE January 1967 WRITER Stephen Stills PRODUCER Charles Green, Brian Stone LABEL Atco UK CHART PEAK/WEEKS – US CHART PEAK/WEEKS 7/15

America's generation gap was never wider than in November 1966, when Los Angeles teenagers battled police for the right to hang out on the trendy Sunset Strip. Although Buffalo Springfield member Stephen Stills had those riots in mind when he wrote **For What It's Worth**, its lyrics were universal, pinpointing the tensions that divided the nation during that tumultuous time. One verse contains the line 'a man with a gun', which Atco-Atlantic label head Ahmet Ertegun wanted to remove, but was talked into letting it remain.

Hardly a typical protest number, **For What It's Worth** *didn't moralize or choose sides: rather, it laid out the facts in black and white and urged restraint.* **Compilation, Rolling Stone, September 1988**

For Your Love

ARTIST The Yardbirds RELEASE DATE March 1965 (UK)/May 1965 (US) WRITER Graham Gouldman PRODUCER Giorgio Gomelsky, Paul Samuel Smith LABEL Columbia (UK)/Epic (US) UK CHART PEAK/WEEKS 3/12 US CHART PEAK/WEEKS 6/12

UK blues boomers the Yardbirds had tended to recycle Chicago blues numbers as they worked the south-east circuit, taking over the Crawdaddy residency from the Stones and then moving on to the Marquee. This was an original, written by future 10 cc member Graham Gouldman, a commercial track he had created for his own band, the Mockingbirds. Maybe it was too commercial: Eric Clapton, the Yardbirds's guitarist, left the band shortly after its release, his purist sensibilities offended.

Yardbirds to visit America where their English first hit **For Your Love** *is still rising in the US Top 10. A short film featuring the group playing* **For Your Love** *has been shown in 12 different countries.* **Melody Maker, July 1965**

Freedom

ARTIST Wham! RELEASE DATE October 1984 (UK)/July 1985 (US) WRITER George Michael PRODUCER George Michael LABEL Epic (UK)/Columbia (US) UK CHART PEAK/WEEKS 1/14 US CHART PEAK/WEEKS 3/18

Part of Wham!'s 'classic' period of the mid-Eighties, including 1983's US Number 1 **Wake Me Up Before You Go-Go**, George Michael's solo success **Careless Whisper** and **I'm Your Man** in November 1995, **Freedom** was enormous fun, with Abba-style chord changes and plenty of camp, and George and Andrew wriggling their way through the bouncy dance routine.

From A Jack To A King

ARTIST Ned Miller RELEASE DATE February 1963 (UK)/December 1962 (US) WRITER Ned Miller PRODUCER – LABEL London (UK)/Fabor (US) UK CHART PEAK/WEEKS 2/21 US CHART PEAK/WEEKS 6/13

From A Jack To A King is another song in a country music tradition of songs with a playing card metaphor. In this case, Ned Miller isn't singing about gambling or religion – romance is on his mind. It is a betting man's tale of love: the chorus explains how the husky voiced Ned transformed himself from, well, a jack to a king, from loneliness to a wedding ring. He knavishly proclaims 'I gambled an ace and I won a queen.'

Ned's slow ballad **From A Jack To A King** *has entered the NME chart at Number 29. His name may be new to disc fans in this country, but he is no stranger in America, where he has been an established performer for some time.* **Ian Dove, NME, March 1963**

From Me To You

ARTIST The Beatles RELEASE DATE April 1963 WRITER John Lennon, Paul McCartney PRODUCER George Martin LABEL Parlophone UK CHART PEAK/WEEKS 1/21 US CHART PEAK/WEEKS 0/0

The Beatles's first Number 1, **From Me To You**, also charted in America – but not for The Beatles. Del Shannon heard it while on tour with the Fab Four and rushed to record it when he returned home. His version reached Number 77 on *Billboard*'s Hot 100 in July 1963 – the first Lennon & McCartney song to make the chart. The Beatles's version would not hit there until the following year, after Beatlemania hit, when it reached Number 41.

The Beatles have made it again! Today, the big beat boys from Liverpool have smashed their own disc sales record and leaped into the hit parade at Number 19. The Song **From Me to You** *is another composition by the hit-writing Beatles John Lennon and Paul McCartney.* **Melody Maker, April 1963**

Funky Town

ARTIST Lipps Inc RELEASE DATE May 1980 (UK)/March 1980 (US) WRITER Steve Greenberg PRODUCER Steve Greenberg LABEL Casablanca (UK & US) UK CHART PEAK/WEEKS 2/13 US CHART PEAK/WEEKS 1/23

Funky Town pulled out all the stops. The opening seconds are sung by disco androids, electronic voices intoning: 'Gotta make a move that's right for me' before the track opens up and out with Cynthia Johnson soulfully urging: 'Won't you take me to funky town'. The instrumentation is equally diverse, dropping a saxophone solo onto a raft of up-tempo percussion, setting drum beats against maracas and a purring electric guitar. Despite its diversity it is still a disco stomper.

Categorising popular music is not a good idea, but there are a lot of disco records in the chart still. If disco has peaked somebody ought to tell the kids.... **Martyn Sutton, Melody Maker, June 1980**

Gangsta's Paradise

ARTIST Coolio Featuring LV RELEASE DATE October 1995 (UK)/August 1995 (US) WRITER Artis Ivey Jr, Larry Sanders, Douglas Rasheed PRODUCER Douglas Rasheed LABEL Tommy Boy (UK)/MCA Soundtracks (US) UK CHART PEAK/WEEKS 1/20 US CHART PEAK/WEEKS 1/38

Coolio presaged the murders of Tupac Shakur and the Notorious B.I.G. with *Gangsta's Paradise*, his morose meditation on the nihilistic life of an inner-city gangsta. It was based on a sample of Stevie Wonder's *Pastime Paradise*. Although the song does not condone the gangsta world, Coolio discovered that many listeners thought it was a design for living. To be on the safe side, he said, he doesn't let his kids listen to his records.

An oddly reserved frustratingly MEAGRE moment. Coolio is, generally speaking, among the lusher, more intriguing gangsta rappers.... Gangsta's Paradise limps a bit. Nice ominous looped choir. Fits a little too comfortably on America's Top 10. **Taylor Parkes, Melody Maker, October 1995**

Geno

ARTIST Dexy's Midnight Runners RELEASE DATE March 1980 WRITER Kevin Rowland, Kevin Archer PRODUCER Pete Wingfield LABEL Late Night Feelings UK CHART PEAK/WEEKS 1/14 US CHART PEAK/WEEKS –

The group based their tough street-gang image on the Martin Scorsese film *Mean Streets* and their first single, *Dance Stance*,

peaked at Number 40. Their second, *Geno*, written about one of Kevin Rowland's heroes Geno Washington – who, with his group the Ram Jam band, had been a Sixties club favourite – gave the group their first UK Number 1 in 1980. However, after a couple of further UK hits the original line-up split.

The most boring band of 1979 burst forth again with this erratic and tuneless tribute to their hero, Geno Washington, who would probably keep his earplugs if he heard it. Now, if they had stuck to wearing their flowery shirts and supporting Kleenex.... **Robbi Millar, Sounds, March 1980**

Georgy Girl

ARTIST The Seekers RELEASE DATE February 1967 (UK)/December 1966 (US) WRITER Jim Dale, Tom Springfield PRODUCER – LABEL Columbia (UK)/Capitol (US) UK CHART PEAK/WEEKS 3/11 US CHART PEAK/WEEKS 2/16

The title song from the film of the same name, starring Lynn Redgrave in her first major role, was the biggest US hit for the Australian group; their mentor Tom Springfield co-wrote the number with actor-singer and Carry On regular Jim Dale. It was their last big chart success and shortly afterwards lead singer Judith Durham went solo, leaving the way open for the creation of the New Seekers.

I don't like them, but they always get a hit. I admit they are good for the type of stuff they do, but it doesn't do anything for me at all.... This will be a hit, I'm afraid. **Alan Blakeley, Melody Maker, February 1967**

Get Back

ARTIST The Beatles RELEASE DATE April 1969 (UK)/May 1969 (US) WRITER John Lennon, Paul McCartney PRODUCER Glyn Johns LABEL Apple (UK & US) UK CHART PEAK/WEEKS 1/121/17 US CHART PEAK/WEEKS 1/12

The Beatles's first single since *Hey Jude*, *Get Back* was intended to herald a new musical era for them: one which would return to the stripped-down, straight-ahead style of their Liverpool days. To that end, they enlisted American R&B organist Billy Preston, who became the only artist ever to receive a 'The Beatles with...' label credit. It entered the British charts at Number 1 and broke records in the US by entering *Billboard*'s Hot 100 at Number 10.

Always the same reaction to a new Beatles record: when it comes out you are a bit disappointed, then after five plays you realize how good it is. This is very simple, with a Chuck Berry guitar riff going, chk, chk, chk. **John Peel, Melody Maker, April 1969**

Get It On

ARTIST T. Rex RELEASE DATE July 1971 WRITER Marc Bolan PRODUCER Tony Visconti LABEL Fly Bug UK CHART PEAK/WEEKS 1/13 US CHART PEAK/WEEKS 0/0

Get It On was Bolan's second UK Number 1 – another four to the bar foot-tapper and his glam rock following was secure in Britain – but it was the first to make the US Top 10 and became his biggest hit internationally. The track was renamed *Bang A Gong* in the States to avoid a clash with another *Get It On*, released by the jazz-

rock outfit Chase. Bizarrely, the singer of Chase also died in a car crash.

Bolan's Boogie. It's an understated shuffle beat, monotonous but compulsive. Marc sings mysteriously and is backed by stomping drums and grumbling guitar … typical of the new Rex with its roots in classic pop. **Chris Welch, Melody Maker, July 1973**

Get Ready

ARTIST Rare Earth RELEASE DATE March 1970 WRITER William 'Smokey' Robinson PRODUCER Rare Earth LABEL Rare Earth UK CHART PEAK/WEEKS 0/0 US CHART PEAK/WEEKS 4/20

Upon signing with Motown's rock subsidiary Rare Earth, Detroit rockers the Sunliners took on the same name as the label and reached Number 4 in the US with their first release, *Get Ready*. Smokey Robinson had written and produced the original recording by The Temptations in 1966. Rare Earth's version was edited down from the entire first side of their first album, and demonstrated both the group's musical strengths and latent longwinded tendencies.

Get Up I Feel Like Being A Sex Machine (Part 1)

ARTIST James Brown RELEASE DATE October 1970 (UK)/July 1970 (US) WRITER James Brown, Bobby Byrd, Ron Lenhoff PRODUCER James Brown LABEL Polydor (UK)/King (US) UK CHART PEAK/WEEKS 32/7 US CHART PEAK/WEEKS 15/9

Sex Machine remains one of James Brown's most inventive and influential recordings. It was his first record to feature future Parliament-Funkadelic member William 'Bootsy' Collins on bass, providing a down-and-dirty accompaniment to Brown's up-and-dirty vocals. Although it fell short of the Top 10 on both sides of the Atlantic, it was a massive R&B dancefloor hit, becoming Brown's first million-seller of the Seventies.

This is not one of the best he has done rhythmically. He has always got something to say…. The intricacy of rhythm is beautiful and I have respect for him. **Jack Bruce, Melody Maker, September 1970**

Ghost Town

ARTIST The Specials **RELEASE DATE** June 1981 **WRITER** Jerry Dammers **PRODUCER** John Collins **LABEL** 2 Tone **UK CHART PEAK/WEEKS** 1/14 **US CHART PEAK/WEEKS** –

Ghost Town was one hell of a timely swan song, coinciding as it did with Britain's inner-city riots of 1981. Jerry Dammers stoked up the lyrics, and Terry Hall provided the vocals, recorded in the suitably urban setting of a flat in north London's Tottenham. The single was a UK Number 1 and broke the Specials in the States, but internal arguments over the group's image that belied their 2-Tone ideals were beginning to cast doubt over their future.

Ghost Town
Why?
Friday Night Saturday Morning

Gimme All Your Lovin'

ARTIST ZZ Top **RELEASE DATE** September 1983 (UK)/April 1983 (US) **WRITER** Bill Gibbons, Dusty Hill, Frank Beard **PRODUCER** Bill Ham **LABEL** Warner Brothers (UK)/Warner (US) **UK CHART PEAK/WEEKS** 61/3 **US CHART PEAK/WEEKS** 37/12

ZZ Top deliver Texas rock with a 10 gallon hat and cowboy boots – and a couple of long, long beards. The trio had been slogging round the Texan circuit for years with their brand of metallic blues 'n' boogie, never quite capturing their live feel on record. But with the arrival of MTV in the early Eighties, their world view of Ford Coupes, luscious babes and downhome fun found a perfect visual outlet on promos supporting singles like the million-selling **Gimme All Your Lovin'**.

Enough beef in this brazenly sour celebration of a Texan egomaniac to forewarn of a second rising of the Confederacy, even if the cortex is wired to a supremely lurid crotch fetish. Discipline! **Richard Cook, NME, May 1983**

A Girl Like You

ARTIST Edwyn Collins **RELEASE DATE** November 1994 (UK)/October 1995 (US) **WRITER** Edwyn Collins **PRODUCER** Edwyn Collins **LABEL** Setanta (UK)/Bar None (US) **UK CHART PEAK/WEEKS** 42/3 **US CHART PEAK/WEEKS** 32/9

The former leader of Orange Juice had a tough time getting a UK hit with **A Girl Like You**. Only after it had become a hit in 10 other countries did the tide begin to turn. Collins's label re-issued the single and album, and it became one of the biggest hits of the summer of 1995. Collins crowed: ' ... they'll all be saying, "Oh, he's the greatest thing since sliced bread".' Also ... the NME had to re-review *Gorgeous George* and make it their lead review.

There is always someone with fond memories, it seems, who's prepared to sign up former Orange Juice's Collins…. Sadly over the past few years he has proved something of a diminishing return. **Susie Boone, Vox, October 1994**

CYNDI LAUPER

GIRLS JUST WANT TO HAVE FUN

A3943

Girls Just Want To Have Fun

ARTIST Cyndi Lauper **RELEASE DATE** January 1984 (UK)/December 1983 (US) **WRITER** Robert Hazard **PRODUCER** Rick Chertoff **LABEL** Portrait (UK & US) **UK CHART PEAK/WEEKS** 2/12 **US CHART PEAK/WEEKS** 2/25

Cyndi (Cynthia) Lauper first recorded with the group Blue Angel without success. She went solo and recorded this bouncy track which was helped by an equally bouncy video. The single just failed to top both the US and UK charts. In 1994, the track was re-mixed and re-issued under the longer title of **Hey Now (Girls Just Wanna Have Fun)** and made the Top 5 in the UK.

Glad All Over

ARTIST The Dave Clark Five **RELEASE DATE** November 1963 (UK)/February 1964 (US) **WRITER** Dave Clark, Mike Smith **PRODUCER** Dave Clark **LABEL** Columbia (UK)/Epic (US) **UK CHART PEAK/WEEKS** 1/19 **US CHART PEAK/WEEKS** 6/14

It may be hard to believe, but there was a time when the Dave Clark Five were The Beatles's most formidable rivals. *Glad All Over* was the breakthrough hit for the boys from Tottenham, knocking The Beatles' *I Want To Hold Your Hand* from Number 1 on the UK charts. It featured the pounding drums which would become the group's trademark. While Clark was a capable live drummer, when producing the DC5 he preferred to rely on studio drummers such as Bobby Graham.

… the same criticism applies here as it did for the Fourmost and The Hollies. It is all right, but how many more groups can this sound take? If I were starting a new group I would aim for originality. **Pete Murray, Melody Maker, November 1963**

Go Your Own Way

ARTIST Fleetwood Mac **RELEASE DATE** February 1977 (UK)/January 1977 (US) **WRITER** Lindsey Buckingham **PRODUCER** Richard Dashut, Lindsey Buckingham, Chris Norris, Ken Caillat **LABEL** Warner Bros (UK)/Warner (US) **UK CHART PEAK/WEEKS** 38/4 **US CHART PEAK/WEEKS** 10/15

The 1977 album **Rumours** has been described as a rock soap opera depicting the stresses and strains of couples John and Christine McVie and Lindsey Buckingham and Stevie (Stephanie) Nicks. If so, then **Go Your Own Way**, must be the most vitriolic and heartfelt of all the tracks it contains. It was the first track played to the record label which, amazingly, hadn't wanted to release a single in case a flop would damage sales.

Not quite as instantaneously hit-sounding as I had been led to believe. The endless repetition of 'You can go your own way' is tedious: a desert of lyrical ineptitude; but the backbone of the track is an outstanding bass and drum riff. **Caroline Coon, Melody Maker, February 1977**

God Only Knows

ARTIST The Beach Boys **RELEASE DATE** July 1966 (UK)/August 1966 (US) **WRITER** Tony Asher, Brian Wilson **PRODUCER** Brian Wilson **LABEL** Capitol (UK & US) **UK CHART PEAK/WEEKS** 2/14 **US CHART PEAK/WEEKS** 39/8

Brian Wilson says that the beginning of his **God Only Knows** melody was inspired by a John Sebastian tune. His then lyricist Tony Asher came up with the first line, and, two and a half hours later, the song was complete. Wilson was concerned that radio would not play it because of the mention of God, but Asher convinced him it wouldn't make a difference. In England it hit Number 2. In America, where Capitol relegated it to B-side status, it stalled at Number 39 on *Billboard*'s Hot 100.

One of the best The Beach Boys have recorded…. Bryan Wilson has excelled himself in arranging the lush, symphonic orchestra and the church choir voicing. **Melody Maker, July 1966**

God Save The Queen

ARTIST The Sex Pistols **RELEASE DATE** June 1977 **WRITER** Johnny Rotten, Paul Cook, Steven Jones, Glen Matlock **PRODUCER** Chris Thomas **LABEL** Virgin **UK CHART PEAK/WEEKS** 2/9 **US CHART PEAK/WEEKS** –

1977 was Queen Elizabeth II's Jubilee Year: the celebrations proved a ripe target for punk's own aristocracy to attack. After leaving EMI, the band had moved to A&M, signing outside Buckingham Palace, but were fired six days later, with 25,000 copies of **God Save The Queen** already pressed. Virgin picked up the pieces, including the problems. Everything from the lyrics to designer Jamie Reid's safety-pinned Queen was guaranteed to cause controversy. Though banned by BBC Radio 1 and some chains, the record shifted 150,000 in five days.

There's nothing anyone could say about the Pistols that hasn't been said and contradicted thousands of times before. **Carol Clerk, Melody Maker, December 1980**

Going Underground/Dreams of Children

ARTIST The Jam RELEASE DATE March 1980 WRITER Paul Weller PRODUCER Vic Coppersmith-Heaven LABEL Polydor UK CHART PEAK/WEEKS 1/9 US CHART PEAK/WEEKS –

The Woking trio's first UK chart-topper, *Going Underground* (technically a double A-side with *Dreams Of Children*) was their tenth single and entered at the top, displacing one-hit wonder Fern Kinney. The band received this news while at the Sunset Marquis hotel in Hollywood on their fourth US tour, and their celebrations managed to earn them a ban from a legendary establishment where, in their own words, 'suites in the swimming pool were de rigueur.'

Weller's plain voice dourly furthers his own simple man persona, this time threatening to beat the retreat from communications blitzes, excessive taxes, etc.; but it does have an accumulative, emotional impact, especially when it's set off by those melancholy sweet guitar lines he's so good at. **Chris Bohn, Melody Maker, March 1980**

Golden Brown

ARTIST The Stranglers RELEASE DATE January 1982 WRITER Jean-Jacques Burnel, Hugh Cornwell, Jet Black, David Greenfield PRODUCER Steve Churchyard LABEL Liberty UK CHART PEAK/WEEKS 2/12 US CHART PEAK/WEEKS –

Golden Brown was a long way from the sometimes loutish new wave attitude of The Stranglers in the mid-Seventies. Written by Hugh Cornwell about heroin – he'd spent some time at Her Majesty's pleasure in 1980 for possession – the track was a lolloping waltz with a Sixties-feel harpsichord riff and bags of melody. It became the Strangler's most successful single, denied the UK Number 1 spot by The Jam's **A Town Called Malice**.

Gonna Make You A Star

ARTIST David Essex RELEASE DATE October 1974 WRITER David Essex PRODUCER Jeff Wayne LABEL CBS (UK)/Columbia (US) UK CHART PEAK/WEEKS 1/17 US CHART PEAK/WEEKS 0/0

Far from the overnight sensation he appeared, David Essex had worked long and hard for the success he achieved in the mid-

Seventies. The self-penned *Gonna Make You A Star* was full of references to the vagaries of the entertainment business, and gives an insight into why Essex has survived when almost all his peers have long since faded into obscurity. Catchy and well crafted, with a dash of characteristic humour, it topped the UK charts for three weeks in late 1974.

Extremely catchy cut from a British rocker who is riding the top of the English charts with this one. More of a big band style than he has used previously, and double tracked vocals give a more powerful overall sound. **Billboard, 1974**

Gonna Make You Sweat (Everybody Dance Now)

ARTIST C&C Music Factory RELEASE DATE December 1990 (UK)/November 1990 (US) WRITER R. Clivilles, F B Williams PRODUCER Robert Clivilles, David Cole LABEL CBS (UK)/Columbia (US) UK CHART PEAK/WEEKS 3/12 US CHART PEAK/WEEKS 1/25

Their name couldn't have been more descriptive: 'C&C' stood for topflight dance producers Robert Clivilles and David Cole, and they were a hit factory during their brief existence, until Cole died of spinal meningitis in 1995. *Gonna Make You Sweat (Everybody Dance Now)*, which featured rapper Freedom Williams, was their biggest hit, a smash on both sides of the Atlantic in January 1991.

… Their impressive track record in the over and underground club scene…. Infectiously hyper-active. **Isabel Appio, Vox, April 1991**

Good Golly Miss Molly

ARTIST Little Richard RELEASE DATE February 1958 (UK & US) WRITER Robert Blackwell, John Marascalco PRODUCER – LABEL London (UK)/Speciality (US) UK CHART PEAK/WEEKS 8/9 US CHART PEAK/WEEKS 10/10

Little Richard's records reflect the extravagance of his appearance. He played 'the devil's music' and he lived the decadent lifestyle. But his father and grandfather were Seventh Day Adventist preachers. His life was pulled between religion and Satan's Rock 'n' Roll. He had a wild intense piano style, bashing out notes with his feet and his songs were risqué, sung out with feral howls. *Good Golly Miss Molly* speeded along on a screaming falsetto.

The news of Little Richards' retirement from the music business gives added impact to his latest release…. Miss Molly is dressed up in boogie-woogie framework. **Laurie Hernshaw, Melody Maker, March 1958**

Goodbye Yellow Brick Road

ARTIST Elton John RELEASE DATE September 1973 (UK)/October 1973 (US) WRITER Elton John, Bernie Taupin PRODUCER Gus Dudgeon LABEL DJM (UK)/MCA (US) UK CHART PEAK/WEEKS 6/16 US CHART PEAK/WEEKS 2/17

The double LP of which this was the title track topped both the US and UK charts in 1973, but the single couldn't follow suit. It spent three weeks at Number 2 in the US, two behind Charlie Rich's *The Most Beautiful Girl.* The song, like its companions, had been written in a Jamaican hotel room and recorded in France after the island's recording facilities were found wanting.

So obvious a hit that there's little point in talking about the song. Nice strings, with touches of Eltonian falsetto. Nigel Olsson's drum's add sway to what would, in less knowing hands, be a plodding beat. **Geoff Brown, Melody Maker, September 1973**

Goodnight Girl

ARTIST Wet Wet Wet RELEASE DATE January 1992 WRITER Graeme Clark, Tom Cunningham, Neil Mitchell, Marti Pellow PRODUCER Wet Wet Wet LABEL Precious Jewel UK CHART PEAK/WEEKS 1/11 US CHART PEAK/WEEKS 0/0

By the end of the Eighties, critics were consigning Wet Wet Wet to the wastebin, but after the song had received national TV coverage with its inclusion in a *Coronation Street* Christmas special, a shrewd piece of marketeering, *Goodbye Girl* spent four weeks at Number 1 in the UK, and sparked another lease of life for the Scottish band.

Good Vibrations

ARTIST The Beach Boys RELEASE DATE November 1966 (UK)/October 1966 (US) WRITER Mike Love, Brian Wilson PRODUCER Brian Wilson LABEL Capitol (UK & US) UK CHART PEAK/WEEKS 1/13 US CHART PEAK/WEEKS 1/14

Many critics think this is the greatest single of all time. At the very least, it was in its time the most musically and technologically sophisticated single that rock had ever produced. During 17 sessions over six months, using four studios, Brian Wilson created his 'pocket symphony'. The group's first eight-track recording, featuring such unconventional instruments as the Theramin, it cost $50,000 to make – nearly as much as the entire **Sgt. Pepper** album.

This record took 90 hours and four different recording studios before it was completed. The record is an obvious progression on Wilson's **Pet Sounds** *LP … incorporating a myriad of voices – sounding like the swinging singers at times.* **Melody Maker, October 1966**

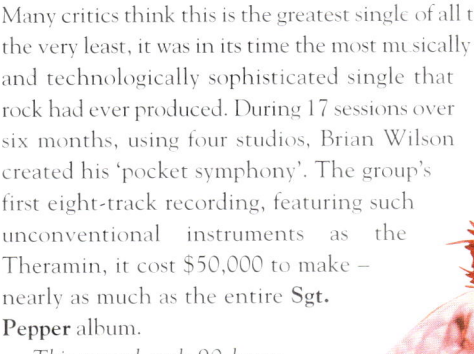

Grease

ARTIST Frankie Valli RELEASE DATE August 1978 (UK)/May 1978 (US) WRITER Barry Gibb PRODUCER Barry Gibb, Albhy Galutan, Karl Richardson LABEL RSO (UK & US) UK CHART PEAK/WEEKS 3/14 US CHART PEAK/WEEKS 1/22

Having been able, like Rod Stewart with the Faces, to maintain simultaneous group and solo careers, Valli split with the Four Seasons in 1977, despite the group's over eighty-five million record sales. The following year he had his biggest solo success with the Barry Gibb-penned *Grease*, the title track of the Olivia Newton-John/John Travolta-starring movie of the same name.

Both Andy Gibb and Frankie Valli's airwave luftwaffle compositions are from the magic papermate of Barry Bee Gee. Both suffer from lousy brash intros but after repeated playing they reveal the layered melodies and haunting choruses that have made radio a joy for Betty Baker's boy recently. **Danny Baker, NME, August 1978**

The Greatest Love Of All

ARTIST Whitney Houston RELEASE DATE April 1986 (UK)/March 1986 (US) WRITER Linda Creed, Michael Masser PRODUCER Michael Masser LABEL Arista (UK & US) UK CHART PEAK/WEEKS 8/11 US CHART PEAK/WEEKS 1/18

Written by Michael Masser and Linda Creed for the 1977 Muhammad Ali biopic *The Greatest*, **Greatest Love Of All** peaked at a respectable Number 24 in the hands of singing guitarist George Benson. Included as the B-side to Whitney Houston's debut single **You Give Good Love**, the amount of radio airplay the track received persuaded Arista to release it as a single in its own right and the reward was a transatlantic top 10 hit.

Beautiful song, but somehow lacking the sincerity of George Benson's wondrous recital. Any suggestion of a little feeling is immediately dispelled as Miss Houston affords the pedestrian arrangement automatically clinical treatment – it lasts forever, and the string section might bring tears to your mother's eyes. Any more, I cannot say. **Will Smith, Melody Maker, April 1986**

Green Green Grass Of Home

ARTIST Tom Jones RELEASE DATE November 1966 (UK)/December 1966 (US) WRITER Curly Putnam PRODUCER – LABEL Decca (UK)/Parrot (US) UK CHART PEAK/WEEKS 1/22 US CHART PEAK/WEEKS 11/12

The 1950 film *The Asphalt Jungle* inspired Claude Putman to write this song about a convicted criminal waiting to die. Porter Wagoner took it to the US country charts, although Tom Jones decided to cover it after he heard a version by Jerry Lee Lewis. The song, the UK's Christmas Number 1 of 1966, gave the Welshman his second UK chart-topper after the very different **It's Not Unusual** and his third Top 20 single in the US.

'It's a nice Country & Western song, and reminds me of Wales, which is what attracted me to it' (Tom Jones). The cry has gone up 'It's not the Tom Jones we know: it's too slushy.' **Melody Maker, November 1966**

Green Onions

ARTIST Booker T & The MG's RELEASE DATE December 1979 (UK)/August 1962 (US) WRITER Steve Cropper, Al Jackson, Lewie Steinberg, Booker T. Jones PRODUCER Booker T. Jones, Steve Cropper LABEL Atlantic (UK)/Stax (US) UK CHART PEAK/WEEKS 7/12 US CHART PEAK/WEEKS 3/16

The classic Sixties soul instrumental, **Green Onions** was a US Number 3 hit for Booker T. & the MG's in 1962. It did not hit in the UK until 17 years later, when it appeared on the soundtrack to *Quadrophenia*. Booker T. & the MGs were Stax Records's house band during the Sixties, defining the label's sound with their tight, sharp groove. **Green Onions** was actually the B-side of their first single, re-issued as an A-side after DJs started flipping it over.

Another quintessential mod anthem and one of the very first hits for Stax records back in 1962, although – to our eternal shame – it was never a chart hit in Britain. A masterpiece of tense, understated, bluesy funk…. **Alan Lewis, Sounds, December 1979**

Groove Is In The Heart

ARTIST Deee-Lite RELEASE DATE August 1990 (UK)/September 1990 (US) WRITER J. Davis, Deee-Lite, H. Hancock PRODUCER Super DJ Dmitry, Jungle Towa, Kirby Kier LABEL Elektra (UK & US) UK CHART PEAK/WEEKS 2/13 US CHART PEAK/WEEKS 4/23

The retro-chic dance band Deee-Lite – Lady Miss Kier, Super DJ Dmitry, and Jungle DJ Towa Towa – scored a major hit in 1990 with their debut single, **Groove Is In The Heart**. Although the group was from New York City, **Groove** hit first in England before going on to be a smash in America. Its commercial fortunes were helped no end by its throbbing bass line, provided by Parliament-Funkadelic's Bootsy Collins.

A multinational outfit, Deee-Lite have supported De-La-Soul, which is a clue to their 'Gum Charms', playing that same colourful psyche-a-funka-delic party sound, but this hooks in better with the current Stateside funk revival schtick and then onto a sweater funk loop … a total toothache. **John Robb, 1990**

Groovin'

ARTIST The Young Rascals **RELEASE DATE** May 1967 (UK)/April 1967 **WRITER** Felix Cavaliere, Eddie Brigati **PRODUCER** Tom Dowd, Arif Mardin **LABEL** Atlantic (UK & US) **UK CHART PEAK/WEEKS** 8/13 **US CHART PEAK/WEEKS** 1/13

A second US Number 1 for the Young Rascals, *Groovin'* (*…On A Sunday Afternoon*) had summer sunlight spilt all over its major 7th chordings and Latin rhythms. The afternoon in question referred to the only time founder member Felix Cavaliere, as a working musician, could get to spend some time with a young lady of his acquaintance. Other original member Eddie Brigati and his brother David reprised the song on the 1991 multi-talented *New York Rock And Soul Revue*.

I have never liked this group, but this is a super record. It is a great number … it certainly deserves to be a hit. **Peter Murray, Melody Maker, May 1967**

Halfway To Paradise

ARTIST Billy Fury **RELEASE DATE** May 1961 **WRITER** Gerry Goffin, Carole King **PRODUCER** – **LABEL** Decca **UK CHART PEAK/WEEKS** 3/23 **US CHART PEAK/WEEKS** –

The song had originally been a US Top 40 hit in 1961 for Tony Orlando and was written by Carole King. Billy Fury had first charted in the UK in 1959 with his own composition **Maybe Tomorrow**. Fury's version of **Halfway To Paradise** became the second of 11 UK Top 10 hits and is his best-known song, even though *Jealousy* went one place higher in the UK. He died in 1983.

Hang On Sloopy

ARTIST McCoys **RELEASE DATE** September 1965 (UK)/August 1965 (US) **WRITER** Bert Russell, Wes Farrell **PRODUCER** Rick Gottehrer, Bob Feldman, Jerry Goldstein **LABEL** Immediate (UK)/Bang (US) **UK CHART PEAK/WEEKS** 5/14 **US CHART PEAK/WEEKS** 1/14

The McCoys's snappy song *Hang On Sloopy* knocked *Eve of Destruction* off the top of the charts. Its bubble gum pop was sweet, unpretentious and totally without any kind of message.

The McCoys were a garage band of the mid-Sixties, who used speedy light instrumentation to give their songs sweep and sway. *Hang On Sloopy* has roller-coasting harmonies and a sing-along tune. It was also the first success for pop supremo Andrew Loog Oldham.

Hangin' Tough

ARTIST New Kids On The Block **RELEASE DATE** September 1989 (UK)/July 1989 (US) **WRITER** Maurice Starr **PRODUCER** Maurice Starr **LABEL** CBS (UK)/Columbia (US) **UK CHART PEAK/WEEKS** 52/4 **US CHART PEAK/WEEKS** 1/17

Maurice Starr, musical veteran and entrepreneur, had already been responsible for New Edition – New Kids On The Block were created to be a white version of the teen group. They were a musical hybrid, mixing rap with pop, but in a safe, sanitized way. *Hangin' Tough* saw them as urban, street wise dudes, rapping and moving through slick dance routines. In 1990 *Rolling Stone* magazine readers picked them as the Worst Band, *Hangin' Tough* as the Worst Single – but they had a huge fan base.

… NKOTB are not the worthless bubble gum boy bimbos reactionary 'serious' music journalists diss-miss them as either…. Contextually their music is certainly as good as most of the other fluff cluttering the chart weekly. **Ralph Traitor, Sounds, October 1989**

Happy Birthday

ARTIST Altered Images **RELEASE DATE** September 1981 **WRITER** Altered Images **PRODUCER** Martin Rushent **LABEL** Epic **UK CHART PEAK/WEEKS** 2/17 **US CHART PEAK/WEEKS** –

Led by the crush-inspiring Claire Grogan, Altered Images got off to a shaky start in early 1981 when they unwisely chose to release for their first single a tune called **Dead Popstars**. They said they recorded it before December 8, 1980, but that meant little to listeners still in shock from John Lennon's murder. After that disc stalled at Number 67, they bounced back with their second release, **Happy Birthday**, which would remain the biggest hit of their brief career.

Not to be confused with the brilliant Stevie Wonder single, this is a woefully shallow song given a disco beat and an inspired production job, which does its best but can't foist off tedium. **Colin Irwin, Melody Maker, August 1981**

Happy Talk

ARTIST Captain Sensible **RELEASE DATE** June 1982 **WRITER** Oscar Hammerstein II, Richard Rodgers **PRODUCER** Tony Mansfield **LABEL** A&M **UK CHART PEAK/WEEKS** 1/8 **US CHART PEAK/WEEKS** –

The 27-year-old lead singer of The Damned scored a Number 1 hit first time out with this faithful rendering of a tune from the Rodgers and Hammerstein musical *South Pacific*. If ever there was a runaway hit, this was it: in its second week on the charts, it made a record-breaking leap from Number 33 to Number 1.

Happy Xmas (War Is Over)

ARTIST John Lennon & The Plastic Ono Band **RELEASE DATE** December 1972 (UK)/December 1971 (US) **WRITER** John Lennon **PRODUCER** John Lennon, Phil Spector **LABEL** Apple (UK & US) **UK CHART PEAK/WEEKS** 2/26 **US CHART PEAK/WEEKS** 1/10

When originally released in 1972, this seasonal standard was actually credited to John Lennon and Yoko Ono, the Plastic Ono Band and the Harlem Community Choir and peaked at Number 4. Following John Lennon's death in December 1980, the

song was re-released and went two places better, failing to dislodge *Imagine* from Number 1 in the UK charts, as the country mourned the passing of a legend.

This was the track put out by John and Yoko last year which, for absurd and complicated reasons, never reached our shores; luckily 12 months later, it is in time again. I welcome it wholeheartedly. **Penny Valentine, Sounds, November 1972**

A Hard Day's Night

ARTIST The Beatles RELEASE DATE July 1964 (UK & US) WRITER John Lennon, Paul McCartney PRODUCER George Martin LABEL Parlophone (UK)/Capitol (US) UK CHART PEAK/WEEKS 1/13 US CHART PEAK/WEEKS 1/13

The title of The Beatles' first film, for which this theme was written, was taken from a comment Ringo Starr made at the end of a day on the set: 'That was a hard day's night, that was.' Disproving the notion that drummers can't read, Starr borrowed the line from Lennon, who had used it in his book *In His Own Write*. The song's grabbing opening chord signified that, even at this early stage in their career, The Beatles were eager to stretch the boundaries of pop.

On this new one, the instrumental sound is very unusual. I like it very much, really. It's The Beatles, and it will be very big. But you would never have thought of A Hard Day's Night for a song title, would you? **Dave Clark, Melody Maker, July 1964**

Have I Told You Lately

ARTIST Rod Stewart RELEASE DATE June 1993 (UK)/April 1993 (US) WRITER Van Morrison PRODUCER Patrick Leonard LABEL Warner Bros (UK)/Warner (US) UK CHART PEAK/WEEKS 5/9 US CHART PEAK/WEEKS 5/22

This luscious Van Morrison ballad – from Van's **Avalon Sunset** album and an FM radio play favourite – was included in Rod

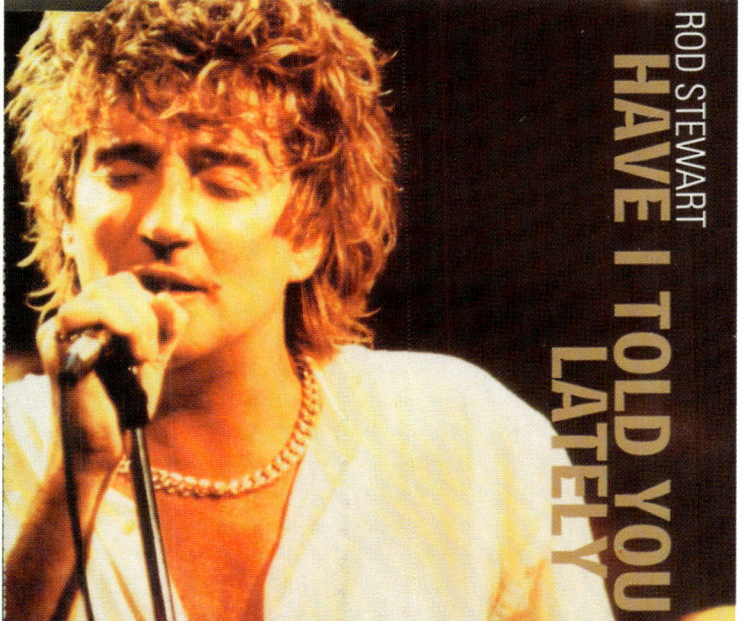

Stewart's February 1993 **Unplugged** session at Universal Studios, Universal City, alongside Stewart favourites like **Gasoline Alley** and **Maggie May**. An album followed and this cover, dedicated to Stewart's wife Rachel Hunter, was released as a single. He performed the song at the World Music Awards in Monaco in May 1993, when collecting an award for his life-long contribution to the music industry.

Rod's raspy pipes sound a little weathered here, but that lends some necessary roughness to a sweetly romantic cover of a nugget from Van Morrison's vast song-writing catalogue. This tune is lifted from his current **Unplugged** *album.* **Billboard, 1993**

Have You Ever Really Loved A Woman

ARTIST Bryan Adams RELEASE DATE April 1995 (UK & US) WRITER Bryan Adams, Robert John 'Mutt' Lange, Michael Kamen PRODUCER Robert John 'Mutt' Lange, Bryan Adams LABEL A&M (UK & US) UK CHART PEAK/WEEKS 4/9 US CHART PEAK/WEEKS 1/24

After his prolonged chart success with **(Everything I Do) I Do It For You,** the theme from Kevin Costner's mega-grossing film *Robin Hood: Prince Of Thieves*, Bryan Adams found Hollywood to be a ready market for his AOR ballads. **All For Love**, from a limp 1994 remake of *The Three Musketeers*, reached US Number 1 and UK Number 2, and the following year he provided this song – featuring the flamenco guitar work of Paco De Lucia – for the soundtrack of the Johnny Depp vehicle Don Juan DeMarco. Nominated for an Oscar (Adams performed it at the 1996 awards ceremony), it missed out on the top honour, but Adams could console himself with an Ivor Novello Award later that year.

Adams at his most plaintive – which is bad news as Adams at his least plaintive is a whinge too far for most. Apparently poor Bazza's been in love and it's all gone wrong. Well join the club, you big Jessie. **Barbara Ellen, NME, April 1995**

Have You Seen Her

ARTIST Chi-Lites RELEASE DATE January 1972 (UK)/October 1971 (US) WRITER Eugene Record, Barbara Acklin PRODUCER Eugene Record LABEL MCA (UK)/Brunswick (US) UK CHART PEAK/WEEKS 3/12 US CHART PEAK/WEEKS 3/14

Hailing from Chicago, the Chi-Lites (pronounced CHY-lites) were together for 11 years before they had their first Top 10 hit, **Have You Seen Her**. Written by the group's lead singer and producer, Eugene Record, the song was originally intended only for their album **(For God's Sake) Give More Power To The People**. It was released as a single only after disc jockeys picked up on it. Seventies soul balladeering at its best, the song became an unlikely hit for MC Hammer in 1990.

It's what one might call unemotional over dramatics. You've got to watch yourself when you start talking lyrics over music because if you ain't careful you can sound outrageously daft. **Roy Hollingworth, Melody Maker, December 1971**

He Ain't Heavy He's My Brother

ARTIST The Hollies **RELEASE DATE** October 1969 (UK)/December 1969 (US) **WRITER** Bob Russell, Bobby Scott **PRODUCER** Ron Richards **LABEL** Parlophone (UK)/Epic (US) **UK CHART PEAK/WEEKS 3/15 US CHART PEAK/WEEKS 7/18**

Having topped the British charts in 1965 with *I'm Alive*, the Hollies had to wait 23 years to repeat the feat – and it was a 19-year-old song picked up by Miller lager for a TV ad campaign that did it for them. Elton John, once signed to the band's publishing company Gralto (Graham-Allan-Tony), was the session piano-player. Righteous Brother Bill Medley competed with a cover version that was featured in *Rambo III*.

Untypical Hollies, but repeated plays prove it has charm and verve. Much sadness: cascading strings and a lead voice projects with clarity and conviction. In the final analysis, one feels obliged to report a palpable hit. **Chris Welch, Melody Maker, September 1969**

He'll Have To Go

ARTIST Jim Reeves **RELEASE DATE** March 1960 (UK)/December 1959 (US) **WRITER** Joe Allison, Audrey Allison **PRODUCER** – **LABEL** RCA (UK)/RCA Victor (US) **UK CHART PEAK/WEEKS 12/31 US CHART PEAK/WEEKS 2/23**

Shortly after he signed a new five-year deal with RCA, 'Gentleman' Jim Reeves, the Texan country crooner, had his biggest US hit and his first UK Top 20 entry with *He'll Have To Go*. The song had earlier been recorded by Billy Brown and later became a hit for R&B singer Solomon Burke. Among many answer versions it inspired was the Top 5 hit by Jeannie Black, *He'll Have to Stay*.

Hitherto unknown in this country, Jim is a prominent figure on the Stateside country & western scene and He'll Have A Go recently took him to second place in the American charts. His first British hit. **Pat Twitty, NME, April 1960**

He's So Fine

ARTIST The Chiffons **RELEASE DATE** April 1963 (UK)/February 1963 (US) **WRITER** Ronnie Mack **PRODUCER** Hank Medress, Jay Siegel **LABEL** Stateside (UK)/Laurie (US) **UK CHART PEAK/WEEKS 16/12 US CHART PEAK/WEEKS 1/15**

A song written by Ronnie Mack, a poor aspiring writer who enlisted the Chiffons, a group of high schoolers, to sing on a demo which he took to the Tokens, who had recently become producers. Impressed by Mack's conversational lyrics, they had the Chiffons record *He's So Fine*, its 'doo-lang' opening suggested by the engineer. Sadly, although it became the Chiffons's first and biggest hit, Mack's songwriting career was over. Stricken with Hodgkins disease, he received his gold record in the hospital and died shortly after.

He's So Fine, the disc by the Chiffons, a coloured all girl group with The Shirelles-type sound, looks set to confirm the prophecy of Bob Schwartz, boss of America's Laurie Records, who said: 'I'll sell a million'. **Ian Dove, NME, April 1963**

He's The Greatest Dancer

ARTIST Sister Sledge **RELEASE DATE** March 1979 (UK)/February 1979 (US) **WRITER** Bernard Edwards, Nile Rodgers **PRODUCER** Bernard Edwards, Nile Rodgers **LABEL** Atlantic/Cotillion (UK)/Cotillion (US) **UK CHART PEAK/WEEKS 6/11 US CHART PEAK/WEEKS 9/19**

A hit from the potent combination of the creative force behind the Chic Organisation, Nile Rodgers and Bernard Edwards, and the foursome of sisters from Philadelphia – this was the first of a pair of disco hits in 1979, the other being *We Are Family*. Sister Sledge began to fade in the States during the early Eighties but maintained their popularity in the UK, where they came back strongly, taking *Frankie* to Number 1 in 1985.

The awesome rhythm guitar, the stunning bass lines, the beautifully controlled yet fiery build, the sense of variation and jubilation that increases throughout: they all connect with riveting style – anyone who doesn't immediately should have there ears syringed. **Ian Birch, Melody Maker, March 1979**

Heart Of Glass

ARTIST Blondie **RELEASE DATE** January 1979 (UK & US) **WRITER** Debbie Harry, Chris Stein **PRODUCER** Mike Chapman **LABEL** Chrysalis (UK & US) **UK CHART PEAK/WEEKS 1/12 US CHART PEAK/WEEKS 1/21**

For many of Blondie's fans, *Heart of Glass* was their sell-out record – but for many more, especially in America, it was the one that put them on the map. It seemed that for every new wave fan that Blondie lost, they gained two disco addicts. The disc was the third single from their third album, **Parallel Lines**, it was the one that put which would go on to sell over twenty million copies world-wide.

A 12 inch with the instrumental version on the other side. Talking Heads-style Blondie with a near-opening production from Mike Chapman. **Simon Frith, Melody Maker, January 1979**

Heartbreak Hotel

ARTIST Elvis Presley RELEASE DATE March 1956 (US)/May 1956 (UK) WRITER Mae Boren Axton, Tommy Durden, Elvis Presley PRODUCER Steve Sholes LABEL HMB Pop (UK)/RCA Victor (US) UK CHART PEAK/WEEKS 2/21 US CHART PEAK/WEEKS 1/27

Elvis's first US Number 1 single and UK Number 2, marking his ascendancy into international phenomenon and crowning him king of rock 'n' roll. **Heartbreak Hotel** originated from a front page newspaper story about a suicide victim who left a one-line note: 'I walk a lonely street.' Mae Axton, who handled Colonel Parker's PR in Florida suggested to co-writer Tommy Durden that at the end of that lonely street was a heartbreak hotel.

Elvis discovered this song himself whilst on a personal appearance in Florida: he was given the tune by Mae Axton (Hoyt's mother). He liked it immediately…. **Anne Fulchino, NME, February 1976**

Heaven Knows I'm Miserable

ARTIST The Smiths RELEASE DATE June 1984 WRITER Steven Morrissey, John Marr PRODUCER John Porter LABEL Rough Trade UK CHART PEAK/WEEKS 10/8 US CHART PEAK/WEEKS –

Some of the major record chains in the UK banned the single from their racks: its B-Side **Suffer Little Children** had provoked complaints from the families of the children killed by the Moors murderers Ian Brady and Myra Hindley. The main track's title was a clear nod of affection and admiration towards Morrissey icon Dusty Springfield's **Heaven Knows I'm Missing You Now**, who'd covered the Smiths's own **Hand In Glove**.

This record is well put together and nicely produced and everything, and I think The Smiths are on their way to making really good records – but this is not it. Morrissey has actually got a good voice, he has got a very wide range … but I'm always weary of singers who try to croon. **Rat Scabies, Melody Maker, May 1984**

Hello

ARTIST Lionel Richie RELEASE DATE March 1984 (UK)/February 1984 (US) WRITER Lionel Richie PRODUCER Jon Anthony Carmichael, Lionel Richie LABEL Motown (UK & US) UK CHART PEAK/WEEKS 1/15 US CHART PEAK/WEEKS 1/24

Originally written by Richie for his first solo album after leaving The Commodores, **Hello** was ultimately rejected. It was only at the insistence of his wife Brenda that it was included in his second album, **Can't Slow Down**, eventually becoming his fourth US Number 1 single. The success of this sweet, sentimental ballad was perhaps helped by the accompanying video in which Richie, as a teacher of sculpture, falls in love with a blind student.

The one flaw in all of Richie's music is its lack of personal assertion, its rampant tastefulness. Pleasant enough to hear, but rarely missed in its absence. **Kurt Loder, Rolling Stone, December 1984**

Hello Goodbye/I Am The Walrus

ARTIST The Beatles RELEASE DATE November 1967 WRITER John Lennon, Paul McCartney PRODUCER George Martin LABEL Parlophone (UK)/Capitol (US) UK CHART PEAK/WEEKS 1/12 US CHART PEAK/WEEKS 1/11

Hello Goodbye, the lyrically simple but highly commercial side of this double A disc was a huge Christmas hit, holding off the double EP taken from their surreal film *Magical Mystery Tour*. **I Am The Walrus** contained some of their most far-out psychedelic sound ideas, including whoops and hollers from the Mike Sammes Singers, and snatches of King Lear taped live from BBC radio.

No doubt the more times you hear **Hello, Goodbye** *and* **I Am The Walrus** *the more the subtleties come to light.* **Nick Jones, Melody Maker, November 1967**

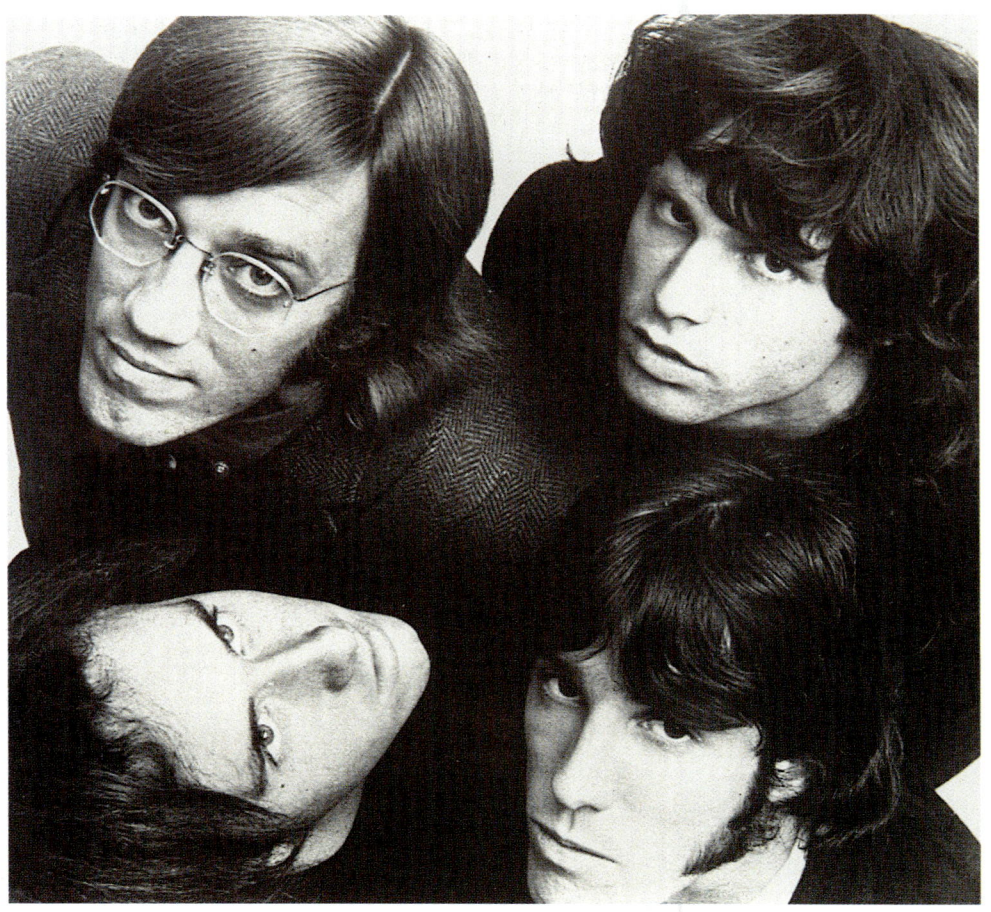

afterwards that its lyrics really were a cry for help. He was in what he would later call his 'fat Elvis' period: bloated and full of insecurity. McCartney's B-side, ***I'm Down***, provided the perfect emotional complement to Lennon's song.

They always find a new chord progression … there is some pretty obvious double-tracking there. It doesn't strike you as immediately as the last one, but it's certainly very clever and certain to be a hit. **Keith Relf, Melody Maker, July 1965**

Help Me Rhonda

ARTIST The Beach Boys **RELEASE DATE** June 1965 (UK)/April 1965 (US) **WRITER** Brian Wilson **PRODUCER** Brian Wilson **LABEL** Capitol (UK & US) **UK CHART PEAK/WEEKS** 27/10 **US CHART PEAK/WEEKS** 1/14

The opening line of this hit has confused listeners for some time; for the record, it is, 'Since she put me down, I've been out doin' in my head.' Al Jardine's first chance at the mike on a Beach Boys A-side, ***Help Me Rhonda*** was their second US Number 1. They originally recorded the song for their album **The Beach Boys Today**. When they heard that producer Gary Usher was planning a cover version, they went back and recorded the more commercial single version.

This big American hit will do well for them over here too. Clever title catch-phrase, and the jaunty harmony is the winning formula. **Melody Maker, May 1965**

Hello, I Love You

ARTIST The Doors **RELEASE DATE** August 1968 (UK)/July 1968 (US) **WRITER** Robbie Krieger, Jim Morrison, John Densmore, Ray Manzarek **PRODUCER** Paul Rothchild **LABEL** Elektra (UK & US) **UK CHART PEAK/WEEKS** 15/12 **US CHART PEAK/WEEKS** 1/12

The Doors's third album **Waiting For The Sun** contained many songs reflecting US youth's disaffection with Vietnam. But it was this non-confrontational song that got the nod as a single which gave the band its second US chart-topper and their best ever UK chart placing. Like ***Light My Fire***, it presented the Doors and their leather-clad lead singer Jim Morrison less as a threat to society than as pop stars, pure and simple.

Somebody has been listening to The Kinks. What have they done! They've gone commercial. Three cheers for the Doors…. What will John Peel say? I don't think he'll even play it. **Andy Fairweather, Melody Maker, August 1968**

Help

ARTIST The Beatles **RELEASE DATE** July 1965 (UK)/August 1965 (US) **WRITER** John Lennon, Paul McCartney **PRODUCER** George Martin **LABEL** Parlophone (UK)/Capitol (US) **UK CHART PEAK/WEEKS** 1/14 **US CHART PEAK/WEEKS** 1/13

After it was agreed that The Beatles' second film would be called *Help!*, John Lennon and Paul McCartney set about writing a theme song with that title. Lennon, who wrote most of the song, said

Heroes

ARTIST David Bowie **RELEASE DATE** October 1977 (UK & US) **WRITER** David Bowie **PRODUCER** David Bowie, Tony Visconti **LABEL** RCA (UK & US) **UK CHART PEAK/WEEKS** 24/8 **US CHART PEAK/WEEKS** 0/0

Although ***Heroes*** is today one of Bowie's best-remembered records, at the time of its release it made only a modest impression on the charts. It was the title track of the second album in the trilogy that he recorded with Brian Eno, coming after **Low** and before **Lodger.** At Bowie and Eno's invitation, Robert Fripp added some guitar fire to the song's cool synth textures.

I think that his time has been and gone. This just sounds weary. Then again, maybe the ponderous heavy riff will be absorbed on the radio, and the monotonous feel may just be hypnotic enough to drag people into buying it. I hope not. **Charlie Gillett, NME, October 1977**

Hey Joe

ARTIST Jimi Hendrix **RELEASE DATE** January 1967 (UK & US) **WRITER** Dino Valenti **PRODUCER** Chas Chandler **LABEL** Polydor (UK)/Reprise (US) **UK CHART PEAK/WEEKS** 6/10 **US CHART PEAK/WEEKS** 0/0

Ex-Animals bassist Chas Chandler had heard Tim Rose's version of this folk song nine months earlier and was determined Hendrix would cover it. It took three sessions to complete, thanks to problems with the female backing vocals. They didn't have the money to cut a B-side, and when Hendrix suggested **Land Of 1000 Dances** Chandler said: 'If anyone makes publishing-money it's gonna be you.' Thus, paired with the trio's first recording was **Stone Free**, the first Experience song Jimi ever wrote.

Hendrix leads Stones in pop song race. Jimi Hendrix – the newest name in pop excitement this week, the phenomenal guitarist and singer, discovered by ex-animal Chas Chandler – has pushed aside The Rolling Stones. **Melody Maker, February 1966**

Hey Jude

ARTIST The Beatles **RELEASE DATE** September 1968 (UK & US) **WRITER** Paul McCartney **PRODUCER** George Martin **LABEL** Apple (UK)/Capitol (US) **UK CHART PEAK/WEEKS** 1/23 **US CHART PEAK/WEEKS** 1/19

Julian Lennon may have been the intended audience for **Hey Jude**: as John Lennon was divorcing Julian's mother to marry Yoko Ono, McCartney, who initially called the song 'Hey Jules', felt the boy's pain. But, as Lennon observed in the single's B-side, **Revolution**, there were others suffering in 1968. With the deaths of Martin Luther King, Robert F. Kennedy, and thousands in Vietnam, the world grew more cynical every day. **Hey Jude**'s message of hope resonated deeply around the globe, selling over nine million copies.

It is not staggering, but it could grow on you. The slow, heavy, piano-ridden beat, sensuous vocals and nice thumpy drums from Ringo, plus a sad soulful atmosphere, lead one to the conclusion 'Top Hole'. **Chris Welch, Melody Maker, August 1968**

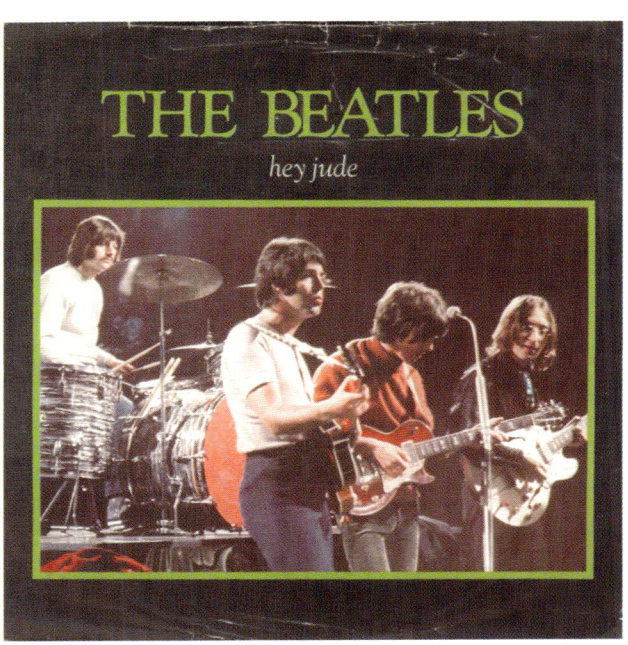

Hey There

ARTIST Rosemary Clooney **RELEASE DATE** September 1955 (UK)/July 1955 (US) **WRITER** Richard Adler, Jerry Ross **PRODUCER** – **LABEL** Philips (UK)/Columbia (US) **UK CHART PEAK/WEEKS** 4/11 **US CHART PEAK/WEEKS** 1/27

Hey There, from the Broadway hit musical *The Pyjama Game*, was the fifth million-seller for Rosemary Clooney and Number 1 in the US for six weeks. The 28-year-old singer first rose to fame in 1951 with her hit recording of **Come On-A My House** which was written by the most unlikely pair of tunesmiths you are likely to find: Chipmunks mastermind Ross Bagdasarian (a.k.a. David Seville) and his cousin, author William Saroyan.

It is unusual for two vocal records of the same label to be issued by the same record company – even more unusual is that **Hey There** *by Rosemary Clooney and John Ray's version are both leading the field in Britain.* **The Alley Cat, NME, November 1955**

(Hey There) Lonely Girl

ARTIST Eddie Holman **RELEASE DATE** October 1974 (UK)/December 1969 (US) **WRITER** Salatore Adamo **PRODUCER** – **LABEL** ABC **UK CHART PEAK/WEEKS** 4/13 **US CHART PEAK/WEEKS** 2/14

This classic romantic ballad was originally written by Earl Shuman and Leon Carr and recorded in 1963 by Ruby and the Romantics, who made the US Top 30 under the title of **Hey There Lonely Boy**. Soul singer Eddie Holman changed the sex when he covered it in 1969 in a style reminiscent of Michael Jackson and it peaked at Number 2 in the US for one week in February 1970. The song made the UK Top 5 in 1974.

Hi-Ho Silver Lining

ARTIST Jeff Beck RELEASE DATE March 1967 (UK & US) WRITER Scott English, Lawrence Weiss PRODUCER Mickie Most LABEL Columbia (UK & US) UK CHART PEAK/WEEKS 14/14 US CHART PEAK/WEEKS 0/0

Jeff Beck's first hit after leaving the Yardbirds was written by the team of Scott English and Larry Weiss, who later wrote the American Breed/Amen Corner hit **Bend Me, Shape Me**. He not only played lead guitar on it, but also sang lead, something he would rarely do again. Although it only reached Number 14, it remains one of the more popular discs of its era: a real period piece with a super-catchy chorus.

It's simple and the lyrics are very amusing. It could get off the ground very well. It seems all the new artists are getting off the ground! **Engelbert Humperdink, Melody Maker, March 1967**

Hit Me With Your Rhythm Stick

ARTIST Ian Dury & The Blockheads RELEASE DATE December 1978 WRITER Ian Dury, Chas Jankel PRODUCER Chas Jankel LABEL Stiff Buy UK CHART PEAK/WEEKS 1/15 US CHART PEAK/WEEKS –

The invisible man behind Ian Dury's success was the multi-talented Chas Jankel, whose guitar, keyboard, co-writing and production talents could be heard on all the loveable Cockney's early records. This was the one that brought him commercial success to match critical acclaim, and saw him add lyrics to a disco instrumental Jankel had written. Jankel would later find favour with Quincy Jones, who covered the similarly flavoured but not as cheeky **AI No Corrida**.

A couple of times it seems that Ian Dury is not familiar with his own lyric, but all can be forgiven because of the middle break … awash with African Jazz percussion and cranky sax runs. **Danny Baker, NME, December 1978**

Hit The Road Jack

ARTIST Ray Charles RELEASE DATE October 1961 (UK)/September 1961 (US) WRITER Percy Mayfield PRODUCER Sid Feller, Ray Charles LABEL HMV Pop (UK)/ABC Paramount (US) UK CHART PEAK/WEEKS 6/12 US CHART PEAK/WEEKS 1/13

Hit The Road Jack, Ray Charles's third million-seller was written by his friend and fellow soul singer-pianist Percy Mayfield. Coming at the dawn of the civil rights movement it was, for many, not just an R&B sing-along but a powerful anthem of rebellion. Charles himself not only talked the talk but walked the walk, providing financial support for the efforts of Dr Martin Luther King, Jr and other civil rights leaders.

Hit The Road Jack *is a groovy beat song in a minor key that continues the twin – and rare – qualities of musicianship and potent juke box appeal.* **Melody Maker, October 1961**

Hold My Hand

ARTIST Don Cornell RELEASE DATE November 1954 WRITER Jack Lawrence, Richard Myers PRODUCER – LABEL Coral UK CHART PEAK/WEEKS – US CHART PEAK/WEEKS 2/18

Having had many hits in the 1940s, Cornell's biggest success shared the same title as the song by The Beatles. There was another connection: he recorded the original version of **Mailman Bring Me No More Blues**, which Buddy Holly covered – The Beatles heard it from Holly and performed it in their Cavern days. **Hold My Hand**, a decidedly less bluesy affair, was from the soundtrack of the Debbie Reynolds/Dick Powell film *Susan Slept Here*, and reached Number 2 in the States.

Hold Tight

ARTIST Dave Dee, Dozy, Beaky, Mick & Titch RELEASE DATE March 1966 WRITER Ken Howard, Alan Blaikley PRODUCER Steve Rowland LABEL Fontana UK CHART PEAK/WEEKS 4/17 US CHART PEAK/WEEKS –

Dave Dee, Dozy, Beaky, Mick & Titch were the kind of group that could not have existed at any other time but the Sixties. Their fun-loving sensibility earned them a largely teenage following, and for a time they were the closest thing Britain had to the Monkees. However, Dave Dee etc. (as they were called) wore better clothes and took themselves much less seriously. **Hold Tight**, their first Top 20 hit, was transformed into a popular football chant during the summer 1966 World Cup tournament.

Holding Back The Years

ARTIST Simply Red **RELEASE DATE** November 1985 (UK)/April 1986 (US) **WRITER** Mick Hucknall, Neil Moss **PRODUCER** Stewart Levine **LABEL** Elektra (UK & US) UK CHART PEAK/WEEKS 51/4 US CHART PEAK/WEEKS 1/23

The song had been co-written by Mick Hucknall in pre-Simply Red days when he was lead singer with the Manchester new wave outfit, the Frantic Elevators. Resuscitated for Simply Red's debut **Picture Book** album, the single did little on its 1983 release, but eventually US radio picked up on its potential and second time around, three years later, the ballad, with the sheen of Crusaders producer Stewart Levine evident, made the top of the US charts.

And still the treasure seems to trickle through Simply Red's fingers…. Subtle and soulful to be sure, but that's not really enough. **Professor Irwin, Melody Maker, May 1986**

Holiday

ARTIST Madonna **RELEASE DATE** January 1984 (UK)/October 1983 (US) **WRITER** Curtis Hudson, Lisa Stevens **PRODUCER** Jon Benitez **LABEL** Sire (UK & US) UK CHART PEAK/WEEKS 6/11 US CHART PEAK/WEEKS 16/21

Madonna Louise Veronica Ciccone is the epitome of 'Girl Power' – the ultimate modern pop star, fully in control of her image and her material. Her early years were spent dancing with Patrick Hernandez's

disco revue in Paris, and scrabbling around in New York, surviving on popcorn and working in a doughnut shop in Times Square. Then in 1983 she released her third single, *Holiday*, a simple dance groove with a Euro-disco feel. It was a club hit and offered a hint of what was to come.

The lady with the biblical name may not have the raunchy tonsil power of Tina Turner but she manages to inject more than a soupçon of slick soulfulness into that sweet and girlish voice of hers. **Tony Mitchell, Sounds, January 1984**

Homeward Bound

ARTIST Simon & Garfunkel **RELEASE DATE** March 1966 (UK)/February 1966 (US) **WRITER** Paul Simon **PRODUCER** Bob Johnston **LABEL** CBS (UK)/Columbia (US) UK CHART PEAK/WEEKS 9/12 US CHART PEAK/WEEKS 5/12

One of the best known 'stories behind the songs' in pop history is how Paul Simon, touring small clubs in the UK following the poor sales of his debut album with Art Garfunkel, found himself on the platform of Widnes station, near Manchester. Missing the States and his girlfriend Kathy Chitty he turned his emotional pain into a song. Released as a follow-up to **The Sound Of Silence**, its heartfelt emotion and strong melody gave the pair their first UK hit.

It is a relaxing voice … a relaxing record, good lyrics, but not a hit here…. It's better on second hearing. I like it. **Alan Clark, Melody Maker, March 1966**

Honey

ARTIST Bobby Goldsboro RELEASE DATE April 1968 (UK)/March 1968 (US) WRITER Bobby Russell PRODUCER Bob Montgomery LABEL United Artists (UK & US) UK CHART PEAK/WEEKS 2/15 US CHART PEAK/WEEKS 1/15

Having served as harmony singer and co-songwriter to Roy Orbison for two and a half years, Goldsboro had been reluctant to leave the fold. But when his first solo release **See The Funny Little Clown** entered the chart in 1963 he knew he wouldn't have to take up the Big O's offer to hold his job open. This chart-topper five years later established Bobby as a major star. It was penned by country songwriter Bobby Russell.

Sounds like Simon & Garfunkel with that guitar going da-da-dee. Do you know what it sounds like? A drive-in movie in Minnesota. That's what it means to me. It is tripe, trash. **Arlo Guthrie, Melody Maker, April 1968**

Honky Tonk

ARTIST Bill Doggett RELEASE DATE August 1956 WRITER Henry Glover, Bill Doggett, Billy Butler, Shape Sheppard, Cliff Scott PRODUCER – LABEL King UK CHART PEAK/WEEKS 0/0 US CHART PEAK/WEEKS 2/29

A supporting musician for so long, latterly in Louis Jordan's Tympani 5, keyboardist Doggett was in the right place at the right time as rock 'n' roll began – and this jogging instrumental, playing off Billy Butler's guitar against Cliff Scott's sax, would be his first major hit at the tender age of 40! Doggett and his band benefited from earlier exposure on the all-star Top 10 *R&B Show* and were voted Most Promising Instrumental Group of the year.

Honky Tonk Woman

ARTIST The Rolling Stones RELEASE DATE June 1969 (UK)/July 1969 (US) WRITER Mick Jagger, Keith Richard PRODUCER Jimmy Miller LABEL Decca (UK)/London (US) UK CHART PEAK/WEEKS 1/17 US CHART PEAK/WEEKS 1/15

Honky Tonk Woman, the Stones's 15th British hit and the opening track of **Let It Bleed**, spent five weeks at the top of the charts, longer than any of their seven other hits. It was also their eighth and final Number 1 in the UK. Sadly, Brian Jones, who had been replaced by guitarist Mick Taylor a month earlier, was found dead in his swimming pool at the time the record was racing up the charts.

An important single for The Stones, but a disappointment for us. The supposedly gutsy **Honky Tonk Woman** *fails to make much impact and the drum and the guitar sound is rather unconvincing. A big mistake is the failure to maintain a strong bass line.* **Chris Welch, Melody Maker, July 1969**

Hopelessly Devoted To You

ARTIST Olivia Newton-John RELEASE DATE November 1978 (UK)/July 1978 (US) WRITER John Farrar PRODUCER – LABEL RSO (UK & US) UK CHART PEAK/WEEKS 2/11 US CHART PEAK/WEEKS 3/19

Olivia Newton-John's perfect pitch and purity of tone sent **Hopelessly Devoted To You** spiralling into the charts. It also helped that she starred opposite the suavely handsome John Travolta in *Grease*, and sang the song when things weren't going too well in their on-screen romance. The film was a Fifties pastiche, full of quiffed hair and billowing circle skirts. Olivia played the blushing ingenue and sang **Hopelessly Devoted To You** with quiet histrionics against chest heaving orchestration. It was kinda cool.

That old Olivia has made the transition from Chanteuse to Actress with as much grace as anyone has ever mustered. This is wet rubbish…. **Julie Burchill, NME, October 1978**

A Horse With No Name

ARTIST America RELEASE DATE December 1971 (UK)/February 1972 (US) WRITER Lee Bunnell PRODUCER Jeff Dexter, Ian Samwell LABEL Warner Bros (UK & US) UK CHART PEAK/WEEKS 3/13 US CHART PEAK/WEEKS 1/14

Despite its name, America actually formed in England, its members being sons of US Air Force servicemen stationed there. Their debut disc, **A Horse With No Name**, hit in Britain before it topped the US charts. Considered a Neil Young soundalike, it ironically bumped Young's **Heart of Gold** from Number 1 in the States. The group would show its individuality on future US hits like **Ventura Highway** and the George Martin-produced **Sister Golden Hair**.

A maxi single from a band we'll hopefully be hearing much more of. A really beautiful track with shades of Neil Young about the vocals and an almost sensuous rapport on the harmony and guitar work. **Penny Valentine, Sounds, November 1971**

Hot Stuff

ARTIST Donna Summer **RELEASE DATE** May 1979 (UK)/April 1979 (US) **WRITER** Pete Bellotte, Harold Faltermeyer, Keith Forsey **PRODUCER** Giorgio Moroder, Steve Bellotte **LABEL** Casablanca (UK & US) **UK CHART PEAK/WEEKS** 11/10 **US CHART PEAK/WEEKS** 1/21

Her album **Bad Girls** had taken fans and critics by surprise, adding a tougher rocking guitar sound to the disco formula that had worked so well through the late Seventies. This single, co-written by Pete Bellotte – who had nurtured Summer along with his partner Giorgio Moroder – was, like the title track off the album, a US Number 1, where it remained for three weeks and was the singer's first two million seller.

Dirty, aggressive, she-slut Donna, on heat and working up an appetite: the guitar solo is excruciating, but it's still an irresistible single. Donna's not just a sex symbol, y'know. **Gavin Martin, NME, May 1979**

Hotel California

ARTIST The Eagles **RELEASE DATE** April 1977 (UK)/February 1977 (US) **WRITER** Don Felder, Don Henley, Glenn Frey **PRODUCER** Bill Szymczyk **LABEL** Asylum (UK & US) **UK CHART PEAK/WEEKS** 8/10 **US CHART PEAK/WEEKS** 1/19

The last chart-topper to feature the bass playing of Randy Meisner, **Hotel California** is regarded as a classic. Recording took place in Miami after the group members had listened to a tape of Don Felder's original instrumental idea. The dominant writing partnership of Henley and Frey then ran with it, creating a song many think sums up the decadence of the LA scene, but it was Felder and guitar partner Walsh whose sparring on the outro made it memorable.

Title track from the album which Francis Rossi told me turned him on to The Eagles. **Caroline Coon, Melody Maker, April 1977**

Hot Love

ARTIST T. Rex **RELEASE DATE** February 1971 (UK)/May 1971 (US) **WRITER** Marc Bolan **PRODUCER** Tony Visconti **LABEL** Flybug (UK)/Reprise (US) **UK CHART PEAK/WEEKS** 1/17 **US CHART PEAK/WEEKS** 72/6

Hot Love was the first Number 1 for Marc Bolan's re-vamped T. Rex (formerly known as the hippy duo Tyrannosaurus Rex, but now a quartet, snappier and definitely more commercial) after their UK Number 2 hit **Ride A White Swan**. By now Bolan had also got rid of his mythical lyric style – he said he wrote **Hot Love** because he wanted to write a rock record, but with a little touch of him in it, bless him.

Marc Bolan rushes back into the chart battle with a sound that will appeal to all pop purists…. It's how we remember the hits of our youth. The 'la, la, la,' chorus will shortly be booming from juke boxes, where the new ten pence's will fit in the slot. **Chris Welch, Melody Maker, February 1971**

Hound Dog

ARTIST Elvis Presley RELEASE DATE August 1956 (UK & US) WRITER Jerry Leiber, Mike Stoller PRODUCER – LABEL HMV Pop (UK)/RCA Victor (US) UK CHART PEAK/WEEKS 2/23 US CHART PEAK/WEEKS 1/28 (Double A Side with Don't Be Cruel)

Elvis's double-A side was a US Number 1 hit for 11 weeks, longer than any other record in the rock era. Originally written by Leiber and Stoller as a country song for blues belter Big Mama Thornton, when Elvis heard a comic version by Freddie Bell & The Bellboys, he added it to his repertoire. He first performed it on Milton Berle's TV show, singing in tuxedo and blue suede shoes to a sad-eyed basset hound.

I think that **Don't Be Cruel** *and* **Hound Dog** *are the best R&R records to be made in years, and I cannot see any other record holding it when it is released in Britain.* **John Davidson, NME, August 1956**

House Of Fun

ARTIST Madness RELEASE DATE May 1982 WRITER Michael Barson, Lee Thompson PRODUCER Clive Langer, Alan Winstanley LABEL Stiff Boy UK CHART PEAK/WEEKS 1/9 US CHART PEAK/WEEKS 0/0

The Nutty Boys shoved Nicole's Eurovision winner **A Little Peace** off the Number 1 position. It is a comic tale of coming of age and teenage misunderstandings about contraceptives in the local chemist shop. Suggs sung it in a jaunty conversational style with the music adding a discomforting bite. The video saw them whizzing around a fairground, and heading for 'The House of Fun' with comic leers on their faces.

House Of The Rising Sun

ARTIST The Animals RELEASE DATE June 1964 (UK)/August 1964 (US) WRITER Alan Price PRODUCER Mickie Most LABEL Columbia (UK)/MGM (US) UK CHART PEAK/WEEKS 3/9 US CHART PEAK/WEEKS 1/11

The traditional folk tune *House of the Rising Sun* had been recorded by Bob Dylan, but Animals bassist Chas Chandler, who suggested the group record it, knew it from Josh White's version. With Eric Burdon's intense delivery and Alan Price's bedazzling organ swirls, the record became an instant classic. A massive influence on rock, it inspired Bob Dylan to go electric and gave songwriter Graham Gouldman a blueprint for his Yardbirds hit *For Your Love*.

This is the sort of record I would have for my personal collection. I have no idea who it is singing but I like it a lot, I'll have a guess: Jackie Wilson? I like the build up there, they deserve a big, big hit. That's great. **Brian Poole, Melody Maker, June 1964**

How Am I Supposed To Live Without You

ARTIST Michael Bolton RELEASE DATE February 1990 (UK)/October 1989 (US) WRITER Michael Bolton, Doug James PRODUCER Michael Omartian LABEL CBS (UK)/Columbia (US) UK CHART PEAK/WEEKS 3/10 US CHART PEAK/WEEKS 1/23

After 20 years in the music business, white pseudo-soul singer Michael Bolton earned his first US Number 1 with this cover of a song that had hit Number 12 six years earlier for Laura Branigan. Two months after Bolton's version peaked in the US, it became his

first UK Top 10, much to the chagrin of critics, who had hoped Britain would be spared from Boltonmania.

There should be a law about ugly records like this: syrupy ballad with receding hairline and sagging chops. Actually forget the law, vigilante justice will do. **Caren Myers, Melody Maker, February 1990**

How Can You Mend A Broken Heart

ARTIST The Bee Gees RELEASE DATE June 1971 (UK & US) WRITER Barry and Robin Gibb PRODUCER Barry, Robin and Maurice Gibb, Robert Stigwood LABEL Polydor (UK)/Atco (US) UK CHART PEAK/WEEKS – US CHART PEAK/WEEKS 1/15

For the Bee Gees this song was as much about mending broken fences as it was about mending broken hearts. It was the first song that Barry and Robin Gibb wrote together since Robin returned to the group after a 15-month split. Not released as a single in England, it became their biggest hit yet in America, where it topped the Hot 100 for four weeks.

An interactive question. I'd ask this lot if I wasn't in danger of getting replies I couldn't handle…. Very intriguing sound, with Robin's voice nicely pained and a rather warm romantic overtone. **Penny Valentine, Sounds, June 1971**

How Deep Is Your Love

ARTIST The Bee Gees RELEASE DATE October 1977 (UK)/September 1977 (US) WRITER Barry, Maurice and Robin Gibb PRODUCER Albhy Galutan, Karl Richardson, Barry Gibb LABEL RSO (UK & US) UK CHART PEAK/WEEKS 3/15 US CHART PEAK/WEEKS 1/33

One of the strongest ballads of the Bee Gees's disco era, ***How Deep Is Your Love*** was the first song from the *Saturday Night Fever* soundtrack to make the charts. It reached Number 3 in the UK before the film was even released. In the States, it topped *Billboard's* Hot 100 for three weeks and spent a record-breaking 17 consecutive weeks in the Top 10.

Archetype smoothie disco muzak for deejays everywhere. You can practically hear your favourite radio bore talking over it as soon as the intro comes on. Instant smash. 'Oo you calling a cynic John? **Charles Shaar Murray, NME, October 1977**

I Believe

ARTIST The Bachelors RELEASE DATE March 1964 (UK)/June 1964 (US) WRITER Ervin Drake, Jimmy Shirl, Irvin Graham, Al Stillman PRODUCER – LABEL Decca (UK)/London (US) UK CHART PEAK/WEEKS 2/17 US CHART PEAK/WEEKS 33/8

The Bachelors have largely been written out of British pop history because, during a time when beat groups were king, they were essentially beatless. Yet the smooth-voiced Irish trio, which began life as a harmonica band, were enormously popular in their time: the second biggest UK singles act of 1964. Their cover of the Frankie Laine standard ***I Believe*** sold over 600,000 copies in the UK and 300,000 in America, with global sales of over a million.

This is like a re-hash, but the group know how to sing it. The trouble is, you can't do much to it. I don't think it will be a hit, so it will probably be a smash. **Chris Roberts, Melody Maker, March 1964**

I Can Never Go Home Anymore

ARTIST The Shangri-Las **RELEASE DATE** November 1965 (UK & US) **WRITER** George Morton, Jerry Grimaldi **PRODUCER** George Morton, Jeff Barry, Ellie Greenwich **LABEL** Red Bird (UK & US) **UK CHART PEAK/WEEKS** 0/0 **US CHART PEAK/WEEKS** 6/11

With the successful sound of the motorbike on their 1964 hit **Leader Of The Pack** revving in their ears, the Shangri-Las' set about creating more melodramatic mini-epics. Their producer, George Morton, thought this 1965 release was their best: a major tearjerker in which a teenager runs away from home over a boy, leaving her mother to die of a broken heart. Untrained vocalist Mary Weiss was only 16, but her pained 'Momma' in the middle of the track was unforgettable.

I Can See Clearly Now

ARTIST Johnny Nash **RELEASE DATE** June 1972 (UK)/September 1972 (US) **WRITER** Johnny Nash **PRODUCER** Johnny Nash **LABEL** CBS (UK)/Epic (US) **UK CHART PEAK/WEEKS** 5/15 **US CHART PEAK/WEEKS** 1/20

Johnny Nash used his high, clear voice for two different styles of songs: in the Fifties he was a teen ballad star, but in the Seventies he had hits with reggae tinged material and was the first American artist to record Bob Marley's songs. In 1971 the lilting melody of **I Can See Clearly Now** was sung with the sweetness of an old ballad, and the sway of a warm sunny day, when the rain has gone.

A kind of clip-cloppy beat…. He has a unique voice and the accompaniment is both original and funky. **Chris Welch, Melody Maker, June 1972**

I Can't Stand The Rain

ARTIST Anne Peebles **RELEASE DATE** April 1974 (UK)/September 1973 (US) **WRITER** Donald Bryant, Anne Peebles, Bernard Miller **PRODUCER** Willy Mitchell **LABEL** London (UK)/Hi (US) **UK CHART PEAK/WEEKS** 41/3 **US CHART PEAK/WEEKS** 38/21

Anne Peebles' raunchy, intense voice was all but forgotten with the arrival of dance and jazz funk. Her sweet, soulful notes were drowned out by the disco beats. **I Can't Stand The Rain** had a distinctive grainy feel to it, with hints of Peebles's gospel singing background adding weight to the notes. The song dealt with the break up of a relationship – a common enough theme, but her voice was vivid and expressive, full of a regret and heartbreak that makes it memorable.

It was either John Lennon or Snowy who said something to the effect that **I Can't Stand The Rain** *was the best record since Ketty Lester's* **Love Letters***. It certainly was a genius and it still sounds great after several hundred plays.* **John Peel, Sounds, June 1974**

I Can't Stop Loving You

ARTIST Ray Charles **RELEASE DATE** June 1962 (UK)/May 1962 (US) **WRITER** Don Gibson **PRODUCER** Sid Feller, Ray Charles **LABEL** HMV Pop (UK)/ABC Paramount (US) **UK CHART PEAK/WEEKS** 1/17 **US CHART PEAK/WEEKS** 1/18

Ray Charles's only British Number 1, a cover version of country star Don Gibson's **I Can't Stop Loving You**, appeared on his landmark album **Modern Sounds in Country and Western Music**. Many years before genre-hopping became common, Charles proved that a black R&B singer could not only sing country music, but be phenomenally successful at it. The album sold over a million copies, and the single over two million.

This folksy ballad doesn't seem the sort of material to pack such momentous hit parade potential, and it's a sure Number 1. Strange to find Ray Charles making a disc that could have come out of the Country & Western stable. **M. M. Panel, Melody Maker, June 1962**

I Don't Like Mondays

ARTIST The Boomtown Rats **RELEASE DATE** July 1979 (UK)/February 1980 (US) **WRITER** Bob Geldof **PRODUCER** Phil Wainman **LABEL** Ensign (UK)/Columbia (US) **UK CHART PEAK/WEEKS** 1/12 **US CHART PEAK/WEEKS** 73/5

The punk movement was socially conscious, to be sure, but **I Don't Like Mondays** was more than social commentary, and it was more than a catchy pop song. Masterfully arranged, it did what all great records are supposed to do: create a feel, an entire world for the listener to step into. Bob Geldof accomplished that with his true-life tale of Brenda Spencer, the young woman who one day shot at children from her bedroom window because, she said, she didn't like Mondays.

The story behind the song is riveting: the girl in America last year who took her father's rifle, went to school and proceeded to wipe out everyone in her way. When asked why she had done it, she replied, 'I Don't Like Mondays'. **Ian Birch, Melody Maker, July 1979**

With her producers she's created an atmospherical synthesis of futuristic space-drama and old world romance. Her voice adds the earth dimension to sounds that would otherwise beat heartlessly. Already a disco hit. Should cross over into the pop chart. **Caroline Coon, Melody Maker, June 1977**

I Get Around/Don't Worry Baby

ARTIST The Beach Boys RELEASE DATE July 1964 (UK)/May 1964 (US) WRITER Brian Wilson PRODUCER Brian Wilson LABEL Capitol (UK & US) UK CHART PEAK/WEEKS 7/13 US CHART PEAK/WEEKS 1/15

The spring of 1964 was not the greatest time to be a rock band in America. Even one of the most successful acts, The Beach Boys, could see that it would be difficult to buck the British invasion. Brian Wilson wrote *I Get Around* to meet that challenge. It became their first US Number 1 and a UK smash. Its B-side, the luminescent *Don't Worry Baby*, was also an American hit and a UK turntable fave.

I wouldn't buy it really. Don't think a chance at the Top 10 with this one. It sounds too much like a baby song for me – like a Christmas baby song. I would not buy it for heavens sake! **Millie, Melody Maker, June 1964**

I Feel For You

ARTIST Chaka Khan (Rufus) RELEASE DATE October 1984 (UK)/September 1984 (US) WRITER Prince PRODUCER Arif Mardin LABEL Warner Bros (UK)/Warner (US) UK CHART PEAK/WEEKS 1/16 US CHART PEAK/WEEKS 3/26

Chaka Khan came to prominence fronting the multi-racial Rufus, but it was her solo career that brought her UK chart breakthrough in 1978. Six years later, a cut with Rufus hit the Top 10 for the first time, and later the same year *I Feel For You* was released, featuring contributions from Grandmaster Flash, Melle Mel (rap) and Stevie Wonder (harmonica) and written by Prince. *I Feel For You* exploded on radio, selling over a million copies in the US alone.

I Feel Love

ARTIST Donna Summer RELEASE DATE July 1977 (UK)/August 1977 (US) WRITER Donna Summer, Giorgio Moroder PRODUCER Giorgio Moroder, Pete Bellotte LABEL GTO (UK)/Casablanca (US) UK CHART PEAK/WEEKS 1/11 US CHART PEAK/WEEKS 6/23

It is not too far fetched to suggest that Donna Summer and Giorgio Moroder – who, with partner Pete Bellotte had discovered Summer singing backing vocals at the Musicland Studios in Munich – invented disco with the orgasmic *Love To Love You Baby* in 1976. *I Feel Love* pushed the disco genre to its metronomic best, sitting at Number 1 in the UK charts for four weeks, selling over half a million copies and reaching the US Top 10 later in the year.

I Get The Sweetest Feeling

ARTIST Jackie Wilson **RELEASE DATE** July 1972 (UK)/July 1968 (US) **WRITER** Van McCoy, Alicia Evelyn **PRODUCER** Jackie Wilson **LABEL** MCA (UK)/Brunswick (US) **UK CHART PEAK/WEEKS** 9/13 **US CHART PEAK/WEEKS** 34/8

More than 10 years after he released *Reet Petite,* this Jackie Wilson single didn't figure that highly on its first outing, only making US Number 34 – not that Wilson had necessarily lost his touch, as 1967's *Higher And Higher* had been his third million-selling single. But *I Get The Sweetest Feeling* didn't make an impression until its 1972 re-release reached the UK Top 10, and charted again in 1975 as a double A-side with *Higher And Higher*.

I Got You (I Feel Good)

ARTIST James Brown (And The Famous Flames) **RELEASE DATE** February 1966 (UK)/November 1965 (US) **WRITER** James Brown **PRODUCER** James Brown **LABEL** Pye Int. (UK)/King (US) **UK CHART PEAK/WEEKS** 29/6 **US CHART PEAK/WEEKS** 3/12

James Brown's signature tune started life as *I Found You,* a disc he wrote and produced for singer Yvonne Fair in 1962. Three years later he recorded it himself as his follow-up to *Papa's Got a Brand New Bag*. The song sold a million copies in America, topping *Billboard*'s R&B chart for six weeks. On *Billboard*'s pop chart, it only made Number 3. The Godfather of Soul has never had a Number 1 in the US or Britain.

It's a good record, and I like it very much. They have been a long time over releasing that. It was out in America months ago. Great sound but not as good as his last two. **Mick Jagger, Melody Maker, February 1966**

I Got You Babe

ARTIST Sonny & Cher **RELEASE DATE** August 1965 (UK)/July 1965 (US) **WRITER** Sonny Bono **PRODUCER** Sonny Bono **LABEL** Atlantic (UK)/Atco (US) **UK CHART PEAK/WEEKS** 1/12 **US CHART PEAK/WEEKS** 1/14

Sonny Bono – working in the early Sixties as PA/gopher to Phil Spector – persuaded his boss to use the vocal talents of one Cherilyn Sakisian La Pierre, whom he met in 1963 and married in 1964. Sonny and Cher did some backing vocals for Spector, and Bono had chart success as a writer with *Needles And Pins* for the Searchers before the couple recorded *I Got You Babe*. It installed the kookily dressed couple into hippy aristocracy.

… very Dylan-ish – a sort of dry statement. Great recording technique. A huge sound … fabulous, fabulous. **Keith Relf, Melody Maker, July 1965**

I Hear You Knocking

ARTIST Dave Edmunds **RELEASE DATE** November 1970 (UK)/December 1970 (US) **WRITER** Dave Bartholomew, Pearl King **PRODUCER** Dave Edmunds **LABEL** MAM (UK & US) **UK CHART PEAK/WEEKS** 1/14 **US CHART PEAK/WEEKS** 4/12

This 12-bar R&B classic had already been a hit in the US, reaching Number 2 for Gale Storm in 1955 and is most often associated with Smiley Lewis, whom Edmunds gives a namecheck to in this version. It gave the multi-instrumentalist, who had previously found chart success in 1968 with *Love Sculpture*, his first solo hit in the UK where it leapt to Number 1 in its second week in the charts.

The Fats Domino speciality is revived. There's an insistent slow boogie beat, punctuated by startling cymbal crashes, plus an aura of authenticity and earthiness, which probably stems from the fact that it was recorded in a barn in Wales. **Derek Johnson, NME, November 1970**

I Heard It Through The Grapevine

ARTIST Marvin Gaye **RELEASE DATE** February 1969 (UK)/November 1968 (US) **WRITER** Norman Whitfield/Barrett Strong **PRODUCER** Norman Whitfield **LABEL** Tamla Motown (UK)/Tamla (US) **UK CHART PEAK/WEEKS** 1/15 **US CHART PEAK/WEEKS** 1/15

Songwriter and producer Norman Whitfield's policy of wringing every last possible sale out of his songs often paid dividends for Motown. Marvin's version was held back, allowing Gladys Knight to enjoy a US Top 3 hit. Whitfield then reworked elements of

Marvin's version and saw it top the transatlantic charts. The song returned to the UK Top 10 in 1986 following a Levi Jeans ad campaign and was also used in the films *The Big Chill* and *The Walking Dead*.

A song of such eerie majesty that it seemed to overpower anything else on Motown, or indeed any of the other material recorded under the burgeoning umbrella of soul. **Colin Irwin, Melody Maker, April 1984**

I Just Called To Say I Love You

ARTIST Stevie Wonder RELEASE DATE August 1984 (UK & US) WRITER Stevie Wonder PRODUCER Stevie Wonder LABEL Motown (UK & US) UK CHART PEAK/WEEKS 1/26 US CHART PEAK/WEEKS 1/26

Motown's biggest ever single in the UK, *I Just Called To Say I Love You* horrified many critics with its potential schlock rating, but as usual Wonder had his finger right on the pulse. The ballad, which he had started writing in the Seventies, featured in the Gene Wilder movie *Woman In Red* and brought Wonder 1985's Best Song Oscar: at the ceremony he dedicated the award to Nelson Mandela, promptly ensuring the single was banned from all official South African radio stations.

I Just Want To Be Your Everything

ARTIST Andy Gibb RELEASE DATE June 1977 (UK)/April 1977 (US) WRITER Barry Gibb PRODUCER Barry Gibb, Albhy Galuten, Karl Richardson LABEL RSO (UK & US) UK CHART PEAK/WEEKS 26/7 US CHART PEAK/WEEKS 1/31

The fourth Bee Gee, Andy Gibb, was gifted this song by brother Barry who had given him his first ever guitar when still a pre-teen. The original debut single **Love Is Thicker Than Water** had come out of the same writing session in Bermuda and, written by Andy and Barry together, would be a follow-up hit. Having taken 14 weeks to ascend the Hot 100, ... **Everything** was ousted from top spot by the Emotions, but then claimed it back as disco fever ruled.

Without those harmonies, Gibb's music doesn't amount to much. But then you could say that about a lot of what's making the rounds at the moment. **Dave Marsh, Rolling Stone, June 1977**

I Love Rock 'N' Roll

ARTIST Joan Jett And The Blackhearts RELEASE DATE April 1982 (UK)/February 1982 (US) WRITER Jake Hooker, Alan Merrill PRODUCER Kenny Laghuna, Richie Cordell LABEL Epic (UK)/Boardwalk (US) UK CHART PEAK/WEEKS 4/10 US CHART PEAK/WEEKS 1/20

Having come to fame in manufactured all-girl rock band the Runaways, Jett toured heavily with her own band the Blackhearts to prove she was a genuine musician. This song was originally the B-side, but the co-writer Jake Hooker, a personal friend, encouraged her to record it again, with dramatic results. The song had been conceived in just half an hour as an answer song to The Rolling Stones's *It's Only Rock 'n' Roll.*

I overheard DLT having a bet with someone that this single wouldn't make the Top 10. I would like to join in on this bet and say that it will definitely not make Top 10. I think that records like this should only be released in America. **Fun Boy Three, Melody Maker, April 1982**

I Love You Because

ARTIST Jim Reeves **RELEASE DATE** February 1964 (UK & US) **WRITER** Leon Payne **PRODUCER** – **LABEL** RCA (UK)/RCA Victor (US) **UK CHART PEAK/WEEKS** 5/39 **US CHART PEAK/WEEKS** 0/0

Jim Reeves's voice was pitched somewhere between country and pop, with a warmth, smoothness and depth that has secured his popularity among the 'easy-listening' market years after his death. With *I Love You Because*, his revival of the romantic 1950 Leon Payne/Ernest Tubb country ballad, he spent 47 weeks in the UK charts. The song had been a US Top 10 hit for Al Martino a year earlier.

Intro sounds like the start to a Goon's record. American singer? It's Jim Reeves. This could get into the chart. This sort of stuff's very popular at the moment. He has a great voice, Yes, it could do very well…. Lovely. **Adam Faith, Melody Maker, February 1964**

I Never Loved A Man (The Way I Love You)

ARTIST Aretha Franklin **RELEASE DATE** March 1967 **WRITER** Ronnie Shannon **PRODUCER** Jerry Wexler **LABEL** Atlantic **UK CHART PEAK/WEEKS** – **US CHART PEAK/WEEKS** 9/11

Although Aretha's vocal talent was obvious from an early age, her career did not explode as anticipated and her arrival at Atlantic from CBS, disillusioned but still confident, heralded a rebirth. Aretha herself discovered the song and informed producer Jerry Wexler she wished to record it, although release was delayed as she had been unable to finish the B-side. Acetates of the A-side had already been circulated to radio by the time she returned to the studio, resulting in her eventual chart breakthrough.

The song was an immediate success. Aretha's first ever US Top 10 record, and served as a springboard for an unbroken series of Stateside hits over the next five or six years. **Bob Woffinden, NME, February 1976**

I Only Have Eyes For You

ARTIST Art Garfunkel **RELEASE DATE** September 1975 (UK)/August 1975 (US) **WRITER** Al Dubin, Harry Warren **PRODUCER** Richard Perry **LABEL** CBS (UK)/Columbia (US) **UK CHART PEAK/WEEKS** 1/11 **US CHART PEAK/WEEKS** 18/18

It took the former Simon & Garfunkel vocalist five years to register his first solo hit in Britain, during which time Paul Simon, who wrote the songs, had scored two Top 10 entries and a pair of lesser hits. None, however, did as well as this retread of a Thirties song that had already found pop success in the US for the Flamingos in 1959. The pure-toned Garfunkel would continue to split his time between musical and film careers.

The fact that the Moonglows' version is generally considered an archive piece will do Art no end of good. Expect to see it staggering around in the charts somewhere soon. **Ian MacDonald. NME, September 1975**

I Owe You Nothing

ARTIST Bros **RELEASE DATE** June 1988 **WRITER** Matt and Luke Goss **PRODUCER** Nicky Graham **LABEL** CBS **UK CHART PEAK/WEEKS** 1/11 **US CHART PEAK/WEEKS** –

Bros (pronounced 'bross') consisted of a pair of platinum-haired twin brothers who looked like grown-up versions of the *Village Of The Damned* kids, and a friend who was not quite so dreamy. They originally released *I Owe You Nothing* in 1987, but nothing happened. A year later, after the group had hit with **When Will I Be Famous** and **Drop That Boy**, they tried again with a remixed version. It became their first and only Number 1.

Gee, that's kinda ginchy! This disc has three different sleeves so you can have your favourite Broster on the cover, or if you are a truly devoted Brosberry, you can have the set! Wow!!!! **Bob Stanley, NME, June 1988**

I Pretend

ARTIST Des O'Connor **RELEASE DATE** May 1968 **WRITER** Les Reed, Barry Mason **PRODUCER** – **LABEL** Columbia **UK CHART PEAK/WEEKS** 1/36 **US CHART PEAK/WEEKS** –

Des O'Connor was an all round entertainer, who had worked in Butlins before he made it to the hit parade. He had a lick at the rock 'n' roll lolly pop, but only as a compere. He was the linkman for Buddy Holly's only British tour. But it wasn't until 1967 that his records began to sell. Within three years he had seven Top 10 hits, including the ballad **I Pretend** which stayed in the charts for 36 weeks.

*'People said that **Careless Hands** was a sing along fluke, but it was meant that way. It got me started. I could have done another like that, but I came up with something different,' said Des.* **Alan Jones, NME, 1968**

I Remember You

ARTIST Frank Ifield **RELEASE DATE** July 1962 (UK)/September 1962 (US) **WRITER** Victor Schertzinger, Johnny Mercer **PRODUCER** – **LABEL** Columbia (UK)/Vee-Jay (US) **UK CHART PEAK/WEEKS** 1/28 **US CHART PEAK/WEEKS** 5/11

Born in Coventry but raised in Australia, Frank Ifield returned to his homeland in 1959 in an attempt to break into the pop market. After initial success in 1960 with **Lucky Devil**, which reached Number 22 in the UK, the hits disappeared. It wasn't until he recorded **I Remember You** that the singer with the yodelling voice hit the top. It was the first of four UK chart-toppers for Ifield in the next 12 months.

The greatest surprise for years: the disc took off like something from Cape Canaveral and is now firmly in Orbit at Number 1. **Chris Roberts, Melody Maker, July 1962**

I Say A Little Prayer

ARTIST Aretha Franklin **RELEASE DATE** August 1968 (UK & US) **WRITER** Burt Bacharach, Hal David **PRODUCER** Jerry Wexler **LABEL** Atlantic (UK & US) **UK CHART PEAK/WEEKS** 4/14 **US CHART PEAK/WEEKS** 10/11

Many critics believed it was Dionne Warwick who lifted Burt Bacharach and Hal David's songs to greatness. In truth, it was the combination of simple yet effective writing coupled with an excellent voice – particularly true of **I Say A Little Prayer**. The musical accompaniment is sparse, the story simple, the rhyming couplets exceptional and the vocal delivery powerful, adding up to one of the all time great songs. That Aretha should manage to surpass Dionne's original version speaks volumes for her vocal delivery.

I like her a lot but I thought her last one was more commercial. I much prefer the Dionne Warwick version of this. She sings it well, but she mucks about with the tune and it doesn't need it. It is a lovely song. **Tony Blackburn, Melody Maker, August 1968**

I See The Moon

ARTIST Stargazers **RELEASE DATE** February 1954 **WRITER** Meredith Wilson **PRODUCER** – **LABEL** Decca **UK CHART PEAK/WEEKS** 1/15 **US CHART PEAK/WEEKS** –

The Stargazers were the most popular British vocal group of the Fifties, fronted by Marie Benson, and became the first native act to get a UK Number 1 with **Broken Wings**. This single, first recorded by inter-racial US outfit the Mariners, was backed by Julius La Rosa's party hit **Eh, Cumpari**, and produced by Dick Rowe – 'the man who turned down The Beatles'.

I have in the past so often sounded the praises of the Stargazers that I can best review two sides by saying that the Gazers are supreme. No guards R.S.M. ever drilled and rehearsed his regiment better than this group drill themselves! **Geoffrey Everitt, NME, February 1954**

I Shot The Sheriff

ARTIST Eric Clapton **RELEASE DATE** July 1974 (UK & US) **WRITER** Bob Marley **PRODUCER** Tom Dowd **LABEL** RSO (UK & US) **UK CHART PEAK/WEEKS** 9/9 **US CHART PEAK/WEEKS** 1/14

Clapton loved his recording of this Bob Marley tune, but didn't want to release it for fear of obstructing Marley's career. Somehow, it got out anyway, and Marley was indeed angry when stations played Clapton's release – even in Jamaica – while he himself couldn't get his latest single on the air. He reportedly even threatened a Jamaican DJ over it and police got involved. But all ended well: when Clapton visited Jamaica Marley treated him warmly, happy for the attention the record brought him.

There was always something of a soft-centre about Eric, something that didn't just quite grab, technique apart. The single, like the album, is a bit off target but will no doubt meet with success. **Jeff Ward, Melody Maker, July 1974**

I Should Be So Lucky

ARTIST Kylie Minogue **RELEASE DATE** January 1988 (UK)/May 1988 (US) **WRITER** Mike Stock, Matt Aitken, Pete Waterman **PRODUCER** Mike Stock, Matt Aitken, Pete Waterman **LABEL** PWL PWL (UK)/Geffen (US) **UK CHART PEAK/WEEKS** 1/16 **US CHART PEAK/WEEKS** 28/14

Kylie Minogue became famous as Charlene in the Australian soap

Neighbours. She was invited to sing at a football game where she performed Little Eva's hit **The Locomotion**, and this led to a recording contract. **I Should Be So Lucky** is a light, pop confection with a disco beat. In the mid-Nineties her work became more edgy. She ditched the bubble gum for something sad and slow, singing the haunting **Wild Rose** with noirish Nick Cave.

Look, I'm as ferocious a campaigner as the next man for less profundity, more disposability in the Top 40 pop, but the line has to drawn somewhere, and this is where I am drawing it. Kylie Sucks. Truly. **Caroline Sullivan, Melody Maker, July 1988**

I Still Haven't Found What I'm Looking For

ARTIST U2 **RELEASE DATE** June 1987 (UK & US) **WRITER** U2 **PRODUCER** Brian Eno, Daniel Lanois **LABEL** Island (UK & US) **UK CHART PEAK/WEEKS** 6/11 **US CHART PEAK/WEEKS** 1/17

The band's second US Number 1 was reprised on the *Rattle And Hum* film of 1989 with U2 rehearsing and performing at Madison Square Garden with Harlem's New Voice of Freedom gospel choir – and the Christianity of the band (Adam Clayton notably excepted) was apparent in the song's soul-searching fervour. The Chimes's cover version charted again in 1990.

It would be terribly easy for us to shoot down U2 for their sanctimonious posturing and their pompous ceremony but it'd be like slagging off Coca-Cola for being a multinational – obvious and dumb. The indisputable fact is that U2 and multinationals are brilliant at what they do.... **The Stud Brothers, Melody Maker, May 1987**

I Swear

ARTIST All-4-One **RELEASE DATE** June 1994 (UK)/April 1994 (US) **WRITER** All-4-One **PRODUCER** David Foster **LABEL** Atlantic (UK)/Blitz Atlantic (US) **UK CHART PEAK/WEEKS** 2/18 **US CHART PEAK/WEEKS** 1/30

After hitting the US Top 5 with their debut single, a remake of the Tymes's 1963 doo-wop hit **So Much In Love**, All-4-One had the biggest US hit of 1994 with **I Swear**, which topped *Billboard*'s Hot 100 for eleven weeks. Their record label made much of the fact that none of the group's members were professionally trained vocalists; they had gained the bulk of their singing experience from performing in their church choirs.

I Walk The Line

ARTIST Johnny Cash RELEASE DATE September 1956 WRITER Johnny Cash PRODUCER – LABEL Sun UK CHART PEAK/WEEKS – US CHART PEAK/WEEKS 17/22

After his first two singles only made the country charts, Johnny Cash enjoyed his first across-the-board success with his million-selling *I Walk the Line*. Cash had originally conceived it as a slow-paced number, but his producer, Sun label head Sam Phillips, insisted he make it up-tempo. That rockabilly beat, combined with Cash's stoic delivery and instantly recognizable voice, became the blueprint of a style which would earn Cash continued popularity over the ensuing decades.

I Wanna Sex You Up

ARTIST Color Me Badd RELEASE DATE April 1991 WRITER Dr Freeze PRODUCER Dr Freeze LABEL Giant UK CHART PEAK/WEEKS 1/14 US CHART PEAK/WEEKS 2/23

From the soundtrack of the movie *New Jack City* came *I Wanna Sex You Up*, the debut single for Color Me Badd and an international smash. The group met while attending high school in Oklahoma City and would harmonize on old doo-wop songs that they learned from Levi's commercials. They were discovered by Robert 'Kool' Bell of Kool & the Gang, who brought them to New York and hooked them up with their record label.

A dash of Stevie Wonder there, a little Lionel Richie, a lot of George Michael, with Eighties stubble and impossibly clear complexion…. Color Me Obvious, Color Me Cruel, Color Me Unnecessary but true: This is crap. **Damon Wise, Vox, September 1991**

I Want To Break Free

ARTIST Queen RELEASE DATE April 1984 (UK & US) WRITER John Deacon PRODUCER Mac Reinhold, Queen LABEL EMI Queen (UK)/Capitol (US) UK CHART PEAK/WEEKS 3/15 US CHART PEAK/WEEKS 45/8

A wry and affectionate male riposte to Women's Lib, the release of *I Want To Break Free*, written by Queen's bass player John Deacon, was supported by a video directed by David Mallet: Mercury sang of his yearning to break free of the chains of domesticity whilst operating a vacuum cleaner and wearing a false chest, with drummer Roger Taylor portrayed as a sexy blonde teenager, guitarist Brian May in a nightie with hair in curlers and Deacon as an elderly grandmother.

Cover is rotten – well, it is Queen – and Freddie Mercury's as oafish as ever. I suppose it is preferable to **Bohemian Rhapsody** *– but what isn't?* **Lyndan Barber, Melody Maker, April 1984**

I Want To Hold Your Hand

ARTIST The Beatles RELEASE DATE December 1963 (UK)/January 1964 (US) WRITER John Lennon, Paul McCartney PRODUCER George Martin LABEL Parlophone (UK)/Capitol (US) UK CHART PEAK/WEEKS 1/24 US CHART PEAK/WEEKS 1/15

America's brand of Beatlemania seemed to sprout spontaneously – in fact, it was carefully planned. Lennon and McCartney wrote *I Want To Hold Your Hand* after manager Brian Epstein asked them to have the American market in mind. Since they already liked the Brill Building pop that ruled America's charts, that was no problem. But while American teens found the song's structure familiar, they knew that the recording would change pop forever. It took America's music industry a little longer to realize that fact.

A sizzling seven from the unbeatable Beatles, who leaped effortlessly to Number 1 in the Top 50 this week with their million-seller **I Want To Hold Your Hand**. *It pushes their first million-topper* **She Loves You** *into second place – an unequalled achievement in the record world.* **Melody Maker, December 1963**

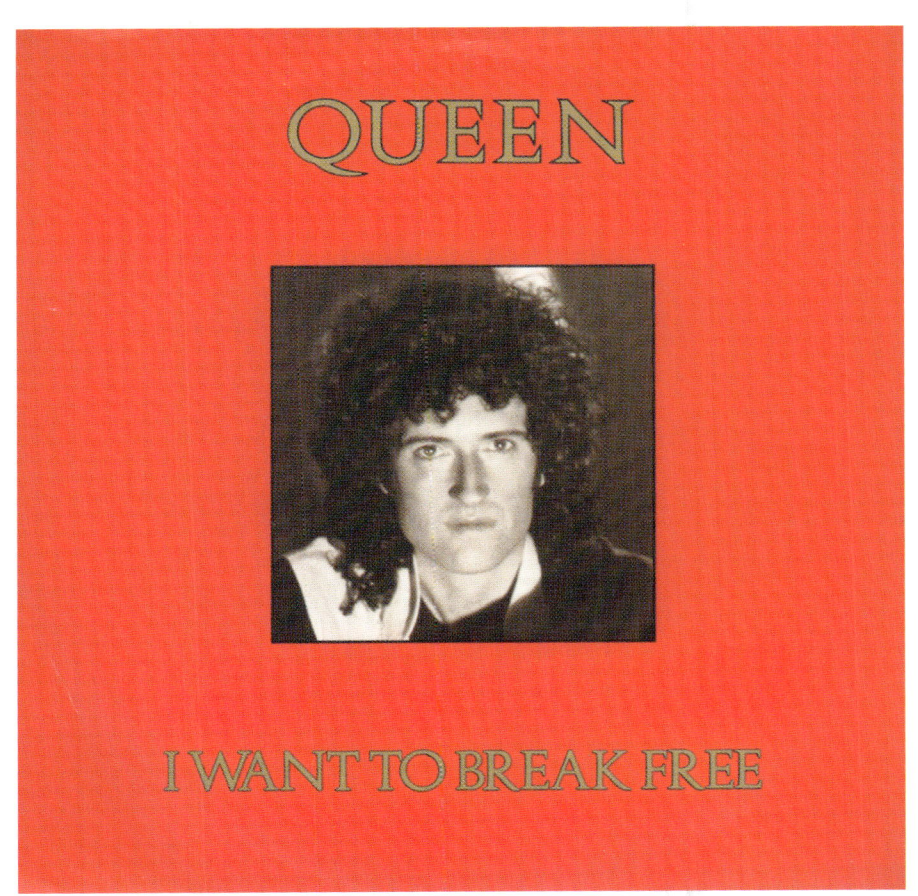

QUEEN

I WANT TO BREAK FREE

I Want To Know What Love Is

ARTIST Foreigner RELEASE DATE December 1984 (UK & US) WRITER Mick Jones PRODUCER Mick Jones, Alex Sadkin LABEL Atlantic (UK & US) UK CHART PEAK/WEEKS 1/16 US CHART PEAK/WEEKS 1/21

The AOR group formed in New York in 1976 around the nucleus of Londoner Mick Jones and New Yorker Lou Gramm. They had hit the US Top 10 five times before this gospel flavoured ballad became their first transatlantic Number 1 single. Tom Bailey (of the Thompson Twins), Jennifer Holliday (star of *Dream Girls*) and the New Jersey Mass Choir guested on the single. The LP, which featured the single **Agent Provocateur**, also spent three weeks at the top of the UK charts.

One of those ludicrously self-regarding, bloated ballads that make the group consistently disagreeable.... The swelling choir that accompanies the lurid chorus is a typically modest touch. I'd rather be eaten by voles than have to listen to this shit again. **Allan Jones, Melody Maker, December 1984**

I Want You Back

ARTIST The Jackson Five RELEASE DATE January 1970 (UK)/November 1969 (US) WRITER Freddie Perren, Al Mizell, Deke Richards, Berry Gordy Jr PRODUCER The Corporation LABEL Tamla Motown (UK)/Motown (US) UK CHART PEAK/WEEKS 2/13 US CHART PEAK/WEEKS 1/19

Originally penned with Gladys Knight And The Pips in mind, this song would become Motown's first US chart-topper of a new decade from a brand-new group and was the only single to be released from the boy wonders' debut album. They followed with **ABC** and **The Love You Save**, all from the same songwriting quartet known as The Corporation.

Here is the most energetic piece of soul music since Aretha's **Respect**. *A very rapid and urgent bass line supports the moaning and crooning of young Michael, the other Jacksons shout their support and give every evidence that they too can sing.* **Langdon Winnie, Melody Maker, March 1970**

I Will Always Love You

ARTIST Whitney Houston RELEASE DATE November 1992 (UK & US) WRITER Dolly Parton PRODUCER David Foster LABEL Arista (UK & US) UK CHART PEAK/WEEKS 1/23 US CHART PEAK/WEEKS 1/26

One of the most successful singles of all time was originally written by Dolly Parton, who had a US Number 53 with the song in 1982. The song was included in the soundtrack of the 1992 movie *The*

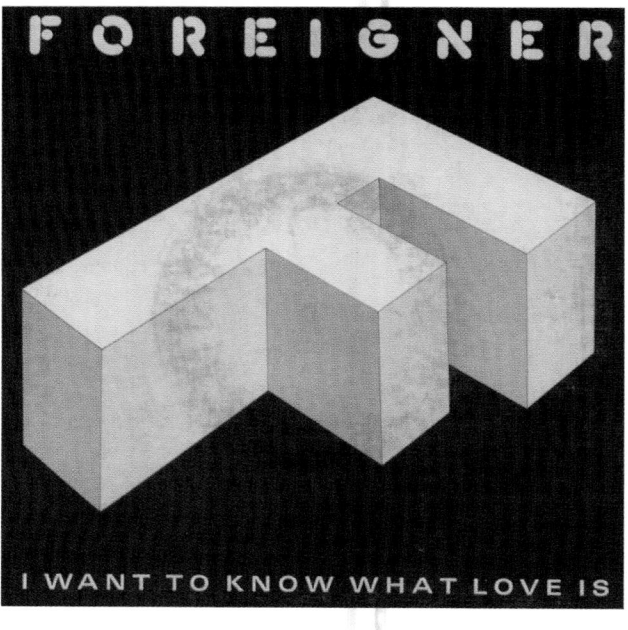

FOREIGNER

I WANT TO KNOW WHAT LOVE IS

Bodyguard at star Kevin Costner's suggestion. Sung by his co-star in the film it clocked up almost 400,000 sales in one week in December 1992, and became the longest US chart topper, taking the title from Boyz II Men's **End Of The Road**.

(This) cover of a Dolly Parton song is bolstered by a remarkably restrained, ultimately effective vocal by Houston. She builds a dramatic, heartfelt conclusion that makes sense given the usually slow building created by producer David Foster. Will please loyalists, while likely bringing more than a few previous defectors to the fold. **Billboard, November 1992**

I Will Survive

ARTIST Gloria Gaynor RELEASE DATE February 1979 (UK)/December 1978 (US) WRITER Dino Fekaris, Freddie Perren PRODUCER Freddie Perren, Dino Fekaris LABEL Polydor (UK & US) UK CHART PEAK/WEEKS 1/15 US CHART PEAK/WEEKS 1/27

This song of defiance against the odds had real meaning for disco diva Gloria Gaynor who, in the few months before recording it, had suffered both hospitalization for spinal surgery and the death of her mother. The New Jersey native was undaunted, however, and let the world know about it with help from writer-producers Dino Fekaris and Freddie Perren. Amazingly it was originally slated as the B-side to **Substitute**, but discos flipped it and found gold – not to mention a future karaoke classic!

Yawn. Predictable 'song' from forthcoming 'album', please don't bother.... I can see why all these lame disc-inflamed 45s are pressed on injection-moulded smashable plastic: they aren't meant to last more than a week. **Sandy Robertson, Sounds, January 1979**

I Write The Songs

ARTIST Barry Manilow RELEASE DATE November 1975 WRITER Bruce Johnston PRODUCER Ron Dante, Barry Manilow LABEL Arista UK CHART PEAK/WEEKS – US CHART PEAK/WEEKS 1/20

Barry Manilow has been dismissed by critics as a 'peroxide puppet' and a 'stuffed dummy', but for millions Barry's middle of the road croon has nestled into their hearts. **I Write The Songs** is a swoony ballad, with a twinkling piano accompaniment, a perfect vehicle for his tacky charm. Before reaching the pinnacle of his success, Barry wrote advertising jingles and was a piano player in a gay venue, accompanying Bette Midler, where he developed his inimitable camp aesthetic.

The idea of Manilow has always chilled me to the bone. A devastatingly awful EP in the easy listening, Neil Diamond-encrusted mould. His phenomenal success in the States (five albums simultaneously in the charts) remains a mystery. **Ian Birch, Melody Maker, July 1977**

along. They split, and The New Seekers were formed a couple of years later.

Written by four people, including the perennial Greenaway and Cook, this will take the Jolly New Seekers into the chart pretty effortlessly. Personally, I found it twee and undeniably catchy, with a kind of very light gospel feel. **Penny Valentine, Sounds, December 1971**

I'll Be Home

ARTIST Pat Boone RELEASE DATE April 1956 (UK)/February 1956 (US) WRITER Ferdinand Washington, Stan Lewis PRODUCER – LABEL London Hld (UK)/Dot (US) UK CHART PEAK/WEEKS 1/24 US CHART PEAK/WEEKS 4/22

Pat Boone enjoyed his only UK Number 1 with a song that didn't make it to the top in the States, *I'll Be Home*. It followed his pattern of covering songs by R&B groups, this one by doo-wop legends The Flamingos. Three years later, The Flamingos would hit in the US with the original version of what would be Art Garfunkel's UK Number 1, *I Only Have Eyes For You*.

Things to come? Will bet that Boone's latest disc I'll Be Home has all the slushy ingredients to reach the best sellers…. **The Alley Cat, NME, April 1956**

I'll Be Missing You

ARTIST Puff Daddy And Faith Evans RELEASE DATE 1997 WRITER Sting, Faith Evans, T. Gaither PRODUCER Sean Combs, Stevie J. LABEL Bad Boy UK CHART PEAK/WEEKS 0/0 US CHART PEAK/WEEKS 1/0

Fourteen years after Sting's *Every Breath You Take* gave Police their 1983 transatlantic Number 1 hit, rap impresario Sean 'Puffy' Coombs revamped the song with new lyrics to call it *I'll Be Missing You* and included it in **No Way Out**, the album he recorded under his Puff Daddy pseudonym; it hit Number 1 in August 1997. The song, in which he duetted with Faith Evans, is an elegy to the murdered rap artist Notorious B.I.G..

I'd Like To Teach The World To Sing (In Perfect Harmony)

ARTIST The New Seekers RELEASE DATE December 1971 (UK & US) WRITER – PRODUCER – LABEL Polydor (UK)/Elektra (US) UK CHART PEAK/WEEKS 1/21 US CHART PEAK/WEEKS 7/11

I'd Like To Teach The World To Sing bounced along with bubbly harmonies and fizzy melodies. It was a revamp of an advertizing jingle which had hummed: 'I'd like to buy the world a Coke', and which The New Seekers turned into a hit record. The Seekers had been a commercial folk group, specializing in tight harmonies, with a pure, lead vocal carrying the song

TRIBUTE TO THE NOTORIOUS B.I.G.

Boyz II Men's second US Number 1 was masterminded by Babyface, who had produced and co-written their first chart-topper, **End of the Road**. With that disc, the Boyz had set a record for the longest stay at Number 1 – 13 weeks. It was broken the following year by Whitney Houston's **I Will Always Love You**. **I'll Make Love to You** evened the score, equalling Houston's 14-week run.

Silky harmonies waft over a well measured arrangement chockfull of bright, glistening percussion. Lovely sing-a-long chorus, initially will remind many of past glories, but the single ultimately will provide a refreshing cool breeze to any of the numerous radio formats it graces. **Billboard, August 1994**

I'm A Believer

ARTIST The Monkees **RELEASE DATE** January 1967 (UK)/December 1966 (US) **WRITER** Neil Diamond **PRODUCER** Jeff Barry **LABEL** RCA (UK)/Colgems (US) **UK CHART PEAK/WEEKS** 1/17 **US CHART PEAK/WEEKS** 1/15

The Monkees were formed in the wake of Beatlemania. Richard Lester's film *Help* was used as a template, and an ad was placed in Variety asking for: 'four insane boys, age seventeen to twenty four.' Davy Jones, Mickey Dolenz, Peter Tork and Mike Nesmith were the lucky quartet. The show was a quirky, innocent take on the day-to-day life of a pop band. **I'm A Believer** was a Neil Diamond song, transformed by the Monkees into a classic piece of pop.

It has that groovy American folk oriented pop group sound, like the Mamas & Papas…. It'll be a hit. They sound like a folk group that have done well in turning to pop…. **Julie Felix, Melody Maker, 1967**

I'll Be There

ARTIST The Jackson Five **RELEASE DATE** November 1970 (UK)/September 1970 (US) **WRITER** Bobby West, Hal Davis, Willie Hutch, Berry Gordy Jr **PRODUCER** Hal Davis **LABEL** Tamla Motown (UK)/Motown (US) **UK CHART PEAK/WEEKS** 4/16 **US CHART PEAK/WEEKS** 1/6

This ballad capped a history-making sequence of four US chart-topping singles in four attempts since the Five signed to Motown. The hit hat-trick having been obtained, label boss Berry Gordy decided to show the Five had more in their armoury than dance music, and the result was Motown's biggest-selling 45 to that date. Though the Jacksons would never hit Number 1 again as a group, Michael, and later Janet, would keep the family flag flying through the Eighties and Nineties.

Group hit Number 1 with their first three discs, and this dynamite funky beat blues ballad has to meet with the same smash success. Strong sound. **Billboard, 1970**

I'll Make Love To You

ARTIST Boyz II Men **RELEASE DATE** September 1994 (UK)/August 1994 (US) **WRITER** Babyface **PRODUCER** Babyface **LABEL** Motown (UK & US) **UK CHART PEAK/WEEKS** 5/12 **US CHART PEAK/WEEKS** 1/33

I'm Gonna Be

ARTIST The Proclaimers **RELEASE DATE** August 1988 (UK)/June 1993 (US) **WRITER** Charles Reid, Craig Reid **PRODUCER** Pete Wingfield **LABEL** Chrysalis (UK & US) **UK CHART PEAK/WEEKS** 11/11 **US CHART PEAK/WEEKS** 3/20

A pair of fervent Scots Nationalist identical twins, the Proclaimers produced one of the unlikeliest hits of the 1980s. Part of a short-lived acoustic wave that included Tracy Chapman and Tanita Tikaram, they produced one of the few genuinely catchy sounds of the period. The duo's clear poppy harmonies and taut folk guitar settings were given a slightly uncanny edge, courtesy of the 'Joe 90' specs and smiley semi-belligerence of their image.

Naturally, though we'll never listen to them again, we grudgingly approve – just as we approve of bus-passes, meals-on-wheels and sheltered accommodation. Jolly good show chaps. **The Stud Brothers, Melody Maker, August 1988**

I'm Into Something Good

ARTIST Herman's Hermits RELEASE DATE August 1964 (UK)/October 1964 (US) WRITER Gerry Goffin, Carole King PRODUCER Mickie Most LABEL Columbia (UK)/MGM (US) UK CHART PEAK/WEEKS 1/15 US CHART PEAK/WEEKS 13/13

This sunny pop song caught the public's imagination in the summer of 1964, catapulting it to the top of the British charts. Peter Noone, a buck-toothed northern actor who had starred in *Coronation Street*, picked up on the song originally recorded by Cookies lead singer Earl Jean which launched his career with his group the Heartbeats. It would be writers Goffin and King's first and only UK Number 1.

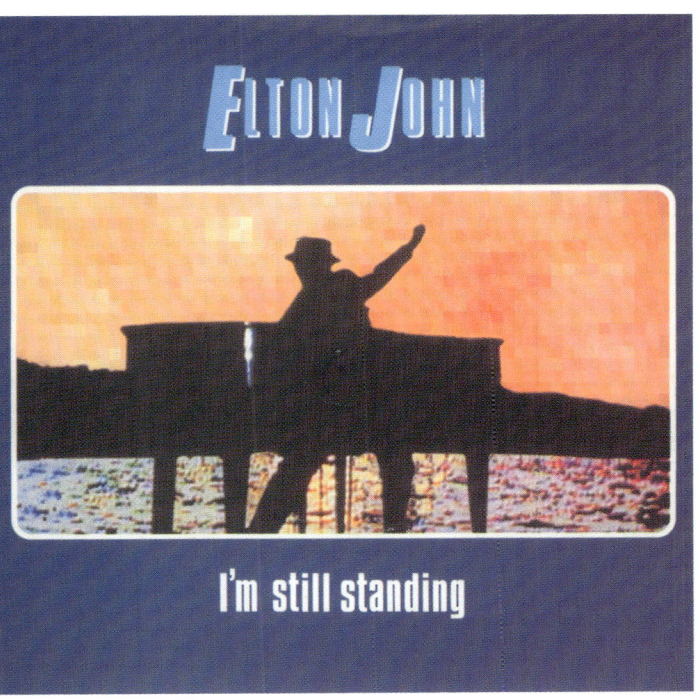

The group's sound is styled on the American surfing sound, which we all like very much, and we intend to do more of the surfing type of numbers. **Peter Noone interviewed by Chris Roberts, Melody Maker, September 1964**

I'm Not In Love

ARTIST 10 cc RELEASE DATE May 1975 (UK & US) WRITER Graham Gouldman, Eric Stewart PRODUCER 10 cc LABEL Mercury (UK & US) UK CHART PEAK/WEEKS 1/11 US CHART PEAK/WEEKS 2/17

Of the band's entire output this song will probably be the longest remembered if only for the reason that it ended every disco in the late Seventies and early Eighties as an invitation for a final smooch. Despite tongues being lodged firmly in cheeks, the group's vocal work coupled with innovative and expressive use of mixing desk faders made this Gouldman/Stewart number a slender but beautifully multi-layered piece of pop irony that picked up three Ivor Novello awards in 1976 and gave them their first US hit.

I'm Still Standing

ARTIST Elton John RELEASE DATE July 1983 (UK)/May 1983 (US) WRITER Elton John, Bernie Taupin PRODUCER Chris Thomas LABEL Rocket (UK)/Geffen (US) UK CHART PEAK/WEEKS 4/11 US CHART PEAK/WEEKS 12/16

This single was released from **Too Low For Zero**, Elton's first UK Top 10 LP for five years, and gave him a second consecutive Top 5 hit in the UK. An upbeat, bouncy number with an equally memorable video to accompany it, it became something of a theme tune as the singer wrestled with problems with his personal life, and featured in his first performance for the Prince's Trust in 1986 – the year before he would become embroiled in court battles with the tabloid *Sun* newspaper.

One to go to a desert island of the mind with…. This dynamically pretty song is his best record since **Your Song**. *Fabulous.* **Barney Hoskins, NME, July 1983**

I'm The Leader Of The Gang (I Am)

ARTIST Gary Glitter RELEASE DATE July 1973 WRITER Gary Glitter, Mike Leander PRODUCER Mike Leander LABEL Bell UK CHART PEAK/WEEKS 1/12 US CHART PEAK/WEEKS 0/0

Rock 'n' Roll (Part 2) started a run of 11 consecutive UK Top 10 hits for Gary Glitter. However, having had three of his first four releases stall at Number 2, it was *I'm The Leader* which took him all the way to the top in 1973. It was another Glitter/Leander composition and became his anthem. It was also the seventh best selling single of the year. His follow-up *I Love You Love Me Love* entered the UK charts at Number 1.

Gary attempts to lose surplus poundage in a spirited attempt at rhythmic excitement, claimed by many dieticians to be the best possible way to keep man and gut in hipsters. **Chris Welch, Melody Maker, July 1973**

I'm Too Sexy

ARTIST Right Said Fred RELEASE DATE July 1991 (UK)/December 1991 (US)
WRITER F. Fairbrass, R. Fairbrass, R. Manzoli PRODUCER Tommy D LABEL Tug
Snog (UK)/Charisma (US) UK CHART PEAK/WEEKS 2/16 US CHART
PEAK/WEEKS 1/21

The tongue-in-cheek fun dance record *I'm Too Sexy* was the
product of the Fairbrass brothers, Richard and Fred. Together with
Rob Manzoli, they make up Right Said Fred, named after a 1962
novelty record by actor/comedian Bernard Cribbins. Appealing
both to a gay and straight audience, in the States it topped the
charts for three weeks, but only reached Number 2 in the UK.

*You wonder what spirit they made it in, and it's amazing how Radio 1
DJs will still happily attach themselves to records like this. You think they've
made some progress in the last few years and then you get this. I doubt
whether this could be a hit anywhere else but in Britain.* **Miles Hunt,
NME, December 1991**

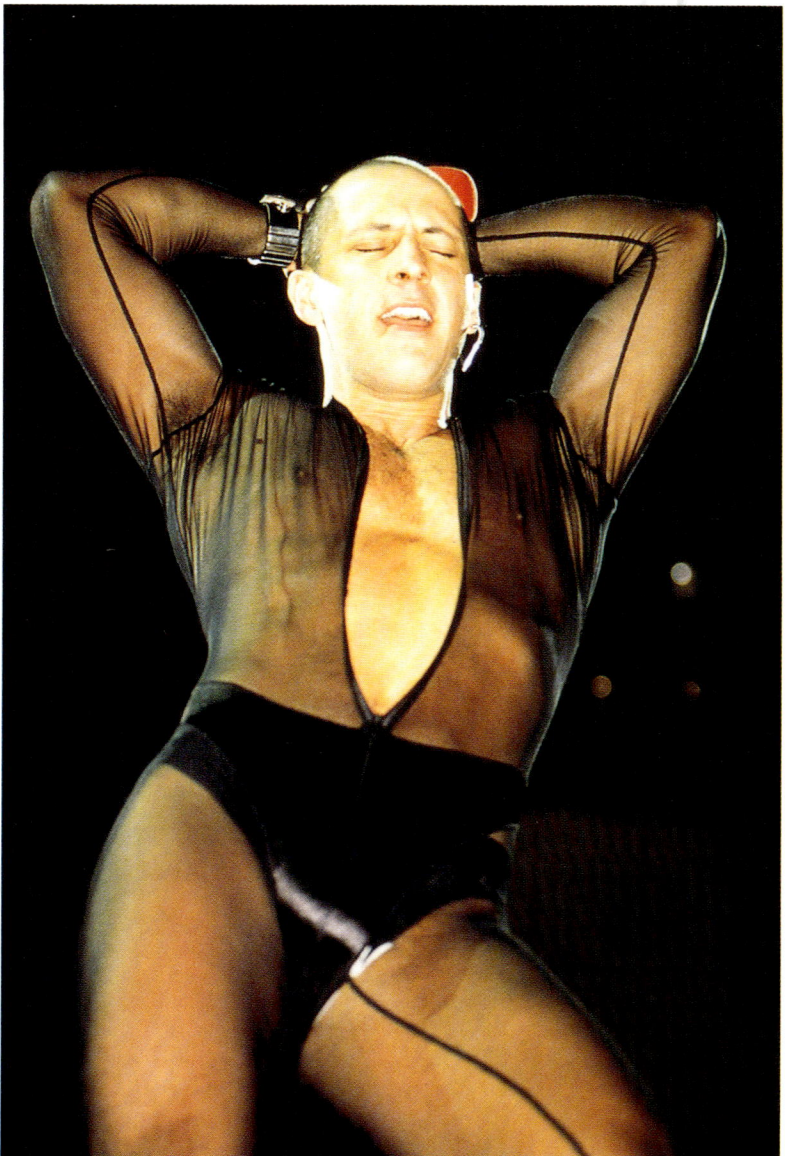

I've Got You Under My Skin

ARTIST Frank Sinatra & Bono RELEASE DATE December 1993 WRITER Cole
Porter PRODUCER – LABEL Island UK CHART PEAK/WEEKS 4/9 US CHART
PEAK/WEEKS –

The song was recorded by Sinatra with the Nelson Riddle orchestra
in 1956, as part of the session for **Songs For Swingin' Lovers.** The
take was live, with Sinatra in a booth next to the band, and a small
audience were invited to watch, and applaud after the
performance. First released as a single in 1964, it charted again in
the UK when Sinatra and U2 frontman Bono produced a version
for Sinatra's **Duets** project.

*Although it appears to be an odd union, Sinatra and Bono's voices
actually are a good match. Hearing Bono belting and whooping in front
of a traditional Jazz/swing band is jarring at first, but it ultimately works
just fine. On the whole, the track is a pleasant surprise that will please
long term Sinatra fans – and rockers in an adventurous
quirky mood.* **Billboard, 1993**

Ice Ice Baby

ARTIST Vanilla Ice RELEASE DATE November 1990
(UK)/September 1990 (US) WRITER Earthquake, Vanilla Ice
PRODUCER Tommy Quon, Vanilla Ice LABEL SBK (UK & US)
UK CHART PEAK/WEEKS 1/13 US CHART PEAK/WEEKS 1/21

Spurned by the hard-core rappers who deemed him
a pretty white boy with questionable talent trying to
come over as a gangsta, Robert Van Winkle
nonetheless picked up a less discriminating
constituency of fans who responded to the easy
chorus and the bass line – sampled from David
Bowie and Queen's 1981 collaboration **Under
Pressure – of Ice Ice Baby**, taken from Vanilla Ice's
breakthrough album **To the Extreme.**

*Six months ago Paula Abdul and MC Hammer were
singing the praises of his dancing, Public Enemy, and
Chuck D encouraging their producer to sign him ... How
could this fabulously photogenic rapper from Miami fail?*
Pete Lewis, Vox, January 1991

If

ARTIST Bread RELEASE DATE March 1971 WRITER David
Gates PRODUCER David Gates LABEL Elektra UK CHART
PEAK/WEEKS 0/0 US CHART PEAK/WEEKS 4/12

This is one of those songs that people back in the
early Seventies would learn to play and sing on
acoustic guitar so that they could appear sensitive.
It was the third US Top 10 hit for the Los Angeles
trio (later a quartet) led by singer/songwriter David
Gates. In the UK it didn't chart at all until it was
covered in 1975 by *Kojak* star Telly Savalas, who for
the most part recited rather than sang it.

*Opens like the run into one of those American movies
that tells a tale of true, beautiful love – The walking
through Central Park feeling, scrunching Autumn leaves*

and that trip…. Slow, languid, pure pop ballad, and done by Bread – that's nice…. **Roy Hollingworth, Melody Maker, June 1971**

If I Could Turn Back Time

ARTIST Cher RELEASE DATE September 1989 (UK)/July 1989 (US) WRITER Diane Warren PRODUCER Guy Roche, Diane Warren LABEL Geffen (UK & US) UK CHART PEAK/WEEKS 6/14 US CHART PEAK/WEEKS 3/23

Written by hitmaker Diane Warren, *If I Could Turn Back Time* was Cher's biggest US chart hit since *Dark Lady* 18 years ago. She promoted it with a big-budget video that showed her in a naval setting. However, unlike the days of the Sonny and Cher TV show, few viewers noticed her navel. Sartorially speaking, she appeared to want to turn back time to the moment she was born.

(If Paradise Is) Half As Nice

ARTIST Amen Corner RELEASE DATE January 1969 WRITER Lucio Battasti, Jack Fishman PRODUCER Shel Talmy, Andy Fairweather-Low LABEL Immediate UK CHART PEAK/WEEKS 1/11 US CHART PEAK/WEEKS –

This song is what is known as 'chorus-intensive'. It has a couple of verses, but no one can remember them. What made it Number 1 was its hook-filled chorus, propelled by percussive acoustic guitars, sung with abandon by Andy Fairweather-Low, and repeated ad infinitum. The production was surprisingly expansive for Shel Talmy, better known for the raw, intense sounds he sparked out of the Kinks, The Who, and others.

If You Don't Know Me By Now

ARTIST Simply Red RELEASE DATE April 1989 (UK)/May 1989 (US) WRITER Leon Huff, Kenny Gamble PRODUCER Stewart Levine LABEL Elektra (UK & US) UK CHART PEAK/WEEKS 2/10 US CHART PEAK/WEEKS 1/22

An affectionate cover version of a Philly classic, first recorded by Teddy Pendergrass, then released in 1973 by Harold Melvin and the Blue Notes. Mick Hucknall's interpretation was knocked by many as insipid cocktail jazz, cynically aimed at the adult contemporary market. Perhaps Hucknall took consolation not only from its chart position, but also from the award of a Grammy for Best R&B Song.

If You Leave Me Now

ARTIST Chicago RELEASE DATE October 1976 (UK)/August 1976 (US) WRITER Peter Cetera PRODUCER James William Guercio LABEL CBS (UK)/Columbia (US) UK CHART PEAK/WEEKS 1/16 US CHART PEAK/WEEKS 1/21

By the time Chicago released *If You Leave Me Now*, their first Number 1, they had come a long way since their early days, when they were the Chicago Transit Authority. In 1969, Chicago mayor Richard Daley forced the band to shorten its name to avoid conflict with the real CTA. In 1976, a few months before *If You Leave Me Now* peaked, the same mayor awarded them the city's Medal of Merit.

Chicago's gentle If You Leave Me Now stayed at Number 1 for six weeks, making it the single of the year. **Caroline Coon, January 1977**

Imagine

ARTIST John Lennon & The Plastic Ono Band **RELEASE DATE** November 1975 (UK)/October 1971 (US) **WRITER** John Lennon **PRODUCER** Phil Spector, John Lennon **LABEL** Apple (UK & US) **UK CHART PEAK/WEEKS** 1/24 **US CHART PEAK/WEEKS** 3/9

Co-produced by Phil Spector and extracted from the LP of the same name, *Imagine* originally charted in 1971 in the US when it made the Top 3 but was only released in the UK four years later. Its vision of a world at one has come to be considered his personal creed. It was re-issued following his murder in 1980 and gave him his second posthumous UK Number 1 single in January 1981.

The idealist at his most idealistic. 'Imagine no possessions': he was denounced a hypocrite over that line. **Melody Maker, November 1975**

In Between Days

ARTIST The Cure **RELEASE DATE** July 1985 (UK)/February 1986 (US) **WRITER** Robert Smith **PRODUCER** Dave Allen, Robert Smith **LABEL** Fiction (UK)/Elektra (US) **UK CHART PEAK/WEEKS** 15/10 **US CHART PEAK/WEEKS** 99/1

When Cure leader Robert Smith penned *In Between Days*, he could just as well have called it 'In Between Members'. During the eight years since the group's inception, nearly a dozen musicians had passed through the group. The single is notable for being the first Cure song to hit in America, although it just squeaked in at Number 99 on the Hot 100.

A bit of a disappointment, because some Cure singles of late have been quite good, but this just sounds like Robert Smith's borrowed the Bernie Albrecht 100 guitar riffs. **Stephen Mallender, Melody Maker, July 1985**

In The Air Tonight

ARTIST Phil Collins **RELEASE DATE** January 1981 (UK)/May 1981 (US) **WRITER** Phil Collins **PRODUCER** Phil Collins, Hugh Padgham **LABEL** Virgin (UK)/Atlantic (US) **UK CHART PEAK/WEEKS** 2/10 **US CHART PEAK/WEEKS** 19/17

This, Phil Collins's first solo single, made the Top 10 twice in two different years. It first hit in early 1981, reaching Number 2 and generating so much interest in Collins's upcoming album **Face Value** that the album debuted at Number 1. Seven years later, the use of the song in a Mercury Communications TV commercial spurred the release of a remixed version, which made Number 4.

In The Air Tonight sees the down to earth more acceptable face of Genesis dawdling through a fairly atmospheric, vaguely haunting piece. All I can say is that it's alright. **Paul Du Noyer, NME, January 1981**

In The Still Of The Nite (I'll Remember)

ARTIST Boyz II Men **RELEASE DATE** February 1993 (UK)/November 1992 (US) **WRITER** F. Parris **PRODUCER** – **LABEL** Motown (UK & US) **UK CHART PEAK/WEEKS** 27/4 **US CHART PEAK/WEEKS** 3/20

After the enormous success of *End of the Road*, Boyz II Men paid tribute to their influences with a cover of the Five Satins's *In the Still of the Nite*. Although the Five Satins's version only made it to Number 24 in *Billboard*, it would become the most popular doo-wop record of all time, a reported multi-million seller. Its recording quality may be primitive, and the singers not in perfect tune, but it compensates with an intangible charm, capturing the essence of teenage romance.

An acappella doo wop work-out with some excellent singing and absolutely no instrumentalisation…. There's nothing to hate here, unless you think love songs are insincere or you're an unreconstructed rocker with no vision beyond what you know. **Dele Fadele, NME, February 1993**

In The Summer Time

ARTIST Mungo Jerry RELEASE DATE June 1970 (UK)/July 1970 (US) WRITER Ray Dorset PRODUCER – LABEL Dawn (UK)/Janus (US) UK CHART PEAK/WEEKS 1/20 US CHART PEAK/WEEKS 3/13

Band leader, vocalist and laboratory researcher Ray Dorset wrote the guitar riff for *In The Summer Time* one night and polished off

the words at work the next day. The band's record company thought it would be a hit. When the acetate was pressed they were still called Good Earth, but after a group ballot they renamed themselves after a cat in a T. S. Eliot poem. The single would go on to top the charts in 26 countries.

A good try from a cheerful jug and boogie band with a 33 ⅓ rpm so called maxi single, which reminds me that the EP is now a discarded concept. Unfortunately they tend to sound amateurish. **Chris Welch, Melody Maker, May 1970**

In The Year 2525

ARTIST Zager & Evans RELEASE DATE August 1969 (UK)/June 1969 (US) WRITER Rick Evans PRODUCER Denny Zager, Rick Evans LABEL RCA (UK)/RCA Victor (US) UK CHART PEAK/WEEKS 1/13 US CHART PEAK/WEEKS 1/13

Rick Evans had written this number in 1964 and in 1968 produced it in a Texas studio with his fellow Nebraskan Denny Zager for $500, running off a thousand copies for their own label Truth Records. RCA's Ernie Altschuler picked it up and the futuristic nostalgia song became a transatlantic Number 1. Sadly for the pair their own success barely continued into the Seventies, let alone until 2525.

Here's one for all you science fiction addicts! It tells you not only what to expect in 2525 AD, but also much further into the distant future. Compellingly derived, it is set to a sort of Gypsy hora rhythm, with shimmering strings and a strumming beat. **Derek Johnson, NME, July 1969**

Informer

ARTIST Snow RELEASE DATE March 1993 (UK)/January 1993 (US) WRITER Michael Grier, Terri Moltke, Darrin O'Brien, Edmond Leary PRODUCER M. C. Shan LABEL East West America (UK & US) UK CHART PEAK/WEEKS 2/15 US CHART PEAK/WEEKS 1/25

Reggae fan Darrin O'Brien, a.k.a. Snow, picked up his Jamaican rapping technique at parties thrown by black friends in Toronto. *Informer*, from his debut album **12 Inches Of Snow**, made Number 1 while Snow himself was languishing in jail, charged with murder (he was later acquitted). On release he couldn't travel to promote the single, but it didn't seem to matter.

The Israelites

ARTIST Desmond Dekker And The Aces RELEASE DATE March 1969 (UK)/May 1969 (US) WRITER Desmond Dacres, Leslie Kong PRODUCER Syd Bucknor, Lol Gellor LABEL Pyramid (UK)/Uni (US) UK CHART PEAK/WEEKS 1/14 US CHART PEAK/WEEKS 9/10

Desmond Dekker was the first reggae artist to become an international star. He first hit the UK charts in 1967 when his **007 (Shanty Town)**, a Number 1 hit for him in Jamaica, made Number 14. *Israelites* was his biggest smash, a hit not only in Britain, but also in America, which was much more resistant to reggae. It hit the British charts again in 1975, re-issued by the Cactus reggae label, reaching Number 10.

room studio in a house in Dagenham and Suggs, singing over the top, is slow and dreamy. In the same month he got married, so romance truly was in the air.

The arrangement alone is gold star quality. A thumping piano here, an ebullient thrust of strings there, sax breaks at the most unexpected moments, and tempo changes where tempo changes rarely tread. All offset by a deadpan desultory vocal. **Colin Irwin, Melody Maker, November 1981**

It Must Have Been Love

ARTIST Roxette RELEASE DATE June 1990 (UK)/April 1990 (US) WRITER Per Gessle PRODUCER Clarence Ofwerman LABEL EMI UK CHART PEAK/WEEKS 3/14 US CHART PEAK/WEEKS 1/25

Roxette, also a Swedish export, was more popular in the US than Abba was. Whereas Abba were purveyors of pure pop, Roxette specialized in big power ballads, tinged with HM: none more so than their 1990 hit *It Must Have Been Love*. Originally a Swedish Christmas hit in 1988 it was partly rewritten by Per Gessle to omit the Christmas references. Featured in the Richard Gere/Julie Robert movie *Pretty Woman*, the success of the single revived interest in their **Look Sharp** album.

Ever heard of a little ditty called 'Take My Breath Away'? Combine that with every other overblown, soppy ballad ever written and you have it. It must have been desperate. **Andrew Smith, Melody Maker, June 1990**

It Doesn't Matter Anymore

ARTIST Buddy Holly RELEASE DATE February 1959 WRITER Paul Anka PRODUCER Norman Petty LABEL Coral Q UK CHART PEAK/WEEKS 1/21 US CHART PEAK/WEEKS 13/14

The first of nearly a dozen posthumous chart-toppers of the pop era, the Paul Anka-penned *It Doesn't Matter Anymore* had been recorded in Coral Records's New York studio backed by violins, violas and cellos less than four months before Buddy Holly's untimely death. It was also notable because, with the B-side, *Raining In My Heart*, written by Felice and Boudleaux Bryant, it would be the only single released before his death that did not contain a Holly composition.

The song demonstrates Holly's mastery of the pop ballad, and its appeal lies with the rockability flavour of the vocal, which owes nothing to the style favoured by Tuxedoed crooners. **Bob Edmonds, NME, September 1976**

It Must Be Love

ARTIST Madness RELEASE DATE December 1981 (UK)/August 1983 (US) WRITER Labi Siffre PRODUCER Clive Langer, Alan Winstanley LABEL Stiff (UK)/Geffen (US) UK CHART PEAK/WEEKS 4/12 US CHART PEAK/WEEKS 33/12

It Must Be Love was a hit for Labi Siffre in 1972, and Madness revived it. They recorded its backing track in nine hours in a front

It Started With A Kiss

ARTIST Hot Chocolate RELEASE DATE July 1982 WRITER Errol Brown PRODUCER Mickie Most LABEL RAK UK CHART PEAK/WEEKS 5/12 US CHART PEAK/WEEKS 0/0

Despite singer Errol Brown's songwriting ability, Hot Choc's biggest hits, **So You Win Again** and **No Doubt About It**, have been outside compositions. *It Started With A Kiss*, the 26th of a run of 30 UK Top 75 hits (charting every year from 1970 to 1984) was a more typical self-penned effort, produced as ever by popmeister Mickie Most. It re-charted in early 1993 on re-issue. Four years later they were back in vogue with their music featuring in the film *The Full Monty*.

It's all soft and soupy; no incision at all, but this is the price we have to pay for unconscious, common genius. It louses up every other single. **Dave McCullough, Sounds, July 1982**

It's A Shame

ARTIST The (Motown) Spinners **RELEASE DATE** November 1970 (UK)/July 1970 (US) **WRITER** Stevie Wonder, Lee Garrett, Syreeta Wright **PRODUCER** Stevie Wonder **LABEL** Tamla Motown (UK)/V.I.P. (US) **UK CHART PEAK/WEEKS** 20/1 **US CHART PEAK/WEEKS** 14/15

After a relatively hit-free decade in the Sixties, this single, written and produced by fellow Motown artist Stevie Wonder, finally gave the hometown quintet a breakthrough in the US. In the UK they made the Top 20 with this song as the Motown Spinners, so nobody could confuse them with the folkier Liverpool group also called The Spinners. Rapper Monie Love's cover version *It's A Shame (My Sister)*, with True Image, was a 1990 UK hit.

It's All In The Game

ARTIST Tommy Edwards **RELEASE DATE** October 1958 (UK)/August 1958 (US) **WRITER** Charles Gates Dawes, Carl Sigman **PRODUCER** – **LABEL** MGM **UK CHART PEAK/WEEKS** 1/17 **US CHART PEAK/WEEKS** 1/22

Initially written in 1912 by future American Vice-President Charles Gates Dawes as the instrumental *Melody In A Major*, it was only after songwriter Carl Sigman added the lyrics nearly 40 years later that Tommy Edwards took it to the US Top 20 in October 1951. With the advent of stereo and in need of resurrecting his career, Edwards re-recorded *It's All In The Game* in 1958 and was rewarded with a transatlantic Number 1 which sold more than three million copies worldwide.

It's All In The Game marks a comeback for Tommy who, like so many other singers of his calibre, experienced something of a slump during the height of the rock 'n' roll craze – but you can't keep a good singer down for very long. **Bruce Charlton, NME, October 1958**

It's Different For Girls

ARTIST Joe Jackson **RELEASE DATE** January 1980 **WRITER** Joe Jackson **PRODUCER** David Kershenbaum **LABEL** A&M **UK CHART PEAK/WEEKS** 5/9 **US CHART PEAK/WEEKS** 0/0

The former Portsmouth nightclub bandleader struck gold with this single from his second album **I'm The Man**. Its desperate yet plaintive appeal from the male side of the gender divide was ideal for radio and captivated even those to whom his 'Spiv-Rock' image did not appeal. His dissolution of his excellent band after the late 1980 **Beat Crazy** signalled a retreat from the pop world that saw him investigate jump blues, jazz and finally classical music.

English rocker turns in another look at soured relationships. Though the lyrics may be scathing … the backup singers provided nice harmonies. **Billboard, November 1979**

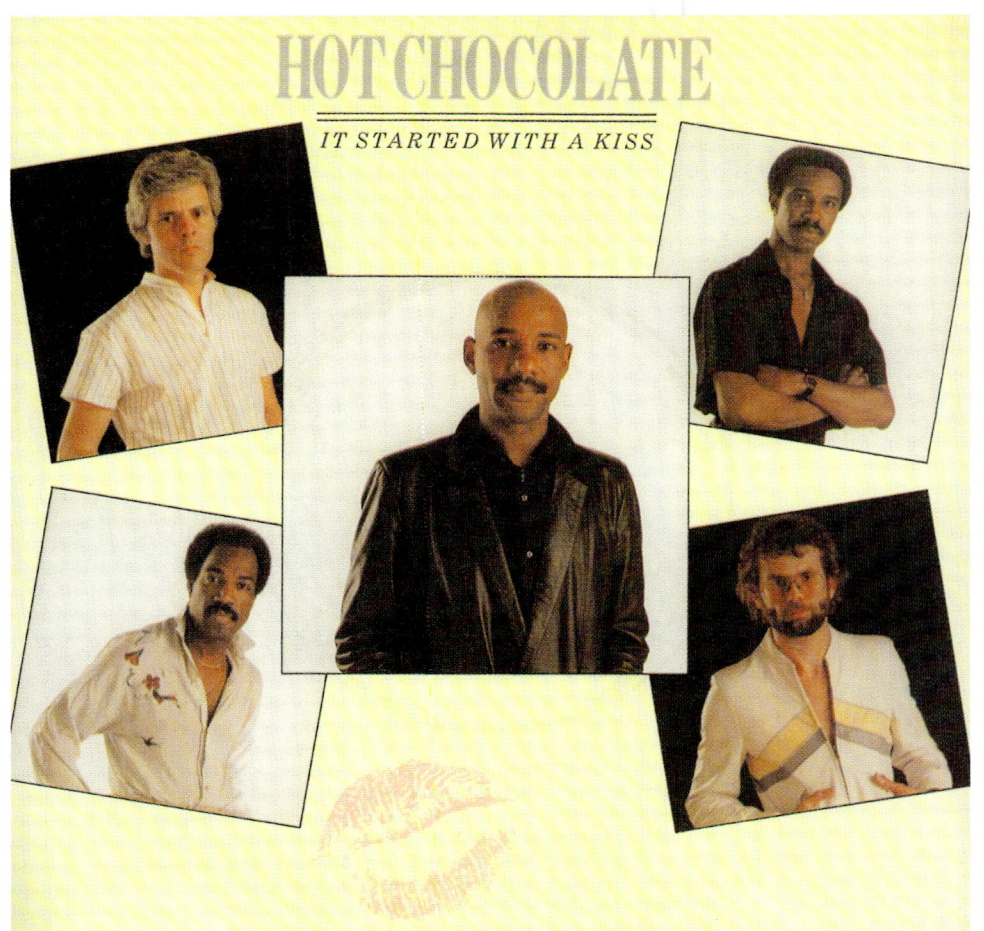

HOT CHOCOLATE

IT STARTED WITH A KISS

It's My Party

ARTIST Lesley Gore **RELEASE DATE** June 1963 (UK)/May 1963 (US) **WRITER** Herb Weiner, Wally Gold, John Gluck Jr. **PRODUCER** Quincy Jones **LABEL** Mercury **UK CHART PEAK/WEEKS** 9/12 **US CHART PEAK/WEEKS** 1/13

Plucked from teenage obscurity to record four songs for Mercury Records, Lesley Gore was catapulted to overnight success with the Quincy Jones-produced *It's My Party*. Rush-released to beat a Crystals version, 17-year-old Gore became the third youngest solo female to top the US charts behind Little Peggy March and Brenda Lee. Although not as successful in the UK in its original version, Dave Stewart and Barbara Gaskin's cover would redress the balance in 1981.

It's My Party is currently Number 1 In America. Very much a teen beat number, good for a not-too-energetic twist, good too for our own Top 30, though far from being a number one I fear. **Keith Fordyce, NME, June 1963**

It's Not Unusual

ARTIST Tom Jones RELEASE DATE February 1965 (UK)/April 1965 (US) WRITER Gordon Mills, Les Reed PRODUCER – LABEL Decca (UK)/Parrot (US) UK CHART PEAK/WEEKS 1/14 US CHART PEAK/WEEKS 10/12

Tom Jones burst on to the scene in early 1965 with the Les Reed/Gordon Mills-composed *It's Not Unusual*. Originally written for future Eurovision winner Sandie Shaw, Jones added his distinctive vocal power to the already impressive arrangement to kick-start a career that is still going strong in the Nineties. The song was re-issued in 1987 and reached a respectable Number 17 in the UK, still embodying the much parodied hip-swivelling appeal that is Jones' stock-in-trade.

22 year old ex-builder's labourer and vacuum cleaner salesman currently high on the hit parade with his second record; the title is: **It's Not Unusual**, *and it is one of the best solo pop releases for a long time.*
Ray Coleman, Melody Maker, February 1965

It's Now Or Never

ARTIST Elvis Presley RELEASE DATE November 1960 (UK)/July 1960 (US) WRITER Aaron Schroder, Wally Gold PRODUCER Steve Sholes, Chet Atkins LABEL RCA (UK)/RCA Victor (US) UK CHART PEAK/WEEKS 120

Elvis's biggest-selling single was Number 1 for eight weeks in Britain and marked a change from pure rock 'n' roll to a more operatic sound. It also gave Elvis a new audience through the easy listening stations, who had never previously played his records. Based on an Italian song, **O Sole Mio,** popularized by Mario Lanza, it was released later in the UK than in the US due to copyright disputes.

It's Now Or Never finds Elvis Presley in mainly romantic mood. There is a vocal support group and the accompaniment is mainly piano and rhythm. Presley's discs have been hits but this one is unquestionably the best he has done in the quieter style. **Keith Fordyce, NME, October 1960**

It's Oh So Quiet

ARTIST Björk RELEASE DATE November 1995 WRITER Hans Lang, Erich Meder, Bert Reisfeld PRODUCER Nellee Hooper LABEL One Little Indian UK CHART PEAK/WEEKS 4/15 US CHART PEAK/WEEKS 0/0

On Björk's first Top 5 disc, she paid tribute to actress/singer Betty Hutton, who did the original recording of *It's Oh So Quiet* in 1948. Björk used a 20-piece orchestra to give her version a period feel. By that point in her recording career, she knew how to get the sounds she wanted. Even though she was only 30 years old, she had made records for nearly 20 years, having been a child prodigy in her native Iceland.

It's Only Rock 'N' Roll (But I Like It)

ARTIST The Rolling Stones RELEASE DATE August 1974 WRITER Mick Jagger, Keith Richard PRODUCER The Glimmer Twins LABEL Rolling Stones UK CHART PEAK/WEEKS 10/7 US CHART PEAK/WEEKS 16/10

Taken from the album of the same name which peaked at Number 2 in the UK and heralded by a graffiti campaign throughout London, *It's Only Rock 'n' Roll* marked the first production credit for 'The Glimmer Twins' – a pseudonym for Mick Jagger and Keith Richard. After the pressures of touring forced guitarist Mick Taylor to quit at the end of 1974, saying he needed to 'move on and do something new,' the Stones started a lengthy search for a replacement.

It's lean, muscular and blunt, with a Jagger double tracked to effect, with a guitar break that will ease stubborn cases of constipation and with a dancing beat that will snap the legs off the more delicate among you.
John Peel, Sounds, July 1974

It's Over

ARTIST Roy Orbison RELEASE DATE April 1964 WRITER Roy Orbison, Bill Dees PRODUCER – LABEL London (UK)/Monument (US) UK CHART PEAK/WEEKS 1/18 US CHART PEAK/WEEKS 9/11

From 1960 to 1964, Roy Orbison scored hit after hit as he moved through a metaphorical vale of tears, dressed in black, with only his guitar for company. But they would later fill a bitter cup of personal tragedy: the death of his wife in a road accident in 1966 and a house fire that killed two of his children two years later. His creativity was drained; here, however, using the full range of his terrific voice, Orbison seemed untouchable.

A dramatic weepie becomes this week's top pop in the thick of the beat age, and Orbison becomes the first American Artist to reach Number 1 since Elvis Presley's **Return to Sender** *in the last week of December, 1962.* **Peter Walsh, Melody Maker, May 1964**

It's Raining Men

ARTIST The Weather Girls **RELEASE DATE** August 1983 (UK)/January 1983 (US) **WRITER** Paul Jabara, Paul Shaffer **PRODUCER** Bob Esty, Paul Jabara **LABEL** CBS (UK)/Entertainment Co (US) **UK CHART PEAK/WEEKS** 2/14 **US CHART PEAK/WEEKS** 46/11

Martha Wash and Izora Armstead never had a hang-up about their size, dubbing themselves Two Tons Of Fun when singing backing vocals for disco pioneer Sylvester in the late Seventies. Working with songwriter/producer Paul Jabara, the Weather Girls' cheery, cheeky, celebratory single was a huge dance club hit and adopted as something of a gay anthem.

Some crazy pre-holocaust cosmic fantasy to be sure and a nice way to finish for the ladies. Both this and **Survival** *have the buzz, should be irresistibly BIG hits and are further proof of the single's capacity to convey any sort of world.* **Gavin Martin, NME, December 1982**

It's Too Late

ARTIST Carole King **RELEASE DATE** August 1971 (UK)/May 1971 (US) **WRITER** Tom Stern, Carole King **PRODUCER** Lou Adler **LABEL** A&M (UK)/Ode (US) **UK CHART PEAK/WEEKS** 6/12 **US CHART PEAK/WEEKS** 1/17

Queen of the bedsit bards, Carole King epitomized the introspective strain of singer-songwriting that proved hugely popular as the Sixties ended and a new, uncertain decade began. The album from which this and the equally billed *I Feel The*

Earth Move came from was **Tapestry**: a 15-week chart-topper which sold fifteen million worldwide and brought her four Grammys. One was specifically for this song.

Now here we do have something worth writing home about, or sending a carrier pigeon for that matter. Miss King is a singer that brings me out in a rash of superlatives. **Penny Valentine, Sounds, May 1971**

Itchycoo Park

ARTIST The Small Faces **RELEASE DATE** August 1967 (UK)/November 1967 (US) **WRITER** Steve Marriott, Ronnie Lane **PRODUCER** Steve Marriott, Ronnie Lane **LABEL** Immediate **UK CHART PEAK/WEEKS** 3/14 **US CHART PEAK/WEEKS** 16/17

The Mod band was sharp of dress and razor-sharp of attitude, and featured in the UK singles charts consistently for three years. Then in the Summer of Love they broke ranks and experimented with a tongue-in-cheek piece of psychedelia: all phased cymbals and spaced-out harmonies. They created a hippy, trippy, flower power classic that went on to influence the Raspberries and Prince. Re-released in 1976, it reached the UK Top 10 for a second time.

Another joint effort by Mister Stephen Marriott and Ronald Lane, who seem to be achieving their aim, to get the Faces together as a powerful force in the happy, creative field of pop music. This is a complete gas-lyrics.... **Chris Welch, Melody Maker, August 1967**

Jailhouse Rock

ARTIST Elvis Presley **RELEASE DATE** January 1958 (UK)/October 1957 (US) **WRITER** Jerry Leiber, Mike Stoller **PRODUCER** Steve Sholes **LABEL** RCA (UK)/RCA Victor (UK) **UK CHART PEAK/WEEKS** 1/14 **US CHART PEAK/WEEKS** 1/27

The title song from Elvis's third movie, *Jailhouse Rock* was also the first of his records to enter the UK charts at Number 1, selling 500,000 copies in three days. Perhaps the wildest, most belted-out rock 'n' roll performance he recorded, it was made more popular by the stunningly produced choreography of his film performance of the song – still one of the greatest 'pop videos', not just of the Fifties but of all time.

*In **Jailhouse Rock** Elvis seems to be trying to outdo Little Richard. **Treat Me Nice** follows the pattern of Presley's best selling **Teddy Bear**. This one should do as well.* **Laurie Hernshaw, Melody Maker, April 1958**

Jamming/Punky Reggae Party

ARTIST Bob Marley And The Wailers **RELEASE DATE** December 1977 **WRITER** Bob Marley **PRODUCER** Bob Marley And The Wailers **LABEL** Island **UK CHART PEAK/WEEKS** 9/12 **US CHART PEAK/WEEKS** 0/0

This exuberant, disco-tinged reggae dance number was released only a year after Marley had been shot and wounded by unknown gunmen during the violence surrounding the 1976 elections in Jamaica. At this point in their career the Wailers no longer included Peter Tosh, who moved on to a solo career, whilst Marley was moving towards further pop success with crossover classics like *Is This Love* and *Could You Be Loved* before his premature death from cancer at the age of 36 in 1981.

Jamming's great, so if you do not have the album, lay some money down and get happy. **Charles Shaar Murray, NME, November 1977**

Je T'Aime, Moi Non Plus

ARTIST Jane Birkin and Serge Gainsbourg **RELEASE DATE** July 1969 (UK)/November 1969 (US) **WRITER** Serge Gainsbourg **PRODUCER – LABEL** Fontana **UK CHART PEAK/WEEKS** 2/11 **US CHART PEAK/WEEKS** 58/10

Anyone who has heard this disc doesn't need to be told that Jane Birkin and Serge Gainsbourg were lovers. Gainsbourg originally recorded the song with his ex, Brigitte

Bardot, but she reportedly barred its release, deciding she did not want to be identified with such an erotic tune. Birkin, on the other hand.... The disc made it to Number 1, despite being banned by the BBC, and its own label, Fontana, stopped sales as it climbed the charts and sold it to Major Minor.

'It is such a beautiful song, I can't see that anyone could take exception to it,' says Jane, and she firmly denies any suggestion that the intention was to make a risqué recording with an eye on its commercial sales potential.... **Jane Birkin interviewed by Laurie Hernshaw, Melody Maker, August 1969**

Jealous Guy

ARTIST Roxy Music **RELEASE DATE** February 1981 **WRITER** John Lennon **PRODUCER** Rhett Davis, Brian Ferry **LABEL** EG Roxy **UK CHART PEAK/WEEKS** 1/11 **US CHART PEAK/WEEKS** 0/0

Following John Lennon's tragic murder in December 1981, many songs associated with him were released; this cover version of one of his most poignant and lyrical songs was also one of the most impressive tributes to him. *Jealous Guy* was Roxy Music's only Number 1. While Roxy was known for its stylish idiosyncrasies, they nevertheless stuck respectfully to the original arrangement on **Imagine,** right down to the whistled chorus.

We may be fooled but we won't forget. Brian Ferry plays a sincere tribute the way he knows how, quavering in the smoke-filled wings, casually ruffled, yet comfortable with the choking kind of unhappiness. **Max Bell, NME, February 1981**

The Jean Genie

ARTIST David Bowie **RELEASE DATE** December 1972 (UK)/November 1972 (US) **WRITER** David Bowie **PRODUCER** Ken Scott, David Bowie **LABEL** RCA (UK)/RCA Victor (US) **UK CHART PEAK/WEEKS** 2/13 **US CHART PEAK/WEEKS** 71/5

Bowie wrote **The Jean Genie** in 1972 while touring the US with his *Ziggy Stardust* revue and recorded it at his final stop, New York City, where he also made his Carnegie Hall debut. His popularity continued to increase as listeners began to seek out all his albums, even those that had previously flopped. Re-issues of his **Space Oddity** album and **The Man Who Sold The World** were charting for the first time in both the US and the UK.

*I was, if you recall, rather disappointed with **John I'm Only Dancing**.... This track, on the other hand, is far more biting and hard with guitar and harmonica wheeling and building up behind his almost talking lyrics into something steely and feverish.* **Penny Valentine, Sounds, November 1972**

Johnny B. Goode

ARTIST Chuck Berry RELEASE DATE April 1958 WRITER Chuck Berry PRODUCER Leonard Chess LABEL Chess UK CHART PEAK/WEEKS 0/0 US CHART PEAK/WEEKS 8/15

No-one has ever captured the essence of rock 'n' roll, both in words and music, better than Chuck Berry. A singer-songwriter before the term was invented, he used his songs to create scenarios, inviting the listener to jump in. *Johnny B. Goode* in particular so embodies rock's spirit that it seemed only natural when NASA included it on the Voyager capsule's Interstellar Record as a sample of what Earth music sounds like.

To keep pace is my most earnest desire because this R&B is a music for dancing. I like people to dance, yes, because you cannot dance without hearing and feeling. **Chuck interviewed by Max Jones, Melody Maker, November 1964**

Jesus To A Child

ARTIST George Michael RELEASE DATE January 1996 (UK)/February 1996 (US) WRITER George Michael PRODUCER George Michael LABEL Virgin (UK)/Dreamworks (US) UK CHART PEAK/WEEKS 1/13 US CHART PEAK/WEEKS 7/14

Jesus To A Child was a starker, more introspective song than was usual for George Michael. It was released following months of legal wrangling with Sony, his record label, because he believed they didn't do much to promote his last album and that the giant electronics company treated their artists as pieces of software, instead of individuals. He came out of the experience world weary, and it bled into the sophisticated melancholia of this single.

The second coming as a wool-knit Interflora bouquet for the middle-aged? Yes sir! Disappointing really with all those zillions still available and a new lease of life opening beyond the 'horrid' confines of the 'nasty' Sony 'beast'. **Roger Morton, NME, January 1996**

Jive Talkin'

ARTIST The Bee Gees RELEASE DATE June 1975 (UK)/May 1975 (US) WRITER Barry, Robin and Maurice Gibb PRODUCER Arif Mardin LABEL RSO UK CHART PEAK/WEEKS 5/11 US CHART PEAK/WEEKS 1/17

The Bee Gees's comeback after four dry years; they wrote this song while driving back from a session, taking its rhythm from the sound the car made while going over a set of bumps. It was originally called 'Drive Talking,' but they changed it to *Jive Talkin'* even though they weren't sure what jive talking was. When they presented the song to their producer, Arif Mardin, he explained it to them, and they changed some of the lyrics accordingly.

Whispered vocals are used to reasonable affect and though this still lacks immediate impact it is nice to see them stepping beyond the seemingly never ending trail of woeful anguished ballads. It might even break through via the disco market. **Colin Irwin, Melody Maker, May 1975**

Joy To The World

ARTIST Three Dog Night RELEASE DATE May 1971 (UK)/March 1971 (US) WRITER Hoyt Axton PRODUCER Richard Podolor LABEL Probe (UK)/Dunhill ABC (US) UK CHART PEAK/WEEKS 24/9 US CHART PEAK/WEEKS 1/17

Danny Hilton came up with the Three Dog Night concept: a band with an eclectic range of music fronted by three vocalists including himself, specializing in cover versions. And it worked, becoming one of the most commercially successful US rock acts of the early Seventies, and pushing the careers of young singer/songwriters including Harry Nilsson, Laura Nyro, Randy Newman, and the tyro pairing of Elton John and Bernie Taupin. *Joy To The World*, by Hoyt Axton, was their second Number 1 after *Mama Told Me (Not To Come)*.

Three Dog Night's **Joy To The World** *was Number 1 for so long it was gold by the time it gave way to* **Brown Sugar***.* **Paul Gambaccini, Rolling Stone, July 1971**

Jump

ARTIST Van Halen RELEASE DATE February 1984 (UK)/January 1984 (US) WRITER Eddie Van Halen, Alex Van Halen, Michael Anthony, David Lee Roth PRODUCER Ted Templeman LABEL Warner Bros. (UK)/Warner (US) UK CHART PEAK/WEEKS 7/13 US CHART PEAK/WEEKS 1/21

By 1984 the band based around Eddie Van Halen's dazzling guitar vocabulary and the flamboyant charisma of David Lee Roth had delivered five platinum albums. This song, written by Eddie, had been rejected by the rest of the band, but then Roth added a lyric inspired by a news item about a man threatening to leap off a skyscraper. Their video, shot on home equipment for around $6,000, won an award at MTV's Video Music Awards.

Jump

ARTIST Kriss Kross RELEASE DATE May 1992 (UK)/April 1992 (US) WRITER Jermaine Dupree PRODUCER Jermaine Dupree LABEL Ruff House UK CHART PEAK/WEEKS 2/8 US CHART PEAK/WEEKS 1/21

Chris Mack Daddy Kelly and Chris Daddy Mack Smith, both 13, had been discovered by Jermaine Dupree (himself only 19) and signed to New York rap label Ruff House. Borrowing the bass line to the Jackson 5's *I Want You Back* and with an identifiable image that involved them wearing all their clothes back to front, *Jump* became the fastest-selling single for 15 years in the US, shifting over four million and topping the charts for eight weeks.

Jump, performed by a pair of pre-pubescents and Number 1 in the States for 12 weeks, hits just the right spot by taking the rhythms of gangster rap but not making the mistake of letting the kids struggle with that music's familiarly ugly concerns. **Danny Kelly, NME, May 1992**

Jumpin' Jack Flash

ARTIST The Rolling Stones RELEASE DATE May 1968 (UK)/June 1968 (US) WRITER Mick Jagger, Keith Richard PRODUCER Johnny Miller LABEL Decca (UK)/London (US) UK CHART PEAK/WEEKS 1/11 US CHART PEAK/WEEKS 3/12

Jumpin' Jack Flash can be viewed not just as a radical return to the Stones's R&B roots after the experimental **Their Satanic Majesties Request**, but almost as a benchmark for all their future work. Under the production skill of Jimmy Miller the Stones welded together elements of R&B, rock, soul and a funky 'Southern' feel. The power and authority of the sound still buzzes with energy.

Mick Jagger denies it was a deliberate move backwards, but it certainly stirs memories of the group a year or two back – wild, exciting, bluesy with that massive furry sound. **Bob Dawbarn, Melody Maker, May 1968**

(Just Like) Starting Over

ARTIST John Lennon RELEASE DATE November 1980 WRITER John Lennon PRODUCER John Douglas, John Lennon, Yoko Ono LABEL Geffen UK CHART PEAK/WEEKS 1/15 US CHART PEAK/WEEKS 1/22

In 1975 John Lennon temporarily retired following the birth of his son Sean. His comeback LP, **Double Fantasy**, was released in November 1980. *Just Like Starting Over* was the first single released from the LP and had already peaked at Number 8 in the UK when, on 8 December 1980, the ex-Beatle was shot dead. The record then halted its descent and leapt from 21 to Number 1, though for only one week. In the US, the record climbed to the top and stayed there for five weeks.

Lennon at 40 has a middle-aged idea of rock 'n' roll. Opens with wimpish sentiments and damp acoustic guitar over oooohing back-up vocals. The listener's stomach flips over and hits the carpet. This man wrote 'ver blues', you know. **Allan Jones, Melody Maker, October 1980**

Just The Way You Are

ARTIST Billy Joel **RELEASE DATE** February 1978 (UK)/November 1977 (UK) **WRITER** Billy Joel **PRODUCER** Phil Ramone **LABEL** CBS (UK)/Columbia (US) **UK CHART PEAK/WEEKS** 19/9 **US CHART PEAK/WEEKS** 3/27

Despite having attained the status of a MOR standard, this song of unconditional love was, surprisingly, not one of Billy Joel's three US chart-toppers, though it charted twice in Britain, eight years apart, and both times within a week of Valentine's Day: the reprise a double A-side with *She's Always A Woman*. Barry White had the greatest UK success, his deep-soul version following 10 months after the original and ending up seven places higher.

Singer-songwriters are rather unfashionable these days, and a lot of very talented ones have flopped in the past. But there are people saying nice things about Billy Joel at the moment. Enjoyable stuff, dunno about it being a hit.... **Sandy Robertson, Sounds, January 1978**

Just Walkin' In The Rain

ARTIST Johnnie Ray **RELEASE DATE** October 1956 (UK)/September 1956 (US) **WRITER** Johnny Bragg, Robert S. Riley **PRODUCER** – **LABEL** Philips (UK)/Columbia (US) **UK CHART PEAK/WEEKS** 1/19 **US CHART PEAK/WEEKS** 2/28

Johnnie Ray enjoyed a string of hits from 1952 to 1960 and occupies a unique place in pop history: bridging the era between early post-war Sinatra and Elvis's ascendancy. He put so much feeling into his songs of heartbreak that he literally cried the words, earning him such nicknames as 'Cry Guy' and 'Prince of Wails'. *Just Walkin' In The Rain*, probably his most well-known single, was Number 1 in the US in 1956. His closest UK equivalent was Frankie Vaughan.

Compared with the high octane stuff that's flying around this week, this sad fellow sounds as potent as a milkshake. Surrounded by all this heat treatment, Johnnie Ray doesn't rock or roll. A determined stagger is about the nearest he gets. **Alex MacIntosh, NME, October 1956**

Karma Chameleon

ARTIST Culture Club **RELEASE DATE** September 1983 (UK)/December 1983 (US) **WRITER** George O'Dowd, John Moss, Michael Craig, Roy Hay, Philip Pickett **PRODUCER** Steve Levine **LABEL** Virgin (UK)/Virgin/Epic (US) **UK CHART PEAK/WEEKS** 1/20 **US CHART PEAK/WEEKS** 1/22

Culture Club's biggest hit, and deservedly so, it was Number 1 for six weeks during the autumn of 1983. The song was co-written by Phil Pickett, a former member of Sailor who also played keyboards on the disc. *Karma Chameleon* went on to win the 1983 Brit award for Best British Single, while Culture Club won as the Best British Group.

It's peace and love, team; perky, free and easy, clever and crafty and this country's very next number one hit single. I love it pretty much to pieces and seem to play it all the time. **Danny Baker, NME, September 1983**

Kayleigh

ARTIST Marillion RELEASE DATE May 1985 (UK)/October 1985 (US) WRITER Marillion PRODUCER Chris Kimsey LABEL EMI (UK)/Capitol (US) UK CHART PEAK/WEEKS 2/14 US CHART PEAK/WEEKS 74/8

Marillion swished on to the stage in loon pants and face paints and harked back to Seventies' progressive rock. They got their name from a Tolkien novel and wrote long, complex songs. In 1982 their self indulgence was quelled on the concept album **Misplaced Childhood**: a moody exploration of the loss of innocence. *Kayleigh* was a love song sung straight from Fish's heart, and it gave them mainstream success. Eventually Fish went solo, and Marillion continued with a new vocalist.

A ballad: 'Do you remember barefoot on the lawn, with shooting stars? Do you remember, love on the floor in Belsize Park? Do you remember dancing in stilettos in the snow?' Must have something to do with the fluoride in the water north of the river. Oddly compelling, certainly compellingly odd, and not bad. **Caroline Sullivan, Melody Maker, May 1985**

Keep On Truckin' (Part 1)

ARTIST Eddie Kendricks RELEASE DATE November 1973 (UK)/August 1973 (US) WRITER Frank Wilson, Leonard Caston, Anita Poree PRODUCER Frank Wilson, Leonard Caston LABEL Tamla Motown (UK)/Tamla (US) UK CHART PEAK/WEEKS 18/14 US CHART PEAK/WEEKS 1/19

Announcing his departure following the Temptations's **Just My Imagination**, great things seemed in store for Eddie Kendricks – but he struggled to find a distinctive solo style. Success came with more up-tempo material aimed at the burgeoning disco scene rather than ballads. *Keep On Truckin'* was perhaps Motown's first acknowledgement of disco music, but it certainly worked. The only pity is that the single predated the 12 inch format, for the full unedited version is one of Motown's best dance tracks.

Instrumentally it's much as you might expect: the best in contemporary Motown – lots of clarinet, crisp bass and slightly Norman Whitfield-ish strings. Production is excellent … and it was a happy idea to feature vibes so prominently. Good Vibes, man. **John Peel, Sounds, October 1973**

Killer Queen

ARTIST Queen RELEASE DATE October 1974 (US)/February 1975 (US) WRITER Freddie Mercury PRODUCER Roy Thomas Baker LABEL EMI (UK)/Elektra (US) UK CHART PEAK/WEEKS 2/12 US CHART PEAK/WEEKS 12/19

The band's first UK Top 3 single taken from their third album **Sheer Heart Attack**. The literary high camp lyrics of *Killer Queen* borrows as much from Noel Coward as from science fiction: 'Caviar and cigarettes/Well versed in etiquette/Extraordinarily nice/She's a killer queen/... Dynamite with a laser beam/Guaranteed to blow your mind/Any time.' The production has all the classic Queen hallmarks: mock-Mozartian piano chords, falsetto chorus overdubs and phased guitar.

Killer tries very hard to be sophisticated and intelligent, but merely substitutes a tasteless and not very clever manipulation of standard images for those qualities. **Allan Jones, Melody Maker, October 1974**

Killing Me Softly With His Song

ARTIST Roberta Flack RELEASE DATE February 1973 (UK)/January 1973 (US) WRITER Norman Gimbel, Charles Fox PRODUCER Joel Dorn LABEL Atlantic UK CHART PEAK/WEEKS 6/14 US CHART PEAK/WEEKS 1/16

The song was originally inspired by Don McLean of **American Pie** fame. Folk singer Lori Lieberman saw his performance and asked writers Norman Gimbel and Charles Fox to finish and arrange the song, which she then recorded. Soul singer Roberta Flack heard her recording and covered the song, which was released in 1973 and was her second US Number 1. In 1996, the Fugees covered the song which became the year's best-selling single in the UK.

While it has its own kind of gentle beauty … the vocal is more sifting, the backing slightly more subtly funky and I think the whole thing may be a bit too classy for the charts. **Penny Valentine, Sounds, February 1973**

PRINCE AND THE REVOLUTION/KISS

Kiss

ARTIST Prince And The Revolution **RELEASE DATE** March 1986 (UK)/February 1986 (US) **WRITER** Prince **PRODUCER** Prince **LABEL** Paisley Park **UK CHART PEAK/WEEKS** 6/9 **US CHART PEAK/WEEKS** 1/18

Less successful than its predecessor **Purple Rain**, Prince's second movie, *Under The Cherry Moon*, nevertheless had a superb soundtrack which went platinum on its release and included this falsetto-sung funky masterpiece. **Kiss** became Prince's third US Number 1, selling over a million at the same time as another of his songs, **Manic Monday**, was a hit for The Bangles. In 1988 The Art Of Noise, with guest vocalist Tom Jones, who shares a birthday with Prince, had their biggest hit with a cover version of this song.

It's official, he has gone this time! The world's most deluded fruitcake, now glaring from the picture like a midget Mercury, is scaling new heights of falsetto, while a seriously undernourished arrangement jiggles and twitches bony hips, oblivious to the preposterous squeaks of its lord and master. **Carol Clerk, Melody Maker, March 1986**

Knock On Wood

ARTIST Amii Stewart **RELEASE DATE** April 1979 (UK)/January 1979 (US) **WRITER** Eddie Floyd, Steve Cropper **PRODUCER** Barry Leng **LABEL** Atlantic/Hansa (UK)/Ariola America (US) **UK CHART PEAK/WEEKS** 6/12 **US CHART PEAK/WEEKS** 1/20

The original was recorded by Stax recording artist Eddie Floyd, who co-wrote the Memphis classic with Booker T. And The MG's guitarist Steve Cropper for Otis Redding. Covered innumerable times (including a live version by David Bowie in 1974) it was given a chart-topping disco twist by actress/singer Amii Stewart, the aunt of Sinitta.

Knockin' On Heaven's Door

ARTIST Bob Dylan **RELEASE DATE** October 1973 (UK)/September 1973 (US) **WRITER** Bob Dylan **PRODUCER** Gordon Carroll **LABEL** CBS (UK)/Columbia (US) **UK CHART PEAK/WEEKS** 14/9 **US CHART PEAK/WEEKS** 12/16

Written by Dylan as one of three vocal contributions to the soundtrack of the movie *Pat Garrett And Billy The Kid*, it would become his most covered post-Sixties song. Eric Clapton had a hit with it in 1975, while 13 years later Guns N' Roses attempted a heavy-metal version, possibly casting themselves as a modern Jimi Hendrix Experience. For Bob himself, it was his biggest-selling single since 1969's **Lay Lady Lay**.

Knowing Me, Knowing You

ARTIST Abba **RELEASE DATE** February 1977 (UK)/May 1977 (US) **WRITER** Stig Anderson, Benny Andersson, Bjorn Ulvaeus **PRODUCER** Benny Andersson, Bjorn Ulvaeus **LABEL** Epic (UK)/Atlantic (US) **UK CHART PEAK/WEEKS** 3/12 **US CHART PEAK/WEEKS** 14/15

After reaching Number 3 with **Money Money Money**, Abba revisited a subject which had hit for them in the past – relationships – and returned to the top with **Knowing Me, Knowing You**. The disc kicked off their second series of three straight Number 1s. By that time, Abba was well on its way to becoming the biggest-selling group in recorded history, a title they held for several years until The Beatles regained first place.

This isn't an instant hit sound, as most Abba hot-shots. Perhaps because it grows on you it will become one of their best loved. A hit. **Caroline Coon, Melody Maker, February 1977**

Kung Fu Fighting

ARTIST Carl Douglas **RELEASE DATE** August 1974 (UK)/October 1974 (US) **WRITER** Carl Douglas **PRODUCER** Biddu **LABEL** Pye (UK)/20th Century (US) **UK CHART PEAK/WEEKS** 1/13 **US CHART PEAK/WEEKS** 1/18

Originally recorded as the B-side of the Larry Weiss-penned *I Want To Give You My Everything,* this novelty track rocketed Jamaican-born Carl Douglas to international recognition amid the martial arts crazy Seventies. Douglas had written lyrics which were augmented in the studio by a melody written by producer Biddu. Released at the height of Bruce Lee mania, the timing was perfect and the single went on to sell almost ten million copies.

La Bamba

ARTIST Los Lobos **RELEASE DATE** July 1987 (UK)/June 1987 (US) **WRITER** Ritchie Valens **PRODUCER** Steve Berlin, Mitchell Froom **LABEL** Swash **UK CHART PEAK/WEEKS** 1/11 **US CHART PEAK/WEEKS** 1/21

Los Lobos started out as a Top 40 covers band, but changed track and began exploring their Chicano musical heritage. They used guitars, accordions, banjos and saxophones to creates a jazzy Tex-Mex sound, and also wrote some gorgeous folk ballads. In 1987 they contributed music to *La Bamba*, the film based on the life of Ritchie Valens, a Chicano pop star. Los Lobos did a spirited rendition of the traditional wedding song *La Bamba*, with jaunty percussion and a sing-along rhythm.

You know the song – there's a lot of noise and then everyone yells 'La Bamba' and throws their nachos in the air before doing it all over again. **Sam King, Melody Maker, July 1987**

Lady

ARTIST Kenny Rogers **RELEASE DATE** November 1980 (UK)/October 1980 (US) **WRITER** Lionel Richie **PRODUCER** Lionel Richie **LABEL** United Artists (UK)/Liberty (US) **UK CHART PEAK/WEEKS** 12/12 **US CHART PEAK/WEEKS** 1/25

The collaboration between Lionel Richie as writer/producer and Kenny Rogers as singer created the only solo Number 1 of Rogers's recording career: *Lady*. 'The idea,' Rogers said later, 'was that Lionel would come from R&B and I'd come from country, and we'd meet somewhere in pop.' *Lady* was important for both men, establishing Rogers as a crossover superstar and for Richie, still a member of The Commodores, opening up the way for his later success as a solo artist.

As pop figure-heads go Kenny is pleasant enough: he's not arrogant and he regularly attempts to extend his range. **Ken Turner, Rolling Stone, October 1980**

The Lady In Red

ARTIST Chris De Burgh **RELEASE DATE** July 1986 (UK)/February 1987 (US) **WRITER** Chris De Burgh **PRODUCER** Paul Hardiman **LABEL** A&M **UK CHART PEAK/WEEKS** 1/15 **US CHART PEAK/WEEKS** 3/26

It took Chris De Burgh 11 years and eight albums, but he finally went to Number 1 in 1986 with *The Lady in Red*. Written about his wife, it was the first single from his 1986 album **Into The Light** and quickly became a romantic standard. It continues to be one of the most played songs on soft-rock stations.

CHRIS DE BURGH
THE LADY IN RED

Lady Marmalade (Voulez-vous Coucher Avec Moi Ce Soir)

ARTIST LaBelle RELEASE DATE March 1975 (UK)/January 1975 (US) WRITER Bob Crewe, Kenny Nolan Helfman PRODUCER Alan Toussaint LABEL Epic UK CHART PEAK/WEEKS 17/9 US CHART PEAK/WEEKS 1/18

Bob Crewe had been a long-time songwriter for the Four Seasons, so it was ironic that when LaBelle topped the US chart in March 1975 with one of his songs they should knock off Seasons singer Frankie Valli with another Crewe/Nolan song, *My Eyes Adored You*. But *Lady Marmalade* was an altogether steamier song, set in New Orleans and produced by Allen Toussaint. The French chorus 'Voulez-vous coucher avec moi ce soir?' was literally a hook line, being delivered by a hooker!

The Last Time

ARTIST The Rolling Stones RELEASE DATE March 1965 WRITER Mick Jagger, Keith Richard PRODUCER Andrew Loog Oldham LABEL Decca (UK)/London (US) UK CHART PEAK/WEEKS 1/13 US CHART PEAK/WEEKS 9/10

The Stones's sixth hit single and third Number 1 was the first A-side to be written by Jagger and Richards and, although there is resemblance to *Maybe The Last Time* by The Staple Singers, the memorable guitar riff that runs through the track from the very opening is pure Keith Richard. The record was the group's first transatlantic Top 10 entry.

Lay Lady Lay

ARTIST Bob Dylan RELEASE DATE September 1969 (UK)/July 1969 (US) WRITER Bob Dylan PRODUCER Bob Johnston LABEL CBS (UK)/Columbia (US) UK CHART PEAK/WEEKS 5/12 US CHART PEAK/WEEKS 7/14

The makers of the film *Midnight Cowboy* commissioned this song, then apparently rejected it – which is their loss, because this extract from the country-tinged **Nashville Skyline** album gave Dylan his first Top 10 single for three years and, nearly three decades later, his last big 45. With no hidden messages, this perfect seduction song has been covered by artists as diverse as Kevin Ayers, the Everly Brothers and Melanie without threatening the original.

Layla

ARTIST Derek And The Dominoes RELEASE DATE August 1972 (UK)/March 1971 (US) WRITER Eric Clapton, James Beck Gordon PRODUCER Tom Dowd LABEL Polydor (UK)/Atco (US) UK CHART PEAK/WEEKS 7/11 US CHART PEAK/WEEKS 10/25

Eric Clapton used the name Derek and the Dominoes to avoid the hype that he had experienced before when he was part of supergroup Blind Faith. The song was originally recorded in 1970, being the title track of the group's LP **Layla And Other Assorted Love Songs**. Layla was Patti Boyd's (then Mrs George Harrison) nickname; Eric married her in 1979. Duane Allman played slide guitar on this track which gave Clapton his first UK and US Top 10 hit.

Lazy Sunday

ARTIST The Small Faces **RELEASE DATE** April 1968 **WRITER** Steve Marriott, Ronnie Lane **PRODUCER** Steve Marriott, Ronnie Lane **LABEL** Immediate UK CHART PEAK/WEEKS 2/11 US CHART PEAK/WEEKS 0/0

The Small Faces' biggest hit felt as if it could have been written by the Kinks' Ray Davies, with its mix of music hall observation on an indolent hippie lifestyle, all delivered in Steve Marriott's cockney, nay mockney, vocals, backed by sound effects of birdsong, surf and, bizarrely, flushing loos.

Oddly enough, I played this at five a.m. in Walthamstow last week at full volume and not only did the neighbours knock on the wall, some nutter picked up a dustbin and emptied it all over the garden. So good luck Faces, you have got a winner. **Chris Welch, Melody Maker, April 1968**

Le Freak

ARTIST Chic **RELEASE DATE** November 1978 (UK)/October 1978 (US) **WRITER** Bernard Edwards, Nile Rodgers **PRODUCER** Bernard Edwards, Nile Rodgers **LABEL** Atlantic UK CHART PEAK/WEEKS 7/16 US CHART PEAK/WEEKS 1/25

Chic were turned down by the A&R department of Atlantic Records and signed only after label president Jerry Greenberg personally intervened on their behalf. After their first single, *Dance, Dance, Dance (Yowsah, Yowsah, Yowsah)*, made the Top 10, the follow-up, *Le Freak*, topped the Hot 100 for six weeks. With five million copies sold, it was the biggest-selling single in Atlantic history. It remains one of the most memorable and much imitated songs of the disco era.

Half way through, the strings take off, thereby transforming (I've done science you know) a merely functional dance track into something inspirational. You never can tell with these foreigners.... **Paul McCrea, Sounds, November 1978**

The Leader Of The Pack

ARTIST Shangri-Las **RELEASE DATE** January 1965 (UK)/October 1964 (US) **WRITER** George Morton, Jeff Barry, Ellie Greenwich **PRODUCER** George Morton, Jeff Barry, Ellie Greenwich **LABEL** Red Bird UK CHART PEAK/WEEKS 11/9 US CHART PEAK/WEEKS 1/12

The Shangri-Las' hit the big time when they hooked up with producer George 'Shadow' Morton. *Leader Of The Pack*, a tale of love, parental disapproval, and death by motorbike, used sound effects and took them to new heights. With the girls' heavy twang from their home borough Queens in New York City and the sound of a real bike (the engineer's Harley Davidson) providing the revs, it became a delinquent classic.

The self-righteous lunacy happened again with Ready, Steady, Go! *banning the great new single,* **Leader Of The Pack**. **Michael Mergeson, Melody Maker, January 1965**

Lean On Me

ARTIST Bill Withers RELEASE DATE August 1972 (UK)/April 1972 (US) WRITER Bill Withers PRODUCER Bill Withers, James Gadson, Melvin Dunlap LABEL A&M (UK)/Sussex (US) UK CHART PEAK/WEEKS 18/9 US CHART PEAK/WEEKS 1/19

Bill Withers began composing seriously while working in a Los Angeles aerospace factory. His playing and singing came to the attention of Booker T. Jones, who produced and arranged Withers' debut release in 1971 when the singer was 32. That single, *Ain't No Sunshine*, hit US Number 3 and won a Grammy. His second album, *Still Bill*, produced the self-written *Lean On Me*, a strong, rhythmic, gospel-influenced track that topped the US charts, and headed them again in 1987, revived by Club Nouveau.

Bill sings soulfully a fragmented song that … warms the cockles of one's heart. A wonderful song deserved of hit status. **Chris Welch, Melody Maker, June 1972**

Leaving On A Jet Plane

ARTIST Peter, Paul And Mary RELEASE DATE January 1970 (UK)/October 1969 (US) WRITER John Denver PRODUCER Albert Grossman, Milt Okun LABEL Warner Bros. (UK)/Warner (US) UK CHART PEAK/WEEKS 2/16 US CHART PEAK/WEEKS 1/17

Peter, Paul And Mary were one of the first folk revival groups to aim at mass market success, and they popularized the music of Bob Dylan and Gordon Lightfoot. They lead the singing at Martin Luther King's civil rights march on Washington. Their clear voices and sweet melodies lifted the John Denver number *Leaving On A Jet Plane* into the charts. It was simple and soulful, full of farewell and longing, and the last song that the group would record together.

Lovely song, beautiful treatment. The lyric is wistful and spellbinding and the melody, particularly the repetitive hook-line, clings long after the disc has stopped playing. One of the trio's best-ever discs. **Derek Johnson, NME, November 1969**

Let's Dance

ARTIST David Bowie RELEASE DATE March 1983 WRITER David Bowie PRODUCER Nile Rodgers, David Bowie LABEL EMI America UK CHART PEAK/WEEKS 1/14 US CHART PEAK/WEEKS 1/20

On Bowie's **Let's Dance** album and its title track, he presented himself as a serious romantic, dancing in the moonlight. Despite the single's minor-key verses, it was relaxed and upbeat, turning away from the dark and edgy textures that had marked much of his previous work. Stevie Ray Vaughan's lead guitar work added the feel of spontaneity to the super-slick Nile Rodgers production.

The shards of inspiration which litter Let's Dance – the humorous thick-ear opening and subsequent finely spaced harmonies, the flashbulb reflexes, the baroque, twisting horn and guitar solos – seem to mock the language of the disco-mix while rejoicing in their employment. The reverberations won't stop moving. **Richard Cook, NME, March 1983**

Let's Get It On

ARTIST Marvin Gaye RELEASE DATE September 1973 (UK)/July 1973 (US) WRITER Ed Townshend, Marvin Gaye PRODUCER Marvin Gaye, Ed Townsend LABEL Tamla Motown (UK)/Tamla (US) UK CHART PEAK/WEEKS 31/7 US CHART PEAK/WEEKS 1/19

Having enjoyed success with **What's Going On**, Marvin turned to a more earthier subject matter for **Let's Get It On**. And while the former had shown off the jazzier side of his style, **Let's Get It On** was a welcome return to R&B. The result was Marvin's first American chart-topper since … *Grapevine* five years previously and the perfect way to kick off the album promotion. More importantly, **Let's Get It On** has since gone on to enjoy folklore status for its seductive powers!

In the first two weeks of its release the whole of America bought this record. And who can blame 'em. A mid paced ballad; a loose, roomy feel with Marv's let's get it together appeals floating to the top. **Geoff Brown, Melody Maker, September 1973**

Let's Stay Together

ARTIST Al Green RELEASE DATE January 1972 (UK)/December 1971 (US) WRITER Al Green, Willie Mitchell, Al Jackson PRODUCER Willie Mitchell LABEL London (UK)/Hi (US) UK CHART PEAK/WEEKS 7/12 US CHART PEAK/WEEKS 1/16

Artists as diverse as Edwyn Collins and Talking Heads have covered Al Green songs, but no-one does it quite like the man himself. The year after this, his only US pop chart-topper, he would be 'born again' and, like Little Richard before him, be thenceforth torn between gospel and 'the Devil's music'. His co-writers here were producer Willie Mitchell – who Wet Wet Wet would seek out in the Eighties – and drummer Al Jackson Jr from Booker T and the MGs.

Al Green sings without any effort at all. Putting his voice in and out of all kinds of marvellous seamy trickery, with a really uptight brass section and a lovely velvety touch about the whole thing. **Penny Valentine, Sounds, December 1971**

Let's Talk About Sex

ARTIST Salt 'N' Pepa **RELEASE DATE** August 1991 **WRITER** Fingerprints **PRODUCER** Herby Lovebug **LABEL** FFRR (UK)/Next Plateau (US) **UK CHART PEAK/WEEKS** 2/13 **US CHART PEAK/WEEKS** 13/20

The US and UK charts at the end of 1991 were given a funky lift by Cheryl James and Sandy Denton's up-front single. With DJ Dee Dee Spinderella they had established themselves, and with their raunchy 1988 hit single **Push It**, became the principal female rap act. **Let's Talk About Sex**, a catchy, witty manifesto for, well ... talking about sex, was re-recorded by the act in 1993 as **Let's Talk About AIDS** for a safe sex campaign.

Let's Twist Again

ARTIST Chubby Checker **RELEASE DATE** August 1961 (UK)/June 1961 (US) **WRITER** Kal Mann, Dave Appell **PRODUCER** – **LABEL** Columbia (UK)/Parkway (US) **UK CHART PEAK/WEEKS** 2/30 **US CHART PEAK/WEEKS** 8/23

Both **The Twist** and its sequel **Let's Twist Again** came out in Britain at the same time they were released in the US, but neither made much of an impact. Then, shortly after **The Twist** topped the Hot 100 for the second time (the only record ever to do so), both singles were reissued in the UK with Chubby Checker over to promote them: **The Twist** peaked at Number 14 and **Let's Twist Again** at Number 2.

Twist is a frantic R&B Rocker that has already climbed to a prominent position in the Stateside chart. Checker sings his juke-box natural with tremendous urge against a potent beat. Flip slows down the tempo a bit, but that Checker beat is still there. **Melody Maker, August 1961**

The Letter

ARTIST Box Tops **RELEASE DATE** September 1967 (UK)/August 1967 (US) **WRITER** Wayne Thompson **PRODUCER** Dan Penn **LABEL** Stateside (UK)/Mala (US) **UK CHART PEAK/WEEKS** 5/12 **US CHART PEAK/WEEKS** 1/16

The Letter was the biggest hit for The Box Tops, a Memphis quartet led by the 16-year old Alex Chilton, who would later co-found the highly influential Big Star. It remains the shortest US Number 1, clocking in at 1:58. Chilton's vocal on **The Letter**, grittier than on most of his other work, was achieved after coaching at length by his producer and proven hit-maker, Dan Penn.

The all British Mindbenders have also recorded this, which was a Stateside hit for the Box Tops, and naturally one hopes this will be an all British hit here, but the Box Tops have a very strong version of the tune. **Chris Welch, Melody Maker, September 1967**

Life On Mars

ARTIST David Bowie **RELEASE DATE** June 1973 **WRITER** David Bowie **PRODUCER** Ken Scott **LABEL** RCA **UK CHART PEAK/WEEKS** 3/13 **US CHART PEAK/WEEKS** 0/0

From David Bowie's 1971 album **Hunky Dory**, RCA did not release **Life on Mars** until 1973, when it gained popularity through Bowie's performing it on his Ziggy Stardust tour. A few months later, Bowie's old label, Decca, likewise released an old recording to capitalize on his current fame. Decca, however, did RCA one better, scoring with a song that didn't even have the advantage of being in Bowie's stage set – **The Laughing Gnome**.

It is indeed a fascinating production, filled with such lines as 'now the workers have struck for fame', and 'rule Britannia is out of bounds' – and I love the echo-delayed drum beat ... Question: Is there life on Mars? **Chris Welch, Melody Maker, June 1973**

Light My Fire

ARTIST The Doors **RELEASE DATE** August 1967 (UK)/June 1967 (US) **WRITER** Jim Morrison, Robbie Krieger, Ray Manzarek **PRODUCER** Paul Rothchild **LABEL** Elektra **UK CHART PEAK/WEEKS** 49/1 **US CHART PEAK/WEEKS** 1/17

Trimmed from an original six-minute track on the Doors' eponymous debut album to a two and a half minute single, **Light My Fire** topped the US chart, and through radio exposure elevated them to the spokesmen of a generation. Despite the abilities of lead singer and shaman Jim Morrison, it was written by guitarist Robbie Krieger and relied on organist Ray Manzarek's driving, spiralling patterns for its appeal. That said, it got the word 'higher' with its drug connotations on the radio – and if that's not subversive....

Doors are a beautiful group designed solely for nice people, and they make pretty records. If this ever becomes a Number 1 smash hit ... then we might consider ourselves saved. **Chris Welch, Melody Maker, July 1967**

Lightnin' Strikes

ARTIST Lou Christie **RELEASE DATE** February 1966 (UK)/December 1965 (US)
WRITER Lou Christie, Twyla Herbert **PRODUCER** Charles Calello **LABEL** MGM
UK CHART PEAK/WEEKS 11/8 **US CHART PEAK/WEEKS** 1/15

Ten months before the Beach Boys' 'pocket symphony' *Good Vibrations* made the charts, Lou Christie struck with this schizophrenic suite about love and lust. American listeners already knew his stratospheric falsetto from hits like *The Gypsy Cried*. After *Lightnin' Strikes* topped Billboard's Hot 100, two of his former labels sensed he was hot and released singles of his early material. In fact, he was 'lightning' hot. He became the first artist since The Beatles to have three discs simultaneously on the Hot 100.

Many people who listen to this compare it with the Four Seasons, because Lou sings very high falsetto à la Frankie Valli on the record.
Melody Maker, March 1966

Like A Prayer

ARTIST Madonna **RELEASE DATE** March 1989 **WRITER** Patrick Leonard,
Madonna **PRODUCER** Patrick Leonard, Madonna **LABEL** Sire **UK CHART
PEAK/WEEKS** 5/10 **US CHART PEAK/WEEKS** 1/16

By the time of *Like A Prayer* Madonna's vocal style had matured: the up-tempo breathlessness replaced by a surer, more melodic swoon. The lyrics explored her fascination with Catholicism and eroticism whilst a great gospel choir swelled out the dance beat. It is pop perfection, but not without controversy: its promo video was banned by the Vatican for its 'blasphemous' imagery – Madonna kissing a black Christ. It won the Best Viewers Choice Video at the MTV Awards.

… one more great dance trifle, the latest in the line of unruffled classics … and that superbly innocent yet carnal voice at the centre.
Ian Gittins, Melody Maker, March 1989

LIKE A PRAYER

Like A Rolling Stone

ARTIST Bob Dylan **RELEASE DATE** August 1965 (UK)/July 1965 (US) **WRITER** Bob Dylan **PRODUCER** Tom Wilson **LABEL** CBS (UK)/Columbia (US) **UK CHART PEAK/WEEKS** 4/12 **US CHART PEAK/WEEKS** 2/12

Although he has never had a chart-topping single in either the US or UK, Bob Dylan came closest with this six-minute track from the LP **Highway 61 Revisited**. Fuelled by Al Kooper's organ, it reached Number 2 in the US in 1965 and made him a star in his own right. He had already made an impression in the US charts as a writer, Peter, Paul and Mary having taken his songs **Blowin' In The Wind** and **Don't Think Twice, It's Alright** to the Top 10.

A great song! I'm not sure that it's really Top 10. If it's going to do a Beatles or a Stones I think it might be. **Mike Clark, Melody Maker, August 1965**

Like A Virgin

ARTIST Madonna **RELEASE DATE** November 1984 **WRITER** Billy Steinberg, Tom Kelly **PRODUCER** Nile Rodgers **LABEL** Sire **UK CHART PEAK/WEEKS** 3/18 **US CHART PEAK/WEEKS** 1/19

Madonna exploded across the pop world like a supernova with the release of *Like A Virgin* and the film *Desperately Seeking Susan*. She swanked across the silver screen with peroxide hair, bright red lipstick, and a knowing street look. On record she was a vamp breathing: 'Like a virgin, touched for the very first time' over a dance beat. The world's media immediately latched onto her saucy, sexy image and the risqué words of the single and made her a star.

The sugar-sweet tones of Madonna will always need a great song and a fat production to really hit home and here she is lucky enough to be blessed with one of these two crucial components, courtesy of the genius of Nile Rodgers. **Barry McIlheney, Melody Maker, November 1985**

Lily The Pink

ARTIST Scaffold **RELEASE DATE** November 1968 **WRITER** Roger McGough, Mike McGear, John Gorman **PRODUCER** Paul McCartney **LABEL** Parlophone **UK CHART PEAK/WEEKS** 1/24 **US CHART PEAK/WEEKS** 0/0

For a while the Scaffold whipped up a saleable mix of poetry, humour and impeccable Scouse credentials – member Mike McGear was Paul McCartney's brother. *Lily The Pink*, an infectious piece of nonsense promoting a spurious 'medicinal compound' was based on a traditional rugby song *Lydia Pinkham*. The French version *Le Sirop Typhon* was a hit for one Richard Anthony.

It is a traditional song which has been adapted to the commercial market place with more acceptable words – the thumping toe tapping beat is guaranteed to liven up any party – must stand at least a 50-50 chance of success. **Derek Johnson, NME, October 1968**

Lipstick On Your Collar

ARTIST Connie Francis **RELEASE DATE** July 1959 (UK)/May 1959 (US) **WRITER** Edna Lewis, George Goegring **PRODUCER** – **LABEL** MGM **UK CHART PEAK/WEEKS** 3/16 **US CHART PEAK/WEEKS** 5/17

Connie had already scored two UK Number 1s when *Lipstick On Your Collar* reached the Top 5 in both the US and UK. She had a troubled life, being raped in her motel room in 1974 and suffering long-term illness, but resumed performing in the Eighties. She obtained a new recording contract with Sony in 1993 as *Lipstick* rode the charts once more thanks to the Denis Potter TV series of the same name using it as its theme.

A teenage special with a fast beat that will bring a blush to the cheeks of many a feller who has been caught out by the tell-tale traces. There's a load of punch and drive in the presentation. **Keith Fordyce, NME, June 1959**

Listen To The Music

ARTIST The Doobie Brothers **RELEASE DATE** March 1974 (UK)/September 1972 (US) **WRITER** Tom Johnston **PRODUCER** Ted Templeman **LABEL** Warner Bros. (UK)/Warner (US) **UK CHART PEAK/WEEKS** 29/7 **US CHART PEAK/WEEKS** 11/13

Taking their name from the slang for a marijuana cigarette, the Doobies formed in 1969 and hit pay-dirt three years later with the platinum album **Toulouse Street** from which this cut came. Its success in Britain was delayed and by the time they got over in late 1973 they had a new album out, **The Captain And Me**, which more accurately reflected their hard-rocking stage act.

Quite definitely the most commercial single this week. New American band ... who sound full of black dynamics but ain't. Really tight instant stuff – watch it move by golly. **Penny Valentine, Sounds, October 1972**

Little Arrows

ARTIST Leapy Lee **RELEASE DATE** October 1968 **WRITER** Albert Hammond, Mike Hazlewood **PRODUCER** – **LABEL** Decca **UK CHART PEAK/WEEKS** 2/– **US CHART PEAK/WEEKS** 16/14

Real name Lee Graham, Leapy was given his nickname because he was always leaping about. He had originally started out as an actor and had even performed at the London Palladium when, in 1968, he found this Hammond/Hazlewood composition which he recorded in gimmicky pop style. The result was his only Top 20 hit in either the UK or the US. In Britain, the song reached Number 2 for one week behind Mary Hopkin's **Those Were The Days**.

Leapy Lee is a compulsive comedian – a sort of pop singer's answer to Kenneth Williams. 'With **Little Arrows** *I've bridged the gap between* **Boiled Beef And Carrots** *and the commercially ridiculous,' says Leapy.* **Keith Altham, NME, September 1968**

Little Darlin'

ARTIST The Diamonds **RELEASE DATE** May 1957 (UK)/March 1957 (US) **WRITER** Maurice Williams **PRODUCER** – **LABEL** Mercury **UK CHART PEAK/WEEKS** 3/17 **US CHART PEAK/WEEKS** 2/26

This Canadian vocal group formed in 1953 had twice made the US Top 20 before releasing their best known song **Little Darlin'** in 1957. Written by Maurice Williams (who later had a US Number 1 single, **Stay**, with his group the Zodiacs), it spent eight weeks at Number 2 in the US, seven of which were behind Elvis's **All Shook Up**. The Diamonds re-formed in the Eighties as a country act.

Little Darlin' *is already a best-seller in the States. It has the necessary ingredients to make it a hit here too ... This song has been buzzing around in my ears with persistence....* **Laurie Hernshaw, Melody Maker, June 1957**

Little Things Mean A Lot

ARTIST Kitty Kallen **RELEASE DATE** July 1954 **WRITER** Edith Lindemann, Carl Stutz **PRODUCER** – **LABEL** Brunswick **UK CHART PEAK/WEEKS** 1/23 **US CHART PEAK/WEEKS** 1/5

The original one-hit wonder of the UK chart, 21-year-old American songstress Kitty Kallen hit the top with a song composed by the Richmond-based duo of DJ Carl Stutz and 56-year-old newspaper editor Edith Lindemann. Kallen had previously enjoyed Stateside success with various Big Bands, including those led by Jack Teagarden and Jimmy Dorsey, and had indeed already scored a US Number 1 with **I'm Beginning To See The Light** in 1945.

This song was an immediate success in the States. Now it's beginning to do every bit as well in Britain. Musicians and critics may complain that once honest she has degenerated into yet another gimmick hound. The paying customers disagree. **Rex Morton, NME, July 1954**

THE BEAUTIFUL SOUTH
A LITTLE TIME

A Little Time

ARTIST The Beautiful South **RELEASE DATE** October 1990 **WRITER** Paul Heaton, David Rotheray **PRODUCER** Mike Hedges **LABEL** Go! Discs **UK CHART PEAK/WEEKS** 1/– **US CHART PEAK/WEEKS** –

A Little Time reached Number 1 in October 1990, aided by a video that dramatized the song's theme of marital strife. An easygoing duet, with strings and muted horns, it is the biggest hit to date for the group, which was formed in 1989 by former Housemartins singer Paul Heaton. Singer Brian Corrigan left and was replaced by Jacqueline Abbott in 1994.

The lyric is a dialogue, whereby a wronged girl boots out her lying lover and doesn't repay close scrutiny. The sleeve seems to depict wallpaper.... the record is its aural equivalent. **Ian Gittins, Melody Maker, October 1990**

Live Forever

ARTIST Oasis **RELEASE DATE** August 1994 (UK)/January 1995 (US) **WRITER** Noel Gallagher **PRODUCER** Mark Coyle **LABEL** Creation (UK)/Creation Epic (US) **UK CHART PEAK**/**WEEKS** 10/16 **US CHART PEAK**/**WEEKS** 39/18

Described as a cross between the Sex Pistols and the Small Faces, the music press loved Oasis, and each gig brought new fans. *Live Forever* was recognized as the band's one incontrovertible classic long before it was released. Despite owing a debt to the melodic strengths of mid-period Beatles, it struck a chord beyond its retro stylings, setting the tone for the huge-selling album, **Definitely Maybe**, and marking the beginning of the rise of the 'mad Mancs' to rock superstardom.

There's no point in theorising or pontificating about Oasis. You either get it or you don't … if their anthemic guitars roll over you in an orgasmic rush and Liam's narcissistic stoner drawl kicks dirt in your eyes and carves holes in your heart … you've got it. **Sara Manning, Melody Maker, August 1994**

Livin' For The City

ARTIST Stevie Wonder **RELEASE DATE** January 1974 (UK)/November 1973 (US) **WRITER** Stevie Wonder **PRODUCER** Stevie Wonder **LABEL** Tamla Motown (UK)/Tamla (US) **UK CHART PEAK**/**WEEKS** 15/9 **US CHART PEAK**/**WEEKS** 8/17

One of the highlights of Wonder's 1973 album **Innervisions**, *Living For The City* was a gritty, epic tale, complete with urban sound effects, describing the injustice of black life in modern America. Despite the socially conscious subject matter it was a classic piece of Wonder magic, still unrestrainedly funky.

If you think that he is going to just sing another black ghetto song, hear the way he hits the word 'city' the first time around. In fact his vocal performance will curl those rather attractive small hairs you have on the back of your neck…. **John Peel, Sounds, December 1973**

Livin' On A Prayer

ARTIST Bon Jovi **RELEASE DATE** October 1986 (UK)/December 1986 (US) **WRITER** Jon Bon Jovi, Ritchie Sambora, Desmond Caild **PRODUCER** Bruce Fairburn **LABEL** Vertigo (UK)/Mercury (US) **UK CHART PEAK**/**WEEKS** 4/15 **US CHART PEAK**/**WEEKS** 1/21

Named after lead singer and songwriter Jon Bon Jovi, the group were formed in 1983 in New Jersey, a state they so revered that they even named one of their albums in its honour. *Livin' On A Prayer* was their second US Number 1 and their first disc to make the UK Top 10. It came from their third album, the international smash **Slippery When Wet**, which sold over eight million copies in the US alone.

I was under the impression that Bon Jovi ROCKED – Ha! This record is boring; Van Halen does it better. **Andy Hurst, Sounds, October 1986**

Living Doll

ARTIST Cliff Richard **RELEASE DATE** July 1959 (UK)/September 1959 (US) **WRITER** Lionel Bart **PRODUCER** – **LABEL** Columbia (UK)/ABC Paramount (US) **UK CHART PEAK**/**WEEKS** 1/24 **US CHART PEAK**/**WEEKS** 30/13

The Loco-Motion

ARTIST Grand Funk RELEASE DATE February 1971 (UK)/March 1971 (US) WRITER Gerry Goffin, Carole King PRODUCER Todd Rundgren LABEL Capitol UK CHART PEAK/WEEKS 40/1 US CHART PEAK/WEEKS 1/20

America's heaviest band and a song Carole King penned for her babysitter, Little Eva, back in the early Sixties was hardly an obvious combination, but it resulted in Michigan-based Grand Funk's second US chart-topping single, and the second song to hit Number 1 twice by different artists – the first, **Go Away Little Girl**, was performed by Steve Lawrence in 1963 and Donny Osmond in 1971.

*The arrangement to **Loco-motion** is a goof, the singing is awful, and the production is based on a good idea gone out of control – and yet I turn the radio up whenever it comes on.* **Jon Landau, Rolling Stone, June 1974**

Lola

ARTIST The Kinks RELEASE DATE July 1970 (UK)/August 1970 (US) WRITER Ray Davies PRODUCER Ray Davies LABEL Pye (UK)/Reprise (US) UK CHART PEAK/WEEKS 2/14 US CHART PEAK/WEEKS 9/14

As the Sixties drew to a close, the Kinks found themselves increasingly at odds with prevailing musical trends. In 1970 they enjoyed a welcome, if brief, renaissance, reaching Number 2 with this peculiar paean to the ambiguous appeal of **Lola.** Amazingly, **Lola** was the subject of a BBC ban, when the Corporation made it clear that its reference to 'Coca-Cola' would render it unplayable – the words 'cherry cola' proved an acceptable substitute.

It's nice – full of Ray's always disturbing lyrics. Do they have some strange significance? He remains enigmatic like Fred Lisa – Mona's brother. Not too sure if it can be a hit, but by jove, it'll get a few spins on my acoustic gramophone. **Chris Welch, Melody Maker, June 1970**

The Long And Winding Road

ARTIST The Beatles RELEASE DATE May 1970 WRITER John Lennon, Paul McCartney PRODUCER George Martin LABEL Apple UK CHART PEAK/WEEKS 0/0 US CHART PEAK/WEEKS 1/10

From the **Let It Be** soundtrack, Paul McCartney's plaintive ballad **The Long and Winding Road** topped Billboard's Hot 100 for two weeks in the mid-Seventies. Despite its massive US popularity, it was not released as a single in Britain. The track was originally produced by George Martin, but the version released was overhauled by Phil Spector, who added a choir and an orchestra. Paul McCartney did not hide his distaste for the results, saying Spector never gave him the opportunity to approve or disapprove it.

Living Doll was originally written by Lionel Bart for the film *Serious Charge*, which starred Cliff. Bruce Welch, of Cliff's backing group The Drifters (later The Shadows), thought of slowing it down for a re-recording – it went to Number 1, marking Cliff's departure from pure rock 'n' roll. Twenty-seven years later he took it back to Number 1 when it was re-recorded with the cast of the TV comedy series *The Young Ones* in aid of Comic Relief.

A quiet and easy paced song with a strumming guitar accompaniment which gives us the first opportunity of hearing Cliff's voice as it really is without the enforced racing and belting of the rock format which has been his sole material so far. **Keith Fordyce, NME, July 1959**

The Living Years

ARTIST Mike And The Mechanics RELEASE DATE January 1989 (UK & US) WRITER Mike Rutherford, B. A. Robertson PRODUCER Mike Rutherford, Chris Neil LABEL WEA (UK)/Atlantic (US) UK CHART PEAK/WEEKS 2/11 US CHART PEAK/WEEKS 1/20

For Mike Rutherford, the bass player with Genesis, Mike and the Mechanics was a way of escaping from the routine of creating multi-million sellers every couple of years. He didn't give up the day job, however, but used the spin-off group to create some of his most personal work. This, written in response to his father's death, was an attempt to say all the things he hadn't found the time to say during **The Living Years**.

Long Tall Sally

ARTIST Little Richard **RELEASE DATE** February 1957 (UK)/April 1956 (US) **WRITER** Enotris Johnson, Richard Penniman, Robert Blackwell **PRODUCER** – **LABEL** London (UK)/Speciality (US) **UK CHART PEAK/WEEKS** 3/16 **US CHART PEAK/WEEKS** 6/19

Long Tall Sally made John Lennon speechless when he played it in his bedroom as a teenager. Its belting rhythm and Little Richard's screeching vocals made even Elvis Presley seem tame. Old crooners like Perry Como, were ousted as the teenage revolution took place, and Little Richard was just the King or Queen to replace him. His music crossed all racial and sexual boundaries, and his sensual, theatrical appearance was inspirational. Even turning from rock to religion couldn't conceal his raucous energy and drive.

A belated review arrival: **Long Tall Sally/Tutti Fruttie** *Little Richard is billed 'The Dean of Rock 'n' Roll'. He certainly preaches his creed with uninhibited fervour.* **Laurie Hernshaw, Melody Maker, February 1967**

The Look Of Love

ARTIST ABC **RELEASE DATE** May 1982 (UK)/September 1982 (US) **WRITER** ABC **PRODUCER** Trevor Horn **LABEL** Neutron (UK)/Mercury (US) **UK CHART PEAK/WEEKS** 4/12 **US CHART PEAK/WEEKS** 18/25

The Look Of Love hearkens back to that time in the early Eighties when it seemed that any problem could be solved by the right haircut. It was the second and biggest hit for the trio from Sheffield, which began life as Vice Versa. Heavy airplay of the song's video on the newly-formed MTV made it a hit Stateside as well.

Losing My Religion

ARTIST R.E.M. **RELEASE DATE** March 1991 (UK)/April 1991 (US) **WRITER** Bill Berry, Peter Buck, Mike Mills, Michael Stipe **PRODUCER** Scott Litt **LABEL** Warner Bros. (UK)/Warner (US) **UK CHART PEAK/WEEKS** 19/9 **US CHART PEAK/WEEKS** 4/21

Although it peaked at Number 4 in the US charts, R.E.M.'s biggest-ever single remains one of the best radio songs of the post-punk era. The simple acoustic arrangement, coupled with an effective and soul-searching vocal, launched R.E.M. on a five year rule as the biggest band in the world. Massive audience and critical acclaim earned them a string of awards in Europe and America, including six on the MTV Video Awards, two Grammys and Top Album and Top Artist in Billboard.

R.E.M. meant stupid when I was a kid. No-one could accuse Stipe & Co. of that, although the strummy **Losing My Religion** *is oddly dispassionate for a band notorious for commitment. A subdued and pleasant couple of minutes, but no more than that.* **Ian McCann, NME, March 1991**

Lost In Your Eyes

ARTIST Debbie Gibson **RELEASE DATE** January 1989 **WRITER** Debbie Gibson **PRODUCER** Debbie Gibson **LABEL** Atlantic **UK CHART PEAK/WEEKS** 34/7 **US CHART PEAK/WEEKS** 1/19

Debbie Gibson had the ultra-romantic **Lost In Your Eyes** in her stage set when her first album was climbing the chart, and its familiarity to fans helped it become her second chart-topper when extracted from the **Electric Youth** LP. The fact that she wrote and produced it gave the lie to her image as a teen bimbo, and her potential would be confirmed when Motown legend Lamont Dozier was recruited as co-songwriter for her third album.

How come I never get the flouncy Debbie Gibson records, I always get the ballads? Here Debbie, or Deborah as she is referred to on the production credits, goes all gooey over a soppy bloke. Lovely simple voice as usual, but a rubbish song. **Steve Lamacq, NME, January 1989**

Louie Louie

ARTIST The Kingsmen **RELEASE DATE** January 1964 (UK)/November 1963 (US) **WRITER** Richard Berry **PRODUCER** Gerry Dennon **LABEL** Pye Int. (UK)/Wand (US) **UK CHART PEAK/WEEKS** 26/7 **US CHART PEAK/WEEKS** 2/16

Originally written by R&B singer Richard Berry and recorded by his group the Pharaohs, this classic track, built around the minimum three chords, was covered by The Kingsmen and spent

six weeks at Number 2 in the American charts. The song was a US Top 30 hit for the Sandpipers in 1966 and has also provided minor US hits for John Belushi (1978) and the Fat Boys (1988).

Jack Ely, the voice of **Louie Louie**, *was forced out after that first hit, but apart from the Top 5 novelty* **The Jolly Green Giant**, *most of the Kingsmen's later output consisted of desperate attempts at recapturing the* **Louie** *magic.* **J. D. Considine, Rolling Stone, August 1991**

Love And Affection

ARTIST Joan Armatrading RELEASE DATE October 1976 WRITER Joan Armatrading PRODUCER Glyn Johns LABEL A&M UK CHART PEAK/WEEKS 10/9 US CHART PEAK/WEEKS –

Although Joan Armatrading had been making records since 1972, the British public at large heard her distinctive vocal and acoustic guitar stylings for the first time on her breakthrough hit, **Love and Affection**; it established her presence on the British pop landscape. One sign of her enduring popularity was when **The Very Best Of Joan Armatrading** reached Number 9 in 1991, nearly 20 years after her first record.

… Has that compelling touch of a truly original artist who has absorbed all the right styles and then transplanted her own urgent stamp. **Ray Coleman, Melody Maker, September 1977**

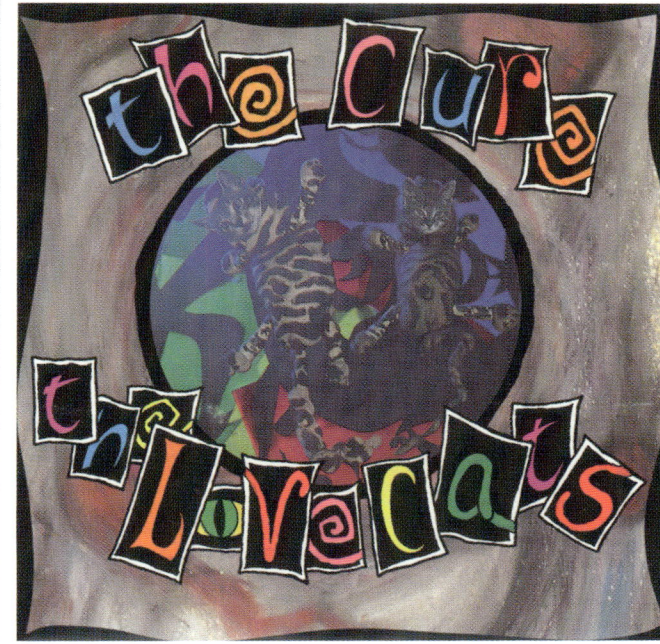

The Love Cats

ARTIST The Cure RELEASE DATE October 1983 WRITER Robert Smith PRODUCER Chris Parry, Phil Thornally LABEL Fiction UK CHART PEAK/WEEKS 7/11 US CHART PEAK/WEEKS –

Five years into The Cure's recording career they finally scored a Top 10 hit with **The Love Cats**. Cure fans had waited a year for a new release. Lead singer and songwriter Robert Smith had lost interest in the group and moved on to other projects. It was only after The Cure were invited to play on BBC-TV's *The Oxford Roadhouse* in April 1983 that Smith decided to reactivate the group, recording **The Love Cats** in a Paris studio.

Brushes on the drums and a slippery-sliding doghouse bass, sparse piano and sound-effect guitar from Citizen Smith and a considerable amount of miaows all stew up very nicely … a record that can most definitely be filed under nifty. **Charles Shaar Murray, NME, November 1983**

Love In An Elevator

ARTIST Aerosmith RELEASE DATE September 1989 WRITER J. Perry, Steven Tyler PRODUCER Bruce Fairbairn LABEL Geffen UK CHART PEAK/WEEKS 13/8 US CHART PEAK/WEEKS 5/16

Nearly 20 years into its career Aerosmith finally earned a gold single with **Love In An Elevator**. It sold better than any of their other singles, aided by a racy video of the kind that had already become their trademark. While it reached only Number 13, its parent album, **Pump**, became the group's first Top 10 album, reaching Number 3.

When everyone was getting into punk and you threw away all your old rock dinosaur records, Led Zeppelin or whatever, I kept all of my Aerosmith records…. This single isn't bad – it sounds good, but it's one of the weakest tracks off the new album – which is brilliant. **Patricia Morrison, NME, September 1989**

Love Is All Around

ARTIST Wet Wet Wet **RELEASE DATE** May 1994 (UK)/July 1994 (US) **WRITER** Reg Presley **PRODUCER** Wet Wet Wet **LABEL** Precious (UK)/London (US) **UK CHART PEAK/WEEKS** 1/37 **US CHART PEAK/WEEKS** 41/20

Sixties garage band The Troggs had a Top 10 US and UK hit with this song in 1967, but after its inclusion in the film *Four Weddings And A Funeral*, sung by Marti Pellow and the Wets, it nearly beat Bryan Adams' record for the longest stay at Number 1 in the UK. Although it did not reach the US Top 40, it charted in 14 territories and earned writer Reg Presley a belatedly hefty chunk of songwriting royalties.

Magnificent. Gorgeous. Sumptuous. All the more so because NOBODY agrees with me about the splendid Wets and the indescribably astute vocalising of the horribly smug Marti Pellow ... I don't care if he's the Antichrist – close your eyes and he's the voice of warm loving sex. **Chris Roberts, Melody Maker, May 1994**

Love Is Blue (L'Amour Est Bleu)

ARTIST Paul Mauriat And His Orchestra **RELEASE DATE** February 1968 (UK)/January 1968 (US) **WRITER** Andre Popp **PRODUCER** – **LABEL** Phillips **UK CHART PEAK/WEEKS** 12/14 **US CHART PEAK/WEEKS** 1/18

Love Is Blue is bachelor pad music, full of strange speeds and ripples of doodling sound. The main instrument is a harpsichord, twinkling through a scale of notes in a vague harmony. It fits in well with the Nineties revival of Lounge Core, a movement dedicated to reviving past masters of syncopated rhythms, orchestration and novel keyboard sounds.

I think there are far too many versions of this number. Someone told me there were 14. Orchestral pieces are not usually for me, but this is a good song. Just the thing for crazy fireside listening. **Georgie Best, Melody Maker, April 1968**

Love Is The Drug

ARTIST Roxy Music **RELEASE DATE** October 1975 (UK)/December 1975 (US) **WRITER** Roger Lewis **PRODUCER** Chris Thomas **LABEL** Island (UK)/ATCO (US) **UK CHART PEAK/WEEKS** 2/10 **US CHART PEAK/WEEKS** 30/14

Epitomizing the decadent feel of the band's 'middle period', Roxy Music's first and only US hit, **Love Is The Drug** became a disco and singles-bar favourite. Untethered by Eno's earlier electronic experimentation, Bryan Ferry began writing songs you could dance to. From the sound of footsteps and a car starting up – 'Late at night I park my car/Stake my place in the singles bar' – and you can guess the rest....

Hesitant bass guitar which dominates the whole track, apart from rare moments when Andy McKay blasts forth with his electronic horn and Phil Manzanera takes on his 2 guitar riffs.... **Chris Charlesworth, Melody Maker, October 1975**

Love Letters In The Sand

ARTIST Pat Boone **RELEASE DATE** July 1957 (UK)/May 1957 (US) **WRITER** Nick Kenny, Charles Kenny, J. Fred Coots **PRODUCER** – **LABEL** London (UK)/DOT (US) **UK CHART PEAK/WEEKS** 2/21 **US CHART PEAK/WEEKS** 1/34

Pat Boone may be known for his white-bread covers of R&B tunes, but his biggest ever hit was a song written before Little Richard was even born. **Love Letters in the Sand** was an old Tin Pan Alley tune, originally done in 1931 by Ted Black. It topped *Billboard's* Hot 100 for seven weeks, with sales of over three and a half million.

Recommend it I do, as one of the best of that category of song that is utterly simple, quite corny, and at the same time irresistible. Combine these with the brilliant vocalising of Mr Boone and you have a dead cert. **Keith Fordyce, NME, July 1957**

Love Me Do

ARTIST The Beatles **RELEASE DATE** October 1962 (UK)/April 1964 (US) **WRITER** John Lennon, Paul McCartney **PRODUCER** George Martin **LABEL** Parlophone (UK)/Tollie (US) **UK CHART PEAK/WEEKS** 17/26 **US CHART PEAK/WEEKS** 1/14

The Beatles' first single, **Love Me Do** had been a staple of their live set, and producer George Martin had them record it at their first session. Originally, after Lennon and McCartney sang 'please', Lennon sang 'Love me ...' and then, omitting the 'do', pulled out his harmonica to play the trademark riff. George Martin found this intolerable and persuaded McCartney to sing the line 'love me do' while John played harmonica. McCartney was extremely nervous at being suddenly thrust into the spotlight, which, he later said, is why his voice was shaking.

Don't forget music is part of our lives - we played it because we loved doing it, not just for the loot. Some groups came to London to try to break through. We didn't till **Love Me Do** *– then we had to.* **John Lennon interviewed by Ray Coleman, Melody Maker, August 1963**

Love Me For A Reason

ARTIST The Osmonds **RELEASE DATE** August 1974 **WRITER** Johnny Bristol, Wade Browd Jr, David Jones Jr **PRODUCER** – **LABEL** MGM **UK CHART PEAK/WEEKS** 1/9 **US CHART PEAK/WEEKS** 10/13

The Osmonds stuck very close to their winning formula for their final Number 1. **Love Me For A Reason** was a Johnny Bristol composition, one of the finest Motown writer/producers of the late Sixties, but the Osmonds recorded it as a squeaky clean pop ballad. Boyzone revived it with swinging melodies and teenage girl appeal.

After nearly a year without a release, the Osmonds are back with a strongly soul influenced tune making almost a complete turnaround from previous singles. This powerful ballad should gather new audiences for the group. **Billboard, August 1974**

Love Me Tender

ARTIST Elvis Presley **RELEASE DATE** December 1956 (UK)/October 1956 (US) **WRITER** Elvis Presley, Vera Matson **PRODUCER** Steve Sholes **LABEL** HMV Pop (UK)/RCA Victor (US) **UK CHART PEAK/WEEKS** 11/9 **US CHART PEAK/WEEKS** 1/23

Presley's rendition of **Love Me Tender**, based on the 1861 folk ballad *Aura Lee*, in 20th Century-Fox's western was so persuasive, the producers decided to rename the movie after the song. A month later, Presley made his historic appearance on *The Ed Sullivan Show*, shown only from the waist up to spare audiences his torrid hip movements. He was watched by an estimated third of the American population, and the subsequent deluge of advance orders made the single, according to Billboard, 'a hit before it was ever released … '.

Listening to **Love Me Tender**, *in which he is consistently off pitch, underlines my conviction that Presley's singing is on par with his guitar playing – and believe me he is no Reinhardt.* **Laurie Henshaw, Melody Maker, December 1956**

The Love Shack

ARTIST The B-52's **RELEASE DATE** March 1990 (UK)/September 1989 (US) **WRITER** The B-52's **PRODUCER** Don Was **LABEL** Reprise **UK CHART PEAK/WEEKS** 2/13 **US CHART PEAK/WEEKS** 3/27

In 1989, the B-52's took the music world by surprise when they scored their biggest hit yet with **Love Shack**, from their album **Cosmic Thing**. Their previous album, 1987's **Bouncing Off Satellites**, had been a flop, and they hadn't had a chart single in four years, save for the UK reissue of **Rock Lobster/Planet Claire**. **Love Shack**, inspired by an Atlanta nightclub, returned them to the limelight, paving the way for their other million seller from **Cosmic Thing, Roam**.

The B-52's are still pretty much making the same frivolous music they always have. **Caren Myers, Melody Maker, February 1990**

Love Train

ARTIST The O'Jays **RELEASE DATE** March 1973 (UK)/January 1973 (US)
WRITER Kenny Gamble, Leon Huff **PRODUCER** Kenny Gamble, Leon Huff
LABEL CBS (UK)/Philadelphia (US) **UK CHART PEAK/WEEKS** 9/13 **US CHART
PEAK/WEEKS** 1/14

The O'Jays' records had movement built into their sound: a dance-floor cacophony of car horns and French horns, vibraphones and vehicles, rushing past on the freeway. Love Train steamed along with a stomping beat and the O'Jays' sweet, charismatic vocals over the top. They were part of Gamble and Huff's Philadelphia International Records, a label that had been set up to promote black artists. The 'Philly Sound' moved away from polished doo-wop and antiseptic ballads to sounds full of urban bite and pounding rhythm sections.

Love Will Tear Us Apart

ARTIST Joy Division **RELEASE DATE** June 1980 **WRITER** Joy Division **PRODUCER**
Martin Hannett **LABEL** Factory **UK CHART PEAK/WEEKS** 13/16 **US CHART
PEAK/WEEKS** –

This song, already a moving new-wave anthem in embryo, gained a new poignancy when singer Ian Curtis was discovered hanged at his home four days before their debut US tour in May 1980. The song was issued regardless of the tragedy and would become Joy Division's first hit, charting again in 1983 and, in remix form, in 1995. Ex-Q-Tips frontman Paul Young would also include an interesting 'white soul' styled version on his 1983 chart-topping solo debut album **No Parlez**.

Divorced from emotions such as sympathy, this record offers a taster of their forthcoming album ... a powerfully original piece of Eighties music. **Martyn Sutton, Melody Maker, June 1980**

Lovely Day

ARTIST Bill Withers **RELEASE DATE** January 1978 (UK)/December 1977 (US)
WRITER Bill Withers, Bill Scarborough **PRODUCER** Bill Withers, Clarence
McDonald **LABEL** CBS (UK)/Columbia (US) **UK CHART PEAK/WEEKS** 7/8 **US
CHART PEAK/WEEKS** 30/12

After his success with **Ain't No Sunshine** and **Lean On Me**, Bill Withers continued his relationship with Booker T. Jones on this hypnotic, uplifting single. Remixed by Dutch DJ Ben Leibrand, it made UK Number 4 in 1988. Like so many classic singles from the Sixties and Seventies, it was introduced to a new audience when it was used in a TV commercial.

Lovin' You

ARTIST Minnie Riperton **RELEASE DATE** April 1975 (UK)/January 1975 (US)
WRITER Minnie Riperton, Richard Dudolph **PRODUCER** Stevie Wonder **LABEL**
Epic (UK & US) **UK CHART PEAK/WEEKS** 2/10 **US CHART PEAK/WEEKS** 1/18

Blessed with an extraordinary five-octave vocal range, Minnie Riperton's death from lymph cancer at the age of 31 in 1979 was a tragic loss to the music world. However, she left a wealth of recorded songs with, among others, The Gems (an all-female group signed to Chess), The Rotary Connection (integrating R&B with psychedelic rock), and collaborations with Stevie Wonder. It was Wonder who produced her Number 1 single **Lovin' You** from the album **Perfect Angel**.

Of the many emergent American Chanteuse-songwriters, the glowingly soignée Minnie Riperton stands out both for her vocal range and her deft touch with an arrangement ... It's nice and easy and mellow as a chocolate liqueur. **Angie Errics, NME, July 1975**

Lyin' Eyes

ARTIST The Eagles RELEASE DATE November 1975 (UK)/September 1975 (US) WRITER Glenn Frey, Don Henley PRODUCER Bill Szymczck LABEL Asylum (UK & US) UK CHART PEAK/WEEKS 23/7 US CHART PEAK/WEEKS 2/14

The creative balance of the Eagles had shifted over time and by their fourth album, **One of These Nights**, the Henley-Frey writing team had taken control: six of the nine cuts carried their credit. Founder guitarist Bernie Leadon reacted by quitting the studio for three days, and leaving for good after the album was released. All three singles would hit the US Top 5: this Frey-sung effort, the second of the trio, hit Number 2 behind Elton John.

*If **One of these nights** highlighted the hard side of The Eagles, then this song, already a huge hit in America, illustrates the acoustic side of the band…. Should make some kind of impression on the British singles charts.* **Steve Clarke, NME, October 1975**

MacArthur Park

ARTIST Donna Summer RELEASE DATE October 1978 (UK)/September 1978 (US) WRITER Jim Webb PRODUCER Giorgio Moroder, Pete Bellotte LABEL Casablanca (UK & US) UK CHART PEAK/WEEKS 5/10 US CHART PEAK/WEEKS 1/20

The Jimmy Webb classic had been recorded by actor Richard Harris in 1968, and all its bizarre imagery – why was the park melting in the rain, and who the hell left that cake out? – was transformed into a disco vehicle for Summer, taken from her double album **Live And More**. *MacArthur Park* brought Summer her first Number 1.

A gloriously daft string quartet and beefy choir stand Donna as she warbles about lakes in the rain and so forth. Then – yeees! – a synth drum twitches into life, Donna Screams 'aaah!' and we're off… .**Ian Birch, Melody Maker, October 1978**

Mack The Knife

ARTIST Bobby Darin RELEASE DATE September 1959 (UK)/August 1959 (US) WRITER Kurt Weill, Bertholt Brecht, Mark Blitzstein PRODUCER Ahmet Ertegun LABEL London (UK)/Atco (US) UK CHART PEAK/WEEKS 1/18 US CHART PEAK/WEEKS 1/26

Starting out as a rocker, Bobby Darin is best known for his nightclub persona, which he introduced with the transatlantic chart-topper *Mack the Knife*. At the time, it was daring for a rocker to attempt a show tune, especially one that was already an 'oldie'. While Darin's main audience from then on was the cabaret crowd, he recorded folk, country and blues as well as pop. His untimely death in 1973 deprived the music world of one of its most uncompromising artistes.

Written by Kurt Weill for the stage musical The Three Penny Opera, *Mack The Knife is an intriguing song, and Bobby's distinctive treatment, which begins quietly and blends to a roaring climax, lends an added fascination.* **Keith Goodwin, NME, September 1959**

Maggie May

ARTIST Rod Stewart RELEASE DATE September 1971 (UK)/August 1971 (US) WRITER Rod Stewart, Martin Quittenton PRODUCER Rod Stewart LABEL Mercury (UK & US) UK CHART PEAK/WEEKS 1/19 US CHART PEAK/WEEKS 1/17

Rod Stewart joined the (Small) Faces to replace the departed Steve Marriott, but on the understanding that he would develop a parallel career as a solo singer. *Maggie May* was Rod at his heart- on-sleeve best, hoarse voiced as ever, with Ron Wood on slide guitar. The song and the album it came from, **Every Picture Tells A Story**, were Number 1 in both the States and the UK – the first time an artist had managed a simultaneous double double whammy.

This enticing story of a schoolboy's liaison with a hooker did the trick for him, and in October 1971 he held the Number 1 albums and singles spot simultaneously, both here and in the States. **Bob Woffinden, NME, February 1976**

Make It Easy On Yourself

ARTIST The Walker Brothers **RELEASE DATE** August 1965 (UK)/October 1965 (US) **WRITER** Burt Bacharach, Hal David **PRODUCER** Johnny Franz **LABEL** Philips (UK)/Smash (US) **UK CHART PEAK/WEEKS** 1/14 **US CHART PEAK/WEEKS** 16/10

The original version of this tear-jerking Bacharach & David song, recorded by Jerry Butler, had reached the US Top 20 in 1962. The Walker Brothers' cover improved on that position, but really hit the jackpot in the UK where the three Americans, Scott (Engel), John (Maus) and Gary (Leeds), topped the charts, became teen idols and were named the Brightest Hopes of 1965 by *Melody Maker*.

The Walker Brothers are epic in a dim kind of way. Pretty boys having nervous breakdowns behind curtains, that Spectoresque sound like a depressed ice-cream man driving his van through the labyrinth corridors of Hades. **Julie Churchill, NME, October 1980**

Make Love To Me

ARTIST Jo Stafford **RELEASE DATE** May 1954 **WRITER** Bill Norvas, Allan Copeland, Leon Rappolo, Paul Manes, Ben Pollack, George Brunies, Mel Stiad, Walter Melrose **PRODUCER** – **LABEL** Philips (UK)/Columbia (US) **UK CHART PEAK/WEEKS** 8/1 **US CHART PEAK/WEEKS** 0/0

During the late Forties and early Fifties, Stafford, a solo singer with the Tommy Dorsey band and a member of the Pied Pipers vocal group, had four Number 1 singles. Deemed a female Sinatra, and blessed with a vibrato-free contralto, she brought an intensity of performance to the lyrics of her songs, including this suggestive 1954 hit, derived from the 1923 jazz instrumental *Tin Roof Blues*.

Although **You Belong To Me** *was a dual hit on both sides of the Atlantic, it's strange that her big follow up* **Make Love To Me**, *which topped the charts in the States and won her a golden disc, didn't rate so highly over here.* **Derek Johnson, NME, June 1959**

Make Me Smile (Come Up And See Me)

ARTIST Steve Harley And The Cockney Rebel **RELEASE DATE** February 1975 (UK)/February 1976 (US) **WRITER** Steve Harley **PRODUCER** Alan Parsons, Steve Harley **LABEL** EMI (UK & US) **UK CHART PEAK/WEEKS** 1/9 **US CHART PEAK/WEEKS** 96/3

Former journalist Harley enjoyed a love-hate relationship with the media, and early Rebel line-ups had been deliberately non-rock in outlook. By their first and only chart-topper, they had become more conventional and the singer had taken star billing, but the success story only had a few more months to run. Harley's solo career failed to take off as planned. Duran Duran covered the song for a B-side, and Harley joined them on stage to relive former glories.

The vocals are still excruciatingly stylized and, if anything, that's what'll bring it down … isn't bad. **Colin Irwin, Melody Maker, February 1975**

Making Plans For Nigel

ARTIST XTC **RELEASE DATE** September 1979 **WRITER** Colin Moulding **PRODUCER** Steve Lillywhite **LABEL** Virgin **UK CHART PEAK/WEEKS** 17/11 **US CHART PEAK/WEEKS** –

The Swindon-based band were always linked to the new wave of 1977, by virtue of signing with Virgin in that year, but their music was much quirkier, blending poppy hooks to art rock and a sideways world view. Off the third album **Drums And Wires** in 1979, produced by Steve Lillywhite and written by bassist Colin Moulding, *Making Plans For Nigel* – a typically wry prod at over-dominant parents – set the tone for their biggest hit, 1982's *Senses Working Overtime*.

While the hapless Nigel bawls at the back of the mix, and the whip-crack sound effects punctuate his pain, the parents are making plans for a future in the Steel Industry. This has a grabby start, quite sinister lyrics and really is an inventive, careful piece of work. **Susan Hill, Melody Maker, September 1979**

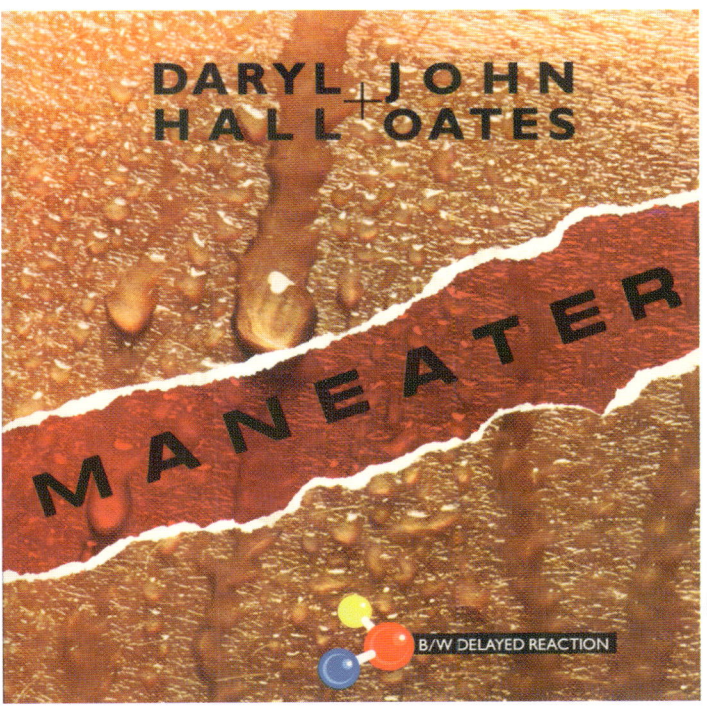

Mama Weer All Crazee Now

ARTIST Slade **RELEASE DATE** September 1972 (UK)/November 1972 (US) **WRITER** Noddy Holder, James Lea **PRODUCER** Chas Chandler **LABEL** Polydor (UK & US) UK CHART PEAK/WEEKS 1/10 US CHART PEAK/WEEKS 76/10

After some years as a nondescript covers-heavy Midlands band, the members of Slade came to the notice of ex-Animals Chas Chandler. Persuaded by Chandler to cash in on the skinhead cult, Slade concocted the formula of a bit of glam, lots of energy and twee working class credentials (check out those misspelt titles). After *Coz I Luv You*, their first UK Number 1 in 1971, *Mama* was the third of five further chart-leaders.

The lads are in for another Number 1. Better, I feel, this is than their last success. Owes more than I can say to The Stones (Catch that ***Brown Sugar*** *Riff) and the early Who. Can't be bad.* **Penny Valentine, Sounds, August 1972**

Mamma Mia

ARTIST Abba **RELEASE DATE** December 1975 (UK)/May 1976 (US) **WRITER** Stig Anderson, Benny Andersson **PRODUCER** Benny Andersson, Bjorn Ulvaeus **LABEL** Epic (UK)/Atlantic (US) UK CHART PEAK/WEEKS 1/14 US CHART PEAK/WEEKS 32/9

At a time when most artists wanted their recordings to reflect their studio bills, Abba's quirky arrangements hid their high gloss beneath a coat of seeming spontaneity. Ear candy filled the grooves – Mamas and Papas-style harmonies; a Brian Wilson bass line; buoyant, Ringo-loving drums. The disc became Abba's second chart-topper. Coming 18 months after *Waterloo*, it proved conclusively that there was life after Eurovision.

More efficient, hygienic, Scandinavian pop, guaranteed to make the Radio 1 play list. **Alan Lewis, Sounds, November 1975**

Maneater

ARTIST Hall And Oates **RELEASE DATE** October 1982 (UK & US) **WRITER** Daryl Hall, John Oates, Sara Allen **PRODUCER** Daryl Hall, John Oates **LABEL** RCA (UK)/RCA Victor (US) UK CHART PEAK/WEEKS 6/11 US CHART PEAK/WEEKS 1/21

Shamelessly derivative of the Sixties Motown sound, *Maneater* gave the golden duo their fourth of five US chart-toppers in the decade – six overall. So formulaic was it that Lamont Dozier, writer with the Holland brothers of *You Can't Hurry Love*, was certain it was his song they had covered, whereas in fact it was a combination of Oates (chorus), Hall (verse) and lyricist Sara Allen. The Philadelphian pair would reproduce their pop success in the R&B chart, showing that black audiences liked their style too.

The idea behind the song – that these rich, tanned, smooth 'n' strong Adonises are having their hearts whipped up like a meringue filling by a cruel bitch on heat – may be a cute marketing ploy, but it hardly registers on the credibility meter. **Gavin Martin, NME, October 1982**

Man With The Child In His Eyes

ARTIST Kate Bush **RELEASE DATE** June 1978 **WRITER** Kate Bush **PRODUCER** Kate Bush **LABEL** EMI (UK)/EMI America (US) UK CHART PEAK/WEEKS 6/11 US CHART PEAK/WEEKS 84/4

Kate Bush followed *Wuthering Heights* with a song that she had previously recorded for the demo that earned her a record deal, *The Man With the Child In His Eyes*. At the time she wrote the lyrics, she was more like a child with a woman's eyes – she was a 14-year-old schoolgirl at the St Joseph's Convent Grammar School.

A clever follow-up in what must have been a difficult decision. This showcases the softer, more reflective side – in direct descent from Joni Mitchell's 'Blue' period. Should be monstrous, despite a few cringe-worthy words. **Ian Birch, Melody Maker, June 1978**

Mandy

ARTIST Barry Manilow **RELEASE DATE** February 1975 (UK)/November 1974 (US) **WRITER** Scott English, Richard Kerr **PRODUCER** Ron Dante, Barry Manilow **LABEL** Arista (UK)/Bell (US) **UK CHART PEAK/WEEKS** 11/9 **US CHART PEAK/WEEKS** 1/16

Mandy is unblushingly romantic, with Barry's clear, bright tenor calling out over the notes of piano-led anguish. It is a dynamic version of Richard Kerr's and Scott English's song. Barry may not be rock 'n' roll, but he has the most fervent of fan bases, who revel in every chocolate box moment of this tale of true love spurned, and then regretted. Aahh.

Manilow's most effective vocal ploy is a crack in the voice at moments of dramatic climax … Enjoyable if one accepts its stagy self-pity. **Stephen Holden, Rolling Stone, January 1975**

Mary's Boy Child

ARTIST Harry Belafonte **RELEASE DATE** November 1957 (UK)/December 1956 (US) **WRITER** Jester Hairston **PRODUCER** – **LABEL** RCA (UK)/RCA Victor (US) **UK CHART PEAK/WEEKS** 1/19 **US CHART PEAK/WEEKS** 12/5

Harry Belafonte's only Number 1 hit to date, *Mary's Boy Child* stayed on top for seven weeks, longer than any other Christmas song has done before. It was actually a year old, having reached Number 12 in the US the previous December. Twenty-one years later, it became a Christmas Number 1 for Boney M, who combined it in a medley with *Oh My Lord*.

Belafonte is unique in that he is surely the first folk or minstrel singer to command such an immense following. The secret of his enormous appeal lies in his simplicity and sincerity…. The record buying public over here has boosted **Mary's Boy Child** *into hit proportions.* **Derek Johnson, NME, November 1957**

Mashed Potato Time

ARTIST Dee Dee Sharp **RELEASE DATE** March 1962 **WRITER** G. Dobbins, R. Bateman, W. Garrett, Frederick Gorman, Brian Holland **PRODUCER** – **LABEL** Cameo **UK CHART PEAK/WEEKS** – **US CHART PEAK/WEEKS** 2/18

After a stint as a backing vocalist for the Cameo-Parkway labels, Sharp added extra oomph as an uncredited vocalist on Chubby Checker's 1962 *Slow Twistin'*, but got her own name check on this novelty dance single. For a while she was lumbered with a culinary tag (a subsequent single was *Gravy (For My Mashed Potato)* but came back in the Seventies as a vocalist for TSOP and Philadelphia International – husband Kenny Gamble's label.

Massachusetts

ARTIST The Bee Gees **RELEASE DATE** September 1967 (UK)/November 1967 (US) **WRITER** Barry, Maurice and Robin Gibb **PRODUCER** Barry, Maurice and Robin Gibb, Robert Stigwood **LABEL** Polydor (UK)/Atco (US) **UK CHART PEAK/WEEKS** 1/17 **US CHART PEAK/WEEKS** 11/8

After conquering their adoptive home of Australia, the Bee Gees, who then included drummer Colin Petersen and guitarist Vince Melouney, scored their first UK Number 1 with this paean to the Bay State. It was also their first A-side on which the quavery Robin Gibb sang lead. It became an international smash.

The Bee Gees are very big in America, and certainly much of their material seems aimed to create Stateside interest. There is a Scott McKenzie feel about this gentle groover, complete with soft strings which involve mental pictures of warm weather and sunshine. **Chris Welch, Melody Maker, September 1967**

Material Girl

ARTIST Madonna **RELEASE DATE** March 1985 (UK)/February 1985 (US) **WRITER** Peter Brown, Robert Rans **PRODUCER** Nile Rodgers **LABEL** Sire (UK & US) **UK CHART PEAK/WEEKS** 3/10 **US CHART PEAK/WEEKS** 2/17

Material Girl could have been a theme tune for the wealth-obsessed Eighties. The video for the song saw Madonna as Marilyn Monroe in a *Diamonds Are A Girl's Best Friend* routine, dripping with jewels. The song itself was not as sparkly – more a jokey purr. But it showed Madonna's playfulness, and her capacity for imaginative re-invention, which hallmarks her career.

Burly stuff from the world's first virginal singer! 'I am a material girl' confesses Madonna, who is glimpsed on the cover, clutching a blue satin sheet to her naked personage: rrrr! The music, meanwhile (if anyone's still interested) is catchy enough, with a purposeful throb in its step. **Adam Sweeting, Melody Maker, February 1985**

Merry Xmas Everybody

ARTIST Slade RELEASE DATE December 1973 WRITER Noddy Holder, James Lea PRODUCER Chas Chandler LABEL Polydor UK CHART PEAK/WEEKS 1/25 US CHART PEAK/WEEKS –

The band's biggest-selling single and, along with Wizzard's *I Wish It Could Be Christmas Everyday*, one of the great and probably the best loved of all upbeat Christmas singles. Recorded in New York while the band were on a tour of the States, the UK made it the Christmas single of December 1973 ... 1981 ... and 1986. Over a million copies sold when first released – quarter of a million on the first day of release.

... this 'pop' group have a cheerful dash of style that reminds me of the Move in their heyday ... it could well be a hit by the end of December.
Chris Welch, Melody Maker, December 1973

Mellow Yellow

ARTIST Donovan RELEASE DATE February 1967 (UK)/November 1966 (US) WRITER Donovan Leitch PRODUCER Mickie Most LABEL Pye (UK)/Epic (US) UK CHART PEAK/WEEKS 8/8 US CHART PEAK/WEEKS 2/12

The presence of Paul McCartney on 'whispered' vocal on Donovan's first 1967 offering did its sales potential no harm at all. Macca was repaying the Scots-born strummer for joining in the singing on The Beatles' *Yellow Submarine*, but the exchange undoubtedly helped Don more. Arranged by future Led Zeppelin man John Paul Jones, the single soared, particularly in the States despite a ban in Boston for allegedly having an abortion theme.

At least if it goes in to the chart they will stop playing it in the clubs! ... By the time they release Donovan's records (especially if they have already been American hits) you're already sick to death with them.
John Entwhistle, Melody Maker, February 1967

Memories Are Made Of This

ARTIST Dean Martin RELEASE DATE February 1956 (UK)/December 1955 (US) WRITER Terry Gilkyson, Rich Dehr, Frank Miller PRODUCER – LABEL Capitol (UK & US) UK CHART PEAK/WEEKS 6/8 US CHART PEAK/WEEKS 1/24

The actor Dean Martin was also a romantic crooner, specializing in treacly, sentimental love songs delivered with an easygoing charm and a slurry drawl. **Memories Are Made Of This** was a catalogue of song, listing out all those precious moments in a romantic affair and a life, with a cabaret flourish and an almost conversational vocal. His style was undemanding: an old fashioned middle-of-the-roadster, appealing to the older generation and not the hip, young things.

Throughout Dean's vocal, there is a group singing the title behind him, and one can't help but notice some fine playing by the rhythm section. Which includes some lovely bass and guitar work. **Geoffrey Everitt, NME, February 1956**

Midnight Train To Georgia

ARTIST Gladys Knight And The Pips **RELEASE DATE** May 1976 (UK)/September 1973 (US) **WRITER** Jim Weatherly **PRODUCER** Tony Camillo **LABEL** Buddah (UK & US) **UK CHART PEAK/WEEKS** 10/9 **US CHART PEAK/WEEKS** 1/19

Songwriter Jim Weatherly conceived the song as 'Midnight Plane To Houston' after a chance conversation had inspired him. But when an Atlanta producer suggested a title change he didn't object. Cissy Houston, mother of Whitney, didn't hit with that version recorded in 1972 but it reached the ears of Gladys Knight who, now free of the constraints of Motown, was able to pick and choose her material. She chose well, and this won a Grammy for Best R&B Vocal Group performance.

Isn't it a bit mingy of Pye to release GK and the Pip's new single with **Midnight Train To Georgia** *on both sides – considering the amount of great material she records.* **Caroline Coon, Melody Maker, May 1976**

The Message

ARTIST Grandmaster Flash And The Furious Five **RELEASE DATE** August 1982 (UK)/October 1982 (US) **WRITER** Edward Fletcher, Melvin Glover, Sylvia Robinson, Clifton Chase **PRODUCER** – **LABEL** Sugar Hill (UK & US) **UK CHART PEAK/WEEKS** 8/9 **US CHART PEAK/WEEKS** 62/7

Grandmaster Flash And The Furious Five were not overly impressed with *The Message* when they first heard it in demo form, but the finished article, which presented a stark view of life at the time, gave a wondrous vision of black music's future. Its subsequent success – it sold over a million despite little American pop chart achievement – has since gone on to provide a blueprint for rap music, with the likes of Ice Cube and NWA.

… a vividly graphic account of the dirty day-to-day struggle down at the roots of black American ghetto life. It might be the hardest, most militant instalment of the rap playback since the last Gil Scott-Heron album. **Adrian Thrills, NME, October 1982**

Message In A Bottle

ARTIST Police **RELEASE DATE** September 1979 (UK)/November 1979 (US) **WRITER** Sting **PRODUCER** Nigel Gray, Police **LABEL** A&M (UK & US) **UK CHART PEAK/WEEKS** 1/11 **US CHART PEAK/WEEKS** 74/7

Message In A Bottle is an anthemic number, with clean, sparse guitars, a jaunty, drawling chorus with stripped-down drum beats that comes in waves. Shortly afterwards *Quadrophenia*, featuring Sting in the role of Ace, premiered. He was immediately offered numerous film parts, including the villain in the Bond movie, **For Your Eyes Only.**

A multi-phased record with a dipping and very hooky lead riff underlying throughout. The phoney West Indian vocals and back-beat end up working well; clean and flat across the complex structure of the song. As mild as paint stripper and the neighbours will probably complain. **Susan Hill, Melody Maker, September 1979**

Mirror In The Bathroom

ARTIST Beat **RELEASE DATE** May 1980 **WRITER** David Steele, Roger Charley, Andy Cox, Everett Morton **PRODUCER** Bob Sargeant **LABEL** Go Feet **UK CHART PEAK/WEEKS** 4/9 **US CHART PEAK/WEEKS** –

The Beat started out on the Specials' Jerry Dammers' 2-Tone label, but by the time they hit with **Mirror In the Bathroom** they were recording for their own subsidiary of Arista: Go Feet. While they enjoyed several hits between 1973 and their break-up in 1983, they made their greatest social impact with their strong support of leftist and anti-racist causes.

The Beat, if not the most colourful live band to come out of the new age, are certainly the most progressive – and the veteran sax player's Jazz-tinged sax motifs are simply exquisite. **Adrian Thrills, NME, April 1980**

Miss You Much

ARTIST Janet Jackson RELEASE DATE September 1989 (UK & US) WRITER Jimmy Jam, Terry Lewis PRODUCER Jimmy Jam, Terry Lewis LABEL Breakout (US)/A&M (US) UK CHART PEAK/WEEKS 22/7 US CHART PEAK/WEEKS 1/20

The first single to be extracted from Janet Jackson's second album, **Rhythm Nation 1814** – the year relating to the birth of America's national anthem. The backing vocals of **Miss You Much** had been recorded during September 1988, but Janet did not return to complete the song until February the following year. Its release would provide her with her second US chart-topper and the first of seven singles to be extracted, three more of which would hit the top Stateside.

Jackson addressed her constituency the way a politician might, abandoning the narrow 'I' for the universal 'We' and instructing us to do the same: Dancers of the world unite. **Vince Aletti, Rolling Stone, October 1989**

Mississippi

ARTIST Pussycat RELEASE DATE August 1976 WRITER Werner Thevissen PRODUCER Edy Hilberts LABEL Sonet UK CHART PEAK/WEEKS 1/22 US CHART PEAK/WEEKS –

In August 1976 the UK charts were stormed by a new Dutch group, Pussycat. The vocal/instrumental group, which was made up of male and female talent, had a surprise Number 1 hit with **Mississippi**, written by Werner Thevissen. Four months later at Christmas, the group had another UK chart hit with **Smile**, this time however, the group's success was limited – the highest chart position the single achieved was Number 24. **Smile** heralded the end of Pussycat's shortlived UK career.

Jonathan King has covered this and will probably hit with it despite Pussycat's inclusion on the Radio 1 play list. It is not too bad a song, if you like Country, but if there was to be a Euro-pop category on this page, **Mississippi** *would probably be on it.* **Chris De Whalley, Sounds, August 1976**

Money For Nothing

ARTIST Dire Straits RELEASE DATE July 1985 (UK & US) WRITER Mark Knopfler, Sting PRODUCER Mark Knopfler, Neil Dorfsman LABEL Vertigo (UK)/Warner (US) UK CHART PEAK/WEEKS 4/16 US CHART PEAK/WEEKS 1/22

The second song to be extracted from the mega-selling **Brothers In Arms** album, **Money For Nothing** became unforgettable for its computer-engineered video. The 'I want my MTV' repeated refrain came courtesy of former Police vocalist Sting who happened to be holidaying in Montserrat while Dire Straits were recording. Though it sounds dated now, the song set the tone for the follow-ups which brought the group massive public and critical acclaim.

The song is insulting to women, and probably everybody. It's a typical piece of rock arrogance, that sounds like a Stones album track … and I can't think of anything that's worse than that … ! **Shane MacGowan, Melody Maker, July 1985**

Monster Mash

ARTIST Bobby Pickett And The Crypt-Kickers RELEASE DATE September 1973 (UK)/September 1962 (US) WRITER Gary Paxton, Bobby Pickett PRODUCER Gary Paxton LABEL London (UK)/Garpax (US) UK CHART PEAK/WEEKS 3/13 US CHART PEAK/WEEKS 1/37

It was a ghoulish title for the Crypt-Kickers but **Monster Mash** was no deadly slow song. Bobby Pickett and his boys made this novelty rock 'n' roll in the early Sixties. Their voices were grave deep: striking baritones with cemetery echoes and haunted bass. The record was engineered by Charles Underwood, who had been very involved with Sun Records, in Memphis.

The 32-year-old part time New York cab driver was awakened at 4 am by the phone. It was a friend from California calling with news that a Number 1 record the cabbie had made 11 years ago was selling again, in the thousands. **Paul Gambaccini, Rolling Stone, August 1973**

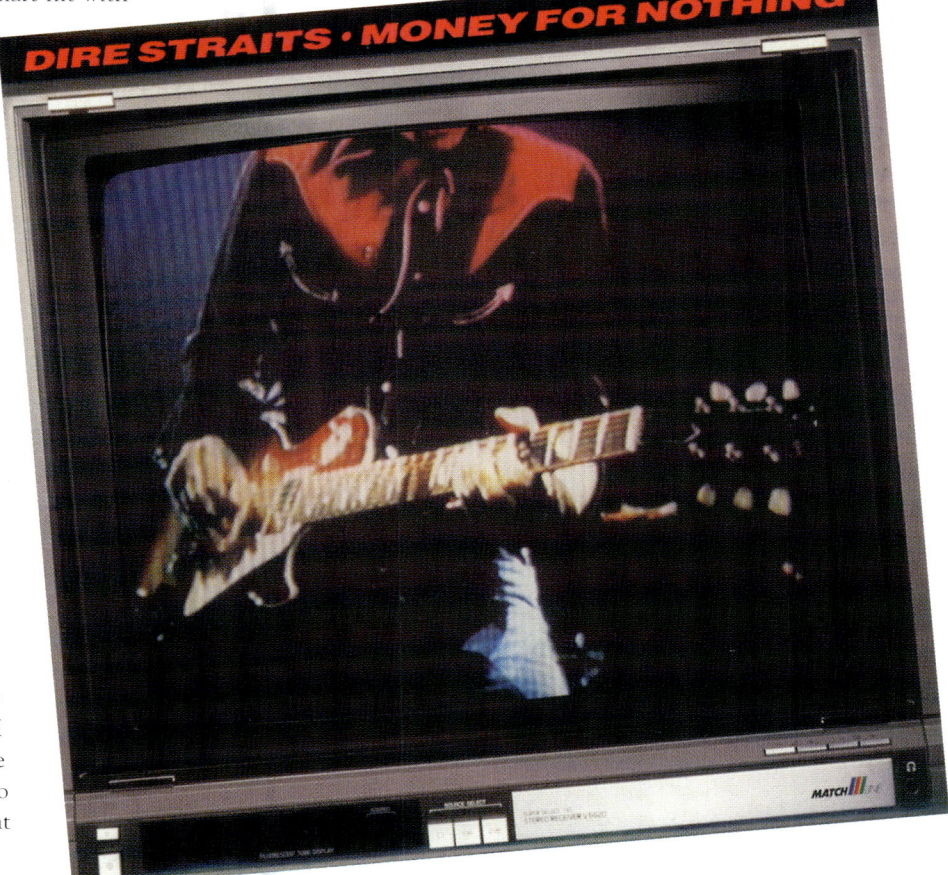

More Than A Feeling

ARTIST Boston **RELEASE DATE** January 1977 (UK)/September 1976 (US)
WRITER Tom Scholz **PRODUCER** John Boylan, Tom Scholz **LABEL** Epic (UK &
US) **UK CHART PEAK/WEEKS** 22/8 **US CHART PEAK/WEEKS** 5/19

Boston leader Tom Scholz lived a dream of being a rock star. An
M.I.T. graduate with a master's degree in mechanical engineering,
he was a senior product designer for Polaroid. He interested Epic
in a demo his band had recorded in his 12-track basement studio
– endeth his day job. Boston's first single, *More Than a Feeling*,
became a smash and their debut album became the third biggest-
selling album of all time in the US.

*Question: How does a good but not original heavy Rock LP become
the fastest seller in history? Answer: I don't know. Listeners to this single,
which somehow reminds me of early Argent, may be similarly mystified.*
Alan Lewis, Sounds, January 1977

More Than Words

ARTIST Extreme **RELEASE DATE** July 1991 (UK)/March 1991 (US) **WRITER**
N. Bettencourt, G. Cherone **PRODUCER** Michael Wagener **LABEL** A&M (UK &
US) **UK CHART PEAK/WEEKS** 2/11 **US CHART PEAK/WEEKS** 1/24

This tender acoustic ballad, the third single from the **Pornograffitti**
album, featured just two of Extreme's four members: guitarist
Bettencourt and vocalist Cherone. It was also a far cry from the
band's usual HM thunder and ensured follow-ups would fall well
short of its near-transatlantic chart-topping performance. The
band split in the mid Nineties, with Cherone signing up as Van
Halen's new singer.

*Extreme were weaned on Van Halen! The mystery is what else they
grew up on.* **More Than Words**, *a placid duet, suggests The Beatles
… Extreme is helping to drag hard rock, kicking and screaming, into the
Nineties.* **Kim Neeley, Rolling Stone, October 1990**

Morning Train (9 To 5)

ARTIST Sheena Easton **RELEASE DATE** July 1980 (UK)/February 1981 (US)
WRITER Florrie Palmer **PRODUCER** Christopher Neil **LABEL** EMI (UK)/EMI
America (US) **UK CHART PEAK/WEEKS** 3/15 **US CHART PEAK/WEEKS** 1/21

Scots lass Sheena Easton got her big break when the BBC featured
her on *The Big Time*. Although her first release, **Modern Girl**, failed
to crack the Top 40 in 1980, her second, **9 To 5**, made Number 3.
As a result of this, **Modern Girl** re-entered the charts to give
Sheena two simultaneous entries in the Top 10. In 1981, the latter
track spent two weeks topping the US charts, retitled **Morning
Train (9 To 5)** to avoid confusion with Dolly Parton's recent
Number 1.

The Most Beautiful Girl
In The World

ARTIST Charlie Rich **RELEASE DATE** February 1974 (UK)/September 1973 (US)
WRITER Rory Bourke, Billy Sherrill, Norris Wilson **PRODUCER** Billy Sherrill
LABEL CBS (UK)/Epic (US) **UK CHART PEAK/WEEKS** 2/14 **US CHART
PEAK/WEEKS** 1/22

A country singer who achieved pop crossover success, Rich began
his career as a session keyboard player for Sam Phillips' legendary
Sun Records. In the late Sixties he was groomed by Billy Sherrill

at Epic in the early days of 'countrypolitan', the easy-listening country style for the MOR market. His first Number 1 was **Behind Closed Doors** and in the same year **The Most Beautiful Girl In The World** achieved Number 1 in both pop and country charts in the US and Number 2 in the UK.

Mouldy Old Dough

ARTIST Lieutenant Pigeon **RELEASE DATE** September 1972 **WRITER** Nigel Fletcher, Robert Woodword **PRODUCER** – **LABEL** Decca **UK CHART PEAK/WEEKS** 1/19 **US CHART PEAK/WEEKS** –

Stavely Makepeace was formed by three school boys in Coventry. They released one unsuccessful single **Edna**, and thought that a change of name would help their careers. They plumped for Lieutenant Pigeon and recorded **Mouldy Old Dough**. The single took eight months to reach the top of the charts, and had almost no vocals except for the words 'mouldy old dough' repeated over and over again, and was recorded in a front room. Their next single was **Desperate Dan**.

Hilda's front room in her semi in Coventry was the scene of the crime. We didn't use the best equipment – it was recorded on a domestic machine. We find we get a better sound using the front room. **Nigel Fletcher (drummer) talking to Julie Webb, NME, October 1972**

ᴹPeople moving on up.

Moving On Up

ARTIST M People **RELEASE DATE** September 1993 **WRITER** M People **PRODUCER** Paul Heard, Mike Pickering **LABEL** Deconstruction **UK CHART PEAK/WEEKS** 2/11 **US CHART PEAK/WEEKS** –

M People's **Search For The Hero** has become synonymous with a certain car ad campaign, but this single became associated with a campaign of another kind when it was chosen as the election night

theme tune of the Labour Party in 1997 (the band are reportedly a favourite of the Blairs). Essentially a joyful paean to self-improvement, it is a fine example of the terrific build quality of all the band's single successes: combining skilful production, a fine vocal performance and a euphoric chorus.

People are getting fed up with grooves and beats, I can see it when I go DJing. Slam in a song and they go mad ... I don't think we're a dance band to be honest. It sounds awful but I think we're a mainstream band. **Mike Pickering interviewed by Johnny Dee, NME, September 1993**

Mr Sandman

ARTIST The Chordettes **RELEASE DATE** December 1954 (UK)/October 1954 (US) **WRITER** Pat Ballard **PRODUCER** – **LABEL** Columbia (UK)/Cadence (US) **UK CHART PEAK/WEEKS** 11/8 **US CHART PEAK/WEEKS** 1/20

In the history of girl groups, the Chordettes are the link between the Andrews Sisters and the Shirelles. Before the Chordettes, female groups generally sang in barbershop-style harmony. The Chordettes were closer to jazzy male groups, like the Ink Spots. Their plea to **Mr Sandman** was their breakthrough hit. They pulled out all the stops, navigating key changes and rhythmic shifts, alternating between simple harmonies and overlapping vocals, all the while emoting the lyrics as if they meant it.

Mr Sandman has all the makings of a first class hit. It is cute, clever and pleasant to listen to. The arranger should also take a bow, for his originality has enabled the group to make an excellent disc. **Geoffrey Everitt, NME, November 1954**

Mr Tambourine Man

ARTIST The Byrds **RELEASE DATE** June 1965 (UK)/May 1965 (US) **WRITER** Bob Dylan **PRODUCER** Terry Melcher **LABEL** CBS (UK)/Columbia (US) **UK CHART PEAK/WEEKS** 1/14 **US CHART PEAK/WEEKS** 1/13

On **Mr Tambourine Man**, the sparkling tones of Jim McGuinn's 12-string Rickenbacker guitar told the world that the words 'folk' and 'rock' were no longer mutually exclusive. McGuinn and the rest of The Byrds learned the song directly from Bob Dylan's demo. Although The Byrds were already famous in the L.A. nightclub world for their jangly guitars and three-part harmonies, producer Terry Melcher wasn't convinced of their playing abilities. McGuinn ended up recording the single with session musicians.

The Byrds roared into prominence with this song, a Bob Dylan composition so haunting that it was a natural hit from the moment an opportunist group put it out as a single. **Melody Maker, July 1965**

Mrs Robinson

ARTIST Simon & Garfunkel **RELEASE DATE** July 1968 (UK) April 1968 (US) **WRITER** Paul Simon **PRODUCER** Paul Simon, Ray Hallee, Art Garfunkel **LABEL** CBS (UK)/Columbia (US) **UK CHART PEAK/WEEKS** 4/12 **US CHART PEAK/WEEKS** 1/13

Simon & Garfunkel were commissioned to supply songs for the soundtrack of Mike Nichol's movie **The Graduate** – four were retreads of existing releases, but Simon created one original, **Mrs Robinson**. The score for the film picked up a Grammy Award and the chirpy single was an instant hit, covered by the Lemonheads in 1992.

Bloody brilliant. Excuse this foul language, but one has to resort to violence now and then to bring to wider attention the works of talented ones. From the film The Graduate *and includes some impish guitar and delicate harmonizing.* **Chris Welch, Melody Maker, July 1968**

Mull Of Kintyre/Girls School

ARTIST Paul McCartney And Wings **RELEASE DATE** November 1977 **WRITER** Paul McCartney, Denny Lane **PRODUCER** Paul McCartney **LABEL** Capitol **UK CHART PEAK/WEEKS** 1/17 **US CHART PEAK/WEEKS** 33/11

Paul McCartney's first post-Beatles Number 1 in the UK was inspired by the Kintyre Peninsular, not far from the McCartney's house in Campbell Town. The single, which stayed at the top for nine weeks, becoming the biggest UK selling single until **Do They Know It's Christmas?** was co-written by McCartney and Wings member Denny Laine. The States remained resistant to the sentiment of the Scottish isles – the single, a double A-side with **Girls School**, failed to make any serious impression.

***Mull** lies somewhere between a traditional folk song (the pipes and drums of the Campbell Town Pipe Band are enlisted to full malt flavour). A scarf waving chant (in the Rod Stewart vein) and a late night at the boozer.* **Ian Birch, Melody Maker, November 1977**

Music

ARTIST John Miles **RELEASE DATE** March 1976 (UK)/May 1976 (US) **WRITER** John Miles **PRODUCER** Alan Parsons **LABEL** Decca (UK)/London (US) **UK CHART PEAK/WEEKS** 3/9 **US CHART PEAK/WEEKS** 88/3

Punk rock was fermenting in seditionary London at the time John Miles was appearing, seated at a piano, to sing this MOR classic on **Top Of The Pops**. It was the biggest of four hits by the talented multi-instrumentalist. Although he hit the Top 10 again with *Slow Down*, the New Wave would soon consign his own work to 'music of the past'.

A fashionably lengthy epic opus – sound sections, ranging from the mildly lyrical to film soundtrack slush. It's a contrived, self-conscious, over-produced 45. Oh well, in the world of rock we are always liable to get rolled. Some people enjoy the experience. **Caroline Coon, Melody Maker, March 1976**

My Baby Just Cares For Me

ARTIST Nina Simone **RELEASE DATE** October 1987 **WRITER** Walter Donaldson, Gus Kahn **PRODUCER** – **LABEL** Charly **UK CHART PEAK/WEEKS** 5/11 **US CHART PEAK/WEEKS** 0/0

Nina Simone was a multi-talented pianist and arranger, including jazz, R&B, black protest songs and traditional ballads in her repertoire. **My Baby Just Cares For Me**, with its deceptively simple piano lines, showed just how well she could craft and deliver a pop song, and its belated success in 1987 – off the back of a TV ad campaign for Chanel No. 5 – proved the point.

My Boy Lollipop

ARTIST Millie Small **RELEASE DATE** March 1964 (UK)/May 1964 (US) **WRITER** Johnny Roberts, Morris Levy **PRODUCER** Chris Blackwell **LABEL** Fontana (UK)/Smash (US) **UK CHART PEAK/WEEKS** 2/18 **US CHART PEAK/WEEKS** 2/12

My Boy Lollipop was a love song for the prepubescent sung by a teenager. Millie's voice was naive and young as she trilled out 'You make my heart go giddy-up'. Millie's romantic song life was not destined to a have a happy ending though. On her second single she was asking: 'And who will marry me? Sweet William will.' By her third and final single she was obviously older and wiser and full of tears – the record was called **Bloodshot Eyes**.

Remember blue-beat? and pills down the Flamingo? Not that I have ever taken any. Always gave me the rabbits. The massive hit that helped to launch Island Records, not to mention West Indian music in Britain. **Chris Welch, Melody Maker, April 1963**

My Cherie Amour

ARTIST Stevie Wonder RELEASE DATE July 1969 (UK)/May 1969 (US) WRITER Stevie Wonder, Henry Cosby, Sylvia Moy PRODUCER Henry Cosby LABEL Tamla Motown (UK)/Tamla (US) UK CHART PEAK/WEEKS 4/15 US CHART PEAK/WEEKS 4/14

Along with *You Are The Sunshine Of My Life* – originally titled 'Oh My Marcia' – this was one of Stevie Wonder's great ballad singles. Released first as the B-side of *I Don't Know Why*, when the main track dropped out of the US Top 40, the flip turned into one of his biggest Sixties hits, proving how well Wonder could handle potentially cloying sentiment and make it irresistible.

Stevie's written many truly lovely melodies like **My Cherie Amour**. *He's more concerned with pure sound and melody than with the meaning of words….* **Gersten, Rolling Stone, January 1972**

My Ding-A-Ling

ARTIST Chuck Berry RELEASE DATE October 1972 (UK)/August 1972 (US) WRITER Chuck Berry PRODUCER Esmond Edwards LABEL Chess UK CHART PEAK/WEEKS 1/17 US CHART PEAK/WEEKS 1/17

The only Number 1 for the man whom many consider the father of rock 'n' roll was a novelty tune which bore little relationship to his classic work. Berry recorded **My Ding-A-Ling** in February 1972,

live at the Lanchester Arts Festival in Coventry, backed by a group that included Average White Band members Robbie McIntosh and Onnie McIntyre. He did it unaware that he was being recorded.

Disc took a hefty hot 100 chart jump with Top 40 radio addition listed this week…. **Billboard, 1972**

My Generation

ARTIST The Who RELEASE DATE November 1965 (UK)/January 1966 (US) WRITER Pete Townshend PRODUCER Shel Talmy LABEL Brunswick (UK)/Decca (US) UK CHART PEAK/WEEKS 2/13 US CHART PEAK/WEEKS 74/5

As the band's reputation grew in the Shepherd's Bush area of West London, Pete Townshend delivered the song that clinched their role as spokesmen for … a generation. With its trademark stuttering delivery from Roger Daltrey, **My Generation** pinned down Sixties teenage frustrations, and its success persuaded Daltrey to stay with the band after a fight with Keith Moon. But even Mods grow old and uncool: in 1977 Generation X responded with *Your Generation (Don't Mean A Thing To Me)*.

This is a group I really shouldn't like, but I do. This has a wild beat. I think that it might offend a few people though. **Pete Murray, Melody Maker, October 1965**

My Girl

ARTIST The Temptations **RELEASE DATE** March 1965 (UK)/January 1965 (US) **WRITER** William 'Smokey' Robinson, Ronald White **PRODUCER** Smokey Robinson **LABEL** Stateside (UK)/Gordy (US) **UK CHART PEAK/WEEKS** 43/1 **US CHART PEAK/WEEKS** 1/13

When the Elgins – as they were then – signed to Berry Gordy Jr's label in 1962 there were no hits, just flops, until David Ruffin joined and they began working with Smokey Robinson; his **The Way You Do The Things You Do** set them on their way. **My Girl** was another Smokey tune he had intended to record himself with the Miracles, but having heard Ruffin's vocal he let the Temptations take it – all the way to Number 1 in the States. In the UK Otis Redding's cover got the chart honours.

Oh, I love his voice – I'll buy this one. With what is happening on the scene now it could well be a hit…. He is a very professional singer, who has been around a while, and can make a hit record whenever he wants. **Chris Andrews, Melody Maker, November 1965**

My Love

ARTIST Paul McCartney And Wings **RELEASE DATE** April 1973 **WRITER** Paul and Linda McCartney **PRODUCER** George Martin **LABEL** Apple **UK CHART PEAK/WEEKS** 9/11 **US CHART PEAK/WEEKS** 1/18

Paul McCartney was the most prolific of the ex-Beatles, turning his songwriting abilities towards light love songs, some soft pop, and the occasional howler. In 1971 he formed Wings, including his wife Linda and Denny Laine, the ex-Moody Blues guitarist. Their first couple of singles were unassuming, but **Give Ireland Back To The Irish** was banned. This overtly political stance did not last and it was back to the sentimental pop ballad style of **My Love**.

A tender, misty vocal with nice solid unobtrusive backing from Wings, and a good guitar solo midway. Everything is tempered with the kind of professional touch that McCartney always used to show in his work. **Penny Valentine, Sounds, April 1973**

My Sharona

ARTIST The Knack **RELEASE DATE** June 1979 **WRITER** Berton Averre, Pedro Berrios **PRODUCER** Mike Chapman **LABEL** Capitol **UK CHART PEAK/WEEKS** 6/10 **US CHART PEAK/WEEKS** 1/22

With their thin ties and dark jackets, The Knack were American new wave – an unthreatening alternative to punk that owed more to The Beatles than the Sex Pistols. Their success was somewhat manufactured, and inspired a 'Knuke the Knack' campaign within the industry, but the simple, catchy **My Sharona**, written in an afternoon, was the best-selling US single of the year. Cheap and cheerful was the maxim: the whole album took just 11 days and cost $18,000.

This is definitely us white boys make love, jerk-and-bang, as opposed to the svelte, backbone-slipping black guys have (I mean judging by the naughty rhythms of the music) … apart from a stoogy guitar break, this is really active, well-nigh irresistible. **Phil Sutcliffe, Sounds, June 1979**

My Sweet Lord

ARTIST George Harrison **RELEASE DATE** January 1971 (UK)/November 1970 (US) **WRITER** George Harrison **PRODUCER** Phil Spector, George Harrison **LABEL** Apple **UK CHART PEAK/WEEKS** 1/17 **US CHART PEAK/WEEKS** 1/14

George Harrison became the first Beatle to have a solo Number 1 in the UK and US with a song co-produced with Phil Spector and inspired by the Edwin Hawkins Singers' version of **Oh Happy Day**. However, the publishers of **He's So Fine** (a US Number 1 for the Chiffons in 1963) felt that there had been an infringement of copyright. Harrison lost the court case and wrote the less successful **This Song** to put across his side of the story.

The acoustic guitars at the beginning are reminiscent of the old Beatles, but as the bottleneck comes in, the sense of the present grows until we find ourselves in the middle of a huge contemporary production. **Jon Landau, Rolling Stone, December 1970**

My Way

ARTIST Frank Sinatra **RELEASE DATE** April 1969 (UK)/March 1969 (US) **WRITER** Paul Anka, Jacques Revaux **PRODUCER** – **LABEL** Reprise **UK CHART PEAK/WEEKS** 18/122 **US CHART PEAK/WEEKS** 27/8

The Sinatra anthem started life as **Comme d'habitude**, a release for French singer Claude François. Paul Anka decided the melody was perfect for a lyric he wanted to arrange for Sinatra, and **My Way** was born. Although it only scraped into the US Top 30, it appeared in the UK charts on eight occasions for a total of 124 weeks. Within two years there were some 200 versions by everyone from Sid Vicious to Elvis, whose first posthumous hit this was.

Well, this is going to be a hit. As I was saying to Bugs and Lefty only the other night, if the boss could lay another ballad on the mugs – I mean the public – he'd be right back in there shooting up the chart. **Chris Welch, Melody Maker, March 1969**

Mystery Train

ARTIST Elvis Presley **RELEASE DATE** February 1957 (UK)/September 1955 (US) **WRITER** Sam C. Phillips, Herman Parker Jr **PRODUCER** Sam Phillips **LABEL** HMV Pop (UK)/Sun (US) **UK CHART PEAK/WEEKS** 25/5 **US CHART PEAK/WEEKS** 11/~

'It was the greatest thing I ever did on Elvis,' said Sam Phillips, the owner of Sun Records, of this Elvis recording. Phillips had first cut the record two years earlier with Little Junior Parker & The Blue Flames. The song itself was of a driving rhythm-based blues which Elvis, Scotty Moore and Bill Black had first applied to **That's All Right** a year earlier. Their experience of playing together for a year gave **Mystery Train** a more refined feel.

*This is slow Rock 'n' Roll and lacks the excitement of **Hound Dog** and other Presley platters. Elvis still shows up as an outstanding R&R singer but I prefer my rock really to rock, and by that I mean: Go, go, go.* **Keith Fordyce, NME, February 1957**

Natural Born Bugie

ARTIST Humble Pie **RELEASE DATE** August 1969 **WRITER** Steve Marriott **PRODUCER** Peter Frampton, Steve Marriott **LABEL** Immediate **UK CHART PEAK/WEEKS** 4/10 **US CHART PEAK/WEEKS** –

The band's only hit single, **Natural Born Bugie** had more than a hint of The Rolling Stones about it. Featuring Steve Marriott, formerly of The Small Faces, and Peter Frampton, fresh from The Herd and later to achieve brief but massive success as a solo artist, **Natural Born Bugie** rose to Number 4 in the UK in the autumn of 1969. Subsequent releases saw Humble Pie move more towards an HM approach, but **Bugie** exhibits a pleasingly lighter touch.

It is a slice of yer real, old fashioned rock 'n' roll, complete with boogie woogie piano … My guess is that it will be a massive hit. **Bob Dawbarn, Melody Maker, August 1969**

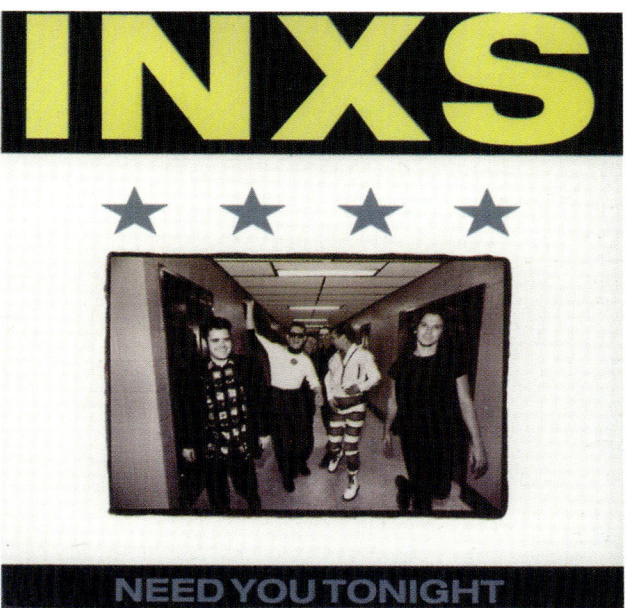

Need You Tonight

ARTIST INXS **RELEASE DATE** October 1987 (UK)/November 1987 (US) **WRITER** Andrew Farriss, Michael Hutchence **PRODUCER** Chris Thomas **LABEL** Mercury (UK)/Atlantic (US) **UK CHART PEAK/WEEKS** 58/3 **US CHART PEAK/WEEKS** 1/25

Need You Tonight gave INXS, formed in 1977, their only US Number 1 when released in November 1987. Based around an Andrew Farriss riff to which Hutchence added lyrics, it took a reissue a year later to break into the UK Top 10, a feat they failed to repeat. Hutchence's November 1997 suicide in a Sydney hotel room brought the curtain down on a 20-year career which had seen the group enjoy worldwide success without ever threatening to reach the level of superstardom.

A tasteful absorption of funk that unhelpfully dries out all the wet, sassy elements … this might as well be white, mid-seventies rock, which is the sad, natural state to which it reverts to in the end. **David Stubbs, Melody Maker, November 1988**

Needles And Pins

ARTIST The Searchers **RELEASE DATE** January 1964 (UK)/March 1964 (US) **WRITER** Sonny Bono, Jack Nitzsche **PRODUCER – LABEL** Pye (UK)/Kapp (US) **UK CHART PEAK/WEEKS** 1/15 **US CHART PEAK/WEEKS** 13/10

This Sonny Bono-Jack Nitzsche number had been a minor hit in the States for Jackie DeShannon, but did much better for the clean-cut Merseyside group, whose first UK Number 1, *Sweets For My Sweet*, John Lennon called the best single ever from a Liverpool group. They learnt *Needles And Pins* from Cliff Bennett & The Rebel Rousers and it became their biggest transatlantic hit. Smokie covered the song in 1977 and reached the UK Top 10.

*Oh! Who's that? One of the well known groups. Could it be The Searchers? I did not go mad for **Sugar and Spice** but I do like them. I liked **Sweets for my Sweet** a lot. This One? A strong hit in the Top 5.* **Helen Shapiro, Melody Maker, January 1964**

Never Can Say Goodbye

ARTIST Gloria Gaynor **RELEASE DATE** December 1974 (UK)/November 1974 (US) **WRITER** Clifton Davis **PRODUCER** Tony Bongiovia, Meco Monardo **LABEL** MGM **UK CHART PEAK/WEEKS** 2/13 **US CHART PEAK/WEEKS** 9/17

The song was originally written by Clifton Davis for the Jackson Five, who took it to Number 2 in the US for three weeks in 1971. While the song made the UK Top 40, it only became a major UK hit when covered by disco diva Gloria Gaynor and released at the end of 1974. The song peaked at Number 2 in January 1975 having already made the US Top 10.

… sounds unremarkable the first time through. But there is a push to its dance beat that could keep the discos playing it longer than its rivals, and the tune's catchy enough for the radio. **Charlie Gillett, NME, November 1974**

Never Gonna Give You Up

ARTIST Rick Astley **RELEASE DATE** August 1987 (UK)/December 1987 (US) **WRITER** Mike Stock, Matt Aitken, Pete Waterman **PRODUCER** Mike Stock, Matt Aitken, Pete Waterman **LABEL** RCA **UK CHART PEAK/WEEKS** 1/18 **US CHART PEAK/WEEKS** 1/24

The biggest British hit of 1987 was the debut solo by Rick Astley, the lead singer of a soul band called F.B.I., when he was spotted by Pete Waterman of Stock/Aitken/Waterman. He worked as a tape operator in the SAW studio for two years, singing on others' discs and learning the trade, before the production trio penned and produced *Never Gonna Give You Up*, kicking off a string of smashes.

The most awesomely ordinary pop star ever, ever, ever. As he himself said: 'Just a spotty northern git really.' **Melody Maker, December 1987**

Never Understand

ARTIST The Jesus And Mary Chain RELEASE DATE March 1985 WRITER William and Jim Reid PRODUCER William and Jim Reid LABEL Blanco Y Negro UK CHART PEAK/WEEKS 47/4 US CHART PEAK/WEEKS –

Having obtained them a contract with the hip, WEA-backed Blanco Y Negro (sic) label with the indie single **Upside Down**, Creation Records supremo Alan McGee had Jesus and Mary Chain release this, their second 45, in the very month that a spectacularly short, feedback-drenched gig at the North London Polytechnic sparked a riot. Three months after that WEA pressing, factory plants refused to make the next single due to an 'obscene and blasphemous' B-side – **Jesus Sucks**.

Good old-fashioned racket from pop's latest loud old fashioned bad boys. Not unpleasant, skilfully amateurish production by unaccredited back room boys. **Adam Sweeting, Melody Maker, February 1985**

Night Fever

ARTIST The Bee Gees RELEASE DATE April 1978 (UK)/February 1978 (US) WRITER Barry, Maurice and Robin Gibb PRODUCER Albhy Galutan LABEL RSO UK CHART PEAK/WEEKS 1/20 US CHART PEAK/WEEKS 1/20

The Bee Gees wrote **Night Fever** for a disco film Robert Stigwood was producing. Stigwood expressed disappointment that he did not have a theme for the film, which was to be called **Saturday Night.** The Bee Gees pointed out that one of their songs was called **Night Fever,** so after much deliberation and forehead-scratching, the decision was taken to change the film's title to – *Saturday Night Fever.*

The Night Has A Thousand Eyes

ARTIST Bobby Vee RELEASE DATE February 1963 (UK)/December 1962 (US) WRITER Buddy Bernier, Jerry Brainin PRODUCER Ed Freeman LABEL Liberty (UK & US) UK CHART PEAK/WEEKS 3/12 US CHART PEAK/WEEKS 3/14

This was the last Top 10 hit of the Sixties for the teen idol whose freakish break came in 1959 when Vee's band, The Shadows (not Cliff's mates), stepped in to fill the gap left by Buddy Holly's death at a gig a few days later. His first US Number 1 was *Take Good Care Of My Baby* in 1961; this track was originally the B-Side of **Anonymous Phone Calls**, but forced its way to the Top 3 in the UK and US.

*I tip **The Night Has A Thousand Eyes** by Bobby Vee, it's just that Bobby Vee and I think that this will get to the top as it is a lot better than his last record* **A Forever Kind Of Love**. **Janice Nicholls in 'O'll give it foive', Melody Maker, February 1963**

A Night To Remember

ARTIST Shalamar RELEASE DATE June 1982 (UK)/April 1982 (US) WRITER Donna Meyers, Charmaine Sylvers, Nidra Beard PRODUCER Leon Sylvers III LABEL Solar UK CHART PEAK/WEEKS 5/12 US CHART PEAK/WEEKS 44/10

When Dick Griffey set up his own label Solar (Sound of Los Angeles Records) he found Shalamar, dancers from the US TV show *Soul Train*, and signed them to produce his synth-driven, funky-bassed hits. Success came with **The Second Time Around**, **Make That Move** and this hit from the album **Friends**, with a powerful performance from Jackie Wilson's goddaughter Jody Watley, who went on to have a strong solo career.

I Can Make You Feel Good was great – this is not. **X. Moore, NME, June 1982**

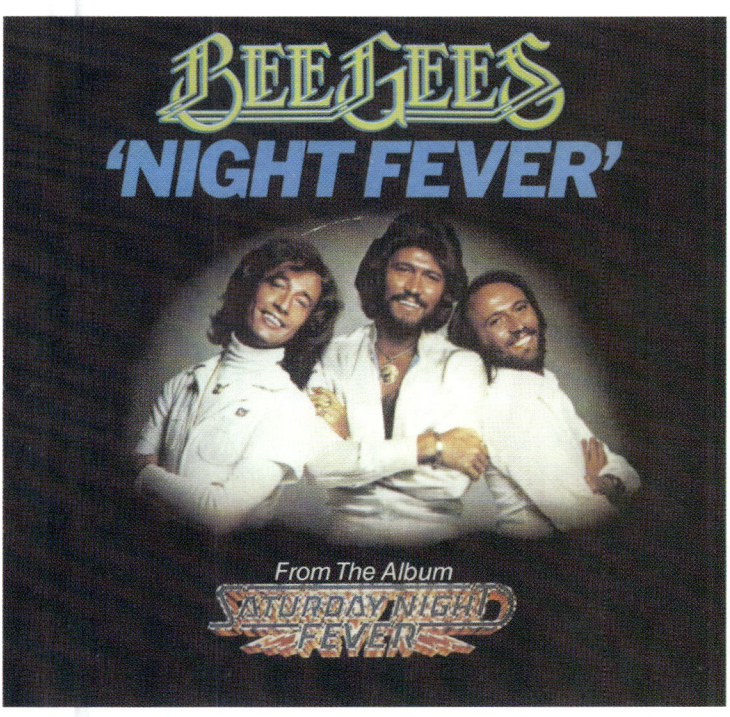

Nights In White Satin

ARTIST The Moody Blues RELEASE DATE December 1967 (UK)/August 1972 (US) WRITER Justin Hayward PRODUCER Tony Clarke LABEL Deram UK CHART PEAK/WEEKS 9/34 US CHART PEAK/WEEKS 2/18

The Moody Blues were originally a British Beat group, who supported The Beatles on tour in America. They turned away from the succinct hook of rhythm and blues when the hits dried up for them. Their new style embraced the rambling lyrics, guitar solos and long songs of progressive rock. **Nights In White Satin** had dreamy poetic imagery for lyrics, meandering against string and flute instrumental passages. It was wildly romantic and overblown.

I do not know who this is. That's a very big sound – a lot of effort has been put into this. I don't think it'll be a hit though. Who is it then. Oh! The Moody Blues; nice group. **Gary Taylor, Melody Maker, November 1967**

19

ARTIST Paul Hardcastle RELEASE DATE May 1985 (UK)/June 1985 (US) WRITER Paul Hardcastle PRODUCER Paul Hardcastle LABEL Chrysalis UK CHART PEAK/WEEKS 1/16 US CHART PEAK/WEEKS 15/14

There were many protest records about the Vietnam war, but keyboard-playing Londoner Paul Hardcastle's was not only different but a long way after the event. This collage of electro-funk backing and the voices of US TV commentators was particularly striking when combined with a video of war footage, the title, reproduced in a stuttering way, being the average age of US soldiers sent to south-east Asia.

As fascinating/depressing as the presentation of wartime statistics is, as good a chunk of funk as this certainly is, it's contemporary relevance is lost on me. As artefact, its interest value is marginal. What's he trying to do? **Caroline Sullivan, Melody Maker, May 1985**

1999

ARTIST Prince And The Revolution RELEASE DATE January 1983 (UK)/October 1982 (US) WRITER Prince PRODUCER Prince LABEL Warner Bros. (UK)/Warner (US) UK CHART PEAK/WEEKS 25/7 US CHART PEAK/WEEKS 12/27

The Artist Formerly Known As Prince continued to dazzle and baffle with his prodigious and prolific output. His creation of the Minneapolis sound – a keyboard-dominated hybrid of rock, pop and funk with sometimes blatantly sexual lyrics – was epitomized in this, the title track of his 1982 multi-platinum album, **1999**. A major turning point in his cross-over career, this funky, fatalistic view of what was then the not-quite-so-near future became his biggest hit to date.

Prince calls his 12-piece band The Revolution – an odd choice for a singer who has virtually withheld any politics from his writing. Apart from the apocalyptic strum of **1999**, *there is very little in his music to quench your thirst for social commentary.* **Stuart Cosgrove, NME, April 1986**

No Limit

ARTIST 2 Unlimited RELEASE DATE January 1993 WRITER Jean-Paul De Coster, Phil Wilde, Anita Doth, Ray Slijngaard PRODUCER Phil Wilde, J. P. De Costa LABEL PWL Continental (UK)/Radikal/Critique (US) UK CHART PEAK/WEEKS 1/16 US CHART PEAK/WEEKS 0/0

Two Dutch rapper/songwriters, Ray Slijngaard and Anita Doth, had met on the Amsterdam club circuit. They linked up with Belgian producers-DJs Jean-Paul De Coster and Phil Wilde, who had been behind the 1990 Bizz Nizz hit *Don't Miss The Partyline*. *No Limit*, a Number 1 in 25 countries, was one of a string of hits in the early Nineties before Doth quit the outfit.

No More Heroes

ARTIST The Stranglers RELEASE DATE September 1977 WRITER The Stranglers PRODUCER Martin Rushent LABEL United Artists UK CHART PEAK/WEEKS 2/9 US CHART PEAK/WEEKS –

In 1975 The Stranglers were still advertising for a keyboard player to join their 'soft rock' group. By the end of 1976 they'd become one of the first new wave/punk bands to sign a record contract with one of the majors – two albums out, and *No More Heroes* reached Number 2 in the UK charts. At their most aggressive and challengingly misogynist in 1977, *Peaches* got a BBC ban for its offensive lyrics. *No More Heroes* led to comparisons with The Doors.

As usual, Dave Greenfield's keyboards overlay the distinctive Stranglers sound. The Ray Manzareu comparison is undeniable, but Greenfield defrosts the icy door and injects warmth, richness & exuberance. Surrealism in a fairground setting. **Ian Birch, Melody Maker, September 1977**

No Particular Place To Go

ARTIST Chuck Berry RELEASE DATE May 1964 (UK)/June 1964 (US) WRITER Chuck Berry PRODUCER – LABEL Pye Int. (UK)/Chess (US) UK CHART PEAK/WEEKS 3/12 US CHART PEAK/WEEKS 10/11

No Particular Place To Go was Chuck Berry's comeback record, his first Top 10 hit after serving two years of a three-year sentence for 'transporting a minor across a state line for immoral purposes'. Because his songwriting grew inconsistent after this disc, some have speculated that he wrote it while in prison, when he was still in the grip of the muse that brought his early hits.

It sounds like the other one he made, School's Out. I like all his work and I think he is great. He's not normally a great big hit, but his tour may push it up further – I hope it does. **Ray Ennis, Melody Maker, May 1964**

No Woman, No Cry

ARTIST Bob Marley And The Wailers RELEASE DATE September 1975 WRITER Vincent Ford PRODUCER Chris Blackwell LABEL Island UK CHART PEAK/WEEKS 22/7 US CHART PEAK/WEEKS –

No Woman, No Cry climbed the UK charts in 1975. Covers of Marley songs had already been successful on both sides of the Atlantic: Johnny Nash's version of *Stir It Up* had made the Top 20 in America and Eric Clapton had made the UK Top 10 in 1974 with *I Shot The Sheriff*. They suggested that the quality of Marley's writing could cross over to a white audience. *No Woman, No Cry* helped Marley become the first reggae superstar.

No Woman No Cry is the one the white audience will go for – if only for the fact that it stirs racial memories of both Percy Sledge and A Whiter Shade Of Pale. A fine song. Its new, slower context should make it available to all. **Ian MacDonald, NME, September 1975**

Nobody Does It Better

ARTIST Carly Simon RELEASE DATE August 1977 (UK)/July 1977 (US) WRITER Carole Bayer Sager, Marvin Hamlisch PRODUCER Richard Perry LABEL Elektra (UK & US) UK CHART PEAK/WEEKS 7/12 US CHART PEAK/WEEKS 2/25

Out of the Top 10 since 1974's *Mockingbird*, Carly Simon was given an opportunity to spring back when she joined the ranks of Bond movie songsters – this track, written by Marvin Hamlisch and Carole Bayer Sager, was the theme for *The Spy Who Loved Me* with Roger Moore as 007, and Richard Kiel as Jaws.

Jeez, how they go down hill....This is the theme tune to the new James Bond movie, The Spy Who Loved Me, and if the movie is as devastatingly tedious as this single, then you'll pardon me if I go see Rocky again. **Harry Doherty, Melody Maker, July 1977**

Nothing Compares 2 U

ARTIST Sinead O'Connor **RELEASE DATE** January 1990 (UK)/March 1990
WRITER Prince **PRODUCER** Sinead O'Connor, Nellee Hooper **LABEL** Ensign (UK
& US) UK CHART PEAK/WEEKS 1/14 US CHART PEAK/WEEKS 1/21

Sinead O' Connor's voice shimmered through people's hearts when
she sang **Nothing Compares 2 U**, and a single tear glistened down
her cheek. She was a controversial figure with her beautiful shaven
head and her unsmiling face. But this cover version of a little-
known Prince song was pure, blistering and beguiling. The
controversy continued when she tore up a picture of the Pope on
national television.

*Her voice is brilliant, but this is a pointless and embarrassing over-
sentimental paw. The billions of strings don't help – they do not add
poignancy.… Sad in a way which was not intended; a waste of talent.*
Push, Melody Maker, June 1990

Nothing's Gonna Stop Us Now

ARTIST Starship **RELEASE DATE** April 1987 (UK)/January 1987 (US) **WRITER**
Dianne Warren, Albert Hammond **PRODUCER** Narada Michael Walden **LABEL**
Grunt (UK & US) UK CHART PEAK/WEEKS 1/17 US CHART PEAK/WEEKS 1/22

As Jefferson Starship, Grace Slick and Paul Kantner had evolved
the Airplane's late Sixties San Francisco sound into an eclectic mix
of influences including one staggeringly gorgeous single in 1975's
Miracles, sung by Marty Balin. By the mid Eighties, even the
Jefferson had been jettisoned (Kantner took the name when he
departed in 1984) with commercial power ballads becoming
Starship's fodder, typified by **We Built This City** and this single

used in the 1987 movie *Mannequin* – the second biggest single of
the year in Britain.

*One pill makes you larger and one pill makes you small, and the ones
that your mother gives you don't do anything at all … Grace Slick sounds
like she is up to 40 Castellas a day, but this song isn't that bad, it's just
more of that MTV valium.* **Paul Temple, Melody Maker, April
1987**

Nutbush City Limits

ARTIST Ike And Tina Turner **RELEASE DATE** September 1973 (UK & US) **WRITER** Tina Turner **PRODUCER** Ike Turner **LABEL** United Artists (UK & US) **UK CHART PEAK/WEEKS** 4/13 **US CHART PEAK/WEEKS** 22/15

Tina grew up in Nutbush and although she had never been the songwriter in the partnership with Ike, her autobiographical song was the last hit the Turners would have together. They had had a run of successes in the early Seventies, including a cover version of Creedence Clearwater's **Proud Mary**, but with Ike's subsequently well-documented behaviour, their relationship later declined dramatically, and their joint career was doomed.

The nearest the Turners ever got to capturing the live excitement of their photographs. **Tony Parsons, NME, November 1978**

Ob-La-Di-Ob-La-Da

ARTIST Marmalade **RELEASE DATE** December 1968 **WRITER** John Lennon, Paul McCartney **PRODUCER** Mike Smith **LABEL** CBS **UK CHART PEAK/WEEKS** 1/20 **US CHART PEAK/WEEKS** –

Marmalade were a Scottish band, singing beat tunes and covering US soul classics. **Ob-La-Di Ob-La-Da** was a Beatles-penned song, a bouncy reggae-tinged number, with a catchy chorus, and chug-along bass and guitar. It is sweet and simple: the words tell the story of an on-the-street romance with a calypso-style vocal that sweeps it along nicely. It is very representative of Marmalade's style – a well-crafted pop song, with a mainstream, commercial slant.

A great battle is on for the hit cover version of The Beatles's song, and it has to be said: the Marmalade's is best. Marmalade are a jolly group who always release highly professional products.... **Chris Welch, Melody Maker, November 1968**

Ode To Billy Joe

ARTIST Bobbie Gentry **RELEASE DATE** September 1967 (UK)/August 1967 (US) **WRITER** Bobbie Gentry **PRODUCER** Kelly Gordan, Bobby Panis **LABEL** Capitol (UK & US) **UK CHART PEAK/WEEKS** 13/11 **US CHART PEAK/WEEKS** 1/14

The song was written and recorded by Bobbie in 1967 and spent four weeks at the top of the US charts. The enigmatic lyric tells of Billy Joe Macallister, who mysteriously jumps off the Tallahatchie Bridge, and the casual way the suicide is discussed around the dinner table. In 1976 the song was adapted for a film; Bobbie re-recorded the theme but it only peaked at Number 65 second time round.

Deeply enhanced by the emotion aroused by the string backing ... this makes for a powerful song with an absorbing story line. Could catch on like a sandstorm in a dustbowl.... **Nick Jones, Melody Maker, September 1967**

Oh Carol

ARTIST Neil Sedaka **RELEASE DATE** November 1959 (UK)/October 1959 (US) **WRITER** Neil Sedaka, Howard Greenfield **PRODUCER** Al Nevins, Don Kirshner **LABEL** RCA (UK)/RCA Victor (US) **UK CHART PEAK/WEEKS** 3/17 **US CHART PEAK/WEEKS** 9/18

This was Neil Sedaka's affectionate tribute to his teenage sweetheart Carol Klein, better known to the world as singer/songwriter Carole King. This fourth single marked the start of a sequence of Top 20 singles over four years or so, marked by his boyish vocals, syncopated rhythms and strong melodies. Carole King replied with her own composition, the little known **Oh! Neil**.

*If you jump to the conclusion that **Oh! Carol** is an early Christmas release then I hasten to reassure you that the Carol in this case is a girl. Strongly recommended to those who are looking for a spot of really good Rock 'n' Roll.* **Keith Fordyce, NME, October 1959**

Oh Pretty Woman

ARTIST Roy Orbison **RELEASE DATE** September 1964 (UK)/August 1964 (US) **WRITER** Roy Orbison, Bill Dees **PRODUCER** Wesley Rose **LABEL** London (UK)/Monument (US) **UK CHART PEAK/WEEKS** 1/18 **US CHART PEAK/WEEKS** 1/15

Oh Pretty Woman took all of 40 minutes to compose – the time it took Orbison's wife, Claudette, to pop in to town for some shopping and return. And for Orbison it was upbeat, celebrational even, the walking guitar riff mirroring a feline stroll and the verse suggesting that this chance encounter with a beauty on the street might bring something other than heartbreak. This, however, was a revision of the original ending 'She's gone and walked away from me/But there's other fish in the sea'.

Mick: 'I don't like the beat there, if he had stuck to it for the middle eight it would have been o.k. It is a good record.' Pete: 'Great, it's a changed style but it's got Orbison's sound.' **The Kinks, Melody Maker, September 1964**

Oliver's Army

ARTIST Elvis Costello **RELEASE DATE** February 1979 **WRITER** Elvis Costello **PRODUCER** Nick Lowe, Elvis Costello **LABEL** Radar **UK CHART PEAK/WEEKS** 2/12 **US CHART PEAK/WEEKS** –

It seems surprising, but even though Elvis Costello is considered one of the greatest singles artists of the past 20 years, he did not hit the Top 10 until two years into his recording career. **Oliver's Army** was his breakthrough, although he was already well known to listeners through his best-selling albums and high media profile.

Costello cherishes the diversity and power of words, yet paradoxically his appeal partly lies in the fact that he hasn't yet been able to master his ebullient wordplay, and so the occasional clutter of phrases becomes as provocative as the more controlled set pieces. **Ian Birch, Melody Maker, February 1979**

On My Own

ARTIST Patti LaBelle And Michael McDonald **RELEASE DATE** May 1986 (UK)/March 1986 (US) **WRITER** Burt Bacharach, Carole Bayer Sager **PRODUCER** Michael Stokes **LABEL** MCA (UK & US) **UK CHART PEAK/WEEKS** 2/13 **US CHART PEAK/WEEKS** 1/23

This US chart-topper almost wasn't: having promised the song to Patti LaBelle, husband and wife team Carole Bayer Sager and Burt Bacharach discovered her producer Richard Perry was less than impressed. They cut their own backing track, but still no go until ex-Doobie Brother McDonald was persuaded to contribute. Both song and video were cut without the artists meeting, Patti in New York (video) and Philadelphia (song) and McDonald in LA.

Next to this, Alexander O'Neal wears a codpiece. The platinum end of more soul, so airbrushed by Burt Bacharach and Carole Bayer Sager that it will manifest on the radio turntables of the world. It will not need a plugger. **David Swift, NME, May 1986**

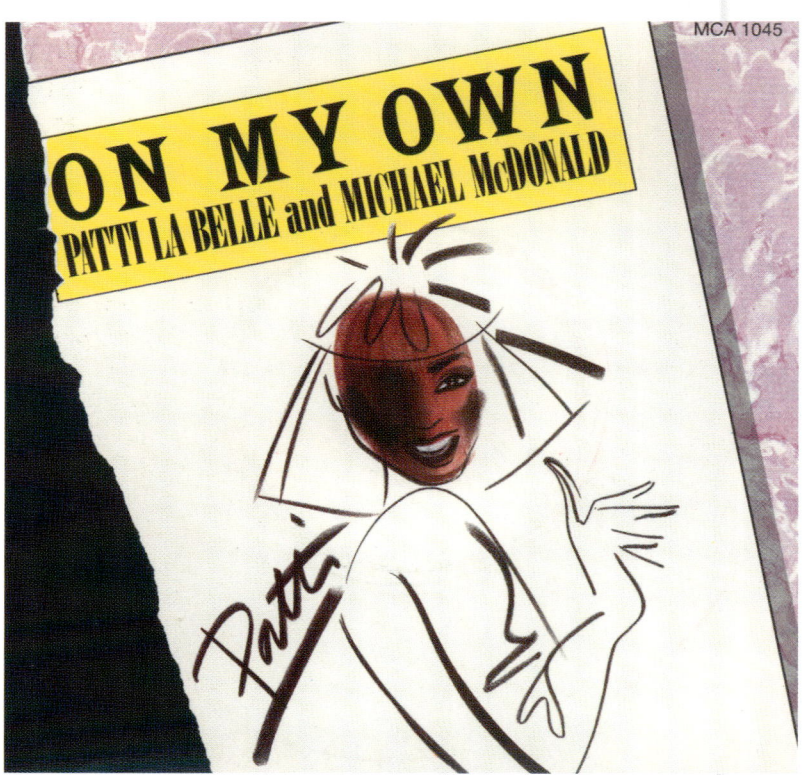

MCA 1045

On The Radio

ARTIST Donna Summer **RELEASE DATE** February 1980 (UK)/January 1980 (US) **WRITER** Donna Summer, Giorgio Moroder **PRODUCER** Giorgio Moroder **LABEL** Casablanca (UK & US) **UK CHART PEAK/WEEKS** 32/6 **US CHART PEAK/WEEKS** 5/17

This track was the only new song on Summer's 1979 compilation album **On The Radio – Greatest Hits, Volumes I and II**, which included all the Summer/Giorgio Moroder hits from *Love To Love You Baby* through the US Number 1 duet with Barbra Streisand *No More Tears (Enough Is Enough)*. Featured in the Jodie Foster-starring movie *Foxes*, the single was a US Top 5 but performed disappointingly in the UK.

1-2-3

ARTIST Len Barry **RELEASE DATE** November 1965 (UK)/September 1965 (US) **WRITER** John Madara, David White, Leonard Borisoff, Brian Holland, Lamont Dozier, Edward Holland **PRODUCER** – **LABEL** Brunswick (UK)/Decca (US) **UK CHART PEAK/WEEKS** 3/14 **US CHART PEAK/WEEKS** 2/15

Born Leonard Borisoff in Philadelphia, Len Barry scored his first US hits as the lead singer of the Dovells, going solo after they broke up in 1963. **1-2-3**, his biggest solo hit, was an international smash, reportedly selling over 1,500,000 copies in the US and 250,000 in the UK. Barry wrote the song with the team of Madara and White, who also penned Lesley Gore's *You Don't Own Me*.

Mr Excitement! The Bombshell! James Brown the second! His first disc **Lip Sync** *did not do very much for him, but already* **1-2-3** *has made the Top 20 in the States. And now Len seems set for a big hit in Britain.* **Norrie Drummond, NME, October 1965**

One More Night

ARTIST Phil Collins **RELEASE DATE** April 1985 (UK)/February 1985 (US) **WRITER** Phil Collins **PRODUCER** Phil Collins, Hugh Padgham **LABEL** Virgin (UK)/Atlantic (US) **UK CHART PEAK/WEEKS** 4/9 **US CHART PEAK/WEEKS** 1/18

While Phil Collins has done very well as a solo artist in his native country, he is much more successful in America, where he has had seven Number 1 singles. **One More Night** was his second, topping Billboard's Hot 100 for two weeks and selling over a million copies. It came from his **No Jacket Required** album, which ascended to Number 1 even faster than did Michael Jackson's **Thriller**.

This one seems more than likely to do the job, but really, if he was playing outside the front door I think I'd still have to pull the blinds. **Barry McIlheney, Melody Maker, April 1985**

One Nation Under A Groove

ARTIST Funkadelic **RELEASE DATE** December 1978 (UK)/September 1978 (US) **WRITER** George Clinton, Gary Shieder, Walter Morrison **PRODUCER** George Clinton **LABEL** Warner Bros. (UK)/Warner (US) **UK CHART PEAK/WEEKS** 9/12 **US CHART PEAK/WEEKS** 28/14

George Clinton's Parliament and Funkadelic had been largely responsible for shaping funk music in the Seventies, with Parliament scoring a succession of American hits. Funkadelic had concentrated on a fusion of rock and funk that had earned them a large following and some album success, but Clinton did not appear to be interested in singles until **One Nation Under A Groove**. Introducing a Parliament influence, reducing the rock element and with a lyric taken up as a call to arms by soul fans across the country, it gave Funkadelic a surefire hit.

The united disco troop are marching across the decibel frontier, fighting for danceable solutions. It's a super-snap sonic attack on your rhythm control…. A great record that's also very boring. **Andy Courtney, Sounds, November 1978**

Boyz II Men, it was Carey's tenth US Number 1 in five years.

The second single from Carey's glorious **Daydream** *opus is a quietly rhythmic pop/R&B ballad that has already snagged widespread airplay as an album cut. Its success will be much deserved, as Carey's increasingly mature and soulful delivery effectively melts into Boyz II Men's wall to wall trademark harmonies.* **Billboard, November 1995**

Only The Lonely

ARTIST Roy Orbison RELEASE DATE July 1960 (UK)/June 1960 (US) WRITER Roy Orbison, Joe Melson PRODUCER Fred Foster LABEL London (UK)/Monument (US) UK CHART PEAK/WEEKS 1/24 US CHART PEAK/WEEKS 2/21

By the time Roy Orbison moved to Nashville to become a songwriter in the late Fifties, he had already had a hit record. But the rockabilly classic *Ooby Dooby*, which made the US charts in 1956, gave little indication of the singer's future direction. He had already written songs for the Everly Brothers and Jerry Lee Lewis when he struck gold with the self-penned *Only The Lonely*, the song that would establish his reputation as a balladeer without peer in the early Sixties.

He … explained how he formulated hits like **Only The Lonely** *… 'I sit down with a guitar and a tape recorder, sing the number over and that's it.' He works out arrangements later on.* **Melody Maker, June 1962**

One Night In Heaven

ARTIST M People RELEASE DATE June 1993 WRITER Paul Heard, Mike Pickering PRODUCER Paul Heard, Mike Pickering LABEL Deconstruction UK CHART PEAK/WEEKS 6/11 US CHART PEAK/WEEKS –

With their smooth commercial sound, M People made the whole dance-soul-pop crossover thing look easy. What set them apart was the opulent vocal stylings of singer Heather Small, who grew up in London's Ladbroke Grove. She was a down-the-line soul singer before she hooked up with former DJ and Happy Mondays producer Mike Pickering – the M stands for Mike's People. Since then, the pop Svengali has steered the group to huge success.

So why do M People light everyone's fire? Maybe it's their accessibility. M People are the exact point where studiously hip club culture meets Top Shop. Their lovely deep garage rhythms have won over dance aficionados, but M People also make cracking pop singles. **Ian Gittins, Melody Maker, March 1994**

One Sweet Day

ARTIST Mariah Carey And Boyz II Men RELEASE DATE December 1995 (UK & US) WRITER Mariah Carey, Walter Afanasieff, Boyz II Men PRODUCER Walter Afanasieff, Boyz II Men, Mariah Carey LABEL Columbia (UK & US) UK CHART PEAK/WEEKS 6/11 US CHART PEAK/WEEKS 1/27

More like 112 sweet days. That's how long this disc topped Billboard's Hot 100 – 16 weeks, breaking the 14-week record that Whitney Houston set with *I Will Always Love You*. (Boyz II Men had tied Houston's record with their own *I'll Make Love To You*). Written by Mariah Carey, her co-producer Walter Afanasieff and

The Only Way Is Up

ARTIST Yazz And The Plastic Population **RELEASE DATE** July 1988 (UK)/November 1988 (US) **WRITER** George Jackson, John Henderson **PRODUCER** Coldcut **LABEL** Big Life (UK)/Elektra (US) **UK CHART PEAK/WEEKS** 1/15 **US CHART PEAK/WEEKS** 96/4

Ex-model and dancer Yasmin Evans added lead vocals to **Doctorin' The House**, Coldcut's 1988 hit, leading to a solo deal with Big Life and a re-emergence with a cover of the Otis Clay soul track. With Yazz's powerful interpretation energizing the arrangement, **The Only Way Is Up** became 1988's best-selling single. The subsequent release **Stand Up For Your Love Rights** was a Yazz original.

*The foghorn that commenced **The Only Way Is Up** was probably the single most powerful sound of 1988. Not only was it capable of instilling deep fits of depression into sensitive young men, but it was equally likely to glean shouts of 'Wa's that your drinking, Wend? Bacardi? On its own?' from the burly white-socked types.* **David Cavanagh, Sounds, January 1989**

Opportunities (Let's Make Lots Of Money)

ARTIST Pet Shop Boys **RELEASE DATE** May 1986 (UK & US) **WRITER** Neil Tennant, Chris Lowe **PRODUCER** Stephen Hague, Nicholas Froome, J. Jeczalik **LABEL** Parlophone (UK)/EMI America (US) **UK CHART PEAK/WEEKS** 11/8 **US CHART PEAK/WEEKS** 10/16

The second single from Pet Shop Boys Neil Tennant and Chris Lowe went the same way as the first – it failed to chart. But, after the success of the reissued **West End Girls**, it too was remixed and reissued, charting strongly in 1986. The group's electronic dance beat was more hard edged at this stage, the instrumentation less lush, but the trademark dry humour of Neil Tennant's vocal styling was already there: 'I've got the brains/You've got the looks/Let's make lots of money'. Tongue-in-cheek but prophetic.

This is the story of two kids on a pop YTS course, who search for cash to fill their colostomy bag, but finish their scheming with more effluence than affluence…. Blue rinse music for the Laundromat. **Ted Mico, Melody Maker, May 1986**

Opposites Attract

ARTIST Paula Abdul **RELEASE DATE** April 1990 (UK)/December 1989 (US) **WRITER** Oliver Leiber **PRODUCER** Oliver Leiber **LABEL** Siren (UK)/Virgin (US) **UK CHART PEAK/WEEKS** 2/13 **US CHART PEAK/WEEKS** 1/23

Opposites Attract, a collaboration with the Wild Pair which featured a rap from the Soul Purpose's Derrick Delite, was Paula Abdul's fourth US Number 1. It proved all too true the following year, when Abdul married actor Emilio Estevez, only to split up two years later. Estevez was far from the only person attracted to Abdul at the time; *Rolling Stone*'s readers voted her the Sexiest Female Rock Artist in the magazine's 1989 poll.

This kicks off with a smart little rap, then Paula jumps in and tip-taps her way through sounding happy: naive and full of herself, like the homecoming queen out on her first real date. She can do no wrong. It must be love. **The Stud Brothers, Melody Maker, April 1990**

Our House

ARTIST Madness **RELEASE DATE** November 1982 (UK)/May 1983 (US) **WRITER** Carl Smith, Christopher Foreman **PRODUCER** Clive Langer, Alan Winstanley **LABEL** Stiff (UK)/Geffen (US) **UK CHART PEAK/WEEKS** 5/13 **US CHART PEAK/WEEKS** 7/19

Madness got bitten by the nostalgia bug in 1983, with **Our House**. The nutty sound had been mellowed down into a kind of wistful meditation on home comforts and the not-too-distant past. It was still distinctively Madness though, with saxophones and piano crammed into the gentle tune. Suggs' vocal had a beguiling melancholy and the single won the Best Pop Song at the Ivor Novello Awards. Madness continued releasing singles until 1986, when they split up.

One of Madness's greatest assets is their ordinariness … they are still very much the Hampstead boys, the downbeat earthiness of their subject matter a sign of just how little they have strayed from their North London roots. **Adrian Thrills, NME, October 1982**

Paint It Black

ARTIST The Rolling Stones RELEASE DATE May 1966 (UK & US) WRITER Mick Jagger, Keith Richard PRODUCER Andrew Loog Oldham LABEL Decca (UK)/London (US) UK CHART PEAK/WEEKS 1/10 US CHART PEAK/WEEKS 1/11

Brian Jones' sitar dominates the sound of this somewhat macabre, Indian-influenced song that became The Stones' sixth and last UK Number 1 for two years and, curiously enough, resurfaced at the top of the Dutch Top 10 in 1990. Mick Jagger lifted the hook line 'I turn my head until my darkness goes' from James Joyce's *Ulysses*.

A glorious Indian raga rock riot that will send The Stones back to Number 1 and probably give pop the biggest punch up the Punjab since Peter Sellers met Sophia Loren. **Melody Maker, May 1966**

Panic

ARTIST The Smiths RELEASE DATE August 1986 WRITER Steven Morrissey, John Marr PRODUCER John Porter LABEL Rough Trade UK CHART PEAK/WEEKS 11/8 US CHART PEAK/WEEKS –

Morrissey was listening to Radio 1: immediately after a news item on Chernobyl, the DJ played Wham!'s *I'm Your Man*. Panic was the Smiths's response: 'Hang the DJ,' declared the chorus. Other 'anti-disco' lyrics got Morrissey into a few problems when a US journalist decided they were detrimental comments on black music. The song was re-recorded for single release to give it an exclusive tag. After a string of unsuccessful and lengthily titled singles, *Panic* was a welcome change.

A stunning astute critique of pop-culture under late capitalism leads Morrissey to the conclusion that terrorism is the answer….Whilst our support of The Smiths in this instance must be critical, it is also whole-hearted and without reservation. **Stephen Wells, NME, July 1986**

Papa Don't Preach

ARTIST Madonna RELEASE DATE June 1986 (UK & US) WRITER Madonna, Brian Elliot PRODUCER Patrick Leonard, Stephen Bray, Madonna LABEL Sire (UK & US) UK CHART PEAK/WEEKS 1/14 US CHART PEAK/WEEKS 1/18

Madonna began to move away from slick pop to songs with more resonant themes. **Papa Don't Preach** is about a father-daughter relationship, the unmarried daughter is pregnant and explaining to her dad that she is, 'gonna keep [her] baby'. The singing is almost conversational, with an emotional thread pulling the lush music along with it, but still had the catchy sing-along chorus that ensured chart success.

A remarkable featureless frump of a fillip which seems afraid to go to the toilet on its own in case it comes across something really dangerous and attack-minded: like toilet paper. Frightfully bland. The Eighties woman indeed! **Chris Roberts, Sounds, June 1986**

Papa Was A Rolling Stone

ARTIST The Temptations RELEASE DATE January 1973 (UK)/October 1972 (US) WRITER Norman Whitfield, Barrett Strong PRODUCER Norman Whitfield LABEL Tamla Motown (UK)/Gordy (US) UK CHART PEAK/WEEKS 14/8 US CHART PEAK/WEEKS 1/16

Throughout the Sixties The Temptations had been consistently churning out hits for Motown; by the end of the decade they were flirting with Sly Stone-like psychedelic soul, and key members, including David Ruffin and Eddie Kendricks, left to go solo. But the hits didn't go away. This song was an 11-minute plus album track cut down to single length but losing none of its power. The R&B classic, The Temptations' last US Number 1, was later covered by Was (Not Was).

… perhaps the most chilling piece of black pop ever made … Paul Riser's superbad post-Shaft arrangements have never been equalled and set the standard for proto-disco. A brave and haunting achievement, and Norm Whitefield's finest hour. **Barney Hoskyns, NME, October 1983**

Papa's Got A Brand New Bag

ARTIST James Brown **RELEASE DATE** September 1965 (UK)/July 1965 (US) **WRITER** James Brown **PRODUCER** James Brown **LABEL** London (UK)/King (US) **UK CHART PEAK/WEEKS** 25/7 **US CHART PEAK/WEEKS** 8/13

'The Godfather of Soul', 'The Hardest Working Man in Show Business', 'Soul Brother Number 1', 'Mr Dynamite' – one could fill a book with James Brown's nicknames alone. Although he began his recording career in 1956 with the classic **Please, Please, Please**, many listeners first experienced his music via **Papa's Got a Brand New Bag**. The funky dance number rejected many pop music conventions, but still drew listeners to its powerful rhythm. It would be Brown's first US Top 10 and his first UK hit.

It is interesting to note the way the bass, drums and guitar links work together in a way that pre-staged reggae. He may well have been a considerable influence on the style. Brown at his best – compact and not over indulgent. **Chris Welch, Melody Maker, February 1973**

Paperback Writer

ARTIST The Beatles **RELEASE DATE** June 1964 **WRITER** John Lennon, Paul McCartney **PRODUCER** George Martin **LABEL** Parlophone (UK)/Capitol (US) **UK CHART PEAK/WEEKS** 1/11 **US CHART PEAK/WEEKS** 1/10

It was a time when each Beatles single contained experimentation, and **Paperback Writer** was no exception. McCartney's bass, for one, was more prominent than ever before. EMI nearly sent the recording back because they feared it would make listeners' styluses jump. Its B-side, **Rain**, with its snatch of backwards vocals, was even more innovative and greatly influenced the psychedelic movement.

Towards Indian-pop using waking harmony and dipping bass lines. A very swinging track with a lot of impact, some vicious sounds and almost disconcerting vocal harmonies. **Melody Maker, June 1966**

Paranoid

ARTIST Black Sabbath **RELEASE DATE** August 1970 (UK)/November 1970 (US) **WRITER** Tony Iommi, Bill Ward, Geezer Butler, Ozzy Osbourne **PRODUCER** Roger Bain **LABEL** Vertigo (UK), Warner (US) **UK CHART PEAK/WEEKS** 4/18 **US CHART PEAK/WEEKS** 61/8

Beneath the crunchy guitars and sensational lyrics and furious lead vocal, the song itself is nothing if not catchy. Which explains why, 30 years after Black Sabbath's formation, **Paranoid** is still one of the first songs that pubescent would-be guitar gods learn on their Japanese-made Flying V copies. The only Black Sabbath song to make the Top 10, **Paranoid** is from their album of the same name, which has sold over four million copies over the years in the US alone.

Played at full volume on a massive stereo, this is definitely the hard rock single of the week. Black Sabbath have not come across on record before, but this is the Birmingham group at their best. **Mark Plummer, Melody Maker, August 1970**

Paranoid Android

ARTIST Radiohead **RELEASE DATE** 1997 **WRITER** Radiohead **PRODUCER** Nigel Godrich, Radiohead **LABEL** Parlophone UK **CHART PEAK/WEEKS** – US **CHART PEAK/WEEKS** –

Paranoid Android, the first single from Radiohead's best-selling album, **OK Computer**, was an unlikely release and initially disappointed their record company who wanted a hard-rocking follow-up to the successes of **The Bends**. Its vivid musical range is astonishing, with echoes of Pink Floyd at their best, the Stones at their rawest, Björk and Johnny Cash, all welded together in a taut, disillusioned, maelstrom. It confirmed the group as a major innovative force on the late 1990s rock scene.

Parklife

ARTIST Blur **RELEASE DATE** September 1994 **WRITER** Damon Albarn **PRODUCER** Stephen Street **LABEL** Food UK **CHART PEAK/WEEKS** 10/7 US **CHART PEAK/WEEKS** 0/0

The tongue-in-cheek title track of Blur's triple-platinum third album marked the pinnacle of Damon Albarn's flirtation with lad culture. It featured a monologue by actor Phil Daniels, who played the lead in the film *Quadrophenia* and also appeared in Mike Leigh's *Meantime*, both major influences on the band. Its buoyant horns and Daniels' Cockney talk were intended to echo The Small Faces who, along with The Kinks, were very much on Blur's mind during the recording sessions for the album.

It is a really good song and it's humorous: something that's sadly lacking elsewhere. Is it as good as **Girls And Boys**? *I didn't like* **Girls And Boys**. **Girls And Boys** *was a definite attempt at 'it', whereas this is just Blur being Blur which is better.* **Thom E. Yorke of Radiohead, Melody Maker, August 1994**

People Are People

ARTIST Depeche Mode **RELEASE DATE** March 1984 (UK)/May 1985 (US) **WRITER** Martin Gore **PRODUCER** Daniel Miller, Depeche Mode **LABEL** Mute (UK)/Sire (US) **UK CHART PEAK/WEEKS** 4/10 **US CHART PEAK/WEEKS** 13/18

Although many regarded the lyrics of Depeche Mode's fourth UK Top 10 single as a touch on the clumsy side, there is no doubting their sincerity. A straightforward plea for tolerance and peaceful co-existence, *People Are People* saw the band come of age with a much more industrial sound, which was to characterize their work in the decade that followed. Mode were getting serious, shaking off their image as purveyors of lightweight synth-pop and beginning to make thought-provoking music.

This one sounds really desperate … all of a sudden it seems imperative that they be thought of as profound. Yeah, it's a bit silly really. **Steve Severin, Melody Maker, March 1984**

Pass The Dutchie

ARTIST Musical Youth **RELEASE DATE** September 1982 (UK)/December 1982 (US) **WRITER** Jackie Mitto, Fitzroy Simpson. Robbie Lynn, Lloyd Ferguson, Leroy Sibbles, Headley Bennett **PRODUCER** Peter Collins **LABEL** MCA **UK CHART PEAK/WEEKS** 1/2 **US CHART PEAK/WEEKS** 10/18

Musical Youth were all pupils at Duddeston Manor school in Birmingham and their ages ranged from 16 right down to 11. *Pass The Dutchie* was a reggae anthem, based on an old Mighty Diamonds' song *Pass The Kutchie*. Kutchie was slang for marijuana, and so 'dutchie' was substituted as a different kind of pot, this one for cooking in. Musical Youth stirred together a mixture of teen tunes and Jamaican patois before disappearing from the pop scene.

One could argue that all the Youth do is assemble a collection of the reggae clichés we have known and loved for years … but the fact is, they put those clichés across with a conviction and style that gives them a new freshness. **Adrian Thrills, NME, September 1982**

Peggy Sue

ARTIST Buddy Holly **RELEASE DATE** December 1957 (UK)/November 1957 (US) **WRITER** Norman Petty, Jerry Allison, Buddy Holly **PRODUCER** Norman Petty **LABEL** Coral **UK CHART PEAK/WEEKS** 6/7 **US CHART PEAK/WEEKS** 3/22

From late 1957 to the end of 1958, Buddy Holly would release records under both his own name (on Coral) and that of his group the Crickets (Brunswick), even though the same personnel played on both. *Peggy Sue* had originally surfaced as *Cindy Lou*, but the bespectacled bard decided to rename it in honour of Peggy Sue Gerron, a Lubbock High School pupil Crickets drummer Jerry Allison was dating. The result was a million seller that registered his first solo UK and US hit.

Features Holly's distinctive hiccuping vocal style (upon which Adam Faith later built his entire pop career). The driving drums of Jerry Allison were a major factor in the song's success, particularly since country & western singers (including at one time, Elvis) felt that drums were an unnecessary frill. **Bob Edmonds, NME, September 1976**

People Got To Be Free

ARTIST The Rascals **RELEASE DATE** July 1968 **WRITER** Felix Cavaliere, Edward Brigati Jr. **PRODUCER** Tom Dowd **LABEL** Atlantic UK CHART PEAK/WEEKS – US CHART PEAK/WEEKS 1/14

One of the top selling bands of the late 60s, the Rascals jostled for chart position with the likes of The Beach Boys, The Beatles, and The Rolling Stones. Their brand of soulful pop kept them riding high in the charts but this song was nearly held back by their record company because of its political content. An anguished lament over the deaths of Robert Kennedy and Martin Luther King Jr, *People Got To Be Free* became their third in a row to sell over a million and established their credentials as right-thinking campaigners.

The Rascals proved on Friday night, playing to a crowd of over 17,000 at the Hollywood Bowl, that they are, by far, one of the finest American concert attractions today. **June Harris, NME, August 1968**

Perfect

ARTIST Fairground Attraction **RELEASE DATE** April 1988 (UK)/December 1988 (US) **WRITER** Mark Nevin **PRODUCER** Kevin Maloney **LABEL** RCA (UK)/RCA Victor (US) UK CHART PEAK/WEEKS 1/13 US CHART PEAK/WEEKS 80/6

After splitting the group, Scots singer Eddi Reader called her new band the Patron Saints of Imperfection, showing her distaste for this Number 1 sing-along single. Many now share her view, having heard it once too often as a supermarket TV jingle, but few folk-rock singles top the UK charts, even as novelties. Writer Mark Nevin would later contribute to the careers of Morrissey, Kirsty MacColl and Brian Kennedy, while Reader produced critically acclaimed albums; but this was, commercially at least, their finest four minutes.

Acoustic folksy rockabilly and a brilliant, brilliant woman singing it. A minor triumph, to be sure, but for what it is – perfect. **Tony Reed, Melody Maker, April 1988**

Physical

ARTIST Olivia Newton-John **RELEASE DATE** October 1981 **WRITER** Steve Kipner, Terry Shaddick **PRODUCER** John Farrar **LABEL** EMI (UK)/MCA (US) UK CHART PEAK/WEEKS 7/16 US CHART PEAK/WEEKS 1/26

Physical launched the all-new raunchy Olivia Newton-John. She swapped guileless innocence for a more sweaty, aerobicized image. Dressed in a track suit, she suggested that we 'get physical ... let me hear your body talk'. The sound was tougher, with a harder edge. It was banned by some American radio stations for its supposed sexual innuendo. It still managed to clamber to the US Number 1, despite, or because of, the fuss, and it stayed there for 10 weeks.

The picture sleeve shows Livvy looking great in towelling sports gear, in good old health & efficiency poses. She sings about getting 'Physical' like someone who lives on laxatives. **Vivien Goldman, NME, October 1981**

Pick Up The Pieces

ARTIST Average White Band **RELEASE DATE** February 1975 (UK)/December 1974 (US) **WRITER** Average White Band **PRODUCER** Arif Mardin **LABEL** Atlantic UK CHART PEAK/WEEKS 6/9 US CHART PEAK/WEEKS 1/17

Ex-Delaney & Bonnie singer Bonnie Bramlett gave the Average White Band their name because she was amused that the pale-faced men from Glasgow could perform such convincing R&B. The rest of the world was similarly impressed when the group brought forth its first and biggest hit, **Pick Up The Pieces**. The single and its parent album, **Average White Band**, simultaneously reached Number 1 in America in February 1975.

Infectious sax playing and super percussion, and it is also true that the band are very popular. But somehow I can't see young Rita, who's in the fifth form at school and works in Woolworths on Saturdays, wanting to buy it. **Chris Irwin, Melody Maker, February 1975**

Pinball Wizard

ARTIST The Who RELEASE DATE March 1969 (UK), April 1969 (US) WRITER Pete Townshend PRODUCER Pete Townshend, Kit Lambert LABEL Track (UK)/Decca (US) UK CHART PEAK/WEEKS 4/13 US CHART PEAK/WEEKS 19/11

The vision and ambition of Pete Townshend in creating *Tommy*, the 90-minute rock opera, took The Who away from their previous single driven career. But ***Pinball Wizard*** was a clear hit within the larger opus: released as a curtain raiser to *Tommy* in 1969 it reached UK Number 19, and scored a replay with a 1976 cover version from Elton John out of Ken Russell's film treatment.

This is a track which will appeal to pin-table and Who fans alike. It will also hang up the DJs, as the opening bars consist of a guitar backing recorded at a much lower level than the main introduction. It is quite a shock.... **Chris Welch, Melody Maker, March 1969**

Play That Funky Music

ARTIST Wild Cherry RELEASE DATE October 1976 (UK)/June 1976 (US) WRITER Robert Parissi PRODUCER Robert Parissi LABEL Epic UK CHART PEAK/WEEKS 7/11 US CHART PEAK/WEEKS 1/25

The song everybody remembers – 'Play that funky music, white boy' – and the band few can recall. They were indeed a bunch of white boys, a hard-rock quintet from Ohio, who picked up the phrase when they performed in discos, turned it into a song and got a deal on the back of it. The chant was given another lease of life by Vanilla Ice 15 years later when he chose it as his 1991 follow-up to ***Ice Ice Baby.***

The sheer brute force of Wild Cherry's performance should bulldoze this into the British charts. However, I can't help wondering why on both sides of the Atlantic the full title 'Play that funky music, white boy' was truncated. Surely it wasn't regarded as racially inflammable? Or was it? **Roy Carr, NME, October 1976**

Please Mr Postman

ARTIST The Carpenters RELEASE DATE January 1975 (UK)/November 1974 (US) WRITER Brian Holland, Freddie Gorman PRODUCER Richard Carpenter LABEL A&M UK CHART PEAK/WEEKS 2/12 US CHART PEAK/WEEKS 1/17

Continuing their fascination with oldies – which dated back to their very first single, a cover of The Beatles' ***Ticket to Ride*** – The Carpenters revived this song, an American chart-topper for the Marvelettes in 1961. History repeated itself, only The Carpenters did the Marvelettes one better by not only topping the Hot 100 but also charting in Britain, where it peaked at Number 2.

A diluted pastiche of The Marvelettes's 1961 hit, that is nonetheless pleasant. **Stephen Holden, Rolling Stone, August 1975**

Please Please Me

ARTIST The Beatles RELEASE DATE January 1963 (UK)/February 1964 (US) WRITER John Lennon, Paul McCartney PRODUCER George Martin LABEL Parlophone (UK)/Vee-Jay (US) UK CHART PEAK/WEEKS 2/18 US CHART PEAK/WEEKS 3/13

While The Beatles' first disc, ***Love Me Do***, made a respectable Number 17, their second one, ***Please Please Me***, proved conclusively that Beatlemania was not just a Liverpool phenomenon. Lennon and McCartney originally intended to have a slow, Roy Orbison-type feel, but producer George Martin persuaded them to speed it up. Although today's chart books list it as hitting Number 2, it made Number 1 on three of the four charts used at the time: *Melody Maker, NME,* and *Disc.* Only the *Record Retailer* chart had it at Number 2.

I think that it is better than their last record ***Love Me Do****: more quality in this one. I think that it should do a lot better than* ***Love Me Do****. A lot of people do not like it but I do.* **Janice Nicholls in 'O'll give it foive', Melody Maker, January 1963**

Pony Time

ARTIST Chubby Checker RELEASE DATE March 1961 (UK)/January 1961 (US) WRITER Don Covay, J. Berry PRODUCER – LABEL Columbia (UK)/Parkway (US) UK CHART PEAK/WEEKS 27/6 US CHART PEAK/WEEKS 1/16

After making the big time with his cover of Hank Ballard & The Midnighters' **The Twist**, Chubby Checker checked out the recent R&B releases and found another song with dance craze potential: **Pony Time**, by Don Covay's band, the Goodtimers. His version quickly trounced the original, topping the Hot 100 for three weeks. **Like The Twist**, **The Pony** required couples to dance apart – something still unusual in those days.

Poor People Of Paris

ARTIST Les Baxter And His Chorus And Orchestra RELEASE DATE February 1956 WRITER Maguerite Monnot, Rene Rouzard, Jack Lawrence PRODUCER – LABEL Capitol UK CHART PEAK/WEEKS 0/0 US CHART PEAK/WEEKS 1/24

Band leader Les Baxter topped Billboard's Hot 100 for six weeks with this instrumental version of a tune originally recorded by Edith Piaf as 'La Goualante Du Pauvre Jean'. Winifred Atwell had the hit with it in the UK, her second Number 1.

Pop Muzik

ARTIST M RELEASE DATE April 1979 (UK)/August 1979 (US) WRITER Robin Scott PRODUCER Robin Scott LABEL MCA (UK)/Sire (US) UK CHART PEAK/WEEKS 2/14 US CHART PEAK/WEEKS 1/24

It might have been a one-hit wonder, but it was still memorable. M was Robin Scott who combined an electro sound with disco beats in a homage to pop. It had a certain novelty value, but its synthesized sound and Scott's unemotional conversational vocal was inventive and catchy.

Pop Muzik throws in everything but the kitchen sink: Euro references, disco beat, 'La-la-la' chorus, even mildly subversive touches. It's a mistake to be too obvious in fooling some of the people some of the time. **Jon Savage, Melody Maker, March 1979**

The Power Of Love

ARTIST Celine Dion RELEASE DATE January 1994 (UK)/November 1993 (US) WRITER C. De Rouge, G. Mende, J. Rush, M. Applegate PRODUCER David Foster LABEL Epic UK CHART PEAK/WEEKS 4/10 US CHART PEAK/WEEKS 1/33

Celine Dion's decision to learn English (she had been born in the French-speaking part of Canada) opened an expansive market following her 1988 victory in the Eurovision Song Contest representing Switzerland with **Ne Partez Pas Sans Moi.** Likewise, the selection of the popular **The Power Of Love**, a 1985 UK chart-topper for Jennifer Rush, was important, for American audiences took to Celine's version and put it at the chart summit for two weeks.

The Power Of Love

ARTIST Huey Lewis And The News RELEASE DATE August 1985 (UK)/June 1985 (US) WRITER Huey Lewis, John Hayes, John Collar PRODUCER Huey Lewis LABEL Chrysalis UK CHART PEAK/WEEKS 11/10 US CHART PEAK/WEEKS 1/19

Lewis and Sean Hopper, former members of country rock outfit Clover (who had masqueraded as 'The Shamrocks' to back Elvis Costello on his debut album **My Aim Is True** in 1977) got together with some jamming buddies in 1980 to form the News. Becoming a firm favourite act with American heartland rock audiences, they topped the US chart with this million seller, which was written as the theme to Steven Spielberg's time travel fantasy film *Back To The Future*.

Huey Lewis is rock's equivalent to Listerine: what every regular kid should gargle with three times a day, on flossy radio, in the disco and via the car stereo. **Neil Taylor, NME, August 1986**

Pray

ARTIST Take That **RELEASE DATE** July 1993
WRITER Gary Barlow **PRODUCER** Steve Vervier
LABEL RCA **UK CHART PEAK/WEEKS** 1/11 **US
CHART PEAK/WEEKS** 0/0

By mid 1993 the five-piece boy band had
got close to the Number 1 slot in the UK,
with **Could It Be Magic** and **Why Can't I
Wake Up With You**, both Top 3. The Gary
Barlow written **Pray**, with its superb
hookline and a touch of gospel choir,
finally delivered the goods, picking up Best
Single and Video at the 1994 Brits and
bringing Barlow a coveted Ivor Novello
award for songwriting.

*I'm not particularly keen on that song … I
think they've got more than most teen bands.
They've shown they can write good pop songs,
so there's no reason why they can't get more
hits. That audience won't remain for long, but
they're not completely manufactured and
they could last.* **Mark Lamarr, NME,
December 1993**

Pretty Vacant

ARTIST The Sex Pistols **RELEASE DATE** July 1977
WRITER Paul Cook, Steve Jones, Glen Matlock,
Johnny Rotten **PRODUCER** Chris Thomas **LABEL**
Virgin **UK CHART PEAK/WEEKS** 6/8 **US CHART
PEAK/WEEKS** –

Sid Vicious was a fully fledged Pistol by the
time they released **Pretty Vacant** – this
was the first single he'd performed on –
during 1977's summer of punk, when the country was up in arms,
or so the media liked to state, over the scorn and impudence of
punk. With this, by Pistols' standards, positively melodic single,
the band finally got to appear on BBC's *Top Of The Pops*.

*On replay, the grand old masters sound just as fine and stirring and
magnificent as they ever did, Rotten's sneer unmatched by anyone before
or since.* **Carol Clerk, Melody Maker, December 1980**

Pride (In The Name Of Love)

ARTIST U2 **RELEASE DATE** September 1984 (UK)/October 1984 (US) **WRITER**
Larry Mullen, David Evans, Adam Clayton, Paul Hewson **PRODUCER** Brian Eno,
Daniel Lanois **LABEL** Island (UK & US) **UK CHART PEAK/WEEKS** 3/11 **US
CHART PEAK/WEEKS** 33/15

This was U2's first single release after a break of a year and a half;
in the meantime the band had completed a packed agenda
including the live album **Under A Blood Red Sky**, a world tour,
setting up their own record label, and the recording of
Unforgettable Fire, from which this was the first single release.
Bono later said it had originally been written about the
Reaganesque pride that might cause nuclear war, but he then
converted it to a tribute to Martin Luther King.

Prince Charming

ARTIST Adam And The Ants RELEASE DATE September 1981 WRITER Adam Ant, Marco Pirroni PRODUCER Chris (Merrick) Hughes LABEL CBS (UK)/Epic (US) UK CHART PEAK/WEEKS 1/12 US CHART PEAK/WEEKS 0/0

The second of Adam Ant's three Number 1s, *Prince Charming* was aided in its progress by a highly memorable video. Continuing with the pantomime theme which he had established in his *Stand And Deliver* video, Ant played the title role in the Cinderella-based *Prince Charming* clip. For the role of the Fairy Godmother, he enlisted his boyhood idol, Diana Dors.

Opening with a series of wails, the song moves into a thick percussiveness surrounded by dense, dramatic texture, bagpipe guitars and layers of vocals, building up gradually to a stirring, disturbing conclusion: 'Ridicule is nothing to be scared of,' he sings. **Carol Clerk, Melody Maker, September 1981**

Proud Mary

ARTIST Creedence Clearwater Revival RELEASE DATE May 1969 (UK)/January 1969 (US) WRITER John Fogerty PRODUCER John Fogerty LABEL Liberty (UK)/Fantasy (US) UK CHART PEAK/WEEKS 8/13 US CHART PEAK/WEEKS 2/14

Although acid-rock jams were the norm in the San Francisco of the late Sixties, of those who bucked the trend only Creedence was a commercial success, thanks largely to the fiery presence and Everyman songwriting of singer John Fogerty. *Proud Mary*, reflecting Fogerty's fascination with a Bayou lifestyle which he had never experienced, sold over two million copies, establishing Creedence as a definitive singles band. It quickly became a widely covered standard. Ike and Tina Turner's down 'n' dirty 1971 rendition was their only million-seller.

They also happen to be the most exciting new group I have heard in quite a while. Like so much of the best music currently coming from America's West Coast, they are almost impossible to fit into any of the easy pigeon holes. **Bob Dawbarn, Melody Maker, May 1969**

Pump Up The Volume

ARTIST M/A/R/R/S RELEASE DATE September 1987 (UK)/November 1987 (US) WRITER Manuel Kamosi, Thomas De Quincey PRODUCER Dave Dorrell, C. J. Mackintosh, Martin Young LABEL 4AD (UK)/4th And Broadway (US) UK CHART PEAK/WEEKS 1/14 US CHART PEAK/WEEKS 13/23

Pump Up The Volume was a powerful slab of dance beats, which used samples from old records and mixed them through the grooves of an electronic keyboard and some abrasive guitar. Hip-hop artists had been doing this for a while, and now it would be *de rigueur* for dance acts. M/A/R/R/S was a collaboration of Colourbox, Alex and Rudi Kane, DJ Dave Dorrell and champion scratch mixer Chris 'C. J.' Mackintosh. The record involved the band in a legal wrangle about the use of unaccredited samples.

Taking its cue from a swatch of Rahim's 'I know you've got soul' rap, M/A/R/R/S jog round the hip houses with a good idea which isn't completed. At night, topped and tailed by the glow of a couple of brilliant records, it might sound better. **John McCready, NME, August 1987**

Puppet On A String

ARTIST Sandie Shaw RELEASE DATE March 1967 WRITER Phil Coulter, Bill Martin PRODUCER – LABEL Pye UK CHART PEAK/WEEKS 1/18 US CHART PEAK/WEEKS 0/0

Shaw was only just 20 when she won the 1967 Eurovision Song Contest for the UK with this Phil Coulter/Bill Martin number. Three years earlier, Sandra Goodrich had used the gift of her gab to get backstage at an Adam Faith show. Faith's manager signed her, changed her name, and, with barefoot trademark in place, she took her first release, a cover of the Bacharach & David song *(There's) Always Something There To Remind Me* to UK Number 1.

That's terrible, that's embarrassing! Is that for the song contest? It'll lose definitely. Germany will love all that 'oomph' though. That's very funny. It really is a bad record, and she has made some great records.... **Scott Walker, Melody Maker, March 1967**

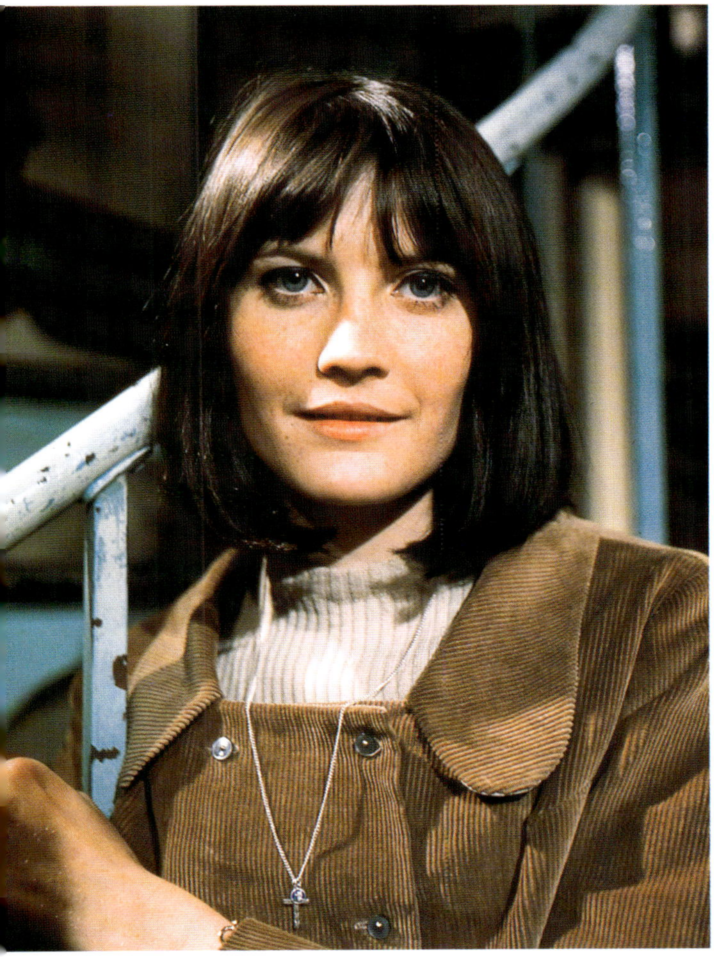

Puppy Love

ARTIST Donny Osmond **RELEASE DATE** June 1972 (UK)/February 1972 (US) **WRITER** Paul Anka **PRODUCER** – **LABEL** MGM (UK & US) **UK CHART PEAK/WEEKS** 5/12 **US CHART PEAK/WEEKS** 3/12

Donny was the teen heart throb, the swoony one from the band of pop star brothers, The Osmonds. In the flush of Jackson Five fever they got a record deal. Because of his clean good looks Donny also recorded solo. ***Puppy Love*** sounded just like an old Fifties ballad, which Donny sang with a tearful quality and a beseeching pathos, not quite able to disguise the sugaring. It was unthreatening and vastly popular.

Purple Haze

ARTIST The Jimi Hendrix Experience **RELEASE DATE** March 1967 (UK)/August 1967 (US) **WRITER** Jimi Hendrix **PRODUCER** Chas Chandler **LABEL** Track (UK)/Reprise (US) **UK CHART PEAK/WEEKS** 3/14 **US CHART PEAK/WEEKS** 65/8

After the volume of Hendrix's amplifier caused neighbours at De Lane Lea studios to complain, The Rolling Stones suggested the guitarist move to Olympic Studies in Barnes, West London where he met engineer Eddie Kramer, who would have a key role in future recordings. His guitar sound benefited from an effects unit known as the Octavia. The unusual guitar effect at the end, panned left and right for extra emphasis, was an Octavia recording played back at a higher speed.

It is very difficult to assess its commerciality ... it's a great record, full of atmosphere and excitement with the dynamic Hendrix personality shining from every groove. **Melody Maker, March 1967**

The Purple People Eater

ARTIST Sheb Wooley **RELEASE DATE** June 1958 (UK & US) **WRITER** Sheb Wooley **PRODUCER** – **LABEL** MGM (UK & US) **UK CHART PEAK/WEEKS** 12/8 **US CHART PEAK/WEEKS** 1/14

Country musician Wooley was an Oklahoma farm boy who'd had some acting success: as the killer in *High Noon* and, notably, as Pete Nolan in *Rawhide*. Wooley came up with this novelty song about visitors from outer space, the single becoming a hit hot on the heels of another novelty, David Seville's in April 1958. ***Witch Doctor***.

Who's going to pilot the space-age ***Purple People Eater*** *into the British best sellers? ... Wooley must have the best chance as, after all, he did write the song and make the original version*. **Dick Hall, Melody Maker, June 1965**

Purple Rain

ARTIST Prince And The Revolution **RELEASE DATE** September 1984 (UK)/October 1984 (US) **WRITER** Prince **PRODUCER** Prince **LABEL** Warner Bros. (UK)/Warner (US) **UK CHART PEAK/WEEKS** 4/15 **US CHART PEAK/WEEKS** 2/16

The title song from the soundtrack album of Prince's highly successful and semi-autobiographical debut movie turned Prince into a star, allegedly selling 1.3 million copies on the day of its release. In a song drenched in high-octane emotionalism, Prince's stunning bravado guitar and vocals reflect the influence of Jimi Hendrix and Little Richard respectively.

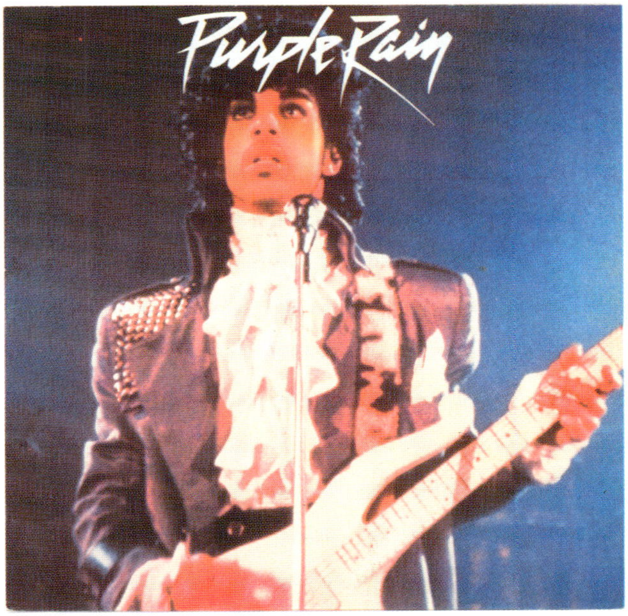

Radar Love

ARTIST Golden Earring **RELEASE DATE** December 1973 (UK)/May 1974 (US) **WRITER** George Kooymans, Barry Hay **PRODUCER** Golden Earring **LABEL** Track (UK)/MCA (US) UK CHART PEAK/WEEKS 7/13 US CHART PEAK/WEEKS 13/20

Dutch band Golden Earring are always identified with this track, the original version of which was a transatlantic Top 20 hit after they had come under the wing of The Who. They shared both a vocals-guitar-bass-drums line-up and a hard-rocking direction with the ex-Mods who they often supported. Earring re-recorded it in 1977, when it re-entered the UK chart, but America, with the patronage of MTV, would prove kinder to them in the early Eighties.

If their material is, as others have said, a composite of early Sixties styles, that's more than compensated for by their visual side. Golden Earring do seem to exude strong charisma and, according to recent reports, a great deal of spunk on stage. **Rob Makie, Sounds, November 1973**

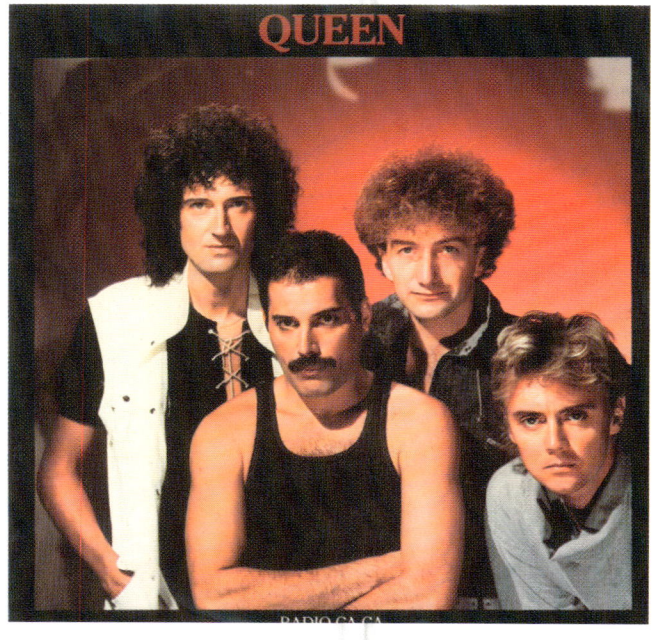

Radio Gaga

ARTIST Queen **RELEASE DATE** February 1984 (UK & US) **WRITER** Roger Taylor **PRODUCER** Mac Reinhold, Queen **LABEL** EMI Queen (UK)/Capitol (US) UK CHART PEAK/WEEKS 2/9 US CHART PEAK/WEEKS 16/13

The first hit single from Queen's 10th album, **The Works**, and carrying the personalized catalogue number 'QUEEN 1', **Radio Gaga** was accompanied by a video incorporating scenes from Fritz Lang's silent movie classic *Metropolis*. The orchestrated fist salute from the crowd in the video, eerily reminiscent of Nazi rallies, was later repeated by fans at live concerts in time to the refrain, 'All we need is Radio Gaga/Radio Googoo ...', leading some to interpret the lyric as a criticism of music radio programming.

Unwinding tediously, on and on, like a roll of Andrex (at least I would wipe my ass with that) **Radio Gaga** *displays a startling lack of substance, invention, cohesion or spirit. Arrogant nonsense. It quite upset my afternoon.* **Carol Clerk, Melody Maker, January 1984**

Rag Doll

ARTIST The Four Seasons **RELEASE DATE** August 1964 (UK)/June 1964 (US) **WRITER** Bob Crewe, Bob Gaudio **PRODUCER** Bob Crewe **LABEL** Philips (UK & US) UK CHART PEAK/WEEKS 2/13 US CHART PEAK/WEEKS 1/12

This song was written about Bob Gaudio's experience with a scruffy little girl who cleaned his car windows as he was stopped at traffic lights. Not having any change to give her he handed over a five dollar note and could not forget the image of disbelief on the girl's face. Having struggled with its composition, *Rag Doll* was eventually completed with help from Bob Crewe and on its release provided the Four Seasons with their last US chart-topper of the Sixties.

This is another of those American sounds that has not made it over here yet. I admire them very much and would like to bring them over again, but I'm afraid I don't see this happening over here, excellent though it is. **Brian Epstein, Melody Maker, August 1964**

Raindrops Keep Falling On My Head

ARTIST B. J. Thomas **RELEASE DATE** February 1970 (UK)/November 1969 (US) **WRITER** Burt Bacharach, Hal David **PRODUCER** Burt Bacharach, Hal David **LABEL** Wand (UK)/Scepter (US) UK CHART PEAK/WEEKS 38/4 US CHART PEAK/WEEKS 1/22

Burt Bacharach and Hal David had intended this song for Ray Stevens, but it was the Oklahoman singer B. J. (Billy Joe) Thomas who landed the job. The track, a backdrop to the bicycle antics in a happy interlude in *Butch Cassidy And The Sundance Kid*, won its writers an Oscar. Thomas went on to record in a pop-country-gospel vein, with chart hits including a second US Number 1: *(Hey Won't You Play) Another 'Somebody Done Somebody Wrong Song'*.

Thomas' recording is nothing less than superb. His delivery is marked by his characteristically ... sensitive approach to a lyric, and he is, of course, supported here by the excellence of the song, production and arrangement – all the responsibility of Burt Bacharach and Hal David. **Jon Landau, Rolling Stone, January 1972**

Raspberry Beret

ARTIST Prince **RELEASE DATE** July 1985 (UK)/May 1985 (US) **WRITER** Prince **PRODUCER** Prince **LABEL** WEA (UK)/Paisley Park (US) UK CHART PEAK/WEEKS 25/8 US CHART PEAK/WEEKS 2/17

The psychedelic influence of The Beatles' Yellow Submarine pervaded both the sound and graphics of **Around The World In A Day,** Prince's follow-up to **Purple Rain** and the first release on his own Paisley Park record label. Though it was critically and commercially not as successful as **Purple Rain**, it did produce a couple of hits, including the funky *Pop Life* and the wistful, Beatles-esque *Raspberry Beret* – a tale of love at first sight between an assistant in a five and dime store and a skimpily dressed customer.

*Prince has managed some brilliant singles, but after **Paisley Park** this tends to confirm his gift is eluding him. It's a fairly miserable, conformist 'Hallmark' record; as it is, though, the name should be enough to guarantee our interest....* **Mick Mercer, Melody Maker, July 1985**

Reach Out (I'll Be There)

ARTIST The Four Tops RELEASE DATE October 1966 (UK)/September 1966 (US) WRITER Brian Holland, Eddie Holland, Lamont Dozier PRODUCER Brian Holland, Lamont Dozier LABEL Tamla Motown (UK)/Motown (US) UK CHART PEAK/WEEKS 1/16 US CHART PEAK/WEEKS 1/15

This song gave The Four Tops international success. Although they had established themselves in the US, and had even topped the chart in 1965 with *I Can't Help Myself*, they were yet to crack the UK Top 20. Motown chief Berry Gordy had great faith in the song which the group thought was just another album track. The song was again a Holland-Dozier-Holland composition and in 1966 topped the US and UK charts for two and three weeks respectively.

It pounds, swells, dips, then thunders onward like a stadium full of people singing into the sky. A record production performance – so totally excellent – cannot be kept down. **Melody Maker, October 1966**

four track ep including four page booklet

Real Gone Kid

ARTIST Deacon Blue RELEASE DATE October 1988 WRITER Ricky Ross PRODUCER Bob Clearmountain LABEL CBS UK CHART PEAK/WEEKS 8/13 US CHART PEAK/WEEKS –

The wistful, acoustic guitar-fuelled *Real Gone Kid* was the first Top 10 hit for Deacon Blue, who took their name from a Steely Dan song. Lead singer Ricky Ross wrote the song about Lone Justice's vocalist Maria McKee, whom he had seen in concert earlier that year. It was the first song Deacon Blue released with Lorraine McIntosh, a.k.a. Ricky Ross' girlfriend, in the band.

Deacon Blue go public in a big way, join the dots, fling out their arms to try and make sense for all of us. An edge like guitar ... tries to summon up Deserts and Oceans as a warm, 'Humane' vocal starts to spell it out.... **Ian Gittins, Melody Maker, October 1988**

Rebel Rebel

ARTIST David Bowie RELEASE DATE February 1974 (UK)/June 1974 (US) WRITER David Bowie PRODUCER David Bowie, Ken Scott LABEL RCA (UK)/RCA Victor (US) UK CHART PEAK/WEEKS 5/7 US CHART PEAK/WEEKS 64/8

After the retirement of Bowie's Ziggy Stardust persona, and the covers album **Pin-Ups**, Bowie was back on track with 1974's **Diamond Dogs**, loosely adapted from George Orwell's *1984*. The hero of Orwell's novel, Julia, described by Winston Smith in the text as a 'rebel from the waist downwards' was transformed into the hot tramp of this single.

Rebel Rouser

ARTIST Duane Eddy **RELEASE DATE** September 1958 (UK)/June 1958 (US) **WRITER** Duane Eddy, Lee Hazlewood **PRODUCER** Lee Hazlewood **LABEL** London (UK)/Jamie (US) **UK CHART PEAK/WEEKS** 19/10 **US CHART PEAK/WEEKS** 6/14

Duane Eddy started to play guitar when he was five and became famous for developing a 'twangy' sound by playing on the bass strings only. In 1955 he began a long association with producer and songwriter Lee Hazlewood with whom he co-wrote this track. *Rebel Rouser* gave Duane his first US and UK Top 20 entry in 1958 and went on to have a string of instrumental hits in both countries.

*It wasn't until he had made **Rebel Rouser** that the American public at large became familiar with his knack of giving a string: driving beat to his music by the predominant use of the single bass string. Now the disc comes here....* **Charles Govey, NME, September 1958**

Red Red Wine

ARTIST UB40 **RELEASE DATE** August 1983 (UK)/January 1984 (US) **WRITER** Neil Diamond **PRODUCER** – **LABEL** Dep Int (UK)/A&M (US) **UK CHART PEAK/WEEKS** 1/14 **US CHART PEAK/WEEKS** 34/15

The reggae education of UB40 included the late Sixties version of this song by Jimmy James & The Vagabonds – they later said they were unaware that the song was originally written and recorded by Neil Diamond. When the band produced their 1983 reggae cover version album **Labour Of Love**, this was an inclusion, and it brought them their first UK Number 1 plus some US chart exposure in a territory notoriously resistant to reggae crossover singles.

*Certainly more listenable to than some of their other more recent stuff, **Red Red Wine** is still far from a spectacular return to form.* **Adrian Thrills, NME, August 1983**

Reet Petite

ARTIST Jackie Wilson **RELEASE DATE** November 1957 **WRITER** Tyran Carlo, Berry Gordy Jr **PRODUCER** – **LABEL** Coral Q (UK)/Brunswick (US) **UK CHART PEAK/WEEKS** 6/14 **US CHART PEAK/WEEKS** 62/10

Wilson signed to a solo career with Motown founder-to-be Berry Gordy Jr. Gordy would write many songs for Wilson, including the classic *Lonely Teardrops* and this R&B belter, which fared far better in the UK than the States on its first release, reaching UK Number 6 in January 1958. Twenty-eight years later the song got to UK Number 1, but Wilson could not enjoy its success – he had died two years earlier after a long illness.

... an unadulterated joy to hear anywhere, anytime – the sound of a man crazed, knotted, overwhelmed by ecstasy ... the swooping harmonies, the heaven piercing horns ... a record of pure genius. **Gavin Martin, NME, October 1982**

The Reflex

ARTIST Duran Duran **RELEASE DATE** April 1984 **WRITER** Duran Duran **PRODUCER** Nile Rodgers **LABEL** EMI Duran (UK)/Capitol (US) **UK CHART PEAK/WEEKS** 1/14 **US CHART PEAK/WEEKS** 1/21

Though it gave Duran Duran their second UK and first US chart-topper, Nick Rhodes had been convinced that *The Reflex* was purely an album track until put in the hands of producer Nile Rodgers. The resulting remix ensured the group (named after a character in Jane Fonda's *Barbarella*) a continued presence in the transatlantic charts that would only come to an end with the split into Arcadia and the Power Station in 1986.

*There is a flamboyant urgency about which makes this their best stab since **Is There Something I Should Know?**, but that is not saying much, and for all the elaborate power of Le Bon's vocals it still sounds like a Nick Heyward B-side.* **Colin Irwin, Melody Maker, April 1984**

Relax

ARTIST Frankie Goes To Hollywood **RELEASE DATE** November 1983 (UK)/April 1984 (US) **WRITER** Peter Gill, William Johnson, Mark O'Toole Trevor Horn **LABEL** ZTT (UK)/Island (US) **UK CHART PEAK/WEEKS** 1/48 **US CHART PEAK/WEEKS** 67/7

Relax was one of the most potent singles of the Eighties. A thumping, pulsating, bass-line married to a catchy chorus and then treated to the most up to date studio techniques, it deserved its chart-topping position. But Mike Read's least favourite record will doubtless be remembered most as a prime example of the power of shrewd and aggressive marketing, and, by the few who saw it, for the outrageous excesses of the accompanying but banned video.

Basically a chant over the rhythmic vibration of the very latest digital kitchen sinks.... **Charles Shaar Murray, NME, 1983**

Release Me (And Let Me Love Again)

ARTIST Engelbert Humperdink RELEASE DATE January 1967 (UK)/April 1967 (US) WRITER Eddie Miller, W. S. Stevenson, Bob Harris PRODUCER – LABEL Decca (UK)/Parrot (US) UK CHART PEAK/WEEKS 1/56 US CHART PEAK/WEEKS 4/14

Arnold George Dorsey changed his name at the suggestion of former flatmate Gordon Mills in 1965. His big break came two years later when he was asked to deputize for an ill Dickie Valentine on TV's *Saturday Night At The London Palladium*. He performed the song soon after release and thanks to the exposure it became the year's UK best selling single. The song even broke The Beatles' run of UK chart-toppers, keeping **Penny Lane** from the top slot.

A fine singer, and he drifts through this fine ballad with great expertise and charm. There is some similarity to Tom Jones in his tone and style, but sounds much more relaxed. **Melody Maker, January 1967**

Relight My Fire

ARTIST Take That (Featuring Lulu) RELEASE DATE October 1993 WRITER Gary Barlow PRODUCER Livingston Negro LABEL RCA UK CHART PEAK/WEEKS 1/14 US CHART PEAK/WEEKS –

A shrewd choice of cover – the Dan Hartman original had been a club hit but not so big that everyone knew the original – and the inclusion of the Glasgow bombshell herself, Lulu, added an extra oomph to proceedings. The second Number 1 for Take That was accompanied by a party video shot at the Ministry of Sound in London; Mark Owen got some flak for wearing a T-shirt saying 'Junkie's Baddy Powder'.

Respect

ARTIST Aretha Franklin RELEASE DATE June 1967 (UK)/April 1967 (US) WRITER Otis Redding PRODUCER Jerry Wexler LABEL Atlantic UK CHART PEAK/WEEKS 10/14 US CHART PEAK/WEEKS 1/12

Respect, a song originally written and recorded by the late, great Otis Redding, showed Aretha's ability to take a song, however well known or associated with another artist, and breathe new life and meaning into it. It also marked her British breakthrough and the beginning of a love affair that continues today. Whether trying her hand at disco, recording duets or updating someone else's song, she has earned her right to the title of First Lady of Soul.

It grooves along with Aretha taking you right back into the Soul-Fontella-bass, with that irresistible discotheque sound and the riffing backing vocals and horns. A great club record and very commercial for the American scene – but not in England. **Melody Maker, June 1967**

Respect Yourself

ARTIST The Staple Singers **RELEASE DATE** June 1972 (UK)/October 1977 (US) **WRITER** Mack Rice, Luther Ingram **PRODUCER** Al Bell **LABEL** Stax **UK CHART PEAK/WEEKS** 30/8 **US CHART PEAK/WEEKS** 12/14

Blues' great Pop Staples moved up to Chicago and built a gospel group around the talent in his family, moving into secular R&B in the Sixties with daughter Mavis taking on lead duties. Joining Stax in 1968 they gained success with 1971's *Heavy Makes You Happy* single and in the following year **Respect Yourself** was a gold album with two gold singles – *I'll Take You There* and *Respect Yourself*. Cover versions include the Kane Gang's excellent 1984 treatment and Bruce Willis' slightly less excellent 1987 rendition.

Dynamite funky beat blues swinger with a potent lyric line that will put them back in the selling market of their smash **Makes You Happy.** **Billboard, 1971**

Return Of The Mack

ARTIST Mark Morrison **RELEASE DATE** March 1996 **WRITER** Phil Chill, Mark Morrison **PRODUCER** – **LABEL** WGA **UK CHART PEAK/WEEKS** 1/24 **US CHART PEAK/WEEKS** –

With its languid rhythms and catchy hook, *Return Of The Mack* was the perfect rejoinder to those who claimed that swingbeat couldn't be transplanted from its West Coast origins. Never off the radio during the summer of 1996, the song hovered round and about the top of the UK charts for months. It then surprised everyone by pulling the same stunt in the US. Morrison's subsequent outings have sounded like variations on a theme, but the original has the enduring quality of the perfect pop single.

Mark Morrison looks to maintain the momentum of his hit **Crazy** *with another assured mix of R&B….* **Music Week, February 1996**

Return To Sender

ARTIST Elvis Presley **RELEASE DATE** November 1962 (UK)/October 1962 (US) **WRITER** Otis Blackwell, Winfield Scott **PRODUCER** Steve Sholes **LABEL** RCA (UK)/RCA Victor (US) **UK CHART PEAK/WEEKS** 1/14 **US CHART PEAK/WEEKS** 2/16

A track from the movie and album **Girls! Girls! Girls!**, *Return To Sender*, with its jaunty and infectious baritone sax backing riff, was a highlight in an otherwise forgettable soundtrack and one of Elvis' best singles of the Sixties. Composed by Otis Blackwell, who had previously written such earlier Number 1s as *Don't Be Cruel* and *All Shook Up*, it was Elvis' fifth UK Number 1 in a row.

Elvis echoes some of the light vocal delivery of some of his earlier discs. The shuffle-beat backing, the song sentiments…. It should soon be blasting a path into single figure brackets. **Rat Coleman, Melody Maker, November 1962**

Reunited

ARTIST Peaches And Herb **RELEASE DATE** April 1979 (UK)/March 1979 (US) **WRITER** Dino Fekaris, Freddie Perren **PRODUCER** Freddie Perren **LABEL** Polydor **UK CHART PEAK/WEEKS** 4/13 **US CHART PEAK/WEEKS** 1/23

Peaches And Herb duet with smooth, creamy voices against a muted slow, dance track. *Reunited* is an end of an evening

smoochy number for couples to shuffle awkwardly around to. There is nothing clumsy about the record though. The single was also a reunion for the couple, who once broke up the duo when Francine Baker left to get married and Herb joined the Washington police force.

The Wind of nasty old schmaltzy stuff that they love to play on TOTP, while the presenter tidies up his hair and brushes up on his transatlantic accent. But do people who write things like this sleep at night? Yes, if they listen to it a few times first. **Tony Mitchell, Sounds, April 1979**

Rhiannon (Will You Ever Win)

ARTIST Fleetwood Mac **RELEASE DATE** March 1978 (UK)/March 1976 (US) **WRITER** Stevie Nicks **PRODUCER** Keith Olsen, Fleetwood Mac **LABEL** Reprise **UK CHART PEAK/WEEKS** 46/3 **US CHART PEAK/WEEKS** 11/18

The eponymous 1975 album by Fleetwood Mac was a slow burner that took 15 months to top the US chart, and this, its second single, helped the cause no end. It showcased its writer, American Stevie Nicks, who had joined the band along with one-time boyfriend and fellow front-person Lindsey Buckingham, and underlined the fact that the Mac had changed from 12-bar blues specialists to an AOR hit machine.

Mac's last album has already sold 12 million copies! **Rhiannon** *is from the previous album,* **Fleetwood Mac.** *It is almost impossible to talk about this affluently swathed Stevie Nicks number. The institution has overtaken the band.* **Ian Birch, Melody Maker, February 1978**

Rhinestone Cowboy

ARTIST Glen Campbell **RELEASE DATE** October 1975 (UK)/May 1975 (US) **WRITER** Larry Weiss **PRODUCER** Dennis Lambert, Brian Potter **LABEL** 4/12 UK **CHART PEAK/WEEKS** 1/23 US CHART PEAK/WEEKS –

After five years away from the Top 10 (but by no means away from the spotlight), Glen Campbell returned with *Rhinestone Cowboy*, its soaring melody perfectly suited to his pure, sparkling tenor. In the US it was his first Number 1 hit, topping the pop, country, and easy listening charts. It became his signature tune, and its title used as the title of his 1994 autobiography.

Rhythm Is A Dancer

ARTIST Snap **RELEASE DATE** July 1992 (UK)/August 1992 (US) **WRITER** T. Austin, B. Benites, D. Butler, J. Garrett **PRODUCER** Snap **LABEL** Arista UK **CHART PEAK/WEEKS** 1/19 US CHART PEAK/WEEKS 5/39

Pittsburgh rapper Turbo B, his cousin Jackie Harris and soul vocalist Penny Ford were brought together by a Frankfurt production duo, Luca Anzilotti and Michael Münzing. As Snap they grabbed a UK Number 1 and US Number 2 with the unrelenting *The Power* in 1990, before Thea Austin replaced Ford for the album **The Madman's Return** in 1992. Turbo B left after *Colour Of Love*, the first single from it, flopped, but he might have regretted his move when *Rhythm Is A Dancer* subsequently slipped into Top 5 territory.

Ride A White Swan

ARTIST T. Rex **RELEASE DATE** October 1970 (UK)/January (US) **WRITER** Marc Bolan **PRODUCER** Tony Visconti **LABEL** Fly Bug (UK)/Blue Thumb (US) UK **CHART PEAK/WEEKS** 2/20 US CHART PEAK/WEEKS 76/6

This was the track that launched T-Rextasy, written by Bolan, emerging – just – from the lyrically excessive poetics of his flower power Tyrannosaurus Rex phase. The sound was no longer congas and acoustic twanging, but a bit of Elvis, lots of trundling electric guitar and the birth of glam. It was simple music, with lyrics suggesting myth and science fiction mystique, and Bolan had found his formula.

A second label launched with the magic rock of Mark Bolan and his bongo-beating partner Mickey Finn. And they cunningly recapture the drive and simplicity of Fifties pop. Swan is their most commercial sound to date … this must be a hit or I'll eat my toadstool. **Chris Welch, Melody Maker, October 1970**

Ride On Time

ARTIST Black Box RELEASE DATE August 1989 WRITER Dan Hartman, Mirko Limoni, Daniel Davoli, Valerio Semplici PRODUCER Groove Groove Melody LABEL Deconstruction (UK)/RCA (US) UK CHART PEAK/WEEKS 1/22 US CHART PEAK/WEEKS 0/0

The only Number 1 for this three-man Italian production team, *Ride On Time*'s chart run was marred by the news that the lead vocal was sampled from an unaccredited Loleatta Holloway. The group also recruited a non-English-speaking model to pose as their singer. The ruse was obvious when she had trouble lip-synching the number on shows like *Top Of The Pops*. Black Box, fearing legal action by Holloway, re-released the disc with her vocals removed, replaced by those of a soundalike session singer.

What an amusing gimmick. A high spirited and almost soulful dance track that pisses all over Belgium – whether it pisses over Belgium from a sitting down or standing up position is the only point to be debated. Steven Wells, NME, August 1989

Riders On The Storm

ARTIST The Doors RELEASE DATE October 1971 (UK)/July 1971 (US) WRITER John Densmore, Jim Morrison, Robert Kreiger, Ray Manzarek PRODUCER Bruce Botnik LABEL Elektra UK CHART PEAK/WEEKS 22/11 US CHART PEAK/WEEKS 14/12

The standout track from the Doors' last album **LA Woman**, released just a month before singer Jim Morrison died in Paris in unexplained circumstances, rides on Ray Manzarek's electric piano and not his usual manic organ shrillings. Though untypical, its haunting, mysterious vibe saw it hit the US Top 20 and gain much airplay elsewhere. It finally charted in Britain in 1991, boosted by the Oliver Stone movie *The Doors* with Val Kilmer cast as the ever-enigmatic Morrison.

Possibly one of the most evocative tracks Morrison ever cut. Its opening mournful rain-swept feeling is never lost – something that Jim

Morrison managed to keep going by making his voice rather gentle and doomy to suit the atmosphere. Penny Valentine, Sounds, September 1971

Right Here Waiting

ARTIST Richard Marx RELEASE DATE September 1989 (UK)/July 1989 (US) WRITER EMI-USA (UK)/EMI (US) PRODUCER Richard Marx, David Cole LABEL 2/10 UK CHART PEAK/WEEKS 1/21 US CHART PEAK/WEEKS –

Right Here Waiting marked a hat-trick of US Number 1s for Marx, whose hook-led, hit-making pedigree came from a father who wrote jingles, a mother who sang them, some time as a back-up vocalist for Lionel Richie, and an apprenticeship writing material for the likes of Kenny Rogers, Chicago and Philip Bailey. As a solo artist, a cluster of US Top 10 successes in 1987 and 1988 (including his first Number 1, **Hold On To The Nights**) led up to the 1989 album **Repeat Offender**, which featured four hits, including *Satisfied* – the second of his troika of chart-toppers – and this piano-led ballad.

Black Crows circle the turntable and light bulbs explode as Richard Marx – bouffant-haired and fancy free – croons for all he is worth for the benefit of his President, his country and his natty new scrumpled-look leather jacket. What manner of diseased beast died to produce that thing I wonder? Patricia Morrison, NME, September 1989

Rikki Don't Lose That Number

ARTIST Steely Dan RELEASE DATE March 1979 (UK)/May 1974 (US) WRITER Walter Becker, Donald Fagen PRODUCER Gary Katz LABEL ABC UK CHART PEAK/WEEKS 58/3 US CHART PEAK/WEEKS 4/19

From the opening riff on the flopanda (a kind of marimba) with its affectionate tribute to Horace Silver's **Song For My Father**, to the tremolo on Skunk Baxter's guitar, *Rikki*, the opening track of **Pretzel Logic**, is one of the warmest songs ever recorded by Steely Dan: the gentle bossa beat is seductive and even the lyric verges on the accessible. By now the Dan were not the Dan pictured inside the album sleeve, but a collection of crack sidemen, including Jim Gordon on drums and Michael Omartian on piano.

Ring My Bell

ARTIST Anita Ward RELEASE DATE June 1979 (UK)/May 1979 (US) WRITER Frederick Knight PRODUCER Frederick Knight LABEL TK (UK)/Juana (US) UK CHART PEAK/WEEKS 1/11 US CHART PEAK/WEEKS 1/21

The only big hit for the Memphis-born former gospel singer, *Ring My Bell* had been written by her producer Frederick Knight for Stacy Lattislaw. Ward, who didn't like the track, recorded it under duress as Knight wanted an additional dance track for her debut album. It was a transatlantic Number 1, but Ward and Knight were unable to repeat the coyly suggestive song's success.

Built with only guitar, bass and drums and a lot of work for the synthesized chiming that Rolls Royce captured on **Love Don't Live Here Anymore**, *but the more forgiving of us will soon get accustomed to its shrill party and be reaching for the tropical TK sleeve at least twice a day.* Danny Baker, NME, May 1979

River Deep Mountain High

ARTIST Ike And Tina Turner RELEASE DATE June 1966 (UK)/May 1966 (US) WRITER Phil Spector, Jeff Barry, Ellie Greenwich PRODUCER Phil Spector LABEL London (UK)/Philles (US) UK CHART PEAK/WEEKS 3/13 US CHART PEAK/WEEKS 88/4

While Phil Spector was working on this follow-up to the Righteous Brothers' **You've Lost That Loving Feeling**, he caught the Ike and Tina Turner Revue on Sunset Strip. Spector wanted Tina's voice. The band he brought together contained top sessioneers including Hal Blaine, Leon Russell and Glen Campbell. Tina struggled against the huge arrangement and in frustration ripped off her blouse and did the take in her bra. The track had everything going for it, but although the UK responded, the US ignored it – Spector was crushed and dropped out for three years.

Fantastic sound. I am going to go out and buy this. If there is any justice in the world this will be Number 1: all the sounds are in there. **Wayne Fontana, Melody Maker, March 1966**

Rivers Of Babylon

ARTIST Boney M RELEASE DATE April 1978 (UK)/June 1978 (US) WRITER Frank Farian, G. Reyam, B. Dowe, F. McNaughton PRODUCER Frank Farian LABEL Atlantic (UK)/Sire (US) UK CHART PEAK/WEEKS 1/40 US CHART PEAK/WEEKS 30/17

The first Number 1 for the studio group formed by future Milli Vanilli mastermind Frank Farian, **Rivers of Babylon** was already familiar to reggae fans in its original version, by the Melodians. It was a runaway success, hitting Number 1 in its third week on the chart. For a time, it was the second biggest-selling disc in British history, superseded only by **Mull Of Kintyre**.

Boney M crown the crumbling coup (in which they toppled Donna Summer) with a ragged disco reggae effort. It's mildly offensive, but no more so than old Bob Marley is when mouthing commercial slush while pausing for Matthew, Mark, Luke and John all rolled into one. **Tony Parsons, NME, April 1978**

The Road To Hell

ARTIST Chris Rea RELEASE DATE October 1989 WRITER Chris Rea PRODUCER Jon Kelly, Chris Rea LABEL WEA (UK)/Geffen (US) UK CHART PEAK/WEEKS 10/9 US CHART PEAK/WEEKS 0/0

The MOR rocker from Middlesbrough was always more successful in Europe than in his home country. **Road To Hell** saw Rea use his gruff, easy blues vocal style to maximum effect on this acerbic comment on modern life, with a graphic description of London's M25 rush-hour traffic that leads the listener down darker paths of imagery. The eponymous album made a feature of Rea's sub-Mark Knopfler guitar tones in unfashionably long but effective guitar solos.

The latest in a lengthy series of fine songs with excellent slide guitar playing. **David Cavanagh, Sounds, October 1989**

Road To Nowhere

ARTIST Talking Heads RELEASE DATE October 1985 WRITER David Burne, Chris Frantz, Tina Weymouth, Jerry Harrison PRODUCER Talking Heads LABEL EMI (UK)/Sire (US) UK CHART PEAK/WEEKS 6/16 US CHART PEAK/WEEKS 0/0

The first and only Top 10 success in the UK for the critically acclaimed, never conventional new wave band came eight years after their first single *Psycho Killer* had – surprisingly, considering its immense later popularity among Talking Heads fans – only scraped into the very lowest echelons of the US Top 100. The Cajun-tinged *Road To Nowhere* did not make any impact in the States, where *Burning Down The House* was their biggest hit.

The title of this aimless slab of multi track is wholly apt – I rest my case, which is becoming rather heavy. **Adam Sweeting, Melody Maker, October 1985**

Roadrunner

ARTIST Jonathon Richman And The Modern Lovers RELEASE DATE July 1977 WRITER Jonathan Richman PRODUCER Greg Kolotkin, Matthew 'King' Kaufman LABEL Beserkley UK CHART PEAK/WEEKS 11/9 US CHART PEAK/WEEKS 0/0

Critics regard Jonathan Richman's career, from its brilliant Velvet Underground/Lou Reed-influenced Boston origins to an apparent fixation with banal ditties in the late Seventies and Eighties, as following a downward trajectory. Even so, the album, mainly recorded with The Modern Lovers in 1971 but released in 1976, and entitled **The Modern Lovers**, was years ahead of its time – and its most famous single, *Roadrunner*, is THE classic of 'driving all night with the radio ON'.

*Roadrunner is arguably one of the three best rock singles of the Seventies, and by the same token comes close to eclipsing both **Fun, Fun, Fun** and **I Get Around** as the ultimate crusin' anthem.* **Roy Carr, NME, July 1977**

Rock 'N' Roll Part 2

ARTIST Gary Glitter RELEASE DATE June 1972 (UK)/July 1972 (US) WRITER Gary Glitter, Mark Leander PRODUCER Mark Leander LABEL Bell UK CHART PEAK/WEEKS 2/15 US CHART PEAK/WEEKS 7/11

Real name Paul Gadd, Glitter had originally recorded in the early Sixties under the name of Paul Raven. In 1967 he met Mike Leander and in 1971 signed to Bell Records. He changed his name to hitch a ride on the glam-rock bandwagon and the pair's first release, the near-instrumental B-side being favoured by radio, was an immediate success. The song spent three weeks at Number 2 in the UK and peaked at Number 7 in the US.

A few people were getting together some joke names – like Apricot Crumble, Terry Tinsel and Horace Hydrogen – and Gary

Glitter was one of them. I remember thinking at the time, that it was good for a laugh. **Gary Glitter interviewed by Julie Webb, NME, July 1972**

Rock And Roll Waltz

ARTIST Kay Starr RELEASE DATE February 1956 (UK)/December 1955 (US) WRITER Roy Alfred, Shorty Allen PRODUCER – LABEL HMV Pop (UK)/RCA Victor (US) UK CHART PEAK/WEEKS 1/20 US CHART PEAK/WEEKS 1/25

Starr, born on an Indian reservation in Oklahoma, sang on some local radio stations before moving to Memphis and singing with jazz violinist Joe Venuti and band leaders Bob Crosby and Glenn Miller. A successful film actress, she had a number of hits in the mid Fifties including this transatlantic Number 1 – a topical cash-in by Tin Pan Alley's mainstream.

Rock Around The Clock

ARTIST Bill Haley And The Comets RELEASE DATE January 1955 (UK)/May 1954 (US) WRITER Max C. Freedman, Jimmy De Knight PRODUCER – LABEL Brunswick (UK)/Decca (US) UK CHART PEAK/WEEKS 1/36 US CHART PEAK/WEEKS 1/38

The song many believe to be the first rock 'n' roll record was originally titled 'Dance Around The Clock' by writers Jimmy De Knight and Max Friedman. It did not exactly set the world alight when originally released. Indeed, only its inclusion in Glenn Ford's 1955 *The Blackboard Jungle* movie prompted the re-release that within weeks resulted in a transatlantic chart-topper. Tragically, guitarist Danny Cedrone would die after a fall down some steps just three weeks after the recording session.

America Decca (Brunswick) pulled off a very smart stroke by having Haley's song similarly featured in The Blackboard Jungle … thus giving Bill his third really big seller, on both sides of the Atlantic, in considerably less than twelve months. **Rex Morton, NME, November 1955**

Rock Your Baby

ARTIST George McCrae RELEASE DATE June 1974 WRITER Harry Casey, Richard Finch PRODUCER Harry Casey, Richard Finch LABEL Jayboy (UK)/TK (US) UK CHART PEAK/WEEKS 1/14 US CHART PEAK/WEEKS 1/17

George McCrae was a veteran R&B singer looking for a hit, and he hit the target with **Rock Your Baby**. Its easy insistent beat and George's high ethereal tenor mingling with a siren synth made it one of the first disco hits. It was sexy, it was fun and most importantly of all, you could dance to it. McCrae stomped the disco wave which emerged in the Seventies.

This is one of those How can it fail? records. The tune is quite unforgettable – the 'Take me in your arms and love me baby' will be zinging about in your small, pointed heads for aeons. **John Peel, Sounds, July 1974**

Rocket Man

ARTIST Elton John **RELEASE DATE** April 1972 (UK)/May 1972 (US) **WRITER** Elton John, Berne Taupin **PRODUCER** Gus Dudgeon **LABEL** DJM (UK)/UNI (US) **UK CHART PEAK/WEEKS** 2/13 **US CHART PEAK/WEEKS** 6/15

One of Elton's best known hits, this was taken from the LP **Honky Chateau**. It gave him his US breakthrough, topping the charts there for five weeks; it peaked at Number 2 in the UK. The single would find a new lease of life in 1991 when it was covered by Kate Bush for the **Two Rooms** tribute album and, extracted as a single, reached Number 12. Lyricist Bernie Taupin admits he stole the title from US singer Tom Rapp.

It's good. Elton returns with a fine new composition, packaged on a useful maxi single, taken from his forthcoming album, **Honky Chateau. Chris Welch, Melody Maker, April 1972**

Rockin' All Over The World

ARTIST Status Quo **RELEASE DATE** October 1977 **WRITER** John Fogerty **PRODUCER** Pip Williams, Status Quo **LABEL** Vertigo **UK CHART PEAK/WEEKS** 3/16 **US CHART PEAK/WEEKS** –

Indelibly associated with Status Quo, and Live Aid – they opened the proceedings at Wembley with this appropriate number – this was neither a new song (they'd first released it 1977) nor even a group original as Creedence Clearwater Revival leader John Fogerty had recorded it in 1975, although it could have been written especially for the Quo.

I loved Quo during their **Price Driver/Hello/Quo** *phases: every concert a gnashing delight of 12 bar boogie that had the subtlety of a pneumatic drill; however this is a let down.* **Ian Birch, Melody Maker, October 1977**

Roll Over Beethoven

ARTIST Chuck Berry RELEASE DATE June 1956 WRITER Chuck Berry PRODUCER – LABEL Chess UK CHART PEAK/WEEKS 0/0 US CHART PEAK/WEEKS 29/5

Although **Roll Over Beethoven** only reached Number 29 on Billboard's Hot 100 and didn't even chart in the UK, it remains one of Chuck Berry's best loved and most influential songs. Beneath the urgent beat and insouciant lead guitar are some of Berry's wittiest lyrics.

You know they never ever brought the record out in the States. It was released only in Canada and they were bringing the record over the border. **Chuck Berry, interviewed by Ren Geratt, Melody Maker, April 1964**

Roll With It

ARTIST Steve Winwood RELEASE DATE June 1988 WRITER Steve Winwood, W. Jennings PRODUCER Steve Winwood, Tom Lord-Alge LABEL Virgin UK CHART PEAK/WEEKS 53/4 US CHART PEAK/WEEKS 1/18

Winwood's Hammond organ and white soul vocals had been at the heart of the Spencer Davis Group, then Traffic, and then the ephemeral super-group Blind Faith. By the time he went solo in 1977, punk was making his bluesy music look passé and it wasn't until **Higher Love** in 1986 that he topped the US singles charts. **Roll With It**, a slice of vintage Winwood pop-soul, and the title song of his first Virgin album, was another America Number 1, but ignored in the UK.

For those who remember the days when Steve Winwood's music was rough, greasy and a little wild, **Roll With It** *is a tantalising reminder of what used to be. The toughest, funkiest he has recorded in years.* **Stephen Holden, Rolling Stone, December 1973**

Roll With It

ARTIST Oasis RELEASE DATE August 1995 WRITER Noel Gallagher PRODUCER Mark Coyle LABEL Creation (UK)/Epic (US) UK CHART PEAK/WEEKS 2/11 US CHART PEAK/WEEKS 0/0

This was the record that was to have provided the battlefield for the Blur v Oasis spat that seemed to obsess the British media in the summer of 1995. Its basic rock-out style never looked likely to beat Blur's poppy **Country House** to the

Number 1 spot but it announced Oasis' new heavyweight sound, which would make **(What's The Story) Morning Glory** easily the best-selling album of the year and provide the platform for an assault on the American charts.

… this isn't the mounting cascade of manna and adrenaline that was **Some Might Say** *or* **Acquiesce**. *It's subdued by comparison; a light shower after that musical thunderstorm, something for us to kick through the puddles to until their next mighty moment of precipitous pop.* **David Stubbs, Melody Maker, August 1995**

Romeo And Juliet

ARTIST Dire Straits RELEASE DATE January 1981 WRITER Mark Knopfler PRODUCER Mark Knopfler, Jimmy Iovine LABEL Vertigo (UK)/Warner (US) UK CHART PEAK/WEEKS 8/11 US CHART PEAK/WEEKS 0/0

Originally considered too long for airplay, this near six-minute album track was selected as a single even though, being keyboard-based, it swam against the perception of Dire Straits as a guitar band. The lyric was about Mark Knopfler's affair with American singer Holly Beth Vincent of new wavers Holy and the Italians, and the singer-guitarist deserves much credit for a great arrangement: he took co-production credit on this and the album **Making Movies** from which it came.

A very straight love song that deserves a bucket of water over the head rather than a red rose. It's not even saved by the boy's lyrical guitar, which only enters stage left in the last act. **Ian Pye, Melody Maker, November 1980**

Rose Marie

ARTIST Slim Whitman **RELEASE DATE** July 1955 **WRITER** Rudolf Frimi, Otto Harbach, Oscar Hammerstein II **PRODUCER** – **LABEL** London (UK)/Imperial (US) **UK CHART PEAK/WEEKS** 1/19 **US CHART PEAK/WEEKS** 0/0

The 1924 musical show Rose Marie (with lyrics co-written by a young Oscar Hammerstein) provided an unlikely source for country and western singer Whitman to find two smash hits. *Indian Love Call* was his first success in 1948 and the title song proved to be his third million seller: it sat at Number 1 in the UK for 11 weeks, a record only beaten by Bryan Adams in 1991.

They say that lightning never strikes twice in the same place. But it can come pretty close to doing this. Slim Whitman made a hit record in America three years age with **Indian Love Call** *from a musical comedy – he's just released* **Rose Marie** *– the title song.* **Rex Morton, NME, July 1955**

Roses Are Red (My Love)

ARTIST Bobby Vinton **RELEASE DATE** August 1962 (UK)/June 1962 (US) **WRITER** Al Byron, Paul Evans **PRODUCER** – **LABEL** Columbia (UK)/Epic (US) **UK CHART PEAK/WEEKS** 15/8 **US CHART PEAK/WEEKS** 1/15

After US Army service, band leader's son Vinton put together a group and landed a spot down the bill on a 1960 tour featuring Chubby Checker and Brenda Lee. After signing to Epic, two albums failed to sell but, owing the record company two singles, Vinton recorded this country-sounding number which promptly went to Number 1 in the US, shifting three million copies. Although it broke into the UK Top 20, it was outsold in Britain by a cover from Ronnie Carroll.

Roxanne

ARTIST Police **RELEASE DATE** April 1979 (UK)/February 1979 (US) **WRITER** Sting **PRODUCER** Police **LABEL** A&M **UK CHART PEAK/WEEKS** 12/9 **US CHART PEAK/WEEKS** 32/13

Police were one of the biggest pop groups of the Eighties. They stitched white reggae rhythms to fuzzed guitars to create catchy tunes. Sparkle was added with clever, witty lyrics. It was Sting who held the whole outfit together: blonde haired, with a bee-striped yellow and black jumper and a husky voice he had a way with words. *Roxanne,* a song about a hooker, was sung with a sore throat harshness and a self-possessed verve that was very distinctive.

Talk about a change of style! Amazing really. It's wiry, main stream rock with plenty of open spaces and one of those high-pitched deliveries. Could even be a minor hit if A&M do the groundwork. **Ian Birch, Melody Maker, April 1978**

Runaround Sue

ARTIST Dion **RELEASE DATE** November 1961 (UK)/September 1961 (US) **WRITER** Dion Di Mucci, Ernest Maresca **PRODUCER** Gene Schwartz **LABEL** Top Rank (UK)/Laurie (US) **UK CHART PEAK/WEEKS** 11/9 **US CHART PEAK/WEEKS** 1/14

Dion's first major solo success was co-written by Ernie Maresca and was actually about a girl named Roberta. The song gave him his only US Number 1 for two weeks in 1961. However, once knocked off the top spot, it then spent a further four weeks at Number 2 behind Jimmy Dean's *Big Bad John*. The song reached the UK Top 20 and was later covered by popsters Racey, giving them their last Top 20 UK hit.

A bright rocker that has a big hit parade sound about it, **Runaround Sue***, recorded on Top Rank by Dion. The tune and the hand clapping beat are first class – the sort of presentation that you will like from the first time you hear it.* **Keith Fordyce, NME, October 1961**

Runaway

ARTIST Del Shannon RELEASE DATE April 1961 (UK)/March 1961 (US) WRITER Del Shannon, Max Crook PRODUCER H. Balk, I. Micahnik LABEL London (UK)/Big Top (US) UK CHART PEAK/WEEKS 1/22 US CHART PEAK/WEEKS 1/17

Runaway was Shannon's debut hit, written on stage in a Michigan club after keyboard player Max Crook noodled up an interesting chord progression. With record company interest they drove to New York and back on a chill winter day to record the track, including Crook's solo on his Musitron, a prototype synthesizer. Shannon released a live version of *Runaway* in 1967 with an easy beat feel, but it wasn't a patch on the original.

'The public,' Del insists, 'should get what they want to hear, if the people want Rock 'n' Roll who has the right to say they shouldn't have it?' … Enthusiasm for his work has been demonstrated through the success of Runaway. **Nat Hentoff, NME, June 1961**

Running Up That Hill

ARTIST Kate Bush RELEASE DATE August 1985 (UK)/September 1985 (US) WRITER Kate Bush PRODUCER Kate Bush LABEL EMI (UK)/EMI America (US) UK CHART PEAK/WEEKS 3/11 US CHART PEAK/WEEKS 30/20

The tribal drums of *Running Up That Hill* marked Kate Bush's return to the music world after two years of self-imposed exile. It was her biggest hit since *Wuthering Heights*, and also cracked the US Top 40. Interested in spiritual themes, she originally wanted to call it 'A Deal With God', but her record label insisted she change it.

This woman is either a witch or a hallelujah merchant, though either way she is precocious, dated and dull. This record is dismally uninteresting; she caterwauls something about making a deal with God, – ho hum. In olden times they would have burned her at the stake for less than this. **Helen Fitzgerald, Melody Maker, August 1985**

Sacrifice

ARTIST Elton John RELEASE DATE November 1989 (UK)/January 1990 (US) WRITER Elton John, Bernie Taupin PRODUCER Chris Thomas LABEL Rocket (UK)/MCA (US) UK CHART PEAK/WEEKS 55/3 US CHART PEAK/WEEKS 18/17

The song was officially a double A-side with *Healing Hands*. Both tracks, from his LP **Sleeping With The Past**, had already been separately released as singles in the US, peaking at 13 and 18 respectively, but had proved less popular in Britain. As a result of strong reaction from radio play by Radio 1 breakfast DJ Steve Wright, Rocket re-released the two tracks with the emphasis on *Sacrifice* to give Elton his first ever solo UK Number 1.

Sacrifice really is an excellent song. It is an exceedingly dignified sound, and his finest composition in ages – serene, delicate and the embodiment of elegance. A pristine production by Chris Thomas … a master-piece of understatement. **Andy Ross, Sounds, October 1989**

Sailing

ARTIST Rod Stewart **RELEASE DATE** August 1975 (UK)/October 1975 (US) **WRITER** Gavin Sutherland **PRODUCER** Tom Dowd **LABEL** Warner Bros. (UK)/Warner (US) **UK CHART PEAK/WEEKS** 1/34 **US CHART PEAK/WEEKS** 58/7

Written by Gavin Sutherland of Sutherland Brothers and Quiver, **Sailing** made two UK Top 3 appearances, the first in its own right, the second after it had been used as the theme tune for *Sailor*, a BBC documentary about the aircraft carrier HMS Ark Royal. Stewart was on the verge of leaving the Faces at this point – he'd been pursuing a simultaneous solo career since joining – and this gave him a great launch pad for flying completely solo.

A song behind which drags everything you most despise about England … the Daily Star crossword, tinned lager, New Year's Eve at the pub, etc…. **David Stubbs, Melody Maker, March 1987**

Samba Pa Ti

ARTIST Santana **RELEASE DATE** September 1974 **WRITER** Carlos Santana **PRODUCER** Carlos Santana, Fred Catero **LABEL** CBS (UK)/Columbia (US) **UK CHART PEAK/WEEKS** 27/7 **US CHART PEAK/WEEKS** 0/0

This track, from the Latin-blues fusion band's 1970 album **Abraxas**, was not deemed single material at the time by either Santana or their label, but was finally released as part of the UK promotion for a 1974 Greatest Hits compilation. A Carlos Santana original, unlike their earlier cover version hits **Black Magic Woman** (Fleetwood Mac) and **Oye Como Va** (a Tito Puente salsa number), **Samba Pa Ti** was a sensual showcase for the leader's sweet sustained guitar soaring over some groovy latin percussion.

I like the title and that's about all…. Well-played, as they say. **Allan Jones, Melody Maker, September 1974**

San Francisco (Be Sure To Wear Some Flowers In Your Hair)

ARTIST Scott McKenzie **RELEASE DATE** July 1967 (UK)/May 1967 (US) **WRITER** John Phillips **PRODUCER** Lou Adler, Jon Phillips **LABEL** CBS (UK)/Ode (US) **UK CHART PEAK/WEEKS** 1/17 **US CHART PEAK/WEEKS** 4/12

San Francisco (Be Sure To) was meant to be a theme song for the Monterey Pop Festival: a gentle, wistful ballad celebrating peace and love; but it also sounds like an instruction guide for tourists to get the definitive hippy look: 'be sure to wear some flowers in your hair'. It was John Phillips, of the Mamas and Papas, who crafted the melody to **San Francisco**.

It's all about the west coast hippies – the beautiful people…. Won't mean a thing over here because for it to mean anything you have got to love beautiful beaches and sunshine. **Gary Brookes, Melody Maker, June 1967**

(I Can't Get No) Satisfaction

ARTIST The Rolling Stones **RELEASE DATE** August 1965 (UK)/June 1965 (US) **WRITER** Mick Jagger, Keith Richard **PRODUCER** Andrew Loog Oldham **LABEL** Decca (UK)/London (US) **UK CHART PEAK/WEEKS** 1/12 **US CHART PEAK/WEEKS** 1/14

Perhaps the most covered Jagger/Richard song – including hit versions by Otis Redding (1966) Aretha Franklin (1967), Bubble Gum, a Jonathan King pseudonym (1974) and Devo (1978) – the record was recorded and first released in the US. It became the Stones' fourth UK Number 1 in a row and their first US Number 1. The song's opening riff was inspired by the Martha & The Vandellas's hit **Dancing In The Street** – which Mick Jagger recorded with David Bowie 20 years later for Live Aid.

Keith Richard initially conceived the basic riff for horn (as can be detected from his use of the Gibson Fuzz Box throughout) and it's Richard's opinion that, in certain respects Otis Redding's re-work was closer to how he envisaged it. **Roy Carr, NME, February 1976**

Saturday Night

ARTIST Whigfield **RELEASE DATE** September 1994 **WRITER** Larry Pignagnoli, Davide Riva **PRODUCER** Larry Pignagnoli, Davide Riva **LABEL** Systematic **UK CHART PEAK/WEEKS** 1/18 **US CHART PEAK/WEEKS** –

Whigfield was a Danish model who had relocated to Barcelona. **Saturday Night** had been a Number 1 in Spain for 11 weeks before its summer Euro success transferred to the UK, where in one week it sold more copies than any single since Band Aid, giving Whigfield the rare distinction of a debut single going straight in at UK Number 1.

Saturday Night's Alright For Fighting

ARTIST Elton John **RELEASE DATE** July 1973 (UK)/August 1973 (US) **WRITER** Elton John, Bernie Taupin **PRODUCER** Gus Dudgeon **LABEL** DJM (UK)/MCA (US) **UK CHART PEAK/WEEKS** 7/9 **US CHART PEAK/WEEKS** 12/12

The first track to be released from the double LP **Goodbye Yellow Brick Road**, this untypical rocker gave Elton his fifth UK Top 10 single and his sixth Top 20 single in the US where the LP spent eight weeks at Number 1. He recorded the song standing up to give his vocal more 'oomph', the piano being added later; and it took The Who to deliver a comparable cover version for the 1991 tribute album **Two Rooms**.

… a jumpy bass line, storming rhythmic togetherness and Elton singing right out of Noddy land – bit of the stomp-along rocking. Saturday Night's Alright is the hook line which comes over and over again, and the record's alright, but not much more than that. Steve Peacock, Sounds, June 1973

Save A Prayer

ARTIST Duran Duran **RELEASE DATE** August 1982 (UK)/February 1985 (US) **WRITER** Duran Duran **PRODUCER** Colin Thurston, Nick Rhodes **LABEL** EMI (UK)/Capitol (US) **UK CHART PEAK/WEEKS** 2/9 **US CHART PEAK/WEEKS** 16/14

The outstanding cut from 1982's **Rio** album, this was Duran Duran's most successful single at the time. There had always been a strong melodic element to Duran Duran's music, but ***Save A Prayer*** stood head and shoulders above previous efforts. With its memorable synth hooks, unusual vocal harmonies and poignant story line about a brief sexual encounter, this was lush without being overpowering, and is rightly regarded as a classic.

Save The Best For Last

ARTIST Vanessa Williams **RELEASE DATE** March 1992 (UK)/February 1992 (US) **WRITER** P. Galdston, J. Lind, W. Waldman **PRODUCER** K. Thomas **LABEL** Polydor (UK)/Wing (US) **UK CHART PEAK/WEEKS** 3/11 **US CHART PEAK/WEEKS** 1/27

The first black Miss America – who had generated a certain amount of unwanted publicity after shots of her appeared in Penthouse – had majored in musical theatre, and developed her singing career with a debut album, **The Right Stuff**, in 1989, from which ***Dreamin'*** got frequent airplay. Off the follow-up album **The Comfort Zone**, ***Save the Best For Last*** became a huge ballad hit: a US Number 1 on the pop, R&B and contemporary adult charts.

After a pair of dance-oriented singles, Williams drops the tempo for this nicely orchestrated pop/soul ballad. The tune proves that she is possibly best suited to such soothing fare, as her crystalline voice is caressed by soft and wafting strings. A beautiful offering from the excellent **Comfort Zone** *collections.* Billboard, January 1992

Save The Last Dance For Me

ARTIST Drifters **RELEASE DATE** November 1960 (UK)/September 1960 (US) **WRITER** Jerome Doc Pomus, Mort Shuman **PRODUCER** Jerry Leiber, Mike Stoller **LABEL** London (UK)/Atlantic (US) **UK CHART PEAK/WEEKS** 2/18 **US CHART PEAK/WEEKS** 1/18

Contracted to put the Drifters on at Harlem's Apollo Theater, manager George Treadwell persuaded existing group the Five Crowns to rename themselves following the dissolution of Clyde McPhatter's original outfit. In lead singer Benjamin Nelson (better known as Ben E. King), they had the perfect voice for this Leiber and Stoller composition that was rumoured to have benefited from the assistance of a young Phil Spector. King left after ***Save The Last Dance For Me*** and the group went through innumerable personnel changes during their career.

Save Your Kisses For Me

ARTIST Brotherhood Of Man **RELEASE DATE** March 1976 (UK)/May 1976 (US) **WRITER** Tony Hiller, Martin Lee, Lee Sheridan **PRODUCER** – **LABEL** Pye **UK CHART PEAK/WEEKS** 1/16 **US CHART PEAK/WEEKS** 21/11

The original Brotherhood Of Man, a studio group formed by producer Tony Hiller, broke up not long after their 1970 **United We Stand** hit. Six years later, Hiller and his writing partners Lee Sheridan and Martin Lee needed an act to perform their song in the Eurovision contest. Remembering he already owned the Brotherhood Of Man's name, a new group was assembled, and Martin Lee himself sang lead on the prize-winning song that would become their 'comeback' hit.

Brotherhood of Man's ***Save All Your Kisses For Me***, *a Eurovision song contest blueprint for success, sat at the top of the charts for four weeks.* Caroline Coon, Melody Maker, January 1977

Saving All My Love For You

ARTIST Whitney Houston RELEASE DATE November 1985 (UK)/August 1985 (US) WRITER Michael Masser, Gerry Goffin PRODUCER Michael Masser LABEL Arista UK CHART PEAK/WEEKS 1/16 US CHART PEAK/WEEKS 1/22

With a pedigree including mother Cissy and aunt Dionne Warwick, Whitney Houston's singing ability was never in doubt and after numerous offers she signed to Arista in 1983. Two years later her eponymous debut album broke records worldwide for a female artist, eventually selling more than thirteen million. This yearning ballad, the second single to be extracted, hit a chord with her audience who rewarded her with a transatlantic chart-topper shortly after her 22nd birthday.

Arista trying to break an American chart-topper in England for the third or fourth time. Here the sweet-voiced girl is on a saccharine slouch with a genteel maturity that doesn't become one so young. **Gavin Martin, NME, November 1989**

Say Hello Wave Goodbye

ARTIST Soft Cell RELEASE DATE February 1982 WRITER Marc Almond, David Ball PRODUCER M. Thorne LABEL Some Bizarre UK CHART PEAK/WEEKS 3/9 US CHART PEAK/WEEKS –

After **Tainted Love** and **Bedsitter**, this, surprise, surprise, melodramatic little number was a third UK Top 5 release for art school technopopper Lancastrians Marc Almond and David Ball. The mix of sleazy synth stylings and Almond's mincing, wailing torch singer vocals was quintessential Soft Cell.

Say Say Say

ARTIST Paul McCartney RELEASE DATE October 1983 WRITER Paul McCartney, Michael Jackson PRODUCER George Martin LABEL Parlophone (UK)/Columbia (US) UK CHART PEAK/WEEKS 2/15 US CHART PEAK/WEEKS 1/22

Say Say Say was Paul McCartney's second duet with Michael Jackson. The first had been **The Girl Is Mine**, a musical argument about a girlfriend. **Say Say Say** was a tuneful ballad, making the most of each of the singers's distinctive voices. The friendship between Paul and Michael eventually went out of tune when Jackson bought the rights to McCartney's Beatles compositions.

Far closer to a Wingsoid rocker than anything that Jackson has attempted over the past few years, **Say Say Say** *packs in percussion, vocodor, and even a harmonica but still falls short of even the pitiful standard set by last year's collaboration.* **Adrian Thrills, NME, October 1983**

School Day

ARTIST Chuck Berry **RELEASE DATE** June 1957 (UK)/April 1957 (US) **WRITER** Chuck Berry **PRODUCER** – **LABEL** Columbia (UK)/Chess (US) **UK CHART PEAK/WEEKS** 24/4 **US CHART PEAK/WEEKS** 3/26

The oft-misspelled title of this song is *School Day*, singular, not to be confused with those dear old golden rule days. Chuck Berry's description of high school life resonated strongly with American youth, who bought over a million copies of the disc. It is a mark of his talent that he could capture the experience so accurately, for he was in fact 30 years old at the time, well past his own school day (s).

The controversy over the future of R & R still rages on. Some say that it's finished, others declare it's here to stay. Chuck Berry gives a boost to the latter view as he sings long live Rock 'n' Roll. That is a line from **School Day**. **Keith Fordyce, NME, June 1957**

School's Out

ARTIST Alice Cooper **RELEASE DATE** July 1972 (UK)/June 1972 (US) **WRITER** Alice Cooper, Michael Bruce **PRODUCER** Bob Ezrin **LABEL** Warner Bros. (UK)/Warner (US) **UK CHART PEAK/WEEKS** 1/12 **US CHART PEAK/WEEKS** 7/13

The name 'Alice Cooper' originally applied to an entire group, and not just its singer, Vincent Furnier. But by the time of *School's Out*,

Furnier had resigned himself to the role of 'Alice'. Not that he minded. A born showman, he constantly devised new ways to shock audiences with outrageous make-up and chicken-swallowing stunts. *School's Out*, written by Cooper with guitarist Michael Bruce, was his first Top 10 hit. He got the title from a line in a Bowery Boys film.

A dramatic, exciting production, destined to be a Number 1 hit, and one of the great rock classics. Much as I dislike them it has to be said: the record is effective. **Chris Welch, Melody Maker, July 1972**

Seasons In The Sun

ARTIST Terry Jacks **RELEASE DATE** March 1974 (UK)/January 1974 (US) **WRITER** Rod McKuen, Jacques Brel **PRODUCER** Terry Jacks **LABEL** Bell (UK & US) **UK CHART PEAK/WEEKS** 1/12 **US CHART PEAK/WEEKS** 1/21

Rejected by The Beach Boys after they had recorded a version, Terry Jacks decided to release *Seasons In The Sun* himself following the death of a friend. The reworking of what was Jacques Brel's *Le Moribond* ('The Dying Man') remained on the back burner for over a year before being issued on his own Goldfish label. It sold over six million copies worldwide. His only other UK Top 40 entry would be another Brel cover, *If You Go Away*, which reached Number 8 later the same year.

Jacks has enjoyed considerable success with **Seasons In The Sun**, *although curly-haired Terry is more than a passing reminder of the sweet voiced post Holly singers…. That in itself isn't a bad thing and it's fashionable to be old fashioned.* **Colin Irwin, Melody Maker, May 1974**

Secret Love

ARTIST Doris Day **RELEASE DATE** April 1954 **WRITER** Paul Francis Webster, Sammy Fain **PRODUCER** – **LABEL** Phillips **UK CHART PEAK/WEEKS** 1/29 **US CHART PEAK/WEEKS** –

Doris Day was on top of the entertainment world when she hit with *Secret Love* in the spring of 1954. She was not only the most popular female singer around, but also a major box office draw. *Secret Love* was featured in the film *Calamity Jane*, in which she played the title role opposite Howard Keel. It originally made Number 1 for one week, and then returned after a two-week absence, staying on top for eight more weeks.

See Emily Play

ARTIST Pink Floyd **RELEASE DATE** June 1967 **WRITER** Roger Barrett **PRODUCER** N. Smith **LABEL** Columbia **UK CHART PEAK/WEEKS** 6/12 **US CHART PEAK/WEEKS** –

The sound of the Summer of Love was crystallized perfectly in Pink Floyd's second single, *See Emily Play*. The band's enigmatic leader, Syd Barrett (born Roger), was an art school product, interested in realizing the concept of music in colour. He condensed all the trippy weirdness of the band's psychedelic stage set into three minutes of pop and scored an unlikely hit. Shortly after, Barrett left the band, suffering a breakdown, supposedly from taking too much acid; the Floyd would never sound the same again.

They are the only people doing this kind of scene, and they have a very distinctive sound. I have not heard this record before but I could tell it was Floyd almost immediately.... I wouldn't call them psychedelic, they have gone above it really. **Gary Brookes, Melody Maker, June 1967**

See My Baby Jive

ARTIST Wizzard RELEASE DATE April 1973 WRITER Roy Wood PRODUCER Roy Wood LABEL Harvest UK CHART PEAK/WEEKS 1/17 US CHART PEAK/WEEKS –

Ex-Move member and Electric Light Orchestra founder Roy Wood entrusted ELO to Jeff Lynne in 1972 and formed Wizzard as a rock 'n' roll revival vehicle for his Phil Spector-ish production numbers. Wood's larger-than-life hair and star-spangled make-up created a visual image that helped project this bouncing number and *Angel Fingers* to UK Number 1 – and *I Wish It Could Be Christmas* to its status as the other great mid-Seventies Christmas hit.

*Roy Wood's professed aim for Wizzard ... is to play all forms of music and then merge them into one.... Be awed by **See My Baby Jive**, where the group does put the pieces together to brilliant effect.* **Paul Gambaccini, Rolling Stone, July 1973**

September

ARTIST Earth, Wind & Fire RELEASE DATE December 1978 (UK)/November 1978 (US) WRITER Allee Willis, Maurice White, Albert McKay PRODUCER Maurice White LABEL CBS (UK)/April (US) UK CHART PEAK/WEEKS 3/13 US CHART PEAK/WEEKS 8/17

By 1978 Earth, Wind & Fire were safely ensconced as the most successful black group in the world, with a string of hit albums and singles in their wake. This paved the way for a **Best Of** compilation which featured a selection of new tracks, including *September*. This stood head and shoulders above the rest, and its release saw EW&F rewarded with their first UK Top 5 hit. Its success in clubs in particular was a crossover for them.

*The track is hurled into greatness by the instantly familiar ... high melody harmonies which appear to repeat **Barney Owl**.... They maintain the crispest drum sound in captivity.* **Danny Baker, NME, December 1978**

Setting Sun

ARTIST The Chemical Brothers RELEASE DATE October 1996 WRITER Tom Rowlands, Edmund Simons, Noel Gallagher PRODUCER The Chemical Brothers LABEL Junior Boys Own UK CHART PEAK/WEEKS 1/7 US CHART PEAK/WEEKS –

Tom Rowlands and Ed Simons met at Manchester University, bonding over a shared love of old-school hip-hop and My Bloody Valentine. In 1995, long-time acquaintance and fan Noel Gallagher offered to record with them. Coincidentally, they just happened to have a track lying around which they had done in the style of The Beatles' *Tomorrow Never Knows*. The rest, as they say, is electronica history.

WAAANGH WAAANGH WAAANGH! ... Jesus, it sounds like a nuclear war siren! And then KERCHUNGG!! KERCHWAAANGGG!! The drums shatter the wailing. A train has been re-routed through your front room. Through the debris a looping metallic voice intones 'You're the devil in me I brought in from the cold ...'. **Ted Kessler, NME, October 1996**

7 Seconds

ARTIST Youssou N'Dour & Neneh Cherry **RELEASE DATE** June 1994 (UK)/October 1994 (US) **WRITER – PRODUCER** J. Dollar, B. Bear **LABEL** Columbia (UK)/Chaos/Columbia (US) **UK CHART PEAK/WEEKS** 3/25 **US CHART PEAK/WEEKS** 98/4

Neneh Cherry stomped across the stage with indie-funk band Rip, Rig and Panic, but it was the **Buffalo Stance** that made her famous, a sassy, hip-hop inspired track. In 1994 she teamed up with the Senegalese artist Youssou N'Dour to record **7 Seconds**, a multilingual duet. N'Dour's voice was startlingly beautiful, a clear stream of sound that washed over the dance beat; Cherry provided a melodic counterpoint to a single that was rich and haunting.

Layers of expressive keyboards ride a submerged hip-hop beat at mid-tempo and everything is polished until you can see your reflection. The voices are pearls at 300 feet below sea level…. Subtlety is the key. **Dele Fadele, NME, June 1994**

Sex 'N' Drugs 'N' Rock 'N' Roll

ARTIST Ian Dury & The Block Heads **RELEASE DATE** August 1977 **WRITER** Ian Dury, Chas Jankel **PRODUCER** P. Jenner **LABEL** Stiff **UK CHART PEAK/WEEKS** 0/0 **US CHART PEAK/WEEKS** –

Early copies of crafty cockney Dury's debut solo album **New Boots And Panties** didn't have this classic single on them – a fault rectified later. It wasn't a hit, but it gave the Stiff label and their infamous 1977 Package Tour their ensemble encore number: a hedonistic hymn unthinkable in the AIDS-aware Nineties. The single B-side **Razzle In My Pocket**, about stealing a porno mag from the top shelf and being caught red-handed, was equally fab.

A classic if ever I have heard one, I mean with lyrics like 'Sex, Drugs and Rock 'n' Roll are all I need!' are all very good indeed, together with ludicrous references to his tailor, Simon, how could it fail? **Ian Birch, Melody Maker, September 1977**

Sexual Healing

ARTIST Marvin Gaye **RELEASE DATE** October 1982 (UK & US) **WRITER** Marvin Gaye **PRODUCER** Marvin Gaye **LABEL** CBS (UK)/Columbia (US) **UK CHART PEAK/WEEKS** 4/14 **US CHART PEAK/WEEKS** 3/21

After falling out with Motown, Marvin was coaxed back to music by CBS executive Larkin Arnold. **Sexual Healing** was a triumphant return, but in the UK it was decided the title was a little risqué and the word 'sexual' was placed in brackets. Author David Ritz was mentioned as having come up with the title but later legal action sought to prove he had been responsible for much more.

Sh-Boom (Life Could Be A Dream)

ARTIST The Crew-Cuts **RELEASE DATE** October 1954 (UK)/August 1954 (US) **WRITER** Carl & Claude Foster, James Keyes, J. Edwards, Floyd McCrae **PRODUCER** – **LABEL** Mercury (UK & US) **UK CHART PEAK/WEEKS** 12/9 **US CHART PEAK/WEEKS** 1/9

In the United States, this is generally considered the first rock 'n' roll record ever to hit Number 1. And it didn't just hit the top – it stayed there for over two months. Unfortunately, it also marked another beginning: that of white rock acts covering black acts' material and blowing the original versions off the charts. However, the Chords, who did the original Sh-Boom, held up surprisingly well in the ensuing chart battle, with their disc going all the way to Number 5.

*In my opinion **Sh-Boom** is the worst side I have listened to since I started writing in the NME several months ago. It is an American record that I understand was once in the hit parade of American best sellers.* **Geoffrey Everitt, NME, September 1954**

Shakin' All Over

ARTIST Johnny Kidd And The Pirates RELEASE DATE June 1960 WRITER Johnny Kidd, Gus Robinson PRODUCER – LABEL HMV Pop UK CHART PEAK/WEEKS 1/19 US CHART PEAK/WEEKS –

The transformation of Freddie Heath And The Nutters into Johnny Kidd And The Pirates was closely followed by their signing to HMV Records in 1959. Some minor chart action preceded their biggest hit, *Shakin' All Over*, written by Kidd and manager Gus Robinson. Despite the rhythm section jumping ship to the Tornados after two more chart entries, Kidd continued to enjoy further success, before his fatal 1966 car accident. Covered by the Guess Who, The Who and countless others, this remains a British rock landmark.

Johnny has the ability to sing in a particularly sinister fashion, with a cold approach. Which is quite an asset, because it makes a distinguishing feature with which to pick him out from other singers. A deliberate song with a steady beat that could do well. **Keith Fordyce, NME, June 1960**

She Drives Me Crazy

ARTIST Fine Young Cannibals RELEASE DATE January 1989 (UK & US) WRITER R. Gift, D. Steele PRODUCER Andy Cox, David Steele LABEL London (UK)/IRS/MCA (US) UK CHART PEAK/WEEKS 5/11 US CHART PEAK/WEEKS 1/23

This spin-off group from Birmingham 2-Tone ska discoveries The Beat did what the parent group never managed: had two chart-topping singles in the States – the second was *Good Thing*, which would peak less than three months later. Both featured the vocals of newcomer Roland Gift as well as the ex-Beat duo of Steele, who co-wrote the song, and Cox. But it was Gift's falsetto that was the selling point in a land where Al Green was still revered.

Why did they bother getting together for another LP? This is pretty weak dance fodder when compared to **Johnny Come Home** *or the stuff they did in Barry Levinson's* Tin Men, *not a hit, me thinks.* **Terry Staunton, NME, January 1989**

She Loves You

ARTIST The Beatles RELEASE DATE August 1963 (UK)/January 1964 (US) WRITER John Lennon, Paul McCartney PRODUCER George Martin LABEL Parlophone (UK)/Swan (US) UK CHART PEAK/WEEKS 1/36 US CHART PEAK/WEEKS 1/15

Number Four in The Beatles' pronoun series – *Love Me Do*, *Please Please Me*, *From Me To You* – *She Loves You* had the world

going, 'yeah, yeah, yeah!'. Written in a Newcastle-upon-Tyne hotel room, The Beatles' second Number 1 was notable for its unusual 6th-chord ending. It took some convincing to get producer George Martin to leave it in, as he thought it was 'too like the Andrews Sisters'.

The lyrics are fatuous and erratic. If this is The Beatles, they're heading downwards … although there was something about their other records that was good, they have descended to the general mire. **Clifford Beven, Melody Maker, August 1963**

She's Not There

ARTIST The Zombies RELEASE DATE August 1964 (UK)/October 1964 (US) WRITER Rod Argent PRODUCER Ken Jones, The Zombies LABEL Decca (UK)/Parrot (US) UK CHART PEAK/WEEKS 12/11 US CHART PEAK/WEEKS 2/15

Ken Jones, manager of the St Albans formed band, wanted them to produce an original number and keyboardist Rod Argent duly supplied *She's Not There*, using a minor to major chord change he'd heard on *Sealed With A Kiss*. The Zombies became part of the Brit invasion of the States. The band split in 1967 but a year later *Time Of The Season* was a million seller and Number 1 in the US and Japan – but no reunions occurred until 1997.

Mike: 'It's The Zombies or something – I heard about them recently.' Billy: 'This could be a big hit, this is very good.' Brian: 'I like it and it could be a hit – I don't know. Is that their pianist? If it is he is very good.' **The Fourmost, Melody Maker, August 1964**

Sherry

ARTIST The Four Seasons **RELEASE DATE** October 1962 (UK)/August 1962 (US) **WRITER** Bob Gaudio **PRODUCER** Bob Crewe, Frank Slay **LABEL** Stateside (UK)/Vee-Jay (US) **UK CHART PEAK/WEEKS** 8/16 **US CHART PEAK/WEEKS** 1/14

Written in a flash by Frankie Valli in the days before the tape recorder, the Four Seasons' lead singer had to keep humming the song as he drove to meet the other members. The original 'make weight' lyrics were found to be suitable, so it was released in the summer of 1962 and quickly became the first of more than 20 Top 20 entries the group would enjoy in the coming three decades.

Shiny Happy People

ARTIST R.E.M. **RELEASE DATE** May 1991 (UK)/July 1991 (US) **WRITER** Bill Berry, Peter Buck, Mike Mills, Michael Stipe **PRODUCER** Scott Litt, R.E.M. **LABEL** Warner Bros. (UK)/Warner (US) **UK CHART PEAK/WEEKS** 6/11 **US CHART PEAK/WEEKS** 10/15

R.E.M. lead singer Michael Stipe was a friend of Kate Pierson's of The B-52s from way back. She was the first-ever guest vocalist on an R.E.M. record: *Shiny Happy People*. 'We keen together,' Stipe commented. 'We both have these high, keening voices and incredible lungs and we can just go on and on forever.' The recording went so well that she added backing vocals to two other tracks on the hugely successful **Out Of Time** album.

When we started out the average radio listeners would have found us totally unapproachable. Now we have **Shiny Happy People** *which is so relentlessly upbeat that you want to throw up.... Sometimes it feels good to do something naive.* **Peter Buch, NME, June 1991**

Should I Stay Or Should I Go

ARTIST The Clash **RELEASE DATE** September 1982 (UK)/July 1982 (US) **WRITER** The Clash **PRODUCER** The Clash **LABEL** CBS (UK)/Epic (US) **UK CHART PEAK/WEEKS** 17/9 **US CHART PEAK/WEEKS** 45/13

For a band that raged against capitalism and conformity, it is ironic that The Clash's only Number 1 hit the top as a result of being featured in a Levi's jeans commercial. *Should I Stay Or Should I Go*, from the Clash's most successful album, **Combat Rock**, peaked at Number 17 when it was first released, in 1982. Although it barely edged into the US Top 50, it has continued to receive a lot of airplay on American radio.

Shout

ARTIST Tears For Fears **RELEASE DATE** December 1984 (UK)/June 1985 (US) **WRITER** Roland Orzabal/Ian Stanley **PRODUCER** Chris Hughes **LABEL** Mercury (UK & US) **UK CHART PEAK/WEEKS** 4/16 **US CHART PEAK/WEEKS** 1/19

On their second album, **Songs From The Big Chair**, Roland Orzabal and Curt Smith found their most successful mix of synths, hook lines and literate lyrics. The previous album had produced three Top 5 hits in the UK, but this was their US breakthrough: after *Everybody Wants To Rule The World*, **Shout** delivered a second consecutive US Number 1.

Former wimp boys make a second tough single.... Shock! Like **Mothers Talk** *this is something of a chant, but it has its power and presence. Very soon it could actually be respectable to say you like Tears For Fears.* **Ian Pye, Melody Maker, November 1984**

Show Me Heaven

ARTIST Maria McKee **RELEASE DATE** September 1990 **WRITER** Maria McKee, Jay Rifkin, Eric Rackin **PRODUCER** P. Asher **LABEL** Epic **UK CHART PEAK/WEEKS** 1/14 **US CHART PEAK/WEEKS** 0/0

Maria McKee's voice called and sighed and soared in this power driven ballad. McKee's band, Lone Justice, put youth and energy back into the country music scene in America, but her solo album

hadn't done so well. She relocated to Ireland and was sent the tape of a song intended for the new Tom Cruise film. She only agreed to record it if she could change the lyrics. The result was an overwhelmingly emotive love song, and the theme tune for *Days Of Thunder*.

The sort of musical Budweiser which we really oughtn't to be taking seriously, if you ask me. Soundtrack to a film and it shows.… As for Maria: 'If you know what it is to dream a dream/Then hold my hand tight' – Ugh! Always a mistake to listen to lyrics. **David Stubbs, Melody Maker, 1990**

The Show Must Go On

ARTIST Queen RELEASE DATE October 1991 WRITER Queen PRODUCER D. Richards, Queen LABEL Parlophone UK CHART PEAK/WEEKS 16/10 US CHART PEAK/WEEKS 0/0

Innuendo entered the UK charts at Number 1 at the same time that rumours of Freddie Mercury's AIDS sickness were spreading.

The release of the single from the album, *The Show Must Go On*, – with its bleak lyrics 'Inside my heart is breaking/My make-up may be flaking/But my smile still stays on' – coincided with Mercury's death at the age of 45, making its chart entry a certainty.

*… Laugh? Sob? Queen hip? … this is f***ing Wagner for 1991 mate.* **Chris Roberts, Melody Maker, February 1991**

Side Saddle

ARTIST Russ Conway RELEASE DATE February 1959 WRITER Trevor Stanford PRODUCER – LABEL Columbia UK CHART PEAK/WEEKS 1/30 US CHART PEAK/WEEKS –

When Russ Conway was in the Royal Navy an accident with a bread slicer lost him the first joint of the third finger of his right hand. He was, however, still able to play the piano, so well that he was signed to EMI in 1957 as a sort of white male Winifred Atwell. He quickly established his own style with *Side Saddle*, the first of a string of hits.

Ross offers a composition by Terry Stanford. Once again it's light-hearted piano entertainment intended to induce a cheerful mood, which it does quite easily. Whether it induces one to buy the record, I'm not so sure. **Keith Fordyce, NME, January 1959**

The Sign

ARTIST Ace Of Base RELEASE DATE February 1994 (UK)/January 1994 (US) WRITER Jonas 'Joker' Bergren PRODUCER D. Pop LABEL London (UK)/Arista (US) UK CHART PEAK/WEEKS 2/16 US CHART PEAK/WEEKS 1/41

A Swedish quartet built around the Bergren siblings, Ace Of Base received countless comparisons to their country's Seventies supergroup, Abba. In truth, while their biggest-selling disc, *The Sign*, bore similarity to Abba's *One of Us*, the reggae-inspired dance group was very much a product of the Nineties. *The Sign* became Arista Records' most successful Billboard chart single in the label's history. It sold over nine million copies in America, in addition to topping charts around the world.

Year after year, some Euro-group or other is catapulted over from Malmo, or in Ace Of Base's case, Gothenburg and land … at the top of the British charts. Our Euro neighbours know the secret of a hit single, you see. Pop is instinctive and spontaneous. **Martin Townsend, Vox, August 1993**

Sign Your Name

ARTIST Terence Trent D'Arby **RELEASE DATE** January 1988 (UK)/May 1988 (US) **WRITER** Terence Trent D'Arby **PRODUCER** Martyn Ware, Terence Trent D'Arby **LABEL** CBS (UK)/Columbia (US) **UK CHART PEAK/WEEKS** 2/10 **US CHART PEAK/WEEKS** 4/21

Trent D'Arby left the US Army with plenty of cocky confidence. He signed to CBS in 1986 off a strong demo. His first single **If You Let Me Stay** reached the UK Number 10, followed by **Wishing Well** which made US Number 1 and UK Number 4. The romantic ballad **Sign Your Name**, also taken from his debut album **Hardline**, was only kept off the top of the UK charts by Belinda Carlisle's **Heaven Is A Place On Earth**.

Tel dips once more into the deep 'n' mysterious wishing well for this near-oriental beat. 'The Thought just caved me in,' he coos, and it's enough to give you butterflies. That voice! Those Peepers! **Bob Stanley, NME, January 1988**

Sincerely

ARTIST The McGuire Sisters **RELEASE DATE** July 1955 (UK)/January (US) **WRITER** Harry Fuqua, Alan Freed **PRODUCER** – **LABEL** Vogue Coral (UK & US) **UK CHART PEAK/WEEKS** 14/4 **US CHART PEAK/WEEKS** 1/21

The McGuire Sisters sang light-hearted songs which they delivered in neat, crisp, vocal harmony style. They actually were sisters and their ambition was to have a hit record and remain inseparable. The hit came with **Sincerely**. It was a cover version of a Moonglows record, a black rhythm and blues number which had been a huge smash on the streets of New York.

Singing The Blues

ARTIST Guy Mitchell **RELEASE DATE** December 1956 (UK)/October 1956 (US) **WRITER** Melvin Endsley **PRODUCER** – **LABEL** Philips (UK)/Columbia (US) **UK CHART PEAK/WEEKS** 1/22 **US CHART PEAK/WEEKS** 1/26

Guy Mitchell could have been a typical big voiced balladeer, slicking out in middle of the road sentimentality. But he had a joshing good humour that sparkled through his notes. His **Singing The Blues** does not sound sad and bluesy: his is a more dapper kind of melancholy, with chirpy whistles and a shruggy 'ah well' tone of voice. Ray Conniff's Orchestra adds oomph with the strings.

*'Mitchell is enjoying one of his quickest moving hits in quite a while,' reports the latest Billboard … **Singing The Blues** – a new song with an old title … Anyhow, we'll be watching the progress with interest….* **Rex Morton, NME, October 1956**

Sir Duke

ARTIST Stevie Wonder **RELEASE DATE** April 1977 (UK & US) **WRITER** Stevie Wonder **PRODUCER** Stevie Wonder **LABEL** Motown (UK)/Tamla (US) **UK CHART PEAK/WEEKS** 2/9 **US CHART PEAK/WEEKS** 1/17

Songs In The Key Of Life was the album that Wonder produced after renewing his Motown contract for the then record fee of $13 million. The all-star jazz horns he brought in were in their element on this tribute to Duke Ellington and other jazz pioneers, so imaginatively arranged that the 16 repeats of 'You can feel it all over' didn't grate. It was stopped from becoming a double Number 1 by Deniece Williams' **Free** in the UK.

No question about it: the texture here is a sound perfectionist's dream, but the song, if it didn't have the Wonder star-making machine behind it, would be dismissed by most as the worst soul-less disco drivel. A hit. **Caroline Coon, Melody Maker, April 1977**

Sit Down

ARTIST James **RELEASE DATE** March 1991 **WRITER** Tim Booth, Larry Gott, Jim Glennie, Gavan Whelan **PRODUCER** S. Power **LABEL** Fontana **UK CHART PEAK/WEEKS** 2/10 **US CHART PEAK/WEEKS** –

Manchester band James had their biggest hit, **Sit Down**, in their set as early as 1988. When the catchy indie anthem ended up nestling behind Chesney Hawkes' **The One And Only** in the April 1991 UK chart, **Gold Mother** was promptly withdrawn 11 months after first appearing. Tim Booth and friends could not come up with anything quite as compelling again.

You can hear the thugs yelling it now 'Oi, that's that poof James whatsit. Hallo James, thassit! I can dance better'n what you can. Oi siddown, Oi siddown!' The confessional Tim Booth will have a new set of problems to discover, confront and write about soon. **Ian McCann, NME, April 1991**

Sixteen Tons

ARTIST Tennessee Ernie Ford **RELEASE DATE** January 1956 (UK)/November 1955 (US) **WRITER** Merle Travis **PRODUCER** – **LABEL** Capitol (UK & US) **UK CHART PEAK/WEEKS** 1/11 **US CHART PEAK/WEEKS** 1/22

Written by country and western star Merle Travis in 1947 and based on his coalminer father, whose favourite saying, 'Another day older and deeper in debt,' became part of the catchy chorus. *Sixteen Tons* was Tennessee Ernie Ford's second UK and only US chart-topping single. Already a regular on daytime television, Ford's high profile undoubtedly aided the song's meteoric rise as it shifted over a million copies in less than a month.

Capitol records have signed Tennessee Ernie Ford to a solid five year contract at maximum royalty – six months before his existing pact expires … Sixteen Tons has already passed the two million mark in the States. British sales are likely to add a further half million. **The Alley Cat, NME, January 1956**

Slave To The Rhythm

ARTIST Grace Jones **RELEASE DATE** October 1985 **WRITER** Bruce Woolley, Simon Darrow, Stephen Lipon, Trevor Horn **PRODUCER** Trevor Horn **LABEL** ZTT (UK) Manhattan (US) **UK CHART PEAK/WEEKS** 12/8 **US CHART PEAK/WEEKS** 0/0

Grace Jones began as a model, drifted into films, flirted with music, went back to music and returned to films again, always leaving the impression of unfinished business. While her early disco recordings were unremarkable, a blossoming ability as a songwriter in her own right paid higher dividends. *Slave To The Rhythm* was superbly overseen by producer Trevor Horn and should have heralded Grace's arrival as a major player in the music stakes, but all too soon she drifted off to pursue other interests.

Great track – a watchful prowl made exquisite with all the right things: wafty drums fill the air, plenty of space for the rhythm guitar to roam in, general air of purring confidence – though how it took four people to write it is a bit of a teaser. **Adam Sweeting, Melody Maker, October 1985**

Sledgehammer

ARTIST Peter Gabriel **RELEASE DATE** April 1986 (UK)/May 1986 (US) **WRITER** Peter Gabriel **PRODUCER** Peter Gabriel, Daniel Lanois **LABEL** Virgin (UK)/Geffen (US) **UK CHART PEAK/WEEKS** 9/11 **US CHART PEAK/WEEKS** 1/21

By the mid Eighties the distinction between the music and the accompanying video had all but disappeared, making it increasingly difficult to assess one without the other. Rarely, though, was sound and vision of a sufficiently high standard to make the

distinction unnecessary: but *Sledgehammer* is a case in point – the superb song stands perfectly well on its own, but its vivid images were interpreted via a brilliant combination of stop-frame animation and photographic images which made this an unforgettable audio-visual treat.

Something is up in Pete's world of silly monkey make-up and arch gestures – he has been played a Phil Collins record, and he has watched amazed as his little bearded chum, the cheery little drummer from halcyon days of sell-out college gigs, has turned into every Renault Five's cassette pet. **David Quantich, NME, April 1986**

Sloop John B

ARTIST The Beach Boys **RELEASE DATE** April 1966 (UK & US) **WRITER** Brian Wilson **PRODUCER** Brian Wilson **LABEL** Capitol (UK & US) **UK CHART PEAK/WEEKS** 2/15 **US CHART PEAK/WEEKS** 3/11

Beach Boy Al Jardine made no secret of his love of folk music. He tried to get the group to record the traditional *Sloop John B* for a couple of years before they finally acquiesced. As usual, Brian Wilson rose to the task, giving the song a dense arrangement with an ear-catching acapella break. While Capitol was thrilled to see it become a runaway hit, Wilson was somewhat less pleased when the label insisted he include it on the group's next album, **Pet Sounds**.

It's a knock out man – a knock out! Beach Boys great…. They are the best group in America. **Christian St Peters, Melody Maker, April 1966**

Smells Like Teen Spirit

ARTIST Nirvana **RELEASE DATE** November 1991 (UK)/December 1991 (US) **WRITER** K. Cobain, Nirvana **PRODUCER** Butch Vig **LABEL** DGC (UK & US) **UK CHART PEAK/WEEKS** 7/6 **US CHART PEAK/WEEKS** 6/20

Smells Like Teen Spirit fixed a fine melodic sensibility to the battering ram of heavy metal chords, and the song exploded into the UK charts at the end of 1991. The success of the single and the album **Nevermind** confirmed the 'grunge' sound of bands from Seattle as rock's Next Big Thing. But it also exposed Cobain to the pressures of stardom that would ultimately play a part in his suicide in April 1994.

… you start wondering if the world's turned mad, that people like Axl and Farrell and the Cure can only dig something so poppy, as puritanical, as passionate as this. **Everett True, Melody Maker, November 1991**

Smoke On The Water

ARTIST Deep Purple **RELEASE DATE** April 1977 (UK)/May 1973 (US) **WRITER** Richard Black-More, Ian Gillian, Roger Glover, Jon Lord, Ian Paice **PRODUCER** Deep Purple **LABEL** Purple (UK)/Warner (US) **UK CHART PEAK/WEEKS** 21/2 **US CHART PEAK/WEEKS** 4/16

Smoke On the Water is based on the true story of an incident that happened in December 1971 at a concert at the Montreux Casino where Deep Purple shared the bill with Frank Zappa's Mothers of Invention. A fire broke out while the Mothers were on, burning the building to the ground. The song was a hit in America in 1972 and gained attention again 25 years later when Pat Boone put it in a lounge setting.

Now this is something the Chelsea shed boys could really get their feet into. If smashing in Luton store fronts is now considered de rigueur, Purple's posthumous maxi-single (all live cuts) will have them laying into OAPs in no time. **Monty Smith, NME, April 1977**

Smooth Operator

ARTIST Sade **RELEASE DATE** September 1984 (UK)/March 1985 (US) **WRITER** Helen Folasade Adu, Ray St John **PRODUCER** Robin Millar **LABEL** Epic (UK)/Portrait (US) **UK CHART PEAK/WEEKS** 19/10 **US CHART PEAK/WEEKS** 5/20

Helen Folasade Adu, a Nigerian studying at St Martin's School of Art in London, co-wrote this track for her band Arriva, and it featured in their live set around 1980. Three years later, she had a solo deal with CBS/Epic and had already reached UK Number 6 with her debut single *Your Love Is King*. She revived *Smooth Operator*, and Sade's sultry vocal attitude and the song's sax-edged bossa feel caught the UK's mid-Eighties imagination.

The Feline Latin pulse is very nice, and so is the greasy introductory Saxophone. Sade also sings quite a bit better that pop-stars are supposed to. **Adam Sweeting, Melody Maker, September 1984**

The Smurf Song

ARTIST Father Abraham And The Smurfs **RELEASE DATE** June 1978 **WRITER** Pierre Kartner **PRODUCER** – **LABEL** Decca **UK CHART PEAK/WEEKS** 2/17 **US CHART PEAK/WEEKS** –

The Smurfs are small blue gnome-like creatures created by Pierre Payo Culliford in 1958 for a comic strip. The song was written by Pierre Kartner and in 1978 became a huge hit all over Europe. BP then obtained the UK rights to use them in their advertising campaign. The record spent six weeks at Number 2, being unable to shift Travolta and Newton-John, but had the consolation of being the year's fifth best-selling single. The Smurfs resurfaced to terrorize another generation in the Nineties.

Incidentally, what's green, goes 'smuuuuurf' and travels backwards at 100 miles an hour? A smurf's runny nose. **Bob Edmonds, NME, December 1978**

Solitaire

ARTIST Andy Williams **RELEASE DATE** May 1974 **WRITER** Neil Sedaka, Phil Cody **PRODUCER** Richard Perry **LABEL** CBS (UK)/Columbia (US) **UK CHART PEAK/WEEKS** 4/18 **US CHART PEAK/WEEKS** 0/0

The only game in town for Andy Williams was smooth crooning, which brought him huge worldwide album sales. He started off his singles chart career with 1956's **Canadian Sunset**, continued with hits like **Can't Get Used To Losing You** (a US Number 2) and ended it with this lonesome lost-love ballad, written by Neil Sedaka, and re-covered in 1983 by New Yorker Laura Branigan.

It has the melodic strength, opulence and percussive force to be a monster…. Behind all the glitter, however, Andy Williams' singing is as bland as ever. He is Mr Relaxation for Mr and Mrs America…. **Stephen Holden, Rolling Stone, December 1973**

Somebody To Love

ARTIST Queen **RELEASE DATE** November 1976 (UK & US) **WRITER** Freddie Mercury **PRODUCER** Roy Thomas Baker **LABEL** EMI (UK)/Elektra (US) **UK CHART PEAK/WEEKS** 2/9 **US CHART PEAK/WEEKS** 13/15

Somebody To Love has something of the flavour of a rock barber-shop quartet song – of which no doubt Freddie Mercury was well aware when he inserted his credit: 'vocal, piano, Choir Meister, Tantrums' on the sleeve of the album **A Day At The Races**, from which the single came. Like the album's highly successful predecessor, **A Night At The Opera**, it was a homage to the Marx Brothers and, also like its predecessor, it topped the UK album chart.

Surprisingly, although this single is about love, Freddie darling does sound as if he is having great difficulty finding it. The feel is reassuringly churchy, but it is more Black gospel than Catholic Cathedral. **Caroline Coon, Melody Maker, November 1976**

Softly, Softly

ARTIST Ruby Murray **RELEASE DATE** January 1955 **WRITER** Pierre Dudan, Paddy Roberts, Mark Paul **PRODUCER** – **LABEL** Columbia **UK CHART PEAK/WEEKS** 1/22 **US CHART PEAK/WEEKS** –

Ruby Murray was a Belfast charmer who crooned out reassuring ballads in the years when women sang with restrained delivery and in lavish dresses. Many of her songs had an Irish theme, **Danny Boy** and **When Irish Eyes Are Smiling**, but her real forte was heartfelt melodies all about love. **Softly, Softly** was a clean sentimental tune, sung with a whispery air, backed by a lush orchestra and was eminently suitable as family entertainment.

*Released this month, **Softly, Softly** has already reached ninth position in the NME's chart of best selling records. Ruby is no fly-by-night success. She has personality, style and a whole heap of talent.* **Pip Wedge, NME, January 1955**

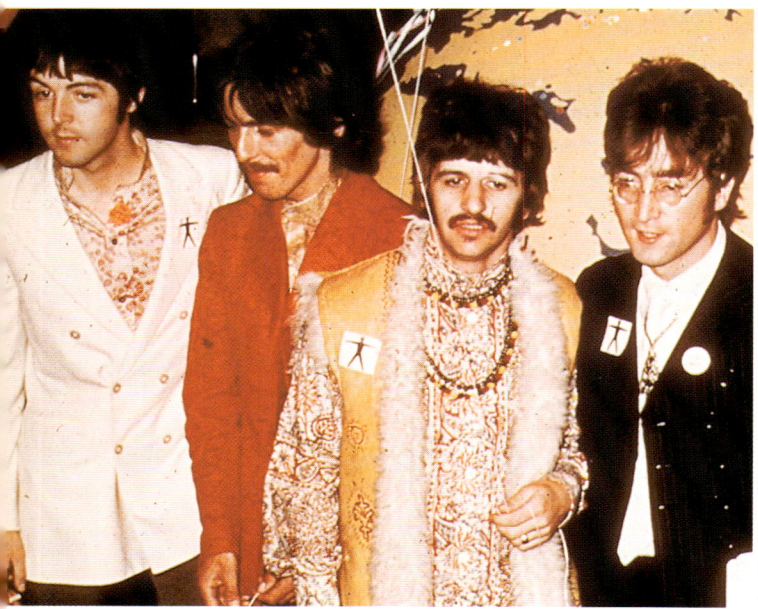

Something/Come Together

ARTIST The Beatles RELEASE DATE November 1969 (UK)/October 1969 (US) WRITER George Harrison PRODUCER George Martin LABEL Apple (UK & US) UK CHART PEAK/WEEKS 4/12 US CHART PEAK/WEEKS 3/16

Something, the first Beatles A-side penned by George Harrison, was an instant classic. One of The Beatles's most covered tunes, it was even done by Frank Sinatra, who called it the greatest love song of the past 50 years. The flip, **Come Together** (the A-side in the States), was a song that John Lennon built around Chuck Berry's **You Can't Catch Me**, a fact which later caused Lennon much grief when Berry's publisher sued him.

What I was waiting for was the guitar solo because George Harrison is just about the only guitar player I know of who can play a solo so it doesn't sound as though it is planned, and I like the drummer – whoever he is. **Keef Hartley, Melody Maker, November 1969**

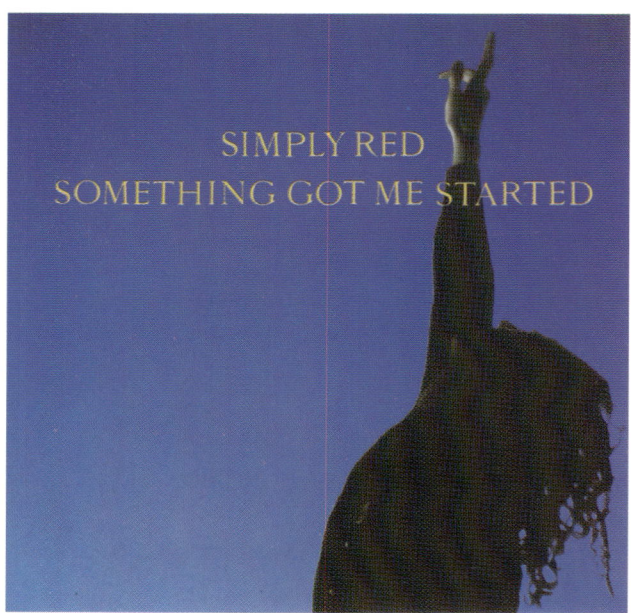

Someone, Someone

ARTIST Brian Poole And The Tremeloes RELEASE DATE May 1964 (UK)/September 1964 (US) WRITER Violet Petty, Edwin Greines PRODUCER Mike Smith LABEL Decca (UK)/Monument (US) UK CHART PEAK/WEEKS 2/17 US CHART PEAK/WEEKS 97/2

Rivals of The Searchers and Freddie And The Dreamers and part of the early 60s British beat movement, Brian Poole and the Tremeloes were signed to Decca in favour of The Beatles. Their version of the former Crickets B-side, **Someone, Someone**, was a wistful, sentimental ballad that just missed out on the top slot in May 1964. Surprisingly, the Tremeloes enjoyed greater success as a group in their own right after Poole's departure in 1966. His daughters, Karen and Shelley, would later burst into the charts in the mid-1990s as the Dave Stewart-produced Alisha's Attic.

I did not know that it was Brian, but I think it will be a big hit for him. It is a smashing song and he does it well. It's great to see him experimenting with different types of stuff. **Ray Ennis, Melody Maker, May 1964**

Somethin' Stupid

ARTIST Frank & Nancy Sinatra RELEASE DATE March 1967 (UK & US) WRITER Carson Parks PRODUCER J. Bower, Lee Hazlewood LABEL Reprise (UK & US) UK CHART PEAK/WEEKS 1/18 US CHART PEAK/WEEKS 1/13

Both father and daughter had enjoyed transatlantic Number 1 hits in just under a year and a half – Frank with **Strangers In The Night** and Nancy with **These Boots Are Made For Walking**. This cute piece of MOR, an early example of eight-track recording, gave them both another Number 1. Sinatra senior was really only guesting on the song, but by the end of the song his performance, not surprisingly, dominated proceedings.

*I do not know why he is doing it – he doesn't need the money. He had some beautiful records out before **Strangers In The Night** and my God he went mad after that.* **Scott Walker, Melody Maker, March 1967**

Something Got Me Started

ARTIST Simply Red RELEASE DATE September 1991 (UK & US) WRITER Mick Hucknall, Fritz McIntyre PRODUCER Steve Levine LABEL East West (UK & US) UK CHART PEAK/WEEKS 11/8 US CHART PEAK/WEEKS 23/14

After the release of a, for some, too MOR cover version of **If You Don't Know Me By Now**, Simply Red came back on song, following a year or so off, with the album **Stars**, opening the album with the massive groove, from long time Hucknall aide Fritz McIntyre's keyboard, and insistently repeated chorus line of 'Something Got Me Started'. The album was a gold mine: three other hits came off it.

So wrapped up is Mick Hucknall in the self-professed brilliance of his voice, that you can just imagine him running to his manager with a copy of The Three Tenors and saying, 'What do they mean Three? Where was my invite?' **Martin Townsend, Vox, September 1991**

Something In The Air

ARTIST Thunderclap Newman RELEASE DATE June 1969 (UK)/September 1969 (US) WRITER John Keene PRODUCER Pete Townshend LABEL Track (UK & US) UK CHART PEAK/WEEKS 1/12 US CHART PEAK/WEEKS 37/10

Thunderclap Newman was the creation of Pete Townshend. He pulled together bearded trad jazz pianist Andy Newman, a whizz-kid on guitar, 16-year-old Jimmy McCulloch, and a singer-songwriter-drummer who used to roadie for John Mayall – John Keen. The Who guitarist engineered and arranged the track, which went to Number 1 in the UK. But the band couldn't deliver live and within a year they were filed under 'One Hit Wonders' – but a wonderful wonder all the same.

Simply, **Something In The Air** knocks me out, as does its flip, the Newman-himself-composed **Wihelminia**: a polka-based drinking song in which T/Clap proves to have a marveilously clumsy Ringo Starrish voice and sense of humour. **John Mendelson, Rolling Stone, October 1969**

Something's Gotten Hold Of My Heart

ARTIST Marc Almond With Gene Pitney RELEASE DATE January 1989 WRITER Roger Cook, Roger Greenaway PRODUCER B. Kraushaar LABEL Parlophone UK CHART PEAK/WEEKS 1/12 US CHART PEAK/WEEKS 0/0

Marc Almond originally invited Gene Pitney to make a brief cameo on his cover of Pitney's 1968 hit **Something's Gotten Hold of My Heart**. The legendary American singer was so enthused that Almond asked him to share lead vocals. Incredibly, while the disc was Number 1 in the UK and many other countries, EMI refused to release it in Pitney's home country. reasoning that, since America's youth were unfamiliar with Almond and Pitney, they would think it was a gay love duet.

To tell the truth, I'm not too keen on anyone trying Gene Pitney songs, although I have been known to attempt **Town Without Pity** myself while waiting for a cab in Harlesden with nought but a half empty bottle of flat Dos Equis for company. **Terry Staunton, NME, January 1989**

Somewhere My Love

ARTIST The Mike Sammes Singers RELEASE DATE September 1966 WRITER Paul Francis Webster, Maurice Jarre PRODUCER – LABEL HMV Pop UK CHART PEAK/WEEKS 14/38 US CHART PEAK/WEEKS –

At the heart of David Lean's 1965 epic Doctor Zhivago was a tumultuous affair between Zhivago (Omar Sharif) and Lara (Julie Christie) – the lilting song used as a leitmotif for their relationship is perhaps better known as **Lara's Theme**. It became a UK hit for the Mike Sammes Singers, regular purveyors of MOR backing vocals for recording sessions and BBC light entertainment shows, seeing off a rival interpretation from Manuel And His Music Of The Mountains. In the States, a version by songwriter Ray Conniff reached the Top 10.

MARC ALMOND

Somethings Gotten Hold Of My Heart

Featuring Special Guest Star

GENE PITNEY

Son Of A Preacher Man

ARTIST Dusty Springfield RELEASE DATE December 1968 (UK)/November 1968 (US) WRITER John Hurley, Ronnie Wilkins PRODUCER Tom Dowd, Arif Mardin, Jerry Wexler LABEL Philips (UK)/Atlantic (US) UK CHART PEAK/WEEKS 9/9 US CHART PEAK/WEEKS 10/12

Taken from what many considered her best ever recording session – in Memphis with the pick of the local musicians – **Son Of A Preacher Man** was Springfield's last hit until she teamed up with the Pet Shop Boys for 1987's **What Have I Done To Deserve This**. The production team included Jerry Wexler, who had been responsible for many of Atlantic's finest R&B moments.

It's a medium slow and very bluesy ballad, in which our gal is backed by gospel-ish chanting. This is Dusty at her very best, though maybe not at her most commercial. I feel confident that it will be a hit. **Derek Johnson, NME, November 1968**

Son Of My Father

ARTIST Chicory Tip RELEASE DATE January 1972 (UK)/March 1972 (US) WRITER Georgio Moroder, Pete Bellotte, Michael Holme PRODUCER Giorgio Moroder LABEL CBS (UK)/Epic (US) UK CHART PEAK/WEEKS 1/13 US CHART PEAK/WEEKS 91/3

Son of My Father was originally a European hit for Giorgio Moroder, the Italian producer who would later become the king of Eurodisco. His early solo singles had a California bubble gum feel, like the Beach Boys crossed with the Ohio Express. Chicory Tip's note-for-note cover prevented him from having a UK hit with this song. Their version was the first Number 1 to feature a synthesizer, in this case a Moog, played by engineer/future star producer Chris Thomas.

An immensely catchy number with an infectious hand-clapping beat, it also has an irresistible sing-along hook chorus, and probably the biggest sales factor of all is the nagging and insistent riff that runs through it. **Derek Johnson, NME, January 1972**

Song For Guy

ARTIST Elton John RELEASE DATE December 1978 WRITER Elton John PRODUCER Elton John, Clive Franks LABEL Rocket UK CHART PEAK/WEEKS 4/10 US CHART PEAK/WEEKS 0/0

Like *Candle In The Wind*, this was another of Elton's songs about a real person – Guy Burchett, a motorcycle messenger who worked for Elton's record label Rocket and who was killed in an accident at the age of 17. The single, a haunting piano instrumental apart from a few lyrics at the end, made the UK

Top 5 in 1978 and was featured on his LP **A Single Man**, which was released the same year.

A tasteful, reverent tribute to one of Elton's employees killed in a road accident…. The catchy bit comes right at the end, when Elton intones the opinion that 'Life isn't everything'; as for eternal life – it is OK but it does go on a bit. **Bob Edmonds, NME, December 1978**

Sorry Seems To Be The Hardest Word

ARTIST Elton John RELEASE DATE November 1976 (UK & US) WRITER Elton John PRODUCER Gus Dudgeon, Elton John LABEL Rocket (UK)/MCA/Rocket (US) UK CHART PEAK/WEEKS 11/10 US CHART PEAK/WEEKS 6/14

This haunting ballad first appeared on the double LP **Blue Moves**, the promotion party for which involved the guests drinking blue liquids and eating blue food. The song followed his recent Number 1 with Kiki Dee, ***Don't Go Breaking My Heart***, into the US charts and became his tenth US Top 10 single there. It also became a concert favourite, and one such version was featured on the B-side of his 1987 'live' recording of ***Candle In The Wind***.

Elton's new single is so ludicrous – piano-strings-and-heartbroken-quavery – that I nearly drowned in my own tears…. **Charles Shaar Murray, NME, November 1976**

Soul Man

ARTIST Sam And Dave RELEASE DATE November 1967 (UK)/September 1967 (US) WRITER Isaac Hayes, David Porter PRODUCER Isaac Hayes, David Porter LABEL Stax (UK & US) UK CHART PEAK/WEEKS 24/14 US CHART PEAK/WEEKS 2/15

Brought up on a diet of gospel music, Sam And Dave went for secular fame, but only clicked when a move to Atlantic/Stax teamed them with songwriters Isaac Hayes and David Porter. When the word soul became voguish, Hayes and Porter created ***Soul Man***, the duo's first Top 10 and a Grammy-winning release. The Blues Brothers 1979 version gave them a career boost, and Sam re-recorded the number with Lou Reed for the 1986 film *Soul Man*.

*Once Sam And Dave succeed in registering a hit in Britain, I reckon they will be here to stay, because they have few, if any, equals as R&B duetists. **Soul Man** has not much tune to it, but it's loaded with feeling – thoroughly groovy.* **Derek Johnson, NME, September 1967**

The Sound Of Silence

ARTIST Simon & Garfunkel **RELEASE DATE** November 1965 **WRITER** Paul Simon **PRODUCER** Tom Wilson, Paul Simon **LABEL** CBS (UK)/Columbia (US) **UK CHART PEAK/WEEKS** 0/0 **US CHART PEAK/WEEKS** 1/14

Lacklustre sales on the act's 1964 debut album **Wednesday Morning 3am** split the pair, Simon crossing to the UK for a series of folk gigs. In his absence producer Tom Wilson heard that a Boston radio station was giving the track *The Sound Of Silence* airplay. He re-mixed the song, adding drums, bass and guitar, and lo and behold, the Simon & Garfunkel folk-rock sound was born. A swift return to the States by Simon and reunion with Garfunkel followed.

Folk Singers Paul Simon and Art Garfunkel presenting their big American hit written by Simon. A moving, depthy disc with some Byrds-type guitar accompaniment. Interesting harmonies and backing might make this a popular record in English Folk circles. **Melody Maker, December 1965**

Space Oddity

ARTIST David Bowie **RELEASE DATE** September 1969 (UK)/January 1973 (US) **WRITER** David Bowie **PRODUCER** Gus Dudgeon **LABEL** Philips (UK)/RCA Victor (US) **UK CHART PEAK/WEEKS** 5/14 **US CHART PEAK/WEEKS** 15/14

The title of Bowie's first hit was a twist on *2001: A Space Odyssey*. He first recorded it for a short film he was making, but Mercury Records got wind of it and invited him to re-cut it for release as a single. Produced by Gus Dudgeon, later famous for his work with Elton John, it hit Number 5 in 1969. When it was reissued six years later, after Bowie had become a superstar, it made it to Number 1.

Mr Bowie has never really surfaced from his own underground line. This Bee Geeian piece of music and poetry is beautifully written, sung and performed. Strangely, it could be a hit and escalate Bowie to the top. **Chris Welch, Melody Maker, July 1969**

Spaceman

ARTIST Babylon Zoo **RELEASE DATE** January 1996 **WRITER** Jas Mann **PRODUCER** Jas Mann, S. Power **LABEL** EMI **UK CHART PEAK/WEEKS** 1/14 **US CHART PEAK/WEEKS** –

Jas Mann formed Babylon Zoo – essentially a studio group centred around himself – after the demise of his high school band, the Sandkings. Their debut single, the techno-glam pastiche *Spaceman*, was bookended by sped-up vocals reminiscent of the Chipmunks. It reportedly sold 250,000 copies throughout Europe within its first week of release, making it EMI's fastest selling single since The Beatles's **She Loves You**.

All together now, consumers 'Spaaaaaacemennnnnn' to the sound of some overproduced we-are-melanik-dancing-syndromes, woorgly voices and even more woorgly synths. Hands up those who think superior life forms really want to hear more Gary Numan. **Jennifer Nine, Melody Maker, January 1996**

Spanish Flea

ARTIST Herb Alpert And The Tijuana Brass **RELEASE DATE** December 1965 (UK)/March 1966 (US) **WRITER** Julius Wechter **PRODUCER** – **LABEL** Pye Int. (UK)/A&M (US) **UK CHART PEAK/WEEKS** 3/20 **US CHART PEAK/WEEKS** 27/7

Spanish Flea, the first and biggest UK smash for Herb Alpert And The Tijuana Brass in January 1966, did not hit in Alpert's home country until four months later, after it was used as the theme for the popular TV show *The Dating Game*. The song was written by Alpert's labelmate Julius Wechter, who had some success as the marimba-playing leader of the Baja Marimba Band.

*Herb Alpert (Pye), and his Tijuana Brass Band make exciting instrumental tracks of lollipops and roses, butter ball, green peppers, love potion. **Spanish Flea** is their first in England.* **Allen Evans, NME, January 1966**

Spanish Harlem/First Taste Of Love

ARTIST Ben E. King **RELEASE DATE** February 1961 (UK)/December 1960 (US) **WRITER** Jerry Leiber, Phil Spector **PRODUCER** Jerry Leiber, Phil Spector **LABEL** London (UK)/Atco (US) **UK CHART PEAK/WEEKS** 27/11 **US CHART PEAK/WEEKS** 10/16

Born Benjamin Nelson, the singer decided to change his name when he joined The Drifters, and having clocked up three years in that well-known vocal group the equally legendary producer Phil Spector worked closely with him after he went solo in 1960. He co-wrote and co-produced the track *Spanish Harlem* which gave King his first solo US Top 10 hit. It was covered and made the UK Top 20 for Jimmy Justice in 1962 and Aretha Franklin in 1971.

Ben … seems completely at home and projects great personality against this muttering rhythmic backdrop. It certainly knocks the rock. **Melody Maker, December 1961**

Spirit In The Sky

ARTIST Norman Greenbaum **RELEASE DATE** March 1970 (UK)/February 1970 (US) **WRITER** Norman Greenbaum **PRODUCER** Erik Jacobsen **LABEL** Reprise (UK & US) **UK CHART PEAK/WEEKS** 1/20 **US CHART PEAK/WEEKS** 3/15

The song was originally recorded in 1970 by Massachusetts-born Norman Greenbaum who had little chart success prior to this release. However, it went all the way to Number 1 in the UK and also reached the Top 3 in the US. Its quasi-religious feel may well have inspired the likes of rock operas *Godspell* and *Jesus Christ Superstar* that were soon to follow.

Greenbaum eh? There must be a cure for that. Norman Normals together with fuzz-toned boogie make me want to cut a rug and jive heavily. He could be the new 'in' name of 1970, ranking with Ramsay Macdonald and Tennessee Ernie Ford. **Chris Welch, Melody Maker, February 1970**

St Elmo's Fire (Man In Motion)

ARTIST John Parr **RELEASE DATE** September 1985 (UK)/June 1985 (US) **WRITER** John Parr, David Foster **PRODUCER** David Foster **LABEL** London (UK)/Atlantic (US) **UK CHART PEAK/WEEKS** 6/13 **US CHART PEAK/WEEKS** 1/22

The archetypal American power pop rocker, *St Elmo's Fire* channels zestful energy into a song that sounds epoch defining, at least for somebody, somewhere. Of course, that might be down to its association with the film *The Breakfast Club*, the coming of age flick that brought several movie brat packers to light. The film was actually pretty dire. The title of John Parr's song refers to the spectral light sometimes seen around a ship's mast.

Doncaster's answer to Bryan Adams comes across as a kind of male Bonnie Tyler. His voice has an amiable if slightly preposterous quality that gave momentum to that schlock movie St Elmo's Fire.... **Alan Jackson, NME, January 1986**

Stagger Lee

ARTIST Lloyd Price **RELEASE DATE** February 1959 (UK)/December 1958 (US) **WRITER** Lloyd Price, Harold Logan **PRODUCER** – **LABEL** HMV Pop (UK)/ABC Paramount (US) **UK CHART PEAK/WEEKS** 7/14 **US CHART PEAK/WEEKS** 1/21

In the time-honoured tradition of rock 'n' roll, this million-selling classic was a reinterpretation of an earlier song, *The Ballad Of Stack O' Lee*. The 'cheerful rendition of the old folk tune', according to *Rolling Stone*, stuck firmly at Number 1 in the US for 4 weeks. Coming from the swinging melting pot of New Orleans, Price had a personality as big as his talent. With early cuts featuring Fats Domino, he piled up a stack o' hits during the 50s, touring in the Biggest Show of Stars alongside Bo Diddley and the Coasters.

As an 'explosion of beat music' this is spot on: the beat thumps out madly, the saxes go crazy and the chorus helps out with those elusive words. A nightmare for the squares, and a winner for the rock fans. It's great! **Keith Fordyce, NME, January 1959**

Stand And Deliver

ARTIST Adam And The Ants **RELEASE DATE** May 1981 **WRITER** Adam Ant, Marco Pironi **PRODUCER** Chris (Merrick) Hughes **LABEL** CBS **UK CHART PEAK/WEEKS** 1/15 **US CHART PEAK/WEEKS** –

Like former Generation X leader Billy Idol, Adam Ant made an effortless transition from punk to teen idol. *Stand And Deliver*, recorded with his band the Ants, was the first of his three Number 1s. The song's galloping beat was used to dramatic effect in its widely seen video, which featured Adam Ant as a dashing highwayman.

Cue haunting horn sound of a galloping horse and the best whinny – old Adam is at it again with his funny sound effects, gurgling voice and the heaviest war drums since Rorke's Drift. **Brian Harrigan, Melody Maker, May 1981**

Stand By Your Man

ARTIST Tammy Wynette RELEASE DATE April 1975 (UK)/November 1968 (US) WRITER Tammy Wynette, Billy Sherrill PRODUCER Billy Sherrill LABEL Epic (UK & US) UK CHART PEAK/WEEKS 1/12 US CHART PEAK/WEEKS 19/16

Hillary Clinton did Tammy Wynette an injustice when, on the campaign trail in 1992, she said she was not 'some little woman standing by my man like Tammy Wynette'. Wynette got a public apology, but it reinforced the superficial impression left by this song. Written by Wynette with her producer Billy Sherrill in about 20 minutes in 1968, at the time of her wedding to the wild-living country star George Jones, the lyric belied Wynette's personal toughness in surviving a turbulent life.

Star Man

ARTIST David Bowie RELEASE DATE June 1972 (UK)/July 1972 (US) WRITER David Bowie PRODUCER David Bowie, Ken Scott LABEL RCA (UK)/RCA Victor (US) UK CHART PEAK/WEEKS 10/11 US CHART PEAK/WEEKS 65/9

After David Bowie had his first Top 10 single with the Number 5 hit *Space Oddity* in 1969, it would be three years before he would make the Top 10 again. He finally did it with another space-themed single, *Starman*, from his album **The Rise And Fall Of Ziggy Stardust And The Spiders From Mars.** The album, his first one that hit, helped make the early Seventies bearable for millions of rock fans who felt alienated by the dry post-Beatles musical landscape.

Starman is, as nearly all his tracks these days, a perfect example of David's very under-rated talents. In many ways it's atmospherically comparable to **Space Oddity***, with the mellotron and guitar work that came to light on that lauded track.* **Penny Valentine, Sounds, April 1974**

Stand By Me

ARTIST Ben E. King RELEASE DATE June 1961 (UK)/May 1961 (US) WRITER Ben E. King, Jerry Leiber, Mike Stoller PRODUCER Jerry Leiber, Mike Stoller LABEL London (UK)/Atco (US) UK CHART PEAK/WEEKS 50/1 US CHART PEAK/WEEKS 4/14

Former Drifters lead singer King followed Jackie Wilson's **Reet Petite** to Number 1 in early 1987, his catalyst the use of the song in a TV jeans ad. The same factor had sent two other soul classics, **When A Man Loves A Woman** and **I Heard It Through The Grapevine**, soaring. It had just hit again in the States thanks to a Rob Reiner film using it as its title song.

A decent but totally superfluous note-for-note rip off of a Stylistics greatest moment, which will get him precisely nowhere.... Finally looks set to go to Top 1 ... thanks to the combined might of a Hollywood movie, a Levi's ad and natural justice. **Kris Kirk, February 1987, Melody Maker**

Stars

ARTIST Simply Red **RELEASE DATE** November 1991 (UK)/January 1992 (US) **WRITER** Mick Hucknall **PRODUCER** Steve Levine, Mick Hucknall **LABEL** East West (UK & US) **UK CHART PEAK/WEEKS** 8/10 **US CHART PEAK/WEEKS** 44/14

The title track of their fourth album, recorded in Venice, was the clearest lyrical marker of the inspiration Mick Hucknall had drawn from the concept of the European Community. The EC's star symbol was tattooed on the singer's arm, though undoubtedly most UK fans never picked up the allusion, just happy that Hucknall and his band were back on form after a fallow period.

No less predictable, cosy, soothing, corporate or vacuous [than Level 42], just with a far more exciting singer … Simply Red were far more diverting when money was too tight to mention, when Mick could almost fit his hair under his cap. The supertax bracket does not become him.
Andrew Collins, NME, October 1991

Stay

ARTIST Shakespears Sister **RELEASE DATE** January 1992 (UK)/July 1992 (US) **WRITER** Marcella Detroit, Siobhan Fahey, J. Guiot, M. Levy **PRODUCER** Alan Moulder, Shakespears Sister **LABEL** London (UK & US) **UK CHART PEAK/WEEKS** 1/16 **US CHART PEAK/WEEKS** 4/20

Marcella Detroit, half of the duo who took their name from a Smiths song with a designer-introduced spelling mistake, already had a songwriting track record: while a backing singer with Eric Clapton she'd co-written **Lay Down Sally**. Ex-Bananarama member Siobhan Fahey had her own songwriting contacts, namely husband Dave Stewart, who co-wrote this second hit for the pair – following 1989's **You're History** – boosted by a memorable video featuring Fahey as a witch and Detroit as a heroine.

… it's like they raided the dressing-up box firsthand then wrote the song to match the costumes…. Until their music is as inspiring as their outfits, I won't want to rush home to listen to one of their records.
Sally Margaret Jay, Melody Maker, January 1992

Stay (I Missed You)

ARTIST Lisa Loeb And Nine Stories **RELEASE DATE** September 1994 (UK)/May 1994 (US) **WRITER** Lisa Loeb **PRODUCER** Juan Patino **LABEL** RCA (UK)/RCA Victor (US) **UK CHART PEAK/WEEKS** 6/15 **US CHART PEAK/WEEKS** 1/30

This single proved that clever, literary songwriting in the tradition of Joni Mitchell, Suzanne Vega and, yes, Bob Dylan could still bring chart success. Even Lisa Loeb's black-haired, bespectacled appearance had the look of Sixties coffee-shop boho culture, but she carried off her folk troubadour pose with wit and aplomb, bringing folk up to date for the Nineties.

Stay Another Day

ARTIST East 17 **RELEASE DATE** December 1994 **WRITER** Tony Mortimer, Dominic Hawken, Rob Kean **PRODUCER** Phil Harding, Ian Curnon, Rob Kean **LABEL** London **UK CHART PEAK/WEEKS** 1/22 **US CHART PEAK/WEEKS** –

The first Number 1 for the boy band named after the Walthamstow area of London from which they originated would also be their last. They'd come close with **If You Ever**, a late-1996 duet with singer Gabrielle, but the expulsion and then reinstatement of lead singer Brian Harvey due to reported pro-Ecstasy remarks followed by the late 1997 departure of songwriter Tony Mortimer ensured this yearning ballad, a perfect Christmas hit, would remain their swansong.

Forget the East 17/Take That feud; as every adult knows, the Walthamstow boys consistently out class the competition…. Stay Another Day, a piano accompanied ballad complete with multi-tracked, choir effect chorus and chiming bells, is the inevitable Christmas single. **Lisa Verrico, Vox, December 1994**

Stay With Me

ARTIST Lorraine Ellison **RELEASE DATE** October 1966 **WRITER** Lorraine Ellison **PRODUCER** J. Ragovoy **LABEL** Warner **UK CHART PEAK/WEEKS** 0/0 **US CHART PEAK/WEEKS** 64/8

There are probably only a handful of songs which have remained firmly in the public consciousness despite never hitting the charts.

Lorraine Ellison's *Stay With Me*, rightly regarded as one of the key singles which defined deep soul, with a vocal delivery that still shakes the listener to the core, is a prime example. Writer and producer Jerry Ragavoy inspired one of the most impassioned pleas ever recorded. A Bette Midler cover was a standout of the 1979 film *The Rose*.

Stayin' Alive

ARTIST The Bee Gees RELEASE DATE February 1978 (UK) December 1977 (US) WRITER Barry, Maurice and Robin Gibb PRODUCER Barry Gibb, Albhy Galutan, Karl Richardson LABEL RSO (UK & US) UK CHART PEAK/WEEKS 4/12 US CHART PEAK/WEEKS 1/27

Considering how effectively this song was used in *Saturday Night Fever*, it is surprising that the Bee Gees wrote it without ever seeing the script. Its title would later be appropriated for the film's sequel. The Bee Gees were already moving in an R&B-oriented direction by the time of the *Saturday Night Fever* soundtrack, but *Stayin' Alive* introduced the falsetto-heavy sound that would become their trademark.

A highly charged disco rocker full of pounding, pulsating rhythms with the highly identifiable Gibb Brothers' falsetto voices cascading up and down throughout. An almost irresistible dance tune. **Billboard, December 1977**

Still Got The Blues

ARTIST Gary Moore RELEASE DATE May 1990 (UK)/February 1991 (US) WRITER Gary Moore PRODUCER Gary Moore, Ian Taylor LABEL Virgin (UK)/Charisma (US) UK CHART PEAK/WEEKS 31/7 US CHART PEAK/WEEKS 97/3

Belfast-born Gary Moore had always been musically under the shadow of his mate Phil Lynott. The pair had been together in the band Skid Row before Lynott left to form Thin Lizzy. Among stints with other bands, Moore briefly joined Lynott again, but finally gained commercial success under his own steam in 1979 with the guitar virtuosity of *Parisian Walkways*. He found his true niche a decade later with this blues number that sold over three million copies worldwide.

Stop! In The Name Of Love

ARTIST The Supremes RELEASE DATE March 1965 (UK)/February 1965 (US) WRITER Brian Holland, Lamont Dozier, Edward Holland PRODUCER Brian Holland, Lamont Dozier LABEL Tamla Motown (UK)/Motown (US) UK CHART PEAK/WEEKS 7/12 US CHART PEAK/WEEKS 1/12

Another Dozier-Holland-Dozier composition for the Supremes, this song grew out of an incident in Lamont Dozier's life – during a heated argument with his girlfriend, she was about to walk out on him, when the phrase 'stop in the name of love' entered his head, and like any good songwriter he knew a great hook line wherever and whenever it cropped up. Its Number 1 US success was the Supremes's fourth successive chart-topper.

Easily their best since the great **Where Did Our Love Go?**. *It has an irresistible sledgehammer beat, those attractive girlie voices, and a good lyric, with the Supremes heading for Britain to push it. This song should re-establish them high in the charts.* **Rat Coleman, Melody Maker, March 1965**

Straight Up

ARTIST Paula Abdul **RELEASE DATE** March 1989 (UK)/December 1988 (US) **WRITER** Elliott Wolf **PRODUCER** K. Cohen, Elliot Wolf **LABEL** Siren (UK)/Virgin (US) **UK CHART PEAK/WEEKS** 3/13 **US CHART PEAK/WEEKS** 1/25

Former child actor and one of the most sought-after choreographers in LA, Abdul's long client list includes George Michael, Janet Jackson and Tracey Ullman. Abdul was propelled into the spotlight as a performer with the release of **Straight Up**, taken from her first album **Forever Your Girl**. She has become the most successful of the dance-pop artists who followed in the wake of the Madonna phenomenon, her acceptance measured by TV performances with The Muppets and her own fitness video Get Up and Dance.

… neo-gap band, Art of Noise scam-door beat whacks and slippery melody … American rock disco at its most genuinely convincing. **Paul Lester, Melody Maker, February 1989**

Strangers In The Night

ARTIST Frank Sinatra **RELEASE DATE** May 1966 (UK & US) **WRITER** Charles Singleton, Eddie Snyder, Bert Kaempfert **PRODUCER** – **LABEL** Reprise (UK & US) **UK CHART PEAK/WEEKS** 1/20 **US CHART PEAK/WEEKS** 1/15

The song that gave Sinatra his only transatlantic Number 1 marked a return to form for a number of people. German composer/conductor Bert Kaempfert, whose tune this was, had written the music for Elvis' 1961 Number 1 **Wooden Heart**, and the ballad also brought producer Jimmy Bowen and arranger Ernie Freeman their first Top 20 hit since the Fifties, when Bowen had had a US hit as a country singer and Freeman had been the pianist on the R&B classic **Nut Rocker**.

An attractive medium-tempo ballad, very nice lyrics and gentle climaxes with not over-dramatic lyrics. Polished, cool performance which must please Frank fans. **Melody Maker, May 1966**

Strawberry Fields Forever/ Penny Lane

ARTIST The Beatles **RELEASE DATE** February 1967 (UK & US) **WRITER** John Lennon, Paul McCartney **PRODUCER** George Martin **LABEL** Parlophone (UK)/Capitol (US) **UK CHART PEAK/WEEKS** 2/11 **US CHART PEAK/WEEKS** 8/9

This disc ended The Beatles' string of 11 Number 1s. It peaked at a mere Number 2, kept from the top by Engelbert Humperdinck's **Release Me**. Both McCartney's **Penny Lane** and Lennon's **Strawberry Fields Forever** were inspired by places in Liverpool. McCartney had long intended to write a song called Penny Lane, simply because he liked the way it sounded. Lennon named his song after Strawberry Field, a Salvation Army home where he attended parties as a boy. Both songs included much experimentation.

I like the other side best. I hated both of them first of all and thought they'd gone down the pan, but **Penny Lane** *gets better every time I hear it.* **Alan Blakely, Melody Maker, February 1968**

The Streak

ARTIST Ray Stevens RELEASE DATE May 1974 (UK)/April 1974 (US) WRITER Ray Stevens PRODUCER Ray Stevens LABEL Janus (UK)/Barnaby (US) UK CHART PEAK/WEEKS 1/12 US CHART PEAK/WEEKS 1/17

Stevens had been a chart presence since the early Sixties, getting tagged with a novelty act reputation pretty quickly after 1962's *Ahab The Arab*. The formula followed on *Bridget The Midget*, and then during that mid-Seventies moment of madness when streaking was in vogue (hard to believe but true) Stevens' bit of whistly, country-style nonsense was as naked a piece of commercialism as the fad that inspired it. Stevens then went all schmaltzy, with 1975's *Misty*.

Ray's the lad who did **Ahab The Arab**, **Bridget The Midget**, *aeons ago and he was mildly amusing in those days. He's still mildly amusing, but nothing more, and I'm surprised this record went to Number 1 in the States.* **John Peel, Sounds, June 1974**

Streets Of London

ARTIST Ralph McTell RELEASE DATE December 1974 WRITER Ralph McTell PRODUCER – LABEL Reprise UK CHART PEAK/WEEKS 2/12 US CHART PEAK/WEEKS –

Ralph McTell's songs were a little like stories. He was a typical 'outsider', coming from a broken home, and dropping out of school and the army. In *Streets of London* he takes the listener on a tour of the city, but he doesn't sing about tourist attractions, he gives voice to the underdog, focusing his attention on the lost and lonely, the homeless. The acoustic guitar ripples along and his voice captures the fragments and impressions of a less than gentle life.

Newcomer to these shores; struck it big at the Isle Of Wight last Summer. The British composer-performer, in his paramount debut, offers a strong folk ballad – and he could easily prove another Taylor or Lightfoot. **Billboard, 1974**

Stuck On You

ARTIST Elvis Presley RELEASE DATE April 1960 (UK & US) WRITER Aaron Schroeder PRODUCER – LABEL RCA (UK)/RCA Victor (US) UK CHART PEAK/WEEKS 3/14 US CHART PEAK/WEEKS 1/16

Stuck On You was Elvis' first post-army single and the first to be released in stereo. Anticipation of the new single had reached such a peak that, even before the song title was known, RCA racked up orders of over 1.25 million – the highest advance sale of any single to date. The good-time feel of *Stuck On You* ensured it three weeks at Number 1 in the US, but it only reached Number 3 in the UK.

Stuck On You (RCA) shows that Elvis has lost none of his former fire, drive and inherent rhythm. It's a medium paced hunk of solid rock, handled in that mean and moody manner which has become his trademark. **Derek Johnson, NME, April 1960**

Stupid Girl

ARTIST Garbage RELEASE DATE March 1996 (UK)/July 1996 (US) WRITER Garbage PRODUCER Butch Vig LABEL Mushroom (UK) / Almo Sounds (US) UK CHART PEAK/WEEKS 4/7 US CHART PEAK/WEEKS 24/20

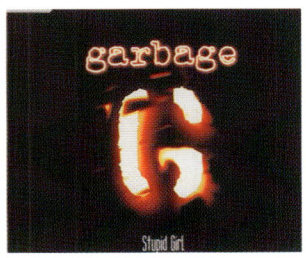

Less stark and un-settling than *Queer*, this simple but effective ode to a nihilistic, disaffected attention seeker proved to be a winner. Like much of the band's debut album, from which it is taken, this has a threatening seductiveness, with mangled guitars and all manner of strange electronic noises lurking in the shadow of the deceptively poppy production. Shirley Manson never once raises her voice, but captivates the listener regardless, giving *Stupid Girl* an infectious, unforgettable quality.

She sounds like a sexier Courtney Love. It's an addictive song, even though it's a little monotonous. I really like it, apart from the slightly Bonnie Tyler-esque lyrics. The Red Snapper mix is more eclectic and eccentric and more interesting for that. **Louise (Sleeper), Melody Maker, March 1996**

Substitute

ARTIST The Who RELEASE DATE March 1966 WRITER Peter Townshend PRODUCER Kit Lambert, Pete Townshend LABEL Polydor (UK)/Decca (US) UK CHART PEAK/WEEKS 5/13 US CHART PEAK/WEEKS 0/0

A brilliant lyric from Pete Townshend was the band's fourth single release, capturing all their onstage energy, but it nearly didn't get heard, as former producer Shel Talmy slapped an injunction on the release. Polydor got round the problem by pressing it with a new B-side called *Waltz For A Pig*, but eventually the injunction was lifted and Talmy replaced by Kit Lambert.

Opens with reverberating guitar, storming rhythm and tambourine, then switches to a double time shuffle. Personally, I don't like it as much as **My Generation**, *but it's a great hunk of commercial beat by Pete Townsend.* **Derek Johnson, NME, March 1966**

199

Subterranean Homesick Blues

ARTIST Bob Dylan **RELEASE DATE** April 1965 (UK & US) **WRITER** Bob Dylan **PRODUCER** T. Wilson **LABEL** CBS (UK)/Columbia (US) **UK CHART PEAK/WEEKS** 9/9 **US CHART PEAK/WEEKS** 39/8

This single marked Dylan's first US Top 40 entry in a year full of incident: a stormy UK tour helped the song breach the Top 10 in May, and at the end of the month was seen in the context of **Bringing It All Back Home**, an album with an acoustic and an electric side. In June, The Byrds' **Mr Tambourine Man** went Number 1. Dylan was booed off at the Newport Folk Festival for his use of electric guitar – and the die was cast, for him and popular music.

Much more commercial sound with harmonica, amplified guitars and a big, big beat. It should prove that the sound is more important than the lyric…. **Tom Sticks, Melody Maker, April 1965**

Suedehead

ARTIST Morrissey **RELEASE DATE** February 1988 **WRITER** Steven Street, Stephen Morrissey **PRODUCER** Steven Street **LABEL** HMV Pop **UK CHART PEAK/WEEKS** 5/6 **US CHART PEAK/WEEKS** –

Stephen Patrick Morrissey had lead Manchester band The Smiths to iconic fame. Johnny Marr provided the shimmering guitars and Morrissey had given his all as an ironic lyricist, pitched in worry. The Smiths were dead, and Stephen was on his own, with a solo deal with EMI. *Suedehead*, the name taken from a Richard Allen novel about post skinhead gangs, warbled with ironic melodrama, but this time the guitars were played by Vini Reilly from Drutti Column.

Fettered with models of impossibly unrequitable love, all he could do

was put a few allusions in his diary. A nation of Smiths fans have since followed suit. A fine, fine record with considerable involvement from the perfectly named Steven Street…. **Andy Darling, Melody Maker, February 1988**

Sugar Shack

ARTIST Jimmy Gilmer And The Fireballs **RELEASE DATE** November 1963 (UK)/September 1963 (US) **WRITER** Keith McCormack, Faye Voss **PRODUCER** Jeff Barry **LABEL** London (UK)/Dot (US) **UK CHART PEAK/WEEKS** 45/8 **US CHART PEAK/WEEKS** 1/15

Hired for a scheduled tour after the original lead singer had quit, Jimmy Gilmer, at the suggestion of producer Norman Petty, fronted The Fireballs for the majority of the Sixties. One of three new Keith McCormack compositions aired on the road, *Sugar Shack* received such an audience response that a decision was made to record and release it as a single. After a slow start, sales picked up and by October 1963 it was Number 1.

Sugar, Sugar

ARTIST The Archies **RELEASE DATE** October 1969 (UK)/July 1969 (US) **WRITER** Jeff Barry, Andy Kim **PRODUCER** Jeff Barry **LABEL** RCA (UK)/Calendar (US) **UK CHART PEAK/WEEKS** 1/16 **US CHART PEAK/WEEKS** 1/22

Based on comic book characters, the Archies were borne of Monkees creator Don Kirshner's desire to create a group that would never talk back to him. Production tasks were handled by Jeff Barry, who wrote *Sugar, Sugar* with singer Andy Kim. With its catchy melody and irresistible beat, *Sugar, Sugar* was the Archies' biggest hit and the best-selling single of 1969.

Sukiyaki (Ueo Muite Aruku)

ARTIST Kyu Sakamoto **RELEASE DATE** June 1963 (UK)/May 1963 (US) **WRITER** El Rohsuke, Hachdai Nakamura **PRODUCER** K. Kusano **LABEL** HMV Pop (UK)/Capitol (US) **UK CHART PEAK/WEEKS** 6/13 **US CHART PEAK/WEEKS** 1/14

Sakamoto, who was successful in Japan as both singer and actor, had a hit with this song there as *Ueo Muite Aruko* ('Walk With Your Chin Up'). It was re-titled as the snappier *Sukiyaki* because jazz trumpeter Kenny Ball wanted to cover the track in the UK – he reached the Top 10. Sakamoto's own version became the first big transatlantic chart success for a Japanese artist, and was later covered by Taste Of Honey in 1981 and 4PM in 1994.

Kyu certainly conveys a nostalgic atmosphere on this song, but he's far from being a sad person in real life: in fact he is a comedian. Sakamoto, when translated means 'Don't look down when you walk on the street'. **Alan Smith, NME, July 1963**

Summer Breeze

ARTIST The Isley Brothers **RELEASE DATE** May 1974 (UK)/March 1974 (US) **WRITER** James Seals, Darrell Crofts **PRODUCER** The Isley Brothers **LABEL** Epic (UK)/T-Neck (US) **UK CHART PEAK/WEEKS** 16/8 **US CHART PEAK/WEEKS** 60/7

One of the first black groups to form their own label, The Isley Brothers were pioneers who injected rock influences into their music (an early member being Jimi Hendrix) and were not afraid to record cover versions. Such an attitude was, by 1973, beginning to reap dividends, with **3+3** winning them a new white audience. Aside from **That Lady**, the standout cut was **Summer Breeze**, a revival of American soft-rockers Seals and Crofts' 1972 smash.

Last year's pop hit is given a soft soul rendition this time around, and the Brothers do a convincing job. It's a nice change for them. **Billboard, March 1974**

Sultans Of Swing

ARTIST Dire Straits **RELEASE DATE** March 1979 (UK)/February 1979 (US) **WRITER** Mark Knopfler **PRODUCER** M. Winwood **LABEL** Vertigo (UK)/Warner (US) **UK CHART PEAK/WEEKS** 8/11 **US CHART PEAK/WEEKS** 4/15

When broadcaster Charlie Gillett played the demo of this song on his Radio London show in July 1977 between Bonnie Raitt and Ry Cooder, every A&R man listening ran to the phone to find out more and guitarist-singer Mark Knopfler's career was off and running. The song would be re-recorded for single release, then again for the album, the 45 being deliberately raw like the demo to get on to the punk-infested airwaves. Whatever, *Sultans* remains Dire Straits' signature tune.

They are already household obsessions in places like Germany, Holland and Australia. The song remains a gem: taut, sensuous, witty and insidious, if marginally under produced. The first Platinum stars of the late Seventies. **Ian Birch, Melody Maker, 1979**

Summer Holiday

ARTIST Cliff Richard **RELEASE DATE** February 1963 **WRITER** Bruce Welch, Brian Bennett **PRODUCER** – **LABEL** Columbia **UK CHART PEAK/WEEKS** 1/18 **US CHART PEAK/WEEKS** 0/0

With such lyrics as 'We're going where the sun shines brightly/We're going where the sea is blue', **Summer Holiday** epitomizes Cliff's perennial clean-cut image. His 20th single, it was the title track of the film of the same name, starring Cliff and The Shadows in which they sallied forth to the seaside in a London Transport double-decker bus. Ironically, both film and song have become immortalized by an episode of TV's *The Young Ones* in which the bus careers over the white cliffs of Dover into the English Channel.

Another single from the Summer Holiday *film, presents Cliff Richard on the catchy title song, backed by Dancing Shoes – a fine record.* **Melody Maker, February 1963**

Summer In The City

ARTIST Lovin' Spoonful RELEASE DATE July 1966 (UK & US) WRITER John Sebastian, Mark Sebastian, Steve Boon PRODUCER Erik Jacobsen LABEL Kama Sutra (UK & US) UK CHART PEAK/WEEKS 8/11 US CHART PEAK/WEEKS 1/11

The American/Canadian Lovin' Spoonful combined the jangle of the British Beatles with the eclectic energy of the Greenwich village folk scene. John Sebastian was a fine songwriter, and his warm, clear singing made *Summer In the City* an atmospheric word painting of New York City on a warm sunny day. Street noises and booming drums added to the appeal. The members of the Spoonful auditioned for the roles of The Monkees, but did not get them.

Tremendous sound-painting from The Spoonful. There is powerful organ, drums and guitar, dramatic breaks and clever use of effects, including car horns and pneumatic drills. **Melody Maker, July 1966**

Summer Nights

ARTIST John Travolta And Olivia Newton-John RELEASE DATE September 1978 (UK)/November 1978 (US) WRITER Warren Casey, Jimmy Jacobs PRODUCER – LABEL RSO (UK & US) UK CHART PEAK/WEEKS 1/19 US CHART PEAK/WEEKS 5/16

A wittily written and arranged duet from the movie *Grease*, in which the two young lovers recount a beach date to their respective friends from different angles – Newton-John's version depicts a candyfloss romantic tryst, while Travolta, trying to be cool, invents a horny, lusty encounter. This was one of three hits for Newton-John from the movie along with *You're The One That I Want* (also with Travolta) and *Hopelessly Devoted To You*.

If you still enjoy hearing a song that's been Number 1 for eight weeks, then it must be a great pop single, and if you hear a song three times, and each time it grates on you more horribly than the last.... **Chris Brazier, Melody Maker, September 1978**

Summer Of '69

ARTIST Bryan Adams RELEASE DATE August 1985 (UK)/June 1985 (US) WRITER Bryan Adams PRODUCER Bryan Adams, Bob Clearmountain LABEL A&M (UK & US) UK CHART PEAK/WEEKS 42/7 US CHART PEAK/WEEKS 5/17

When Canadian singer-songwriter Bryan Adams broke through to the American market, some critics dismissed him as a mere Springsteen copy. It was an extremely image-oriented time. But it didn't take long for Adams to prove himself an original. The extremely catchy *Summer of '69*, his fifth US Top 10, paired his throaty tenor with evocative lyrics and a melody that hit just the right note of wistful nostalgia. It was all over America's airwaves during the summer of '85.

Moonwalks; New Jersey.... The Summer of '69 I remember was positively pastoral compared to Bryan's – that was when the luscious, pouting axe hero 'got his first six string' and well ... the rest is History. **Caroline Sullivan, Melody Maker, August 1985**

Theme From 'A Summer Place'

ARTIST Percy Faith And His Orchestra RELEASE DATE March 1960 (UK)/January 1960 (US) WRITER Mack Discant, Max Steiner PRODUCER – LABEL Philips (UK)/Columbia (US) UK CHART PEAK/WEEKS 2/30 US CHART PEAK/WEEKS 1/21

Despite having severely burned his hands putting out a fire on his sister's clothes while a teenager, Canadian Percy Faith still enjoyed great success as a composer and conductor. Hired as an arranger for Columbia in 1950, he was also free to record his own songs: his version of the Max Steiner film score was ranked by Billboard as the Number 1 song of 1960. Faith would release a re-recording as disco fever hit in 1976, the year of his death from cancer.

All too often fans take little or no notice of the man behind the music on a hit record, but once in a while the tables are turned.... This week it is the turn of Percy Faith, whose interpretation of the theme from Summer Place has leaped into the British best sellers. **Keith Goodwin, NME, March 1960**

Summertime Blues

ARTIST Eddie Cochran RELEASE DATE November 1958 (UK)/August 1958 (US) WRITER Eddie Cochran, Eddie Capehart PRODUCER – LABEL London (UK)/Liberty (US) UK CHART PEAK/WEEKS 18/6 US CHART PEAK/WEEKS 8/16

There's real teen frustration in this protest classic, also a hit for Blue Cheer and The Who. While Eddie Cochran is known as a pioneering American rocker, at the time he wrote *Summertime Blues* Liberty Records was trying mightily to turn him into a crooner, making *Summertime Blues* a mere B-side to the ballad *Love Again*. Fortunately, disc jockeys knew better, bypassing *Love Again* in favour of its flip. Before the summer of 1958 was over *Summertime Blues* was in the US Top 10.

*Now let's make way for an even more successful newcomer, who is busily repeating his Stateside success in this country. Eddy has hit the jackpot in a big way with *Summertime Blues*, which looks like giving him winter time cheer on both sides of the Atlantic.* **Bruce Charlton, NME, November 1958**

The Sun Ain't Gonna Shine Anymore

ARTIST The Walker Brothers RELEASE DATE March 1966 (UK)/April 1966 (US) WRITER Bob Crewe, Bob Gaudio PRODUCER Johnny Franz LABEL Philips (UK)/Smash (US) UK CHART PEAK/WEEKS 1/11 US CHART PEAK/WEEKS 13/19

This ballad of lost love, a previous Frankie Valli recording, was laced with plenty of drama, and featured Scott Walker's baritone. It brought The Walker Brothers their second Number 1 in the UK in six months, but proved to be the American-born act's last US Top 20 hit and the trio's final UK Top 10 until 1976's comeback single **No Regrets**.

Thumping tambourine leads into Scott's flexible vocals. John and Gary chant in the background, and Ivor Raymond fronts an enormously loud orchestra. **Melody Maker, February 1966**

Sunny

ARTIST Bobby Hebb RELEASE DATE September 1966 (UK)/June 1966 (US) WRITER Bobby Hebb PRODUCER J. Ross LABEL Philips (UK & US) UK CHART PEAK/WEEKS 12/9 US CHART PEAK/WEEKS 2/15

Even if Bobby Hebb had never hit the charts he would still be assured his place in history, for at the age of 12 he had become the first black performer to appear at Nashville's world famous Grand Ole Opry. He came from a musical family, with brother Hal (a member of The Marigolds killed in a mugging) providing the inspiration for Bobby's debut hit. Although Bobby returned to the UK charts seven years later, his crowning glory remains this sad and poignant tribute to his murdered brother.

Sunny, which reached Number 2 in Billboard in the States, is typical of his output. And what an output it is! Bobby has written over 3,000 songs during his 25 years…. No wonder they call him the 'Song-a-day-man.' **Derek Johnson, NME, September 1966**

Sunny Afternoon

ARTIST The Kinks RELEASE DATE June 1966 (UK)/August 1966 (US) WRITER Ray Davies PRODUCER Shel Talmy LABEL Pye (UK)/Reprise (US) UK CHART PEAK/WEEKS 1/13 US CHART PEAK/WEEKS 14/11

Perhaps the best song on the Kinks's 1966 album **Face To Face**, the vaudevillian *Sunny Afternoon* provided their third UK Number 1. Ray Davies was rapidly establishing himself as one of the most gifted songsmiths of his generation. *Sunny Afternoon*'s portrayal of a bankrupt, lamenting the loss of his luxurious lifestyle while lazing in the sunshine, is set against a languid musical backdrop which perfectly captures the mood, and continues the observational style established in **Dedicated Follower Of Fashion**, its immediate predecessor.

Starts with a long bass rundown … Ray takes lead vocal in a ridiculously lazy slurring style based over a rather corny progression. **Melody Maker, June 1966**

Sunshine Of Your Love

ARTIST Cream RELEASE DATE October 1968 (UK)/January 1968 (US) WRITER Eric Clapton, Jack Bruce, Peter Brown PRODUCER Felix Pappalardi LABEL Polydor (UK)/Atco (US) UK CHART PEAK/WEEKS 25/7 US CHART PEAK/WEEKS 5/26

In the late Sixties, especially in America, if you were a typical rock fan given a bathroom wall and a pen, the odds are you would write three simple words: 'Clapton is God.' *Sunshine of Your Love* supported that proposition. Surprisingly, the Cream single reached only Number 36 on the Hot 100 upon its release in January 1968. Six months later, after the double live album **Wheels of Fire** topped America's album chart, *Sunshine* blazed back onto the singles chart, peaking at Number 5.

It is a most memorable track and has been a hit single twice in America…. It is one of those riffs that keeps running through your ears, and you can't remember where it came from. **John Peel, Melody Maker, September 1968**

Superstition

ARTIST Stevie Wonder RELEASE DATE February 1973 (UK)/November 1972 (US) WRITER Stevie Wonder PRODUCER Stevie Wonder LABEL Tamla Motown (UK)/Motown (US) UK CHART PEAK/WEEKS 11/9 US CHART PEAK/WEEKS 1/16

By the early Seventies Wonder wanted a new direction for his music. Checking out synth band Tonto's Expanding Mind Band at Hendrix's Electric Lady studios he got them to run his clavinet through their synth and loved the results. As Wonder developed the backing track he knew it was a good 'un, but Jeff Beck wanted the funky song as the gift he was promised for his work on **Talking Book**. Motown vetoed the present. As a result Wonder had his first US Number 1 since 1963.

Dig that drum introduction! and into the Wah-Wah electronic piano. As Stevie jogs along a great track from an even better album, **Talking Book***: it's a marvellous piece of work, from the stomping rhythm to the funky brass phrasing.* **Chris Welch, Melody Maker, January 1973**

Surfin' USA

ARTIST The Beach Boys RELEASE DATE July 1963 (UK)/April 1963 (US) WRITER Brian Wilson, Chuck Berry PRODUCER Nick Venet LABEL Capitol (UK & US) UK CHART PEAK/WEEKS 34/7 US CHART PEAK/WEEKS 3/17

After **Surfin'**, **Surfer Girl**, and **Surfin' Safari** had swelled the Californian surf-rock craze, Brian Wilson returned to the theme with this adaptation of Chuck Berry's **Sweet Little Sixteen**, adding surf-related lyrics to the chugging rock 'n' roll number. The single was The Beach Boys' first to hit British shores and gave them their first Top 10 record in the US, reaching Number 3.

Sweet Child O' Mine

ARTIST Guns N' Roses RELEASE DATE August 1988 (UK)/June 1988 (US) WRITER Guns N' Roses PRODUCER – LABEL Geffen (UK & US) UK CHART PEAK/WEEKS 24/8 US CHART PEAK/WEEKS 1/24

Lead singer Axl Rose seems to receive his greatest inspiration from the ladies in his life. Erin Everly, daughter of Don, was the subject of this, their first chart-topper, and the couple married 18 months later; but within a month Rose was filing for divorce. The video *November Rain* featured a dream-sequence wedding with supermodel and then girlfriend Stephanie Seymour, but again the relationship would not last.

Many will be disappointed by this self-penned statement of woofterish intent. We find ourselves strangely gratified. Now run along petals…. **The Stud Brothers, Melody Maker, August 1988**

Sweet Dreams (Are Made Of This)

ARTIST Eurythmics RELEASE DATE February 1983 (UK)/May 1983 (US) WRITER Annie Lennox, Dave Stewart PRODUCER Dave Stewart LABEL RCA (UK)/RCA Victor (US) UK CHART PEAK/WEEKS 2/14 US CHART PEAK/WEEKS 1/26

A fated first tour as Eurythmics in the winter of 1981 had left Dave Stewart and Annie Lennox, both ex-Tourists, physically and mentally exhausted. Having recovered, they leased a London warehouse and concentrated on songwriting and recording on an obsolete eight-track machine, often waiting for a nearby noisy timber factory to shut for the day. Their video-friendliness helped this, the title track of their second album, top the US charts two years after that awful tour.

Comparisons with Yazoo aside, **Sweet Dreams** *is a cracker; it is probably the best example of the range and depth of Lennox's voice, and it deserves chart action.* **Paul Strange, Melody Maker, January 1983**

Sweet Talkin' Guy

ARTIST The Chiffons RELEASE DATE May 1966 (UK & US) WRITER Doug Morris, Elliot Greenberg, Barbara Baer, Robert Schwartz PRODUCER – LABEL Stateside (UK)/Laurie (US) UK CHART PEAK/WEEKS 31/8 US CHART PEAK/WEEKS 10/10

Nearly three years after their last Top 10 hit, The Chiffons made a stunning comeback with **Sweet Talkin' Guy**. By 1966, the girl group era was long over. Yet The Chiffons somehow managed to hit with this utterly charming pop tune, perfectly suited to their angelic vocal blend. It was compatible with their earlier hits and yet had contemporary touches, such as the overlapping vocals and unusual suspended-chord backing.

SWEET DREAMS
«·are made of this·

Dave & Annie

E U R Y T H M I C S

Sylvia's Mother

ARTIST Dr Hook **RELEASE DATE** June 1972 (UK)/April 1972 (US) **WRITER** Shel Silverstein **PRODUCER** – **LABEL** CBS (UK)/Columbia (US) **UK CHART PEAK/WEEKS** 2/13 **US CHART PEAK/WEEKS** 5/15

This was the first of five singles to make the US Top 100 for the New Jersey group in 1972 under the name of Dr Hook And The Medicine Show. The song reached the Top 5 in the US, and only Donny Osmond's **Puppy Love** prevented it from topping the UK chart. The group's best-known members were its vocalists Ray Sawyer, often mistaken for 'Dr Hook' because of his eye-patch, and Dennis Locorriere.

If you look at the pictures and read the stories, you'll have guessed that Dr Hook is a bunch of lascivious layabouts. If these guys would relax and become a straight pop group, they'd wipe the Osmonds and the Partridge Family off the boards. **Charlie Gillett, Rolling Stone, March 1973**

*Back by demand and sounding as sweet as ever with another groove, **One Fine Day**, on the flip side. For many of the younger kids who didn't hear them first time around. These songs still stand up strong.* **Danny Holloway, NME, March 1972**

Sylvia

ARTIST Focus **RELEASE DATE** January 1973 (UK)/July 1973 (US) **WRITER** Thijs Van Leer **PRODUCER** – **LABEL** Polydor (UK)/Sire (US) **UK CHART PEAK/WEEKS** 20/10 **US CHART PEAK/WEEKS** 89/5

Jan Akkerman and Thijs van Leer were the featured performers in this Dutch quartet who owed their UK success to exposure on TV's *Old Grey Whistle Test*. This track made the US Top 100, whilst in the UK, when Sylvia peaked at Number 4, their follow-up, taken from their **Moving Waves** album, *Hocus Pocus*, was peaking at Number 20. It is rare for any artist to have two simultaneous Top 20 hits and even rarer for this to happen with two instrumentals.

Tainted Love

ARTIST Soft Cell RELEASE DATE August 1981 (UK)/January 1982 (US) WRITER Ed Cobb PRODUCER M. Thorne LABEL Some Bizzare (UK)/Sire (US) UK CHART PEAK/WEEKS 1/16 US CHART PEAK/WEEKS 8/43

From the vaults of Northern Soul, *Tainted Love* had been a favourite from Wigan to Widnes in the version by Gloria Jones – Marc Bolan's missus. The other Marc cheekily revamped it to create the best-selling UK single of 1982 and a Number 1 around the world. The song, written by Ed Cobb, was the perfect platform for Almond and David Ball. America proved stubborn but eventually relented, allowing the song to reach the Top 10 – although this was Soft Cell's only hit in the States.

Structurally it has a natural subsidence to a natural floor. Follow it down and stay with it. **Neil Rowland, Melody Maker, August 1981**

Take My Breath Away

ARTIST Berlin RELEASE DATE October 1986 (UK)/June 1986 (US) WRITER Giorgio Moroder, Tom Whitlock PRODUCER Giorgio Moroder LABEL CBS (UK)/Columbia (US) UK CHART PEAK/WEEKS 1/15 US CHART PEAK/WEEKS 1/21

Although Berlin had moderate success with discs like the controversial *Sex (I'm A …)* and *The Metro*, *Take My Breath Away* was the one that took them to the top on both sides of the Atlantic. The Los Angeles trio, which centred around singer Terri Nunn, recorded the song for the soundtrack of *Top Gun*. It was produced and co-written by Eurodisco master Giorgio Moroder.

The Berlin wall of sound is provided by Giorgio 'Whatever happened to … ?' Moroder, who should be thoroughly ashamed for having anything to do with Top Gun, *to which this is the (irrefutable) Love theme! Gunk, hit.* **Andy Hart, Sounds, October 1986**

Talk Of The Town

ARTIST The Pretenders RELEASE DATE April 1980 WRITER Chrissie Hynde PRODUCER Chris Thomas LABEL Real Are UK CHART PEAK/WEEKS 8/8 US CHART PEAK/WEEKS –

In the wake of the UK chart-topping successes of **Brass In Pocket** and the **Pretenders** album, the group stormed to Number 8 in the UK in April with **Talk Of The Town**. This was the second single to be taken from the album which was mostly produced by Chris Thomas. At this time, The Pretenders made their first visit to the USA and Chrissie Hynde met one of her all-time heroes, Ray Davies of the Kinks, in a New York club. It was the start of a three-year relationship for the couple.

A muddled, over-produced piece that meanders where it ought to lope and slinks where it ought to stride, with Chrissie's voice mixed in such a way as to be both over-prominent and unclear. **Charles Shaar Murray, NME, March 1980**

Tammy

ARTIST Debbie Reynolds RELEASE DATE August 1957 (UK)/July 1957 (US) WRITER Jay Livingston, Ray Evans PRODUCER – LABEL Vogue-Coral (UK)/Coral (US) UK CHART PEAK/WEEKS 2/14 US CHART PEAK/WEEKS 1/31

Once upon a time in the innocent, dawning days of rock 'n' roll, a sweet young teenager called Tammy fell in love with an injured pilot: 'Does my lover feel how I feel/When he comes near?/My heart leaps so joyfully/I wish that he could hear.' And so it was that Debbie Reynolds (singer and Hollywood film star whose actress/writer daughter Carrie Fisher will always be remembered as Princess Leia in *Star Wars*) managed the feat of producing the only Number 1 single by a female between July 1956 and December 1958.

Tammy is an attractive song and Debbie projects it with the natural unaffected charm that is such a part of her personality. But I am somewhat surprized in this gimmick-ridden era that it has rocketed to the Number 1 position in the States. Another welcome sign, perhaps, that gimmicks are on the way out. **Laurie Henshaw, Melody Maker, August 1957**

Tattva

ARTIST Kula Shaker RELEASE DATE May 1996 WRITER Crispian Mills, Kula Shaker PRODUCER – LABEL Columbia UK CHART PEAK/WEEKS 4/8 US CHART PEAK/WEEKS –

Kula Shaker's *Tattva* was a rarity in being sung partly in Sanskrit. The mantra 'acinta bheda bheda tattva' had been uttered to singer Crispian Mills by two different people separated by half the world in the space of a week – and he built a song round it that told of the relationship between God and man. A 2,000-copy limited edition first time round, it was reissued six months later and took the band to the charts in Beatles-esque glory.

The 'hotly tipped' (by WHO?) Kula Shaker ... faff around with the most hackneyed tokens of Sixties psychedelia – they even drag out a sitar ... and reduce it to something that goes 'rrrreeeoooowwww' behind the guitars to make it sound, y'know – exotic. **Taylor Parkes, Melody Maker, June 1996**

Tears

ARTIST Ken Dodd RELEASE DATE September 1965 WRITER Frank Capan, Billy Uhr PRODUCER – LABEL Columbia UK CHART PEAK/WEEKS 31/7 US CHART PEAK/WEEKS –

Buck-toothed comedian Ken Dodd hit his recording peak in 1965 with the release of **Tears**. Written by Billy Uhr and Frank Capano, it saw Dodd dispense with his trademark tickling stick and sidekick Diddymen to reveal a more sombre nature – certainly in contrast to a previous year's hit **Happiness**, which became his theme tune.

Doddy has had big sales in the past with just this sort of sentimental oldie. His many fans will no doubt be queuing outside the record shop. **Melody Maker, August 1965**

Tears In Heaven

ARTIST Eric Clapton RELEASE DATE February 1992 (UK & US) WRITER Eric Clapton, Will Jennings PRODUCER Russ Titelman LABEL Reprise (UK)/Duck Reprise (US) UK CHART PEAK/WEEKS 5/9 US CHART PEAK/WEEKS 2/26

Eric Clapton co-wrote this moving song after his four-year-old son, Conor, fell to his death out of a Manhattan apartment window. Conor had been living with his mother, the Italian model Lori Del Santo. Although it was popularly believed that Clapton wrote the whole song, he in fact wrote only the music. The lyrics were made to order by Wilbur 'Will' Jennings, a song doctor who had previously written for Whitney Houston, among others.

Clapton delivers a soft and effective vocal on this ballad taken from the soundtrack from the film Rush. He swaps his usual guitar for the acoustic picking, creating fluid, evocative lines. This beautiful tune will

receive immediate approval from album, Rock, Top 40, and AC programmers. **Billboard, January 1992**

The Tears Of A Clown

ARTIST Smokey Robinson And The Miracles RELEASE DATE August 1970 (UK)/October 1970 (US) WRITER William 'Smokey' Robinson, Henry Cosby, Stevie Wonder PRODUCER Smokey Robinson LABEL Tamla Motown (UK)/Tamla (US) UK CHART PEAK/WEEKS 1/14 US CHART PEAK/WEEKS 1/16

Smokey Robinson rewrote this original Stevie Wonder and Henry Crosby number. It featured a calliope sound that put Smokey in mind of Pagliacci the clown and inspired his lyrical thought processes. The Miracles first recorded the track on their **Make It Happen** album; when the single was released three years later it shot to Number 1 – the first and only British chart-topper for The Miracles. Released stateside a month later it sold a million copies.

On first listen it is a certain smash, as England confirmed this summer. Soul stations played the cut three years ago, and The Miracles cherished it as they would a hit. Now they will gladly share it with the plebs. **Paul Gambaccini, Rolling Stone, November 1970**

Teenage Kicks

ARTIST Undertones RELEASE DATE October 1978 WRITER Damien John O'Neill PRODUCER Undertones LABEL Sire UK CHART PEAK/WEEKS 31/6 US CHART PEAK/WEEKS –

The Northern Ireland band, led by Feargal Sharkey and John O'Neill, were already highly rated by the time they released this debut single on a small Belfast label, Good Vibrations. John Peel gave the single plenty of airplay and, suddenly, the Undertones were appearing on *Top Of The Pops* and signing to Sire Records, with the re-issued single reaching UK Number 31. The track was further reissued when the band split in 1983. Their most successful single had been **My Perfect Cousin** in 1980.

John Peel is busy losing hair over this single at the moment. Don't fret John, it's just ... Okay, (shrug) ... A loud little bastard this record. **Andy Partridge, Melody Maker, October 1978**

Telegram Sam

ARTIST T-Rex **RELEASE DATE** January 1972 **WRITER** Marc Bolan **PRODUCER** Tony Visconti **LABEL** T-Rex **UK CHART PEAK/WEEKS** 1/12 **US CHART PEAK/WEEKS** –

T. Rextasy was at its height in 1972, and Bolan knew how to put his hits together – this one was recorded at the Rosenberg Studio in Copenhagen, and followed the successful formula: odd lyrics based around Bolan's life with chunky guitar plus a blues tribute to Smokestack Lightning on the fadeout. The magic worked well enough to make Number 1 in the UK, but he would only do it one more time. A subsequent US tour was not a success and the decline started.

Boley piles on the guitar riffs and strings topple around him with rocking menace. **Chris Welch, Melody Maker, January 1972**

Telstar

ARTIST Tornadoes **RELEASE DATE** August 1962 (UK)/November 1962 (US) **WRITER** Joe Meek **PRODUCER** Joe Meek **LABEL** Decca (UK)/London (US) **UK CHART PEAK/WEEKS** 1/25 **US CHART PEAK/WEEKS** 1/16

Tying in with the launch of the first communications satellite, *Telstar* was the first single by a UK group to be Number 1 in the States – selling over five million copies worldwide. The group had previously been the house band for producer Joe Meek, who wrote the track, and also backed Billy Fury on the road. The clavioline and instrumental sound effects made it a spooky little track, the first of four Top 20 hits for the band.

With topicality the only thing to commend it, The Tornados romp through **Telstar***. Billy Fury's backing group ought to be able to produce something less monotonous than this!* **Melody Maker, August 1962**

Temptation

ARTIST Heaven 17 **RELEASE DATE** April 1983 **WRITER** Glenn Gregory, Ian Craig Marsh, Martyn Ware **PRODUCER** Gary Walsh **LABEL** Virgin **UK CHART PEAK/WEEKS** 2/13 **US CHART PEAK/WEEKS** –

When the original Human League line-up split, few gave Ian Craig Marsh and Martyn Ware much of a chance, having lost lead singer Phil Oakey. Four near misses on the Top 40 with new vocalist Glenn Gregory while their erstwhile cohorts (with the benefit of the familiar name) had topped the single and album listings suggested the critics were right – but the powerful vocals of session singer Carol Kenyon grabbed *Temptation* by the scruff of the neck and saw it soar to second place behind Spandau Ballet in a new romantic-dominated chart.

… this isn't [a temptation] and they're not delivering with anything like the panache with which they were launched…. Glenn Gregory's voice still sounds hollow and the synths are tinny and bare. **Charles Shaar Murray, NME, April 1983**

10538 Overture

ARTIST Electric Light Orchestra **RELEASE DATE** July 1972 **WRITER** Jeff Lynne **PRODUCER** Jeff Lynne **LABEL** Harvest (UK)/United Artists (US) **UK CHART PEAK/WEEKS** 9/8 **US CHART PEAK/WEEKS** 0/0

Released almost two years after Move members Roy Wood and Jeff Lynne had initially conceived the project, ELO's first single was well worth the wait. A clever fusion of rock and classical music, *10538 Overture* was Wood's only appearance on an ELO single before he left to form Wizzard. Violins and cellos chugged purposefully away in a manner reminiscent of The Beatles' *I Am The Walrus*, while a neat French horn motif over the closing bars set the seal on an unusual debut.

Bold and adventurous. A beautiful, menacing warring sound, that could be heralding a new dawn or a new era of conflict. A sinister brooding march to the unknown. **Chris Welch, Melody Maker, June 1972**

Tequila

ARTIST The Champs **RELEASE DATE** April 1958 (UK)/February 1958 (US) **WRITER** Chuck Rio **PRODUCER** Dave Burgess **LABEL** London (UK)/Challenge (US) **UK CHART PEAK/WEEKS** 5/9 **US CHART PEAK/WEEKS** 1/19

Named after Challenge Records owner Gene Autry's horse, Champ, The Champs were assembled by A&R man Dave Burgess to record a song of his called *Train to Nowhere*. The song went nowhere, but DJs flipped the disc over and *Tequila* quickly wormed its way up Billboard's Hot 100, reaching Number 1 in its second week on the chart. Though The Champs' only major hit, many future stars passed through the group, including Delaney Bramlett, Glen Campbell, and both halves of Seals & Crofts.

The meteoric rise of **Tequila** *from obscurity to top place was one of the most rapid ever witnessed in the US hit parade. It was surprising, too, for the tune – which takes its title from a potent Mexican drink – was the first ever recorded by the comparatively new Champs.* **Keith Goodwin, NME, April 1958**

That'll Be The Day

ARTIST Buddy Holly **RELEASE DATE** August 1957 **WRITER** Norman Petty, Buddy Holly **PRODUCER** Norman Petty **LABEL** Brunswick **UK CHART PEAK/WEEKS** 1/– **US CHART PEAK/WEEKS** 1/22

Named after a John Wayne line in the 1956 western The Searchers, ***That'll Be The Day*** was the song that began the Buddy Holly legend. Initially a flop in its original 1956 form, Holly and the Crickets persevered in recording an alternative version and were rewarded the following year with a transatlantic Number 1 – their debut chart entry in either country. Less than 18 months later, Holly would perish in the plane crash which also claimed the lives of Ritchie Valens and the Big Bopper.

The song has all the Holly hallmarks: a melody that sticks to your memory like a limpet, economic arrangement, and a vocal that's good humoured without being cloying. Holly's opening chords and rhythm guitar work have been endlessly copied.... **Bob Edmonds, NME, September 1976**

That's Entertainment

ARTIST The Jam RELEASE DATE February 1981 WRITER Paul Weller PRODUCER Vic Coppersmith-Heaven LABEL Metronome UK CHART PEAK/WEEKS 21/7 US CHART PEAK/WEEKS –

Like ***Down In The Tube Station At Midnight***, this track from **Sound Affects** was composed by Paul Weller in a matter of minutes, yet vividly summed up a mood. It described a depressing

walk through a decaying, working-class district in England, the repetitive chorus only accentuating the pain. The song's acoustic mood made it an unlikely single in Britain, but import sales were such that the track became a chart entry.

A hit single by the back import door that, it must be said, has more than a little of **My Sweet Entertainment /He's So Fine** *about the overall structure. And let's face it, overall structures are what singles are all about.* **NME, January 1983**

That's The Way (I Like It)

ARTIST KC And The Sunshine Band RELEASE DATE August 1975 (UK)/October 1975 (US) WRITER Harry Wayne Casey, Robert Finch PRODUCER Harry Wayne Casey, Robert Finch LABEL Jayboy (UK)/TK (US) UK CHART PEAK/WEEKS 4/10 US CHART PEAK/WEEKS 1/16

Harry Wayne Casey, frontman of Florida pop-soulsters KC And The Sunshine Band, toned down the 'uh-huhs' in his song, thinking them too suggestive for airplay in 1975. With that in mind, he must have been bemused when Merseyside electro-pop outfit Dead Or Alive, fronted by the outrageous Pete Burns, made it their UK chart debut nine years later in an infinitely more eyebrow-raising performance. It's arguable the original retains more of its good-time charm than Burns' stylized performance.

The beat-a-pile-driving, percussive groove that's maddeningly repetitive and danceable as hell, and hook lines as simple as the most elemental pop ever conceived. **Joe McEwen, Rolling Stone, February 1977**

That's The Way Love Goes

ARTIST Janet Jackson RELEASE DATE May 1993 (UK & US) WRITER Jimmy Jam, Terry Lewis, Janet Jackson PRODUCER Jimmy Jam, Terry Lewis LABEL Virgin (UK & US) UK CHART PEAK/WEEKS 2/10 US CHART PEAK/WEEKS 1/23

Janet avoided following her brothers into music, preferring to concentrate on an acting career. By 1982, however, family tradition proved too great and she launched her own solo career. Her meteoric rise was coupled with equal accolades for the writing and production team of Jam and Lewis. The move from A&M heightened the need for a smash and *That's The Way Love Goes* delivered. After the dance-orientated material of *1814*, a more mellow side was revealed on her Virgin debut.

La Jackson previews her Virgin debut, **Janet**, *with a gorgeous mid-tempo jam fuelled by warm classic funk and soul instrumental colours. Romantic, almost poetic lyrics, and an instantly memorable caressing, whispered vocal and fluid guitar line.* **Billboard, April 1993**

That's What Friends Are For

ARTIST Dionne Warwick And Friends RELEASE DATE November 1985 (UK & US) WRITER Carole Bayer Sayer, Burt Bacharach PRODUCER Carole Bayer Sager, Burt Bacharach LABEL Arista (UK & US) UK CHART PEAK/WEEKS 16/9 US CHART PEAK/WEEKS 1/23

Released to benefit the American Foundation For AIDS Research at a time when few musicians had yet got involved, the song had first been recorded by Rod Stewart for the 1982 film *Night Shift*, and was co-written by Carole Bayer Sager, ex-wife of Burt Bacharach. Warwick intended her version to be a duet with Stevie Wonder – whose distinctive harmonica is prominent – but then added two more Friends: Aretha Franklin and Elton John. It won the Grammy for Song of the Year in 1987.

The kind of refreshing multi-chart hit that surfaces about once a year.

The La's There She Goes

Its honest well-meaning clichés and uncluttered vocal exchanges between all the singers for the benefit of AIDS research, give the song a Christmas simplicity. **Rob Hoerburger, Rolling Stone, March 1986**

Theme From 'Shaft'

ARTIST Isaac Hayes RELEASE DATE December 1971 (UK)/October 1971 (US) WRITER Isaac Hayes PRODUCER Isaac Hayes LABEL Stax (UK)/Enterprise (US) UK CHART PEAK/WEEKS 4/12 US CHART PEAK/WEEKS 1/13

The rash of 'blaxploitation' movies in the Seventies inspired the occasional classic song, such as Curtis Mayfield's *Superfly*, but they didn't come any bigger than the Grammy-winning *Theme From 'Shaft'*, which was the first performing smash for Isaac Hayes. He was already well known as a backroom boy and with co-writer David Porter had penned hits for major acts like Carla Thomas and Sam and Dave, but this wah-wah guitar-laced stormer won an Academy Award and was the key to a solo career.

I knew it was leading up to something but I didn't want to see what it was leading up to. Nice to drive to. **Emitt Rhodes, Melody Maker, November 1971**

There! I've Said It Again

ARTIST Bobby Vinton RELEASE DATE December 1963 (UK)/November 1963 (US) WRITER Redd Evans, David Mann PRODUCER – LABEL Columbia (UK)/Epic (US) UK CHART PEAK/WEEKS 34/10 US CHART PEAK/WEEKS 1/13

The second successive Number 1 for Vinton was the follow-up to his *Blue Velvet*. Both were cover versions: Tony Bennett first recorded *Blue Velvet*, and *There! I've Said It Again* had been a US Number 1 for Vaughn Monroe in 1945. It was not a major hit in the UK, where The Beatles voted the song a 'miss' on the BBC's *Juke Box Jury*; their own single, *I Want To Hold Your Hand*, would knock it off the top of the US charts.

They don't give them much time to get old before they dig them up! It doesn't seem very long ago that they dug this one up. It's okay, but I can't see it doing very much. **Harry Secombe, Melody Maker, December 1963**

There She Goes

ARTIST The La's RELEASE DATE January 1989 (UK)/July 1991 (US) WRITER Lee Mavers PRODUCER B. Andrews LABEL Go! Discs (UK)/London (US) UK CHART PEAK/WEEKS 59/4 US CHART PEAK/WEEKS 49/10

Noel Gallagher of Oasis credits this as 'the first Brit-pop record' and, if so, confirms that movement's backward-looking philosophy. Produced by Bob Andrews, keyboard-player with American fixated pub-rockers Brinsley Schwarz, the harmonies are Byrds meet Hollies, the plucked guitar riff as nagging as any Sixties Merseybeat ever spawned. It was to be the Liverpudlians' finest three minutes: perfectionist Lee Mavers eventually produced an eponymous album, while bassist John Power flew the coop to form Cast.

Great attitude. Nothing like getting uptight about something so worthless and pointless as re-writing the Sixties in musical form. I'm being serious: if you can't even have control over the things most personal, most precious to you, what point is there to life? **Everett True, Melody Maker, November 1990**

Things Can Only Get Better

ARTIST D:Ream **RELEASE DATE** January 1993 **WRITER** Peter Cunnah, Jamie Petrie **PRODUCER** D:Ream, Tom Frederikse **LABEL** Magnet **UK CHART PEAK/WEEKS** 24/5 **US CHART PEAK/WEEKS** –

D:Ream, who were singer Peter Cunnah and keyboardist Al McKenzie, first charted with it in 1992, reaching Number 40. Two years later, after they had split, their label released a slick remix. This time, it shot to Number 1 and stayed there for four weeks. Three years later, in 1997, Tony Blair adopted the sunny tune as his campaign anthem. Because of the Blair connection, the BBC refused to play it. The disc made the Top 20 anyway, while Blair made it to Number 10.

I know it's only a pop song and I'm being pedantic but this tawdry, smelly pile of shit makes 2 Unlimited sound like Tchaikovsky on amyl nitrate. Come to think of it, that's what I like about 2 Unlimited. **Peter Paphides, Melody Maker, January 1994**

Think Twice

ARTIST Celine Dion **RELEASE DATE** October 1994 (UK)/August 1994 (US) **WRITER** Pete Sinfield, Andy Hill **PRODUCER** Chris Neil **LABEL** Epic (UK)/SSO Music/Epic (US) **UK CHART PEAK/WEEKS** 1/31 **US CHART PEAK/WEEKS** 95/5

Celine's *Think Twice* entered the British Top 40 in early November 1994 and climbed slowly, arriving at the peak in the first week of February and remained there for seven weeks. The near six months residency in the charts meant hundreds of radio plays, media plugs and television appearances, making her a star in Britain.

Think Twice topped the UK Charts for seven weeks, selling more that one million copies.... She is second only to Mariah Carey among female artists, is Sony's current master and she has done it by singing what she wants, and singing it extremely well. **Neville Farmer, Music Week, February 1996**

These Boots Are Made For Walking

ARTIST Nancy Sinatra **RELEASE DATE** January 1966 (UK & US) **WRITER** Lee Hazlewood **PRODUCER** Lee Hazlewood **LABEL** Reprise (UK & US) **UK CHART PEAK/WEEKS** 1/14 **US CHART PEAK/WEEKS** 1/14

Her father had sung *Nancy (With The Laughing Face)* about his eldest child in 1945, but a mini-skirted – and booted – Nancy finally got a hit in her own right, after a succession of unremarkable releases, with this stomping, snarling single, composed for her by producer Lee Hazlewood, who'd written with Duane Eddy. The upfront message of the song over its descending bass line was later given a pro-feminist spin by pundits.

Sounds like a skiffle group.... Hear that double-bass run?... This is unbelievable. Leave it on – either she is bad, or the band is bad. **Steve Winwood, Melody Maker, January 1966**

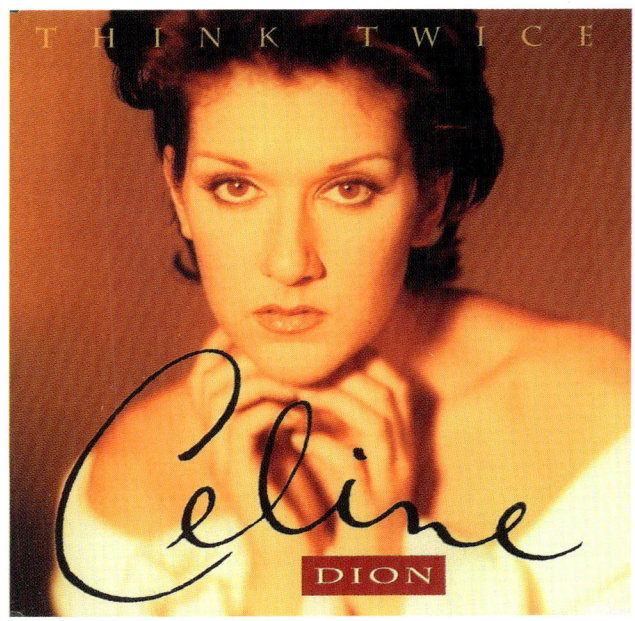

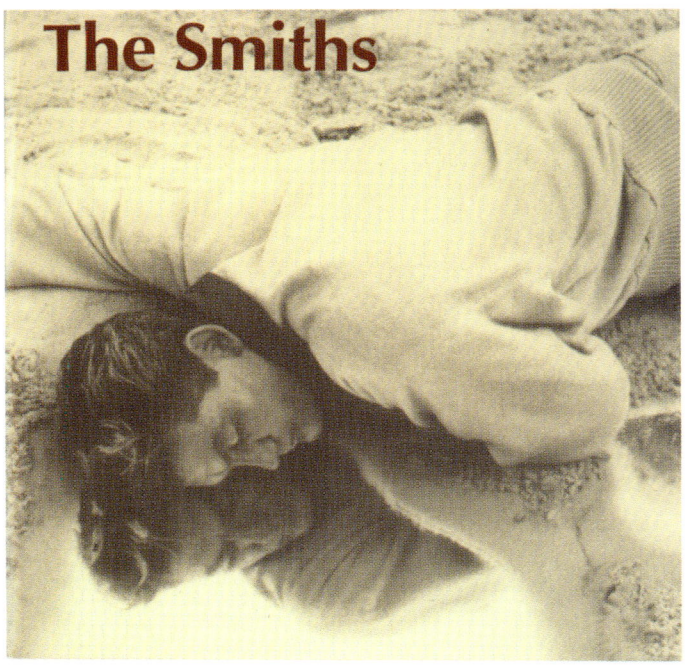

This Charming Man

ARTIST The Smiths RELEASE DATE November 1983 WRITER Morrissey, Johnny Marr PRODUCER J. Porter LABEL Rough Trade UK CHART PEAK/WEEKS 25/12 US CHART PEAK/WEEKS –

Following the indie chart success of their debut single **Hand In Glove**, the Smiths, on their first Rough Trade release, put together the components of Smithsdom. A picture sleeve of a continental art house figure (in this case Jean Marais), the winsome angst of Morrissey permeating the song, and the songwriting chemistry of Morrissey and Johnny Marr. NME declared it one of the best singles of the year, and an extended dance mix by François Kervorkian was released alongside, to The Smiths' annoyance.

Morrissey is serious but he offers us rapture, not dialectics. **This Charming Man** *is an accessible bliss, and seriously moving. This group fully understands that the casual is not enough.* **Paul Morley, NME, November 1983**

This Guy's In Love With You

ARTIST Herb Alpert RELEASE DATE July 1968 (UK)/May 1968 (US) WRITER Burt Bacharach, Hal David PRODUCER – LABEL A&M (UK & US) UK CHART PEAK/WEEKS 3/19 US CHART PEAK/WEEKS 1/14

The first Bacharach/David song to hit Number 1 in the US, **This Guy's In Love With You** remains one of the duo's most popular creations. Herb Alpert took a rare break from his trumpet and recorded it with his band the Tijuana Brass on his tenth album, **Beat of the Brass**. It became a hit after he sang it to his wife on a CBS-TV special.

A disc that's a thumping great hit in the States, probably because it is so totally different from anything Herb Alpert has done before. You see: this is Herb singing. **Derek Johnson, NME, June 1968**

This Is How We Do It

ARTIST Montell Jordan RELEASE DATE May 1995 (UK)/February 1995 (US) WRITER Montell Jordan, Oji Pierce PRODUCER D. Rasheed, O. J. Pierce, Montell Jordan LABEL Def Jam (UK)/PMP/RAL (US) UK CHART PEAK/WEEKS 11/8 US CHART PEAK/WEEKS 1/29

Ever since the Def Jam label first opened its doors in 1985 it has been at the forefront of rap music, signing the likes of LL Cool J and the Beastie Boys. Ten years later and rap had moved on and grown – Def Jam keeping pace with the changes. Sampled from Slick Rick's **Children's Story**, but a more melodic song than we had come to expect from Def Jam, there was little doubt that 6 ft 8 in singer Jordan would score a gigantic hit.

I wrote recently that right now all black music is crap. Montell Jordan's highly successful Stateside single is a case in point – auto-pilot, fast-buck, anthemic swing beat with the usual ring-a-ring-a-roses sing-along chant and partytime chorus. **David Stubbs, Melody Maker, May 1995**

This Old Heart Of Mine (Is Weak For You)

ARTIST The Isley Brothers RELEASE DATE April 1966 (UK)/February 1966 (US) WRITER Brian Holland, Edward Holland, Lamont Dozier PRODUCER Brian Holland, Lamont Dozier LABEL Tamla Motown (UK)/Tamla (US) UK CHART PEAK/WEEKS 3/17 US CHART PEAK/WEEKS 12/12

Although the Isley Brothers' Motown era was not without success, it did not deliver to the extent it had promised, partly because the Holland-Dozier-Holland material they were given was too similar to the Four Tops'. The highlight is undoubtedly **This Old Heart Of Mine**, a cut which enabled the Isleys' gospel and R&B roots to come to the fore.

Great, tremendous, magnificent. One of the cream of Tamla's output over the years, here is one re-release we should welcome. Maybe this time out the Isleys will get the hit that they deserve. **John Wells, October 1968**

This Ole House

ARTIST Rosemary Clooney RELEASE DATE October 1954 (UK)/August 1954 (US) WRITER Stuart Hamblen PRODUCER S. Colman LABEL Philips (UK)/Columbia (US) UK CHART PEAK/WEEKS 1/18 US CHART PEAK/WEEKS 1/27

In the Forties, Stuart Hamblen, hunting in Texas with a friend, found a rundown hut 20 miles from the nearest road. Inside, amidst much trash, lay the dead body of an old man. Hamblen, deeply moved, wrote this song's lyrics on a sandwich bag. No publisher wanted it, so he published it himself – Rosemary Clooney's recording sold over two million in the US alone. Shakin' Stevens' version was a bigger UK hit than Clooney's, topping the chart for four weeks versus her one.

This is a great side in more ways than one…. Miss Clooney has rarely sung better and this style certainly suits her. **Geoffrey Everitt, NME, October 1954**

This Town Ain't Big Enough For The Both Of Us

ARTIST Sparks RELEASE DATE May 1974 WRITER Ron Mael PRODUCER M. Winwood LABEL Island UK CHART PEAK/WEEKS 2/10 US CHART PEAK/WEEKS –

Intriguing, ironic, slightly demented, the brothers Mael crossed the Atlantic and signed to Island. Their 1974 album, **Kimono My House**, showed off the weird wit of elder nerdy-looking brother Ron's lyrics and the manic falsetto of the vaguely Bolanesque Russell, mixed with some art rock extravagance. After a couple more Top 10 singles, the formula fell flat and the group descended into self-parody.

Virtually everything there is to say has been said about this little troupe – Russ's voice reaches ridiculous high notes that you thought were exclusive to opera singers and eunuchs. The lyrics are crazy and prove to be entertaining in their own right. **Pete Makowski, Sounds, June 1974**

Those Lazy-Hazy-Crazy Days Of Summer

ARTIST Nat King Cole RELEASE DATE May 1963 (UK & US) WRITER Charles Tobias, Hans Carste PRODUCER – LABEL Capitol (UK & US) UK CHART PEAK/WEEKS 0/0 US CHART PEAK/WEEKS 6/12

During that last golden summer of Camelot, when American optimism ran high, Nat King Cole scored his final US Top 10 hit with *Those Lazy-Hazy-Crazy Days Of Summer*. It remains a summer radio standard. By the next summer, Cole was no longer performing, due to ill health. He died of lung cancer on 15 February 1965, age 47, leaving behind a long legacy of hits.

Those Were The Days

ARTIST Mary Hopkin RELEASE DATE September 1968 (UK & US) WRITER Gene Raskin PRODUCER Paul McCartney LABEL Apple (UK & US) UK CHART PEAK/WEEKS 1/21 US CHART PEAK/WEEKS 2/14

Signed to Apple following her *Opportunity Knocks* TV appearance, it was Paul McCartney who persuaded Mary Hopkin to record *Those Were The Days*. The single went on to sell four million copies worldwide and ironically knocked The Beatles' **Hey Jude** from the UK chart summit. Though she just failed to displace the Fab Four's **Get Back** to claim a second successive chart-topper with her follow-up, the McCartney-penned **Goodbye**, it would be this song for which the Welsh chanteuse is best remembered.

Pretty Miss Hopkin sings this elderly song with charm that occasionally takes on the extra bite of a Lotte Lenya performance. The backing is of the type that would be described in certain circles as 'Jog-along'.... **Chris Welch, Melody Maker, September 1968**

Three Lions (The Official Song Of The England Football Team)

ARTIST The Lightning Seeds Featuring Baddiel And Skinner RELEASE DATE June 1996 WRITER – PRODUCER – LABEL Epic UK CHART PEAK/WEEKS 1/15 US CHART PEAK/WEEKS –

Football songs are usually naff, tuneless affairs; footballers are nifty on their feet, but their singing is usually fairly clumsy. Ian Brodie of The Lightning Seeds managed to bring his own sweet melodies to England's European Cup anthem. It was a crisp, catchy song, with an understated chorus and added vocals from David Baddiel and Frank Skinner of BBC2 cult programme *Fantasy Football League*. The single sold loads but England were knocked out in the semi-final by Germany.

Three Lions … will nail itself onto your consciousness … and you will be involuntarily humming it like every other sad sucker within a couple of listens. It's no classic and may not figure too highly in critics' end of year polls … but it does the job. **Johnnie Cigarettes and Steve Sutherland, NME, May 1996**

Three Times A Lady

ARTIST Commodores RELEASE DATE August 1978 (UK)/June 1978 (US) WRITER Lionel Richie PRODUCER Jon Anthony Carmichael LABEL Motown (UK & US) UK CHART PEAK/WEEKS 1/14 US CHART PEAK/WEEKS 1/20

Number 1 for five weeks in the summer of 1978, *Three Times a Lady* established Commodores' singer and songwriter Lionel Richie as the soft rock songwriter to beat. Rumour has it that he wrote the song as an all-out commercial move after an embarrassing loss to Leo Sayer at the 1977 Grammy Awards – but it's also said that the song, which he dedicated to his wife, came from the heart, inspired by his parents' 37th anniversary.

Definitely the missing link between The Beatles and Paul McCartney. **Ian Penman, NME, November 1978**

3 am Eternal

ARTIST KLF (Featuring The Children Of The Revolution) RELEASE DATE January 1991 (UK)/June 1991 (US) WRITER J. Cauty, W. Drummond, R. Lyte PRODUCER KLF LABEL KLF Communications (UK)/Arista (US) UK CHART PEAK/WEEKS 1/11 US CHART PEAK/WEEKS 5/19

Originally released three years before it became a chart-topper, this dancefloor smash featured rapper Ricardo and soul singer Maxine Harvey, who appeared to play a bigger part in proceedings than KLF mainmen Jimi Cauty and Bill Drummond. Nevertheless the pair who had already made Number 1 back in 1988 with *Doctorin' The Tardis* under the moniker of the Timelords, would score three more Top 5 singles before retiring and dedicating their royalties to the mysterious K Foundation, whose activities included burning £1 million as an artistic statement.

Nifty sounds, although I'm not convinced about this decent '3 am Eternal' business: could you imagine it? No sunshine (unless you're in Iceland in the summer), no pubs (unless you are in Europe at the time) and you would only be able to shop at the bloody 7-11. **Simon Williams, NME, January 1991**

Thriller

ARTIST Michael Jackson RELEASE DATE November 1983 (UK)/February 1984 (US) WRITER Rod Temperton PRODUCER Quincy Jones LABEL Epic (UK & US) UK CHART PEAK/WEEKS 10/18 US CHART PEAK/WEEKS 4/14

Thriller is widely remembered more for the video than for the music. The album, released almost a year previously, was on its way to sales in excess of 40 million. Four singles had already been lifted and Jackson quickly established himself as the master of the short form video with a 14-minute promo directed by legend John Landis, breaking down MTV's black barriers in the process.

The best thing about hell this week. **Paul Morley, NME, November 1983**

Ticket To Ride

ARTIST The Beatles RELEASE DATE April 1965 (UK & US) WRITER John Lennon, Paul McCartney PRODUCER George Martin LABEL Parlophone (UK)/Capitol (US) UK CHART PEAK/WEEKS 1/12 US CHART PEAK/WEEKS 1/11

For once, The Beatles were following a style instead of starting one – The Searchers had already explored jangly arpeggiated guitars – but they still took it to the edge. Theirs was the first record to pair those guitars with a Phil Spector-style drumbeat, weeks before The Byrds released *Mr Tambourine Man*. Coincidentally, The Byrds' one was recorded first, but neither group had heard the other's recording. Such was the synchronicity between creative rock bands in those days.

The Tide Is High

ARTIST Blondie RELEASE DATE November 1980 (UK & US) WRITER John Holt PRODUCER Mike Chapman, Nicky Chinn LABEL Chrysalis (UK & US) UK CHART PEAK/WEEKS 1/12 US CHART PEAK/WEEKS 1/26

Blondie had their fifth Number 1 with this cover of a song originally recorded by the Paragons and written by their lead singer,

John Holt. Holt himself had charted five years earlier, when his version of Kris Kristofferson's *Help Me Make It Through The Night* made Number 2. Although Blondie never reached Number 1 again, they managed one more Top 10, *Rapture*, which made Number 7 in 1981.

Blondie are far more conversant with this specific genre than this record illustrates, so I find it hard to believe they have unanimously endorsed this toy town travesty. **Roy Carr, NME, November 1980**

Tie A Yellow Ribbon Round The Old Oak Tree

ARTIST Dawn (Featuring Tony Orlando) RELEASE DATE March 1973 (UK)/February 1973 (US) WRITER Irwin Levine, L. Russell Brown PRODUCER D. Appel, H. Medress LABEL Bell (UK & US) UK CHART PEAK/WEEKS 1/40 US CHART PEAK/WEEKS 1/23

This song is based on a modern American myth. It has yet to be proved that it ever happened or that anybody ever tied yellow ribbons around old oak trees to welcome loved ones home. The disc's success, however, is very real. It was massively popular in its time, selling over six million copies to become the biggest record of 1973.

For the fourth week in a row **Tie A Yellow Ribbon Round The Old Oak Tree** *is our top tune. The story, written by a prison inmate asking his girlfriend to show him a sign that she still cares, has given Dawn a new outlook on life.* **Billboard, 1973**

Tiger Feet

ARTIST Mud RELEASE DATE January 1974 WRITER Mike Chapman, Nicky Chinn PRODUCER Mike Chapman, Nicky Chinn LABEL Rak UK CHART PEAK/WEEKS 1/11 US CHART PEAK/WEEKS –

Mud were rockers with a cartoon Teddy Boy sheen. Dressed in drapes and brothel creepers they stomped out rock 'n' roll beats with a good time feel and a novelty twist. *Tiger Feet* was a pacey number, with a shoulder-shaking beat, which started a short-lived dance craze. Mud made their first appearance at the Streatham ice rink in London, singing a hippy-style number, *Flower Power*. They later abandoned the Sixties, adopting a Fifties sound with a sprinkling of rock.

… an irresistible beat, good guitar chunking and proves that Mud are not the duff band it was once believed. Good pop and they seem to be enjoying themselves … **Chris Welch, Melody Maker, January 1974**

Tin Soldier

ARTIST The Small Faces **RELEASE DATE** December 1967 (UK)/March 1968 (US) **WRITER** Steve Marriott, Ronnie Lane **PRODUCER** Steve Marriott, Ronnie Lane **LABEL** Immediate (UK & US) UK CHART PEAK/WEEKS 9/12 US CHART PEAK/WEEKS 73/5

After the cod psychedelia of **Itchycoo Park**, and worried it might typecast them, The Small Faces reverted to the bluesy feel that had brought them most of their chart success and featured P. P. Arnold on backing vocals. Steve Marriott wrote **Tin Soldier**, hoping it would impress his girlfriend Jenny Rylands. It must have done the trick – she married him.

*It is solid as well as being thoughtful, if it doesn't quite have the attraction of **Itchycoo Park** on first listenings at any rate, but the Small Faces are getting better all the time.* **Chris Welch, Melody Maker, December 1967**

To Sir With Love

ARTIST Lulu **RELEASE DATE** September 1967 (UK & US) **WRITER** Don Black, Mark London **PRODUCER** Mickie Most **LABEL** Epic (UK & US) UK CHART PEAK/WEEKS 0/0 US CHART PEAK/WEEKS 1/17

A powerful, versatile voice belted out from Lulu's tiny frame. Her sparky stage presence made her much in demand, and she became a solo act, appearing in pantomimes and clubs. Her single **To Sir With Love**, the title track to the film of the same name, focused on her rhythm and blues influences. In the Nineties she re-invented herself as a disco diva singing alongside the ultimate boy band Take That on **Re-Light My Fire**. She was better than them.

*Lulu has a hit – a big, roaring, bouncing smash hit with **To Sir With Love**, but ironically, although it is her record which is taking off on the charts, it's her screen personality which is beginning to attract more attention in this country.* **Tracy Thomas, NME, September 1967**

Tonight's The Night (Gonna Be Alright)

ARTIST Rod Stewart **RELEASE DATE** June 1976 (UK)/October 1976 (US) **WRITER** Rod Stewart **PRODUCER** Tom Dowd **LABEL** Riva (UK)/Warner (US) UK CHART PEAK/WEEKS 5/9 US CHART PEAK/WEEKS 1/23

This 1976 single, banned extensively on release because of the subject matter – the seduction of a virgin – was the biggest single of the year in the States after its eight weeks at Number 1. The track was taken from the **A Night On The Town** album, on which Stewart had kept the same combination of veteran US producer Tom Dowd and Muscle Shoals sidemen that had worked so well on **Atlantic Crossing**.

In 10 years time the couple who are still together will get rid of the kids for the evening, light the candles and dreamily reminisce about the night when Rod Stewart sang 'Their song' – romanticism with more than just a touch of lustful lechery. A powerful combination, how can you resist? **C. White, NME, May 1976**

Too Much Heaven

ARTIST The Bee Gees RELEASE DATE November 1978 (UK & US) WRITER The Bee Gees PRODUCER The Bee Gees, Albhy Galuten, Karl Richardson LABEL RSO (UK & US) UK CHART PEAK/WEEKS 3/13 US CHART PEAK/WEEKS 1/21

After defining Seventies disco with their contributions to the *Saturday Night Fever* soundtrack, The Bee Gees went for a more timeless sound with the haunting, ethereal **Too Much Heaven**. The first single from their album **Spirits Having Flown**, it was also featured on the benefit compilation **Music For UNICEF**. Brian Wilson sang it upon inducting The Bee Gees into the Rock 'n' Roll Hall of Fame in 1997.

Even the Godfathers of cult, The Brothers Gibb, sound as if they are tired of milking disco on the soft, slow and awkwardly seductive **Too Much Heaven**. *That enhancing whispered vocal which distinguished* **Night Fever** *and* **Jive Talking** *is a bit worn.* **Harry Doherty, Melody Maker, November 1978**

Torn Between Two Lovers

ARTIST Mary MacGregor RELEASE DATE February 1977 (UK)/November 1976 (US) WRITER Peter Yarrow, Philip Jarrell PRODUCER B. Beckett, P. Yarrow LABEL Ariola America UK CHART PEAK/WEEKS 4/10 US CHART PEAK/WEEKS 1/22

This modern retelling of an ancient sexual dilemma obviously struck a chord among two-timers everywhere, as it presented singer Mary MacGregor with her one and only hit. The song's poignant lyrics 'Torn between two lovers/Feeling like a fool/Loving the both of you/Is breaking all the rules' made listening to this the equivalent of going to see a weepie at the pictures.

Mary has taken the US by storm. The quasi-Country song is one of these subtle numbers that initially sounds bland and ordinary, then, after a few plays, you fall for it and it's a fall you don't recover from easily. **Caroline Coon, Melody Maker, February 1977**

Tossin' And Turnin'

ARTIST Bobby Lewis RELEASE DATE April 1961 (UK & US) WRITER Malou Rene, Ritchie Adams PRODUCER Malou Rene LABEL Beltone UK CHART PEAK/WEEKS – US CHART PEAK/WEEKS 1/23

After several unsuccessful auditions and despite the backing of friend Jackie Wilson, Bobby Lewis struck gold when he entered the office of Beltone Records. The already signed Ritchie Adams, lead singer of the Fireflies, recognized Lewis from an earlier gig and suggested he record his composition. It was a marriage made in heaven as **Tossin' And Turnin'** took the US charts by storm. Minor hits followed, including I'm **Tossin' And Turnin' Again**, before Lewis faded from the public eye.

Total Eclipse Of The Heart

ARTIST Bonny Tyler RELEASE DATE February 1983 (UK)/July 1983 (US) WRITER Jim Steinman PRODUCER Jim Steinman LABEL CBS (UK)/Columbia (US) UK CHART PEAK/WEEKS – US CHART PEAK/WEEKS 1/12

Gravel-voiced and husky, the Welsh singer had been spotted by songwriting team Steve Wilfe and Ronnie Scott, who saw her as the ideal front for their 1976 song **Lost In France** (a UK Top 10) and its follow-up **It's A Heartache** in 1978 (a US Number 3 and UK Number 4). In the early Eighties she started working with Meat Loaf producer and writer Jim Steinman. This single, immersed in Steinman's trademark mammoth production, was Tyler's only UK and US Number 1.

Touch Me In The Morning

ARTIST Diana Ross RELEASE DATE July 1973 (UK)/June 1973 (US) WRITER Michael Masser, Ronald Miller PRODUCER Michael Masser, T Baird LABEL Tamla Motown (UK)/Motown (US) UK CHART PEAK/WEEKS 9/13 US CHART PEAK/WEEKS 1/21

By 1972, Ross was making her acting debut in the movie *Lady Sings the Blues*, based on the life of Billie Holiday. Concerned to provide her with a hit vehicle to keep her singing career on the tracks, Berry Gordy Jr teamed novice composer Michael Masser – who went on to have further successes with Ross and Whitney Houston – with the experienced lyricist Ron Miller. The result was a sophisticated lament for lost sexual contact that combined riff elements borrowed from her first solo Number 1, **Ain't No Mountain High Enough**, with spoken parts from Ross.

The perfect choice for a single; it nags with a vengeance. The familiar molasses-like phrasing; the chorus builds as the singers strength wanes; the song becomes a desperate plea. Finally, the two moods merge double-tracked. **Mark Vinning, Rolling Stone, September 1973**

Town Called Malice/Precious

ARTIST The Jam RELEASE DATE February 1982 WRITER Paul Weller PRODUCER P. Wilson LABEL Polydor UK CHART PEAK/WEEKS 1/8 US CHART PEAK/WEEKS –

The Jam's third UK chart-topper owed as much to Motown as its predecessor Start had to The Beatles' *Taxman* – but, as ever, the band infused familiar musical ingredients with a new impetus and inspiration. The live shows also featured covers of classic soul from Chairmen of the Board and Smokey Robinson, all of which added up to a hint of Weller's future direction with the Style Council.

The song sounds better now than it did when it sat proudly at Number 1 for 16 weeks. **Danny Baker, NME, January 1983**

The Tracks Of My Tears

ARTIST Smokey Robinson And The Miracles RELEASE DATE May 1969 (UK)/July 1965 (US) WRITER Smokey Robinson, Warren Moore, Marv Tapplin PRODUCER Smokey Robinson LABEL Tamla Motown (UK)/Tamla (US) UK CHART PEAK/WEEKS 9/13 US CHART PEAK/WEEKS 16/12

When Bob Dylan was asked to name America's greatest living poet he nominated Smokey Robinson. Dylan was not being facetious: Smokey's ability to match lyrics with melody produced an unrivalled number of musical gems for The Miracles and the whole Motown catalogue. One of the most exquisite is this slow, tender, soulful classic described by *Rolling Stone* as 'a triumph of the songwriter's gift for metaphor', in which Smokey's vocal reaches unparalleled expressive heights.

Not a wondrous din I fear: lacking in jollity and menace. The trumpets bray at a great distance, and the men folk intone in a sprightly manner – but one is not moved to great ecstasy. **Chris Welch, Melody Maker, April 1969**

True

ARTIST Spandau Ballet RELEASE DATE April 1983 (UK)/August 1983 (US) WRITER Gary Kemp PRODUCER Steve Jolley, Tony Swain LABEL Reformation (UK)/Chrysalis (US) UK CHART PEAK/WEEKS 1/12 US CHART PEAK/WEEKS 4/18

Having launched the New Romantic look, alongside Duran Duran, with their kilted appearance on *To Cut A Long Story Short*, Spandau's guitarist Gary Kemp came up with a perfect vehicle for Tony Hadley with *True*, a lush soulful sound that was at the heart of Spandau Ballet's moment in the limelight. Its transatlantic success was followed by *Gold*, and in 1991 inspired PM Dawn's US Number 1 *Set Adrift On Memory Bliss*: Hadley made a cameo appearance in their promo video.

'This is the sound of my soul', confesses Gary Kemp in a concentrated drama that is more fascist architecture than music, which reflects about right, I say, for a pop kid who contrives his image on the model of a Fortnum and Mason sales assistant. **Penny Reel, NME, April 1983**

True Blue

ARTIST Madonna RELEASE DATE October 1986 (UK & US) WRITER Steve Bray, Madonna PRODUCER Steve Bray, Madonna LABEL Sire (UK & US) UK CHART PEAK/WEEKS 1/15 US CHART PEAK/WEEKS 3/16

True Blue is a deliciously simple tune, sung with radiant delight. The words are funny and quirky, almost like a nursery rhyme with its pairings of blue and you, love and glove. It has got a hop-skip-jump appeal with a beat that washes up like waves on the shore. And Madonna's voice cool and clean as water on a hot day.

Madonna has provided yet another light, dreamy soupalong soft tease, complete with stock playground lyrics and giggly sentiment. That's its formula, of course, goes without saying…. Still the queen of candy floss pop, it looks like it will take a helluva gal to knock her off that perch. **Paul Elliott, Sounds, September 1986**

True Colors

ARTIST Cyndi Lauper RELEASE DATE September 1986 (UK)/August 1986 (US) WRITER Tom Kelly, Bill Steinberg PRODUCER L. Petze, Cyndi Lauper LABEL Portrait (UK & US) UK CHART PEAK/WEEKS 12/11 US CHART PEAK/WEEKS 1/20

True Colours was the first release from Cyndi's second LP of the same name. Her first LP, **She's So Unusual**, had been a Top 5 success, spawning four US and two UK Top 5 singles, so was a hard act to follow. But this heartfelt ballad gave Cyndi her second US chart-topper, the similarly paced *Time After Time* having been a US Number 1 in 1984.

Impassioned ballad stuff from someone who, not long ago, was extremely fascinating, now she isn't, which is a pity. Thinks: Must stop being so apologetic. **Mr Spencer, Sounds, September 1986**

True Love

ARTIST Bing Crosby And Grace Kelly RELEASE DATE November 1956 (UK)/September 1956 (US) WRITER Cole Porter PRODUCER – LABEL Capitol (UK & US) UK CHART PEAK/WEEKS 4/27 US CHART PEAK/WEEKS 3/31

In the midst of the first upsurge of rock 'n' roll, Bing Crosby and Grace Kelly had a million seller with this Cole Porter tune from the film *High Society*. The film also starred Celeste Holm, Frank Sinatra, and Louis Armstrong and his orchestra. As it happened, Kelly's first hit single was also her last, as she quit the music business just two months after its release to become a princess.

The Cole Porter Songs of the film High Society *provide this week's high spot. The number* **True Love***, pairing Crosby & Kelly, is already a big hit in the States, and is almost sure to one over here.* **Laurie Henshaw, Melody Maker, November 1956**

Turn On, Tune In, Cop Out

ARTIST Freak Power RELEASE DATE October 1993 WRITER Norman Cook PRODUCER Norman Cook, Ashley Slater LABEL Fourth And Broadway UK CHART PEAK/WEEKS 29/5 US CHART PEAK/WEEKS –

This Norman Cook-led project had barely crept into the Top 30 when originally released in 1993, but its selection by Levi to use it in its advertising campaign at the turn of 1995 resulted in the single being re-released and a Top 3 hit. By this time however, Cook had moved on, recording under such monikers as Pizzaman and Fat Boy Slim, adding to an already impressive portfolio that included Beats International and the Housemartins.

Featuring Normon Cook, who is a pop God, this desperately funky bongos 'n' reefer number manages to sound like Richard Fairbrass doing karaoke with Gil Scott Heron's **The Bottle***. Yes, that good!* **Steven Wells, NME, October 1993**

Turn! Turn! Turn!

ARTIST The Byrds RELEASE DATE November 1965 (UK)/October 1965 (US) WRITER Pete Seeger PRODUCER Terry Melcher LABEL CBS (UK)/Columbia (US) UK CHART PEAK/WEEKS 26/8 US CHART PEAK/WEEKS 1/14

The Byrds exploded onto the scene in 1965 with their international chart-topper *Mr Tambourine Man*, an electrified version of a Bob Dylan tune. They introduced the world to folk-rock. After following up with another Dylan tune, **All I Really Want To Do**, they looked to folk legend Pete Seeger. His *Turn! Turn! Turn!*, an antiwar song with lyrics from the book of Ecclesiastes, became The Byrds' second and biggest US Number 1, topping Billboard's Hot 100 for three weeks.

The words of this number are from the book of Ecclesiastes, adapted by folkiest Pete Seeger.... Jangling 12-string guitar, and a falsetto voice. **Melody Maker, October 1965**

The Twist

ARTIST Chubby Checker RELEASE DATE September 1969 (UK)/August 1969 (US) WRITER Hank Ballard PRODUCER K. Mann LABEL Columbia (UK)/Parkway (US) UK CHART PEAK/WEEKS 14/12 US CHART PEAK/WEEKS 1/39

Originally recorded by Hank Ballard & The Midnighters, who performed it on their tours throughout the US, *The Twist* caught on slowly. American Bandstand mogul Dick Clark, seeing the budding interest in Ballard's disc, had Chubby Checker record a sound-alike version. It rocketed to Number 1 in America, starting a dance revolution. Two years later, the song returned to Number 1 after being discovered by the jet set. It was the first rock record to get adults onto the dance floor.

Twist And Shout

ARTIST The Beatles RELEASE DATE March 1964 WRITER Bert Russell, Phil Medley PRODUCER George Martin LABEL Parlophone (UK)/Tollie (US) UK CHART PEAK/WEEKS 0/0 US CHART PEAK/WEEKS 2/26

The Beatles recorded the Isley Brothers' *Twist And Shout* on 11 February 1963, at the very end of the day long session that produced nearly their entire first album. Though not a single in Britain, it was released in the US at the height of Beatlemania and made Number 2 for four weeks running. But what was keeping it out of the Number 1 slot? – *Can't Buy Me Love*, of course.

Despite being recorded on the equivalent of a hip-flask tape machine with about half a battery, the quality is good, and the booze and atmosphere of the Hamburg Star club is captured with not a little authenticity. **Ian Birch, Melody Maker, July 1977**

2-4-6-8 Motorway

ARTIST Tom Robinson Band RELEASE DATE October 1977 WRITER Tom Robinson PRODUCER Vic Maile LABEL EMI UK CHART PEAK/WEEKS 5/9 US CHART PEAK/WEEKS –

The Tom Robinson Band emerged during 1977, and was loosely linked with punk, although Robinson's songs were distinguished by the quality of their melodic and lyrical content – his previous band, Cafe Society, had been signed to the Kinks' Konk label. *2-4-6-8 Motorway* was an appropriately driving dance hit a year before Robinson acquired a 'radical' tag by coming out as overtly as possible on *Glad To Be Gay*. After a brief diversion into post-punk new wave with Sector 27, Robinson eventually rediscovered his touch on the 1983 hit *War Baby*.

TRB are one of the few bands who have managed to locate social/political pith within intestinal Rock 'n' Roll. Motorway is couched in some quasi-Stones, gut searing chords and, indeed, Danny Kustow's lead guitar is beautifully audio throughout. **Ian Birch, Melody Maker, October 1977**

2 Become 1

ARTIST The Spice Girls RELEASE DATE December 1996 WRITER Spice Girls, Richard Stannard, Matt Rowe PRODUCER Richard Stannard, Matt Rowe LABEL Virgin UK CHART PEAK/WEEKS 1/1 US CHART PEAK/WEEKS –

After the immense success of *Wannabe* in summer 1996, industry pundits were looking for proof that The Spice Girls were not a flash in the pan. *2 Become 1*, a warm number featuring Baby Spice in particular, saw off all comers to land the coveted Christmas UK Number 1 that year, and showed that the Spice Girls phenomenon was set to be around forever … well, at least for another 12 months or so.

Two Little Boys

ARTIST Rolf Harris RELEASE DATE November 1969 WRITER Theodore F. Morse, Edward Madden PRODUCER – LABEL Columbia UK CHART PEAK/WEEKS 1/25 US CHART PEAK/WEEKS –

Australian-born artist Harris moved to the UK in the Fifties and became a TV regular in the Sixties. He had already had two UK Top 10 hits early in the decade, but it was this song – originally written in 1903 about an incident that took place during the American Civil War between two childhood pals – that gave him greatest success. It became the Christmas Number 1 of 1969 and Rolf became the first Australian soloist to top the UK charts.

It is difficult for me to start bandying about words like 'childish', 'juvenile' and 'infantile' speaking about a man who was observed running about the Welsh hillsides last week, playing Cowboys and Indians and letting off fireworks. **Chris Welch, Melody Maker, November 1969**

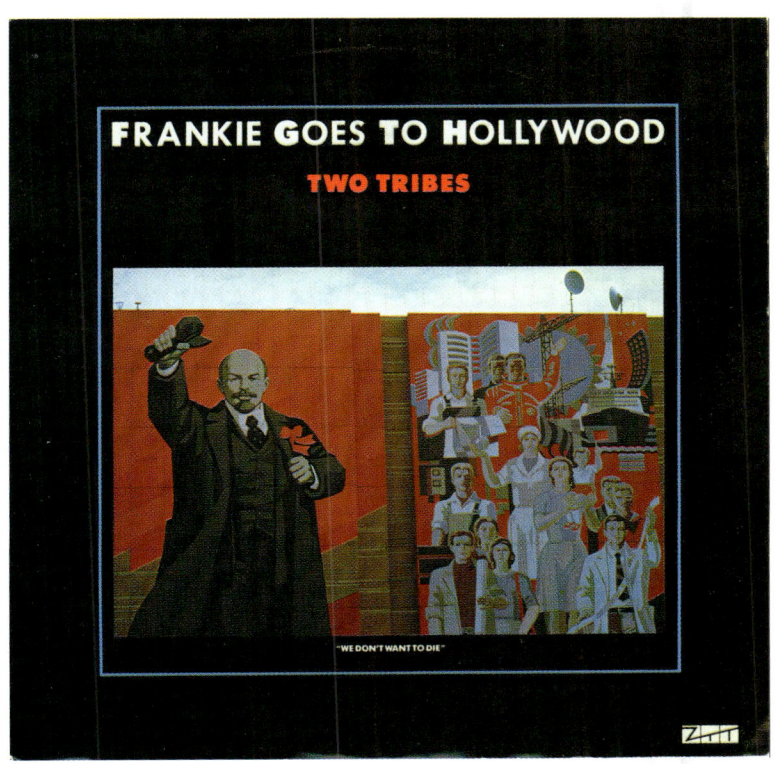

Two Tribes

ARTIST Frankie Goes To Hollywood **RELEASE DATE** June 1983 (UK)/October 1984 (US) **WRITER** Holly Johnson, Peter Gill, March O'Toole **PRODUCER** Trevor Horn **LABEL** ZTT (UK)/Island (US) **UK CHART PEAK/WEEKS** 1/21 **US CHART PEAK/WEEKS** 43/15

Relax was a hard act to follow, but *Two Tribes* was a worthy successor. Another relentless bass line, another distinctive vocal performance from Holly Johnson, and another superb production job from Trevor Horn made it as unstoppable as its predecessor, and gave the Frankies their second UK Number 1 of the year. It stayed there for nine weeks, helped in no small way by another memorable video featuring a no-holds-barred, hand-to-hand fight between Reagan and Andropov lookalikes.

… which goes the whole hog to prove that there is more to them then stolen Ian Dury basslines. It's not just that they are suave or a lovely shade of mauve, it's that they have gone into the Garden Lord and these headaches are going to last a long time. **Mick Mercer, Melody Maker, May 1984**

U Can't Touch This

ARTIST MC Hammer **RELEASE DATE** June 1990 (UK)/April 1990 (US) **WRITER** MC Hammer, Rick James, Alonzo Miller **PRODUCER** MC Hammer **LABEL** Capitol (UK & US) **UK CHART PEAK/WEEKS** 3/16 **US CHART PEAK/WEEKS** 8/17

MC Hammer made his first steps on the way to pop stardom thanks to an investment by baseball players Mike Davis and Dwayne Murphy, selling copies of his first record from the back of his car. A copy found its way to Capitol Records and earned Hammer a recording contract. This combination of a rhythm track based on Rick James's *Super Freak*, coupled with an exuberant dance routine, made the track a winner. It crashed into the American charts at Number 27.

Culturally more popular than sliced bread in the US of A, MC Hammer updates one of the more favoured moments of the dreadful Rick James in a barrage of twiddly synths. **Ben Thompson, NME, 9 June 1990**

Unbelievable

ARTIST EMF **RELEASE DATE** November 1990 (UK)/April 1990 (US) **WRITER** James Atken, Ian Dench, Zachary Foley, Mark DeCloedt, Deran Brownson **PRODUCER** R Jezzard **LABEL** Parlophone (UK)/EMI (US) **UK CHART PEAK/WEEKS** 3/13 **US CHART PEAK/WEEKS** 1/23

Along with Jesus Jones, EMF – the name an acronym for something extremely rude – represented the late Eighties and early Nineties coming together of electro-beat and rock. They hailed from the rural Forest of Dean, but rivalled the then hip Manchester bands for their urban savvy. The song did better Stateside than at home. EMF would cut a record with Reeves and Mortimer, but from then on it was downhill all the way.

Since the debut single, EMF have established themselves as the authentic popstars with attitude. Mingling the considerable angst of the far-flung rural outpost with the received imagery of the contemporary, cosmopolitan dance scene – they appear to have got the lot. **Michael Odell, Melody Maker, December 1990**

Unchained Melody

ARTIST The Righteous Brothers RELEASE DATE August 1965 (UK)/July 1965 (US) WRITER Hy Zaret, Alex North PRODUCER Phil Spector LABEL London (UK)/Philles (US) UK CHART PEAK/WEEKS 14/12 US CHART PEAK/WEEKS 4/13

In 1955 four versions of *Unchained Melody* sat together in the UK Top 20, Jimmy Young's, Al Hibbler's, Les Baxter's and Liberace's – an unbeaten record number of simultaneous chart entries for any song. Ten years later Phil Spector produced the definitive blue-eyed soul version with The Righteous Brothers, to put it back into the Top 20; and 25 years later still, the Spector/Righteous Brothers record again reached Number 1 after being used in the film *Ghost*.

Unchained Melody is an international hit. The duo are in great demand. Already set for appearances on several TV Shows, Hullabaloo and Shindig, the pair plan their first tour of US Colleges in the fall. **Tracy Thomas, NME, August 1965**

Under Pressure

ARTIST Queen And David Bowie RELEASE DATE November 1981 (UK & US) WRITER David Bowie, Queen PRODUCER David Bowie, Brian May, Freddie Mercury LABEL EMI (UK)/Elektra (US) UK CHART PEAK/WEEKS 1/11 US CHART PEAK/WEEKS 29/15

According to Brian May, while David Bowie was living near Mountain Studio, the recording facility which Queen had bought near Montreux, Switzerland, 'He'd often come over to see us, to chat and have a drink'. These friendly visits produced *Under*

Pressure. This dramatic piece of pop angst bewails the destruction of 'some good friends' by pressures on the street (presumably drugs). It became a UK Number 1 and was later sampled in Vanilla Ice's *Ice Ice Baby*.

Oh my god, it really is David Bowie this time, only with Queen. This bombastic drivel should get him shot by some space cadet. Unfortunately, it will also be Number 1. **Melody Maker, October 1981**

Under The Boardwalk

ARTIST The Drifters RELEASE DATE September 1964 (UK)/June 1964 (US) WRITER Arthur Resnick, Kenny Young PRODUCER Bert Berns LABEL Atlantic (UK & US) UK CHART PEAK/WEEKS 45/4 US CHART PEAK/WEEKS 4/14

The group, originally formed in 1953, chose their name from the fact that each member of the group had 'drifted' from group to group. Reaching Number 2 in the US with *There Goes My Baby* six years later, they continued to have consistent Stateside chart success but this was their last Top 5 single in 1964. In the UK, the song failed to reach the Top 20 until Bruce Willis' 1987 cover reached Number 2 behind the Pet Shop Boys' *It's A Sin*.

Mike: 'I like this one – The Drifters, it is fantastic. They deserve a hit.' Dave: 'I don't think this will get them a hit but it is great, sounds a bit like Save The Last Dance For Me, doesn't it?' **The Fourmost, Melody Maker, August 1964**

Under The Moon Of Love

ARTIST Showaddywaddy RELEASE DATE November 1976 WRITER Tommy Boyce, Curtis Lee PRODUCER – LABEL Bell UK CHART PEAK/WEEKS 1/15 US CHART PEAK/WEEKS –

The Sha Na Na of Leicester were an amalgam of local bands who spun together rock 'n' roll revival and plenty of showmanship, including spangly suits and brothel creepers – the works. Their output included tongue-in-cheek but affectionate cover versions of classic tracks, including Eddie Cochran's *Three Steps To Heaven* in 1975 and this loping ballad.

I remember this tune from the first time around, but mercifully forget the artist. This is not as instantly memorable as Three Steps. The last ever Bell single, as it becomes Arista. **John Ingham, Sounds, October 1976**

Unfinished Symphony

ARTIST Massive Attack RELEASE DATE February 1991 WRITER Massive Attack, Shara Nelson PRODUCER Cameron McVey LABEL Wild Bunch UK CHART PEAK/WEEKS 13/9 US CHART PEAK/WEEKS –

Massive Attack lead the trip-hop movement: spaced out on slow grooves that stir in soul, punk, funk and reggae. 3D, Daddy G and Mushroom's *Unfinished Symphony* from their first album **Blue Lines** is classic. The lyrics are edgy and dark, the beats hypnotic and steady and guest vocalist Shara Nelson's smoky, strong voice carries the song across a landscape of samples and scratches. It is the sound of the city, complete with stars and gutters.

An intense, warm blooded dance track…. I liked it for its cheeky sense of melodrama, the nobody gets off the dance floor alive beat and its mood of wilful destruction. **NME, 1991**

Unforgettable

ARTIST Nat King Cole And Natalie Cole RELEASE DATE June 1991 (UK)/July 1991 (US) WRITER Irving Gordan PRODUCER – LABEL Elektra (UK & US) UK CHART PEAK/WEEKS 19/8 US CHART PEAK/WEEKS 14/17

For many, this is Nat King Cole's most unforgettable song, its prominence boosted by the success of his daughter Natalie's 1992 cover. Nat King Cole's original version made little impact in Britain and only reached Number 12 on America's hit parade. Nonetheless, among Cole's fans, it remained one of his best remembered songs. Although not everyone thought Natalie Cole's beyond-the-grave duet with her father was in the best of taste, she did the music world a service by inspiring many to track down the original version.

I've toured with Nat many times, both in America and Britain, and there's only one word to describe him – impeccable. **Ted Heath, NME, February 1965**

Up The Junction

ARTIST Squeeze RELEASE DATE June 1979 WRITER Chris Difford, Glen Tilbrock PRODUCER J. Wood LABEL A&M UK CHART PEAK/ WEEKS 2/11 US CHART PEAK/WEEKS –

A piece of classic Squeeze which borrowed its lyrical mood from the Sixties film starring Suzy Kendall and Dennis Waterman. The vignette of a courting couple, worthy of the Kinks' Ray Davies, was immaculate, but like

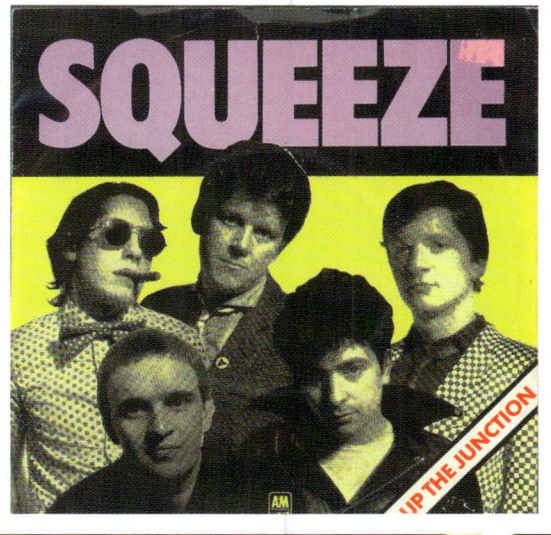

the previous *Cool For Cats*, the single was kept agonizingly off the Number 1 position, this time by Tubeway Army's *Are 'Friends' Electric*.

Squeeze's tale of pain in flowering and fading Clapham is charming. **Simon Frith, Melody Maker, May 1979**

Upside Down

ARTIST Diana Ross RELEASE DATE July 1980 (UK & US) WRITER Bernard Edwards, Nile Rodgers PRODUCER Bernard Edwards, Nile Rodgers LABEL Motown (UK & US) UK CHART PEAK/WEEKS 2/12 US CHART PEAK/WEEKS 1/29

When in 1980 Ross was teamed with Bernard Edwards and Nile Rodgers of Chic, she became unhappy with the session, believing she sounded like a guest star on a Chic album. With help from Motown producer Russ Terrana she remixed every track to bring her vocals forward. The resulting album, **Diana**, went to Number 2 in the US. By September *Upside Down*, a relative sleeper from the album, shot to Number 1, staying there for four weeks, longer than any of her other solo Number 1s.

An out-and-out disco smash from Miss Ross, re-mixed by the lady herself. Should be her biggest hit in years. Great bass and drum and sounds, stunning vocal track and highly accessible hook line. **Martin Sutton, Melody Maker, July 1980**

Uptight (Everything's Alright)

ARTIST Stevie Wonder RELEASE DATE February 1966 (UK)/December 1965 (US) WRITER Sylvia Moy, Stevie Wonder, Henry Cosby PRODUCER H. Cosby, W. Stevenson LABEL Tamla Motown (UK)/Tamla (US) UK CHART PEAK/WEEKS 14/10 US CHART PEAK/WEEKS 3/14

He's been around so long that it's difficult to imagine the impact that Little Stevie Wonder must have had when he landed his first Number 1 on the verge of his teens with *Fingertips (Part 2)* in 1963. Two years later, with the boy Wonder now a mature 15-year-old, *Uptight*, apparently inspired in part by the Stones' *Satisfaction*, featured his manic harmonica playing in a real Motown groove and gave him his first transatlantic Top 20 hit.

Typical thumping bass-line in Tamla vein – but a lot more exciting than a lot of Motown records. Waking vocal and backing hit. Very big in Britain. **Melody Maker, January 1966**

Uptown Girl

ARTIST Billy Joel RELEASE DATE October 1983 (UK)/September 1983 (US) WRITER Billy Joel PRODUCER Phil Ramone LABEL CBS (UK)/Columbia (US) UK CHART PEAK/WEEKS 1/17 US CHART PEAK/WEEKS 3/22

This harmony-laced, Sixties-styled song was Billy Joel's tribute to the Four Seasons from his LP **An Innocent Man**, a collection of musical pastiches that brought him commercial breakthrough in the UK. The track was dedicated to his then girlfriend, supermodel Christine Brinkley, who also appeared in the video. They married in 1985 but separated in 1994.

Venus

ARTIST Bananarama RELEASE DATE May 1986 (UK)/June 1986 (US) WRITER R. Leevonen PRODUCER Mike Stock, Matt Aitken, Pete Waterman LABEL London (UK & US) UK CHART PEAK/WEEKS 8/13 US CHART PEAK/WEEKS 1/19

Bananarama had many more hits in Britain than they did in America, but only America made them Number 1. Their version of **Venus** reached the top of *Billboard*'s Hot 100, the same spot that the Shocking Blue's original had commandeered 16 years earlier. Its synthesized and heavily mechanized dance beat identified it as a the work of Stock Aitken Waterman, the beginning of the producers' long working relationship with Bananarama.

Ah, what I could do with the giggling gaggle on a desert island: I'd lay them side by side, slowly unbuckle their corsets, switch on a tape of their anaemic pap, smother their alabaster skin with maple syrup … and … and … and … and … wait for the ants to arrive. **Ted Mico, Melody Maker, May 1986**

Venus

ARTIST Frankie Avalon RELEASE DATE April 1959 (UK)/February 1959 (US) WRITER Ed Marshall PRODUCER – LABEL HMV Pop (UK)/Chancellor (US) UK CHART PEAK/WEEKS 16/6 US CHART PEAK/WEEKS 1/17

When Bob Marcucci discovered Fifties teen idol Frankie Avalon he was merely an 18-year-old trumpet player in the Philadelphia band Rocco & His Saints. Marcucci convinced Avalon to drop his trumpet and began producing a string of hits for him. **Venus** was the biggest, his first million seller. Nearly two decades later, in 1976, he charted with a disco version of the song, which he reportedly regretted later.

Not so long ago Philadelphia born Frankie topped the US charts for several weeks with his million-selling Venus platter. Now, after a slow start, the disc is beginning to climb the British charts, and has forged ahead of the rival Dickie Valentine version. **Keith Goodwin, NME, May 1959**

Vienna

ARTIST Ultravox RELEASE DATE January 1981 WRITER Midge Ure, Warren Cann, Christopher Cross, William Currie PRODUCER C. Plank, Midge Ure LABEL Chrysalis UK CHART PEAK/WEEKS 2/14 US CHART PEAK/WEEKS –

After Ultravox founder John Foxx left Ultravox for a solo career in 1979, the band looked for a suitable replacement and found one in the shape of ex-Visage, Slik and Rich Kids guitarist/singer Midge Ure. **Vienna** was the title track of the new line-up's 1980 album. The ballad, written by the entire band, and produced by Conny Plank, a German electro wizard, reached its Number 2 position in the UK after strong radio airplay.

*This is an unbearably po-faced track. I'm a sucker for Viennese mythology and history (my Mastermind subject), but there isn't any in **Vienna**. If you see what I mean. In its place is a load of extremely portentous airy fairy nonsense.* **Ian Penman, NME, January 1981**

Ultravox
'VIENNA'

Vincent

ARTIST Don McLean RELEASE DATE May 1972 (UK)/March 1972 (US) WRITER Don McLean PRODUCER Ed Freeman LABEL United Artists (UK & US) UK CHART PEAK/WEEKS 1/15 US CHART PEAK/WEEKS 12/12

Vincent was a highly romantic tribute to Vincent Van Gogh. In 1970, Don McLean spent six weeks singing at primary schools in Massachusetts. While staying at a lodging house he read about the painter, and was so inspired that he wrote a song about him. With its intimate, semi-autobiographical lyrics and genteel instrumentation led by quiet, whimsical guitar, *Vincent* was so popular that it was played daily in the Van Gogh Museum in Amsterdam.

Vincent, syrupy and full of water-colour: tells the story of a painter who most certainly wasn't. You might well dig this very much, but just don't expect another **American Pie** *– and in truth, who could?* **Rory Hollingworth, Melody Maker, May 1972**

Virginia Plain

ARTIST Roxy Music RELEASE DATE August 1972 WRITER Bryan Ferry PRODUCER Pete Sinfield LABEL Island UK CHART PEAK/WEEKS 4/12 US CHART PEAK/WEEKS –

Though they rose in the early Seventies, Roxy stood apart from other Glam Rock bands. Their influence on early Eighties British pop was immense, particularly the New Romantics. *Virginia Plain*, their breakthrough UK hit single, was their clarion call. Bryan Ferry's elastically vibrato warble perfectly complemented Brian Eno's synthesized roller coaster gallop, while Phil Manzanera applied a range of guitar effects from Duane Eddy-esque Fifties to feedback loops and Andy Mackay's percussive oboe hooks seemed to came straight out of *Dr Who*.

There is a good thumping rhythm, nice use of fuzzed guitar and synthesiser, a muddle break slightly reminiscent of the more recent Who singles, and a vocal that 10 years ago would have been dubbed a 'novelty record'. A very good single. **Dave Peacock, Sounds, August 1972**

Virtual Insanity

ARTIST Jamiroquai RELEASE DATE August 1996 WRITER Jay Kay, Toby Smith PRODUCER Jay Kay, Al Stone LABEL Sony UK CHART PEAK/WEEKS 3/11 US CHART PEAK/WEEKS –

As the Eighties wore on, jazz-funk, as exemplified by the likes of Lonnie Liston Smith and Roy Ayers, began to make substantial chart inroads. British acts caught on and Jamiroquai's explosion on to the scene in 1993 saw them gain plaudits from almost all corners. Their third album **Travelling Without Moving** in 1996 was kicked off by the excellent *Virtual Insanity* single; its adventurous video, featuring singer Jay Kay in an ever shifting room, deservedly won an award from MTV.

A grandly squelchy orchestral funk-out with squiggly wah-wah trimmings; it's not quite the retro-trash glitter-ball sex kitten that **Space Cowboy** *was, but it still throbs substantially…. Totally spooned out, dude.* **Stephen Dalton, NME, August 1996**

Volare (Nel Blu Dipinto Di Blue)

ARTIST Dean Martin **RELEASE DATE** August 1958 (UK & US) **WRITER** Michelle Parish, Domenico Modugno **PRODUCER – LABEL** Capitol (UK & US) **UK CHART PEAK/WEEKS** 2/14 **US CHART PEAK/WEEKS** 12/13

The UK charts of October 1958 had a trio of interpretations of *Volare*: one featured the song's writer, Domenico Modugno, who had taken it to the US Number 1, the others were covers by Marino Marini and Dean Martin. The ballad suited Martin's relaxed style. Born Dino Crocetti, he had reminded listeners of his Italian roots with singles including **Mambo Italiano** and **That's Amore**, which re-surfaced on the soundtrack of Norman Jewison's 1987 movie *Moonstruck*.

A wonderful song and a record reviewer's nightmare! The song is sure to be a big hit, but there's such a stock of good recording that the job of picking the second disc to Dean Martin's is more than a little tricky. **Keith Fordyce, NME, August 1958**

Voodoo Chile

ARTIST Jimi Hendrix **RELEASE DATE** November 1970 **WRITER** Jimi Hendrix **PRODUCER** Chas Chandler **LABEL** Track **UK CHART PEAK/WEEKS** 1/13 **US CHART PEAK/WEEKS** –

This single would give Jimi Hendrix the unenviable distinction – along with Otis Redding and Jim Reeves – of having his biggest UK hit single after his death. Buried on 1 October 1970, Hendrix was atop the chart seven weeks later, symbolically deposing Woodstock, Joni Mitchell's anthem for the previous year's peace and love festival of which Jimi had been a star. Its choppy guitar introduction remains one of the most distinctive in rock. The song had appeared twice on the previous year's **Electric Ladyland** album.

Coupled with this memorial single is **Hey Joe**, *the hit that brought Jimi to fame in Britain, and* **All Along the Watch Tower**. *Familiar material to his fans, of course.* **Chris Welch, Melody Maker, October 1970**

Waiting For A Girl Like You

ARTIST Foreigner **RELEASE DATE** December 1981 (UK)/October 1981 (US) **WRITER** Mick Jones, Lou Gramm **PRODUCER – LABEL** Atlantic (UK & US) **UK CHART PEAK/WEEKS** 8/13 **US CHART PEAK/WEEKS** 2/23

After a number of minor UK hits, the Anglo-American hard-rock group at last made the UK Top 10 in January 1982. The track, featuring Thomas Dolby on additional keyboards, was an even more spectacular success in the US, spending 10 consecutive weeks at Number 2, nine of which were behind Olivia Newton-John's **Physical**. The track was a soft ballad which differed from the group's normal output of heavy rock.

I'm not trying to be nasty, yet I've always thought that Foreigner was a group worth ignoring rather than criticising. **Tim White, Rolling Stone, September 1981**

Wake Up Little Susie

ARTIST The Everly Brothers **RELEASE DATE** November 1957 (UK)/September 1957 (US) **WRITER** Felice and Boudleaux Bryant **PRODUCER – LABEL** London (UK)/Cadence (US) **UK CHART PEAK/WEEKS** 2/13 **US CHART PEAK/WEEKS** 1/26

By the mid Fifties, Don and Phil Everly were broke and trying to sell their songs to any interested party. They were picked up by

Archie Bleyer's Cadence label and made their transatlantic Top 10 debut with **Bye Bye Love**. The follow-up was this song written by the husband and wife team of Felice and Boudleaux Bryant. Despite being banned by certain radio stations, who regarded its lyric as somewhat suggestive, **Wake Up Little Susie** nevertheless stormed the charts to give the brothers their first US Number 1 single.

*The **Bye Bye Love** Everly Brothers would seem to have another hit with **Wake Up Little Susie**! This one features a heavy guitar beat. The nasal caterwauling of the Everlys mars the ballad – not the reverse.* **Laurie Hernshaw, Melody Maker, November 1957**

Walk Away Renee

ARTIST The Four Tops RELEASE DATE December 1967 (UK)/February 1968 (US) WRITER Mike Brown, Tony Sansone, Bob Calilli PRODUCER Harry Lookofsky, Steve Jerome, Bill Jerome LABEL Tamla Motown (UK)/Motown (US) UK CHART PEAK/WEEKS 3/11 US CHART PEAK/WEEKS 14/8

This song was originally recorded by New York group the Left Banke and reached Number 5 in the US in 1966. In 1968, the songwriters Holland, Dozier and Holland were in contractual dispute with Motown and The Four Tops, who had relied on these songwriters (along with many other groups in the Motown stable), were forced to change direction. Their cover of **Walk Away Renee** was a Top 20 hit in the US and Top 3 in the UK.

Originally a hit from the Left Bank, and in these spartan days (release wise) after the big guns have fired their best shots for Christmas, it's a welcome sound. It's more than that – it's a marvellous sound. **Chris Welch, Melody Maker, December 1967**

Walk In The Black Forest

ARTIST Horst Janowski RELEASE DATE July 1965 (UK)/May 1965 (US) WRITER Horst Janowski PRODUCER – LABEL Mercury (UK & US) UK CHART PEAK/WEEKS 3/18 US CHART PEAK/WEEKS 12/13

Although Janowski had been voted Germany's top jazz pianist for the last nine years, it was this purely instrumental release that brought international recognition. He had started out backing Caterina Valente on tour in 1952 and later worked with Miles Davis

and Ella Fitzgerald. In 1960, he started his own choir of amateur singers and used it with his orchestra. This record, his own composition, was originally written in 1962 but made the UK Top 3 and US Top 20 three years later.

Walk Like A Man

ARTIST The Four Seasons RELEASE DATE March 1963 (UK)/February 1963 (US) WRITER Bob Crewe, Bob Gaudio PRODUCER Bob Crewe LABEL Stateside (UK)/Vee-Jay (US) UK CHART PEAK/WEEKS 12/12 US CHART PEAK/WEEKS 1/13

Continuing their incredible run of success, The Four Seasons notched up their third US chart-topper in early 1963. Labelled the most successful group in the States at the time, they would soon be pitted against The Beatles' invasion. It was a battle in which Frankie Valli's men came out second best with just one further Number 1 to compare with the Merseysiders' 20 before they split.

*America's Four Seasons turn in a compulsive twister: **Walk Like A Man**, which has topped the US charts but it doesn't look like breaking any British record sales.* **Melody Maker, March 1963**

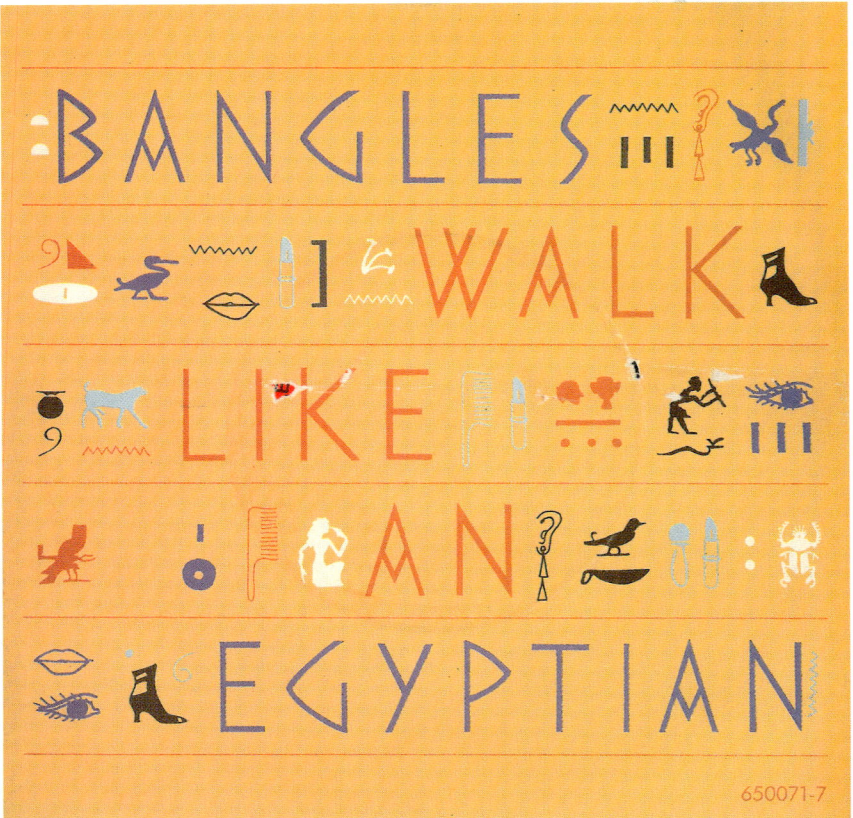

650071-7

Walk Like An Egyptian

ARTIST The Bangles **RELEASE DATE** September 1986 (UK & US) **WRITER** Liam Sternberg **PRODUCER** David Kahne **LABEL** CBS (UK)/Columbia (US) **UK CHART PEAK/WEEKS 3/19 US CHART PEAK/WEEKS 1/23**

When The Bangles recorded *Walk Like An Egyptian*, the song had been around a while. In 1983, it was offered to Toni Basil as a follow-up to **Mickey**, but she rejected it. Perhaps the world was not yet ready for a hit that included the word 'slamdance'. But by 1986, they were, and The Bangles recorded it on their album **Different Light**. Even then, however, it was initially considered something of a novelty. An international smash, it was Number 1 in America for four weeks.

The sound of seashells basking in the heat: a passable update of Faron Young, or more likely, its original source, processed with harmonies (non-guitar) and cloying enough to shrug off dissent. Later you recover from your coma in an old burlap sack under more Californian twilight. Dele Fadele, NME, September 1986

Walk Of Life

ARTIST Dire Straits **RELEASE DATE** January 1986 (UK)/November 1985 (US) **WRITER** Mark Knopfler **PRODUCER** Neil Dorfsman, Mark Knopfler **LABEL** Vertigo (UK)/Warner (US) **UK CHART PEAK/WEEKS 2/11 US CHART PEAK/WEEKS 7/21**

In contrast to the pub musicians of his first hit **Sultans Of Swing**, Mark Knopfler wrote this song to celebrate the street buskers of London, hence the references to **Be-Bop-A-Lula** and **What'd I**

Say, two standards that might be part of such a singer's repertoire. The somewhat throwaway song worked to lighten the mood of **Brothers In Arms** – and one suspects even its writer was surprised when it became a major hit as the fourth single from that multi-platinum album.

Walk Of Life boasts a good country swing, great Hockney guitar and that intangible air of mellowness that to an untrained (or uninterested) ear makes all their songs sound the same. Attractive if not one of their classics. Helen Fitzgerald, Melody Maker, January 1986

Walk On By

ARTIST Dionne Warwick **RELEASE DATE** April 1964 (UK & US) **WRITER** Burt Bacharach, Hal David **PRODUCER – LABEL** Pye Int. (UK)/Scepter (US) **UK CHART PEAK/WEEKS 9/14 US CHART PEAK/WEEKS 6/13**

A Brill Building classic from Burt Bacharach and Hal David brought their protégé Warwick her first transatlantic Top 1 and her first million seller. This track was recorded in the same session as **Anyone Who Had A Heart** and there was some debate over which to issue first. In fact **Walk On By** was the B-side of **Any Old Time Of Day** until legendary DJ Murray The K ran a contest with his listeners to choose the hit side.

I do think that church music has had a big influence on my style.... Burt [Bacharach] comes up with songs and tells me the way he wants me to do it. But it usually comes out the way I want it to. **Interviewed by Bob Dawbarn, Melody Maker, May 1964**

DIRE STRAITS   WALK OF LIFE

Walk On The Wild Side

ARTIST Lou Reed **RELEASE DATE** May 1973 (UK)/February 1973 (US) **WRITER** Lou Reed **PRODUCER** David Bowie, Mick Ronson, Lou Reed **LABEL** RCA (UK)/RCA Victor (US) **UK CHART PEAK/WEEKS** 10/9 **US CHART PEAK/WEEKS** 16/14

Breezing over the social taboos of the time Reed, equally influential as the lead singer/songwriter of cult favourites Velvet Underground, gained his biggest-ever hit with a song about Andy Warhol's seedy, slightly cheesy set of degenerate friends and hangers-on. Ace session bassist Herbie Flowers – later a member of classical-rockers Sky – was paid the princely sum of £17 for playing one of rock's most instantly recognizable bass hooks, which perfectly complemented Reed's seductively dry lyrical delivery. The song was taken from Reed's best album, **Transformer**, which was produced by David Bowie and the underrated Mick Ronson.

It's a gently sinister piece of minor genius which can only have a beneficial effect on the human ear. Dig the backing vocals and the Sax solo – and the vocal of course. A classic of sorts.... **Charles Shaar Murray, NME, May 1973**

Walk This Way

ARTIST Run DMC **RELEASE DATE** September 1986 (UK)/July 1986 (US) **WRITER** Steven Tyler, Joe Perry **PRODUCER** Rick Rubin **LABEL** London (UK)/Profile (US) **UK CHART PEAK/WEEKS** 8/10 **US CHART PEAK/WEEKS** 4/16

At one fell swoop, this single gave hip-hop and rap mass market appeal. With their 1983 debut single *It's Like That* they had been amongst the pioneers who had taken rap from street level to serious vinyl, and on their debut album they'd introduced guitar licks to the drum machine and scratching mix. This last-minute addition to their 1986 album **Raising Hell** (the first platinum rap album) was a speeded-up re-working of Aerosmith's hit from 10 years earlier.

Walk This Way is the fusion of two US cultures: one white, tight, stoogy and stultified, the other robust, moving, willing and black. It's the Ebony and Ivory of aggressive street beat.... A must. **Lucy O'Brien, NME, August 1986**

Walking On Sunshine

ARTIST Katrina And The Waves **RELEASE DATE** May 1985 (UK)/March 1985 (US) **WRITER** Kimberley Rew **PRODUCER** P. Collier **LABEL** Capitol (UK & US) **UK CHART PEAK/WEEKS** 8/12 **US CHART PEAK/WEEKS** 9/21

Fronted by American expatriate Katrina Leskanich and with songs by guitarist Kimberley Rew, formerly of cult rockers the Soft Boys, Katrina And The Waves came up with one of the all-time classic summer sounds. Reissued in 1996, *Sunshine* nearly became a hit all over again, and the band proved their staying power by winning the following year's Eurovision with the anthemic *Love Shine A Light*. Despite that success, this will remain the song they're remembered for.

Katrina And The Waves are the kind of people who write catchy songs, get them played on the radio all the time and eventually get rich. Better get used to it. **Dave Henderson, Sounds, April 1985**

Walking On The Moon

ARTIST Police **RELEASE DATE** December 1979 **WRITER** Sting **PRODUCER** Nigel Gray, Police **LABEL** A&M **UK CHART PEAK/WEEKS** 1/10 **US CHART PEAK/WEEKS** 0/0

Walking On The Moon was another effortless groove. Sting's voice is rough edged, and quiet, singing about love and weightlessness, and about walking home from your loved one's house with 'giant steps'. Summer's charismatic guitar adds texture and depth: fuzzed out with soft distortion, splintered with fragmented chords and built-in delays. There is even a tape loop. The drums provide a dynamic grounding to a song that is in orbit.

Perversely, this is the one Sting vocal performance I actually like, though the peculiarly empty song, based around a stalking bass figure, probably wasn't a smart choice as a single. **Chris Bohan, Melody Maker, November 1979**

The Wanderer

ARTIST Dion **RELEASE DATE** February 1962 (UK)/December 1961 (US) **WRITER** Ernest Maresca **PRODUCER** – **LABEL** HMV Pop (UK)/Laurie (US) **UK CHART PEAK/WEEKS** 10/12 **US CHART PEAK/WEEKS** 2/18

Dion (Di Mucci), American-born of Italian extraction, started his chart career with doo-wop group the Belmonts and first hit the US Top 30 in 1956. He went solo in 1960 and the following year had two major US chart successes. The second of these, *The Wanderer*, eventually peaked at Number 2 in the US and gave him his only UK Top 10 hit. The song was covered by Status Quo in 1984 and reached Number 7 in the UK.

Another HMV artist who is trying to follow up a Top 10 hit is Dion. The Wanderer is a medium paced, rather heavy rocker; quite effective, but if you're expecting the sparkle and exuberance of Runaround Sue I'm afraid you will be disappointed. **Keith Fordyce, January 1962**

Wanderin' Star

ARTIST Lee Marvin RELEASE DATE February 1970 WRITER – PRODUCER –
LABEL Paramount UK CHART PEAK/WEEKS 1/23 US CHART PEAK/WEEKS –

Tough guy Lee Marvin showed he really had gravel for tonsils in
his 'down-to-the-depths-of-the-earth' version of **Wanderin' Star**.
The song was taken from the musical film *Paint Your Wagon*, about
a mining town in California in the late 1840s. It is a great record,
spare and sparse, with Marvin's voice grizzled and appealingly
cantankerous over minimal instrumentation. You can almost
believe that 'hell is in hello' when he sings it.

Wannabe

ARTIST The Spice Girls RELEASE DATE July 1996 WRITER Spice Girls, Richard
Stannard, Matt Rowe PRODUCER Richard Stannard, Matt Rowe LABEL Virgin
UK CHART PEAK/WEEKS 1/24 US CHART PEAK/WEEKS –

The song that launched Girl Power and a thousand endorsements
shook up the pop industry worldwide while it was still bemoaning
the passing of Take That. Though the Spices themselves denied
it vehemently, the group had been constructed brilliantly by
Simon Fuller, and **Wannabe** was a showcase for all five: a mix of
cheek, sassiness, knowing raunch with a monster hook. A
Number 1 just about anywhere young girls existed, the Spice Girls
story began here.

*Get ready for Girl Power! … It doesn't get cuter than this ditty, as
the act conjures up images of such Eighties-era groups as Bananarama,
The Belle Sisters, but with just enough funk grit to get over in the
Nineties…. Anyone with a love of tasty pop hooks, lyrical positivity,
and jaunty rhythms is going to be humming this single for months
to come.* **Billboard, January 1997**

Wanted

ARTIST Perry Como RELEASE DATE June 1954 (UK)/March 1954 (US) WRITER
John Fulton, Lois Steele PRODUCER – LABEL HMV (UK)/RCA (US) UK CHART
PEAK/WEEKS 4/14 US CHART PEAK/WEEKS 1/21

Perry Como was a very wanted man when he released this tune, in
1954. Nicknamed 'the world's most casual singer', he built his
reputation on his relaxed, romantic delivery. **Wanted** was Number 1
in America for eight weeks, but didn't do quite as well in the UK,
due to a competing version by Al Martino.

*It's always a pleasure to listen to Perry Como's easy relaxed singing,
and he is equally at home on a ballad or a beat number.* **Geoffrey
Everitt, NME, April 1954**

War

ARTIST Edwin Starr RELEASE DATE October 1970 (UK)/July 1970 (US) WRITER
Norman Whitfield, Barrett Strong PRODUCER Norman Whitfield LABEL Tamla
Motown (UK)/Tamla (US) UK CHART PEAK/WEEKS 3/12 US CHART
PEAK/WEEKS 1/15

Edwin Starr had delivered R&B hits for Ric-Tic, a small Detroit
label including **Agent Double-O-Soul**. Once Ric-Tic was bought
by Motown and in with the big boys, Starr developed a reputation
for ballsy songs with a message. **War** was as blatant as you could

get, although he may have thought it was just TOO subtle since
the follow-up spelt it out more clearly – **Stop The War Now**. Bruce
Springsteen released a live cover version in 1986.

*Maybe it is intended with sincerity, but this soul anti-war song gives
the impression of clumsy insensibility and unconvincing concern.*
Chris Welch, Melody Maker, October 1970

Waterfalls

ARTIST TLC RELEASE DATE August 1995 (UK)/June 1995 (US) WRITER
Organized Noise, Marqueze Etheridge, Lisa 'Left Eye' Lopes PRODUCER
Organized Noise LABEL LaFace (UK & US) UK CHART PEAK/WEEKS 4/14 US
CHART PEAK/WEEKS 1/34

From the then biggest US album ever by an all-female act – the
spirited *Crazysexycool*, in a style dubbed 'New Jill Swing', reached
nine million sales – *Waterfalls* was performed by TLC at the MTV
Movie Awards in June 1995. A month later it hit the Number 1 in
the US and in August, the UK's Top 5. All this was at a difficult
time for the act, who were involved in a split with their original
mentor Pebbles' production company.

*The third single from the steam rollin *Crazysexycool* is a funk-lined
meditation on taking a more chilled, clear headed path in life. The story
telling verses are pointed and effective, building into a contagious, sing
along chorus that manages to be both melancholy and encouraging. In
any context this is a winner.* **Billboard, June 1995**

Waterloo

ARTIST Abba RELEASE DATE April 1974 (UK)/June 1974 (US) WRITER Stig Anderson, Benny Andersson, Bjorn Ulvaeus PRODUCER Benny Andersson, Bjorn Ulvaeus LABEL Epic (UK)/Atlantic (US) UK CHART PEAK/WEEKS 1/9 US CHART PEAK/WEEKS 6/17

Sweden's pop ambassadors began their career in 1971 as the Engaged Couples (which they were) and then as Bjorn, Benny, Agnetha and Frida, until their manager persuaded them to accept the acronym ABBA. They scored their first international hit in 1973 with **Ring Ring**, which was Number 1 in Holland and Belgium as well as Scandinavia. British success came with their next single, the 1974 Eurovision winner **Waterloo** – it shot to Number 1. An American smash as well, it has reportedly sold over five million copies.

*The cheery lyric of **Waterloo** belies a theme of Brechtian happy acceptance….* **David Quanticu, NME, August 1974**

Waterloo Sunset

ARTIST The Kinks RELEASE DATE May 1967 WRITER Ray Davies PRODUCER Ray Davies LABEL Pye UK CHART PEAK/WEEKS 2/11 US CHART PEAK/WEEKS –

By 1967, Ray Davies had almost completely abandoned writing in the first person, adopting instead the role of bystander. In **Waterloo Sunset** he painted the picture of two lovers meeting at Waterloo Station from the perspective of a lonely onlooker at a nearby window. The style with which the images are conveyed – eloquent, poetic, and distinguished by some of the most delicate vocal harmonies you could ever wish to hear – puts the song in a different league to most of its contemporaries.

Here they are again with that ever-green Kinks sound, noticeably matured, becoming more subtle and less aggressive. This is another colourful Ray Davies composition swaying along with all the hooks and hallmarks of a top disk. **Melody Maker, May 1967**

The Way It Is

ARTIST Bruce Hornsby And The Range RELEASE DATE August 1986 (UK)/September 1986 (US) WRITER Bruce Hornsby PRODUCER Bruce Hornsby, E. Scheiner LABEL RCA (UK)/RCA Victor (US) UK CHART PEAK/WEEKS 15/10 US CHART PEAK/WEEKS 1/22

'I'm sorry, I just don't think it's commercial ...' was Bruce Hornsby's verdict on the song that would give him a US Number 1 on his chart debut. Though the British public failed to appreciate his music to the same extent, *The Way It Is* had been one of four tracks on the original demo tape circulated to various record companies which resulted in him signing to RCA. He'd later combine his career heading backing group The Range with playing keyboards for The Grateful Dead.

The Way We Were

ARTIST Barbra Streisand **RELEASE DATE** March 1974 (UK)/November 1973 (US) **WRITER** Marvin Hamlisch, Alan and Marilyn Bergman **PRODUCER** Michael Paich **LABEL** CBS (UK)/Columbia (US) **UK CHART PEAK/WEEKS** 31/6 **US CHART PEAK/WEEKS** 1/23

Not only did Streisand dominate the 1973 movie *The Way We Were* – a Sydney Pollack-directed melodrama of young love, Hollywood stardom, and McCarthyite witchhunts co-starring Robert Redford – she stamped the title track with her unmistakable emotional oomph. Written by wife and husband team Alan and Marilyn Bergman and Marvin Hamlisch, the song collected a Grammy as Song of the Year and the Oscar for Best Film Song.

The fluke success of the single **The Way We Were** *has revived her recording career, but beneath the posturing she doesn't sound very interested. If she were, she wouldn't have to work so hard to convince.* **Jon Landau, Rolling Stone, June 1974**

The Wayward Wind

ARTIST Gogi Grant **RELEASE DATE** June 1956 (UK)/April 1956 (US) **WRITER** Stan Lebowsky, Herb Newman **PRODUCER** – **LABEL** London (UK)/Era (US) **UK CHART PEAK/WEEKS** 9/11 **US CHART PEAK/WEEKS** 1/28

Los Angeles-based Philadelphian Audrey Arinsberg endured several name changes before settling on the moniker of Gogi Grant and enjoying limited chart success between 1955 and 1956. **The Wayward Wind** had been written by Era Records head Herb Newman with Stan Lebowsky and was originally intended for a male vocalist. Grant realized its potential and recorded her version during a spare quarter of an hour's studio time, dethroning Elvis Presley's **Heartbreak Hotel** to register her only US chart-topper.

Once again the backing stands out in a class of its own, which is perhaps unfortunate in as much as at times it distracts attention from Gogi Grant's singing. Miss Grant is an above average performer, and her singing has a certain warmth about it. **Geoffrey Everitt, NME, May 1956**

We Are Family

ARTIST Sister Sledge **RELEASE DATE** May 1979 (UK)/April 1979 (US) **WRITER** Bernard Edwards, Nile Rodgers **PRODUCER** Bernard Edwards, Nile Rodgers **LABEL** Atlantic/Cotillion (UK)/Cotillion (US) **UK CHART PEAK/WEEKS** 8/10 **US CHART PEAK/WEEKS** 2/19

And indeed they were. Four sisters from Philadelphia whose careers took off under the aegis of Chic-Meisters supreme Nile Rodgers and Bernard Edwards. Their grooves provided plenty of dance energy behind the sibling quartet, allowing the sisters to run up a bunch of disco hits, this one a stomping favourite which was picked up as a theme song for the Pittsburgh Pirates and the gay rights movement.

I like the disco 45s: I like it for the production values … Sister Sledge follow up **He's The Greatest Dancer** *with a slower-grower – the smooth strings hooking you with the anticipation – until the song ends too soon.* **Jon Savage, Melody Maker, May 1979**

We Are The Champions

ARTIST Queen **RELEASE DATE** October 1977 (UK & US) **WRITER** Freddie Mercury **PRODUCER** M. Stone, Queen **LABEL** EMI (UK)/Elektra (US) **UK CHART PEAK/WEEKS** 2/11 **US CHART PEAK/WEEKS** 4/27

Though never rated as highly as **Bohemian Rhapsody**, the obvious triumphalism and anthemic quality of **We Are The Champions** has given it a lasting popularity, particularly among soccer fans. It was Queen's biggest hit of 1977, in the year when **Rhapsody** tied with Procol Harum's **A Whiter Shade Of Pale** as Best British Pop Single 1952–1977, and became Queen's first US Top 5 single as well as their first platinum for a single.

Grisly monomania from Mercury's crew – it is, in effect, Freddie's version of **I Did It My Way**: *a sort of retrospective vindication…. Formless operatic excess for some esoteric reason.* **Ian Birch, Melody Maker, October 1977**

We Are The World

ARTIST USA For Africa RELEASE DATE April 1985 (UK)/March 1985 (US) WRITER Lionel Richie, Michael Jackson PRODUCER Quincy Jones LABEL CBS (UK)/Columbia (US) UK CHART PEAK/WEEKS 1/9 US CHART PEAK/WEEKS 1/18

The success of Bob Geldof's **Band Aid** single in December 1984, inspired Harry Belafonte to create an American response. After the American Music Awards in January 1985, a bevy of stars got down to recording a song written by Michael Jackson and Lionel Richie. Geldof was in the massed chorus of singers backing 21 solo slots; the only celeb to no-show was Prince. The song sold four million copies in the States by April, was a double Number 1, and, combined with the album, went on to raise some $90 million.

We Didn't Start The Fire

ARTIST Billy Joel RELEASE DATE September 1989 (UK)/October 1989 (US) WRITER Billy Joel PRODUCER Billy Joel, M. Jones LABEL CBS (UK)/Columbia (US) UK CHART PEAK/WEEKS 7/10 US CHART PEAK/WEEKS 1/19

Having harboured ambitions to be a history teacher ('but I didn't graduate ... I didn't show up enough'), Joel gave his own potted version of the post-war world and ended up with his third US chart-topper. Joel, who had just turned 40 and was musing on his own mortality, got a lot of approving mail from teachers who said it encouraged kids to take an interest in the subject, and a magazine entitled *Junior Scholastic* licensed it to use as a cover-mounted cassette with lyric sheet.

We Don't Talk Anymore

ARTIST Cliff Richard RELEASE DATE July 1979 (UK)/October 1979 (US) WRITER Alan Tarney PRODUCER – LABEL EMI (UK)/EMI America (US) UK CHART PEAK/WEEKS 1/14 US CHART PEAK/WEEKS 7/2

However sanitized his image as born-again Christian, all-round entertainer and grandmothers' favourite, Cliff still occupies a unique niche in UK pop history, for his longevity in the UK charts and as the most successful of early British Elvis emulators. A great comeback came in August 1979 with this song of jaded love. Its slick use of Todd Rundgrenesque synthesizer and assured vocal made it his best-selling single.

Disappointing, though its sing-along flakiness will get him another residency on that Thursday evening show. **Ian Birch, Melody Maker, July 1979**

The Wedding

ARTIST Julie Rogers RELEASE DATE August 1964 (UK)/November 1964 (US) WRITER Fred Jay, Jonquin Prieto PRODUCER – LABEL Mercury (UK & US) UK CHART PEAK/WEEKS 3/23 US CHART PEAK/WEEKS 10/11

Translated and adapted from **La Novia**, the Argentinian wedding song by Fred Jay, **The Wedding** was originally a US chart success in 1958 for June Valli. When Londoner Julie Rogers recorded it in 1964 it became her only major hit, but it has the distinction of being the first record by a UK female to reach the transatlantic Top 10 in the beat boom era. Such was its popularity at weddings that it sold seven million copies.

Records by people like Julie Rogers should have been burned or smashed the first time around. **Julie Burchill, NME, October 1980**

Welcome Home

ARTIST Peters And Lee RELEASE DATE May 1973 WRITER Jan Dupre, Stanislas Beldone, Bryan Blackon PRODUCER J. Franz LABEL Philips UK CHART PEAK/WEEKS 1/24 US CHART PEAK/WEEKS –

Until they got together in 1970, blind Lenny Peters was a pub piano player and Di Lee a dancer. Opportunity knocked for the duo in the shape of Hughie Green, who put them on his TV programme *Opportunity Knocks*. The audiences loved their gentle middle of the road ballads. *Welcome Home* took almost two months to reach the top of the charts. Lee's sweet quiet voice sighs over the top of the piano chords and the lush orchestration. A choir of singers adds smooth, polished backing.

West End Girls

ARTIST Pet Shop Boys RELEASE DATE November 1985 (UK)/March 1986 (US) WRITER Neil Tennant, Chris Lowe PRODUCER Steve Hague LABEL Parlophone (UK)/EMI America (US) UK CHART PEAK/WEEKS 1/15 US CHART PEAK/WEEKS 1/20

The concept of a two-man synthesizer and vocalist outfit wasn't new: avant-garde US punks Suicide had adopted it to influential effect in the Seventies, while Soft Cell took it to Number 1 in the UK in 1981. But the formula would provide Pet Shop Boys with many years of glorious chart successes. *West End Girls*, their first single, sunk without trace in the UK on its release in 1984, but was subsequently reissued, topping the charts in January 1986.

What A Wonderful World

ARTIST Louis Armstrong RELEASE DATE February 1968 (UK)/February 1967 (US) WRITER George Weiss, George Douglas PRODUCER Bob Thiele LABEL HMV Pop UK CHART PEAK/WEEKS 1/29 US CHART PEAK/WEEKS 12/–

Here's a classic UK Number 1 that almost didn't happen. Bob Thiele, who co-wrote the tune under the pseudonym George Douglas, was recording it with Louis Armstrong when his boss, ABC Records' president, barged in and blew his top: Armstrong had just had a hit with *Hello, Dolly*, and now he was doing a ballad? He ordered everybody out. Thiele screamed in protest. The president finally left but he refused to promote the record. It would not become a hit in America until 1988, when it was on the *Good Morning Vietnam* soundtrack.

Much as we all dig Louis, it has to be said that exercising the gravel voice on a mediocre, nay, sickly song of this ilk isn't going to impress anybody. **Chris Welch, Melody Maker, October 1967**

What Becomes Of The Brokenhearted

ARTIST Jimmy Ruffin RELEASE DATE October 1966 (UK)/August 1966 (US) WRITER Jimmy Dean, Paul Riser, William Witherspoon PRODUCER W. Stevenson, William Witherspoon LABEL Tamla Motown (UK)/Soul (US) UK CHART PEAK/WEEKS 10/15 US CHART PEAK/WEEKS 7/17

Had it not been for this single, Jimmy Ruffin perhaps may have gone down in history as the man who turned down the invitation to join The Temptations. But five years after he first recorded for

Motown he had his first and biggest-selling hit with the massively soulful **What Becomes Of The Brokenhearted**. In the UK the single returned to the Top 10 in 1974 and Dave Stewart's cover version also made the Top 20 in 1980.

… Jimmy Ruffin is in the charts for the first time this week. With **What Becomes Of The Brokenhearted***…. Fellow Tamla artist Levi Stubbs of the Four Tops told me: 'Jimmy Ruffin is a real nice guy.'* **Alan Smith, NME, November 1966**

What Do You Want

ARTIST Adam Faith RELEASE DATE November 1959 WRITER Les Vandyke PRODUCER – LABEL Parlophone UK CHART PEAK/WEEKS 1/19 US CHART PEAK/WEEKS –

Actor and singer Adam Faith's early attempts at pop stardom hardly flourished, but his persistence was rewarded in the late Fifties when **What Do You Want** became his and Parlophone's first Number 1 single. The song was written by former Raindrops vocalist Johnny Worth under the name Les Vandyke, who had met Faith on the set of the Drumbeat TV show. It gave Faith, formerly Terence Nelhams, the first of ten Top 5 hits in the pre-Beatles era.

A mightily attractive song that borrows its inspiration from the rock idiom, but is presented in a completely new way with a brilliant arrangement and backing provided by John Barry. A big bouquet to all concerned. **Keith Fordyce, NME, October 1959**

What Do You Want To Make Those Eyes At Me For

ARTIST Emile Ford And The Checkmates RELEASE DATE October 1959 WRITER Joseph McCarthy, Jimmy Monaco, Howard Johnson PRODUCER – LABEL Pye UK CHART PEAK/WEEKS 1/25 US CHART PEAK/WEEKS –

Sharing top billing for one week with Adam Faith's similarly titled **What Do You Want**, Bahama-born Emile Ford furthered the progress already made by the likes of Shirley Bassey in establishing black singers in Britain. Like many artists around this time. Ford revived a song from a bygone era, in this case 1917, to register a chart success. His follow-up was a cover of Frank Loesser's 1948 **Slow Boat To China**.

It's a rock number with an easy paced beat and a simple catchy tune. The words are good commercial corn, and the disc has enough about it to be a seller if it can get off the ground, surmounting the tricky hurdle of being by an 'unknown'. **Keith Fordyce, NME, October 1959**

What Have I Done To Deserve This

ARTIST Pet Shop Boys And Dusty Springfield RELEASE DATE August 1987 (UK)/December 1987 (US) WRITER Neil Tennant, Chris Lowe, Allee Willis PRODUCER Stephen Hague LABEL Parlophone (UK)/EMI Manhattan (US) UK CHART PEAK/WEEKS 2/9 US CHART PEAK/WEEKS 2/18

This single had been penned three years earlier, at the time of **West End Girls** and **Opportunities**, and its banal chorus line 'What have I?/What have I?/What have I done to deserve this?' reads like the acme of the duo's experiments with emotional reserve. But the collaboration with Dusty Springfield gives it an extra dimension. The song swoops off into new melodic pastures, helped by a breezy, sweet, boppy sound, that saw it soaring up the UK charts to reach Number 2.

For us, Pet Shop Boys define taste in the charts. Actually we are exaggerating, but there is something to be said for Italy, Catholicism, Amanda Lear and sampler. But this is embarrassingly clumsy, it stalls, kangaroos, never really ends, just stops. It's a mess. **The Stud Brothers, Melody Maker, August 1987**

What Is Love

ARTIST Howard Jones RELEASE DATE November 1983 (UK)/April 1984 (US) WRITER John Jones, William Bryant PRODUCER – LABEL WEA (UK)/Elektra (US) UK CHART PEAK/WEEKS 2/15 US CHART PEAK/WEEKS 33/13

One of the few solo stars in an electro-pop age, Southampton-born keyboardist-singer Jones compromised his solo status by using a dancer, Jed Hoile, to illustrate his music on stage. Having found a label, thanks to elaborate demos of this and his first single **New Song**, he hit the Top 3 with both. His was an accidental success: compensation received after a car crash enabled him to buy a synthesizer. By 1987 his hit-making touch deserted him and he entered the restaurant business.

Throughout the centuries, artists by the dozen have tried, through their work, to answer the above question…. None, though, could have done it as facetiously as Howard Jones has done on this eminently disposable record. **Paolo Hewitt, NME, November 1983**

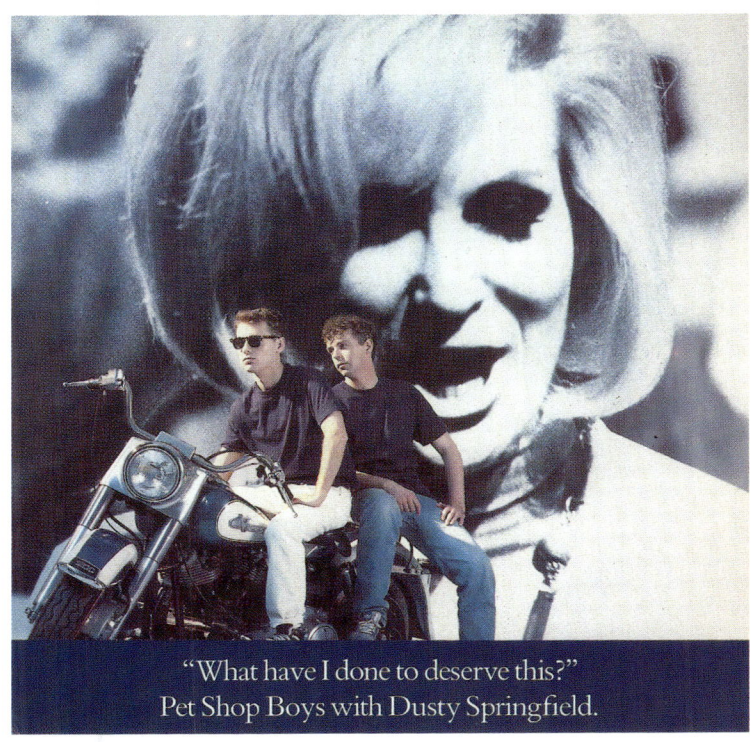

"What have I done to deserve this?" Pet Shop Boys with Dusty Springfield.

What'd I Say

ARTIST Ray Charles **RELEASE DATE** July 1959 **WRITER** Ray Charles **PRODUCER** – **LABEL** Atlantic **UK CHART PEAK/WEEKS** – **US CHART PEAK/WEEKS** 6/15

After eight years as an R&B star Ray Charles finally broke into the pop Top 10 with **What'd I Say**. A mixture of rock, blues, and gospel stylings, it had an enormous impact on the pop music world. Many consider it the beginning of modern soul music. Its influence was so great that, within five years of its release, Jerry Lee Lewis, Bobby Darin and Elvis Presley each recorded it – and all three versions hit the US Top 40.

There's a fast beat with a strong Jazz slant and a vocal that is also a blend of rock and jazz. Not everybody's cup of tea, but at least it gets away from the routine. **Keith Fordyce, NME, July 1959**

What's Going On

ARTIST Marvin Gaye **RELEASE DATE** February 1971 (UK & US) **WRITER** Renaldo Benson, Marvin Gaye, Alfred Cleveland **PRODUCER** Marvin Gaye **LABEL** Tamla **UK CHART PEAK/WEEKS** – **US CHART PEAK/WEEKS** 2/15

Following the death of duet partner Tammi Terrell, Marvin Gaye was coaxed back into the studio thanks to a tune written by Al Cleveland and Renaldo 'Obie' Benson and the seeds of a lyric planted by his brother Frankie's recollections of fighting in Vietnam. Putting the two together and producing himself for the first time resulted in one of the biggest hits Marvin and Motown ever had.

This is rather confused and contrived Gaye and one prefers him in more positive and electro nickel mood. **Chris Welch, Melody Maker, August 1971**

What's Love Got To Do With It

ARTIST Tina Turner **RELEASE DATE** June 1984 (UK)/May 1984 (US) **WRITER** Terry Britten, Graham Lyte **PRODUCER** Terry Britten **LABEL** Capitol (UK & US) **UK CHART PEAK/WEEKS** 3/16 **US CHART PEAK/WEEKS** 1/28

Turner, who had struggled in her solo career since splitting with Ike in 1976, started fighting back in the early Eighties: support slots with the Stones and Rod Stewart, working with Heaven 17 on their BEF project. She reached the top with her huge-selling 1984 album **Private Dancer**, in which Tina left pure R&B behind for harder edged rock. All her raunch and experience emerged on this melodramatic, world-weary number. It was her first US Number 1 for 24 years, and picked up a clutch of Grammys.

At 45, Tina Turner has a voice that's more elemental than ever. Noted in her first hey-day with ex-hubby Ike for her scream, Turner now knocks you out with her intuitive but surgically precise phrasing.... **Kurt Loder, Rolling Stone, December 1984**

Whatever Will Be Will Be

ARTIST Doris Day **RELEASE DATE** June 1956 (UK & US) **WRITER** Jay Livingston, Ray Evans **PRODUCER** – **LABEL** Philips (UK)/Columbia (US) **UK CHART PEAK/WEEKS** 1/22 **US CHART PEAK/WEEKS** 2/27

Doris Day's sixth million seller came from the soundtrack of the Alfred Hitchcock classic *The Man Who Knew Too Much*, in which she starred alongside James Stewart. It would go on to win the Academy Award for Best Song of 1956. Writers Ray Evans and Jay Livingston also penned the ever popular theme song to TV's *Mr Ed*, which Livingston sang.

Now starring in Hitchcock's, The Man Who Knew Too Much, Doris just re-signed to a new contract with American Columbia. Philips here has recorded Evens and Livingston's **Whatever Will Be Will Be** *– also known as 'Que Sera Sera'.* **Mike Butcher, NME, June 1956**

When A Man Loves A Woman

ARTIST Percy Sledge RELEASE DATE May 1966 (UK)/April 1966 (US) WRITER Calvin Lewis, Andrew Wright PRODUCER Quin Ivy, Marlin Greene LABEL Atlantic (UK & US) UK CHART PEAK/WEEKS 4/17 US CHART PEAK/WEEKS 1/13

When A Man Loves A Woman was given passionate treatment by Sledge, backed by Spooner Oldham on organ, Marlin Greene on guitar and an out-of-tune horn section. Atlantic boss Jerry Wexler got top Memphis players to re-record the brass parts. Only trouble was, the master for the single kept the original horns – and they're still there.... In 1991 Michael Bolton proved it WAS possible to cover a classic – by getting it back to US Number 1.

A slowly lifting blues ballad.... You'll go for this in a big way.
Derek Johnson, NME, 1966

When Doves Cry

ARTIST Prince RELEASE DATE June 1984 (UK & US) WRITER Prince PRODUCER Prince LABEL Warner Bros. (UK)/Warner (US) UK CHART PEAK/WEEKS 4/15 US CHART PEAK/WEEKS 1/21

'The most influential record of the Eighties' was how some critics rated **When Doves Cry**, from Prince's semi-autobiographical film *Purple Rain*. It is not hard to see why: with the haunting pathos of its searing vocal delivery and delicate, even spare, production, it showed a new direction to black soul music, selling over two million in the States.

Many of the things that I love about Prince are missing from this record. Here he discovers that pretending that you are married means trading in the Corvette for a Volvo Estate. **When Doves Cry** *could be Prince's* **Good Year For Roses** *– but let's hope that he is back on the streets by sundown.* **Jane Simon, Sounds, June 1984**

When I Fall In Love

ARTIST Nat King Cole RELEASE DATE April 1957 (UK & US) WRITER Edward Heyman, Victor Young PRODUCER – LABEL Capitol (UK & US) UK CHART PEAK/WEEKS 2/20 US CHART PEAK/WEEKS –

When I Fall In Love hit twice for Nat King Cole: first in its original release in 1957, and again 30 years later. The revival was sparked by Rick Astley's faithful cover of the song, which was climbing up the charts when someone at Cole's label thought of reissuing the original version. As a result, Astley's disc stopped just short of Number 1, while Cole's stayed in the lower half of the Top 20 for four weeks.

It is some time since Nat figured high in the hit parade, but this one might restore him to his rightful place.
Melody Maker, April 1957

When I Need You

ARTIST Leo Sayer RELEASE DATE January 1977 (UK)/February 1977 (US) WRITER Carole Bayer Sager, Albert Hammond PRODUCER Richard Perry LABEL Chrysalis (UK)/Warner (US) UK CHART PEAK/WEEKS 1/13 US CHART PEAK/WEEKS 1/20

A follow-up to the disco hit **You Make Me Feel Like Dancing**, also taken from his 1976 US breakthrough album **Endless Flight**, this ballad, written by Carole Bayer Sager and Albert Hammond, has proved durable as a golden oldie radio favourite. Sayer regained the rights to the song in the early Nineties after a legal tussle and reissued it in 1993, though it barely troubled the charts second time around.

Perhaps one of the least annoying tracks of his recent album. Because the Richard Perry production sends you to sleep before the end, Leo Sayer has the same problem as John Miles, if you know what I mean. A miss.
Caroline Coon, Melody Maker, January 1977

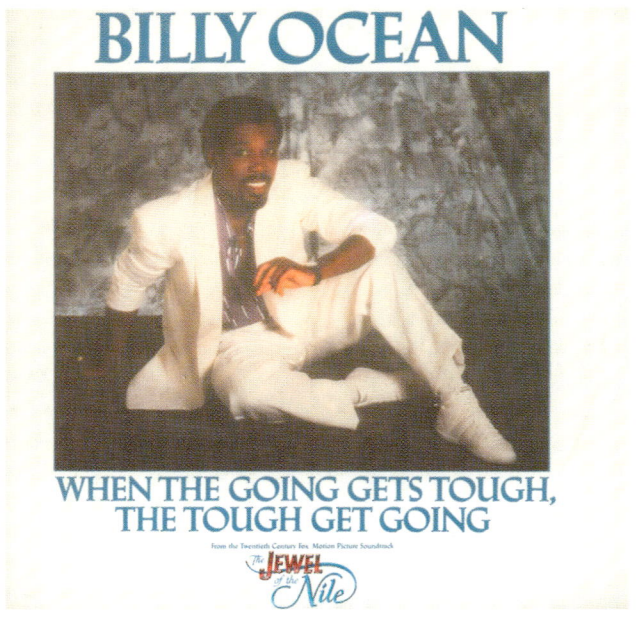

When The Going Gets Tough The Tough Get Going

ARTIST Billy Ocean RELEASE DATE January 1986 (UK)/November 1985 (US) WRITER Wayne Braithwaite, Barry Eastmond, Bob Lance, Billy Ocean PRODUCER William Braithwaite, Barry Eastmond LABEL Jive (UK & US) UK CHART PEAK/WEEKS 1/13 US CHART PEAK/WEEKS 2/13

Fitness coaches everywhere bellow the words, 'When the going gets tough, the tough get going ...' but soulster Billy Ocean crooned them in a smooth voice to a pop beat. The song was featured in the Kathleen Turner and Michael Douglas movie *Jewel Of The Nile* and brought Ocean back into the limelight. For a while his career had been in the doldrums when hits like the soulful **Love Really Hurts Without You** on GTO had dried up, but after signing to a new label, Jive, he started making engaging danceable pop records.

The song rolls along easily enough, straight down without touching the sides. Now you understand how it feels to be a tin of soup in a supermarket display. **Adam Sweeting, Melody Maker, January 1986**

When Will I See You Again

ARTIST Three Degrees RELEASE DATE July 1974 (UK)/September 1974 (US) WRITER Kenny Gamble, Leon Huff PRODUCER Kenny Gamble, Leon Huff LABEL Philadelphia Int (UK & US) UK CHART PEAK/WEEKS 1/16 US CHART PEAK/WEEKS 2/18

After a reasonably successful debut with *Gee Baby (I'm Sorry)* the Three Degrees were taken under the wing of hitmakers Gamble and Huff and formed part of the golden era at Philadelphia International. They had a US Number 1 with **TSOP**, the theme to the *Soul Train* TV show, and a peak year in 1974 with this perky number and **Year Of Decision**. Eventually the trio moved out of mainstream pop onto the cabaret circuit.

Pretty, string-filled ballad from this talented trio. Title serves as a good intro and hook, while lead vocals work well against the vocal back-up. Should move from Soul to Pop with little trouble. **Billboard, 1974**

When You Tell Me That You Love Me

ARTIST Diana Ross RELEASE DATE November 1991 WRITER John Bettis, Albert Hammond PRODUCER P. Asher LABEL EMI UK CHART PEAK/WEEKS 2/11 US CHART PEAK/WEEKS –

Written by John Bettis and Albert Hammond – who between them have written hits for, among others, Madonna, Karen Carpenter, The Pointer Sisters, Whitney Houston and Tina Turner – the warm, sentimental ballad *When You Tell Me That You Love Me*, taken from Ross' **Force Behind The Power** album, was a hit in the UK without, strangely enough, achieving notable sales in the United States.

Miss Ross has spent recent years as a housewife-superstar with a Swiss millionaire, a lifestyle which seems to have taken its toll on her recording career.... Things can only get better from here. **Isabel Appio, Vox, September 1991**

When You're In Love With A Beautiful Woman

ARTIST Dr Hook **RELEASE DATE** September 1979 (UK)/April 1979 (US) **WRITER** Even Stevens **PRODUCER** Ron Haff Kine **LABEL** Capitol (UK & US) **UK CHART PEAK/WEEKS** 1/17 **US CHART PEAK/WEEKS** 6/25

This song, which gave the country-flavoured US group their only UK Number 1, actually topped the UK charts a week early in November 1979. A computer error had resulted in some sales being double-counted and so dethroned Lena Martell's **One Day At A Time**. However, the error was discovered and the chart positions reversed. The following week Dr Hook sold enough singles to reach Number 1 on merit and stayed there for three weeks.

Their usual heart-rending, knickers-wetting for housewives.... **Betty Page, Sounds, September 1979**

Where Did Our Love Go

ARTIST The Supremes **RELEASE DATE** September 1964 (UK)/July 1964 (US) **WRITER** Brian Holland, Edward Holland, Lamont Dozier **PRODUCER** Brian Holland, Lamont Dozier **LABEL** Stateside (UK)/Motown (US) **UK CHART PEAK/WEEKS** 3/14 **US CHART PEAK/WEEKS** 1/14

This Holland-Dozier-Holland song was offered first to The Marvelettes, Motown's top act in the early Sixties, but they rejected it. Lead singer Gladys Horton reportedly said 'I wouldn't sing that junk'! The Supremes, who'd struggled with Motown through the early Sixties, had no such qualms and it brought them their first Number 1 – the first release to feature Diana Ross' inimitable voice.

One of my favourites at the moment, but it might not be a hit here. Could be if someone British records it. I think it is very good; it even has a British sound about it, hasn't it? **Brenda Lee, Melody Maker, August 1964**

Where Do You Go To My Lovely

ARTIST Peter Sarstedt **RELEASE DATE** February 1969 (UK)/April 1969 (US) **WRITER** Peter Sarstedt **PRODUCER** R. Singer **LABEL** United Artists (UK)/World Pacific (US) **UK CHART PEAK/WEEKS** 1/16 **US CHART PEAK/WEEKS** 70/6

Sarstedt, whose brother Eden Kane had a number of UK hits in the early Sixties, came out of the folk scene, started his own recording career as Wes Sands, but reverted to his own name by the time he released this ballad. Its wistful air of vaguely Parisian, bohemian loucheness clicked and went to UK Number 1, although it did little in the States.

On the strength of his last single he has emerged as an impressive folk singing and composing talent. It is a charming melodic song about a girl from the back streets of Naples who becomes an adored member of the millionaire jet set. **Laurie Henshaw, Melody Maker, February 1969**

Where The Streets Have No Name

ARTIST U2 **RELEASE DATE** September 1987 (UK & US) **WRITER** U2 **PRODUCER** Brian Eno, Daniel Lanois **LABEL** Island (UK & US) **UK CHART PEAK/WEEKS** 4/6 **US CHART PEAK/WEEKS** 13/14

Taken from the Brian Eno and Daniel Lanois production **The Joshua Tree**, this was one of three tracks remixed by U2's former producer Steve Lillywhite before release, giving them a more anthem-like feel. The group did a Beatles **Get Back** style rooftop performance while shooting in downtown LA for their *Rattle And Hum* movie. Right on cue, LAPD's finest moved in to break things up when the crowds in the street below got too big.

It is their most likeable effort for quite some time if only for the fact that Bono doesn't see it necessary to pretend to be Jess Yates. It won't last. **Paul Mathur, Melody Maker, August 1987**

Wherever I Lay My Hat That's My Home

ARTIST Paul Young **RELEASE DATE** June 1983 (UK)/October 1983 (US) **WRITER** Marvin Gaye, Norman Whitfield **PRODUCER** L. Latham **LABEL** CBS (UK)/Columbia (US) **UK CHART PEAK/WEEKS** 1/15 **US CHART PEAK/WEEKS** 70/7

The ex-Q Tips vocalist never had any problems with respectful cover versions featuring his (frequently fragile) 'blue-eyed soul' voice. Young's debut solo album, **No Parlez**, featured a version of Joy Division's **Love Will Tear Us Apart**, as well as this revival of a Marvin Gaye B-side which helped win him the award for Best New Male Singer at the Brits in 1985 – the cover formula worked again later that year with Hall & Oates' **Every Time You Go Away**.

Whereas most white soul pretenders usually drown in their overbearing desire to project a sense of epic, Young sounds sufficiently hurt and humble to give his soul creed some real credibility. **Adrian Thrills, NME, June 1983**

Whiskey In The Jar

ARTIST Thin Lizzy **RELEASE DATE** January 1973 **WRITER** Phil Lynott/Eric Bell/Brian Donney **PRODUCER** – **LABEL** Decca **UK CHART PEAK/WEEKS** 6/12 **US CHART PEAK/WEEKS** –

After three years or so playing the club and college circuit, paying their dues in the time-honoured manner, this arrangement of a traditional Irish folk song – which never appeared on a Thin Lizzy studio album – brought them their first UK singles success, though the follow-up *Randolph's Tango* did absolutely nothing and the band had to wait over three years to get another hit with *The Boys Are Back In Town*.

The music is the thing that grabs you in the end. That's what'll grab everybody in the end. The style of presenting it might change. I don't worry about it. I never have. **Phil Lynott interviewed by Harry Doherty, Melody Maker, July 1977**

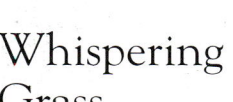

Whispering Grass

ARTIST Windsor Davies And Don Estelle **RELEASE DATE** May 1975 **WRITER** Fred and Doris Fisher **PRODUCER** – **LABEL** EMI **UK CHART PEAK/WEEKS** 1/12 **US CHART PEAK/WEEKS** –

This one knocked Tammy Wynette's *Stand By Your Man* out of Number 1. It came from an album of army party favourites recorded by the cast of TV's *It Ain't Half Hot, Mum*. The show, set in wartime India, starred Windsor Davies as the bullying Battery Sgt. Major Williams and Don Estelle as the meek Private 'Lofty' Sugden. *Whispering Grass* was originally a hit in 1940 for the Ink Spots.

White Christmas

ARTIST Bing Crosby **RELEASE DATE** December 1977 (UK) **WRITER** Irving Berlin **PRODUCER** – **LABEL** MCA (UK)/Decca (US) **UK CHART PEAK/WEEKS** 5/7 **US CHART PEAK/WEEKS** 1/over 50 (various versions)

For 55 years, until the phenomenal success of Elton John's *Candle In The Wind 1997*, this was the biggest selling single of all time. However, with all the seasonal airplay *White Christmas* receives, its copyright remains the most valuable in the world. Originally recorded for the film *Holiday Inn*, it was penned by songwriter extraordinaire Irving Berlin, author of countless other classics, from Always to Alexander's Ragtime Band.

White Lines (Don't Do It)

ARTIST Grandmaster Flash And Melle Mel **RELEASE DATE** November 1983 **WRITER** Sylvia Robinson/Mel Glover **PRODUCER** M. Mel, J. Robinson, S. Robinson **LABEL** Sugarhill **UK CHART PEAK/WEEKS** 7/43 **US CHART PEAK/WEEKS** 0/0

Grandmaster Flash and Melle Mel's second major success was even harder hitting, if possible, than *The Message*. The anti-drug themed *White Lines (Don't Do It)* was superbly crafted, with the clever observations of the legal treatment between black and white, rich and poor and pushers and users particularly relevant. Ironically at least two of the group later descended into drug dependency. It returned to the charts on two further occasions – one a remix and the other a cover by Duran Duran.

The strong stench of dross and desperation.... This, with a backing track as dull as last night's dishwater, is, that's right, a drug song. It is blessed with all the verve and ingenuity of Jimmy Sham singing about going down the pub with his mates. **Gavin Martin, NME, October 1983**

White Riot

ARTIST The Clash **RELEASE DATE** April 1977 **WRITER** Joe Strummer, Mick Jones **PRODUCER** Micky Foote **LABEL** CBS **UK CHART PEAK/WEEKS** 38/3 **US CHART PEAK/WEEKS** –

The Sex Pistols got punk off and running, but it was The Clash who gave it a political agenda, starting

with their very first single, **White Riot**. A self-conscious burst of righteous anger, it made only Number 38 on the charts but was a major influence on other punk acts. They promoted the disc and their ensuing self-titled debut album with the **White Riot** tour, which ended in a real riot at London's Rainbow Theatre when the crowd ripped out the seats.

White Riot isn't a poxy single of the week, it's the first meaningful event all year…. One minute 58 seconds of buzzsaw guitars, Simonon's pumping off-beat bass, an insolent slurred vocal and sheer musical affro. **Tom Robinson, NME, March 1977**

White Wedding

ARTIST Billy Idol RELEASE DATE July 1985 (UK)/May 1983 (US) WRITER Billy Idol PRODUCER Keith Forsey LABEL Chrysalis (UK & US) UK CHART PEAK/WEEKS 6/15 US CHART PEAK/WEEKS 36/13

Sneering peroxide blond Billy Idol had hitched himself to the punk bandwagon as part of the 'Bromley contingent' present at the Sex Pistols' TV confrontation with Bill Grundy that lit the punk touch paper. Splitting his band Generation X in 1981, he relocated to become a major US star. This memorable pop song, delivered with that trademark sneer, was his first hit in his new home.

What a silly sod! **Cath Carroll, NME, July 1985**

A Whiter Shade Of Pale

ARTIST Procol Harum RELEASE DATE May 1967 (UK)/June 1967 (US) WRITER Keith Reid, Gary Brooker PRODUCER Denny Cordell LABEL Deram (UK & US) UK CHART PEAK/WEEKS 1/15 US CHART PEAK/WEEKS 5/12

The musical roots of one of rock's most unlikely hits can be found in Bach's Suite No. 3 in D major. Instantly acclaimed upon its Radio London airing, it took a couple of months to reach the top of the UK chart. Once there, it stayed for 6 weeks and hit Number 5 in the US in July. With surreal lyrical imagery that seemed to reflect the mood of 1967's 'Summer of Love', the song went on to become one of pop's enduring classics with all-time sales topping six million. Annie Lennox's synthesized version in 1995 continued the song's remarkable chart and international success.

Tremendous first record from a new group, the Procol Harum, with a beautiful, sighing ballad which is really too much to take all at once. Mainly featuring a distant angelic organ, the record has a heavenly feel…. **Melody Maker, May 1967**

Whole Lotta Shakin' Going On

ARTIST Jerry Lee Lewis RELEASE DATE September 1957 (UK)/June 1957 (US) WRITER Dave Williams/Sonny David PRODUCER – LABEL London (UK)/Sun (US) UK CHART PEAK/WEEKS 8/11 US CHART PEAK/WEEKS 3/29

Jerry Lee Lewis was a fire ball piano player from Ferriday, Louisiana. He melded together jazz, hillbilly, gospel and rock 'n' roll into outrageous live performances, stoked on pills and drink. He set fire to his piano and hollered out his songs with raw, hysterical energy. **Whole Lotta Shakin' Going On** received little airplay: banned for being vulgar and obscene. But Jerry sang the song on national TV, kicked his piano bench across the stage in a controlled frenzy and record sales soared. He spent the next 40 years rolling through controversy, but abandoned rock for country, his spirit undimmed.

He uses the keyboard in much the same thumping, pounding way that Presley uses his guitar. There is no doubt that Jerry is going to shake up show business a lot more before he is through. **Derek Johnson, NME, October 1957**

A Whole New World (Aladdin's Theme)

ARTIST Peabo Bryson And Regina Belle RELEASE DATE December 1993 (UK)/December 1992 (US) WRITER Alan Menken, Tim Rice PRODUCER Walter Afanasieff LABEL Columbia (UK & US) UK CHART PEAK/WEEKS 12/12 US CHART PEAK/WEEKS 1/23

A Whole New World brought Peabo Bryson and Regina Belle to a whole new echelon. They were established hitmakers by the time they teamed up to record the theme for Disney's *Aladdin*, but that Academy Award-winning recording was the first Number 1 for both of them. However, it was not Bryson's first Oscar, but his second in a row, having won the previous year with his theme for *Beauty And The Beast*, on which he duetted with Celine Dion.

The Whole Of The Moon

ARTIST Waterboys RELEASE DATE November 1985 WRITER Mike Scott PRODUCER M. Scott LABEL Ensign UK CHART PEAK/WEEKS 26/7 US CHART PEAK/WEEKS –

The song, which charted highest as a reissue in 1991 off the back of a Waterboys compilation album, had originally been released in 1985, the guts of the song sketched out earlier that year at New York's Gramercy Hotel when Mike Scott was asked by a girlfriend if it was hard to write a song. It featured the Waterboys' trademarks of acoustic guitar, lyrical intensity, and Anthony Thistlethwaite's sax.

Not really a record at all, but a dream to have while you are awake **The Whole Of The Moon** *sweeps you up in its vast, visionary embrace and swings you at the sky, as soprano saxes scream like shooting stars…. Magnificent.* **Jane Simon, Sounds, October 1985**

Whoomp! (There It Is)

ARTIST Tag Team RELEASE DATE January 1994 (UK)/May 1993 (US) WRITER Stefano Pulga, Cecil Glenn, Stephen Gibson, Luciano Ninzatti, Matteo Bonsante PRODUCER R. Sall LABEL Club Tools (UK)/Life (US) UK CHART PEAK/WEEKS 34/5 US CHART PEAK/WEEKS 2/45

Based on a basketball cheer, Tag Team – Steve Roll'n and DC the Brain Supreme – turned it into a phrase that DC used when DJ-ing at the Magic City club in Atlanta. Added to a Miami bass backing, the sports chant was so successful that Messrs Roll'n and Brain Supreme re-worked it with a bunch of Walt Disney characters for 1994's *Whoomp (There It Went)*.

Who's Sorry Now

ARTIST Connie Francis RELEASE DATE April 1958 (UK)/February 1958 (US) WRITER Bert Kalmar/Harry Ruby/Ted Snyder PRODUCER – LABEL MGM (UK & US) UK CHART PEAK/WEEKS 1/25 US CHART PEAK/WEEKS 4/22

Unlucky not to have a transatlantic Number 1 at any time during her career, Connie Francis had one last throw of the dice before her contract with MGM expired. She was encouraged by her father

to record one of his favourite songs, *Who's Sorry Now*. Her version of the tune, which had enjoyed five different US Top 20 entries in its original 1923 year of release, launched her solo career.

Who's That Girl

ARTIST Eurythmics RELEASE DATE July 1983 (UK)/May 1984 (US) WRITER Annie Lennox, Dave Stewart PRODUCER Dave Stewart LABEL RCA (UK)/RCA Victor (US) UK CHART PEAK/WEEKS 3/10 US CHART PEAK/WEEKS 21/13

This was Dave Stewart and Annie Lennox's third UK Top 10 hit of 1983, a year in which they had shot from cult favourites to chart fixtures. The secret was their eye-catching and arresting videos, in which Lennox would don all manner of disguises to make a point. The clip for this single was no exception, and in fact featured Bananarama singer Siobhan Fahey who, four years later, would become Mrs Stewart. Who's that girl? It's your future wife!

Lennox's voice, an exceptionally rich and fiery instrument, is capable of leaving lasting burns. All it needs is the right song. This cautious electronic simulation of sap soul isn't it. **Chris Bohn, NME, July 1983**

Why

ARTIST Annie Lennox RELEASE DATE March 1992 (UK)/May 1992 (US) WRITER Annie Lennox PRODUCER Stephen Lipson LABEL RCA (UK)/Arista (US) UK CHART PEAK/WEEKS 5/8 US CHART PEAK/WEEKS 34/20

It was clear that Annie Lennox had an assured solo future after Eurythmics split, and this first single from her UK chart-topping debut album **Diva** only underlined the fact. The single peaked at

track will strain at (and should ultimately knock down) the tight boundaries of Top 40 radio. **Billboard, April 1992**

Why Do Fools Fall In Love

ARTIST The Teenagers Featuring Frankie Lymon RELEASE DATE June 1956 (UK)/February 1956 (US) WRITER Frankie Lymon, George Goldner PRODUCER R. Barrett LABEL Columbia (UK)/Gee (US) UK CHART PEAK/WEEKS 1/16 US CHART PEAK/WEEKS 6/21

Frankie Lymon and his friends hung around on street corners singing beautiful vocal harmonies and abandoned school for the music business. The quintet won a local talent competition, and recorded *Why Do Fools Fall In Love*. The song based on an essay written by the 13-year-old Frankie. His pure crystal voice was shiveringly lovely against the deep bass backing vocal and the lilting saxophone. Frankie Lymon had an angelic soprano voice, but his life was dragged into the hell of heroin addiction.

I still like these kids. The trembling treble of young Frankie may drive some folk up the wall, but for me it gives a logical interpretation to Rock 'n' Roll. **Keith Fordyce, NME, November 1956**

Number 5 in April 1992, the month she symbolically unravelled her links with former personal and professional partner David Stewart. Lennox's only previous single under her own name came in 1988, a duet with Al Green on Jackie De Shannon's 1969 hit *Put A Little Love In Your Heart*.

Debut solo single is a soft yet vivid ballad that beautifully showcases the rich and distinctive natural tone of her voice. Sophisticated nature of

Wichita Lineman

ARTIST Glen Campbell RELEASE DATE January 1969 (UK)/November 1968 (US) WRITER Jim Webb PRODUCER – LABEL Ember (UK)/Capitol (US) UK CHART PEAK/WEEKS 7/13 US CHART PEAK/WEEKS 3/15

Although *Wichita Lineman* was not Campbell's biggest seller, over the years it has become his best loved work. Written by Jimmy Webb on request after Campbell hit with his *By The Time I Get To Phoenix*, it is not so much a follow-up as it is a sequel: Webb reasoned that after his hero got to Phoenix, he would continue on to Wichita. It wasn't too difficult for him to get inside his character's head – he'd based the itinerant on himself.

He denies that Wichita Lineman is a Country song. 'It's not strictly a Country song, although a lot of people think of it as such,' said Glen, 'But its chord progression is different ... it's certainly not a Country progression.' **From an interview by Alan Walsh, Melody Maker, March 1969**

Wild Thing

ARTIST Troggs RELEASE DATE May 1966 (UK)/June 1966 (US) WRITER Chip Taylor PRODUCER Larry Page LABEL Fontana (UK)/Atco (US) UK CHART PEAK/WEEKS 2/12 US CHART PEAK/WEEKS 1/11

The Troggs had a choice for their second single: the Lovin' Spoonful's *Did You Ever Have To Make Up Your Mind* or an obscure song sent to the band's manager Larry Page that had been written by Chip Taylor for American act Jordan Christopher and the Wild Ones. *Wild Thing* was their fortunate choice. Replacing a passage of whistling with an off-beat ocarina solo, the Hampshire-based Troggs' stomping version, with echoes of *Louie Louie*, became a transatlantic hit, selling a million copies in the States.

I've got a hunch about this one: I reckon it could make it, if only because it is so gimmick laden. The boys have a sound that's a cross between The Who and The Stones, which is continually interrupted when the leader breaks into romantic speech. **Derek Johnson, NME, April 1966**

Will You Love Me Tomorrow

ARTIST Shirelles RELEASE DATE February 1961 (UK)/November 1960 (US) WRITER Carole King, Jerry Goffin PRODUCER L. Dixon LABEL Top Rank (UK)/Scepter (US) UK CHART PEAK/WEEKS 4/15 US CHART PEAK/WEEKS 1/19

The Shirelles became the first black all-female group to reach the top of the US charts. Their producer Luther Dixon was approached by the new songwriting team of Carole King and Gerry Goffin with this song which the Shirelles first thought was too poppy. Carole King played drums on the track, and the Shirelles started a run of hits including *Soldier Boy*, their second US Number 1. Acts who charted with cover versions include The Four Seasons (1968), Dave Mason (1970) and Dionne Warwick (1983).

Who has sold more records in America than any other artist? No, not Elvis Presley – The Shirelles – hitting the high spots in this country too with their Number 4 placing of **Will You Love Me Tomorrow**. **Derek Johnson, NME, March 1961**

Winchester Cathedral

ARTIST New Vaudeville Band RELEASE DATE September 1966 WRITER Geoff Stevens PRODUCER Geoff Stevens LABEL Fontana UK CHART PEAK/WEEKS 4/19 US CHART PEAK/WEEKS –

Winchester Cathedral is definitely something of an acquired taste. As the band name suggests, their sound was a concentrated update of Twenties and Thirties musical hall bands, with a bit of jazziness thrown in. They used drums, vocals and ooom pah pah effects, with rinky dinky novelty overtones. Paul Maurait also covered *Winchester Cathedral*. Amazingly they did record other singles, *Green Street Green* and the finely named *Dear Rita Hayworth*, none of which were hits.

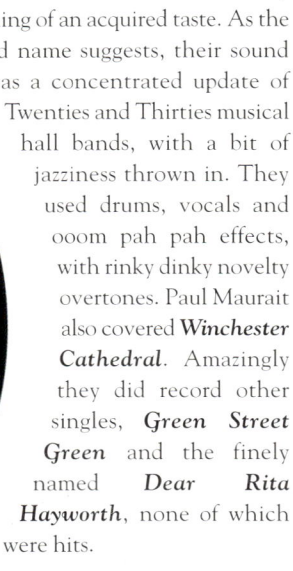

Wind Beneath My Wings

ARTIST Bette Midler RELEASE DATE June 1989 (UK)/March 1989 (US) WRITER Larry Henley, Jeff Silver PRODUCER Arif Mardin LABEL Atlantic (UK & US) UK CHART PEAK/WEEKS 5/12 US CHART PEAK/WEEKS 1/29

Bette Midler talked dirty and camped it up in style in the early days of her career; her nickname was the 'Divine Miss M'. Her big hit *The Wind Beneath My Wings* was a gutsy ballad, packed full of emotion: sentiment sung with a free flowing voice. It won Record and Song of the Year at the Grammy awards. It was a vast achievement for Midler, who had propelled herself from the chorus lines of the Sixties to Hollywood and the hit parade.

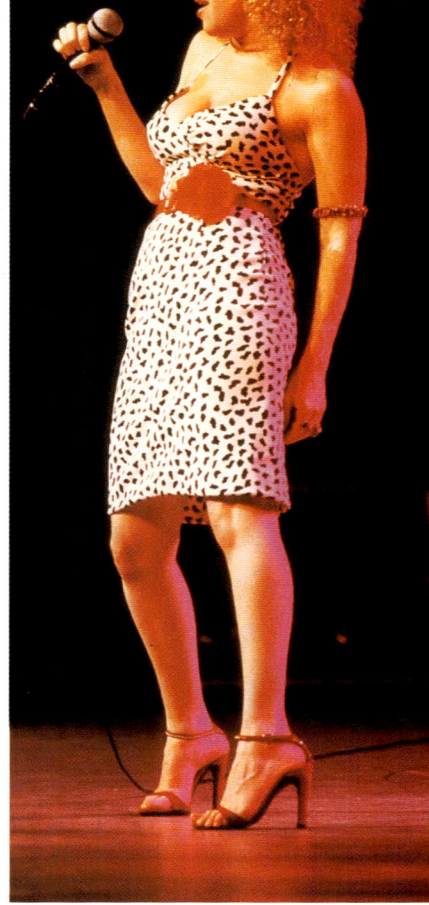

Wind Of Change

ARTIST Scorpions **RELEASE DATE** June 1991 (UK & US) **WRITER** K. Meine **PRODUCER** Ken Olson **LABEL** Vertigo (UK)/Mercury (US) **UK CHART PEAK/WEEKS** 53/3 **US CHART PEAK/WEEKS** 4/25

Sixteen years after the Hanoverian heavy rockers had released their first album, the Scorpions toured the Soviet Union, returning to play the Moscow Music Peace Festival the following year. The experience inspired lead singer Klaus Meine to write this song, completed as the Berlin Wall came down and as social and political changes rolled through Eastern Europe. Meine's anthem, with its poignant whistled motif, picked up a mighty head of steam, with a year-long stay on the German charts and worldwide success.

Everyone was there: the Red Army, journalists, musicians from Germany, from America, from Russia – the whole world on one boat. It was like a vision; everyone was talking the same language. It was a very positive vibe. That night was the basic inspiration for **Wind of Change**. **Klaus Meir interviewed by David Quantick, NME, December 1991**

The Winner Takes It All

ARTIST Abba **RELEASE DATE** August 1980 (UK)/November 1980 (US) **WRITER** Benny Andersson, Bjorn Ulvaeus **PRODUCER** Benny Andersson, Bjorn Ulvaeus **LABEL** Epic (UK)/Atlantic (US) **UK CHART PEAK/WEEKS** 1/10 **US CHART PEAK/WEEKS** 8/26

The Winner Takes It All was an unusually cynical statement for a group known for its bubbly love songs, but it reflected the group's current state of affairs, so to speak: by then, Bjorn had split with Agnetha, and Benny was carrying on an affair that would break up his marriage. Perhaps record buyers sensed the song's honesty, for

it became Abba's eighth chart-topper and their fourth, and last, Top 10 hit in America.

Yet another solid gold hit – it will probably be Number 1. Abba's contribution to popular music has been to take simple musical statements, inject complex arranging and production techniques and produce timeless pop hits that appeal to millions. **Martyn Sutton, Melody Maker, August 1980**

Wishing Well

ARTIST Free **RELEASE DATE** January 1973 **WRITER** Paul Rodgers, Simon Kirke, Tetso Yamauchi, John Bundrick, Paul Kossoff **PRODUCER** Free **LABEL** Island **UK CHART PEAK/WEEKS** 7/10 **US CHART PEAK/WEEKS** –

Taken from **Heartbreaker**, generally regarded as one of Free's weaker LPs, it gave the band their fourth UK Top 20 entry in the opening weeks of 1973. **Wishing Well** was a sympathetic comment on guitarist Paul Kossoff's decline through drug abuse and reached the UK Top 10 as Free undertook their final tour, without Kossoff, before disbanding. Although relatively short-lived, Free were among the most influential of the British blues-based bands, and provided an excellent alternative to the progressive movement that dominated the early Seventies scene.

I must admit this is an excellent little track. It is slightly disconcerting to start with because everything is levelled on a very bass sound, both musically and vocally, but it is so damn solid and funky it really gets hold of you. **Penny Valentine, Sounds, December 1972**

With A Little Help From My Friends

ARTIST Joe Cocker **RELEASE DATE** October 1968 (UK)/November 1968 (US) **WRITER** John Lennon, Paul McCartney **PRODUCER** Denny Cordell **LABEL** Regal-Zonophone (UK)/A&M (US) **UK CHART PEAK/WEEKS** 1/13 **US CHART PEAK/WEEKS** 68/6

The Beatles' refusal to release any singles from **Sgt Pepper** was a gift to artists needing hits. **With A Little Help From My Friends** alone was a hit for three different acts. In 1967, one-hit wonders The Young Idea took it just short of the Top 10. The following year, Joe Cocker took it to the top as his breakthrough hit. Then in 1988, the song was Number 1 again, this time by Wet Wet Wet, as a double A-side with Billy Bragg's **She's Leaving Home**.

Here 'tis the famous Cocker performance of Lennon and McCartney's classic from **Sgt Pepper**: *a favourite among fans of the incredible Joe – his raw voice stamped with sincerity, and it would be pleasing to see this receive a roar of approval....* **Chris Welch, Melody Maker, September 1968**

With Or Without You

ARTIST U2 **RELEASE DATE** March 1987 (UK & US) **WRITER** U2 **PRODUCER** Brian Eno, Daniel Lanois **LABEL** Island (UK & US) **UK CHART PEAK/WEEKS** 4/11 **US CHART PEAK/WEEKS** 1/18

With Or Without You became the band's first US Number 1 and the first ever by an Irish group. The B-side of the American release featured a 33 rpm version of **Luminous Times: Walk To The Water** and hence became an instant collector's item. With the epic feel of **I Still Haven't Found What I'm looking For**, the track **With Or Without You** – unusual for U2, a love song – collected a Viewer's Choice award at the MTV Video Music Awards.

[U2] seem to need to impress upon us just how passionate they are about just about everything. This is why they are so far away from being a soul group. Soul is not about striving for feeling. Soul is simply about feeling…. Boring. **John Wilde, Melody Maker, March 1987**

Without You

ARTIST Nilsson **RELEASE DATE** February 1972 (UK)/December 1971 (US) **WRITER** Peter Ham, Tom Evans **PRODUCER** Richard Perry **LABEL** RCA (UK)/RCA Victor (US) **UK CHART PEAK/WEEKS** 1/20 **US CHART PEAK/WEEKS** 1/19

Without You was an epic ballad, full of extremely emotive vocals and crashing piano chords. Although Nilsson was an accomplished songwriter this was a joint effort from Peter Ham and Tom Evans. The song itself was simple enough, but Nilsson added an element of psycho drama to the tale of a lost love and the ensuing meaningless life. It stopped just short of open weeping. It was, unsurprisingly, his biggest hit.

No trouble with Harry: the ace song writer and performer proves his point … while reminding me of some of Roy Orbison's early work, without Roy's excessively tragic overtones. **Chris Welch, Melody Maker, January 1972**

Woman

ARTIST John Lennon **RELEASE DATE** January 1981 (UK & US) **WRITER** John Lennon **PRODUCER** J. Douglas, John Lennon, Yoko Ono **LABEL** Geffen (UK & US) **UK CHART PEAK/WEEKS** 1/11 **US CHART PEAK/WEEKS** 2/20

The paean to wife Yoko Ono from the LP **Double Fantasy** gave Lennon his second newly recorded hit and became his third posthumous UK Number 1 single in February 1981. In the US, the single narrowly failed to repeat its UK success, spending three weeks at Number 2. The demand for Lennon products at this time was tremendous: Roxy Music's tribute, **Jealous Guy**, a cover of a track from the **Imagine** LP, reached Number 1 in the UK three weeks after **Woman**.

Woman is an album track – from an album even die hard fans agreed couldn't count amongst Lennon's best work. A celebration of life, peace of mind, comfort – some might even say, (or have said), complacency. **Ian Penman, NME, January 1981**

Woman In Love

ARTIST Barbra Streisand **RELEASE DATE** October 1980 (UK)/September 1980 (US) **WRITER** Barry and Robin Gibb **PRODUCER** Barry Gibb, Albhy Galuten, Karl Richardson **LABEL** CBS (UK)/Columbia (US) **UK CHART PEAK/WEEKS** 1/6 **US CHART PEAK/WEEKS** 1/24

In 1978, the Bee Gees were untouchable and it was no surprise that they were hot properties as producers, being approached by both Bob Dylan and Streisand. Only the latter proposal came to fruition in 1980's **Guilty** album, featuring the title song (a hit as a duet with Barry Gibb) and this international Number 1.

Woman In Love expands a melody very similar to Andy Gibb's After Dark – into an aural balloon that wafts Streisand singing right through the stratosphere…. As beautifully crafted a piece of ear candy as I have ever heard. **Stephen Holden, Rolling Stone, December 1980**

Won't Get Fooled Again

ARTIST The Who **RELEASE DATE** July 1971 (UK & US) **WRITER** Pete Townsend **PRODUCER** Glyn Johns, Pete Townshend **LABEL** Track (UK)/Decca (US) **UK CHART PEAK/WEEKS** 9/12 **US CHART PEAK/WEEKS** 15/13

Won't Get Fooled Again was one of the tracks on **Who's Next**. For the first time The Who's sound was underpinned by electronic backing tracks programmed with no little skill by Townshend. Roger Daltrey unleashed a full-blooded scream at the climax of the track, which Pete Townshend described as an anti-anti-song, because 'a revolution is not going to change anything in the long run'.

Most people regard change in a suspicious light, but Won't Get Fooled Again is the epitome of a group moving forward to better things whilst still retaining all the qualities which have served them so well in the past. **Penny Valentine, Sounds, June 1971**

The Wonder Of You

ARTIST Elvis Presley **RELEASE DATE** July 1970 (UK)/May 1970 (US) **WRITER** Baker Knight **PRODUCER** – **LABEL** RCA (UK)/RCA Victor (US) **UK CHART PEAK/WEEKS** 1/21 **US CHART PEAK/WEEKS** 9/12

After a gap of five years Elvis returned to the top of the UK charts in 1970 with this, his biggest single of the year. *The Wonder Of You* was also his last UK hit before his death in 1977. It fared less well in the States, however, where it only reached Number 9. The song, a ballad recorded live at the International Hotel in Las Vegas, was delivered with the full-blooded, no-holds-barred operatic verve of Elvis' later singing-style.

Did you know he has more Uranium Discs than the Beatles ... more talent in his big toe than Sandie Shaw ... made more miles of film than Donald Duck. Come on all you fans let's get him back at Number 1 where he so rightfully belongs. **Chris Welch, Melody Maker, July 1970**

Wonderful Land

ARTIST The Shadows **RELEASE DATE** March 1962 **WRITER** Jerry Lordan **PRODUCER** – **LABEL** Columbia **UK CHART PEAK/WEEKS** 1/19 **US CHART PEAK/WEEKS** –

The Shadows had established their electric guitar instrumental style with *Apache*, their first Number 1, in 1960, and followed it with a run of Top 5 UK hits including *Foot Tapper*, *FBI* and *Kon Tiki*. *Wonderful Land*, by the composer of *Apache*, Jerry Lordan, was the first Shadows track to feature an orchestral backing and brought them a third Number 1 – they had four in total. Another instrumental, *Nut Rocker* by B. Bumble And The Stingers, knocked them off the top.

Credit is due to The Shadows for turning the big beat into music – and this is a fair example. The electrified effects are never overdone and they blend with the string backing. **Melody Maker, February 1962**

Wonderful World

ARTIST Sam Cooke **RELEASE DATE** July 1960 (UK)/May 1960 (US) **WRITER** Barbara Campbell, Lou Adler, Herb Alpert **PRODUCER** – **LABEL** HMV Pop (UK)/Keen (US) **UK CHART PEAK/WEEKS** 27/8 **US CHART PEAK/WEEKS** 12/15

After artists like the Mills Brothers and Nat King Cole made the music world safe for black singers, Sam Cooke made the music world safe for black singers who sounded black. There were others before him, but Cooke had the widest appeal among listeners of all races. *Wonderful World*, which he co-wrote under his wife's maiden name, Barbara Campbell, was the most charming of his many soulful pop gems. Many others have hit with the song, including Herman's Hermits, Art Garfunkel and James Taylor.

A big recording star over in the States, but one who has not had all that much luck over here, is Sam Cooke. I don't reckon he has a winner with **Wonderful World**, *but he's got a lyric there that will ring a bell for lots of listeners.* **Keith Fordyce, NME, June 1960.**

Wonderwall

ARTIST Oasis **RELEASE DATE** November 1995 (UK)/January 1996 (US) **WRITER** Noel Gallagher **PRODUCER** Owen Morris, Noel Gallagher **LABEL** Creation (UK)/Epic (US) UK CHART PEAK/WEEKS 2/32 US CHART PEAK/WEEKS 8/20

Christened after a George Harrison album of the same name, *Wonderwall* is a perfectly poised rock ballad, a grower with real staying power. It hung around the charts for months, then returned in a kitsch version by the Mike Flower's Pops. It also cracked America, proving to be the record that took Oasis into a new league. Ironically it did the same for the band's beloved Manchester City Football Club, where it became a terrace anthem during their relegation season.

*A mesmeric declaration of love – haunting, beautiful and effortlessly simple … **Wonderwall**, to paraphrase the French philosopher Chateaubriand, is the sublime pressed to its farthest limits. And **Round Are Way**, its all-singing, all-dancing all-new B side, isn't far behind.* **Michael Bonner, Melody Maker, November 1995**

Wooden Heart

ARTIST Elvis Presley **RELEASE DATE** March 1961 **WRITER** Berthold Kaempfret, Kay Twomey, Fred Wise, Ben Weisman **PRODUCER** – **LABEL** RCA (UK)/RCA Victor (US) UK CHART PEAK/WEEKS 1/27 US CHART PEAK/WEEKS 0/0

Generally considered to be the record that marked his transition from rebellious rocker to all-round entertainer, Elvis first sang *Wooden Heart* to a puppet in his first post-army film *G.I. Blues*. Based on an old German folk song, the record was considered wrong for the US market by RCA, despite its huge success in Europe. As a consequence several cover versions were released in the States, including one by Joe Dowell which topped the US charts in 1961.

Wooden Heart is an attractive, homely number with a discreet biergarten type accompaniment. Elvis sings this with engaging charm and restraint, and even gives us one chorus in German. **Laurie Hernshaw, Melody Maker, March 1961**

Wooly Bully

ARTIST Sam The Sham And The Pharaohs **RELEASE DATE** June 1965 (UK)/April 1965 (US) **WRITER** Domingo Samudio **PRODUCER** Stan Kesler **LABEL** MGM (UK & US) UK CHART PEAK/WEEKS 11/15 US CHART PEAK/WEEKS 2/18

Domingo Samudio grew up in the Tex-Mex rock 'n' roll tradition. Taking the name Sam from his surname, adding The Sham – a term for a vocalist's jiving – and adopting a bizarre Egyptian outfit, he created The Pharaohs. *Wooly Bully* was a rumbustious novelty dance hit, allegedly referring to Sam's pet cat, and became a classic number for club and bar bands to cover. Like most novelty acts The Pharaohs were ready for embalming by the end of the Sixties.

*The leader of one the hottest groups on both sides of the Atlantic – Sam The Sham – once used to sing in Opera. The Wooly Bully man confided: 'I was a low baritone – just took on small parts.' **Wooly Bully** has got to Number 11 in the NME charts.* **Tract Thomas, NME, July 1965**

Working My Way Back To You

ARTIST The (Detroit) Spinners **RELEASE DATE** February 1980 (UK)/December 1979 (US) **WRITER** Sandy Linzer, Denny Randell **PRODUCER** Michael Zager **LABEL** Atlantic (UK & US) UK CHART PEAK/WEEKS 1/14 US CHART PEAK/WEEKS 2/25

This release was the Spinners' final hit. Thom Bell, the Philadelphia producer had turned the group from a long-time lower league Motown act – which Bell had nonetheless always admired – into a soundscape in which voices were woven together. They had a run of hits from *I'll Be Around* to *If You Wanna Do A Dance*. After Bell and vocalist Phillipe Wynne left, the group teamed up with a new singer, John Edwards, and a new producer, Michael Zager, to record this cover of a Four Seasons 1966 hit.

World In Motion

ARTIST Englandneworder **RELEASE DATE** June 1990 **WRITER** New Order **PRODUCER** Stephen Hague, New Order **LABEL** Factory (UK)/MCA (US) UK CHART PEAK/WEEKS 1/12 US CHART PEAK/WEEKS –

Football records are by definition naff, so the combination of England's World Cup squad with street-credible Mancunians New Order was a departure from the norm. Jamaican-born John Barnes, later to star in Liverpool's *Anfield Rap*, earned his spurs as a rapper on this song, whose lyrics were written by actor Keith Allen. Allen in turn would later link with Black Grape and Joe Strummer for *England's Irie*, an alternative anthem for Euro '96 and still the soundbed for Sky's Football League coverage.

*New Order's World Cup anthem suggests two points: 1: How do you square this amiable knees-up with the sensibility which produced **Ceremony**? 2: Does it really matter, anyway?* **Richard Cook, Sounds, May 1990**

A World Of Our Own

ARTIST The Seekers **RELEASE DATE** April 1965 (UK)/May 1965 (US) **WRITER** Tom Springfield **PRODUCER** Tom Springfield **LABEL** Columbia (UK)/Capitol (US) **UK CHART PEAK/WEEKS** 3/18 **US CHART PEAK/WEEKS** 19/10

Later a country chart Number 1 in the States for Sonny James, who also covered the group's *I'll Never Find Another You*, *A World Of Our Own* was a song from the fertile creative brain of Tom Springfield, Dusty's brother. He wrote for and inspired the Australian singing group who had moved to London the year before. It was their second transatlantic hit in a row.

She has a great voice. It won't be bought as much as the last one, but it's a clever song. It's a lot like country music. **Donovan, Melody Maker, April 1965**

Wuthering Heights

ARTIST Kate Bush **RELEASE DATE** February 1978 **WRITER** Kate Bush **PRODUCER** Kate Bush **LABEL** EMI **UK CHART PEAK/WEEKS** 1/13 **US CHART PEAK/WEEKS** –

'It's me, I'm Cathy, I've come home'. With those words, the voice of 19-year-old Catherine Bush came into the homes of millions of listeners for the first time. It also gave librarians and bookstore owners cause for celebration, as listeners intrigued by Bush's *Wuthering Heights* sought out the original novel. With Bush's haunting soprano surrounded by

orchestration, the disc came out of left moor, so to speak. It exceeded even its own label's expectations, topping the charts for four weeks.

The Theatre influence comes through strongly: from the cover, to every aspect of Kate's song. The orchestration is ornate and densely packed but never overflows it's banks – extraordinary vocals skating in and out, over and above. **Ian Birch, Melody Maker, January 1978**

Y.M.C.A.

ARTIST Village People **RELEASE DATE** November 1978 (UK)/October 1978 (US) **WRITER** Jacques Morali, Henri Belolo, John Willis **PRODUCER** Jacques Morali **LABEL** Mercury (UK)/Casablanca (US) **UK CHART PEAK/WEEKS** 1/16 **US CHART PEAK/WEEKS** 2/26

The troupe of actors, dancers and singers brought together by producer Jacques Morali in 1977 as a collage of gay stereotypes were perfectly chosen. We remember them so well, from the construction worker to the cowboy. They were corny and cynically camp, but they released classic disco tracks until the novelty wore off. **Y.M.C.A.** sold over a million copies in the UK alone and topped the charts for three weeks. A remix of the number reached UK Number 12 in 1993, the year before Morali's AIDS-related death.

At a time when a politician is virtually on trial for alleged homosexuality in the Dailies, this record celebrates Gay sexuality and its gloriously infectiously happy dance music. **Garry Bushell, Sounds, December 1978**

Y Viva Espana

ARTIST Sylvia **RELEASE DATE** August 1974 **WRITER** Leo Caretz, Eddie Rosenstaten **PRODUCER** – **LABEL** Sonet **UK CHART PEAK/WEEKS** 4/28 **US CHART PEAK/WEEKS** –

The 'summer-in-Spain' hit of the Seventies had a complex international history. Written by two Belgians, it had been a massive hit in Belgium for Samantha, in Germany for the Dutch-born Imca Marina and in Sweden for Sylvia. It was Vrethammer's version which charted in the English language, with lyrics by Eddie Seago.

Yakety Yak

ARTIST Coasters **RELEASE DATE** August 1958 (UK)/June 1958 (US)
WRITER Jerry Leiber, Mike Stoller **PRODUCER** Jerry Leiber, Mike
Stoller **LABEL** London (UK)/Atco (US) **UK CHART PEAK/WEEKS** 12/8
US CHART PEAK/WEEKS 1/16

Yakety Yak remains rock's wittiest analysis of parent-teen
relations. Lyrics like 'your father's hip; he knows what cooks'
may sound dated, but the sentiments are timeless. Written
and produced by the team of Leiber and Stoller, it was the
biggest hit for the forever clowning Coasters, one of the first
black groups to enjoy wide acceptance among listeners of
all races and creeds. Scores of British groups covered their
songs, including The Beatles, The Rolling Stones, and The
Hollies.

*It has all the familiar ingredients including a fast beat, a
punchy vocal group and a tooting saxophone. It's the lyric that is
unusual. Instead of dealing with 'lerve/luv/love', it tackles that
social problem of the house work…. Lively and amusing.* **Keith
Fordyce, NME, August 1958**

Yellow River

ARTIST Christie **RELEASE DATE** May 1970 (UK)/July 1970 (US) **WRITER** Jeff
Christie **PRODUCER** – **LABEL** CBS (UK)/Epic (US) **UK CHART PEAK/WEEKS**
1/22 **US CHART PEAK/WEEKS** 23/23

Christie was named for its leader, singer/songwriter Jeff Christie,
who had previously recorded for Deram with a psych-pop group
called the Outer Limits. When the Outer Limits broke up in
1970 Christie wrote *Yellow River* and offered it to the
Tremeloes, who turned it down. Undeterred, he formed a group
and recorded the song himself. The result: a thoroughly likeable
bubble-gum hippy tune that went all the way to the top of the
British charts.

*Michael Blakley: Trying to write music – Vic Elmes: Drink, Coffee
– Jeff Christie: Ambition, Security, Happiness – Common to all:
current hit* **Yellow River.** *Life Lines, NME, June 1970*

The Yellow Rose Of Texas

ARTIST Mitch Miller **RELEASE DATE** October 1955 (UK)/August 1955 (US)
WRITER Don George **PRODUCER** – **LABEL** Philips (UK)/Columbia (US) **UK
CHART PEAK/WEEKS** 2/13 **US CHART PEAK/WEEKS** 1/19

Mitch Miller was one of the most successful recording artists and
producers of the Fifties, with a series of easy listening sing-along
songs, including the *Yellow Rose Of Texas*, a Civil War marching
song. It has a cheerful stomping chorus and galloping rhythm. The
production on this is restrained, but on records for other artists he
included unique sound and dramatic effects He famously hated
rock 'n' roll, and turned down Elvis Presley when he worked at
Columbia.

*The American in Columbia disc wizard who made record stars of
Johnnie Ray, Doris Day and Guy Mitchell, is now a record star
himself. Mitch Miller writes 'I like recording for the British, their
taste and mine get along very well!'.* **Geoffrey Everitt, NME,
October 1955**

Yellow Submarine/Eleanor Rigby

ARTIST The Beatles **RELEASE DATE** August 1966 (UK & US) **WRITER** John
Lennon, Paul McCartney **PRODUCER** George Martin **LABEL** Parlophone
(UK)/Capitol (US) **UK CHART PEAK/WEEKS** 1/13 **US CHART PEAK/WEEKS** 2/9
(Double A side data on Yellow Submarine only)

John Lennon and Paul McCartney wrote *Yellow Submarine* so
that Ringo Starr would have a lead vocal on their upcoming album
Revolver. It became Ringo's first Number 1 as a singer. The
altogether different flip side, *Eleanor Rigby*, was written mostly by
McCartney, who sang it, accompanied by a string octet. The disc
stopped just short of Number 1 in America, where it was held back
by the Supremes' *You Can't Hurry Love*.

Yesterday

ARTIST The Beatles **RELEASE DATE** March 1976 (UK)/September 1965 (US)
WRITER John Lennon, Paul McCartney **PRODUCER** George Martin **LABEL** Apple
(UK)/Capitol (US) **UK CHART PEAK/WEEKS** 8/7 **US CHART PEAK/WEEKS** 1/11

While *Yesterday* bore The Beatles' name, Paul McCartney was the
only group member to play and sing on it, backed by a string
quartet and nothing else. It subsequently became The Beatles' most
covered song, and then one of the most covered songs of all time.
Its ubiquity opened it to criticism, with some deriding it as weepy
and obvious. However, there is no denying that the original
recording marked a great advancement for rock,
paving the way for future experiments
with acoustic and classical
instruments.

*This is a very strange choice
with which to re-promote The
Beatles. It is o.k. as a song,
and the string quartet is
especially imaginative
compared to most pop
strings, but it sounds so
dated.* **John Ingham,
Sounds, March 1976**

Yesterday Once More

ARTIST The Carpenters RELEASE DATE July 1973 (UK)/June 1973 (US) WRITER Richard Carpenter, John Bettis PRODUCER Richard Carpenter LABEL A&M (UK & US) UK CHART PEAK/WEEKS 2/17 US CHART PEAK/WEEKS 2/14

The timing of **Yesterday Once More** couldn't have been better, coming on the eve of the release of American Graffiti. It captured the feelings of many who missed the kind of catchy, simple pop that flourished just a few years earlier but now seemed so far away. Richard Carpenter wrote it with John Bettis, who first worked with him in 1967 when they were both soda jerks at Disneyland's Coke Corner.

I must admit, The Carpenters have risen in my estimation since recent hits and a concert at The Royal Albert Hall sometime back. One can play this for pleasure and not just duty – and believe me that's a rare experience. **Chris Welch, Melody Maker, June 1973**

You Ain't Seen Nothing Yet

ARTIST Bachman-Turner Overdrive RELEASE DATE November 1974 (UK)/September 1974 (US) WRITER Randy Bachman PRODUCER Randy Bachman LABEL Mercury (UK & US) UK CHART PEAK/WEEKS 2/12 US CHART PEAK/WEEKS 1/17

While this Canadian quartet were recording **You Ain't Seen Nothing Yet**, lead singer/songwriter Randy Bachman decided to do a gag version to give to their manager, his brother Gary, who was a stutterer. When B.T.O.'s label heard it by mistake, they insisted on making it a single. A red-faced Randy protested but finally relented, believing it wouldn't be a hit anyway – it was their biggest.

Alright, B.T.O. are about as subtle as an atom bomb and highly commercial, but they make crash-out singles…. The present contender, **You Ain't Seen Nothing Yet**, *is wizard.* **Max Bell, NME, November 1974**

You Can Do Magic

ARTIST Limmie And The Family Cookin' RELEASE DATE July 1973 (UK)/November (US) WRITER Sandy Linzer PRODUCER – LABEL Avco (UK & US) UK CHART PEAK/WEEKS 3/13 US CHART PEAK/WEEKS 84/0

Family trio Limmie And The Family Cookin' was made up of Limmie Snell, Jimmy Thomas and Martha Stewart (not the American Queen of the Domestic Scene) and they threw into the melting pot chunks of groovy harmonies, snappy backing vocals and tingling percussion. **You Can Do Magic** was a delicious mix of speedy vocals and a shimmering 'dance 'til you drop' rhythm. It also had great tambourines and chiming bells, which were used to great effect on **Walking Miracle**, another lip smacking single.

You Don't Bring Me Flowers

ARTIST Barbra Streisand And Neil Diamond RELEASE DATE November 1978 (UK)/October 1978 (US) WRITER Alan And Marilyn Bergman, Neil Diamond PRODUCER Bob Gaudio LABEL CBS (UK)/Columbia (US) UK CHART PEAK/WEEKS 5/12 US CHART PEAK/WEEKS 1/17

Streisand was strong on duets in the late Seventies: following **You Don't Bring Me Flowers Anymore** with Neil Diamond, she released **No More Tears (Enough Is Enough)** with Donna Summer the following year, and linked up with Bee Gee Barry Gibb on 1980's **Guilty**. Diamond, songwriter and superstar in his own right, having sold over ninety million albums worldwide, usually performed solo though he tried another duet with Kim Carnes in 1991 with **Hooked On The Memory Of You**.

The first teaming of the superstars Streisand and Diamond is highlighted by piano and viola-orchestration. The high interplay of vocals brings commanding depth and appeal to the ballad, which first appeared on Diamond's **I'm Glad You're Here With Me Tonight** *album.* **Billboard, September 1979**

You Don't Have To Say You Love Me

ARTIST Dusty Springfield RELEASE DATE March 1966 (UK)/May 1966 (US0 WRITER Nicki Wickham, Simon Napier-Bell, P. Donaggio PRODUCER Johnny Franz LABEL Philips (UK & US) UK CHART PEAK/WEEKS 1/13 US CHART PEAK/WEEKS 4/13

When the Springfields – Dusty, her brother Tom and Tim Field: a kind of British Peter Paul and Mary – broke up in 1963, Tom found success as the Seekers' guru, and Dusty went solo. She launched her career with Bacharach & David's **I Only Want To Be With You**. This ballad was her first and only US Number 1, and her best-selling single, an English version of the powerful ballad that won the San Remo Song Festival in 1965, Io Che Non Vivo (Senzate).

Fabulous intro. It's Dusty all the way for me: a big hit. I've got shivers up and down my spine … she really feels it. **Dave Dee, Melody Maker, March 1966**

(You Gotta) Fight For Your Right (To Party)

ARTIST The Beastie Boys RELEASE DATE February 1987 (UK)/December 1986 (US) WRITER Rick Rubin, The Beastie Boys PRODUCER Rick Rubin LABEL Def Jam (UK & US) UK CHART PEAK/WEEKS 11/11 US CHART PEAK/WEEKS 7/18

With this disc the Beastie Boys made pop history as the first white rap group to make the charts. It was the second major label release for the trio, who started out in 1981 as a hard-core band. Although not consistent hitmakers since then, they continued being a popular album and concert act, notably taking an active role performing in and promoting the Milarepa Fund's benefit concerts for a free Tibet.

This is the record that every five year old should receive when they graduate from play school … an anarchic thrash of utterly gratuitous vileness. **Melody Maker, February 1987**

You Light Up My Life

ARTIST Debby Boone RELEASE DATE December 1977 (UK)/September 1977 (US) WRITER Joseph Brooks PRODUCER – LABEL Warner Bros. (UK)/Warner/Curb (US) UK CHART PEAK/WEEKS 48/2 US CHART PEAK/WEEKS 1/25

The third of Pat Boone's four daughters, Debby, got her start touring with her sisters as the Boones. When they signed with Curb Records, label head Mike Curb wanted to record Debby solo as well. While searching for an appropriate tune, he saw the film *You Light Up My Life* and was hooked by its theme. Debby's recording became America's best-selling record of the Seventies. Utterly inescapable, it was Number 1 for 10 weeks. The British, however, were spared.

You Make Me Feel Like Dancing

ARTIST Leo Sayer RELEASE DATE October 1976 (UK & US) WRITER Leo Sayer, Vini Poncia PRODUCER Richard Perry LABEL Chrysalis (UK)/Warner (US) UK CHART PEAK/WEEKS 2/12 US CHART PEAK/WEEKS 1/21

By this 1976 release Leo Sayer had long abandoned the ultimately annoying pierrot costume and end-of-pier image he'd adopted for his debut release *The Show Must Go On* in 1973. He'd also split

with his songwriting partner Dave Courtney. This track was co-written by Sayer and Vini Poncia and given an LA gloss by Richard Perry (producer for Barbra Streisand and Carly Simon amongst others), and picked up a Grammy for Best R&B Song.

He has been listening to the famous Cliff for some hints about falsetto, but he sounds as if somebody has grabbed him in the wrong place – slightly shocked and uncomfortable. Caroline Coon, Melody Maker, October 1976

You Make Me Feel (Mighty Real)

ARTIST Sylvester RELEASE DATE August 1978 (UK)/January 1979 (US) WRITER James Wirrick, James Sylvester PRODUCER Harvey Fuqua LABEL Fantasy (UK & US) UK CHART PEAK/WEEKS 8/15 US CHART PEAK/WEEKS 36/10

Heading out to San Francisco from LA in 1967, Sylvester was recruited by the Cockettes theatre group, then formed the Hot Band which included future Weather Girls Martha Wash and Izora Armstead. Motown producer Harvey Fuqua discovered them and in 1978 *You Make Me Feel* and *Dance (Disco Heat)* became disco dance high-energy classics, featuring Sylvester's falsetto. The singer died of an AIDS-related disease in 1988 and Jimmy Somerville's tribute cover made UK Number 5 in 1990.

The celebrated black gay who came to fame through the Cockettes, that 'outrageous' late Sixties review in San Francisco. All the ingredients of a huge disco hit, and may be even ripe for the cross over market. **Ian Birch, Melody Maker, August 1978**

You Really Got Me

ARTIST The Kinks RELEASE DATE August 1964 (UK)/September 1964 (US) WRITER Ray Davies PRODUCER Shel Talmy LABEL Pye (UK)/Reprise (US) UK CHART PEAK/WEEKS 1/2 US CHART PEAK/WEEKS 7/15

As the beat boom began to run out of steam, a new generation of British groups emerged, trading in the very R&B style which had originally inspired the groups they were displacing. The Kinks were in the vanguard of the new movement, and this, their third single, became their first hit, reaching Number 1 in

September 1964. Produced by Shel Talmy, it was a seminal slice of rowdy R&B exuberance for which Talmy enlisted session players, including Jimmy Page, to bolster the sound.

The all-time great punk classic, wonderfully snarled by Ray and ... ruined by brother Dave's funny solo. **Chris Bohn, Melody Maker, March 1980**

You Sexy Thing

ARTIST Hot Chocolate RELEASE DATE November 1975 (UK & US) WRITER Errol Brown, Tony Wilson PRODUCER Mickie Most LABEL Rak (UK)/Big Tree (US) UK CHART PEAK/WEEKS 2/12 US CHART PEAK/WEEKS 3/21

One-time protégés of John Lennon, black Britons Hot Chocolate made their UK chart debut in 1970 with **Love Is Life**. **You Sexy Thing**, released in 1975, gave the group their biggest UK hit to date, spending three weeks at Number 2, and would re-chart in 1997 thanks to exposure in the film *The Full Monty*. It also gave the band, fronted by the elastic-voiced Errol Brown, their only Top 3 hit in the US.

You ain't so bad yourself. **Mick Mercer, Melody Maker, January 1987**

You To Me Are Everything

ARTIST The Real Thing RELEASE DATE June 1976 (UK)/July 1976 (US) WRITER Ken Gold, Michael Denne PRODUCER Ken Gold LABEL Pye Int. (UK)/United Artists (US) UK CHART PEAK/WEEKS 1/11 US CHART PEAK/WEEKS 64/8

Liverpool's The Real Thing were the most successful black British group of the Seventies. But although they prided themselves on writing their own material, group members Chris and Eddie Amoo decided they needed to be more commercial just to get radio play. When songwriters Gold and Denne came up with the catchy pop/soul **You To Me Are Everything** in 1976, they found themselves with a Number 1. Ten years later they returned to the Top 5 with a re-mix by DJs Froggy, Simon Harris and KC.

After struggling for years, The Real Thing made it so fast that their record company did not have a chance to mount an expensive promotion campaign. **Caroline Coon, Melody Maker, January 1977**

You'll Never Walk Alone

ARTIST Gerry And The Pacemakers RELEASE DATE October 1963 WRITER Richard Rogers, Oscar Hammerstein II PRODUCER George Martin LABEL Columbia (UK)/Laurie (US) UK CHART PEAK/WEEKS 1/19 US CHART PEAK/WEEKS –

For a song from Rogers and Hammerstein's Carousel show to be adopted as a Liverpudlian anthem takes some believing. After Gerry And The Pacemakers had taken **You'll Never Walk Alone** to the peak in Britain to complete a hat-trick of chart-toppers with their first three releases, it would be picked up by supporters of Liverpool Football Club, recently promoted from the Second Division and just months away from the most consistent run of success the game had ever known.

Absolutely marvellous. You wouldn't expect the song from Gerry, but he makes a great job of it. Imagine it – the beat world doing a ballad ... I like this enormously, it has lots of charm.... **Frankie Vaughan, Melody Maker, October 1963**

You're Having My Baby

ARTIST Paul Anka RELEASE DATE September 1974 (UK)/July 1974 (US) WRITER Paul Anka PRODUCER R. Hall LABEL United Artists (UK & US) UK CHART PEAK/WEEKS 6/10 US CHART PEAK/WEEKS 1/15

Although **You're Having My Baby** has become one of the most maligned discs of the Seventies, it remains beloved by many, particularly those who have a little one on the way. It was Paul Anka's comeback hit after five years out of the American Top 40 and over 13 years out of the US and UK Top 10. However, during that time he had tremendous success writing songs for other artists, including Tom Jones' **She's a Lady** and Frank Sinatra's **My Way**.

This new approach makes you realize just how far he has come. This hit, **You're Having My Baby***, mirrors but doesn't copy a similar sound of the soul group The Stylistics.... This music is still influenced by the earlier rhythm and blues and rock 'n' roll....* **Billboard, December 1974**

You're Sixteen

ARTIST Ringo Starr RELEASE DATE February 1974 (UK)/December 1973 (US) WRITER Dick and Bob Sherman PRODUCER Richard Perry LABEL Apple (UK & US) UK CHART PEAK/WEEKS 4/10 US CHART PEAK/WEEKS 1/15

When The Beatles split in 1970, pundits thought Ringo was 'least likely to succeed' since he'd contributed little in the way of songwriting, his vocal range was limited and even his drumming was a tad lacking. Ringo proved the prophets of doom wrong and ran up a string of US hits, including **Oh My My**, **Photograph** and this reworking of a 1960 Johnny Burnette number, a piece of fun with Harry Nilsson adding vocal backing and Macca himself on kazoo.

The chances are that few Sounds readers will be elderly enough to remember Johnny Burnette's earlier (much earlier) hit. Ringo takes it pretty straight, with a gang of backing singers standing by to smooth off the rough edges. **John Peel, Sounds, February 1974**

You're So Vain

ARTIST Carly Simon **RELEASE DATE** December 1972 (UK & US) **WRITER** Carly Simon **PRODUCER** Richard Perry **LABEL** Elektra (UK & US) **UK CHART PEAK/WEEKS** 3/15 **US CHART PEAK/WEEKS** 1/17

Carly Simon never deigned to reveal who the conceited target of her song was, demurring that it was 'no one in particular'. The daughter of the co-founder of New York publishing house Simon & Schuster, she had begun working with producer Richard Perry after her first two albums, and discovered a new edge and increased confidence in her writing and singing by her third album **No Secrets**, from which this single was taken.

This track from Carly's new London Records album certainly has a lot going for it: there is a nice cross pattern between the back-up produced by Richard Perry, and Carly's piano work on this, which sets the pace racing throughout. **Penny Valentine, Sounds, December 1972**

You're The Best Thing

ARTIST Style Council **RELEASE DATE** May 1984 (UK)/July 1984 (US) **WRITER** Paul Weller **PRODUCER** Paul Weller, P. Wilson **LABEL** Polydor (UK)/Geffen (US) **UK CHART PEAK/WEEKS** 5/8 **US CHART PEAK/WEEKS** 76/5

The pairing of Paul Weller, formerly of The Jam, with ex Mod Mick Talbot to form the Style Council allowed both to explore what was for them the mostly uncharted territory of soul and jazz. **You're the Best Thing**, one of their fondest-remembered hits, was on a double A-side 12 in maxi-single (itself titled **Groovin'**) alongside **Big Boss Groove**. In America it appeared as the follow-up to **My Ever Changing Moods**, which had reached Number 29.

Plenty of get on up, we can make a stamp together etc … **You're The Best Thing** *is lost in a slip-stream of awkward romance.* **Richard Cook, NME, May 1984**

You're The First, The Last, My Everything

ARTIST Barry White **RELEASE DATE** November 1974 (UK & US) **WRITER** Barry White, Tony Sepe, Peter Radcliffe **PRODUCER** Barry White **LABEL** 20th Century (UK & US) **UK CHART PEAK/WEEKS** 1/14 **US CHART PEAK/WEEKS** 2/15

Love Unlimited was the name of his orchestra in the early Seventies, and lurrrve unlimited was what he offered upfront, in singles like **You're The First**, the first solo release under his own name, and **Never, Never Gonna Give Ya Up**. White's husky, rumbling bass voice, sometimes singing, sometimes growling, backed by lush strings and a disco rhythm, revelled in its own excess. A physically massive stage presence, White's sexy seduction numbers were in a league of their own.

He doesn't talk at all on this disc; and though he pushes to make the high notes, Barry White here serves notice he can put his distinctive sound concept across without using the gimmick of long spoken intros every time. **Billboard, October 1974**

You're The One That I Want

ARTIST John Travolta And Olivia Newton-John **RELEASE DATE** May 1978 (UK)/April (US) **WRITER** John Farrar **PRODUCER** John Farrar **LABEL** RSO (UK & US) **UK CHART PEAK/WEEKS** 1/26 **US CHART PEAK/WEEKS** 1/24

Olivia Newton-John's character in *Grease* was Sandy Olsen, the innocent blonde, 'lousy with virginity', who gets sexy – not a million miles from Newton-John's own musical career: **I Honestly Love You** through **Physical**. In *Grease*, **You're The One That I Want** featured a leather-jacketed Newton-John and a yelping John Travolta grooving their way through to the film's finale.

Travolta is frantic throughout in what is obviously a marvellously, sustained pose. Olivia, by contrast, is gentle and yearning. In combination against a relentless beat reciting an irresistible hook, the duo is inspiring. **Paul Gambaccini, Melody Maker, May 1978**

You've Lost That Lovin' Feeling

ARTIST The Righteous Brothers **RELEASE DATE** January 1965 (UK)/December 1964 (US) **WRITER** Barry Mann, Cynthia Weil, Phil Spector **PRODUCER** Phil Spector **LABEL** London (UK)/Philles (US) **UK CHART PEAK/WEEKS** 1/10 **US CHART PEAK/WEEKS** 1/16

Still regarded by many as one of the finest recordings ever made, **You've Lost That Lovin' Feelin'** was The Righteous Brothers' first major hit. Based loosely on The Four Tops' **Baby I Need Your Loving**, the song's co-writer and producer Phil Spector brilliantly layered his unique 'wall of sound' to reach an orgasmic crescendo. The record returned to the UK Top 10 in 1969 and again in 1990.

American soul singing duo The Righteous Brothers on January 30 streaked to the top from Number 18. **You've Lost That Lovin' Feeling** *was immensely popular but only kept that elusive top position for two weeks.* **Melody Maker, July 1965**

Young At Heart

ARTIST Bluebells RELEASE DATE June 1984 WRITER Sara Dallin, Robert Hodgens, Karen Woodwards, Siobhan Fahey PRODUCER C. Fairley, Robert Hodgens LABEL London UK CHART PEAK/WEEKS 8/12 US CHART PEAK/WEEKS –

From Scotland, the Bluebells scored their biggest hit with this fiddle-driven, country-style stomper, written by guitarist Bobby Hodgens, a.k.a. Bobby Bluebell, and his then girlfriend, Bananarama's Siobhan Fahey. It originally reached Number 8 in the UK during the summer of 1984, but got a second life in 1993 when Volkswagen used it in a TV commercial. Reissued then, it made it to Number 1, but by then the group had long since broken up.

Enthusiastic but unadventurous young Country music, the violin makes an occasional brave face, but the rest of them seem a little laid back for Eastenders. **Hugh Fielder, Sounds, June 1984**

Young Girl

ARTIST Union Gap Featuring Gary Puckett RELEASE DATE April 1968 (UK)/March 1968 (US) WRITER Jerry Fuller PRODUCER Jerry Fuller LABEL CBS (UK)/Columbia (US) UK CHART PEAK/WEEKS 1/17 US CHART PEAK/WEEKS 2/15

Formed in 1967, Union Gap named themselves after a battlefield town in Washington State, later styling themselves Gary Puckett And The Union Gap. The ballad *Young Girl*, written and produced by Jerry Fuller, was a warning to a would-be lover of an underage girl of the consequences of him not being able to resist her charms. A Number 1 in the UK, it was the most successful of five singles to enter the US Top 10 for the American Civil War aficionados whose hit machine had run out of ammo by the end of 1969.

Young Guns (Go For It)

ARTIST Wham! RELEASE DATE October 1982 WRITER George Michael PRODUCER S. Brown LABEL Innervision UK CHART PEAK/WEEKS 3/17 US CHART PEAK/WEEKS –

This early success for the Michael/Ridgeley combo was a standout on their first album **Fantastic**. The demo of the (sup)posedly macho track had been put together at Andrew Ridgeley's parents' house before the duo landed a contract and was revived as a follow-up to their debut (flop) single **Wham! Rap**.

If their sound has its lingering traces of the poppy late Seventies soul on which they cut their musical teeth, their lyrics – particularly their

tongue-in-cheek relish for the intricacies of jive talk – resonate with the flippant urgency of the best Sixties pop. **Adrian Thrills, NME, September 1982**

Young Hearts Run Free

ARTIST Candi Staton RELEASE DATE May 1976 (UK & US) WRITER Dave Crawford PRODUCER Dave Crawford LABEL Warner Bros. (UK)/Warner (US) UK CHART PEAK/WEEKS 2/13 US CHART PEAK/WEEKS 20/16

Like many other singers trained in the gospel tradition, Alabama-born Staton swapped to secular music for commercial success, initially singing in a country vein, as the title of her debut single suggested: *I'd Rather Be An Old Man's Sweetheart (Than A Young Man's Fool)*. A move to Warner Brothers in 1974 headed her into the soul-pop field and *Young Hearts* was a hit as disco fever started to build. Staton's next hit was a Bee Gees number, *Nights On Broadway*. In 1991 she had another hit with The Source: *You Got The Love*.

One of the great voices of our time. Disco song (yawn)! Thought this was going to be great, instead it was just O.K. **Vivien Goldman, Sounds, May 1976**

Young Love

ARTIST Tab Hunter RELEASE DATE February 1957 (UK)/January 1957 (US) WRITER Carole Jouner, Rick Cartey PRODUCER – LABEL London (UK)/Dot (US) UK CHART PEAK/WEEKS 1/18 US CHART PEAK/WEEKS 1/21

Tab Hunter was one of the first actors to indulge in a parallel pop career. The song's co-writer Ric Cartey had failed to make a chart impact with the initial release and, at a time when record companies saturated the charts with several artists recording the same tune, both Hunter and country star Sonny James recorded versions. James' effort would stall at Number 2 in the States behind Hunter's debut; singing ultimately proved a less successful long-term career option for the actor.

*Tab Hunter is already well up in the hit parade with **Young Love**, though I feel that the Sonny James version has more 'magic' – as they say in the pop trade.* **Laurie Hernshaw, Melody Maker, February 1967**

Your Song

ARTIST Elton John RELEASE DATE January 1971 (UK)/November 1970 (US) WRITER Elton John, Bernie Taupin PRODUCER Gus Dudgeon LABEL DJM (UK)/UNI (US) UK CHART PEAK/WEEKS 7/12 US CHART PEAK/WEEKS 8/14

Elton John (real name Reginald Kenneth Dwight) obtained his stage name from two fellow members of his first pro group Bluesology, Elton Dean and John Baldry. Chart success started when he teamed up with lyricist Bernie Taupin in 1967 and *Your Song* gave the duo their first UK and US Top 10 hit. The song was on the shortlist for the funeral of Princess Diana, but a rewritten *Candle In The Wind* was considered more suitable.

A pretty McCartneyesque ballad. As hesitant as one might be to own up to it in the light of all the superlative drooling and hive breaking out … Elton John really is a gas. **John Mendelson, Rolling Stone, November 1970**

INDEX OF ARTISTS

Abba, 48, 67, 117, 135, 245, 231
ABC, 128
Abdul, Paula, 154, 198
Ace Of Base, 186
Adam And The Ants, 162, 194
Adams, Bryan, 65, 81, 202
Aerosmith, 129
Alice Cooper, 180
All-4-One, 98
Almond, Marc, With Gene Pitney, 191
Alpert, Herb, 212
Alpert, Herb, And The Tijuana Brass, 193
Altered Images, 80
Amen Corner, 105
America, 88
Animals, The, 90
Anka, Paul, 50, 253
Archies, The, 200
Armatrading, Joan, 129
Armstrong, Louis, 234
Association, The, 13, 41
Astley, Rick, 146
Aswad, 56
Austin, Pattie, And James Ingram, 21
Avalon, Frankie, 224
Average White Band, The, 158
B-52's, The, 131
Babylon Zoo, 193
Bachelors, The, 91
Bachman-Turner Overdrive, 251
Bad Company, 37
Bailey, Philip, With Phil Collins, 60
Bananarama, 224
Band Aid, 52
Bangles, The, 62, 228
Barry, Len, 152
Bassey, Shirley, 18
Baxter, Les, And His Chorus And Orchestra, 160
Bay City Rollers, The, 36
Beach Boys, The, 36, 75, 77, 84, 93, 188, 204
Beastie Boys, The, 252
Beat, The, 138
Beatles, The, 12, 48, 71, 72, 81, 83, 84, 85, 99, 127, 130, 156, 159, 183, 191, 198, 214, 220, 250
Beats International, 59
Beautiful South, The, 125
Beck, Jeff, 86
Bee Gees, The, 91, 113, 136, 147, 197, 217
Belafonte, Harry, 136
Berlin, 206
Berry, Chuck, 113, 143, 149, 174, 180
Billy Idol, 241
Birkin, Jane, And Serge Gainsbourg, 112
Björk, 110
Black Box, 170
Black Lace, 9
Black Sabbath, 156
Black, Cilla, 17
Blondie, 37, 50, 82, 214
Blue Öyster Cult, 54
Bluebells, 255
Blur, 43, 156
Bolton, Michael, 90
Bon Jovi, 126
Boney M, 171
Booker T. & The MG's, 78
Boomtown Rats, The, 92
Boone, Debby, 252
Boone, Pat, 17, 101, 130
Boston, 140
Bowie, David, 18, 84, 112, 121, 122, 165, 193, 195
Box Tops, 122
Boys II Men, 61, 102, 106
Boyzone, 67
Bread, 22, 104
Bros, 96
Brotherhood Of Man, 178
Brown, James, 73, 156
Brown, James, And The Famous Flames, 94
Bryson, Peabo, And Regina Belle, 242
Buffalo Springfield, 71
Bush, Kate, 135, 176, 249
Buzzcocks, The, 63
Byrds, The, 61, 141, 219
C&C Music Factory, 76
Campbell, Glen, 169, 243
Captain & Tennille, 52
Captain Sensible, 80
Cara, Irene, 66, 69
Carey, Mariah, 58, 66
Carey, Mariah, And Boyz II Men, 153
Carnes, Kim, 28
Carpenters, The, 42, 159, 251
Cars, The, 59
Cash, Johnny, 99
Champs, 208
Charles, Ray, 86, 92, 236
Checker, Chubby, 122, 160, 220
Chemical Brothers, The, 181
Cher, 105
Chi-Lites, 81
Chic, 120
Chicago, 105
Chicory Tip, 192

Chiffons, The, 82, 204
Chordettes, The, 141
Christie, 250
Christie, Lou, 123
Clapton, Eric, 98, 207
Clark, Petula, 58
Clash, The, 184, 240
Cline, Patsy, 43
Clooney, Rosemary, 85, 212
Coasters, 250
Cochran, Eddie, 202
Cocker, Joe, 245
Cole, Nat King, 213, 237
Cole, Nat King, And Natalie Cole, 223
Collins, Edwyn, 74
Collins, Phil, 9, 106, 152
Color Me Badd, 99
Commodores, The, 59, 214
Communards, The, 55
Como, Perry, 14, 230
Connell, Don, 86
Conway, Russ, 185
Cooke, Sam, 40, 247
Coolio Featuring LV, 72
Costello, Elvis, 10, 151
Covington, Julie, 54
Crazy World Of Arthur Brown, 68
Cream, 204
Creedence Clearwater Revival, 23, 162
Crew-Cuts, The, 182
Croce, Jim, 23
Crosby, Bing, 240
Crosby, Bing, And Grace Kelly, 219
Cross, Christopher, 18
Crow, Sheryl, 11
Crowded House, 54
Culture Club, 53, 115
Cure, The, 106, 129
D'Arby, Terence Trent, 185
D:Ream, 211
Danny And The Juniors, 19
Darin, Bobby, 133
Dave Clark Five, The, 75
Dave Dee, Dozy, Beaky, Mick & Titch, 86
Davies, Windsor, And Don Estelle, 240
Dawn, Featuring Tony Orlando, 215
Day, Doris, 180, 236
De Burgh, Chris, 118
Deacon Blue, 165
Dean, Jimmy, 28
Dee, Kiki, 14
Deee-Lite, 31
Deep Purple, 188
Dekker, Desmond, And The Aces, 107
Denver, John, 16
Depeche Mode, 62, 157
Derek And The Dominoes, 119
Detroit Spinners, The, 248
Dexy's Midnight Runners, 42, 72
Diamonds, The, 125
Dion, 175, 229
Dion, Celine, 160, 211
Dire Straits, 139, 174, 201, 228
Dixie Cups, 204
Dodd, Ken, 207
Doggett, Bill, 88
Domino, Fats, 31
Donovan, 137
Donovan, Jason, 17
Doobie Brothers, The, 125
Doors, The, 84, 122, 170
Douglas, Carl, 118
Dr Hook, 205, 239
Drifters, The, 178, 222
Duran Duran, 166, 178
Dury, Ian & The Blockheads, 86, 182
Dylan, Bob, 117, 119, 123, 200
Eagles, The, 89, 133
Earth, Wind & Fire, 181
East 17, 196
Easton, Sheena, 140
Eddy, Duane, 24
Edmunds, Dave, 94
Edwards, Tommy, 109
Electric Light Orchestra, 208
Ellison, Lorraine, 196
EMF, 221
Emotions, The, 27
Englandneworder, 248
Erasure, 58
Essex, David, 76
Eurythmics, 204, 242
Everly Brothers, The, 11, 39, 226
Extreme, 148
Fairground Attraction, 158
Faith, Adam, 235
Faith, Percy, And His Orchestra, 202
Fame, Georgie, 24
Father Abraham And The Smurfs, 188
Fifth Dimension, The, 17
Fine Young Cannibals, 183
Flack, Roberta, 69, 116
Fleetwood Mac, 9, 56, 59, 75, 168
Fleetwoods, The, 42
Focus, 205
Ford, Emile, And The Checkmates, 235
Ford, Tennessee, 181
Foreigner, 100, 226
Four Seasons, The, 28, 49, 164, 184, 227
Four Tops, The, 21, 165, 227

Frampton, Peter, 21
Francis, Connie, 124
Francis, Connie, 242
Frankie Goes To Hollywood, 166, 221
Franklin, Aretha, 96, 97, 167
Freak Power, 219
Free, 11, 245
Fury, Billy, 79
Gabriel, Peter, 187
Garbage, 129
Garfunkel, Art, 35, 96
Gaye, Marvin, 94, 121, 182, 236
Gayle, Crystal, 55
Gaynor, Gloria, 100, 146
Gentry, Bobby, 151
Gerry And The Pacemakers, 68, 253
Gibb, Andy, 95
Gibson, Debbie, 128
Gilmer, Jimmy, And The Fireballs, 200
Glitter, Gary, 103, 172
Golden Earring, 164
Goldsboro, Bobby, 88
Gore, Lesley, 109
Grand Funk, 127
Grandmaster Flash And Mellie Mel, 240
Grandmaster Flash And The Furious Five, 138
Grant, Gogi, 232
Green, Al, 121
Greenbaum, Norman, 194
Guns N' Roses, 204
Haley, Bill, And The Comets, 172
Hall And Oates, 135
Hardcastle, Paul, 148
Harley, Steve, And The Cockney Rebel, 134
Harris, Rolf, 220
Harrison, George, 144
Hayes, Bill, 24
Hayes, Isaac, 210
Heart, 138
Heaven 17, 208
Hebb, Bobby, 203
Henderix, Jimi, 10, 85, 163, 226
Henley, Don, 33
Herman's Hermits, 103
Hollies, The, 36, 82
Holly, Buddy, 108, 157, 208
Holman, Eddie, 85
Hopkin, Mary, 213
Hornsby, Bruce, And The Range, 231
Horton, Johnny, 25
Hot Chocolate, 108, 253
Houston, Whitney, 78, 100, 179
Human League, The, 57
Humble Pie, 116
Humperdinck, Engelbert, 167
Hunter, Tab, 255
Ian, Janis, 19
Ifield, Frank, 91
INXS, 145
Iron Maiden, 35
Isley Brothers, The, 201, 212
J. Geils Band, The, 40
Jacks, Terry, 180
Jackson Five, The, 100, 102
Jackson, Janet, 139, 210
Jackson, Joe, 109
Jackson, Michael, 23, 26, 27, 29, 214
Jam, The, 57, 62, 76, 209, 218
James, 186
Jamiroquai, 225
Janowski, Horst, 227
Jesus And Mary Chain, The, 147
Jett, Joan, And The Blackhearts, 95
Joel, Billy, 115, 224, 233
John, Elton, 38, 45, 48, 77, 103, 173, 176, 178, 192, 255
John, Elton & George Michael, 55
John, Elton & Kiki Dee, 54
Jones, Grace, 187
Jones, Howard, 235
Jones, Tom, 49, 78, 110
Jordan, Montell, 212
Joy Division, 132
Kallen, Kitty, 125
Katrina And The Waves, 229
KC And The Sunshine Band, 209
Kendricks, Eddie, 116
Khan, Chaka, 93
Kidd, Johnny, And The Pirates, 183
King, Ben E., 194, 195
King, Carole, 111
Kingsmen, 128
Kinks, The, 10, 127, 203, 253, 231
KLF, Featuring The Children Of The Revolution, 214
Knack, The, 144
Knight, Gladys, And The Pips, 138
Kool And The Gang, 39
Kraftwerk, 19
Kriss Kross, 114
Kula Shaker, 206
La's, The, 210
LaBelle, 118
LaBelle, Patti, And Michael McDonald, 152
Lauper, Cyndi, 74, 219
Lee, Leapy, 125
Lee, Peggy, 141
Lennon, John, & Plastic Ono Band, 80, 106
Lennon, John, 114, 246
Lennox, Annie, 242

Lewis, Bobby, 217
Lewis, Huey, And The News, 160
Lewis, Jerry Lee, 241
Lieutenant Pigeon, 141
Lightning Seeds Featuring Baddiel And Skinner, 214
Limmie And The Family Cookin', 251
Lipps Inc., 72
Little Richard, 76, 128
Loeb, Lisa, And Nine Stories, 196
Los Lobos, 118
Love Affair, The, 63
Lovin' Spoonful, The, 202
Lulu, 216
M, 160
M People, 141, 152
M/A/R/R/S, 162
MacGregor, Mary, 217
Madness, 127, 30, 108, 154
Madonna, 44, 87, 123, 124, 136, 155, 218
Mamas & Papas, 36
Manfred Mann Earth Band, 30
Manfred Mann, 52
Manic Street Preachers, 50
Manilow, Barry, 43, 100, 136
Marcells, The, 30
Marie, Kelly, 67
Marillion, 51
Marley, Bob, And The Wailers, 112, 149
Marmalade, 52
Martha And The Muffins, 60
Martha And The Vandellas, 47
Martin, Dean, 137
Martin, Declan, 226
Martindale, Wink, 49
Marvin, Lee, 230
Marx, Richard, 170
Massive Attack, 27
Mauriat, Paul, And His Orchestra, 130
McCartney, Paul, & Stevie Wonder, 60
McCartney, Paul, 179
McCartney, Paul, And Wings, 25, 142, 144
McCoys, 79
McCrae, George, 172
McGuire Sisters, 186
McGuire, Barry, 63
McKee, Maria, 184
McKenzie, Scott, 177
McLean, Don, 14, 225
McTell, Ralph, 199
Meat Loaf, 49
Melanie, 34
Michael, George, 38, 66, 113
Middle Of The Road, 41
Midler, Bette, 204
Mike And The Mechanics, 127
Mike Sammes Singers, The, 191
Miles, John, 142
Miller, Mitch, 250
Miller, Ned, 71
Minogue, Kylie, 199
Mitchell, Guy, 186
Monkees, The, 48, 152
Moody Blues, The, 148
Moore, Gary, 197
Morrison, Mark, 168
Morrison, Van, 35
Morrissey, 200
Mott The Hoople, 12
Motown Spinners, The, 109
Move, 69
Mud, 215
Mungo Jerry, 107
Murray, Ruby, 189
Musical Youth, 157
N'Dour, Youssou, & Neneh Cherry, 182
Nash, Johnny, 92
Nelson, Willie, 13
New Kids On The Block, 79
New Order, 30
New Seekers, The, 101
New Vaudeville Band, 244
Newton-John, Olivia, 88, 158
Nilsson, 65, 246
Nirvana, 188
Numan, Gary, 39
Numan, Gary, And The Tubeway Army, 18
O'Connor, Des, 97
O'Connor, Sinead, 150
O'Jays, The, 132
O'Sullivan, Gilbert, 13
Ocean, Billy, 238
Ofarim, Esther, And Abi, 41
Orbison, Roy, 45, 110, 151, 153
Orchestral Manoeuvres In The Dark, 62
Osmond, Donny, 163
Osmonds, The, 44, 131
Ottawan, 40
Palmer, Robert, 8
Paper Lace, 29
Parr, John, 194
Patti Smith Group, The, 26
Payne, Freda, 25
Peaches And Herb, 168
Peebles, Anne, 92
Pet Shop Boys, 154, 234
Pet Shop Boys And Dusty Springfield, 235
Peter, Paul And Mary, 121
Peters And Lee, 234

Pickett, Bobby, And The Crypt-Kickers, 139
Pink Floyd, 16, 180
Pointer Sisters, The, 20
Poison, 64
Police, The, 56, 64, 138, 175, 229
Poole, Brian, And The Tremeloes, 190
Prado, Perez, And His Orchestra, 41
Presley, Elvis, 12, 18, 31, 46, 53, 83, 90, 110, 112, 131, 145, 168, 199, 247, 248
Pretenders, The, 34, 206
Price, Lloyd, 194
Prince, 164, 237
Prince And The Revolution, 148, 117, 163
Proclaimers, The, 102
Procol Harum, 241
Prodigy, The, 69
Public Enemy, 53
Puff Daddy And Faith Evans, 101
Pulp, 42, 51
Pussy Cat, 139
Queen And David Bowie, 222
Queen, 31, 44, 99, 116, 164, 185, 189, 232
R.E.M., 44, 156
Radiohead, 44, 156
Rafferty, Gerry, 24
Rare Earth, 73
Rascals, The, 158
Ray, Johnnie, 115
Rea, Chris, 171
Real Thing, 253
Redding, Otis, 53
Reddy, Helen, 15
Reed, Lou, 229
Reeves, Jim, 51, 82, 96
Reynolds, Debbie, 206
Rich, Charlie, 140
Richard, Cliff, 50, 126, 201, 233
Richie, Lionel 83
Richman, Jonathon, And The Modern Lovers, 172
Right Said Fred, 104
Righteous Brothers, The, 222, 254
Riperton, Minnie, 132
Robinson, Smokey, And The Miracles, 207, 218
Roe, Tommy, 51
Rogers, Julie, 233
Rogers, Kenny, 118
Rolling Stones, The, 15, 35, 88, 110, 114, 119, 155, 218
Ronettes, The, 26
Ross, Diana, 9, 40, 217, 223, 238
Ross, Diana, & Lionel Richie, 61
Roxette, 108
Roxy Music, 20, 112, 130, 225
Royal Scots Dragoon Guards, 14
Ruffin, Jimmy, 234
Run DMC, 229
Sade, 188
Sadler, Sgt Barry, 24
Sakamoto, Kyu, 201
Salt 'N' Pepa, 122
Sam And Dave, 192
Sam The Sham And The Pharaohs, 248
Santana, 177
Sarstedt, Peter, 239
Sayer, Leo, 237, 252
Scaffold, 108
Scorpions, 245
Seal, 44
Searchers, The, 146
Sedaka, Neil, 34, 151
Seekers, The, 38, 72, 249
Sex Pistols, The, 14, 75, 161
Shadows, The, 17, 247
Shakespears Sister, 196
Shalamar, 147
Shamen, The, 60
Shangri-Las, The, 92, 120
Shannon, Del, 176
Sharp, Dee Dee, 136
Shaw, Sandie, 162
Shirelles, 244
Showaddywaddy, 222
Silver Convention, 70
Simon & Garfunkel, 32, 34, 87, 142, 193
Simon Park Orchestra, 65
Simon, Carly, 149, 254
Simon, Paul, 61
Simone, Nina, 142
Simple Minds, 10, 57
Simply Red, 87, 105, 190, 196
Sinatra, Frank & Nancy, 190
Sinatra, Frank, & Bono, 104
Sinatra, Frank, 144, 198
Sinatra, Nancy, 211
Singing Nun, The, 53
Sir Mix-A-Lot, 21
Sister Sledge, 82, 232
Slade, 46, 135, 137
Sledge, Percy, 237
Sly & The Family Stone, 65, 66
Small Faces, The, 111, 120, 216
Small, Millie, 142
Smiths, The, 83, 155, 212
Snap, 169
Snow, 107
Soft Cell, 179, 206
Sonny & Cher, 94
Soul II Soul, Featuring Caron Wheeler, 23

Soul, David, 54
Spandau Ballet, 218
Sparks, 213
Specials, The, 74
Spice Girls, The, 220, 230
Springfield, Dusty, 191, 251
Springsteen, Bruce, 32, 47
Squeeze, 42, 223
Stafford, Jo, 134
Stansfield, Lisa, 10
Staple Singers, The, 168
Stargazers, 97
Starr, Edwin, 230
Starr, Kay, 172
Starr, Ringo, 253
Starship, 150
Staton, Candi, 255
Status Quo, 39, 173
Steely Dan, 51, 170
Steppenwolf, 32
Steve Miller Band, The, 8
Stevens, Ray, 199
Stewart, Amii, 117
Stewart, Rod, 47, 81, 133, 177, 216
Sting, 61
Stone Roses, 70
Stranglers, The, 76, 149
Streisand, Barbra, 63, 232, 246
Streisand, Barbra, And Neil Diamond, 251
Style Council, 254
Stylistics, The, 37
Styx, 20
Suede, 16
Summer, Donna, 89, 93, 133, 152
Supergrass, 13
Supertramp, 58
Supremes, The, 22, 197, 239
Survivor, 66
Sweet, 25
Sylvester, 252
Sylvia, 249
T. Rex, 72, 89, 169, 208
Tag Team, 242
Take That, 20, 22, 160, 167
Talking Heads, 154
Taste Of Honey, A, 32
Tears For Fears, 65, 184
Teenagers Featuring Frankie Lymon, The, 243
Temptations, The, 144, 155
10 cc, 57, 103
Thin Lizzy, 33, 240
Thomas, B. J., 164
Three Degrees, 238
Three Dog Night, 114
Thunderclap Newman, 190
TLC, 45, 230
Tom Robinson Band, 220
Tornadoes, 208
Toto, 9
Travolta, John, And Olivia Newton-John, 202, 255
Troggs, 244
Turner, Ike And Tina, 151, 171
Turner, Tina, 27, 237
2 Unlimited, 149
Tyler, Bonny, 217
U2, 70, 98, 161, 239, 246
UB40, 37, 166
Ultravox, 224
Undertones, 207
Underworld, 32
Union Gap Featuring Gary Puckett, 255
USA For Africa, 233
Valli, Frankie, 38, 78
Van Halen, 114
Vandross, Luther, And Janet Jackson, 27
Vanilla Ice, 104
Vee, Bobby, 147
Verve, The, 29
Village People, 249
Vincent, Gene, And His Blue Chips, 26
Vinton, Bobby, 31, 175, 210
Walker Brothers, The, 134, 203
Ward, Anita, 170
Warwick, Dionne, 228
Warwick, Dionne And Friends, 210
Waterboys, 242
Weather Girls, The, 114
Wet Wet Wet, 14, 77, 130
Wham!, 71, 255
Whigfield, 177
White, Barry, 255
Whitman, Slim, 175
Who, The, 143, 159,199, 246
Wild Cherry, 129
Williams, Andy, 189
Williams, Vanessa, 178
Wilson, Jackie, 94, 166
Winwood, Steve, 174
Withers, Bill, 121, 132
Wizzard, 181
Wonder, Stevie, 31, 95, 126,143,186, 204, 224
Wooley, Sheb, 163
Wynette, Tammy, 46, 195
XTC, 134
Yardbirds, The, 71
Yazz And The Plastic Population, 154
Young Rascals, The, 79
Young, Paul, 239
Zager & Evans, 107
Zombies, The, 183
ZZ Top, 74